A History
of Polish
Culture

Cieplice 14. VI 1987

Najukochańszym
            Ludziom na Świecie
Państu TATE - w dowód skromnej
            wdzięczności za
pamiątkę pobytu w Polsce
    rodzina Kaspraków:
Baśka, Józek, Ela, monika

BOGDAN SUCHODOLSKI

A History of Polish Culture

TRANSLATED BY E. J. CZERWIŃSKI

INTERPRESS PUBLISHERS • WARSAW 1986

Designed by Jerzy Kępkiewicz

Illustrations selected and captioned by Maria Suchodolska

Production editor: Maciej Cholerzyński

This is the two thousand one hundred and forty-second publication of Interpress Publishers

This book appears also in Polish and German

Copyright by Polish Interpress Agency, Warsaw 1987

Set, printed and bound by "YUGOSLAVIAPUBLIC" — "BIGZ", Belgrade

ISBN 83-223-2142-2

Table of Contents

Preface

This is the history of the culture of a nation which over a thousand years ago created in the lands between the Vistula and the Odra a state which was for centuries to be a great European power. It is the history of a nation which lost its independence as a result of foreign aggression — although also admittedly through its own errors — but which never ceased throughout the whole period of the partitions to mobilize its forces in the cause of freedom, and became a model of patriotism. And it is the history of a nation which regained its independence and rebuilt its own state, only to lose these again during the tragedy of the World War II. And finally it is the history of a nation which after the war built the state anew, strong and just.

This is the history of the culture of a nation whose chivalrous traditions in the service of great national and cultural ideas have been tried and proved so many times on battlefields: Legnica, the victory at Vienna, the sacrificial struggle "for your freedom and ours" on American and European soil, the barricades of the Paris Commune, the contribution to the victory over Nazism in the Battle of Britain, at Monte Cassino, the route from Lenino to Berlin, and the Polish resistance movement.

This is the history of the culture of a nation whose state — like all the other states of the world — was for centuries a feudal state, but which boldly and independently summoned up all injustices before "the tribunal of reason", searching steadfastly for a system free from prejudices and inequality; of a nation which already at the Council of Constance defended the precepts of fairness and peace in relations among nations and which — especially in the 16th century — became a liberal and tolerant country, giving hospitality to refugees persecuted in the rest of Europe for their beliefs; of a nation which today, while building a country where social justice reigns, at the same time defends peace on earth.

This is the history of the culture of the nation of Copernicus and Chopin; of a nation of scholars and artists, whose creative efforts contributed significantly to the development of world culture; of a nation in which culture became a matter of life itself for the great mass of people, at first within the limits set by the feudal system, next within the broader limits set by the social emancipation movement of peasants and workers, and finally — today — within limits which embrace the entire nation.

This book presents culture as the development of social consciousness, born of the processes occurring in and forming the civilized world. This outer world is dealt with only insofar as is necessary in order to elucidate the birth and operation of the inner world, the world of social consciousness, evolved through centuries and constituting the main theme of this book. The picture of the objective world presents, therefore, only "significant" facts which are open to hermeneutic interpretation.

In short, this book is not an encyclopedia of information about the history of Polish culture, perceived as a totality of all the fields of life. It is not a systematic exposition of political, social, or economic history; it is not a detailed discourse on the history of literature, art, music, education or science. It is not a reference book, which one can reach for when needed: it is a collection of interpretations of occurrences and facts taken from various areas of life — the economy, the social arena, the development of the state, the view of the world and the circulation of culture in society — indicating changes in social consciousness.

This, therefore, is a book intended to stimulate thought about the culture of one of the nations of the world. And, at the same time, thought about the culture of the nation to which, perhaps the reader of these pages may belong. At such a meeting a road of mutual understanding and agreement opens up, a road upon which all the inhabitants of our earth are today setting forth.

THE MIDDLE AGES

Introduction

The Middle Ages represent half our historical existence. From the creation of the Polish state in the 10th century, to the beginnings of the Renaissance, five centuries elapsed which were as rich and varied as the five centuries which followed, and were of fundamental importance in the processes that constituted the state and nation. The uneven distribution of historical source materials creates a false historical perspective shortening the medieval period, and unjustifiably lengthening the age which followed. But, nonetheless, the national consciousness accurately perceived the significance of the era. This is reflected in the widely-held conviction that Poland's greatness stemmed from the period of the Piast and early Jagiellonian Dynasties. National opinion graced only the Piasts with nicknames, such as the Brave, the Bold, the Just, the Honest and the Great; for it was they who built and reinforced the state which was just entering the historical arena occupied for centuries by the papal and imperial powers who ruled the whole world in the name of the cross and the sword. It was during their reigns that the foundations of Polish intellectual and artistic culture were laid, finding their own individual form against the background of medieval universalism. This epoch was recalled by the people of the nation during periods of uncertainty and hardship in Poland's history, especially during the periods of partition and of reconstruction following World War II.

Place in Europe and Historical Consciousness

OPEN FRONTIERS AND THE EMERGENCE OF THE POLISH STATE

The fate of early Poland was determined in the vast areas east of the River Elbe, between the Odra and the Vistula. Traditional tribal ties existed here for centuries. The Polanians inhabited the Warta basin; the Slezanians lived on the River Śleża at the foot of the holy mountain later to be called Sobótka; the Łęczycanians and Wislanians lived in the upper and central Vistula valley; the Mazovians lived in today's Mazovia and the Kujavians inhabited the area in and around Kruszwica; the Opolanians lived in areas between the upper Vistula and Odra, while the Pomeranians inhabited areas between the lower Vistula and Odra. Some of these tribes established early tribal territories. In the South the Wislanians were the first to establish a state, as early as the eighth century. Later, a Polanian state was set up in the North. The Wislanian state fell, while in the ninth century the Polanian state, with its capital at Gniezno, became a focal point integrating other Polish territories and tribes, the basis of the nation's entire future.

This was not an easy task in that "great vastness", as the sixth century Goth historian Jordanes called it, where nature had not designated natural borders. Geographic conditions did not assist in the formation of a state organism within closed borders. These borders needed to be defined and had to be defended. Everything was for the taking and in jeopardy of being lost.

The territorial scope of the state was therefore undefined for a long period. Perhaps it was only at the court of the ruler that anyone had any idea of where the borders ran. The art of charting territories had not been developed to any extent. The map of the country at that time did not reflect, as it does today, the geographical position of the fatherland: the boundaries of the country were only those that were enforceable by the ruler and his retainers, who collected feudal dues. Soon, however, new factors were added to these traditional ones: consciousness of the separate character of the country as against other states, allies and enemies; the awareness of the need for self-defense and, thus, for victory. Under these conditions these factors integrated and influenced the expansion of the Polanian state.

With the acceptance of Christianity by Mieszko I in 966, the Polanian state, now known as Poland, entered into the arena of European affairs.

The introduction of Christianity to Poland, which continued over a long period of time, had a dual political role. On the one hand, it guaranteed the country's independence and protection — at least in principle — against foreign invasions conducted in the name of Christianization. On the other hand, it subordinated Poland to the ever-changing political interests of the Papacy, which often used its religious authority to impose certain political decisions.

Poland's ruling circles took advantage of this situation; it was the first step towards a policy which would bring maximal gains from entrance into Europe's Christian community, as understood by Mieszko I when he committed the country to the Pope's care, while still maintaining his own state interests. The Church's goal was much the same: to have all high ecclesiastical positions occupied by Poles, thus stabilizing its position within the country.

Not until Boleslaus the Brave, the son of Mieszko I, came to power, was the strength of the young country confirmed. It was he — according to the first Polish historian, Gallus Anonymus, voicing the opinions of his contemporaries — who performed the great task of expanding and unifying the country.

The country of Boleslaus the Brave not only attained geographical boundaries, but was also able to defend them, thanks to the ruler's strong military power. The famous meeting between Boleslaus the Brave and the Emperor Otto III in Gniezno in the year 1000, demonstrated and confirmed this power; it was also the victory of a new style of political thinking, as a result of which Poland was to be a sovereign nation the equal of other European powers. The German chronicler, Thietmar of Merseburg, usually unfavorably disposed toward Poland, wrote with genuine grief: "The former tributary has become a lord."

Rome did not accept this independence which,

however, did not weaken Poland's efforts to obtain consent for a coronation. Near the end of his life, in the year 1025, Boleslaus the Brave ordered the Polish bishops to crown him king, and his son assumed the crown upon his father's death. The concept of the crown as a symbol of territorial unity has from that time never been forgotten. When in 1076 Boleslaus the Bold was crowned in Gniezno, the German chronicler, Thietmar, wrote, that he "impudently reached for the royal crown, against the laws of, and to the shame of, our German kingdom." Although the coronation did not bring lasting unification of the country, which was still territorially subdivided, the concept of a certain national unity within the country — *Regnum Poloniae* — remained despite the power of local princes. But a feeling of national separateness and identity was widespread — *gens Polonica* using a common language and with common beliefs and laws. Cracow remained *urbs et sedis regia*, as it was described in the mid-thirteenth century in one of the Lives of Saint Stanislaus.

The fight for the unity of the state was undertaken by the Silesian Piasts, especially Henry IV, who made overtures to Rome to secure consent to his coronation. His death in 1290 brought his efforts to an end, and it was finally Przemysł II who was crowned king of Poland at Gniezno in 1295. The great significance of this act for the national consciousness can be measured by the fact that the Bohemian ruler, Wenceslas II, who reigned over Cracow only temporarily, also had himself crowned in Gniezno in 1300.

After years of further battles for the unification of the country, Ladislaus the Short, having defeated his opponents, was crowned king in Cracow in 1320. He reigned over the ancient Polish lands — although not all of them. He also stressed Poland's ties with Kujavia and Mazovia, upheld the rights of Poland to Western Pomerania and the Lubusz region and conducted wars with the Teutonic Knights.

The crest of Poland, established during the rule of Casimir the Great, was the same as the one used by Przemysł II, and also by the Silesian ruler Henry IV, whose sarcophagus was adorned with two eagles — of Wrocław and Cracow — in a crown. According to Długosz, at the funeral in 1370 of Casimir the Great, the king who ultimately united the kingdom, homage was paid with the eleven banners of the separate lands of the Crown and a twelfth banner of the whole kingdom.

THE BEGINNINGS OF HISTORICAL CONSCIOUSNESS

Poland entered the arena of European affairs as a country without a past history. The existence of society took the form of survival marked by religious rites, tribal links and recurring agricultural activities in areas isolated by forests or water, or by unconquerable distances. Only a knightly adventure might have provided diversion from the steady drone of everyday life. More important and interesting knightly adventures found their way into tales and legends. And excitement could also be found along the trade routes crossing Poland from east to west and from south to north. These incidents were only transitory, however; they would come, then pass, and were not part of the fabric of life.

The country from its very beginnings had its history charted in chronicles. It was worth writing about, and it was written about: the development and rise of the nation went parallel with its historiography, which was the first, and more importantly, truly Polish branch of medieval literature, although written in Latin. Each century had its historian and chronicler: Gallus Anonymus in the twelfth century; Wincenty Kadłubek in the thirteenth; Janko of Czarnków in the fourteenth; and Jan Długosz in the fifteenth. These, as well as many other anonymous chroniclers, wrote varied accounts, but they were united in the belief that the past was worth remembering, and that all traditions contributed to the greatness of a nation.

This belief was manifested for the first time in art, and especially in historiography, in the twelfth century, in a mature form which proved conclusively that it had been developing for a long time. Such works as the Gniezno Doors and the *Chronicle* of Gallus Anonymus date from this period. The *Chronicle* of Gallus Anonymus, the court historian of Boleslaus Wrymouth, was the first piece of Polish historiography, presenting all the previous and contemporary might of Poland. The Gniezno Doors were the first masterpiece of art serving the nation. Scenes from the life of a saint were portrayed on these doors, which were the front gates to the Cathedral of Gniezno. The saint, St. Adalbert, was not only a missionary, but also the first Polish martyr; he sailed from Gdańsk to the Prussian lands, and was murdered by pagans. His holy relics became the foundation of the Cathedral of Gniezno and the Polish metropolitan see, independent of the Archbishop of Magdeburg. For this reason the tale of his life as shown on the panels of the Gniezno Doors ends with scenes depicting the king ransoming the body of the martyr and the solemn translation of his relics to the Gniezno Cathedral.

Wincenty Kadłubek, living and writing a century later than Gallus Anonymus, wanted to include in his *Chronicle* a reconstruction of that part of history on which memory and sources had long been lost or forgotten. The eagerness to have a long and beautiful history was most certainly not Kadłubek's private goal alone. Misappropriating the tools of the historian's craft, Kadłubek created ancient Polish history, thus meeting the requirements of those for whom he wrote. It was this fictional history which was, however, to a great degree accepted by the nation. Throughout the following centuries there remained in the minds of the gentry the idea of an ancient Poland, extending from the Baltic to the Black and Adriatic Seas. The process of bringing to light the falseness of such claims during the Enlightenment was not an easy one. The tale of the dragon of Wawel is to this day known to every child in Poland; and the funeral mounds of Krakus and Wanda are a definite proof, along with the poetry of Norwid and Wyspiański, of the vitality of these legends in contemporary times.

In the fifteenth century Jan Długosz abandoned this mythical place attributed to Poland in European history. Dedicating his work to Zbigniew Oleśnicki, he maintained that historians often undertake their task in an attempt to achieve wealth or fame: "I did not undertake this precarious task, one which requires a great amount of work, for any of such reasons, but solely for the greatness of the past of a nation that still remains in a deep and dark shadow; not for the hope of material gains, but for the love of country: the truest of all feelings manifested by the wish to embellish my native country with all possible splendor, contributing to its growth and well-being, as well as for the love of mankind."

This chronicle by Długosz was the history of all of Poland for two reasons. First, because it particularly strongly stressed the unity of Poland as a kingdom. Writing about the history of Silesia, Długosz criticized the rulers of this land, who swore obedience to the Bohemian king, and expressed the hope that "one day Wrocław will return and unite with the rest of Poland"; he also welcomed the joining of the lands of Pomerania, Chełmno and Michałów with the Kingdom. Secondly, it was the history of the entire society, since it mentioned all of its groups. Długosz spoke with a certain severity about the ruling class, but with sympathy toward the peasants.

And although Długosz's historio-philosophic concept was religious throughout (it was God that watched over the nation, defending "our lands and cities, through the mediation of Saint Stanislaus, our patron saint and the first Polish martyr"), he severely condemned the greed of the clergy and their "terrible corruption." He supported, however, strict and pure theocracy. His beliefs were similar to those of Zbigniew Oleśnicki and contrary to those of the coming period, since soon afterwards Casimir the Jagiellonian himself decided to nominate bishops, and Jan Ostroróg formulated the concept of the independence of national politics from Rome.

The national historical self-knowledge presented by Długosz did not, however, win him recognition among succeeding generations. When in the sixteenth century an entire new historical vision of the fate of Poland up to those times was being created, the work of Długosz, which had survived in manuscript form, came more and more under criticism. For the humanists it was much too medieval in nature; heretics could not forgive Długosz his fanaticism, which led him to write about the burning of Huss and the extermination of the Hussites with joy; orthodox Roman Catholics, who on the whole accepted Długosz's theocratic beliefs, could not forget that in his work he condemned corruption among the clergy and directed various criticisms against some noble families.

HISTORICAL CONSCIOUSNESS AND POLITICS

Awareness of the historical role of Poland was not only an element of national pride, but also and more importantly, it was a means by which political strategy was molded. The idea was again to unite the state, now divided

into principalities, and to guarantee the gentry the privileges which were theirs by tradition. In a letter to Pope John XXII on the subject of the coronation of Ladislaus the Short, the following argument was developed: "In the absence of the king of Poland, riots, disagreement, and the threat of civil war came about among the inhabitants of the Kingdom. Invasions by the Tartars, Lithuanians, Ruthenians, and other pagans occurred repeatedly. These peoples took the newly baptized Poles away in chains, turned them into slaves, and denied them the light of religion in mockery of our Redeemer, forcing them into idolatry. In the absence of defenders, we were deprived of many lands and stronghold towns by foreigners. For these reasons, our kingdom fell from the heights of prosperity to the pits of degradation."

In the minds of society the history of Poland under the first Piasts was becoming a symbol of prosperity and well-being, to which one would refer in times of trouble and despair. The idealization of the past which would be a means of hope and encouragement for future generations was developed in this way.

The cult of St. Adalbert and St. Stanislaus, handed down from generation to generation by word of mouth or hagiographic literature, had a similar character. (These saints were a symbol of the independence and power of the kingdom.) The relics of St. Adalbert led to the founding of an archbishopric in Gniezno. When the Bohemian ruler, Bretislav, reached Gniezno, he returned to Prague with the ashes of St. Adalbert, correctly assuming that in this way he would ultimately defeat Poland. But when Boleslaus Wrymouth came to power, these ashes were found and brought back to the cathedral in Gniezno — where wild animals were by this time sheltering in the ruins. The cathedral was reconstructed, so also was the state.

Gallus Anonymus considered St. Stanislaus a traitor who was deservedly punished by Boleslaus the Bold, but Kadłubek wrote of him as of a martyr, who died fighting for justice. The canonization of Stanislaus, the bishop of Cracow, in 1253, led to the writing of several stories about his life, in which he was portrayed as the symbol of the unity of the Crown. This symbol was often referred to in years to come. Prophecies were heard that the nation would soon be united, thanks to the intercession of the saint whose body had miraculously grown together after dismemberment. In this way, Cracow acquired a certain supremacy over Gniezno.

The role of history in state policy could also be clearly discerned in the conflict between the Teutonic Knights and Poland. The Emperor Charles IV's chancellor commented in the following way on the views of a Polish envoy, Spytek of Melsztyn, in a letter to the Grand Master of the Teutonic Knights (dated 26 April 1357): "He criticized all that the sainted Frederick and others have done for the Order. 'Who, I say', said the villain, 'is your Emperor? To us only a neighbor, but equal to our king.' When we spoke to him about Roman law dealing with imperial power, he answered hastily: 'Where is Rome, in whose hands is it? Answer me! Your Emperor is lower in rank than the Pope; he pays homage to him, while our

14

king wears the crown and holds the sword given to him by the Lord; he honors his own laws and the traditions of his ancestors more than the laws of the Empire.'" The chancellor's letter ended with a cry: "Woe is me — what do they hold sacred?"

Historical knowledge also had a role in the social consciousness of the ruling classes. The nobility growing in power and wealth, could always by referring to the past renew their privileges and acquire new ones as well, always based on tradition. Under these circumstances, the past was thought of as a society of freedom and equality.

This concept of the past and the consequence of such thinking were slowly finding a place in laws and official documents. In the Buda Charter of 1355, Louis of Hungary promised to respect all "old traditions" and "to maintain all liberties held." In the Jedlnia Charter of 1430, Ladislaus Jagiello declared: "The rights declared by both ourselves and our ancestors alike, kings and princes, the true and legal rulers of the Polish Kingdom, we hereby return to their former state, renew, declare, consecrate and state that they are to be enforced in their entirety."

In these statements, interests of individual estates were assured, as was the case in feudal states throughout Europe; the conviction was also expressed that tradition was a model for contemporary society and the highest court of justice.

EXPANSION OF THE STATE
IN THE FOURTEENTH CENTURY

The experience gained in the fight to overcome feudal particularism became in the mind of society a starting point for a new program for the regaining and uniting of all the Polish lands. In the fourteenth century the following phrases were often found in various official documents as well as in speeches: *Corpus Regni* and *Corona Regni* — the Body of the Kingdom and the Crown of the Kingdom. In comparison with earlier definitions of the kingdom, such as *Unicum Regnum,* which is often found in works of Gallus Anonymous, these expressed conviction that the lands which had at the time been united in this state were one and indivisible.

The Košice Charter of 1374 contained the stipulation that the indivisibility of the "Kingdom's Crown" should never be threatened because of dynastic disputes. Louis of Hungary swore, therefore, to "maintain the Kingdom in its present size and not separate any lands from the country, nor diminish it in any way, but try to augment its lands and to recover those once taken away."

The accession of Ladislaus Jagiello, the ruler of Lithuania, to the Polish throne in 1368, united Poland and Lithuania for many centuries, thus creating a powerful and vast state.

Jan Długosz described its territory with pride, mentioning the seven main rivers: the Vistula, Odra, Warta, Dniester, Bug, Niemen and Dnieper, and their basins. The union with Lithuania strengthened Poland in its fight with the Teutonic Knights. In 1410 a great victorious battle was fought at Grunwald, which henceforward became a

symbol of the ability of the nation to defend itself when threatened by an enemy. These struggles did not end until the peace settlement in Toruń in 1466, by which the state of the Teutonic Knights was partitioned, and Poland regained Gdańsk Pomerania, a western strip of Prussia with Malbork and Elbląg and also Warmia and the Chełmno region. Once again we can quote Jan Długosz, always loyal to the Piast traditions, who wrote with great joy: "I am more than happy that the Prussian war is over, that Prussia has been joined with Poland; it pained me that thus far the Polish Kingdom was torn asunder by various peoples and nations; now I and my contemporaries can call ourselves fortunate, for our eyes can once again look upon the nation as a united whole; but I would be even more joyous to see, by the Grace of God, the unification of Silesia, Lubusz and Słupsk with Poland."

This dream did not come true until five hundred years later, when after World War II the Odra and Lusatian Nysa became the western borders of Poland.

Man and the Forces of Production

THE EXPANSION AND INTEGRATION
OF THE POPULATION

Procopius of Caesarea, a sixth century Byzantine historian, wrote about the Slavs that "dispersed, they occupy their lands living far apart from each other." In the next century, Theophylact Simocattes, another Byzantine historian, added to the above, that these peoples did not want to interfere in the bellicose affairs of Europe since they lived on its outskirts, and did not like to travel great distances.

For many centuries these observations held true. Poland, which became involved in European affairs only due to its contacts with the Papacy and the Empire, remained a far off and impassable country, the population of which was dispersed over great areas of land. During the formative period of the Polish state, approximately a million inhabitants lived within a territory of about 250,000 sq. km. Thus the average population density was about four to five persons per square kilometer. Taking into account certain areas, such as the mouth of the River Odra, Kujavia, Central Great Poland, Silesia, Cracow and its surroundings, and Sandomierz, it is possible that other areas had an even lower population density than this average; some swampy areas and those covered by thick forests were completely uninhabited. Villages were very small, usually consisting of about a dozen families. Communication between such villages was difficult and had no social significance. Such villages were self-supporting in terms of food and basic tools.

Trade routes, built and maintained by the rulers and by the lords, represented one factor which could help overcome this isolation and dispersion. Although they did not constitute a very dense communications system, they did offer some glimpses of a different style of life. A good example was Wolin, which was famous throughout Europe. Adam of Bremen wrote the following: "This famous town is a place frequently visited by the Greeks and barbarians ... Since so much has been said to glorify this town, may I add a few words myself ... It is unquestionably the largest of European towns ... It is inhabited by Slavs as well as by other peoples . . . One will not find a more honest and friendly nation in regard to hospitality and customs." Other sources confirm this opinion. Wolin was densely built; it had firm shores, a convenient port, and even a lighthouse, called a "Greek torch"; it had a bridge over the River Dziwna, a church, and fortifications.

In later centuries the central authorities took an interest in and protected the trade routes and many smaller towns asked for the privilege of having these roads directed through them. Casimir the Great laid down routes leading from Toruń to Wrocław, via Radziejów, Konin, Kalisz and Ostrzeszów, and from Toruń to Vladimir, by way of Lublin and Sandomierz. Cracow councillors forwarded a request to the king that the roads to Rus and Silesia should pass through Cracow and that the road to Hungary should lead via Cracow and Sącz.

Another factor combating isolation and the dispersal of the population was the state organization. The prince and his retainers lived in a stronghold town; they built frontier castles; they formed a still weak but, nevertheless, viable administration, which guaranteed the collection of tribute from an ever-widening national territory. This growing communications network was simultaneously becoming a commercial network for trade, of great importance for farmers and craftsmen who would set up their stalls and workshops in the area surrounding the stronghold town. As early as the tenth century large towns developed, such as Szczecin, Kołobrzeg, Gniezno, Poznań, Kruszwica, Kalisz, Wrocław, Cracow and Wiślica. Smaller towns also came into existence, whose names, like Sobótka (from *sobota* meaning Saturday) or Środa (meaning Wednesday), were taken from the day on which markets were held in them. These towns were generally small, with only a few having more than one thousand inhabitants.

But it was only slowly and in restricted areas that these factors introduced change in the primitive conditions of life over the whole vast area of the country. The predominant way of life was still the separated and isolated style, more attuned to nature than to social contacts. This way of life was better expressed in religious rituals and customs than in verbalized, written accounts. Such an existence, in the centuries to come when conditions were radically changed, would be turned into a recurrent dream of a quiet place to live, away from the bustle of the world.

THE BIRTH OF ECONOMIC PRODUCTION

The Archbishop of Magdeburg, Adelgoz, campaigning for the conquest of the Slav lands, in the year 1108 described the natural resources of Poland. His opinion was confirmed by Gallus Anonymus who wrote: "It is true that the country is densely wooded, but it is rich in gold, silver, bread and meat, fish and honey. It deserves to be put before others because, although surrounded by so many Christian and pagan peoples, which all together or each separately have repeatedly fought against it, never has it been subdued in its entirety; it is a land where the air is healthy; the forests are rich in honey; the waters abound in fish; the knights are valiant; the farmers are hardworking; the horses are enduring; the oxen are willing to work; the cows are milk-heavy; the sheep are covered with wool."

But the economy in these areas developed very slowly. The population was relatively small and methods of working the soil, as well as implements in use were still primitive. Therefore it required immense effort to increase the cultivated land area. The problem with communications was another reason why certain areas had a strictly self-supporting economy, that is, producing and growing only that which could be used directly.

Slowly, however, this state of affairs was changing. The organization of the country required an administrative network. The number of ducal stronghold towns was rapidly increasing; these were not only centers of government exacting specified taxes and dues from the population, but also centers for trade, where farmers came in direct contact with craftsmen. The cultivation of the soil was gaining importance in the national economy; it not only produced food but also the means by which one could gain wealth. Those directly interested in its growth were the rulers and the lords, the Church and the monasteries. From the middle of the twelfth century the period of colonization had begun, at first due to settlement of captives; later due to the inflow of free people, to whom good working and living conditions were guaranteed. Of equal importance were the advances made in the modernization of farm implements and the introduction of crop rotation (three-field system), which considerably increased the productivity of the land. It was becoming more and more advantageous to increase the extent of farming land, especially by cutting down forests.

These changes molded a new type of social relations in the villages, much more complicated than those which had existed in the past. The memory of patriarchal times was still vivid, when peasants had direct access to the ruler (Gallus Anonymus described "a poor peasant and some woman" who personally complained to Boleslaus the Brave) but in everyday practice, the interest of the wealthy feudal lords was beginning to take precedence over that of the remaining population. Unavoidably, a structuring of society was taking place with a permanent division of the population into various classes.

THE DEVELOPMENT OF TOWNS

The economic development of the country became more and more intense from the beginning of the thirteenth century. Contemporary Poland was swept by the process of forming new villages and towns, which originated in Silesia. Around the year 1205, Henry the Bearded 16 planned to form a few hundred new villages and settle there about 10,00 families. Although his plan was not carried out, its boldness indicated the scope of his economic endeavors. In Great Poland over a hundred new villages were settled in the thirteenth century; in the area of Dobrzyń, in Kujavia and the Sieradz region, about seventy were created. In the fourteenth century this process was accelerated.

The process of forming new towns took place in a similar way. In some instances it was simply a matter of changing the legal position of already existent towns; in others, it was a matter of building from nothing. Środa in Silesia and Chełmno in Pomerania were examples of this new trend. In Great Poland, in the thirteenth century, 38 cities were founded; in the fourteenth century, 55 were created. This process was shaping up similarly in other parts of the country.

Simultaneously, the population of the towns was growing rapidly. Although the population in most of the towns was still under one or two thousand, some "metropolitan" towns did exist. In the middle of the fourteenth century, Wrocław had 17,000 inhabitants; Cracow had about 14,000; Głogów about 11,000; and Nysa about 6,000. At the same time, new areas, previously uninhabited, were being settled. Due to these changes the population of Poland was increasing and in the middle of the fourteenth century, there were almost 1,800,000 inhabitants. Under these conditions a new type of social communication was being born and along with it, new needs and aspirations.

These new conditions helped change the human attitudes and social relationships formed in the conditions of a natural economy and barter. Money, and along with it, economic initiative, the search for new profitable products and transactions, were gaining in importance.

In the new towns and villages, which were founded on the basis of the new location law, new socio-economic relations were taking shape; the slogans of freedom and independence were being born; a means for claiming one's privileges was enforced; new prospects were opening for broader production and for the increasing of wealth. In these new towns, self-government with fairly wide powers was taking shape. The townsmen were gaining confidence in their importance and their separateness from the remaining population; new forms of coexistence and cooperation among town dwellers were developing.

These new socio-economic tendencies reflected in the policy and politics of Casimir the Great, the first Polish king who was not only the ruler but also the master of his kingdom, who cared for the well-being and prosperity of his subjects. The chronicler Janko of Czarnków, his contemporary, wrote the following: "He saw to it that his peasants and servants sowed the fields on his lands as carefully as possible . . . Seeing how starvation was rampant among his people and the neighboring nations, in various parts of the kingdom he opened up his replete granaries and ordered the starving and the poor to be fed . . . He ordered dams of stone and other structures to be constructed in various parts of the kingdom, not so much for his own gain, as to improve the hard lot of

craftsmen and farmers." The king led a great campaign to build new towns and to raise new fortifications, reshaping Poland, as was often said, from wood to stone. Throughout his reign, some fifty new castles were built and about thirty towns were fortified.

Economic policy molded the people's mentality and the country's administrative system. From now on instead of offering occasional rewards in return for service to the state, attempts were made to offer prospects of a reliable income. A charter of 1354 granted the city of Rzeszów and the surrounding lands, "with full rights of possession with all existing and future settlements and all related profits" to Jan Pakosławowic, for his "admirable merits, deeds, full of good intentions". In addition, so that "the city and the villages belonging to it might flourish abundantly," this charter released it from the jurisdiction od voivodes. The king, in granting this charter, described its social impact: "it is well that a noble head be decorated with noble hands; it befits, therefore, the royal majesty to have wealthy subjects, so that in times of need, they can defend him."

THE EXPLOITATION OF NATURAL RESOURCES AND NEW FORMS OF LABOR

The wealth of the royal court and especially the armor of its knights are proof of the utilization of raw materials and the development of various crafts, especially iron-smelting. In Silesia, the Kielce region and Mazovia, centers for smelting iron ore had existed since ancient times. In the Poland of the Piasts, such production was on a wide scale. Iron was at that time the basic element in farm implements, in reinforcing defensive wooden pales, and in knights' armor. Although a certain amount of armor was imported, the local industry had to supply the majority of materials needed for war or other uses. This was one of the reasons for the growing number of workshops which specialized in the production of metal objects. Some of these workshops could be quite large. A forge founded at Rogoźno in 1326 had to pay a tribute to the king of 104 plows and 52 colters yearly. Water power was utilized increasingly in mills and sawmills.

For many years many Polish monarchs had shown an interest in the efficient utilization of natural resources, especially salt. But in the fourteenth and fifteenth centuries these attempts became more systematic and were carried out with full realization of their importance. Ladislaus Jagiello, giving the Cracow burghers the right to mine sulphur, stated: "Among our other preoccupations our mind also reaches out into the wise utilization of the riches gathered in the mountains or other places underground for our benefit and the benefit of the kingdom, that the virtue of our foresight be praised and the state of the kingdom be praised under our prosperous government." Jagiello encouraged others to "dig, search and to study" in "all other areas and mountains of our kingdom which would give any indication of having an abundancy of minerals", adding that he would take under his protection and care the miners and diggers, sheltering them from lawlessness, violence and oppression.

In the fifteenth century production by craftsmen and miners increased considerably. For example, in Wrocław in 1403, there existed some 30 guilds for 92 trades, including 23 specialized lines dealing with the processing of metals. The art of iron smelting was quickly perfected. The names of the first masters in metallurgy can be found in various documents of the period. More and more materials were being utilized: besides iron ore there were mines of zinc, copper, lead, and gold, especially in the area of Złotoryja. The technique of manufacturing, the machines, the means by which water could be drained from the mines which were built when open-cast mining no longer yielded sufficient returns — all these were much improved. The art of weaving also developed; some of these products were even exported. In Biecz, for example, an enormous bleachery was built, powered by water; in many cities fulling presses were constructed. More and more glass-works were built, especially in Little Poland. The expansion of building, initiated by Casimir the Great, was still going on and demanded new tools and new technology. In the quarries, improved windlasses were used; on various construction sites the challenges of Gothic architecture were being met. Carpenters from the countryside displayed their ability and ingenuity. There is no doubt that the work of such carpenters was highly valued; Jagiello at one point presented Wawrzyniec of Gniezno with a sawmill on the Warta as a reward for his skills.

This evolution of various activities enlivened trade between the town and countryside, between various large towns in Poland, and abroad. Roads through Poland leading north-south and east-west were filled with caravans of merchants. Systematic attempts were made to improve the conditions of these roads and safety on them. As early as the reign of Casimir the Great, attempts were made to make rivers navigable in order that they might be used to transport goods, for example, the River Prosna below the city of Kalisz, the Vistula below Nowy Korczyn and the Odra below Wrocław.

These processes were changing the way that people thought: both those who were directly involved, and also those who were affected only indirectly by new types and methods of production, trade and transport. Traditional work, dependent on the rhythms of nature and intended primarily to satisfy one's own needs, was replaced by a new type of work. This work was meant to bring greater profits; it required specialized training, was frequently linked with artistic skills, and was often related to commercial risk and profit. This work was generally performed in large groups and was regulated in various ways by special laws and guild regulations; thus, it became a social activity.

A direct reflection of this new, skilled, organized, and social work-style could be seen in the art of the time. In Romanesque sculpture and painting, one could see man in his lonely battle with nature, as a hunter, a gardener or a farmer cutting forests or cultivating land; in later times, this picture was changed to include more complicated human work. The culminating point in this area was *Baltasar Behem's Codex* (1505), a great illustrated book, documenting the various types of jobs carried out by the guilds of Cracow, in which the Gothic vision of the organized world and the dignity of work was already merging with a Renaissance mood of beauty and the richness of life.

Social Unrest

THE POPULAR INSURRECTION OF 1037

Feudal oppression began in the eleventh century; this increasingly limited the freedom of the people working on the land and worsened their living conditions. Still fresh in the memory were times when the land belonged to everyone, when he who cultivated the land profited from it and enjoyed wide respect within society. The development of the economy put an end to these relations. More and more the land was becoming the property of the king and the lords, who leased it out only under specified conditions. Thus, great estates were built up by royalty, the knighthood, and the clergy. A new system sprang up, based on oppression and the exploitation of those employed on these estates.

This expansion, to an ever greater degree, threatened the freedom of the agricultural population, a considerable part of which lost its independence. A time came when many peasants deliberately neglected their obligation to work and to render dues; they often ran away and there were local rebellions. The process had already begun at the end of Boleslaus the Brave's reign but intensified considerably immediately after his death.

It reached a nationwide scale in 1037, during the dynastic disputes and the deterioration of royal authority. This anti-feudal rebellion was linked with a return to the ancient, folk religion, which had officially been wiped out, but in reality was still alive.

The defeat of the popular uprising, which never reached the major centers of power in the cities and stronghold towns, was, however, of some significance for the national consciousness. These incidents manifested for the first time the discontent of the people and their fighting spirit, which was bred on the vision of a new and just social order. This spirit was also present in neighboring countries, especially in Rus and Hungary. Criticism was also directed against the Church, as a semi-secular religious organization, with a discrepancy between its "spiritual" role and its role in the secular sphere, that is in politics and the economy.

REBELLIONS IN THE TOWNS

Social conflicts also grew in the towns; they were of varied origin. Great differences existed between townsmen in terms of wealth, ancestry, and occupation. There were struggles for greater profits between the guilds and various wealthy merchants. Local councils often

18

prohibited craftsmen to sell their products themselves: they had to do it through merchants. But at the beginning of the fourteenth century the guilds were already strong enough to take up the struggle with the patrician merchant caste and to play a greater part in the governing of cities. These struggles sometimes turned into true revolutions with demands being made to equalize taxation and to liberalize statutes dealing with trade and production. In 1333 in Wrocław the weavers organized a rebellion against the merchant oligarchy; the rebels gained the support of the poor of the city. About 900 people took part in this rebellion. This resulted in defeat but the causes of the conflict still remained and even increased as more and more people without any particular occupation began to flow into the cities — the escaped serfs, beggars, groups of vagabonds, and ex-soldiers who formed the urban mob.

Toward the end of the fourteenth century town councils passed a number of regulations that bear witness to worsening conflict. Discontent became so widespread that the central government and the church authorities began to take notice of it. The Papal Bull of 1373 claimed a relation between the heretical movements and the process of radicalization among the urban populace; the Polish synods enumerated various examples of how city conflicts had led to attacks on the Church and its clergy.

Other sources of conflicts in the cities included ethnic relations and the changing political situation. A major part of the urban partician caste, especially in Little Poland, was of German descent. During the struggle for the unification of the state, many political viewpoints emerged. In 1311, the Bishop of Cracow, Jan Muskata, and the mayor of the city, Albert, came out against Ladislaus the Short, favoring the rendering of power in Poland to the Bohemian Luxemburg dynasty. Proof of the intensity of the struggle lay in the fact that it continued for almost a year. Ladislaus the Short was victorious, but the privileges of the townspeople and the role of municipal councils were clearly reduced.

The belief developed in the mind of the gentry that they alone defended the interests of Poland, and that the urban patricians — even in the capital city — were enemies of the state.

It was from this time that conflicts between the townspeople and the gentry began to surface. The intensity of these conflicts became apparent through an incident which was quite fortuitous, but which was well known throughout the country for many years.

A Polish magnate, Andrzej Tęczyński, had a disagreement with a Cracow armorer, who had prepared a suit of armor for him for the Prussian war. During the altercation' the nobleman beat him. This story reached the ears of the citizens of the city, who murdered Tęczyński in the sacristy of the Franciscan Church, where he had sought sanctuary. An anonymous nobleman wrote about this event in one of his poems which was circulated throughout Poland, causing resentment toward townspeople.

All these events contributed to awareness of the division between these two estates in the minds of society; this division, with which Poland had not been at all familiar in the past, developed at the end of the Middle Ages and henceforth dominated social condition and the attitudes of the various estates, gentry and burghers alike.

THE HUSSITE MOVEMENT

Together with the political and economic growth of Poland, opposition and social tensions began to grow. In the fifteenth century, disagreements between the gentry and the clergy pertaining to the payment of tithes, the removing of village administrators, the higher dues demanded from the cities and the guilds, the increased exploitation on the great estates of the spiritual and secular lords — all these contributed to the tense situation.

Under these circumstances the Hussite movement gained importance in Poland, particularly in Silesia. Poles, especially the minor gentry and the peasants, took part in the Hussite battles in Bohemia. In 1436, a Pole, Wyszek Raczyński, was executed in Prague as one of the leaders of the Hussite movement. After the defeat of the Hussites, a significant portion of Bohemian refugees came to Poland, spreading news of the events in Bohemia. This encouraged an attempt at armed action, and attacks on the residences of bishops and magnates by the poor gentry and peasants. The peasant insurrection of 1437 in Hungary was contemporaneous with these events. Under these circumstances, Spytek of Melsztyn formed the Great Confederacy in May 1439, in which many representatives of the Polish Hussite movement took part, including groups of the minor gentry, the town poor, and the peasants.

The Act of Confederacy expressed the will of "the entire community of the dignitaries and gentry of the regions of Cracow, Sandomierz, Lublin and Rus" to bring about the removal of those "deficiencies and wrongs", which in the eyes of the Confederates, were leading to the "destruction of the Kingdom of Poland."

The program of the Confederacy was not, however, realized. Spytek died in the great battle of Grotniki; some of his followers were murdered; the rest were dispersed throughout the country. Still, for some time, a Hussite center was maintained in Zbąszyń in Great Poland, but it did not gain nationwide significance. It is true that the Hussite movement did not play a great role in the political history of the country; it was, however, a significant and characteristic symptom of social dissatisfaction. Although its ideology was never clearly defined (Spytek's Act of Confederacy was exceptionally general), it was, nevertheless, a factor in bringing about criticism of the *status quo* and promoted collective action. Though confederacies had already been formed from the fourteenth century — particularly during interregna — they never had as their direct goal the basic reform of the kingdom. In addition they never actually involved the masses nor were they linked with radical religious currents. Furthermore, they never had such international connections as those which united the centers in Melsztyn and Zbąszyń with the traditions of the uprisings of the Taborites in Bohemia and Silesia. In these insurrections the slogan, "For your freedom and ours", which in the nineteenth century was to become the slogan of the oppressed nation, if not yet in defined form, was for the first time put into practice.

The Unification of the State and the Integration of the Nation

THE UNITY OF THE NATION

The first centuries of Polish history provided dramatic lessons in a national way of thinking. The collapse of the state and its restoration took place many times; almost everything was lost and then a new life was built up anew; sometimes the same victories and defeats were repeated over and over again. Despite these obstacles, however, the spirit of persistent aspiration toward goals was not broken.

It is enough to recall the vicissitudes of the history of the Polish crown. The coronation of Boleslaus the Brave took place in 1025 and he died in the same year. His son, Mieszko II, began his reign with a coronation, but a few years later he had to flee the country. Boleslaus the Bold was crowned in 1076 but in 1079 he was driven out. Then for many years Poland did not have a crowned ruler. Even Boleslaus Wrymouth was not able to regain the crown. In 1295 Przemysł II had himself crowned king of Poland, but in the following year he was murdered. It was not until the reign of Ladislaus the Short, crowned in 1320 in Cracow, that royal authority was permanently established over the united country during the thirteen years of his reign.

Coronation, during these three centuries of Poland's history, was a visible symbol of the integration and sovereignty of the state, and of its continued existence. Coronation was therefore the persistent aspiration of many Polish princes, despite opposition from the Empire and reluctance on the part of the Papacy. Various dynastic and regional struggles were also obstacles to coronation. For this reason, the royal seal chosen by Przemysł II bore not only the eagle with a crown, but also an inscription, proclaiming "the restoration of victorious symbols to the Poles".

The basis of these aspirations during the entire period was the developing unity of the nation. It was founded mainly on the ethnic community of the tribes occupying the territory united under the power of the first Piasts. Different sources and chroniclers from that period speak of a Poland and a Polish nation, the customs of the Poles, and the Polish language. The people living in the Vistula and the Odra basins were probably united in language long before the state was established. Under favorable political circumstances this linguistic unity developed, victoriously resisting the pressure of Latin, the language of the Church and the royal chancery. At the end of the thirteenth century efforts were made to develop and to maintain the native language and to give it greater scope and authority. During the synod in Łęczyca in 1285, it was decided that the "headmasters of cathedral and monastic schools were to be chosen from among those who spoke Polish perfectly and could explain the texts to the boys in Polish". This concern with language was an expression of consciousness of national unity, confirmed by various expressions used in contemporary sources: *lingua polonica*, *homines linguae polonicae* and *gens polonica*.

Despite feudal particularism, the same traditional laws and the same customs were preserved over the entire territory of Poland. Some sources speak of *ius Polonicum*. Another element that strengthened the ties between various regions was the existence of a uniform church administration. All the churches in Poland were subject to the authority of the See of Gniezno.

These elements of integration shaped the national and political consciousness of the various social strata. The upper strata, involved in international conflicts of interests, and regional and dynastic conflicts, took different standpoints regarding the idea of national unification at different times and in different provinces. The lower strata, separated from the king's court and its intrigues, felt the ties that united the people of the land much more strongly than factors that divided them. This social consciousness, which was expressed neither in writing nor in political ideology, was directly connected with life, work, customs and everyday existence: to these people the unity of Poland seemed to be obvious. It was for this reason that the peasants, according to historical sources, supported efforts toward unification. Długosz explains that there were more peasants than knights in Ladislaus the Short's army. Even the legend which stated that Ladislaus the Short hid in the caves at Ojcow with the help of peasants, testified to the hope that this social class placed in a "good king", who would be the protector of all the inhabitants and a just judge for rich and poor alike.

THE TARTAR THREAT

During the following three centuries the state that had been created by Boleslaus the Brave was the scene of military expeditions by Poland's neighbors. Peace and safety came to an end. Fighting took place not only along Poland's defenseless borders, but also in the heart of the country.

The most frequent and devastating invasions were those conducted by the Tartars. The first great incursion by the numerically strong and well-trained Mongol army took place in 1241. There were two wings to this attack: one to take Cracow and Opole, the other toward Łęczyca. Cracow was destroyed and burned; at Legnica, the Polish army under the command of Henry the Pious, was defeated. Despite the fate of Cracow and Legnica, the march of the Tartar hordes was halted; Poland and Europe were saved. In 1259 the second Tartar invasion commenced. This time Lublin, Sandomierz and again Cracow were taken; a significant part of Silesia was destroyed. The third invasion in 1287 was halted by new fortifications surrounding Sandomierz and Cracow. The fall of Sandomierz in 1259 had echoed around the country. The *Songs of a Dweller in Sandomierz* 20 are proof of this. They expressed, with great passion, the connection between religious and patriotic beliefs, the consciousness of guilt and confidence in God's protection of Poland, and lastly, the hope for Christian improvement as a condition for peace and safety for the country and its people. All these experiences were confirmed and developed in the historical events of the following centuries.

THE THREAT FROM THE GERMANS AND THE TEUTONIC ORDER

During this difficult period of Polish history, the threat from the Germans and the Teutonic Knights jeopardized the safety of Poland. The heart of the country was not directly threatened but Silesia, Western and Gdańsk Pomerania, Kujavia and Mazovia, were repeatedly centers of heavy fighting.

The victory of Mieszko over the army of Margrave Hodo at Cedynia in 972 was the first link in this long chain of battles that were waged against the Germans by Boleslaus the Brave, from 1004 up to the peace treaty of Budziszyn (Bautzen) in 1018. As a result of this peace treaty, Poland was able to hold on to Lusatia and Milsko and guarantee the safety of her western borders at least for the time being. It was not until 1029 that the Emperor Conrad II again besieged Budziszyn. In 1109 the Emperor Henry V attacked Silesia, and attempted to capture Bytom, Głogów and Wrocław. It was at Psie Pole near Wrocław that he was defeated. The next invasion began in 1146. In 1157, the Emperor Frederick Barbarossa reached as far as Poznań.

In the first half of the thirteenth century, Lubusz, the capital of the Lubusz region, was frequently beleaguered and conquered. In the second half of the thirteenth century, the margraves of Brandenburg captured vast territories in the north of the country. In 1308, they reached Gdańsk. Ladislaus the Short resumed the war with Brandenburg to regain the Lubusz district but, because of the strong pressure from the Teutonic Order, which was becoming the most dangerous arm of the German aggression, he failed in his attempt. The year 1327 marked the beginning of the long-lasting Polish-Teutonic wars. The defense of Kalisz and the victory in 1331 near Płowce failed to halt the Teutonic drive. The "perpetual" peace signed by Casimir the Great at Kalisz in 1343 was a compromise arrangement and did not last very long, especially since it left Gdańsk Pomerania in the hands of the Teutonic Knights.

New conflicts broke out at the end of the fourteenth century; in 1409 the Teutonic Knights made inroads upon the Dobrzyń district. One year later in the great battle near Grunwald, combined Polish and Lithuanian-Ruthenian troops gained a victory which, however, failed to hold back Teutonic aggression. Instead, it marked the beginning of new war plans by the Emperor Sigismund of Luxembourg and the Order, to bring about the total destruction of Poland. The possible partition of the Polish territories among the Teutonic Order, the Empire, the Silesian Princes and the Hungarians was also included in these plans. According to their alliance, each party to the agreement was to obtain that portion of territory which had long belonged to him or to his ancestors. Everything else was to be distributed on the basis of mutual negotiations.

The long history of defending the western borders of the country from the Empire and the Teutonic Order was an important element in national integration. From the very beginning, the war with the Germans was a nationwide war. The German chronicler, Thietmar, described the defense of Niemcza in the following way: "I have never heard of a people who struggled for their defense with greater persistence and resourcefulness." The local people, the peasantry, took part in the ambushes which decimated the emperor's army. The defense of Głogów was similarly a mass operation. Gallus Anonymus clearly speaks of the participation of "dogged peasants" who fought together with Boleslaus Wrymouth's knights. In later struggles with the Germans, the local population — in cities under attack, and the peasants — were always active.

THE SYSTEM OF ESTATES

Poland was a monarchy in which the privileges of some social classes were becoming greater and the limitations of freedom upon other classes more severe. During the reign of Mieszko II, the lords, even in opposition to the central authorities, were able to reach the point where their importance and influence were considerable. By interfering in the internal affairs of the governing dynasty and exploiting royal family quarrels, they strengthened their position. After the death of Mieszko II in 1034, a group of lords removed his son Casimir from power and established feudal lordships in the various regions of the country. True, Casimir returned to Poland in 1039 and restored the significance of the central authority (though Mazovia remained independent for almost another ten years) but the role of the lords was not destroyed.

During the reign of Boleslaus the Bold the lords conspired with the bishop of Cracow against the king. The purpose of this plot was to turn the crown over to the king's brother, Ladislaus Herman. Boleslaus accused the bishop of being a traitor, however shortly thereafter, in 1079, the king was exiled. It was a great triumph for the lords. In alliance with the church hierarchy, they forced the new king, Ladislaus Herman, to change the country's policies.

Power in the country passed more and more to the lords who pursued their own policies. Succession disputes or difficulties were ever more frequently settled by the lords according to their own interests. During the struggle against Mieszko the Old, the so-called "law of resistance against authority" was brought into effect by the lords; and in 1177, they replaced him as king by his younger brother, Casimir the Just. In this way royal power, which in theory was hereditary, was in practice conferred by election by the feudal lords. The congress that convened in Łęczyca in 1180 conferred special economic privileges on this group, especially on the bishops. These privileges significantly supplemented the political power of the lords.

The process of overcoming regional division did not weaken the lords' position; it merely changed its character. While the central authority was strengthening its position, the role of spiritual and secular lords, mainly in the capital, also increased. This group had crucial influence when Louis of Hungary came to power and even after his death (1382) when his daughter Jadwiga (Hedwig), was placed on the throne. In their own view and in reality, the lords became the rulers of the country. Their political power and economic privileges not only made them the highest estate in society but also led them to believe — even more so in the succeeding centuries — that Poland was their own personal property.

POLITICAL ADVANCEMENT OF THE GENTRY

Poland was not however their exclusive property: for some time the gentry had been gaining greater significance and wealth. The gentry now played a much more serious role in the very complicated political life of the country, especially in alliances and conflicts between the king and lords and in regional disputes.

At the end of the thirteenth century hereditary coats-of-arms came into existence; despite the fact that knighthood was not yet a closed caste, the concept that only someone who was born of gentle parents was a member of the gentry began to be all-important. In the statutes of Casimir the Great the following appeared: "Generations of the gentry take their origins from their ancestors, whose successors, issuing from a certain line, will always prove their worth."

The privileges of the gentry began to increase slowly. Louis of Hungary, after receiving in 1374 the promise of the Polish throne for his daughter, decided to grant the gentry special favors. This act of the king, the Košice Charter, limited the gentry's obligations toward the country to only one tax, which was not only an economic privilege but also showed favoritism toward the gentry as an estate. This act also guaranteed that no foreigner would be nominated to high office, which gave the gentry the opportunity to participate in governing the country and united their personal interests and their interests as an estate with national patriotic interests.

After the death of Louis in 1382, the gentry together with the magnates decided on the succession and handed the crown to Louis' younger daughter, Jadwiga. In 1385, the gentry played an important role in effecting the union with Lithuania, choosing Jagiello, the Grand Duke of Lithuania, as husband for Jadwiga and accepting the Lithuanian lords and boyars into their own crests. Casimir the Jagiellonian, son of Ladislaus Jagiello, carrying out a policy against the feudal lords, strengthened even more the political and economic position of the gentry, granting the Nieszawa Charter in 1454. This increased the authority of the regional diets, direct vehicles for the will of the gentry, and brought further power to this estate. In the constitution of 1505, the so-called *Nihil Novi* (Nothing new), the king stated the following: "Because the universal laws and public regulations concern not individuals but the nation as a whole, we have decided that it would be appropriate and wise that in the future no new law be adopted without the common consent of the senators and regional deputies." In this way the gentry, as a privileged estate in society, became both the main source of the country's power and the basis of its existence. The kingdom thus grew into a commonwealth (Polish *Rzeczpospolita:* etymologically identical with Latin *Respublica)*, a commonwealth of the gentry.

View of the World

THE CHRISTIAN LIFE

Since the beginning of Christianity in Poland, religious considerations were the basic and prevailing element in the Polish philosophy of life. This was expressed and strengthened in Romanesque architecture, which pointed out the greatness of God and called upon worshippers to pray; in paintings and sculptures, which represented the powers of good and evil fighting over man's soul, visions of paradise, and damnation; in sermons; in the lives of the saints and martyrs; in written accounts of miracles; and finally, in poetry, which, from its inception, expressed the dramatic lot of man imperiled by death and punishments, but also surrounded by the care of Christ and the Holy Virgin.

We have no evidence to testify that this view of the world was influenced by philosophical literature. The Christianization of Poland brought missionary Christianity, which organized religious practices and encouraged people to adopt a new approach to life, which was opposed to pagan tradition. This view of the world was an amalgam of the beliefs encouraged by priests and the injunctions they gave to the worshippers.

It was for this reason that the main characteristic of this view of the world was its concreteness. Christianity was understood, in this way, not as a metaphysical of ontological system; it was a story about God, especially about Christ and the Holy Virgin, a story about miracles, and the lives of the saints. It was in this way that literature and art presented the Christian view of the world.

Written works have not survived, but we know that many tales and legends were in circulation. A larger number of works of art and books survive from the thirteenth century. These are mostly lives of the saints, particularly Polish saints. The essential elements of the Christian life, like courage and generosity, humility and sacrifice, are presented in the Lives of Saint Adalbert and Saint Stanislaus. Polish kings and princes — Przemysł I, Boleslaus the Pious, Henry the Pious, Boleslaus the Bashful, and many others — are described in a way that underlines their generosity toward the church, their virtues of charity and love. The inscription on the tombstone of Boleslaus the Brave in Gniezno Cathedral explains that he was "Christ's soldier" and had "the soul of a dove."

Women were also presented as examples of the Christian ideal. Kinga (Kunegunda), Jadwiga and Salomea embodied such virtues as godliness and atonement, charity and benevolence, generosity and asceticism. Their lives at their courts and in convents, their consideration for the poor and destitute, and their mystical visions were frequently commented upon.

Many religious orders, in particular the Poor Clares and the Franciscans, disseminated stories about the most holy nuns and monks, as well as legends about miracles. In this way, the cult of miracles became widespread throughout the country.

The lives of the saints exemplified the realization of the Christian ideal in real life. Even adaptations of foreign literature, for example, the *Legenda Aurea,* maintained this simple native character.

But in the last analysis, the Christian life was life devoted to God. The Bible presented the creation of the world, original sin, the birth of Christ, his life and death and his teaching. Worshippers were prohibited from reading the Bible; its contents were explained by priests. The Bible, at that time, was not the object of philosophical analysis. It was the story of miraculous, dramatic and moving events.

In the later Middle Ages this aspect of the Christian religion was also presented in *The Przemyśl Meditations* and *The Dominican Meditations,* two great works which illustrated the sacred story by word and picture. Religion was presented in a similar way through the paintings and sculptures of the period: the birth in the stable and the adoration of the shepherds, the life of Christ and the miracles He performed, His sufferings at Golgotha, the Sorrowing Mother of God, the Feast of the Resurrection and the Assumption, the Last Judgment, the condemnation of sinners, the triumph of the virtuous — these were related with the same simplicity in great cathedrals and small churches, in the same way to the poor as to the rich.

Similar subjects were dealt with in poetry. Polish poetry, which appeared in the fifteenth century, lyrically presents Mary and Christ, the humble birth, the cruel death, and the human suffering of the Mother of the crucified Son. On the other hand, this poetry also presented the history of sinful people, who on their deathbeds suddenly realized that throughout their lives they had been generous only to themselves, but avaricious toward God, that they had sold their souls to the Devil. *The Conversation Between the Master and Death* and *The Complaint of the Dying Man* realistically presented examples of the godless lives of the rich and the poor, of clerics and laymen, and of lords and peasants.

The simple Christian view of the world was confined to these oppositions of sinful and religious lives, of various negative and positive patterns. They were the sole sources of emotion and experiences, common to all the people, regardless of their social status, wealth or education.

RADICAL RELIGIOUS MOVEMENTS

As Christianity spread through the country, and religious belief became authentic and fervent, the problem of contradiction between faith and the church as a social institution became a real one. Opposition of various kinds developed toward the secular power of the church, expressed in papal policy and the participation of church officials in national power struggles, the wealth and glamor of bishops' palaces, and the splendor of church services.

In the middle of the thirteenth century, Silesia, Great Poland, and Little Poland were invaded by processions of flagellants, mainly recruited from among the peasants and the poor. These processions reached their greatest intensity in 1261. The second wave of this movement appeared approximately one hundred years later. At the same time, in the middle of the thirteenth century, the Waldenses come to Poland. They called the official church, "the house of lies". They gained considerable influence in Silesia, Little Poland and in Western Pomerania. They were persecuted by the church and punished by the secular power. In Silesia people were burnt at the stake. In Świdnica, fifty people were burned. In 1318 the Pope appointed two inquisitors for Poland and later a special Dominican tribunal which dealt with people suspected of heresy.

The new movement of Beguines and Beghards had a different character. They professed the Franciscan ideals of poverty and love of mankind in everyday affairs, without attacking the church. But soon this movement was radicalized. The idea that "perfect people" are better than the priests or even the saints of the church and that faith should merely depend on a "free spirit" and should not be administered and exploited by the clergy soon won out. At the beginning of the fourteenth century, the Inquisition carried out a major campaign against this movement in Silesia, intending to wipe it out. But despite persecution by the church, the embers of criticism still smoldered. Popular preachers gave sermons concerning the essence of true faith, the social meaning of Christian morality, the corruption of the church, and the immorality of the clergy.

These were, however, isolated efforts. It was not until the Hussite movement that a new flame spread. It enveloped much wider sections of society than any previous heretical movement. In his *Song of Wycliffe,* Master Andrzej Gałka of Dobczyn, a Cracow scholar and master, not only paid homage to the precursor of the Reformation, Wycliffe, and not only repeated all the accusations formulated against the church hierarchy and the Pope, but also put forward a new program of Christian regeneration. It was he who first created the motto of Polish tolerance — to propagate faith not by the sword but by Christ's word. It was also he who fervently supported the rule that faith is a matter for all people and not only for the clergy. He accused the clergy of concealing the truth because, according to him, they were afraid of the truth. These ideas circulated in Poland for a long time and were reborn in the period of the Reformation.

THE IDEAS OF THE SCHOLARS OF CRACOW

The purpose of religious movements, from the flagellants to the Hussites, was the radical regeneration of Christianity, and also, to an ever greater degree, social revolution. The aspirations of a very small, generous and brave group of seekers after Christian truth expressed ideas, and hopes which were not alien to wider sections of society. However, the latter formulated their ideas in a moderate way that did not interfere with either the social order or the church.

In the fifteenth century, particularly the first half, the University of Cracow was the center of a very active intellectual movement, which took upon itself the reconstruction of scholastic philosophy and theology and voiced new important ideas in the area of social morality, constitutional law and international relations.

This program was inaugurated in 1410 by an anonymous commentary to Artistotle's *Politics.* It was later developed and refined by Mateusz of Cracow, Paweł of Worczyn, Stanisław of Skarbimierz, Paweł Włodkowic, Jan of Ludzisko, Benedykt Hesse, Jakub of Paradyż, and many others. Mateusz of Cracow, in his famous work *De Praxi Romanae Curiae,* strongly criticized the practices of the Roman curia; Paweł Włodkowic upheld the right of councils to remove a Pope who "traffics in devotional articles". Mateusz, in his basic philosophic arguments on the meaning of faith and the church, asserted that the totality of worshippers, and not the Pope or the ecclesiastical hierarchy, forms the true body of the church. All Christians, as *ecclesia militans,* are represented by the church and the church council is *ecclesia repreasentans.* The conciliar movement, which had been defended by the Cracow scholars, expressed the belief that faith is both an individual and a social matter. It is a joint possession of all worshippers and does not belong to a church administration which distributes God's forgiveness and mercy according to material profits and earthly interests.

This approach led to very important conclusions in the area of philosophy. It put aside fruitless, abstract reasoning and held that philosophy should help people to organize their individual and social lives. Ethics and especially the branch of ethics which formulates the social responsibilities of people and their happiness, was recognized as much more important than metaphysics and theology. This was the substance of the argument presend by Paweł of Worczyn and Jakub of Paradyz, whose works had a wide audience in Europe.

Paweł Włodkowic drew political conclusions from these arguments, putting forward a theory which opposed the principle that the law need not be respected in dealings with unbelievers.

The views of the Cracow scholars constituted a characteristic interpretation of faith as an authentic experience, of the church as a community of believers, of the responsibilities of the individual as a member of society and as a citizen of the country, of the relations between people of different religions, and of the unjust war and tolerance. These views were indicative of the great maturity of Christian culture in Poland. They were also proof of a very deep and realistic approach to life and of confidence in the power of human intelligence, capable of guiding both individuals and the country.

THE PARTICULAR VALUE OF JUSTICE

In the area of political criticism, justice had a very special place in Poland. In the popular view a good ruler had to be brave and magnanimous, but above all he had to be just. Gallus Anonymus wrote with great approbation of Boleslaus the Brave, as a leader with such characteristics as "justice and magnanimity", who even though "occupied with important issues and surrounded by numerous groups of magnates and knights", always had time to listen to the complaints brought to his royal throne by a "poor beggar or an old country wife". Wincenty Kadłubek repeatedly underscored in his chronicle the particular value of justice through which the king was able to rise above those who were at variance with one another and protect the weak. Casimir the Just was judged positively from this standpoint, and was described as the guardian and protector of the people's rights. On the other hand, Boleslaus the Bold and Mieszko II were condemned for their conceit and lawlessness.

Other chroniclers used similar means of judging not only kings but also the feudal lords, especially those who held influential positions. Contemporary poetry also underlined the significance of justice.

At the beginning of the fifteenth century, the problem of justice was a pervasive one among the Cracow intellectuals. Jan of Ludzisko, greeting Casimir the Jagiellonian at the University, gave a speech in which he referred to justice in the country, and pointed to the plight of the peasantry. He asked the king to "overthrow hypocrisy which became widespread and was so harmful to the Kingdom", "destroy the servitude of the peasants, and restore freedom to the Christian people, since nature made all men equal".

Stanisław of Skarbimierz not only considered the problem of unjust wars, but also analyzed in detail, in his *Dissertation on the State,* the conditions necessary for justice to reign in the state. The law should be the same for all and available to everyone. Only an increase in equality could assure the development of the state. Only in this way would it be possible to include everyone in the process of reaching common goals.

All these considerations confirmed that the problem of social and state organization was becoming increasingly important. The rise of Christianity in Poland over the centuries was expressed more in the conviction of the importance of this practical and social problem than in the intensity of theological arguments. The basic question was how to live, and especially, how to live together. These questions foreshadowed the future, when the "reform of the Commonwealth" would become the predominant theme of meditation and action.

Consideration of justice did not only involve the construction of ideal models or theoretical analyses of the country's organization and the principles of individual and social morality, but was also frequently connected with direct and critical observation of reality. *The Conversation Between the Master and Death,* from the second half of the fifteenth century, one of the first Polish poetic works, presents the *danse macabre* as satirical entertainment, showing the threat of punishment for all who stray from the norms of justice and honesty.

The Arts

THE CULTURE OF THE WRITTEN LANGUAGE

The culture of pagan Poland was a specific aspect of everyday life, maintained through customs and rites, in the oral tradition, and the festivities of people inhabiting a common territory. Christianity introduced a culture whose form and language were foreign: thus, to be assimilated, these new elements had to be introduced through education and the practical testing of educational precepts. In pagan Poland there was no separate group of priests, although sacrifices were offered to the gods. Christianity, from the very beginning, introduced a differentiation between the clergy and the general mass of believers, a differentiation based, to a great degree, on special education, contrasting the "clergy" with "laymen", i.e. those who were educated with those who were uneducated.

The culture of pagan Poland was a common and existential culture; the Christian culture introduced to Poland was élite and scholastic. That is why the conflict between the two types of culture was reflected both in philosophy and the accepted values, and in the content and the form of expression. Verbal expression was very limited. Latin was, of course, a foreign and difficult language of which only a few individuals had full command. Parchment was very expensive and the immense complexity of the craft of writing meant that only specialists were able to utilize this form. Beautiful manuscripts, much admired today, had few readers. Some of these manuscripts cost as much as several villages. They were the property of monasteries, princes, and bishops. To the masses they were inaccessible, neither material nor tools of cultural life.

The new culture achieved its range of influence in society through different means, that is, through visual forms. The Middle Ages appealed to the visual sense and the imagination because the written word was not yet fully recognized and because pictorial reality was more directly available to the people than was a verbal and abstract education.

The new cultural life of Poland began within the framework of churches, monasteries and castles. These were clear signs of a new order, including the monumental and ceremonious grandeur of temples, the unusual colorfulness of liturgical rites, and the elevated character of mass by candlelight with organ music and the ringing of bells. These signs were also discernible in the splendor of a prince's court and the courts of the lords which dazzled the eye with their magnificence, and the wealth of games, pageants, knights' tournaments, and hunts. The events of everyday life also had a pictorial character at markets and fairs, which always took place on the same day as in ancient times, and when wandering troupes of clowns and jugglers appeared. There were also monks and friars and perhaps occasionally groups of flagellants marching through the countryside.

This direct visual form of culture blended in with the still existing tradition of pagan customs and rites much more readily than did Latin culture. Although the Christian liturgical year did not correspond with the pagan calendar of ceremonies dictated by the rhythms of nature — such as the melting away of winter snow, the welcoming of spring, the equinox, or the harvest-time holiday — it was not entirely in opposition. It enriched the traditional imagery by introducing a new pictorial world — angels and devils — and a new concept of human fate presented in the extraordinary stories from the life of Christ and the saints.

Churches, because of their interior decoration, became an element which shaped the collective and individual imagination. Entering a church meant taking a step into a different world, one which allowed the senses to experience new, different sensations and the imagination to construct new forms. Thus painting and sculpture were especially close to the people and became a source of individual and collective experience. Paintings turned into objects of adoration and prayers; works of art occasionally acquired a specific local character. These images influenced the polychrome paintings and sculptures of the late Middle Ages, especially the figures of Christ and the Virgin Mary.

Slowly the written language gained the social significance which the visual language had already achieved. There was a long and close relationship between both these forms of expression and communication. Testifying to this relationship are the numerous medieval manuscripts where visual depiction and verbal description were complementary. Religious texts for meditation had such a twofold character. *The Dominican Meditations* is the most magnificent, though very late — dating from the beginning of the sixteenth century — example of this creative marriage. The events of Holy Week are depicted by word and picture on 117 pieces of parchment. The left side carries the text; the right is decorated with a miniature, which enriches and visually develops the events which have been related.

During this entire period the scope for utilization of the written language was enlarged. In the beginning the written word was only used to record events that were especially important and worthy of remembrance — *littera sacra, littera perhennis* — and even these very briefly. But from the middle of the twelfth century writing gained a new function, in the chanceries of both secular and clerical officials, as well as for intellectual discussions and exchange of information. A period of epistolographic and oratorical art was inaugurated. In addition to the school program, consisting of grammar, dialectic and rhetoric, a greater mastery of language skills was achieved, of which the beautiful style of Kadłubek is an excellent example.

Language as a means of individual and personal expression was the next stage in the development of culture. The establishment of the University in Cracow in 1364 was the beginning of a dynamic period of development for spoken and written Latin. Latin was utilized in university lectures and at ceremonies; several hundred speeches from the fifteenth century have been preserved. It was also used by the student community, and although in everyday life they spoke their native language, Latin became a second language, capable of expressing emotional and intellectual experiences. An example of this can be found in an anonymous letter written by a student, *Epistola ad Dominicellam*. This is an enchanting letter to his beloved, praising her beauty and declaring his love: *te amavi, te laudavi, te inspexi, te dilexi.*

From the short notes in the early medieval annals, dealing with important events, for example the arrival of Dąbrówka or the bapitism of Mieszko, to the letter of the Cracow student, one can sense the long evolution of the Latin language as a tool and material in the nation's cultural life.

The native language took a different and rather later course of development. While Latin was a foreign language used by the church and the royal chancery, the native language was for everyday speech. Therefore, its development and assimilation into the intellectual and artistic life of the nation followed a different course. While Latin expanded its social range through the educational system, especially university education, because it satisfied and developed intellectual needs and transmitted literary texts, the native language served the emotional and imaginative needs of the people. The native tongue did not deal in philosophical treatises or scientific dissertations but it was used in religious and patriotic songs, like *Bogurodzica* (Mother of God), texts for reflection and meditation which described wonderful miracles, as in *The Dominican Meditations* and *The Przemyśl Meditations*, translations of the Bible, especially the Book of Psalms, and in reports on local and national political events.

The language slowly matured to the point where it was used not only as a medium for passing on information but also as a means of expression which developed an emotional and imaginative richness of its own. Fifteenth century love prose and poetry, though unfortunately preserved only in fragments, provide evidence for this claim. Perhaps the same students who wrote to their beloved in Latin also wrote to them in their native language. It is significant that it is in their native language that they received answers to such declarations: "Love has something about it that seldom or never comes in joy; it is always in sorrow or in longing or in unbearable heart-ache that it lives."

Thus, the social functions of the language were manifold. Serving various ends, the language became richer, more flexible and imaginative, and its value went beyond merely presenting information. It became both the material and a tool for artistic culture.

THE ROMANESQUE STYLE

While the social range of the written word extended, despite some progress, only over a limited area of Poland in the Middle Ages, art, especially architecture, had from the beginning a much greater possibility of developing. Architecture became a visible sign of human greatness — both when it served the state and when it served God.

In the tenth century and in the first half of the eleventh, new structures were raised in stone in a pre-Romanesque style. Such churches were constructed either on a circular plan with apses or on a square plan, for example the Wawel Cathedral in Cracow, at Ostrów Lednicki, Gniezno, Przemyśl, and a few other stronghold towns. The Benedictine buildings, for example at Trzemeszno, were similar. Wars and fires destroyed the first material evidence of the new faith and the new human experiences.

From the middle of the eleventh century when new religious and secular buildings were being built upon the ruins, the Romanesque style began to be used. Although the Romanesque style was imported, it was able to express Polish needs and experiences chiefly because it was the style used to build the churches and castles which laid down new lines for Polish history during this period. Gniezno and Cracow were both centers for the Christianizing of Poland and centers of the secular kingdom. The Romanesque churches and secular buildings became the cradle of the nation and the state. The Gniezno and Wawel Cathedrals — reconstructed and expanded on the pre-Romanesque ruins — assumed the role of monuments of national history in the Romanesque style. Their national and symbolic significance was for centuries associated with this style which dominated the country, from Szczecin and Wolin down to Strzelno, Płock, Łęczyca, Czerwińsk and Wiślica, Wrocław and Cracow. The magnificent Gniezno Doors, dating from 1170, presented in bronze the life and death of Saint Adalbert; they are the best example of how the Romanesque style could express and commemorate important events in Polish history, and strengthen the greatness of the nation; they astounded foreigners, and were renowned among the country's inhabitants.

The Benedictine monks, who began arriving in Poland in the tenth century, built their abbeys at Tyniec, Mogilno, and Płock. Numerous churches of stone were also constructed. Many churches were founded by lords, for example Sieciech, who, at the end of the eleventh century, built St. Andrew's Church for the Benedictine monks in Cracow. But the Silesian lord Piotr Włostowic of the Łabędź-Dunin family surpassed them all; according to legend, in the first half of the twelfth century he founded seventy-seven churches.

The mid-twelfth century saw a blossoming of the fine arts. The interior decoration of churches and residences became more elaborate; the portals were exquisitely carved, as were the friezes, fonts, and keystones. This new image of clerical and secular power became an important element in the shaping of a common culture.

Such was the social role of Romanesque art — the art of great churches, abbeys and cathedrals built throughout the country. Many of these were destroyed by war; some, centuries later, were discovered in ruins; only a few have been preserved. The most important were: the St. Leonard Crypt in the Wawel Cathedral; the reconstructed cathedrals in Poznań and Gniezno; the churches in Czerwińsk, Inowłódz, and Strzelno; and the collegiate church at Kruszwica on Lake Gopło. Of special artistic value was the collegiate church at Tum near Łęczyca, built in the mid-twelfth century.

In the field of Romanesque architecture mention should be made of the Cistercian Order. The Cistercians came to Poland in the middle of the twelfth century; their monasteries and churches were much richer than the architecture of the early Romanesque period. The buildings at Jędrzejów and Sulejów and especially at Wąchock, are some of the most beautiful monuments of Romanesque architecture. During the thirteenth century the Dominicans competed with the Cistercians. The former were active mainly in Cracow and Wrocław, and also in Sandomierz where they built the beautifully embellished St. James' Church. These sacred Romanesque buildings also shaped the religious imagination of the people living outside the major communities, as evidenced by the village church in Kościelec near Proszowice, built in the middle of the thirteenth century.

GOTHIC ART

The Gothic art which sprang to life in Poland in the middle of the thirteenth century was of a different character. It could be seen in both sacral and secular architecture. The great churches in Toruń, Wrocław, Cracow, Frombork and Orneta were Gothic, as were the townhalls in Wrocław, Gdańsk, Toruń, and in many other Polish cities. Some of the churches stood as monuments to Poland's greatness and to the glory of its princes, as, for example, the new Wawel Cathedral or the Church of the Holy Cross in Wrocław, the latter founded by Henry IV, who was later commemorated with a magnificent tomb. The chapel of Prince Boleslaus of Legnica in Lubiąż is another example of the Gothic style.

Although during this period, too, numerous foreign artists and craftsmen came to Poland, the local particularism and the rise in the fourteenth and fifteenth centuries of the affluence and cultural aspirations of the burghers and middling knightly class favored the development of native art. One can trace a very distinct architectural design present throughout Poland during the reign of Casimir the Great. Castles, townhalls, granaries, and churches — which were also to be used for secular purposes — achieved a unified national style.

The development of Gothic art extended beyond architecture. In the severe Romanesque world, a search for new content and new forms of expression began in the middle of the thirteenth century. This process was especially characteristic of the fourteenth and fifteenth centuries. In the religious sphere, the need for a more individualized and personal piety was felt. This need was satisfied by various types of prayer-books and religious songs, which offered considerable choice, depending on the mood of the moment. There was also the need to connect religious meditation with a more vivid experience of the history of holy events. One example of this genre is *The Przemyśl Meditations,* an apocryphal story in prose about the life of Mary and Jesus, which is in part a collection of information and in part a picturesquely moving tale.

Painting and sculpture, which portrayed the religious world as one close to man, expressed and fulfilled these needs. For this reason, Gothic art blended well with Polish life, in a way different from that of Romanesque art. While Romanesque art expressed the great traditions of the state and its historical prospects, Gothic art was connected with the varied and common existence of society, on the level of both the royal court and of the various estates. In religious paintings the figures of benefactors appeared; the beauty of the tombs erected in the churches testified to the virtues of the local clergy and knights. In religious sculpture and painting, themes taken from the simple tales of the life of Christ and His Mother began to dominate — themes which were much closer to the lives and experiences of the people than to eschatological concepts of theology.

The fifteenth century marked the development of humanistic art, filled with tender lyricism. Less often one found great scenes portraying God, the Last Judgment, God the Judge, and God meting out punishment. More often the "human" interpretation of religion appeared. Churches built on knights' estates, or in small towns, and villages were full of this kind of human art, an art which although native in origin was also religious and universal.

This new art was at its best when it presented figures from the Bible endowed with "human" feelings. It showed Christ and the Virgin Mary in different situations, in this way creating certain types which were now to be ingrained in the human consciousness and imagination for centuries, as, for example, Christ in Sorrow, the Madonna with Child, or the Sorrowing Madonna.

This new art, which in many ways became a part of the people, often reached a high artistic level. It ceased to be merely an "illustration" of the holy story and a parable. Beauty itself became of great value in the artistic vision of the world. It was rightfully called an era of "the beautiful style". Numerous figures of Beautiful Madonnas (from Krużlowa, from the Carmelite church in Cracow, from Kazimierz, Czempion and Toruń), sculpted Pietàs (like the Pietà in Wągrowiec), various crucifixes and figures of Christ in Agony (like that in the parish church in Poznań) were created in this new style. A peculiar realism emerged from this art, a realism of human fate hidden in the fate of God on earth (for example, in the Lamentation from Chomranice dating from the mid-fifteenth century).

The high point of achievement of fifteenth century sculpture was Wit Stwosz's (Veit Stoss) altarpiece in St. Mary's Church in Cracow, one of the most magnificent Gothic altarpieces in all Europe. It tells a lyrical and dramatic tale about the lives of Mary and Christ, brought into the world of humanity, full of worldly and psychological diversity, of hope and resignation, love and hypocrisy, cruelty and emotion. The greatness of Wit Stwosz as an artist was unique; the spirit of his art was a reflection of the ideological and artistic atmosphere which was emerging in Poland at the time.

In many works of fifteenth century art a different kind of realism was discernible. It emerged as a result of the artist's close connections with the community in the village or in the town. It was reflected in the use of local scenery and, above all, in an individual mode of expression, whether coarse and macabre, or lyrical and sentimental.

What better way to visualize the road of this evolution which took place in religious expression in medieval Poland, than to compare the majestic, historical and religious portrayals on the Gniezno Doors with the sixteenth century wall paintings in the church in Dębno in the sub-Carpathian region, which depict robbers from the Tatra Mountains, or the portrayal of folk musicians in the church in Grębień?

This movement toward reality and, at the same time, the sensitivity toward human experience, so characteristic of fifteenth century art, can also be seen in literature.

While the scanty information recorded in the annals satisfied the needs of the people during the tenth to the twelfth centuries, later a more elaborate and detailed historical account was needed to satisfy human interest in the world. Thus, numerous chronicles were written during this period in various regions, for example in Great Poland and Silesia, and also by various religious chapters and orders, as, for example, the famous *Księga Henrykowska (Henryków Book)* from Silesia. Information on current and historical events was also supplied by poetry, which described various events, such as, for example, the Tartar raids, the death of Zawisza the Black, the killing of Tęczyński, and the revolt of the Cracow administrator Albert.

Breaking away from traditional models and patterns, poetry individualized events and experiences. Abandoning a moralizing manner, the poets attempted to evoke feelings and emotions. In searching for the meaningful and emotional, they did not confine themselves to simple information.

Religious poems were slowly losing their crude style and awkwardness of prosaic lectures on sins, miracles and the godly life. They gained a new tone, drawing on unusual metaphors, boldly reaching into new depths of expression. The presentation of religious themes was meant to evoke emotions; for this reason the divine was linked with human experience. Religious poems were no longer about God but about man experiencing the fate of God.

Similar changes were noted in love poetry. *Epistola ad Dominicellam* was a direct and personal expression of feelings, a poem about the absorbing power of love, a love full of joy and grief, the only one on this earth. The whole earth was Cracow, and the lady's name was Helen. The author adored her and paid her homage.

Toward the end of the Middle Ages, art often became a link between the old and the new life-styles. The three volume *Gradual of John Albert,* dating from the beginning of the sixteenth century, and the *Pontifical of Erazm*

Ciołek, presenting the splendor of liturgical rites, the sublimity of the mass and the grandeur of royal coronations, are examples of such art. In this art, objective religious themes blend in with personal human experience and the ecclesiastical intertwines with the secular. The traditional life-style began to acquire the characteristic of Renaissance richness and cheerfulness. The renowned *Behem Codex* can also be placed on the borderline between the Middle Ages and the Renaissance.

Culture in Society

THE SPREAD OF CHRISTIANITY

Recalling the campaign of the first Polish Bishop, Jordan, who, in 968, began the Christianization of Poland, Thietmar observed that "it required of him quite an effort". Indeed missionary activity often met great obstacles. Although the positive requirements of the new religion were not difficult to fulfill, the bans it formulated were directed against century-old concepts and customs. The people had to reject gods which were both familiar and close to them, to destroy their statues and the holy groves in which they lived. They were not allowed to offer sacrifices nor pray to the gods for protection; they were not permitted to burn the bodies of the dead nor to hold traditional funeral ceremonies. The new religion was "alien", not only because it came from the outside but also because it was preached by foreigners and the language used in the religious ceremonies was completely incomprehensible. The new religion opposed traditional supernatural beliefs; it did not reach into the everyday world of work in the woods and fields.

However, it was not only the will of the rulers, effected by means of harsh punishment, that fostered the progress of Christianization. This new religion impressed people with its greatness and splendor. The churches that Mieszko and his successors ordered to be built were constructed of stone. Up to that time, such buildings were unknown in Poland. The magnificent masses conducted in these new churches were also something novel. The power of the Church and the clergy seemed to some to insure to a greater extent the benevolence of supernatural forces than did the old sensualistic rites. The abstract and spiritual contents of the new religion were difficult to understand, but perhaps for this reason it was necessary for man to humble himself before it.

Yet for a long time the fate of Poland's Christianization process remained in doubt. In the first half of the eleventh century popular uprisings in Hungary and Rus defended the old faith. This was also true in Poland. Following the death of Boleslaus the Brave in 1025, and especially after the death of Mieszko II in 1034, the cause of Christianization in Poland began to lose ground. Popular revolts, incited by different causes, manifested the pagan sympathies of the people; churches were destroyed and priests were killed. The new groundwork for the reconstruction of the nation's Christianization was created only in the second half of the eleventh century during the rule of Casimir the Restorer, who was brought up in a monastery and well understood the character of missionary work. The transfer of the capital to Cracow was also of significance.

The old churches were reconstructed and new ones were erected. An estimated 130 sacral historic buildings date from this period. A wide network of churches gradually covered the whole country. As pagan traditions subsided, Christian ceremonies were transformed into a new form of participation in a distant, partly foreign and yet native culture.

The church organization was expanding, reaching everywhere and to everyone. Its basic unit was the parish. The eleventh and twelfth centuries witnessed the formation of approximately 1,000 parishes; 2,000 parishes were established in the thirteenth century, and 3,000 in the fourteenth and fifteenth centuries. These figures indicate that the network of parishes was extremely dense. In Silesia, an average parish area amounted to 26 square kilometers, in Little Poland and Great Poland up to 60 square kilometers, and in the eastern territories to over 100 square kilometers. The parish, though sometimes embracing a vast area, played an important role in the life of the local population. Religious discipline, which was then more severe than in later times, required frequent participation in the services and other religious ceremonies. The parish church gradually became the center of social life, of common religious experiences, artistic activity and of artistic emotions of all kinds. Churches were often built in places that had been considered holy sites in pagan times; this was a conscious reference to old traditions and an attempt to fulfill the needs of the people in a new way. As late as in the fourteenth century, Slav nocturnal rites to celebrate the spring were still being held around the monastery on Łysiec Hill. By this time, however, they were no longer a threat to the new religion. Pagan ceremonies in honor of the dead also survived and were still practiced up to the age of Romanticism, but they too could not endanger the well-grounded position of Christianity. They added a more local, popular color to it. The church officially opposed these rites, but the clergy — even the bishops — who had come from that community, were more tolerant. Perhaps they too believed in this moderate form of the Christian faith, adapted to specific conditions, and viewed unfavorably both strict asceticism and Roman universalism.

Such was the beginning of the history of the church in Poland and of the Christian religion which, as Gallus Anonymus perspicaciously noted, manifested "a certain simplicity of faith". From then on it was to last through later centuries in which Polish religiosity reached neither the heights of devotion nor the dramatic ardor of faith; yet it was a part of people's everyday life, giving them comfort through their personal and national vicissitudes.

The church network was complemented by monasteries. At the beginning of the eleventh century, small abbeys, like those in Łęczyca, Trzemeszno and Międzychód, were built. Towards the end of this century, wealthy Benedic-tine monasteries were established at Tyniec near Cracow and at Mogilno. In the early twelfth century, the Canons Regular and the Norbertines built their monasteries and in the mid-twelfth century, the first Cistercian monasteries were established. Numerous feudal lords founded monasteries, like, for example, the one in Wrocław and on Sobótka Hill endowed by Piotr Włostowic.

In the twelfth century only several dozen monasteries were built. Some 150 monasteries were built in the thirteenth century, and about 130 in the fourteenth and fifteenth centuries. A considerable number of these monasteries belonged to the mendicant orders — Dominicans, Franciscans, Augustinian eremites and Carmelites — which established particularly close contacts with the local population who contributed alms for their upkeep. In return, the monks offered religious services in the widest meaning of the phrase. Often the services meant "brotherly help", embracing medical treatment or helping out in work, information about the world or practical advice helpful in everyday life. In general, however, the activity of these orders represented an example of the religious life, ascetic and fairly "human", a life shaped by the vision of an afterlife, and also by unstinting, courageous participation in the everyday, earthly interests and concerns of lay people.

A different role was played by the strict, contemplative orders, the Benedictines in particular. The range of their relations with the local population was not so broad, but having considerable funds, their monasteries maintained a relatively high intellectual and artistic level, especially due to their close contacts with foreign countries. The participation of these monasteries in the life of the Polish nation constantly grew, due to their increasing pastoral activity linked with the patriotic experiences of the population. An example of this is *The Life of Saint Stanislaus*, prepared by the Dominican Wincenty of Kielce. In his verse devoted to Saint Stanislaus, the author beseached him to "send the light of faith upon us."

Finally, a higher level of propagation of the new Christian culture was provided by the arch-episcopal and episcopal curias. Not only did they execute tasks in the sphere of church administration, conduct church policy and interfere in the area of state policy, but they also played an important role as intellectual centers. The rich library collection of the Cracow Cathedral as well as those of other sees, attest to this fact. In the thirteenth century, the practice of legacies to libraries became widespread and these often contained richly illuminated manuscripts. Numerous centers set up scriptoria which enriched their library collections and sometimes also received orders from the courts.

It is estimated that at the beginning of the sixteenth century some 20,000 people worked for various church and monastic institutions which, considering Poland's estimated population of six million, was quite a significant figure. Those employed were not evenly distributed throughout the country. At the beginning of the sixteenth century Cracow and Wrocław each had between 800 and 1,000 clergymen which constituted a relatively high percentage of the population.

GENERAL EDUCATION
AND THE UNIVERSITY OF CRACOW

Education was linked with the church. Its beginning in Poland dates back to the eleventh century. The rule of Ladislaus Herman saw the activity of Otto, later bishop of Bamberg, who probably headed the cathedral school in Gniezno and also the one in Cracow. We know that midway through the twelfth century a school was founded in Płock. At first, these schools were designed to educate clergymen. It was due to these schools that Poland boasted of at least a basic preparation for the senior clergy. Further education was probably gained abroad. Because of this, the Gniezno archbishop, as well as the bishops of Cracow and Poznań, were Poles.

The thirteenth century witnessed the establishment of parish schools. They had a modest curriculum, and, in principle, were to serve everyone, not only those planning to take holy orders. Although providing merely an elementary education, they prepared students to participate in cultural activities, by including writing and rhetoric among the subjects taught. The traditional medieval *trivium* — grammar, logic and rhetoric — made it possible, at least in some better schools, to develop education and shape intellectual culture, especially skills in reasoning and expression. This new range of parish education was expanded in the fourteenth and fifteenth centuries. Since the parish network embraced the whole country, and since 90 percent of the parishes ran schools on their territories, the idea of a "universal" education was implemented quite effectively. This should not be measured by today's standards but by those of the period.

In this feudal society the spheres of activity were precisely laid down for the various estates; the need for education depended on the social function which the members of a particular estate performed. The system of parochial schools insured an education for those on the lower rungs of the social ladder, but, at the same time, it offered possibilities for social advancement across class boundaries which at that time were still not strictly established.

The changing conditions of life in the thirteenth century led to higher educational aspirations, which in many cases provided a guarantee of a personal social advancement. This was the mechanism behind the establishment of higher-level schools — cathedral schools, which were to teach the *quadrivium,* consisting of music, arithmetic, geometry and astronomy.

In the meantime, the development of the state administration created a demand for officials both for the royal chancery in the capital and for town chanceries. The transformation taking place in agriculture also required educated people who would be able to manage the vast church and lay estates, as well as handle the post of village administrators.

The towns also needed educated people. The development of crafts and town councils required people who were appropriately prepared for those tasks. Thus there was growing interest in the school system in the towns. Although the system still remained under the church organization, schools were slowly becoming "town" schools, in the sense that the town supervised equipment, selection of teachers, and even changes in the school curriculum, as, for example in Legnica in 1309. Similar schools were also established in Cracow and Wrocław.

Under these circumstances, the efforts of Casimir the Great to establish a school on the highest level can well be understood. The establishment of the University in Cracow in 1364 opened up new vistas in the history of Polish intellectual culture. The University, especially after its revival in 1400, became an academy — an institution of education and for the promotion of learning, a great center which was to prepare people for public life.

Franciszek of Brzeg, professor at Cracow University in the years 1409—32, said that those who were "uneducated laymen and yokels" could gain the light of truth through the academy and thus become more useful to the country. Indeed, while the establishment and reconstruction of the University attested to the wise policy of the Polish kings, the popularity of the academy throughout the entire Polish nation was proof of the increasing intellectual aspirations of various regions of the country and various social groups and classes.

Over 3,000 students enrolled at the University in the first quarter of the fifteenth century, more than 3,500 in the second quarter, more than 5,000 in the third quarter, and about 6,500 in the last quarter. Both the increase and the total number of students — almost 18,000 — are significant. In addition, the territorial range of the University was quite remarkable. Obviously, most of the students came from Cracow (759). But in the fifteenth century, there were 386 students from Wrocław, 162 from Nysa, 160 from Poznań, 116 from Kościan, and 112 from Gdańsk. Less than a hundred, but more than fifty, students came from other Polish towns, like Głogów, Lvov, Legnica, Kalisz, Toruń, Brzeg, Vilna, Warsaw, Olkusz, Elbląg, Opole, Bochnia, Sandomierz, Nowy Sącz, Wieliczka, and Szamotuły. Students from these towns, however, constituted only 5.5 percent of the total enrollment. The rest of the students — except for the foreigners — came from small Polish towns (more than 200) as well as from rural areas. It is probable that approximately half of the students came from these rural areas.

These figures indicate how vast the territorial range of the University's activity was and how widespread were social aspirations in regard to education. Taking into account the fact that the largest cities in those times — Cracow and Wrocław — had no more than 15,000 inhabitants each, that the structure of society limited access to education and that the great majority of occupational groups had little need of an education, much less a university education, it becomes apparent that the figures quoted here are very high.

The extent of travel abroad in search of education also testifies to the society's educational aspirations. Relatively rare in the thirteenth century, this grew rapidly in the fourteenth century. An overwhelming majority of students headed for the university in Prague. In the fifteenth century the number increased. More and more frequently they began to choose Italian universities. The majority of those studying abroad were sons of the lords and gentry; there were also students with an urban patrician background or, in some cases, with a peasant family background.

Studying abroad was, of course, rather costly and required considerable sums of money. That there were many rich people who could afford these expenditures is not so significant as the fact that they wanted to spend their money for educational purposes. And it is more significant still that quite often those better-off financed study for the poorer, thus becoming patrons to those who could not afford an education.

At the same time, the fifteenth century witnessed an increase in study trips organized by monastic orders, the Dominicans in particular. Annually they sent hundreds of monks to Rome, Paris, and Cologne. Many repeated the trips several times. The practice was similar in other orders. Even when limited to theology, these educational trips testified to the efforts of placing missionary work upon a higher intellectual level and were an expression of the necessity for keeping pace with the growing intellectual demands of society and its general culture. In addition, lay people also followed these same roads which led to the centers of medieval civilization.

CULTURAL CENTERS IN SOCIETY

The church, monastery and school marked only one current of cultural activity. Another current was set by life itself. From the very beginning of Poland's statehood, the ruling class provided a cultural focal point. The ruling circles organized the country by setting up a system of stronghold towns which served as points of support for a prince or a king. These fortified settlements which were governed by castellans and were erected both as strongholds and as trade centers, were also inhabited by craftsmen. As a rule, a stronghold town had a church and sometimes a monastery. The size and facilities of stronghold towns varied; the range of their administrative functions also differed. The largest stronghold towns, like Cracow, Wrocław, Gniezno, and Kruszwica, had become large urban centers as early as the twelfth century.

The stronghold towns constituted centers of power, and their life-styles became models for wide circles of society. It is estimated that prior to the disintegration caused by feudal particularism, there were 150 senior posts in Poland's state and church administration. Some of these high officials gained greater importance and held larger pieces of property than did others. The most influential families were already distinguishable at that time.

While the administrative, trading, military and ecclesiastical significance of the towns was constantly growing, they were simultaneously becoming centers of culture; they promoted novelties in building construction, technology, soil cultivation and handicrafts. They also propagated new forms of life and new forms of missionary work. At the beginning of the tenth century the first stone buildings were constructed in the stronghold towns. Churches and royal residences were the first structures made of stone. They were erected by Boleslaus the Brave, for example at Ostrów Lednicki, and later, by his successors. In the area of fortifications, the wooden and wood-earth defenses were supplemented by stone structures. In the thirteenth century stone building was already widespread. Construction work required numerous, specialized craftsmen.

The royal court was gaining an ever greater importance in the area of culture. The education of the Piasts and Jagiellonians varied greatly: Mieszko II was famous in Europe, due to his education which enabled him, according to Matilda of Lorraine, to praise God not only in his native tongue but also in Latin and Greek; on the other hand, Casimir the Jagiellonian was not very sure how to write. Yet the very functions of the royal court required educated people. The royal chancery had not only to prepare official documents, but had to assess the political situation in Europe, to be aware of dynastic conflicts, especially in the neighboring countries, and had to be knowledgeable about the current state of disputes and alliances between the Papacy and the Empire. Relations of various kinds were important. Official envoys and unofficial informers had to be received and sent abroad. The Polish missions which were sent to Rome, to the Church councils, to various capitals and to the Emperor's court, gained quite a reputation, astonishing foreigners with their refined manners and education. They effectively represented the great kingdom and its just cause in the international forum which was to resolve all conflicts.

The royal court since the very beginning had been a center of instruction in the spirit of native customs. It is difficult to reconstruct that atmosphere, but it is amply reflected in a contemporary story about the Hungarian King Laszló I (Saint Ladislaus), who, having spent his youth at the court of Casimir the Restorer, "became, to some extent, a Pole in regard to customs and life-style". Court education was followed by knightly service in which the sons of the lords became acquainted with both martial arts and public service. The ancient ceremonies of knighting remained alive for a long time, testifying to the social importance of that kind of education. The introduction and consolidation of coats-of-arms became an important element of family integration, in which tradition and honor had the greatest educational significance.

A new trend in the governing of the country and the shaping of its material and spiritual profile was begun in the fourteenth century by Casimir the Great. He created an extensive network of castles, developed municipal facilities, and founded churches which were to be used not only for religious functions, but also to house court sessions and diets. These "royal-state" buildings set an example for the activity of the lords and the clergy. Wealthy knights took part in these undertakings. Churches were founded on the property of numerous knights and these became both centers of religious worship and shrines for family relics. Votive paintings and sculptures began to appear more frequently, as well as sarcophagi of knightly ancestors. These social changes were also reflected in contemporary poetry.

In the fifteenth century the area of culture witnessed

increased burgher class influence. The significance of the burghers in the large cities had already been discerned some time before, but during this century, the small towns also became more animated. The medieval town had various public buildings, the most prominent being the town-hall, usually with a high tower — a symbol of municipal independence. This period marked the construction of huge townhalls in Toruń, Gdańsk, Malbork, Wrocław, Cracow, and Orneta. Equally magnificent were the great houses of the merchants' associations in Gdańsk, Elbląg and Toruń. They were richly ornamented, manifesting the significance and role of the burghers.

The most important structures in medieval cities were fortifications. Such systems began to appear as early as the thirteenth century and continued up to the fourteenth and fifteenth centuries. Huge parish churches, some of them with as many as forty altars, were also constructed. They were sometimes funded by contributions from the townspeople, or endowed by mighty patricians and guilds, and were the pride of the city. Wit Stwosz's altarpiece, funded not only by the urban patricians but also by the populace, was an especially telling expression of the common need to combine religious worship with the beauty of art, presenting man through the perspective of the present and the afterlife. Under these circumstances, large groups of specialized craftsmen found permanent employment on building sites in towns. There was an increasing demand for publishers, wood-carvers, gold-smiths, stone-cutters, carpenters, sculptors, and masons.

Smaller towns too were changing their appearance; here also there were new, ever more magnificent buildings. Kościan, Kalisz, Nowy Sącz, Olkusz, and Tarnów were becoming centers of artistic crafts, which directly served the needs of the town and its inhabitants who wanted to match the larger cities — sometimes ordering replicas of famous altarpieces or paintings. Urban craftsmen, especially from smaller towns, also constructed castles, manor-houses, and richly embellished family chapels, at the request of knights living far from the great cities.

Other bodies that disseminated culture — to an ever greater degree as the economy developed — were the guilds. They constituted important links between craft and technical progress in the cities, as well as being training centers for young people. The guilds were the oldest institutions which combined production with education. This task was not an easy one; the numerous statutes which regulated the activity of the guilds are eloquent testimony to the conflicts between masters and journeymen, between workshops and their customers, as well as between the workshops of various trades. The rules were extremely precise. They regulated everyday life and civic morality: thus, they did not allow journeymen to carry a sword or a knife, except a bread knife; they required the master personally to take his journeymen to bathe; and they warned against making "malicious remarks" at gatherings or "holding meetings were they spoke against the country or against the city".

Despite these conflicts, the guilds conducted a highly complex activity, requiring both skills and knowledge — sometimes guarded jealously — as well as special talents.

This stress on solid work created a specific educational atmosphere, which helped shape the younger generation. In many areas the production of crafts exceeded direct consumer demand and, while preserving their utilitarian character, they took on artistic forms. Gallus Anonymus, when describing the reception accorded the Emperor Otto by Boleslaus the Brave, wrote with admiration of the "golden and silver vessels and utensils", which were changed every day, of the fabrics and tablecloths, as well as of the "decorations hitherto unseen". In later centuries the work of guilds gained ever increasing significance; the objects that they produced, despite their multifarious links with foreign crafts, displayed genuine Polish features. The best workshops enjoyed considerable renown and the royal court, as well as the courts of the lords, competed for their artistc products. The value of such high-quality artistic work gained ever wider recognition, which was reflected in the paintings of the period, showing the craftsmen's work as a model for a man's life.

IN THE SERVICE OF GOD AND COUNTRY

A significant characteristic of the culture of Polish society in the Middle Ages was the connection between religious and patriotic convictions, which was shaped both by the Church, and by secular rulers and the gentry.

Since ancient times the ruling group was interested in everything which maintained and strengthened its significance and splendor and which reflected the greatness and power of the country. The task of extolling the king and the country was entrusted to royal chroniclers. The greatness of Boleslaus Wrymouth's reign was recorded by Gallus Anonymus; Wincenty Kadłubek in his chronicle took into account remarks of Casimir the Just concerning the history of Poland and of the dynasty; Janko of Czarnków praised the fame of Casimir the Great. Lords, knights, their descendants and their fellow-men wished that the significance of their dynasties could be put down on paper. The biography of Piotr Włostowic was recorded in *Carmen Mauri*. In *The Great Poland Chronicle* King Przemysł I was presented not only as a king but also as a knight and a saint. Songs were sung about the great knights, and poems were dedicated to them. Długosz recorded a poem written by Adam Świnka, Canon of Gniezno and Cracow, entitled *A Tombstone for Zawisza the Black*. The poet admiringly spoke of the knight's life and death, for whom all of Poland wept; for he was "a star, no matter where fate led him".

Sermons, and above all the lives of the saints, had a similar patriotic character; among them, the life of Saint Stanislaus inspired patriotic reflections, voiced by anonymous poets and also by Wincenty of Kielce, in the mid-thirteenth century, who saw the unification of Poland in the miraculous fusion of the dead bishop's body.

Patriotism was not only a characteristic of the royal court, the political intentions of which were expressed by the chroniclers, a small intellectual élite in the Middle Ages. It also affected a wider section of society. Everyday 32

1. Section of the reconstructed
   fortified settlement at Biskupin, c. 500 B.C.

2. Aniconic statue Monk
   from Garncarsk, 3rd—1st cent. B.C.

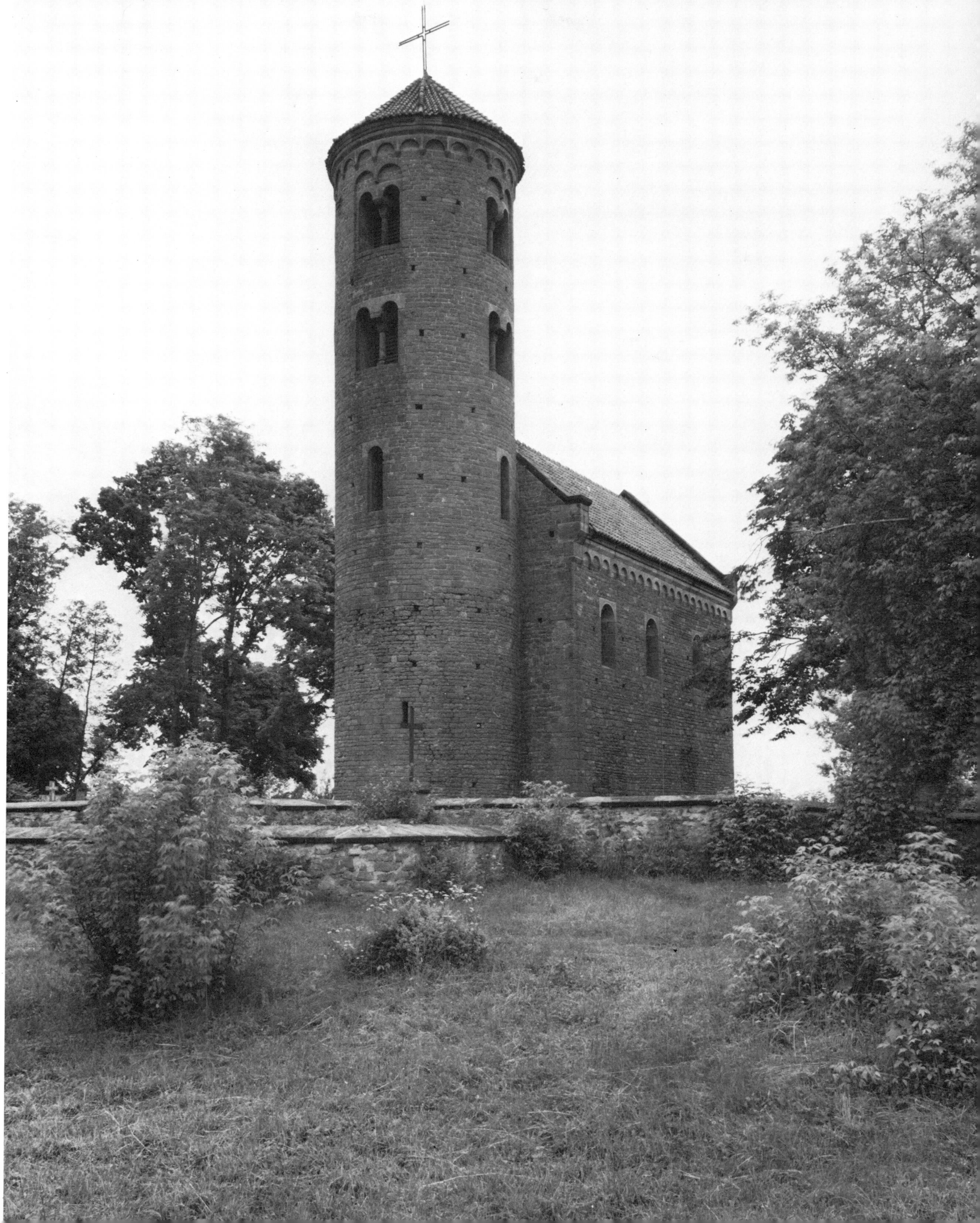

3. St. Giles' church in Inowłódz, 1086

4. Castle chapel in Cieszyn, 11th cent.

5. St. Leonard's crypt
   in Wawel Cathedral, c. 1118

6. Collegiate church of the B.V. Mary
   and St. Alexis at Tum near Łęczyca, 1140—61

8. SS. Peter and Paul's church
in Chełmno, mid-13th cent.

7. St. Leonard's church
in Lubin, 12th cent.

9. Cathedral dedicated to the Assumption of the B.V. Mary in Frombork, 1329—38

10. St. James' church in Toruń, 1309—50

11. SS. Peter and Paul's church
in Strzegom, 2nd half of the 14th cent.

12. St. Mary's church in Wiślica, 1346—50

13. Castle in Będzin, 13th—14th cent.

14. Castle in Czorsztyn, 14th cent.

15. Ruins of the castle
    in Bobolice, mid-14th cent.

16. Townhall in Torun,
    late 13th—early 14th cent.

17. Eastern front of the Chlebnicka Gate in Gdańsk, early 14th cent.

18. Townhall in Wrocław, late 15th—early 16th cent.

19. Townhall in Stargard,
15th—16th cent.

20. Courtyard of the castle
of Warmia bishops in Lidzbark,
2nd half of the 14th cent.

22. Boleslaus the Brave redeeming
the body of St. Adalbert murdered
by Prussians. Bas relief from the right
wing of the Gniezno Doors, mid-12th cent.

23. Rotunda-shaped chapel of Mieszko I.
Bas relief from the left wing
of the Gniezno Doors, mid-12th cent.

21. Gniezno Doors,
mid-12th cent.

24. Courtyard of the Collegium Maius
    in Cracow, 1492—97

25. Tympanon from the former Premonstratensian church
in Strzelno, 12th cent.

26. *Iustitia*. Bas relief on a column
in the Holy Trinity church
in Strzelno, 12th cent.

28. David's Concert, tympanon
of a portal in the former Cistercian church
in Trzebnica, 13th cent.

27. Reconstructed statue of St. John
the Baptist on the wall of
the cathedral in Wrocław, 1160—70

30. Coat-of-arms of the Cracow principality.
Detail of the slab of the sarcophagus
of Henry (IV) Probus, late 13th cent.

31. Coat-of-arms of the Silesian principality.
Detail of the slab of the sarcophagus
of Henry (IV) Probus, late 13th cent.

29. Slab of the sarcophagus
of Henry (IV) Probus, late 13th cent.

32. Detail of the sarcophagus
    of Ladislaus the Short, 2nd quarter
    of the 14th cent.
    Wawel Cathedral in Cracow

33. Detail of the sarcophagus
    of Casimir the Great, 1370—82.
    Wawel Cathedral in Cracow

34 Detail of the sarcophagus
of Ladislas Jagiello, 2nd quarter
of the 15th cent.
Wawel Cathedral in Cracow

35. Detail of the sarcophagus of Casimir the Jagiellonian showing the figure of the king sculpted by Wit Stwosz, 1492—94

36. Detail of the sarcophagus of Casimir the Jagiellonian showing figures of weepers with the emblem of Poland, 1492—94

37. Marian Altar
from St. Elizabeth's church
in Wrocław, c. 1380

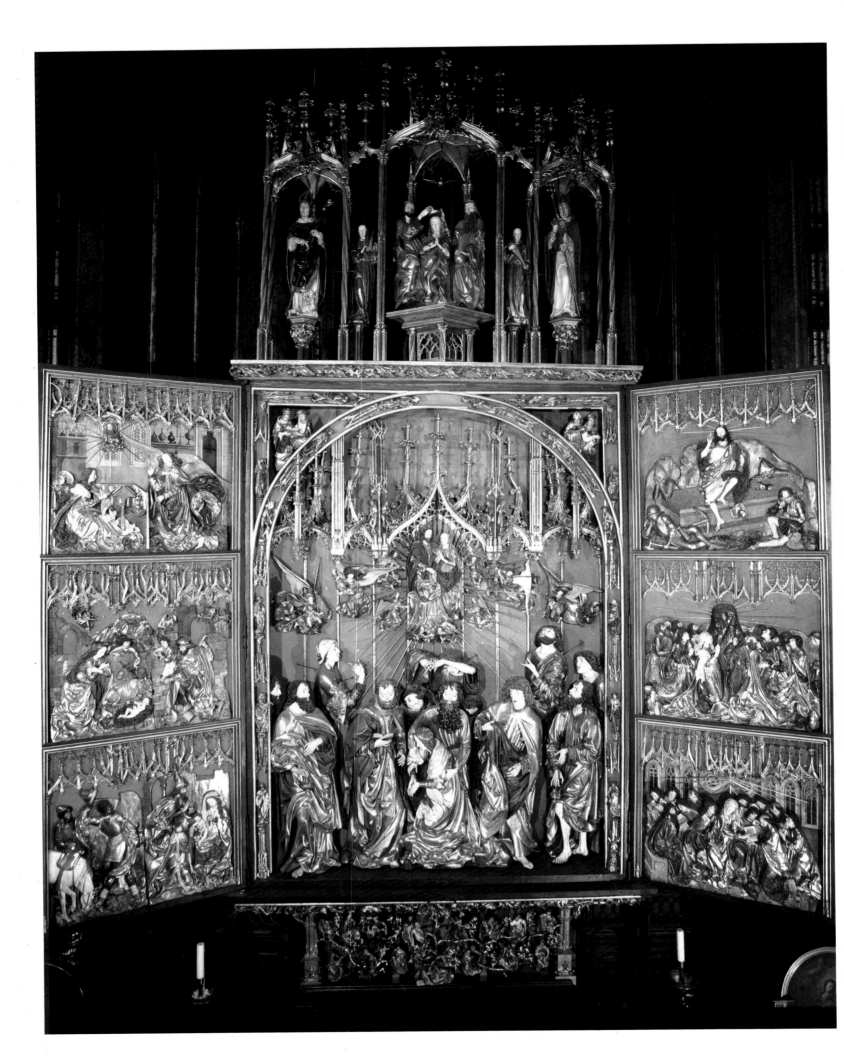

38. Wit Stwosz, Marian Altar,
    1477—89. St. Mary's church in Cracow

39. St. Mary's church in Cracow

40. *Dormition* of the B.V. Mary
    from Wit Stwosz's Marian Altar,
    1477—89. St. Mary's church in Cracow

41. Madonna of Krużlowa (detail), c. 1410

42. *Annunciation.* Polychromed sculpture from St. Elizabeth's church in Wrocław, 1460—70

43. Smith, miniature from a psalter, mid-12th cent.

44. Masons buildings a church in Trzebnica.
Miniature from the *Legend
of St. Hedvig*, 1353

45. Quern. Miniature from
the *Legend of St. Hedvig*, 1353

46. St. Hedvig interceding
with the prince on behalf
of the poor and unfortunate. Miniature
from the *Legend of St. Hedvig*, 1353

47. Coronation scene.
   Miniature from the *Pontifical* of Erazm Ciołek, c. 1510—20

48. Emblems of Queen Jadwiga.
Page from the *Florian Psalter*, late 14th cent.

49. Chivalrous scene.
Detail of a polychromy
in the residential tower
in Siedlęcin, 1st half of the 14th cent.

50. *Legend of St. Hedvig of Silesia.*
Two wings of a triptych
by the Master of the Triptych
of Wielowieś in Silesia, c. 1430

51. Epitaph of Wierzbięta of Branice, 1425

52. *Deposition* from Chomranice, c. 1440

53. *Sacra conversazione.*
Center piece of St. Barbara's altar
in St. Barbara's church in Wrocław, 1447

54. *St. Catherine of Alexandria*
from Biecz, c. 1450

55. **Shepherd and sheep.** Detail of the painting
Deposition from St. John's church in Toruń, 1495

56. Knights and peasants. Detail of the Jerusalem altar
from St. Mary's church in Gdańsk, 1490—97

57. Crown (known as the Sandomierz
    crown) of Casimir the Great, 14th cent.

TYPVS FVNDATIONIS ACAD: CRACOVIEN·
Ex Altari & Epitaphio ad Mausolæum Diui IAGELLONIS.
In Ecclesia Cathedrali Vrbis eiusdem.

IN QVO.

HINC

DIVVS IAGELLO, Rex Poloniæ, alterâ manu trophæa Prussica, alterâ Academiam tenens, suosǵ; Lithuanos ad fidem Catholicam inducens, adstante sibi Sancto STANISLAO, Episcopo Cracouiensi & Martyre:

INDE

D. HEDVIGIS VLADISLAI Coniunx, Regina Poloniæ, alterâ quidem Collegium Crac. sustinens, alterâ ad idem Polonos quasi manu ducens, adstipulante sibi D. LADISLAO Vngariæ Rege, ad viuum effigiati conspiciuntur.

AD HÆC

Sæculi illius ad amussim expresso cultui iuncta est B. CANTII Imago viua, ex antiquis tabulis, quantum fieri potuit, diligentissimè excerpta.

EX PRIVILEGIO FVNDATIONIS.

Si quis autem has nostra Erectionis Study, concessionumǵ, pro ipso Libertatum & Exemptionum, ac Jurium literas, de Successoribus nostris, aut quibuscunque, violare & infringere præsumpserit : iram vindicem districti Iudicis, & miserabilis infelicitatu horridum & inopinatum euentum, nouerit se incursurum.

58. Allegorical representation of the foundation
of the Cracow Academy.
Woodcut dating from 1628 made according
to a lost picture from Wawel cathedral

ptis. Mandatecp sacra eadem Maiestate accu-
ratissime castigatis.

59. Chancellor Łaski presenting King Alexander
the Jagiellonian with a copy of his
Commune incliti regni Poloniae privilegium, 1506

60. Seym debate attended
by King Alexander. Illustration from
Commune incliti regni Poloniae privilegium, 1506

14492/2164/73

oſce/náſzy ſpiewac. A wtym też vcerzono w trąby y w bębny tu potykaniu.
A iż ſtali Pruſowie na wyżſzym mieyſcu á náſzy niżey/ przetoſz gdy puſcili ná
náſze ze dwu dźiał/ſzkody żadney w náſzych nie vczynili/bo przenioſły kule woy-
ſko: lecz im przedśię ráźniey było z gory ſie potykác á niż náſzym z dołu. A w-
ſzákże pod gorą potkawſzy ſie náſzy z nimi/ opárli ſie im nieźle. Zaczym był
wielki grzmot z obu ſtron y chrzeſt zbroie/ tákież łamánie drzewcow: co ták

Pod Tannenberg
Bitwá známieni-
tá. czyli
pod Grunwaldem
1410.

61. *Battle of Grunwald in 1410.*
   Illustration from Marcin Bielski's *Chronicle*, 1597

62. *Mother of God with the Infant Jesus.*
   Detail of the baptismal font in SS.
   Peter and Paul's church in Legnica

63. Marcin Marciniec, Reliquary of St. Stanislaus, 1504

64. Arabian astrolabium of Marcin Bylica,
made in Córdoba in 1054

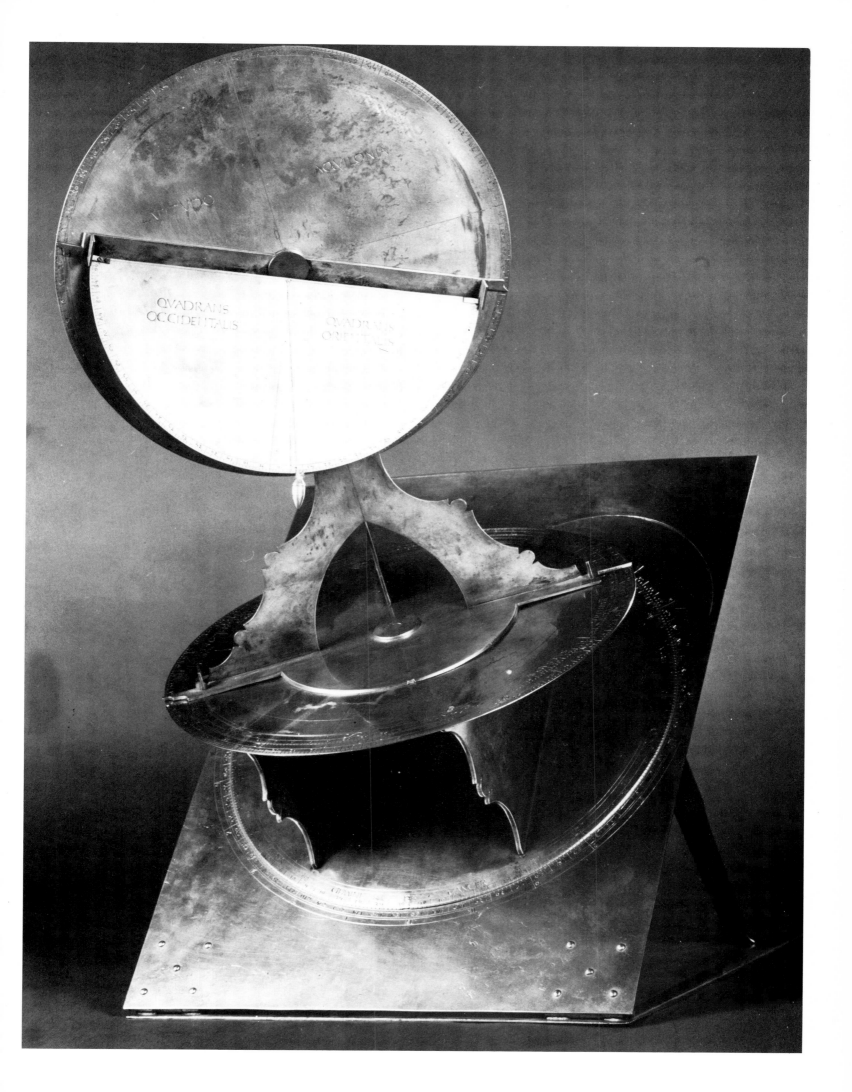

65. Marcin Bylica's torquetum, 1493

reality served as a much more effective tool for such an educational course in patriotism than did the written word which was not accessible to all at the time.

During the struggle for sovereignty and unification against foreign foes, a feeling grew and matured among the knights who fought to restore the "Polish crown" regarding Poland's greatness and the sacred duty to defend it. During the difficult years of the Bohemian invasion, feudal divisions, and Tartar raids which devastated the country and carried Poles into captivity, patriotic sentiments embraced a growing number of people. Amidst such disasters, what a unified and strong Poland could be, became apparent to the burghers and the peasants. While in cities the population, which was only partly of Polish origin, did not always support state policy, large masses of peasants, according to numerous chronicles, aided the knights in defending the country. It was the peasants who helped the armies fighting against the Germans; it was they who helped Ladislaus the Short in his struggle for the throne and when he suppressed the revolt of the Cracow administrator, Albert.

This patriotism became more universal and from the beginning was linked significantly with the process of Poland's Christianization. The struggle for the independence of the Church hierarchy in Poland became, at the same time, a defense of the state's interests. This was indicated in the struggle for the sovereignty of the Gniezno archdiocese. It was also characteristic of the resolution of the synod of Polish bishops in Łęczyca in 1285: the Pope was petitioned to oppose the secession of the Silesian Franciscans and to allow the country to again be "called Poland and not Saxony".

The effect of this diplomatic mission on numerous groups of society gave birth to a feeling of faith and patriotism, as expressed in *Bogurodzica,* the oldest Polish religious and patriotic song dating from the thirteenth century. Such feelings did not extend to the idea of the "bulwark of Christendom", which was created much later and for specific political goals. *Bogurodzica* expressed, most simply, the people's humble request for a "pious life" on earth and, after death, "passage to heaven". It became the hymn of knights going into battle, although how this came about is not certain. Długosz, after a magnificent description of the armies assembled at Grunwald, which included "numerous noblemen skilled in the martial arts", wrote that when "the call to charge was given, all the royal troops sang their native *Bogurodzica,* and then with raised lances rode into battle".

SOCIAL AND PERSONAL CULTURE

The propagation of culture was not only a matter of the educational process; it was also, and primarily, a part of the changes taking place in everyday life-style, in human relationships, and in the tastes and habits of the population. The center for the exercise of such influence was, of course, the royal court. But this was not limited only to the capital, since it was customary that the monarch, in times of peace, should travel throughout the country and remain for certain periods in various castles. This custom expanded the sphere of the court's influence. The courts of the lords also wielded significant influence. During the reign of Ladislaus Herman, Sieciech built two great residences for himself: in Cracow and in Płock. The Silesian court of Piotr Włostowic was filled with foreigners, and the courts of the bishops of Cracow radiated with similar pomp and glamor.

At the same time, the development of the cities created new possibilities for establishing personal contacts and, in general, for enriching life. The academic community in Cracow expressed the need for new experiences with great intensity. Ever larger sections of society became increasingly interested in the new life-style. As examples of this we can cite the popularity of the work, *Antigameratus,* written by Canon Frovinus in the first half of the fourteenth century, dealing with the rules for social behavior. The renowned fifteenth century Polish poem by Słota, on how to behave at table, is another example. It criticized the old vulgar customs, offered advice on how to behave at court and enumerated the forms of courtesy one should use in the company of women. In contrast to western tradition, where relationships with women were viewed by knights in categories of courtly love, the poem stressed the link between courtesy towards women and the worship of the Virgin Mary.

Women, who had, beginning with Dąbrówka, played important roles in Polish history, now returned to private and ordinary human experiences. We find short love poems and letters dating from the fifteenth century in which anonymous poets expressed the blinding force of their feelings and were surprised that their love could be so great. Everything was expressed in these poems and "letters": affection and tenderness, faithfulness and envy, adoration and resignation, sincerity and suffering. These love poems and letters which have been preserved from the fifteenth century reflect — like religious folk art — the evolution of the national consciousness, from monumental and sacred images and historical visions to the acceptance and expression of man's personal needs.

It is rather difficult to reconstruct today the common culture of Polish society of the period. Nevertheless we can quote Długosz, who, on the basis of his own observations, offers us a picture of the everyday lives of various strata of Polish society. Of the gentry he wrote that they were "greedy for fame, inclined to plunder, scornful of danger and death, unreliable in keeping their word, hard on the poor and unfortunate, inconsiderate in their speech, reckless with their wealth, faithful to the ruler, given over completely to agriculture and animal husbandry, kind and considerate to foreigners and guests, and excelling in hospitality over all other nations". About the peasants, Jan Długosz wrote the following: "The village people tend to be drunkards and argumentative, to swear and to murder . . . They never shirk any type of work or any heavy load; they can withstand cold or hunger . . . They are satisfied with poor huts; they lack neither courage nor impudence; they have quick minds; their posture and movements are beautiful."

Foreign Culture in Poland
and Polish Culture in the World

THE NATIONAL VERSION
OF UNIVERSAL CHRISTIAN CULTURE

It is not true that Christianity brought culture to Poland. Pre-Christian Poland, even before it became a state, was a country of wide cultural differentiation. Stronghold towns and settlements, as well as the economically high level of life, made possible the development of an inner culture, reflection of which can be seen both in art and religious and social rites. Iron-smelting, still primitive but effective, permitted the production of weapons and agricultural implements. The conflict between the wealthy and the poor, between the lords and the prince's retainers on the one hand, and the people in general on the other, was only beginning to take form in the social structure. Old family traditions were still alive; the ideals of primitive equality in society, and decision-making in regard to mutual goals were still maintained.

Travelers, acquainting themselves for the first time with Poland, would always remark on the relatively high standard of living and the extreme honesty of the people: "Such is faith among them and social conscience," wrote Herbord about the hospitality of the people of Pomerania in the twelfth century, "that you will never find a thief or a liar among them." And still another, Helmold, noted with surprise that although the country of the Slavs was the "hearth of superstitions", they had, however, "many inborn attributes; they honor, above all, hospitality; and they show their parents proper respect." He went on to say that "neither beggars nor poor exist", since the needy are amply cared for.

At first Christian culture was foreign. The organization of the church was accepted; the models of sacral architecture were imported, as well as the entire liturgy; the clergy was also of foreign descent. Relatively rapidly, however, the process of adaptation of medieval forms to contemporary conditions and local needs began. The concept that the church's sovereignty in Poland must be absolute was systematically defended; such was the character of the archdiocese in Gniezno. More and more clergymen of Polish descent were placed in important positions in the ecclesiastical hierarchy. The Polish episcopal synods took care that the native language was an integral part of all educational and pastoral activities. In the religious life formed by Christianity, one could observe certain local and national characteristics. In the rebuilt city of Gniezno, the cult of St. Adalbert was becoming a symbol of the independence of the state; while the cult of St. Stanislaus, the bishop of Cracow, executed by order of the king, expressed the desire for unification of the kingdom, which was still divided into feudal principalities. Certain other cults of local saints were surfacing: of St. Hedvig in Silesia, of St. Kinga and St. Jacek Odrowąż in Little Poland. The masses especially worshipped St. Florian, the guardian of everyday life.

In the area of artistic expression of the Christian religion, a slightly different process was taking place. Poland was a country of wooden architecture. The church introduced stone architecture, which was more monumental and grand. The Gniezno Cathedral, for example, during the rule of Boleslaus Wrymouth, was forty meters in length and about twenty-four meters in width. The building of churches was mainly funded by the rulers; but sometimes lords also contributed to the building of churches, as, for example, St. Andrew's church in Cracow, which was endowed by Count Palatine Sieciech at the end of the eleventh century. Monasteries, especially those owned by the Benedictines and the Canons Regular, were built in Western architectural style (for example, at Tyniec, Ślęża, Łysiec and many other places). In the twelfth century and at the beginning of the thirteenth century many new churches were built in Wrocław, Cracow, Czerwińsk, Płock, Włocławek, Kruszwica, and in smaller centers, such as Tum, Opatów, Giecz, Prandocin, Jędrzejów, Wąchock, Sulejów, Trzemeszno, Strzelno and Siewierz. These structures, built during an earlier period by expert foreign craftsmen, were similar to those found all over Europe. Even when built completely by local craftsmen, they still retained the European style. Regional characteristics insinuated themselves particularly into interior details: certainly in the wall paintings, destroyed with the passing of time; and in the liturgical vestments, usually woven in noble households, sometimes even at the royal court, in liturgical vessels and decorated altarpieces. The contribution of these local artisans must have been even greater than the relics that have reached us indicate. The famous Gniezno Doors are evidence of how widespread was the process of adapting the Romanesque style and architecture and interweaving it with the sacral and national history of Poland.

Evidence of the growing power of these processes can be found in the Gothic style. Although imported from the West, like the Romanesque style, it gained an ever increasing local character and acceptance. With the change in attitudes regarding building only from stone and with the increasing utilization of bricks in combination with stone, a new architectural form and a unique, truly Polish Gothic style appeared. Many new religious orders, among them the Cistercians, the Franciscans, and the Dominicans, took up the building of churches and monasteries in this style. The great Gothic churches of Cracow, Szczecin, Kamień, Kołobrzeg, Toruń, Gdańsk, Chełmża and Pelplin acquired renown.

The burghers had great influence on the widespread acceptance of this style. Buildings in the Romanesque style were erected as residences of the rich and powerful, but as early as the thirteenth century, and expecially in the fourteenth century, wealthy patricians built their houses both as centers for trade and as living quarters. Burgher houses from Cracow and Wrocław as far as Gdańsk and Szczecin, became the basic element of the Polish urban landscape. Their interior and exterior decorations were done by Polish craftsmen and contained many regional characteristics.

A considerable contribution to architecture was made

by Casimir the Great, founder of many churches, who initiated the building of many castles, cities, and granaries throughout Poland, built, as the chronicler Janko of Czarnków once wrote, for the purpose of helping the starving poor, in a style which even today is regarded as a model of the Polish architectural style.

The Christianization of Poland meant submission to the influence of the universal, Latin culture of the European medieval period. It was this culture which served as the basis for education in the parochial and cathedral schools; this culture was represented in the libraries built up by the bishops; and finally this was the culture which the clergymen and the sons of the lords encountered while seeking an education outside the borders of the country. Latin made possible direct contacts with all of Europe, but on the other hand, prevented the masses from participating in this intellectual culture.

Nevertheless, the process of deeper assimilation of and participation in this culture by the Poles was taking place fairly rapidly. A fine example of this process can be found in the activities of Gallus Anonymus. His chronicle, the first history of Poland, even though written by a foreigner, and in Latin, was imbued with a patriotic spirit. In the same way, the medieval, cosmopolitan erudition of Kadłubek's chronicle provided a very Polish view of the history of the country. During the dawn of Poland's history, Gallus Anonymus was the first in a long succession of foreigners whose polonization served to create a Polish intellectual culture that continued into the succeeding centuries and indeed almost up to the present time.

However, more important examples can be cited from a later time. A center of Polish scholarship developed in Silesia in the fourteenth century, of particular significance in the field of the natural sciences. A university was founded in Cracow, where from the outset the professors were Poles, men who later became famous throughout all of Europe. From the turn of the fourteenth century, the voice of Poland was heard throughout the world in theological and philosophical matters, and was included in important discussions of church and secular politics. During this time Poland was becoming an equal partner in European intellectual culture.

POLAND IN THE EYES OF THE WORLD

Very little, and often confusing information about Poland was provided by geographers and merchants during Roman times, although some spoke of the country between the Odra and the Vistula. Even Ptolemy of Alexandria, although very accurate in his accounts, knew very little. Silence reigned throughout the next few centuries. Only the southern Slavs' expansion into Byzantium aroused interest in these peoples. In the ninth century, references to the country of the Wislanians appeared. More information, although still sketchy, appeared in the tenth century. This was provided by Ibrahim ibn Jacob, a merchant and scholar from Spain, who was an envoy to Otto I, and later by the German chronicler Thietmar and particularly by Adam of Bremen,

and finally by Helmold of Bosau. The latter wrote of the prowess and cruelty of the Slavs, and was enchanted by the greatness and beauty of Wolin. But the Ebstorf map dating from the beginning of the thirteenth century was still very vague. Gervase of Tilbury, at the beginning of the thirteenth century, perhaps thanks to his personal contacts developed during his study in Paris or Bologna, was the first to import more specific information. He already employed the name *Polonia* and explained its roots as stemming from the word *pole* (field). Interest in Poland grew during the period of the Tartar invasions. But only at the beginning of the fourteenth century in Spain and in France in the Franciscan monasteries, did specific information regarding Eastern Europe and Poland emerge. This occurred during the reign of Casimir the Great.

Such scanty information could not be used as a basis for concrete historical generalizations of which there certainly was not a lack of in Western Europe. And thus the history of the Poles was traced back to the Vandals, a point of view which was also willingly accepted by local historiographers. In the *Nibelungenlied,* the Poles are allied with Attila the Scourge of Gods and fight together with the Huns against the knights of the West; according to other sources, the Poles were allied with Alaric during his expedition to Rome. According to the *Chanson de Roland,* Poland was supposed to have been conquered by this knight and offered to Charlemagne. The *Chanson des Saisnes,* another French composition, written in the twelfth century by Jehan Bodel of Arras, described an expedition against Charlemagne undertaken by Widukind and his Polish vassals. For political reasons some of the German writers referred to Poland as a country conquered by Caesar. This would justify the pretensions of the Holy Roman Emperors to rule over Poland. These different, largely fictitious, historical theories, bear witness to how fascinated Western Europe was with Poland, and how much they attributed to it. But at the same time they also prove how difficult it was during the epoch to acquire very concrete information.

This state of affairs underwent only a slight change in the fifteenth century. Although international contacts became much more animated, and Poland's significance in Europe became considerably more evident, the conflict between Poland and the Teutonic Knights still provided an opportunity to formulate many biased and false views. Johann Falkenberg, a defender of the Teutonic Knights with whom Włodkowic debated at the Council of Constance in 1415, called for revenge on and the destruction of the Poles, promising the Knights "eternal life for the extermination of the Poles and their King Jagiello." Poles were, Falkenberg believed, "idolaters", and they were a "social menace" to all of Christianity. He was not alone in making these accusations. It was pointed out that Poland was too tolerant of the Hussite movement; accusations were made regarding the agreement made with Turkey in 1421. Various versions of an apocryphal story were circulating in Germany in 1430, according to which a legendary sultan presiding over the entire Mohammedan world invited the Lithuanian dukes, Jagiello and Olgierd, to his kingdom. It was not until the heroic death of

Ladislaus III at Varna in 1444 that these accusations were stilled.

These false accusations, in the light of which Europe viewed Poland, were ever more frequently contradicted by the accounts of travelers and merchants in the fifteenth century. These accounts were generally unbiased, but superficial. They give details relating to the climate, roads, living conditions, and business opportunities in Poland. The foreigners often praised Poland — Giosafat Barbaro wrote that Poland is a "fine and beautiful country" — but they also pointed out many examples of poor husbandry, and described a very low standard of living.

POLISH CONTRIBUTION TO SCIENCE AND PHILOSOPHY IN THE MIDDLE AGES

Benedykt Hesse of Cracow, a well-known Polish fifteenth century philosopher, differentiated three fields of human knowledge: *ratio naturalis, ratio fidei,* and *ratio philosophica.* In these three fields, medieval Poland brought its own contribution to the development of science and philosophy during this period.

Witelo was one scholar who was very learned, by European standards, in the area of the natural sciences. He lived in Silesia at the end of the thirteenth century, and his treatise on optics was a synthesizing discourse on physics, which also included many new and invaluable observations. For several succeeding centuries this treatise was frequently referred to, and Kepler valued it highly. Witelo was not alone; in the fourteenth century, and particularly in the fifteenth century, the natural sciences were developing mainly in Cracow. Benedykt Hesse designated physics as the "principal philosophy" and commented on Aristotle with reference to Buridan.

Wawrzyniec of Racibórz and Marcin Król contributed considerably to the development of astronomy. At the end of the fifteenth century, Cracow University became one of the most important centers of mathematical and astronomical research in Europe, thanks to scholars such as Marcin Bylica, Jan of Głogów, Wojciech of Brudzew and Mikołaj Wodka. Nicolaus Copernicus was educated in this scientific environment.

In the field of theology, Mateusz of Cracow, who died in 1410, became famous throughout Europe. In his great work entitled *Rationale operum divinorum,* written in the form of a conversation between a father and son, Mateusz attacked deductive philosophy and speculative theology, proving that they did not obey rational principles, and that they were "medicine for the soul", rather than real cognitive disciplines. He also formulated a modern program of careful and critical scientific research. Mateusz aquired great fame in Europe as a result of his firm defense of the principle of conciliarism. Mateusz's arguments penetrated very deeply into the nature of faith and the organization of the church; they suggested that Christians are not the pawn of Church activities, but the subject of ecclesiastical organization. Based on this point of view, the sole head of the Church was Christ and not the Pope.

Polish studies on the subject of the ethics of law and the theory of constitutional law also gained renown in Europe. Paweł of Worczyn, who died in 1430, elaborated upon Mateusz's idea on the subject of the increasing emphasis in philosophy upon ethics, the object of which was to be the happiness of man but not the abstract idea of goodness. Jakub of Paradyż who worked out a social system of ethics in the beginning of the fifteenth century, and who was well known throughout Europe, developed Paweł's concepts further. In the field of constitutional law, war and peace, as well as international relations, similar ideas were put forward by Stanisław of Skarbimierz who analyzed unjust wars, and the Poznań bishop, Andrzej Łaskarz, who attempted to convince his readers that one must not "use the sword of this world" where one is in need of a "heavenly weapon." Finally we come to the most famous of them, Paweł Włodkowic, whose appearance at the Council of Constance in 1415 was discussed throughout Europe. Włodkowic asserted that "it is forbidden to conquer the kingdoms of infidels — even if they did not recognize the Roman Empire — to take their possessions or privileges, because without sin they possess it by holy decree, through Him Who created all for men without distinction." Włodkowic also asserted that "one must not force infidels to accept the Christian faith by force, or by oppression, since these methods are harmful to one's fellowman and because one must not commit evil deeds to achieve goodness." According to these principles, "both Christians and infidels are fellowmen without distinction."

The work of these scholars attested to the fact that Poland not only took part in the intellectual culture of Europe, but also made her own bold contribution. This is evidence of a deep humanitarian feeling of justice and tolerance, of a conviction concerning the equality of people, regardless of their origin or religious beliefs, of a desire for the peaceful resolution of political arguments, and finally of the administrations of the Church by the faithful through councils.

Conclusions

The Middle Ages ended in Poland and the Renaissance began without any revolutionary upheavals, without any marked crisis. During the fifteenth century, different trends, different beliefs, and various aspirations coexisted. Sometimes the achievements of the Middle Ages were a basis for its development. What were these accomplishments?

At the turning point between the period of which we know almost exclusively from excavations, and the period described by the chroniclers, the Polish state was formed as a consequence of a process of uniting different tribes. These tribes, however, were similar enough to make integration feasible. The process of forming a state, and its further development, was never a process of conquest; it was a process of unification. The tribes of Wislanians, Polanians, Mazovians, and Slezanians were ethnically 36 homogeneous. Mieszko had been already the sovereign over the entire territory ("king" of Poland, as he was called by Widukind) and not just the ruler over one of the tribes which conquered others. Feudal divisions did not result from reborn separatism or attempts to emancipate conquered tribes; they were the consequences of arguments and rivalry within the dynasty, as well as of the process of feudal disintegration which encouraged the local lords to procure the rights of sovereignty over their own territory. During this period, the feeling of national unity was not dissipated, nor did the efforts concerning the restitution of central authority which encompassed all of Poland wane. An important factor of unity, alongside integrational concepts, was the organization of the Church which was common to the whole territory, and above all a common language, which was not yet written, but was providing a strong everyday tie. Other factors included common beliefs and customs, which were moreover expressed in the legal system. The law was always defined as *ius polonicum* and not as local or separatist law.

This integration not only acted as an impediment to the feudal process of de-centralization within the country, but characteristically exercised influence over a wider area than the territories of the Polish state, which varied in different periods. In this sense, Western Pomerania and Silesia remained a part of Poland even when in the political and legal sense they were separated from the kingdom. Długosz correctly conveyed the idea of "Poland" as an ethnic and cultural unity extending more widely than the actual national borders. In the trial of the Teutonic Knights, which, on the basis of the Pope's decisions, was conducted in Warsaw in 1338 and 1339, witnesses of the lawlessness of the Knights claimed that in Pomerania "all the people living speak Polish together," and that their princes were Poles.

During this process of integration, an outstanding Polish patriotism, which encompassed all estates, arose and matured. This patriotism was exemplified by the crowning of Polish rulers, as well as by the courage of the knights in battle against their enemies, and by the local people's cooperative resistance in protecting the country. This patriotism relating to the land very early acquired the trait of attachment to a particular national style of life and generally held values. One of the German chroniclers. Widukind of Corvey, explained the obstinacy of their defense against the Germans by the fact that Poles "would endure all poverty for freedom." Similarly Thietmar wrote of Boleslaus the Brave that, "he has regained the honor of freedom for the Poles." Gallus Anonymus stated the same. Boleslaus Wrymouth, in his opinion, was supposed to have said to his knights: "Be prepared to live or to die for the freedom of Poland," and he declared that he would prefer "to lose the Kingdom preserving freedom than to rule it in peace but in disgrace."

The Tartars destroyed the country numerous times, but this only served to strengthen the patriotism of the people. These vicissitudes emphasized the specifically Polish way of life, and particularly strengthened the Christian religion which already had become the common faith. While the pressure of the Germans, who repeatedly referred to alleged rights "ensuing from the tradition of the Roman Empire" and who were often favored by papal politics, provoked conflict between national and ecclesiastic interests, the Tartar aggression consolidated the link between the Polish feeling of patriotism and Catholicism. This is most notably expressed in *Bogurodzica,* and also in the fourteenth century religious and patriotic songs of which fragments still survive.

Because of regional particularism, Poland developed a dual political awareness: the king as "natural heir," as "father of the homeland," holding "complete power" — thus wrote Gallus Anonymus and Kadłubek about Boleslaus the Brave — and "the community of subjects" *(communitas subditorum)* whose meaning for the state and in the state was ever-heightened. Kadłubek, differing from Gallus Anonymus, emphasized the right of the subjects to remove a "tyrant." Casimir the Just had, according to Kadłubek, once uttered the following: "Justly is the right to reign forfeited by the sovereign ruler who abuses it." The king as natural ruler and the king who is given authority to rule — this was the twofold idea, which became in political life and legislation more distinct and ever more contradictory. But the king's reign united in peace and harmony "government by the strong" with wide participation by society in politics, economy, and culture. During the thirty-seven years of Casimir the Great's reign, the national consciousness gained three important new elements: understanding of the national and individual significance of material culture and the economy, an understanding of the role of learning in the life of the nation, and comprehension of the significance of the national or royal administration of justice, standing above the lawlessness of the feudal lords. This development was an essential pre-condition for the further growth of political consciousness as early as the fifteenth century during the reigns of the first Jagiellons.

In a society with well-defined divisions into estates, there was still a certain balance between the privileges of the upper classes and the rights of the other classes. Cities were passing through a period of rapid development and peasant farms still had the chance to develop. The social composition of the Cracow University students, who came from various classes of society, reflected this relative balance of power. There was also a balance between the king as the "lord" and the knightly estate summoned to defend and co-govern the state.

The victory at Grunwald, and the later success in the war against the Teutonic Knights strengthened the state. The Turkish menace, still present despite the defeat at Varna, was averted, and the union with Lithuania opened up new political prospects, although also causing new problems. Increasingly important, as a result of the contrast between Poland and Lithuania, were questions regarding the essence and value of Polish culture and life-style. This found expression in Jan Ostroróg's *Memorial* in which the author elucidated the concept of national sovereignty in the face of papal policy, and defended the Polish national character against German claims.

Science and art, particularly architecture and sculpture, flourished. Scholarship developed in the university and since its political significance was highly valued, it soon became part of the intellectual life of court circles as well. While Romanesque art remained the art of the secular and ecclesiastical ruling groups, Gothic art was much more widely accepted in society. It also became the art of the towns and of manor-houses that combined defense and residential functions. Altarpieces, especially the altarpiece which Wit Stwosz worked on for a period of twelve years, tombstones, murals, paintings, and stained-glass windows, were usually ordered either by the lords or by entire communities, such as town councillors or guilds. However, as soon as these works of art were completed, they began to lead their own lives: they turned out to be "necessary" for everyone at mass on high days and holidays. Art also became a part of daily life among the very rich: in the homes of the lords and in the patrician houses of Cracow, Wrocław, Gdańsk, Poznań, and Toruń.

In these new material and social circumstances, many groups of people found it important not only to be able to subsist but also to value life's beauty, not only existence itself, but also sensible direction of both community and individual life. As early as the middle of the fifteenth century this constituted the background for the development of other new trends which manifested people's desire to search for freedom and happiness during their lifetime on earth.

THE RENAISSANCE

Introduction

The Renaissance, however short-lived, was undoubtedly one of the greatest epochs in the history of Polish culture. Although the beginning of this period can be traced as early as the second half of the fifteenth century, one has to bear in mind that the Middle Ages continued in Poland into the first few decades of the sixteenth century. And even though Renaissance culture can be discerned as late as the beginning of the seventeenth century, the Baroque started to develop in Poland towards the end of the sixteenth century.

This "Golden Age", therefore, lasted for only a few decades. It covered the activities of several generations, thriving during the reign of Sigismund I and Sigismund II, the last two kings of the Jagiellonian dynasty, and the first kings chosen by election.

Nonetheless, within this short period of time substantial changes had been effected in the national conscioussness. The universe became worth exploring, while the Earth was assigned a new place in the system of planets revolving around the Sun. The value of life and the expression of its richness were reflected in art and, in particular, poetry which from then on was expected to enhance the lives of people, to accompany their joys and sorrows, their religious and secular experiences. Economic prosperity began, while the process of changing the medieval *Regnum* into the modern Commonwealth provided a starting point for reflections upon social life and state organization, upon the privileges and duties of citizens, as well as the role of those in power. However, current, day-to-day political considerations turned out to be less important than the tribunal of reason and conscience which was built up. Each citizen, and especially those "who were responsible for the fate of others", had to account for his social activities before this tribunal.

These new achievements and opportunities of the Polish Renaissance formed a lasting national consciousness. This was to be seen on several occasions in the centuries that followed.

Place in Europe and Historical Consciousness

THE STATE FRONTIERS OF THE COMMONWEALTH OF TWO NATIONS

The union of Poland and Lithuania was not a political act completed on one occasion but rather a long-lasting process. This union was ultimately consolidated in Lublin as late as 1569, toward the end of the reign of Sigismund Augustus, the last of the Jagiellonians. The Union Act contended that "the Kingdom of Poland and the Grand Duchy of Lithuania form one, the same and indivisible body... one joint Commonwealth which has grown and fused from the two states and peoples into one state and one nation." After almost two hundred years of attempts at uniting the two states by various ties, after two centuries of rapprochement and conflict, Poland became a commonwealth of two nations. Poland was three times larger within its new boundaries. Its population increased more than two-fold, but it consisted of people who belonged to different ethnic groups. Toward the end of the sixteenth century, the Commonwealth was c. 815,000 square kilometers in area; its population totaled about seven and one half million, including three million people in the Duchy of Lithuania.

The figures themselves are not important: the fundamental changes in the conditions of development and the formation of national consciousness were far more crucial. In the course of almost two centuries, from the moment of Jagiello's accession in 1386 to the time of the eventual consolidation of the Union in Lublin in 1569, a process of transformation slowly took place: previously Poland had been viewed as the state of the Polish nation and everything that composed the national consciousness of the Poles formed an element in the organization of their state. Following the Union, the new state became multinational, although power remained in the hands of the Poles.

The vast incorporated territories required new policies at home and abroad. At the same time they opened prospects for new military activity and for new alliances and conflicts.

The western border of the country remained unchanged. The northern boundaries were also established, after another war against the Teutonic Knights had been brought to an end in 1525 with the Grand Master of the Teutonic Order swearing allegiance to King Sigismund the Old. However, the eastern territories remained unstable because of the Lithuanian-Ruthenian conflict, which forced Poland to get more and more involved in long-lasting wars against Muscovy — wars which were waged by the Poles with varying degrees of success.

In the second half of the fifteenth century Muscovy overcame feudal divisions and became a significant power during the reign of Ivan III; it was heading toward a liberation of Rus which was still dominated by Lithuania. Towards the turn of the fifteenth and sixteenth centuries, the two countries were involved in various wars, during which Muscovy succeeded in gaining new territories; in the years 1507—08, 1512—22 and 1534—37, further wars were waged between Lithuania and Muscovy. In 1535, when Russian armies fought their way as far as Vilna, Poland joined the war to help Lithuania; the outnumbered Polish armies were led by Hetman Jan Tarnowski. While the royal court and the Lithuanian magnates pleaded for Poland's maximum involvement in these wars, the radical movement of the Polish gentry opposed the policy of eastern expansionism.

Similarly, the Livonian War that followed was not accepted favorably in Poland. There were different reasons why the Polish gentry were against participation; contemporary political writers criticized "a decline of the knightly spirit", but one of the main reasons was the fact that the war was to defend territories much too far away, and to expand the territorial possessions of Lithuania. The 40 idea that this would serve the interests of the whole Commonwealth of Poland was not yet so clearly discerned.

The process of making this issue clear seemed particularly difficult and complex. It required a change in patriotic consciousness different from an immediately discernible threat to patriotism based on *raison d'état*. Polish patriotism had been nurtured over several centuries as a response to immediate danger and as a necessity for fighting an enemy who had penetrated deep into the country, ruining the everyday life of the citizens. During the fifteenth century, the battles between the Poles and the Teutonic Order were an expression of such patriotism. These new conflicts, however, were no longer considered an immediate danger nor did they make immediate impact, since they usually broke out on far-away frontiers. The meaning of these conflicts was understood, rightly or wrongly, only by those circles that governed the country, responsible for policy-making as well as for convincing the general public of the correctness of their political decisions. Patriotism had to acquire another dimension under these new conditions. It had ceased to be the patriotism of immediate action, and had to become the patriotism of *raison d'état*.

The understanding of the importance of the northern boundary was formed in a different way. The belief developed that the state frontiers in the Pomeranian provinces were not marked simply by the coast but by the Baltic Sea itself, the sea route providing a window on the world. The idea actually dated back to the Thirteen Years' War (1454—66) against the Teutonic Order. At the battle of Gniew, an important fortress controling the Vistula waterway leading to Gdańsk, the fleet was engaged on both sides. In the Vistula Bay, the fleet of the Teutonic Order was defeated by a considerably outnumbered flotilla belonging to Gdańsk and Elbląg: this battle proved to be a decisive step in the Polish victory. The Poles belatedly learned a valuable lesson from the consequences of this military experience. Between 1517 and 1522 a fleet of privateers was organized in Gdańsk, called "the royal sea-guard". This royal fleet developed rather slowly, since Gdańsk, having its own fleet and fearing this competition, refused to cooperate. The process of building the royal fleet was accelerated during the period of the Livonian War. In 1567 the fleet was made up of seventeen ships. From the foundation of a Marine Commission in 1568, which was the first admiralty in the nation's history, the number of vessels steadily increased. The royal fleet operated in the Baltic Sea and was mainly engaged in battles against the "Narva Navigation", which was founded by Czar Ivan the Terrible, after capturing the Livonian port of Narva in 1558. It was Sigismund Augustus who decided that a strong fleet should be built after the Polish fleet had been almost totally destroyed by the Danes in 1571. As a result, a great galleon, the *Dragon,* and another smaller ship were soon constructed. However, the death of the king brought an end to the whole project.

These varied experiences and intentions were expressed through the idea of *dominum maris Baltici* that was formulated in official sixteenth century documents and presented by the Polish envoys, Marcin Kromer and Dymitr Solikowski, before the Peace Congress of 1570 in Szczecin, which marked the end of the Seven Years' War of the North. The Polish concept of reigning on the sea was met with a certain degree of understanding among the gentry. Although they were hardly interested in the affairs of Livonia, they appreciated the importance of defending the shipping trade and thus were willing to secure Polish interests in Gdańsk.

HISTORIOGRAPHY AND HISTORICAL INTERESTS

Polish society in the early Renaissance period did not have easy access to historical knowledge about the country's past. The chronicles, including those written by Długosz, remained in manuscript form. Nonetheless, Polish society did have a considerable amount of information on the most important events of the past, especially the most recent past, and also a certain range of opinions concerning the historical path it had followed up to that time. The past was now seen as a specific aspect of reality, to be taken seriously in the present that was now being lived through. Society was already aware that its present existence had been shaped by that past and that the place of Poland in the world and the situation of the ruling stratum had been established within these historical perimeters.

And yet before Renaissance historiography embarked on deepening and disseminating historical awareness, Polish art and Latin poetry had been harbingers of these changes. The Polish Latin poets gathered at the courts: Mikołaj Hussowski, for example, lived in the court of Bishop Erazm Ciołek in Rome; Klemens Janicki in the court of Piotr Kmita; Andrzej Krzycki and Jan Dantyszek, the Bishop of Warmia in later years, lived in the royal court. They all presented the historical ideology of the ruling circles. Jan of Wiślica published his epic poem entitled *Belli Pruthencini Libri III* in Cracow in 1516. The poem began with a legendary history of Poland, and in particular, with the story of Krakus and Wanda. The battle of Grunwald was presented, followed by a description of the policies of previous rulers, such as Jagiello, Ladislaus III, Casimir the Jagiellonian and his sons, and Sigismund I. Thus it emerged as a tremendous project and the first epic poem about Polish history. No other Polish Latin poets had ever presented such a wide sweep of national history, although the poetry of Krzycki and Dantyszek contained a number of historical overtones showing the past as important and invigorating. The most famous poet of that group, Klemens Janicki, understood well the vocation of an artist. However, his illness and premature death precluded his poetic dream from coming true. What remained was a series of interesting poems about the lives of the Gniezno archbishops and, in particular, *The Lives of the Polish Kings,* which was re-issued several times in the sixteenth and seventeenth centuries and was also translated into Polish.

That such a poetic program was deeply rooted in the minds of contemporary Polish society is evidenced in its adoption by one of the most famous Polish poets of all times, Jan Kochanowski, after the Latin poets had already disappeared. He expressed interest in national history in many of his poetic works, beginning with the Latin elegy *On Wanda*. A synthesis of the history of Poland was then presentend in *The Pennant,* in which he showed the ceremony of the Grand Master of the Teutonic Order, swearing allegiance to King Sigismund the Old of Poland. This event was depicted against the background of the many battles between the Poles and the Teutonic Order, battles that continued over several centuries.

The task of historians turned out to be much more difficult than that of the poets. The gentry not only expected the greatness of the Polish Kingdom to be presented but they also insisted that their own great genealogy be given appropriate attention. They did not approve of any kind of criticism, whether it was directed against the legendary history of Poland, the families of magnates, or the significance of their own social stratum. Marcin Bielski turned on Kromer when the latter abandoned the theory that the Slavs were descendants of the Vandals, a hypothesis that seemed to Bielski most honorific. The Polish gentry, although praising Kromer, objected to the fact that he overestimated the importance of the burghers in Polish history. Mikołaj Radziwiłł also criticized him on one occasion by saying that "he [Kromer] defiled the reputation of many revered families." The chronicles of Maciej of Miechów were confiscated upon order of the Senate, and only after they had been censored, were they allowed to be reprinted in 1521. In the early seventeenth century, Herburt's edition of Długosz's *History of Poland* was suspended on the order of the King since it contained harsh criticism of the clergy and some "revered Polish families".

Works that met with the approval of both the magnates and the gentry, and which emphasized both the greatness and antiquity of Poland, gained immediate recognition and fame. The social implication of *Sarmatia* (old Poland) seemed to be characteristic of the period. This notion had already been used by fifteenth century writers. Długosz himself employed it to denote various attitudes: thus, in the course of the sixteenth century, the idea acquired an exceptionally dignified connotation. It orginally meant a people, or peoples, as ancient as the Romans but independent of Rome. This theory of independence was to justify the righteousness of the struggle of Piast Poland against the medieval German Empire, with its claims to the entire "Roman" Europe. It also brought up the issue of Poland's past and its cultural integrity, which was to be strongly stressed in the seventeenth century.

The entire discussion concerning Sarmatia was revived by Maciej of Miechów, in the sixteenth century. In his famous geographical treatise, *Tractatus de duabus Sarmatiis Asiana et Europiana* (1517), Maciej emphasized the distinction between two Sarmatias, that is, the European and the Asian. He connected the history of Poland with that of European Sarmatia and, by the same token, was the first to introduce such a geographic and cultural term,

prior to Erasmus of Rotterdam. The book by Maciej of Miechów received wide public acclaim. It was published a number of times in Latin and was later translated into various languages. The Polish translation by Andrzej Glaber was exceptionally popular, and new editions appeared in 1535, 1541, and 1545, of which only one damaged copy has been preserved.

However, these needs and historical interests, so genuinely pursued by a wide circle of the gentry, found an outlet mainly in comprehensive studies devoted to world and Polish histories. Marcin Bielski's *The Chronicles of the Whole World,* published in Cracow in 1551, gained great popularity among readers. During the second half of the sixteenth century many writers followed the path paved by Bielski. Maciej Stryjkowski published his chronicle in 1582, the complete title of which read *Published for the First time Ever — A Chronicle of Poland, Lithuania, Samogitia and All Parts of Ruthenia.* The author outlined the beginnings of the Lithuanian state, from the times of Palemon, who was believed to have escaped from Rome because of Nero's persecutions. Stanisław Sarnicki, a Calvinist, dealt with history in a much more daring fashion; in his *Annales* (1587), he ventured to present Polish history from the times of Lech, whom he acknowledged as a direct descendant of Assarmation-Sarmatian, the son of Noah's brother. Joachim Bielski, Marcin's son, also followed the same trend, and in 1597, he used his father's name to publish an expanded version of the latter's work under the title of *The Polish Chronicle.*

These great world and Polish histories tackled not only national historic events but also recorded biographies of distinguished families. The average reader was particularly responsive to this kind of information. Bartosz Paprocki, the author of numerous books glorifying gentry families, presented what the genealogical pride of the gentry liked and required. In this way the "great" history of the nation was brought down to a "concise" history of a family, in which stories concerning certain ancestors of the gentry would often be contrived in a legendary way.

The commemoration of important current events became still another form of the historical awareness of Polish Renaissance society. Thanks to these reports, great deeds could be saved from falling into oblivion while the protagonists in such events were guaranteed that posthumous fame which they truly deserved.

This type of reporting was started by Stanisław Orzechowski in his journal that covered the years 1548—52. It was published, however, much later, in 1611. Łukasz Górnicki was no more fortunate in publishing his great work, entitled *The History of the Polish Crown,* containing the events between the years 1538 and 1572: it was first printed in 1637.

The first interregnum after the Jagiellonian dynasty died out was followed by important and dramatic events. Many diarists found these times especially interesting. Świętosław Orzelski covered this period in *Interregni Poloniae libri viii;* Jan Dymitr Solikowski in *Commentarius brevis rerum polonicorum;* and Krzysztof Warszewicki in *Rerum polonicorum libri tres.*

The turbulent times of the reign of Stephen Báthory were of equal interest to many historians. Leonard Górecki published an account of the Livonian War and left a manuscript chronicle which recorded at great length the events of the years 1575—82. Jan Łasicki presented the war of Báthory against Gdańsk in his work *Clades Dantiscana,* published in Poznań in 1577, and later in Frankfurt (1584), with the intention of opposing the Habsburgs' anti-Polish activities.

Nonetheless, the most prominent historian of the day turned out to be the secretary in the royal chancery of King Stephen Báthory, Reinhold Heidenstein, who worked on current history at the request of the ruler. He proved to be as deeply interested in history as was his chancellor and the famous leader of the gentry, Jan Zamoyski. Heidenstein gave an account of the Muscovite campaign in his work, *De bello Moscovito commentariorum libri sex,* which he had published in Cracow in 1584. Four years later, the same book appeared in Basel. His voluminous Polish history dating from the death of Sigismund Augustus appeared, however, considerably later; it was printed in Frankfurt am Mein as late as 1672. Heidenstein was also the author of a biography of Jan Zamoyski. Franciszek Bohomolec translated and edited this text and published it in 1775, contributing to the popularity of Zamoyski during the period of the Enlightenment.

In this way, the historians proved that their work was indispensable, and that the great people, whose lives and deeds they recorded, would receive due fame and honors from generations to come.

POLAND PRESENTS ITSELF TO THE WORLD

The Poland of the fifteenth and sixteenth centuries became more and more aware of both its strength and place in Europe. The days when merchants and travelers who had seen it related strange stories about this distant and unknown land were now over; so were the days when the popes intended to Christianize and the emperors to annex this country. Poland counted as a state in the world. Under these circumstances, there was a growing need to work on a Polish history that would reflect the spirit of the epoch and also be able to present the state of which the Poles were justly proud.

By the turn of the fifteenth century, Polish historiography was already criticized among Polish humanists. There were plans to make Filippo Buonaccorsi called Kallimach (Callimachus) responsible for working out a new version of the history of Poland. Such a choice was made in order to gain more attention in Europe, and Kallimach's name, as well as his international repute, could well provide for success on a wide scale. The king, John Albert, encouraged Kallimach to embark on such a work. The original plan was carried out but only on a small scale; Kallimach ended up by giving only an account of the life and death of King Ladislaus of Varna. Sigismund the Old took over John Albert's work and did his best to initiate historical writings within the circle of

contemporary historians. His attempt turned out to be futile. Nor were the attempts made by Maciej of Miechów, Wapowski, or Decius, whose history was to be corrected by Hosius at the request of the king, to achieve any considerable significance.

The most crucial work of the period was written by Marcin Kromer. It was entitled *De origine et rebus gestis Polonorum,* published in Basel in 1555, and reprinted several times later. In his book Kromer presented the ancient Sarmatian origins of Poland and also described Polish history, up to the beginning of the sixteenth century, which he based mainly on Długosz.

This Polish history, written in excellent Latin, gained great acclaim throughout Europe. It was highly praised by an Italian humanist and historian, a great, authoritative voice of that day — Francesco Robortello. Kromer's contributions were also appreciated by the Poles themselves. During the 1580 Seym, the Polish Parliament expressed its gratitude and praise for his work in spite of the fact that Kromer had been a burgher.

Kromer's book turned out to be so highly appreciated by foreign readers that it soon went into several new editions, and in 1571, Jan Herburt published a shortened version of Kromer's Polish history, including additional material that brought it up to the middle of the sixteenth century. At the same time Jan Krasiński published his outline of Polish history, entitled *Polonia* (1573), in Italy; and Aleksander Gwagnin published *Sarmatiae Europeae descriptio,* in 1578. Kromer himself did additional historical research to prepare a kind of guidebook to contemporary Poland. It appeared in Cologne in 1577 and was re-issued several times.

Man and the Forces of Production

THE FEUDAL CONSCIOUSNESS

From the end of the fifteenth century the population of Poland rapidly increased. This increase was due to many factors. For decades Poland had been free of the wars and incursions that earlier had systematically destroyed the population. The country was also spared the mass visitations of the plague, which decimated the populations of other European countries. Local epidemics were successfully combated by the severe winters and also thanks to improved sanitary conditions in the cities; not only the major cities, but also small towns were building water pipes and hospitals; doctors were employed on wealthy estates and in the towns. The various laws passed by the municipal authorities obliged citizens to take better care of hygienic conditions and threatened penalties for any kind of infringements in this field. Conditions in the rural areas also improved, especially in Great Poland.

The population density was increasing. For example, at the end of the sixteenth century, there were about 23 people per square kilometer in Little Poland, 24 in Mazovia and 19 in Great Poland. The population distribution was different in various areas: in Great Poland, 30 percent of the population lived in the towns while the figure for Mazovia was only 18 percent, but a fairly dense network of settlements was beginning to cover the entire country and large tracts of previously unpopulated wilderness were disappearing relatively quickly. This gave impetus to new and more intensive social relationships, based on improved exchange of information and more active participation in public life. It also signaled the beginning of economic change.

During the second half of the fifteenth century and the beginning of the sixteenth century the rural peasant economy developed rapidly. The rents and labor dues which the peasants were required to contribute often left them with a surplus income which they were free to dispose of at will. This resulted in the development of a monetary exchange system and also in the intensification of rural production. The average peasant owned about 16 hectares of land; his livestock consisted of a few horses and cows, with rather more pigs and sheep. It was not unusual for the sons of peasants to study at the universities, to reach high positions and to participate in the development of intellectual and cultural life.

However, this situation changed greatly following the organization of ecclesiastical manors and manors for the *sołtys* (village headman) in the fifteenth century and the development of the manorial farms of the gentry in the sixteenth century. The new organization was based not on rents but upon obligatory feudal services, that is, work on the estates of the ruling stratum. To an ever greater degree the increased strictness of the conditions of labor converted the peasants into the slaves of the lord of the manor, liquidated the possibility of independent farming, and made their participation in the commodity markets impossible.

In the first half of the sixteenth century the price of grain increased considerably; for example, the cost of wheat increased four times, and that of rye three times. Under these conditions the manors of the gentry became more profitable. In 1520, the Seym passed legislation establishing obligatory lengths of forced service for all peasants; in fact, it was a rather liberal law — limiting work to one day a week. At the very end of the century the length of service increased to 3 or 4 days a week, sometimes in practice even to 6 days. This meant the complete utilization of peasant manpower for the benefit of the manors. In addition, the peasants' duties in rendering service to the lord of the manor in his public and private life increased. These included the duty of preparation for war and sometimes even participation in wars.

Craft production also to a considerable extent passed into the hands of the gentry who, taking advantage of peasant manpower, organized it to suit their own needs and for the benefit of local markets. The urban craftsmen were undercut in this way and the standard of craft production also fell, since these products were now being created by unskilled workers.

The owners of manors began to exploit the forests on a large scale. The price of wood was high and the demand for this resource, both for export to Gdańsk and for the domestic trade, was significant. Approximately one hundred sawmills, the majority operated by water power, were used in this production. The production of tar and charcoal also started to expand, the latter being later used in metallurgy. All of these contributed significantly to the ravaging of forest areas.

The burden imposed on the peasants led to protests, or passive resistance, and encouraged them to run away, especially on the manors of the most demanding owners. In order to prevent this form of resistance, the gentry passed a decree at the Seym session in 1496 that no more than one peasant could leave a village each year. The Seym constitutions of 1501, confirmed repeatedly later, prohibited the peasants from leaving the land and undertaking jobs without their master's permission. In 1518 all disputes and contentions between the peasants and their lords were to be judged not by the royal courts as previously, but by the gentry themselves. Only peasants from royal estates were tried by the royal referendary courts, which fact was of some social significance.

This economic system resulted in the peculiar mentality of the slave owner. After a time, it became clear that society divided itself into those who had power and material resources for their own well-being, and those who were forced to obey and to perform the hardest work which barely satisfied their own needs. This second group was not only deprived of civic rights but their rights as human beings as well.

EARLY INDUSTRY

The change in agricultural techniques was accompanied by a change in industrial output. Salt production in the royal mines in Wieliczka and Bochnia steadily increased, thanks to extension of the mine area and new techniques in mining rock-salt, which permitted exploiting deeper layers. Production at Wieliczka was increased three-fold during the first half of the sixteenth century. Private salt-works were also built in eastern Little Poland. The gathering of salt from deep shafts demanded complicated techniques. In addition to manpower, horsepower was also utilized, and the continual improvement of the tread-wheel brought an increase in this power. The number of those employed also grew; at Wieliczka over a thousand people worked the mines at the end of the sixteenth century.

In the Cracow region, thanks to the initiative of Jan Turzon, copper-mining began to develop. In the Mogiła copper works, a new method of extracting copper and silver was introduced at the end of the fifteenth century, a method which was later employed elsewhere in Europe. The draining of the mines was a difficult problem, and failure in this field forced the closing of some mines during this period; during the second half of the fifteenth century this happened to a number of lead and gold mines (Złotoryja, Bytom, Sławków, Trzebinia). At the end of the sixteenth century the exploitation of copper was begun at Miedziana Góra near Kielce. The requirements of the

44

building trade stimulated the development of brick production and stone quarrying. Large stone quarries were to be found in the regions of Chęciny and Pińczów.

The iron industry, however, was of greatest significance. This was concentrated mainly in the Holy Cross (Świętokrzyskie) Mountains and in the Częstochowa Basin. In the second half of the sixteenth century there were over two hundred ironworks in the kingdom. More and more people were employed here, both well trained specialists, and various drifters or runaway peasants. The technical level of the ironworks rose steadily; water-power was employed increasingly often, and the number of smelting furnaces in various works rose significantly.

King Stephen Báthory took a great deal of interest in the development of iron production. At his initiative, the production of iron cannon balls was greatly expanded. During Sigismund III's reign a large ironworks sprang up in Bobrza, specializing in the production of steel; several other ironworks produced guns, cannon balls and muskets. In the same region, the production of copper and lead also expanded. In the second and third decades of the seventeenth century large iron and steel works and lead and copper works were built at Białogon and Samsonów. Mikołaj Wolski built two blast furnaces and produced arms, wire and sheet metal on his property near Częstochowa. Other magnates, as well as members of the gentry, also took up production on their estates, employing serf labor.

However, at the end the century the development of the iron industry slowed down. The take-over of the works by local landowners and the expulsion of free blacksmiths, the employment of peasants in place of paid workers, unwillingness to make major investments, and the difficulty in providing fuel from the denuded forests — all these created unfavorable conditions for the development of metallurgy. The sudden rise in grain prices and the difficulty in selling Polish iron presented an additional reason for closing down a number of works. Only those that satisfied local needs remained.

During this period Walenty Roździeński published an excellent volume, a great defense of the miners, and at the same time proof of the fact that within the broad group of the gentry the miners received faint recognition. The book was entitled *Officina ferraria, or furnaces and workshops with Forges of the Noble Work of Iron* (1612). Roździeński quoted from the Bible and ancient authors in order to present mining as a noble profession. He wrote that "ironware was respectable", discovered by Adam, who used a hatchet and a hoe. From that moment "iron-production was the beginning for everything." In Greek mythology Vulcan and his brother Bacchus were the guardians of smiths; the latter "passed around cool drinks in the torrid swelter". This genealogy, however laudable, did not guarantee those working in the furnaces either recognition or a good life. The only riches of these hard-working people was freedom, understood as the opportunity to do what one wished with oneself. It was, however, freedom only in comparison with the slavery of the serf, freedom to live in poverty, freedom to search for work, and freedom to journey to look "for bread."

Industrial production was relegated to the margins of national economic life; it had developed under difficult conditions during the first half of the sixteenth century, but by the end of the century it was ever more neglected and ruined, and was not part of the social consciousness of the times. Agricultural production took its place in the national consciousness; it was driven to the limits of maximum profits on the manors of the gentry. Neither mining nor metallurgy entered the consciousness of Renaissance Poland, nor did the technical knowledge that was associated with these industries.

DECLINE OF THE CITIES AND THE LANDOWNERS' MENTALITY

Almost from the very beginning the social and cultural role of the cities in Renaissance Poland gave evidence of deterioration: their magnificence did not presage hope for the future.

Throughout an entire century, from the 1550's to the 1650's the number of cities in Poland increased and their wealth was multiplied. Crafts and trade were developing. In Poland itself, about two hundred new cities were built. During Báthory's reign (1576—86), the number of cities in Poland amounted to over a thousand, although they were mainly smaller towns, with a population of 1,000—2,000. Larger towns with greater populations were developing very rapidly into major cities. At the end of the sixteenth century, Cracow had a population of 28,000; Warsaw about 20,000; and Wrocław more than 28,000. Poznań is a good example of a city which had a high rate of increase in population. From a town of 4,000 inhabitants at the end of the fifteenth century it expanded, by the end of the sixteenth century, to a city of over 20,000.

Towns situated on trade routes developed particularly rapidly, especially cities like Sandomierz, Kazimierz, Płock, Włocławek, Toruń, and Elbląg which lay on the River Vistula or its tributaries. Some of the big cities became trade and cultural centers on an international scale. It was here that the intellectual and artistic life of Poland was carried out and where many artists and scholars, both Polish and foreign, lived and worked.

The most important city in this respect was Gdańsk. At the beginning of the sixteenth century it consisted of 30,000 inhabitants; by the end of the same century its population had increased to 50,000. This was an average size for the trade centers of Northern Europe at the time. Amsterdam, for example, in the middle of the sixteenth century had a population of 16,000 people, but by the end of the century, its population had increased to more than that of Gdańsk. A Venetian envoy, Lippomano, wrote in 1597 that it was "the richest city in Poland" and that during the summer its port was visited by from 400 to 500 ships from all over Europe.

The great St. Dominic's Fair in Gdańsk, lasting for a fortnight, became an international trade event. Polish exports of grain increased eight times at the end of the sixteenth century, and ten times during the first decade of the seventeenth century.

For Gdańsk, trade was extremely beneficial. The constantly increasing wealth of Gdańsk had been accomplished, however, at the expense of other cities because the merchants of Gdańsk made contracts with the grain-producers — i.e. the gentry — directly, eliminating all middle-men. This almost monopolistic character of Gdańsk at times brought dissatisfaction, sometimes even among the gentry who attempted to influence the king to revoke Gdańsk's privileges.

This privileged but precarious position of Gdańsk was the main reason why the rich bourgher culture of this port was unable to influence wider areas of Poland. It is true that the gentry appreciated the quality of Gdańsk furniture, clocks and products made of silver and amber, but they remained loyal to their own culture. In terms of social and trade contacts, Gdańsk was like an open window on the world, receiving news from all over Europe. Despite all these facts, the Gdańsk commodity markets did not become markets for ideas.

The vernacular culture of the towns of Central Poland was not approved by the gentry either. Despite the fact that a large percentage of sixteenth century writers and politicians were of burgher origin, the merchant, the craft, and the intellectual cultures of cities were not widely recognized.

The gentry contrasted the advantages of living in cities with the freedom and enjoyment of living in the countryside, which according to their ideas, was the ideal type of existence. These were times when the problems of the life-style of the gentry were widely discussed. Society was beginning to realize that the era of knighthood in Poland was coming to an end. From the fifteenth century, literature was filled with complaints that the spirit of knighthood was disappearing. Despite these literary complaints, more and more people became convinced that the style of life in the countryside was the only way to live peacefully and happily.
'

Social Unrest

PEASANT PROTESTS

Andrzej Frycz Modrzewski wrote of the gentry that "they have as many enemies as they have serfs". Indeed, a great deal of tension existed between the peasants and gentry, as well as between the spiritual and the secular lords. But when other European countries were going through bloody peasant revolts at the beginning of the sixteenth century, social conflicts were less violent in Poland.

The main form of protest for the peasants was escape, refusal of obligatory services (especially when the work on estates was most needed), and the neglect of other obligations.

These forms of resistance were sometimes more serious and widespread. Especially in Southern Poland, in the sub-Carpathian region, there were collective protests,

attacks upon manor-houses and even murders of the most detested feudal lords. Social conflicts were more violent in Silesia. The class struggle in many cities in Silesia, the influence of the Bohemian Brethren, and the continuous spreading of news about peasant insurrections in Germany and Hungary were the main reasons why the resistance of the masses became more active and strong here. But even in these regions the actions did not occur on any grand scale.

Without becoming violent, peasant resistance was still increasing. At the end of the sixteenth century, the most popular form was escape from the owner's land. Because of the vastness of the eastern territories joined with Poland by the act of the Polish-Lithuanian Union, these escapes were very hard to detect and still more difficult to punish. On many farms a large part of the land lay fallow and there were more and more of these "empty corn-fields". Large scale peasant strikes, organized on the estates of various landowners, took place. In 1592 in Podlasie, a strike ended in the execution of more than a dozen peasants.

These were, however, only sporadic events and it was not until the seventeenth century that the violence of these conflicts was to develop on a large scale.

THE SITUATION IN THE CITIES

Similarly, and usually without violence, class struggles began to take place in the cities. The main battle front was between the rich urban patrician class, with their large financial resources and profitable trade transactions, and the ordinary townspeople, mainly the craftsmen associated in various guilds, who demanded certain privileges, to be allowed to sell their products more easily and to take part in the town councils. The second front was between the master craftsmen in the guilds, who wanted to preserve their privileges and rights, and the journeymen, who considered their work in the master craftsman's workshops as a limitation to their freedom and exploitation; they wanted to achieve full emancipation. Sometimes the journeymen established their own unions, which were opposed to the guilds. There were also strong links between the journeymen and the discontented urban poor. The third front was between the settled urban population which had permanent jobs and was relatively prosperous and the poor, consisting of disabled soldiers, deserters, and escaped peasants, who came to the cities to find sanctuary and establish new lives.

These social conflicts took place at various levels during various periods and in different towns. The ordinary townspeople relatively easily obtained the right to participate in city administration, particularly in determining the level of taxation. This took place in Poznań in 1518, in Cracow in 1521, and in Toruń in 1523. But this new form of organization was not easily established everywhere. In Gdańsk, in 1525, a real revolution occurred during which a new program of social reforms was presented, which included limiting the patricians' rights, the abolition of usury, and a universal franchise in electing the city 46 council. The intervention of Sigismund the Old put down this movement, and in the following year the old order was restored with only minor changes.

In various Silesian cities, at the beginning of the sixteenth century, new insurrections broke out, but this time their social structure and ideology were even more complicated, due to miners' revolts, the nationalistic oppression practiced by the German bishops in Wrocław, and Anabaptist propaganda. The insurrection at Tarnowskie Góry, in 1534, was apparently one of the most dangerous.

In many cities, especially during the second half of the sixteenth century, different kinds of rioting occurred and for various reasons. In some towns, the poor constituted half of the population. The urban patricians, who made up less than 10 percent of the total population, were a source of irritation because of their enormous wealth and their luxurious style of living. Deprived of the possibility of participating actively in the economic life of the country, the patrician class became more parasitical than useful. Because of this, the poor demanded all the more that the patricians' luxurious life-style be curtailed and that a higher level taxation be imposed on the rich minority. Varied national and religious relationships were also reasons for the bloody rioting. In Cracow, the Catholic poor attacked the Protestants in 1593; but in Gdańsk, the situation was reversed: the Protestant poor attacked the Catholics.

These social struggles were neither sufficiently well-organized nor well-coordinated to accomplish their ends. They were acts of protest against current and concrete injuries and injustices, which did not, however, turn into a widespread popular movement. Nor did they bring about the formation of burgher class consciousness, which might have been able to oppose the policies of the gentry, which were an increasingly serious threat to the cities. The social life of the towns did not provide an adequate basis for the growth of this class consciousness, for internal divisions and dissent were too strong. No political movement developed among the burghers, and in fact the towns played no significant role in the growth of the state. Without the political back-up, the literary, artistic and intellectual activities of the burghers remained of marginal importance, even though high standards were often achieved in these fields and works were produced which deserved general recognition.

CONFLICT BETWEEN THE GENTRY AND THE MAGNATES

The struggle of the gentry against the princes of the church and state — and against the king when he favored the magnates — were often dramatic and sometimes had considerable impact on a large part of society.

The beginnings of this struggle dated back several centuries. First Louis of Hungary and then Ladislaus Jagiello granted many privileges demanded by the gentry in the area of the economy, administration, and politics.

The charters of Nieszawa, in which the king agreed not to levy any new taxes nor to call a mass levy without the consent of the regional diets, were of crucial significance. They were issued by Casimir the Jagiellonian at the beginning of the Thirteen Years' War in 1454. As a result of this decision, the gentry as a whole acquired greater latitude to express their opinions during conventions, attended in principle by all the gentry. As their role increased, two chambers began to form within the Polish Seym: a chamber of deputies of the regional diets, and a chamber of senators.

From the beginning of the sixteenth century a growing conflict between the gentry and the magnates developed, the latter group being unwilling to share their power. At the Seym at Piotrków in 1504 the gentry led by Jan Łaski, the current chancellor, passed a resolution which prohibited the holding of two high offices by the same person. It also passed a law which placed certain limitations on the king in granting and pledging the crown lands. The Radom Seym, in 1505, ratified these rights of the gentry by incorporating them in the *Nihil novi* Constitution. The gentry were also guaranteed that no new resolution would be made unless a joint agreement of both the Senate and the deputies of regional diets were reached.

The policy of Sigismund the Old, however, was favorable to the magnates; the king was eager to divide lands among them because in this way he was able to win their support for his policies. This was another reason that made the gentry unite and act together. At the Bydgoszcz Seym in 1520, the gentry demanded that "a seym of justice" be called. It was to convene every four years for the next twelve years in order to improve substantially the state of affairs in the country. The plan proved rather difficult to carry out. In 1537, a civil war almost broke out when the gentry, gathered for a campaign in Moldavia, voted for a radical program of reforms, containing thirty-six demands. This rebellion of 1537, disdainfully called "the war of laying hens" by the magnates, resulted in a considerable victory for the gentry.

Another gentry movement initiated at the Seym sessions between 1552 and 1558, under the name of the execution movement, was a continuation of that earlier victory. This movement soon found leaders and its program not only defended the interests of the gentry estate but was used to carry out reforms in the whole Commonwealth as well. The consolidation of the privileges granted to the gentry was no longer the only urgent issue. There were now many more things that mattered, such as justice in the state, the limitation of rights in the church hierarchy, church reform, change in the system of administration, the judiciary, the treasury, and education. Another important matter was to strengthen royal power, as the central executive body of the state, but still to subordinate it to currently existing laws, and, in the final resort, to the collective will.

The king's changing policies, the strength of the magnates' coalition, and the conflicts within the execution movement slowed down the realization of various decisions taken by the consecutive Seyms. They also narrowed the scope of further reforms in the administration, the judiciary, and the military. Thus against this background of partial success and definite defeats, the gentry movement steadily lost its reforming character.

The prospects which the union with Lithuania had opened up, the immediate economic benefits, resulting from the exploitation of serf labor and the limitations of the rights of the burghers, made the rest of the nation realize that the gentry was a privileged estate rather than an estate which accepted responsibility for the country's existence and progress.

IDEOLOGY OF AGREEMENT

All these conflicts and social tensions were relatively mild. Even if more severe controversies occurred, they never lasted very long nor did they become widespread. Steady progress was still possible by means of compromise. This program of agreement and integration was often and deliberately emphasized. The idea of mutual agreement was becoming a slogan of the epoch.

It was Stanisław Łaski who first formulated this slogan in an adress entitled *An Admonition to Poland to Follow the Path of Agreement,* presented in 1545. According to the author "crowns [kingdoms] rise and prosper thanks largely to justice, agreement and love, without which both the army at war and the states at peace could, by no means, last long."

Jan Kochanowski, representing the royal ideology of the time which was formulated in the speeches of two vice-chancellors, Piotr Myszkowski and Filip Padniewski, devoted an entire single work to the problem of agreement and published it as a political leaflet in Cracow in 1564. The program contained a critique of the existing state of affairs, in which everybody "neglected his office": clergy had ceased to be a model of piety, the gentry had abandoned their knightly skills, justice ceased to exist — "courts and law remained silent" — no one was willing to "serve the crown", everyone was possessed by "gluttony and excessive socializing" so that "in this anarchy, the poor waste away in slavery." According to Kochanowski the only condition of agreement was the reformation of all the estates by re-imposing duties which they had thus far neglected.

This concept was not accepted by everybody. It was clear to everyone that in such a vast state as the Commonwealth, there existed serious conflicts between the gentry and the burghers and also between the peasants and the gentry. An excellent lawyer, Jakub Przyłuski, defined a citizen as one who "could hold an office in the state", which meant that both the gentry and the burghers were regarded as citizens, but not the peasants. Kromer had a similar attitude, insisting that *populus polonus* was made up of two estates. This concept was supported by writers who were descended from the burghers. It was also defended by Sebastian Petrycy of Pilzno at the end of the Renaissance.

Modrzewski had a much more radical attitude in this regard: "Gentle birth and common birth are follies of the human mind." He also asked: "Why do the gentry live together with the plebeians in the same Commonwealth if they do not want to share the same rights with them?"

However, there was another viewpoint that eventually dominated. The defender of the gentry's privileges, Stanisław Orzechowski, clearly stated that the Commonwealth of Poland meant "the king and the gentry". It was his conviction that all others, that is the peasants and the burghers, remained outside the range of citizenship. Such a concept was recognized by Sigismund Augustus who made the distinction between "the nation of the gentry" and "the nation of the common people", when he approved the rights and privileges of 1550.

In spite of these developments, there were no acute antagonisms apparent during the sixteenth century. Tranquillity was still maintained. Admittedly, the political rights of the burghers were systematically limited so that they did not participate in elections, which meant that they did not count as citizens who shared the responsibilities of ruling the country. However, owing to the wealth of the cities, their self-government and various cultural institutions, the burghers could still enjoy a decent existence and had ready access to culture and education. Thanks to their activities, the burghers soon entered the Polish cultural scene, although they were barred from entering the circle of citizens. In this way, they were part of the nation in the sense of a cultural community but were not regarded as part of the political community.

Thus, the program of agreement recommended a strategy of compromise so far as social conflicts and struggles were concerned. As a matter of fact, this compromise benefited the ruling class but, due to various changes, managed largely to keep the entire society in balance and in relative harmony.

The history of the Polish Reformation, from the very beginning searching for agreement rather than conflict, proved that the entire program of concord was not merely the cunning tactics of the ruling classes but that it also contained higher and more permanent social aims than simply the *ad hoc* assuagement of conflict. The state authority, in spite of various threats aimed at "heretics", displayed a similar attitude. Even the Arians (Polish Brethren), despite being accused of "crimes" against the state and the social order because of their protests against serfdom and wars, enjoyed all the freedoms in their life and work that the age provided.

When in 1570 representatives of the Lutherans, Calvinists and the Bohemian Brethren (but not the Arians) convened in Sandomierz, they adopted a resolution presenting the principles of national agreement, which they called *fraterna coniunctio.* This fraternal reconciliation allowed each of the parties to maintain its own profession of faith. It even called for discussions and polemics; yet, at the same time, it guaranteed common and mutual tolerance. The principles of the Sandomierz Agreement became famous abroad; they were discussed in Germany and in Bohemia. The Sandomierz Agreement also formed the basis for the resolutions of the Warsaw Confederacy of 1573 which, during the period of the interregnum after the death of Sigismund Augustus, formulated still more radical principles of tolerance that 48 were meant for the entire country. The participants of the Confederacy took it upon themselves not to let blood be shed because of "different professions of faith or different churches", nor to punish anyone, confiscate his property, or send him to prison. The gentry also committed themselves to adhere to these principles and to prevent the authorities from acting against them.

Henri de Valois, who was to accede to the Polish throne, was obliged to take an oath to respect these resolutions of tolerance which were presented to him by the Polish envoy in France. This ceremony took place in Paris, at the Cathedral of Nôtre Dame.

The Commonwealth of Poland

STATE SOVEREIGNTY

It was a long and difficult way that led from the Piast monarchy to the Commonwealth of the Gentry. The reign of Casimir the Jagiellonian (1427—92) became a landmark in understanding state sovereignty and royal power. The treatise by Jan Ostoróg, written between 1474 and 1477, brought broad justification to the ideology of state sovereignty, according to which the king "had no superiors and recognized no one except God as higher in rank than himself." Ostoróg's treatise expressed the will of Casimir the Jagiellonian who, in both his internal and foreign policies, tried to employ the principle of state sovereignty and the supreme sovereignty of royal power. He demanded that the Pope give him the right to grant benefices and nominate candidates to higher-level church offices in Poland. In this way he wanted to become independent of the church hierarchy and have a decisive voice in shaping the latter's development.

Casimir the Jagiellonian consistently aimed to integrate the state and strengthen its central power, although this was a very complex task, since the long-lasting animosities between Great Poland and Little Poland were still profound; Mazovia maintained its autonomous, or perhaps even foreign, character; in the eastern regions Ruthenia differed in many respects from Poland; Polish-Lithuanian antagonisms and prejudices were not decreasing in spite of many political acts and declarations; Gdańsk Pomerania, recently regained, needed special attention. Lastly, the state required modernization, especially in the area of the treasury and the army. The old mass levy, based on widespread and voluntary participation by the gentry in defending the country in times of a threat of war, no longer could guarantee national security. Besides, the mobilized army was weak and inefficient. State funds were insufficient to cover growing expenses; they were even insufficient to support the royal court. It was necessary to carry out more fundamental reforms.

All this — sovereignty over the church, centralization, strengthening of the royal authority, reform of the military, and the treasury — required more than a simple reorganization of the state. It was a crucial change which demanded a new way of thinking, using education as the basis of a new social and legal awareness. Kallimach and Ostoróg served this cause, each, however, in his own way.

In later years Kallimach was considered by the gentry to be the author of *Pieces of Advice.* This advised the king to rule according to his own will, without listening to public opinion. Kallimach's *Pieces of Advice* — authentic or not — were considered by the gentry for decades to be evidence of the danger of a possible transformation of the monarchy into despotic and absolutist rule. Kallimach was not likely to have proclaimed such extreme views, although his way of thinking actually differed greatly from that of the secular magnates and the higher clergy. His viewpoint must have been influenced and later formed as a result of his Italian experiences and political theories which stood in opposition to the medieval tradition. Kallimach claimed that "the basis of the law is not justice but utility", which should be defined in accordance with "the conditions of the time, place, issue and the position of the citizens"; such an evaluation should be conducted by the monarch, responsible for the fate of the country, and for promulgating the law.

This point of view justified the right of the state to free its policies of any ties and limitations and, in particular, to defend its sovereign privileges from being questioned by the church hierarchy — the papal hierarchy in Rome and the local bishops.

Jan Ostoróg, a magnate from Great Poland, agreed with Kallimach's views. His monumental work on bringing order to the Commonwealth, completed in the last quarter of the fifteenth century, *Monumentum . . . pro Reipublicae ordinatione congestum,* postulated that the royal power be independent of Rome. This was to be expressed by renouncing payment of dues to Rome, abolishing the taking of oaths by bishops to the Pope, and by prohibiting appeals to the Roman Curia. In his opinion the church hierarchy should be treated equally with all other citizens, which meant that the church was to share in the same burden in the area of paying taxes and other dues to the state.

At the same time Ostoróg called for internal reforms, thanks to which the king would be able to rule more successfully. It was important to remove outdated laws and regional privileges, to abolish German and canon law, to standardize jurisdiction, to defend the burghers and, in particular, the peasants against feudal exploitation, and lastly to raise taxes and reorganize the army.

Kallimach and Ostoróg laid down — or perhaps only foresaw — the future road towards progress. The consolidation of the state through integration and centralization and by defending and securing its sovereignty became the points in a common program which was pursued by the royal court and by the political parties of Renaissance Poland.

A political struggle for church reforms in the first half of the sixteenth century proved the validity and strength of this program. As a result of a growing conflict between the gentry and the church hierarchy concerning various economic and religious issues, the idea of becoming

49

independent from Rome, which would allow Poles to decide for themselves in the event of religious arguments, gained significant support. The concept of convening a national church council was supported at an early stage not only by dissenters but also by Catholics; even the primate, Jakub Uchański, was in favor of it. At the Seym session in 1552, both deputies and senators joined in attacks against the bishops, and even against the king for his compliance with the latter's wishes. First the suspension of church jurisdiction in matters of faith was achieved. Another achievement was that the district headman *(starost)* was no longer allowed to execute sentences passed by ecclesiastical courts in secular matters. The king did not want to be "the king of conscience", which in practice meant that the state refused to play the role of a secular sword to impose the judgments of the Catholic church or other churches. The state was to guarantee freedom of religion to everybody so that citizens would have the right to argue and dispute ideas, which would eventually lead to agreement.

In this way the great evolutionary circle of ideas concerning the state and the foundations and the basic orientation of its politics steadily closed. While the most immediate need of the mid-fifteenth century was to make the state independent of the church — both of Rome and the political influence of the ecclesiastical hierarchy at home — in the mid-sixteenth century it became possible to make the Church and its affairs at least partly dependent on the state.

THE KING AS RULER
OF THE COMMONWEALTH

The program of defense, consolidation and enlarging of state sovereignty was inseparable from the complex and disputed problem of sovereign power in the country. It was a lively and controversial issue which contemporary society focused on. The king was a symbol of the unity and permanence of the state. He was sanctified by kingship and was the highest authority in the state. He was an arbiter placed above the disputing parties who could turn to him to seek justice and protection. At the same time, however, the king presented a threat of absolute rule, of despotism and tyranny, a source of many fears among the gentry who worried that their freedoms could be limited. The coexistence of these two tendencies characterized the legal-political structures and institutions as well as the political awareness of the whole epoch.

Stanisław Orzechowski expressed current public opinion regarding the unusual character of the political system in those days. In his address to the Polish knights, in the form of a preface to *The Rules and Regulations,* collected and edited by Jakub Przyłuski, Stanisław Orzechowski contended that the Polish political system incorporated elements of all political systems known throughout the world, such as monarchy, aristocracy and democracy. Poland, according to him, was a monarchy, but secured against tyranny; it was an aristocracy, but organized for the benefit of all, and not just a few; it was a democracy,

but one that was free of social unrest and tumult. The king, the Senate and the people constituted a peculiar threefold configuration of power, mutually supportive and delimiting: "neither the reign of one, nor the power of a few, nor the rule by everybody."

REFORM OF THE COMMONWEALTH

The state, organized according to the aforementioned principles, was ever more widely called a Commonwealth, and although the word meant simply a state in Renaissance Europe, the new name was given particular significance in Poland.

The name *Rzeczpospolita* (Commonwealth) — *respublica* — eventually removed and replaced the traditional medieval name of kingdom — *regnum* — in Renaissance Poland. In the eyes of the public and in official nomenclature the state was now a "common wealth", that is, it was owned by everyone, although it still remained a kingdom. This unusual change was made as a result of an enthusiastic approach toward classical antiquity and, in particular, Roman history. It was not an ordinary consequence of this humanist approach, however. Rhetoric was only a form for the substance, which resulted from social processes which increasingly brought the magnates and gentry to greater involvement in ruling the country. Nevertheless, the acceptance of this stylistic convention was not without influence upon the very substance of social experiences.

While the notion of the kingdom was linked with the concept of citizens of a state — *regnicolae* — being the subjects — *subditi* — of the king, the Commonwealth was a common good which required definition in terms of what it was, who it belonged to, and how it should be organized. Jurists and politicians tried to provide answers to these questions, as did philosophers, writers and poets. This issue was of interest to both the deputies of the gentry and the senators, to leaders of various Reformation factions and to the Catholics. They all tried to define what should be reformed in Poland and how it should be done: in the political system, class privileges, jurisdiction, administration and education. The answers differed greatly and those differences revealed the deepest social conflicts of the epoch, which later served as the basis for different visions concerning the future of the country.

Andrzej Frycz Modrzewski assumed a more radical stand on this issue. His social outlook was rooted in the religious idea of the equality of man. Why had society made men unequal when God had made all men equal in the first place? The most evident example of that inequality in Poland was the inequitable punishment imposed for killing a gentleman and killing a peasant. "Why," asked Modrzewski, "were commoners barred from taking high-level offices, even though their virtues and knowledge were impeccable and remarkable?" In this case, did they belong to the Commonwealth or not? The Commonwealth, as Modrzewski understood it, was a commonwealth of equal people of good will, a moral commonwealth enabling everyone to lead an honest life, a commonwealth of a just social order inside the country 50 and peace outside, and a place where different religions existed in reconciliation. The Commonwealth was also to take equal care of the education and welfare of all its inhabitants.

A program of reform formulated in such a way could hardly become popular. The opinion was widespread among the gentry that it was not a program of reforms, which would fit new situations and tasks that really mattered. What the gentry insisted upon was the "reinstitution" of the old order everywhere it had been — in fact, or only in their own view — violated. What actually mattered was not to make a sober analysis of contemporary society but rather to create myths about it through rhetoric and pathos. Thus the model of the Roman tradition was to be imitated and applied to the Polish situation. In this way, these courageous thoughts and plans, based on rational considerations of right and wrong, were opposed by belief in the "natural" course of events, the "wisdom" contained in traditions, faith in old-fashioned principles and institutions, and even sometimes Providence itself, which was supposed to govern contemporary history, and in particular, Polish history.

The speeches of the nobility at Seym sessions and at regional diets, leaflets printed in the course of the interregnum and free elections, various resolutions and manifestoes — these were all aimed to promote this political approach.

Under these circumstances the entire evolution of understanding of the concept of the Commonwealth was directed toward narrowing the scope of the commonwealth and not opening it up for the entire population. It aimed at such transformations of its essential values that would secure the defense of the interests of the privileged groups and not the common good. More and more people began to assert that those who dealt in trade and crafts could not belong to this community. This meant that the Commonwealth was becoming a Commonwealth of the gentry to the exclusion of all others.

THE ARIAN CONCEPT OF EQUALITY AND COMMONWEALTH

The Arians were outsiders in the whole discussion concerning "the common wealth". Their ideology grew from both the Anabaptist traditions and from humanist rationalism. They opposed not only Catholic concepts but also the views of the followers of Luther and Calvin. A large group of Arians, mostly of plebeian descent, was represented by Piotr of Goniądz, Grzegorz Paweł of Brzeziny, Marcin Czechowic, Jan Niemojewski and Paweł of Wizna. Their theological views were severely criticized by all other religious groups; their social views challenged the entire system of the state and its authority. The 1566 Seym, as a result of a motion by Calvinist senators, considered the question of expelling the Arians from the country. The resolution was not adopted, but Hieronim Filipowski, defending the case of the Arians by presenting the argument that the time would come when Christ and not kings would try people, was accused of lese majesty.

Mikołaj Sienicki, speaker of the Seym and also an Arian, won Filipowski's case in court. However, from that time on, the Arian social program became the target of widespread criticism. The Calvinist headman *(wójt)* of Vilna, Augustyn Rotundus, wrote the following about the Arians: "They oppose all authority, all offices, praise Christian freedoms and introduce collective ownership of all property; they would also make all estates equal, both in the church and the state, in order to get rid of all differences between the king and the people, between the ruler and his subjects, and between the gentry and the plebeians."

Indeed, many Arians organized their lives in accordance with the radical requirements of their religion: "There were such," wrote Andrzej Lubieniecki, "who worked as peasants, using their own hands."

In fact these radical concepts were not unanimously recognized in Arian circles. Szymon Budny, for example, represented a more moderate and conformist approach toward the social system and state authority, but the Arian left formulated a social reform program with courage and determination. Their program of social reforms was to provide a paradise on earth — a real Christian Commonwealth.

"Christ, our Lord, did not come down to earth merely to lead His disciples into the world, for them to give counsel or to govern the world, but in order that they should turn aside from the world and feel hatred for it," wrote Marcin Czechowic. According to this program, private property was to be liquidated and serfdom no longer to be tolerated. Paweł of Wizna preached that "a religious man should not keep any serfs, let alone men and women slaves; for only pagans dominate over their brothers, using their blood and sweat." Resolutions were passed at many Arian synods, demanding that ministers "earn their living with their own hands," that they sell their inherited property, which their ancestors were given for "shedding blood", and that the money they made should be given away to the poor. Such a radical ideology insisted on refusal to participate in wars, rejection of the state judicial system and, in particular, condemnation of capital punishment. Many Arians displayed their radical attitude by carrying wooden swords, by resigning their offices, and giving up court cases in which they had been involved. Peasants were released from doing compulsory work and were given back their freedom. Jan Niemojewski resigned his position as district judge, returned his crown lands and sold family estates, giving the money to the poor; after which he earned his living as a craftsman.

As the Arians became more threatened and isolated, their ideas of tolerance proved to be more and more meaningful to the new life-style. As early as the seventeenth century, Jonasz Szlichtyng, an Arian, wrote the following about the problem of religious freedom: "What does freedom of conscience, which is subordinated solely to God, consist in if not in the fact that you think freely about religious matters, freely express your ideas and are able to do anything which does no harm to other human beings?"

In this way, for the first time in the history of Polish culture, there appeared a fundamental ideological and moral conflict between ethical and social radicalism on the one hand and sober consideration on the other. Radicalism was ready to make all possible sacrifices and even risk total annihilation in defending its program. Sober consideration led to compromise, thanks to which it might be possible — though at a risk of losing its Christian purity — to achieve at least the minimum aims of a Christian organization of social life. This conflict between radicalism, or perhaps quixoticism, which led to alienation from social and public life, on the one hand, and conformism, which threatened the rejection of one's own philosophy, on the other hand, was to be ever-present in Polish history in the centuries to come.

FREE ELECTIONS:
A TEST OF POLITICAL MATURITY

The death of Sigismund Augustus without leaving an heir, made it necessary for the community of the gentry to take public affairs into their own hands. So long as the monarch was still alive, the participation of both the gentry and the magnates in ruling the country had a secondary and limited character; the interregnum period was thus a difficult test for this heterogeneous group to prove its maturity and sense of responsibility.

The test became more difficult the more often it was repeated, for in the course of the next fourteen years a new monarch had to be elected three times. The first election of 1573 brought victory to Henri de Valois, who secretly fled the country a year later. Stephen Báthory, who was elected in December 1575, ruled for only ten years. Thus in 1587 another election had to take place. Sigismund III Vasa, disliked from the very beginning by Polish court circles, was elected king of Poland.

These three elections within the lifespan of one single generation, revealed all the severe and difficult problems which the ruling class had to face and deal with. The political writings and leaflets from the period prove that there was a great deal of uneasiness and uncertainty present in contemporary society.

First of all, there was a fundamental discrepancy as to who should rule the country: a foreigner or a "Piast", a native of old Poland? The unfortunate election of de Valois strengthened the position of the political wing that was in favor of a Pole. However, such a solution was opposed for two reasons: firstly, a decision in favor of a Polish-born king violated the principle of the equality of the gentry; for it was not easy to approve of someone who "was one of us" ruling "over us." The second reason was connected with the multinational structure of the Commonwealth. "I do not think there is any way of electing a ruler from among this nation," wrote Jan Dymitr Solikowski, "since the Commonwealth and the kingdom is shared by the Poles, Lithuanians, Prussians, Ruthenians, as well as the people of Samogitia, Livonia, Podlasie, Volhynia and Kiev." Even if these words were meant to be a cunning tactical maneuver, they clearly indicated the complexity of the problem of electing a king from among the citizenry of such a multinational state.

And still the election of a foreigner always made things more complicated in both the internal affairs of the state and in its foreign policy. The latter had to respect the dynastic plans of a foreigner, once he acceded to the Polish throne.

Therefore, people were more than willing to believe that it was still possible "to elect a king from among peers, who had previously been equal with us before the law and had served with us the one Lord, and had the same customs as the rest." However, events developed in a different direction. After de Valois fled the country, Stephen Báthory took over the Polish throne and after his death, he was succeeded by Sigismund, a representative of the Vasa dynasty, about whom the supporters of the Piasts warned, that "the kingdom should not be given to be ruled by such a distant monarch."

In this way there appeared an internal discrepancy in the national consciousness between the concept of the state as an organization of the whole nation, and submission to the highest authority in the state which remained in the hands of a foreigner. This conflict was expressed in Mikołaj Zebrzydowski's rebellion in a way that weighed heavily on the further development of Polish national awareness. Hundreds of elegies, such as *The Elegy of the Polish Crown, A Threnody of the Commonwealth,* and *The Lament,* expressed all the grievances held against Sigismund III. A malicious paraphrase of the Lord's Prayer was addressed to the king: "To Thy Swedish Kingdom Go!" Hundreds of leaflets, speeches, satires, dialogues and treatises described the purposes of the rebellion in terms of defending the Commonwealth and restoring justice to it. This kind of ideology, often filled with pathos and a mystification of reality, and yet effective, became the basis for the differentiation and contrast between the state, which was to be a state of the gentry, and the king who was not to be regarded as a ruler even though he had been chosen through election to govern.

View of the World

THE NEW NATURAL SCIENCES

"Reason itself proves that it is nature which rules" were the words of Biernat of Lublin, expressed in his work, *A Brief Description of Aesop's Life and Some Other Affairs of His.* It was published in Cracow, around 1522. Only one edition from 1578 has been preserved. This work constituted a demarcation line between the medieval and Renaissance views of the world in sixteenth century Poland. These words were pronounced by Aesop when he could not agree with the answer given to a gardener by a philosopher. The former wanted to know why herbs, planted by people, did not grow as fast as wild ones. Having no explanation of his own, the philosopher 52 answered by referring to God, Who had planned the world according to His own will. Aesop felt that things could just as easily be explained in lay terms: "He who makes God responsible for everything does not reveal the real cause of the matter," wrote Biernat. Admittedly, Aesop's explanation was far from being scientific: he made it clear that nature "bears herbs as its own children," that is, it takes greater care of its own offspring than foundlings. But this opened new possibilities for seeking the causes of natural processes within nature itself.

Biernat opened up an analogous method for human reason in the field of religion: "It seems to me that divine judgments are impenetrable and that, except for the Bible, no other regulations ought to be recognized, since they are indiscernible and uncertain," wrote Biernat in a letter to a Cracow bookseller, Szymon, in 1515 — that is, before Luther nailed his 39 theses to the church door in Wittenberg. And although obedience to papal decisions could guarantee "simplicity of religious faith," Biernat believed that "the human mind cannot be suppressed in its search for truth," and that it is hard to believe that "we might fall into the power of sin because of seeking after truth." The letter ended with a brief confession: "I approve of nothing firmly, except faith in Christ."

A new scientific approach and a new program of scientific research, both of them socially very useful, was formed and developed according to the guidelines indicated by Biernat. Though the idea of reason in social service was not a product of Renaissance culture (it had appeared already in medieval Poland, in particular in Cracow circles as well as in international disputes) it, nonetheless, aquired a new substance in the sixteenth century. More important than traditional philosophy were empirical studies, leading to a better grasp of reality and to bold criticism of ancient and scholastic knowledge. Knowledge of natural science, directly useful in practical matters, turned out to be more profitable than the study of law.

From this point of view, attempts were made to learn about the geographical and scientific environment, to study man and protect his health. A book by Maciej of Miechów, *Tractatus de duabus Sarmatiis Asiana et Europiana* (1517), presented the first appropriate picture of Eastern Europe and became one of the most widely read scientific books in contemporary Europe. In the sixteenth century alone it went through eleven new editions. A precise map of Poland was prepared and published in Cracow by Bernard Wapowski in 1526. Jan Stanko from Silesia edited a huge catalogue of Polish flora and fauna, containing 523 species of medicinal herbs and 219 species of animals. Numerous herbal manuals were compiled, pioneered by Stefan Falimirz. His medical-botanical volume, *On Herbs and Their Potency*, published in 1534, was meant primarily to serve areas where people had neither "doctors" nor pharmacies. Adam of Bochynia dealt with the natural resources available in the country; Adam Schröter described the salt-mines of Wieliczka (1553); Stanisław Grzepski was the author of a handbook on geometry, which he defined as a "science of measuring" (1566). Medical studies and medical practice

enjoyed a steady growth, while the medical papers of Józef Struś gained European recognition.

The development of the empirical sciences was accompanied by a steady progress in the field of mathematics and astronomy, especially towards the end of the fifteenth century. Cracow became the center of these studies, attracting scholars and students from all over Europe. The talent of Nicolaus Copernicus developed in this scientific atmosphere. In 1543, in the year of the author's death, his immortal work, *De revolutionibus orbium coelestium*, appeared, providing a turning point not only in the knowledge about the world but also in ways of acquiring this knowledge. The intellectual courage of Copernicus consisted not only in his opposition to the geocentric theory, which was supported by the ancient and medieval authorities, but also in his questioning of the immediate evidence of his eyes, which showed the Sun movable and the Earth stationary. Copernicus' method was the first attempt at combining empirical observation with mathematical calculation. Such a combination made it possible to discover the principles according to which the planets revolved, which could not be discerned by sensory observation but had now been revealed by mathematics. Modern science was born not only in the course of battles against previous authorities, with the help of simple empirical observation, but also, in the course of a battle against narrow-minded sensualism, which did not allow study of the mechanisms of movement and the principles governing nature which, in turn, could only be grasped by a mathematical method.

In this way reason, equipped with mathematical knowledge that was an expression of the essence of reason itself and also the nature of scientific reality, was becoming the highest instance in science. In this sense Copernicus wrote of his method: "We have found by these methods the wonderful orderliness of the world . . . which otherwise would hardly have been discovered."

From the philosophical point of view, Copernicus' theory was not intended, as was then fairly generally thought, to degrade man by degrading the Earth from its privileged, central position in the universe. Copernicus' theory, which made the Earth movable, made at the same time the Sun stationary as well as central in the universe and vital as a life-giving force. The Earth and its inhabitants were thus guaranteed development within the rays of the Sun, around which other planets also revolved. In this sense Copernicus' teachings brought up a concept of new universal harmony, and also, a new interrelation between man and his universe. This great *harmonia mundi* was simultaneously the harmony of man, as a creature equipped with reason, an expression of the mathematical order of the world, within the universe, lit by the Sun.

SOCIAL ISSUES BEFORE
THE TRIBUNAL OF REASON

The turning point regarding man's knowledge about nature ignited another change in the field of social science. The human mind, which managed to penetrate through the veil of superstitions and sensory illusions by uncovering the real essense of nature and its mathematical rules, refused to abandon its privileges in other areas.

Nonetheless, the obstacles that were to be overcome in the social realm, seemed to be much greater than those which had previously made it so difficult to carry out natural research. And yet there was a need for the social sciences which manifested itself quite early. There were frequent arguments championing the value of reason, in both philosophical and theological disputes on the idea of conciliarism. These arguments were also used in legal discussions concerning royal power and state sovereignty. At the close of the Middle Ages, Stanisław Zaborowski wrote about "science, enlightening the whole kingdom."

From the beginning of the sixteenth century there was a proliferation of opinions which postulated that reason be granted more privileges in forming people's lives in society, their conduct and morality and their political system. Understandably, such a tendency was also revealed in literature, although the latter was influenced by humanist ideology only to a small degree. The literary trend was represented by two folk heroes of vernacular literature: Marchołt and Eulenspiegel, as well as two authors, Glaber of Kobylin and Marcin Bielski. In *The Lives of Philosophers* Bielski frequently referred to the actual meaning of learning in man's life. He recalled old thinkers who "had led odd and not very pleasurable lives, and who sacrificed their lives to learning and worship." He argued further that "human reasoning is necessary to man" to teach him how to live in virtue. The words of Bielski, whose *Chronicles of the Entire World* contained a portrait of the scholar and the epigraph "Never against the truth of reason", became the main slogan of the group that fought to reconstruct the political system of the Commonwealth.

A program of such reconstruction was most effectively presented by Andrzej Frycz Modrzewski, whose activities fully expressed the new trends in social reality and a new philosophy on society. As Copernicus observed the movements of heavenly bodies to discover the laws that governed them, Modrzewski studied closely the course of people's lives and society in the Commonwealth in order to define the existing social order. The actual picture of reality became a starting point of criticism and postulates for reform, with the latter based on reason. All conflicting issues were to be considered from this point of view. According to Modrzewski, "everything should be brought before the tribunal of reason instead of being submitted to insolent or deceitful emotions which often run much too high: let those judges take their stand, for whom the good of the whole country and the high office of law are far more important than profits, revenge, and godless arbitrary rule; who would like to see law and the power of good in force in the interests of nature and not of one single estate; who want to bring equal rights to all living in this Commonwealth."

The tribunal of reason was to solve problems of unjust laws allowing the gentry to remain lawless and exploitative while dealing with the peasants. The gentry destroyed the principles of natural and Christian equality of men, allowing intolerance and fanaticism to govern their lives. "The laws require much improvement," wrote Modrzewski, "and their dignity and greatness can surely be restored only by those who really know what they are, since it is only they who can transform things that have not been a science into a science. So far as faith is concerned it cannot be defended without the sound knowledge of the various sciences, and those who believe it can, will certainly discover that they are wrong in a terrible and fatal way; it is easy to fall, like a ship that plunges into icebergs, from such error to criminal conduct; and many people have been taught this lesson by the greatest teacher of all, that is experience."

A combination of the two principles, that is, reason and experience, to examine society, enabled Modrzewski to form a basis for an ideal vision of the Commonwealth, in which the dream that "all citizens may live peacefully and happily" could come true. The leading role in such a Commonwealth was relegated to philosophers who were to "guard the common health and be on guard for truth." "They employ," wrote Modrzewski, "a lively strength of spirit in order to lead people to honesty." "Only if human viciousness destroys this goal" should royal power be allowed "to use sword and force" as a last resort. Schools are the basis for such an order, that is, a lay power of reason and a lay power for using force, that "opened the way to the virtues which provided foundations upon which the laws that governed in the Commonwealth could later be established." Therefore, his treatise *On the Reform of the Commonwealth* devotes an entire volume to education.

THE SECULAR CONCEPT OF HUMAN LIFE

The Renaissance view of the world encouraged everyone to enjoy manifold during his lifetime.

Latin poetry, written in Poland by foreigners, for example, Kallimach or Celtis, showed this Renaissance completeness of individual life by depicting love, enjoyment, and travel. The Polish poets, writing in Latin, such as Andrzej Krzycki, Jan Dantyszek, and Klemens Janicki, developed this concept of life.

The ups and downs of human life were depicted incomparably more richly by the most famous writer of the period, a member of the gentry, Mikołaj Rej, in his *Self-Portrait of a Kind-Hearted Man,* and the later prose work *The Life of a Kind-Hearted Man.* By combining man's life with the changes of the four seasons of the year, Rej managed to show the beauty and richness of such a rhythm which governed the world. He criticized those who rebelled against the passing of time and the seasons: "When the time of bidding one's farewell to the world" nears, "whether it be in one's own room or near the fireplace," it should be a time of great harmony with the all-embracing rhythm of nature, a harmony which allows acceptance of the passing of time, and also admits painless remembrance of events lived through that can now be reflected upon with ease and a quiet mind.

Jan Kochanowski, the great lyric poet, so different from 54

Rej in his basic beliefs, defined life in another, but, in essence, similar way. In his famous epigram *To Mountains and Forests,* the poet, returning to the country of his youth, remembers the course of his life: first, when he traveled as a student, and later as a knight; when he lived "as a courtier in a castle," and later as "a priest in the chapter house", until he came back to his "high mountains and green woods," where his "youthful moments" had passed. This epigram on life ends with the avowal that the wise man grasps things at the right time.

In many of his songs and epigrams, Kochanowski expressed the concept of life as a variety of events and experiences, the value of passing occasions, always full of glamor, as an eternal present that is indifferent to the future and free of worries which ruin the immediacy of experience.

In this "making the most of the present", love was to occupy a special place, and although love was not only the source of joy but heartaches as well, it was able to overcome the viciousness of the world and all its cataclysms.

Love — "the dispenser of griefs and joys" — was the gift of a beloved woman. It was also a source of friendship as, for example, those guests who talked about life in the shadow of a lime-tree. Here good thoughts were born, especially when lute and wine aided conversation.

This concept of life, rich and versatile, was also expressed by Polish Renaissance music. During the second half of the fifteenth century, especially in the academic society of Cracow, it was music that served to express the joy of life, its pastimes and its love affairs. In the sixteenth century it became a permanent component of life, both in the manor-houses and in the towns; it became the irreplaceable companion of people in their everyday life and on holidays — in their homes, on the streets of the towns, and in village inns. A great deal of this music was set down in *The Tablature of Jan of Lublin,* the most voluminous book of organ music in sixteenth century Europe. This can be seen in the titles of these works: "On a Shoemaker, Going Along the Street and Carrying Awls"; or "But There's Venus" or "Eyes Dear to Me". A famous lutanist, Valentin Bakfark, composed similar songs in the royal court. The songs openly expressed men's experiences, their needs, their joys, and their pastimes.

Man proposes, God disposes; and the program of enjoying life was not always carried out in accordance with man's plans. The fates also sent defeats and suffering. The wheel of fortune was a problem that many Polish writers were aware of and anxious to solve. Like their colleagues elsewhere, they tried to find answers to such questions as: How should men live and behave in times of disaster and miseries? From what source were they to regain their strength?

An attitude of resignation, so far as life was concerned, was not approved of. On the other hand, involvement and the courage to challenge one's fate were appreciated. In one of his epigrams Kochanowski wrote: "Let everything be courageously withstood when necessary." In his *Thre-nodies,* he put the following words into a mother's mouth: "Bear your human experiences in a human way." This

advice, known to man in antiquity, was valued by humanists because it proved man's dignity and courage; it expressed the peculiar heroism of a lonely man struggling against his fate.

From this point of view, Roman writers were most often cited, in particular, Cicero and Seneca, and the great humanists of those days, especially Erasmus of Rotterdam. Numerous translations and adaptations proved that such sympathies and affinities existed. Stanisław Koszutski translated Cicero's *De officiis* (1575). In 1561 and 1565 Patrycy Nidecki edited and wrote a critical introduction to four volumes of Cicero's writings that were recognized all over Europe. Cicero was also referred to by Kochanowski on many occasions. The philosophical prose of Seneca was translated by Górnicki, especially *De beneficiis* (1593), and also some of his tragedies.

RELIGION AS CONSOLATION AND CHRIST'S CHALLENGE

However, this humanistic and stoic consolation did not suffice; not everybody was able to produce secular courage in misery. Therefore, the philosophy that was formed in Poland in the sixteenth century, emphasized a religious concept of life. Nevertheless, the church hierarchy was consistently criticized within the framework of this very concept. The church's materialist attitude and its dependence on Rome were the two main reasons for this criticism. The fact was that the matter of faith did not fit in with the position and demands of the clergy, or with the whole organization of the Catholic church. The Reformation, which spread all over Poland during the second half of the century, strengthened the conviction that faith was the private matter of believers and not the province of bishops, parish priests, or vicars.

People needed faith. The intensity of the Reformation revealed that such a need was very strong and widespread. The Counter-Reformation in the Catholic church emphasized the fact by the end of the century. Faith was not needed in matters of the state and its politics, for studying the world or for education, but it was necessary for people who wanted to know how to live. They were looking for the highest and most rigid principles of moral conduct and needed to be assured that everlasting and omnipotent protection was being provided for them from above.

Almost all the writers of the Renaissance served this cause, even in times when they served other causes. Biernat of Lublin not only propagated the sour folk wisdom of Aesop but also was the author of *A Paradise of Souls,* meant to teach man how to live and express his pleas to God: "To destroy the devil's snare and all our enemies." The most important works by Rej — *Postils, Image* and *Mirror* — developed the concept of a "Christian man." Kochanowski translated the *Psalms of David,* the most frequently read Polish poetry of the sixteenth and seventeenth centuries. In his numerous songs, in particular in the *Threnodies,* he presented the religious contemplation of life; when Fortune brings calamities to people, "there is only one Lord of sorrow and of reward," the mother remarks in the *Threnodies.*

Yet these religious experiences evolved in various ways. In the course of several decades of the sixteenth century, this variety of religious experiences was a source, and in a sense, the effect of an extremely rich intellectual trend which expressed itself in hundreds of Synod disputes and books of all kinds.

One of the most prominent Polish Arians, Grzegorz Paweł of Brzeziny, entitled his book, printed in 1568, *The Antihymn of Despised Servants of Christ.* It was a bitter polemic directed against all those who served "an evil world," those who organized official churches and employed theology instead of the Bible.

A comparison of this work with a contemporary hymn by Kochanowski, "What do You Want, Lord, for Your Generous Gifts", that had been published in 1562, indicates that the Polish religious practice of the epoch was polarized. On the one hand, there were Catholics and also heretics, who cherished God's greatness and might, His hatred or love for people, who seemed always small before Him but equal to each other in their smallness. On the other hand, there were the Arians, lonely and persecuted, who revealed the deep conflicts between those who were Christians in name only or by virtue of their office, and those who courageously followed the Way of the Cross, in hope of salvation.

In this ideology of the "despised," widely differing philosophical trends converged. Marcin Czechowic, representing a fairly popular Arian conviction, wrote the following: "God chooses those who are unknown to the world, fools and weaklings in order to confuse the stronger ones, thus rendering human wisdom foolish." Stanisław Wiśniowski contended that "we do not need acts, speculations, and human sciences." Jan Niemojewski preached that an uneducated man with "his understanding based on the simple message of the word of God," heads straight for his goal, while scientists "brood over their speeches and fruitless debates, going round and round in circles."

However, this conflict with theology in defense of the Bible needed some historical and philosophical knowledge. In this regard, "the greatest power can do nothing without reason," wrote Szymon Budny. Thus the history of Polish culture witnessed a symbiosis of irrational needs and forces proved by individual involvement in the crusading war against the "world", and the critical strength of reason, which was called to fight all forms of idolatry even if they were disguised in alleged holiness and the authority of the church.

The Arts

ART AND POETRY

Polish culture during the Renaissance was characterized by a great richness in the means of expression. Sacral and secular architecture remained an expression of monumental assumptions. Its importance consistently increased, since it was to serve not only the needs of the royal court and the ambitions of the lords, but also the aspirations of the gentry and the burghers.

The beginning of Renaissance culture in Poland was marked by the conversion of the Royal Castle at Wawel in Cracow into a splendid Renaissance residence; the end of the era came while the "Tribune of the Gentry", Chancellor Jan Zamoyski, was carrying out ambitious plans to build the Renaissance city of Zamość. Within these time limits, architecture blossomed, inspired and financed by various social groups.

Castles, residences, palaces, mansions, burgher houses, townhalls, churches and monasteries were built. The manor-houses of the gentry were also undergoing reconstruction and improvements. Only village architecture preserved its old style since the peasants were no longer in a position to try any new forms in building.

Many foreign architects and master builders came to Poland, especially from Italy. In time, however, there were increasing numbers of Polish specialists.

In 1512 in Cracow, a new guild of masons and bricklayers was created. Other cities followed Cracow's example. The stone quarries in Pińczów were the main source of building material for the entire country.

Unlike architecture, painting and sculpture produced little of significance. The achievements at the end of the Middle Ages and beginning of the Renaissance, for example, the altarpiece of Wit Stwosz (Veit Stoss) or *Behem's Codex,* were never surpassed. The social significance which art had attained, especially in Cracow, at the end of the fifteenth century, suddenly lost momentum.

Among the various trends during the Renaissance period, literature developed most rapidly and became of increased social importance. During the Renaissance Polish culture became mainly a "culture of words". This was closely connected with both the new possibilities created by the invention of printing and the new character of public life inspired by the movement of the gentry and the Reformation debates.

While in all other areas of creativity — architecture, painting, sculpture and music — the basic structure of relationships between art and society did not noticeably alter during the Renaissance, even when new styles appeared, in the sphere of literature and poetry, fundamental changes took place.

In the sixteenth century, a real revolution occurred — the invention of printing. With the advent of printing, it became relatively cheap to copy texts which were now given a wider range of circulation throughout society. In Poland people began to read and to discuss issues. The speeches at Seyms and regional diets, the discussions taking place during the synods and the conventions, the various political writings at times of interregnum and at elections, and especially church sermons were born of new books and political leaflets; at the same time, they gave rise to new secular books and new political pamphlets. There was an incessant inter-action between the printed and spoken word, which was later recognized as a characteristic of modern culture.

This spoken and written polemics was only a part of the gigantic "culture of the word" that was created during the era of the Renaissance in Poland. During the next few decades a new and exceptionally varied literature came into being — narrative, drama, prose and poetry. Latin and Polish poetry were written; there were also mystery plays, carnival drama, morality plays, satire, novels, aprocryphal religious literature, historical-secular literature, philosophical and moralizing literature, chivalrous literature, and humorous literature, presenting such characters as Marchołt, Aesop, and Eulenspiegel. Historiography, geography and scientific literature also developed. Literary styles were formulated and improved: the lyric, the hymn, the epigram, songs, satire, parable and drama.

But it was poetry that had an outstanding career and gave Polish Renaissance culture its own specific character. It dominated not only the lyric, drama and epic, but also such areas as political and religious writings, various polemics, philosophical treatises, and history. Poetry became something more than the art of writing poems; it seemed to become a very special gift of the muse, which allowed the poet to understand the world better and to describe it more deeply.

Zbigniew Oleśnicki, writing to the Italian humanist Aeneas Silvius Piccolomini in 1453, described the great function of poetry as "luring the souls of the readers" and acquainting them with the "excellent lessons" that poetry can draw from history and nature. This was to be the sense of "poetic fiction", which in later years was sometimes unjustly accused of being spurious.

Grzegorz of Sanok, according to Kallimach, stated that it was "much easier for someone who understands poetry to become acquainted with other disciplines than for someone who is acquainted with other disciplines to understand poetry".

Music, which had already found favorable conditions in which to develop at the court of Ladislaus Jagiello, now began to gain even more significance in expressing religious and secular experiences. At the beginning of the sixteenth century, the royal court was a very important center of muscial life, attracting various foreigners to Poland. For a certain period, Cracow was not only an international center of astronomy and mathematics but also of music. It was in Cracow that the German composer, Heinrich Finck, found a place to study and work. Various composers of religious and secular music gained fame and renown; among these were Wacław of Szamotuły, Marcin Leopolita, Sebastian of Felsztyn, and Mikołaj Gomółka.

At the royal court and also in other social circles, music, which was played at parties and banquets, also won a great deal of popularity. The same is true of lyrical music, dance music and what might be called music for high society, for whom the lute, wine and conversation were the main attractions of life. This was the character of music in both town and countryside.

Ceremonial songs and folk dances, as well as folk musical instruments, had from early times had their own individual character. In the sixteenth century, this type of music gained universal appeal. Many composers borrowed from this source, and created music which was again to return to the daily life and festivals of the small town and countryside. By combining various musical forms a completely new musical culture was created, a culture where the bounds between composers, players, and listeners partly vanished, a culture where new processes of mutual stimulation were born — very similar to what happened in literature amongst authors, printers and readers.

Songs combining this folk and burgher character also gained popularity and were extensively published at the end of the sixteenth and at the beginning of the seventeenth century: songs such as "A Maiden Took a Chicken to Town", "The Lady Had a Really Fine Student", and "Last Night the Fiddlers Sang about the Tailors".

ART CENTERS

Loose groups of intellectuals and artists linked by their mutual interests and frequently working at the court of wealthy patrons — secular or church dignitaries, or rich patricians — formed the nerve centers of cultural creativity.

In the fifteenth century, one such center was the court of the Archbishop of Lvov, Grzegorz of Sanok, at Dunajów; many poets and artists gathered there. Kallimach gives us very valuable information about the philosophical views of Grzegorz of Sanok and about the nature of various disputes that took place in Dunajów. In Cracow, Celtis (Conradus Celtes) established a literary society under the name of Sodalitas Litteraria Vistulana, operating in conjunction with the University. Also in Cracow, Kallimach organized in c. 1490 a new association of humanists; among its participants were professors of the Cracow Academy, Silesian scholars, like Wawrzyniec Corvinus-Rabe, and well-known royal courtiers. Kallimach had an important position at court as the adviser to the king, and his philosophical and artistic views were connected with political ideology, since he advocated strengthening the king's influence and power — to the later disgust of the gentry.

This intellectual circle gave birth to a new generation of patrons of the humanist movement, like Bishop Maciej Drzewicki and Bishop Piotr of Bnin. It is true that a conservative group of Cracow professors was opposed to these new trends but some of the most outstanding, not only from the arts faculty, participated in these meetings. The well-known astronomer and mathematician, Wojciech of Brudzew, who was also Copernicus' teacher, was very enthusiastic about Celtis' activity and even called him "his son". While the group centered around Kallimach was rather élite, and closely connected with the court, the Sodalitas Vistulana had members of burgher and plebeian origin.

Jan Łaski (Johannes a Lasco), a pupil of Erasmus of Rotterdam, became active somewhat later. He and his circle of devotees of Erasmus in Cracow favored the Reformation and the criticism heaped on church institutions. At the same time, a different group of admirers of Erasmus was concentrated around the person of Jost Decius, a burgher and the royal secretary and historian. These, as well as other groups, proved the existence of greater intellectual interests in the country. Krzysztof Szydłowiecki retained close contacts with Erasmus and also gathered a group of enthusiasts around himself. The attitude of this group, however, was completely different from Łaski's circle, which was primarily interested in the Reformation.

Andrzej Trzecieski (the elder) established a different type of artistic and intellectual community. His house in Cracow was a place where famous writers and political personalities met. Among them were Mikołaj Rej, Andrzej Frycz Modrzewski, Stanisław Orzechowski, Jakub Przyłuski, the Primate Jakub Uchański, the later Primate Jan Drohojowski, and Stanisław Hosius. This group also included leaders of the Reformation, like Franciszek Lismanin, Bernard Wojewódka, and others who later joined the heretical movement.

A group established by Joachim Retyk, a friend of Copernicus, was of a different character. The members of this group were basically representatives of the exact sciences from the University in Cracow and from outside. Among those who participated in these activities were: the Scot Martin Fox, the astrologer of Sigismund Augustus; Stanisław Grzepski, a mathematician and the author of a work on measurement; and Andrzej Dudycz, a Hungarian bishop living in Poland. The international character of Retyk's group, and the fact that it continued in existence for more than twenty years, proved that there was serious interest in learning in Cracow — and to a considerable degree outside university circles.

These scientific and literary circles were, during the first half of the sixteenth century, real centers of intellectual and literary activities; frequently, they were more modern than the University and attracted more mature people, not only students. The social role of these informal institutions was frequently more significant than the role of the University. While the University was facing financial difficulties and had to overcome the constantly increasing aversion of the royal court and the gentry and the indifference of its ecclesiastical patrons, the scholarly and literary circles, which included some of the most outstanding figures in Poland, were gaining greater direct significance in the development of opinions and views among secular and ecclesiastical dignitaries. In the late Middle Ages, the only center of intellectual activity had been the University of Cracow and a group of people directly connected with it and partly belonging to the royal court; in the sixteenth century, however, a new authentic society of intellectuals was formed, loosely organized but with a common approach to life and a common vision of the responsibilities to be assumed.

For the first time in Polish history, there was a wider "market" for culture, which in turn inspired the artists. This market was in the form of large numbers of rich courts linked with the new artistic and intellectual trends and their authors. Even if the kind of people grouped around those courts differed from those in the groups and associations mentioned above, they usually brought a new atmosphere, encouraging education, intellectual contacts, discussions, criticism, and literary and poetic interests.

The following court played this role: that of Piotr Tomicki, the Bishop of Cracow and deputy chancellor; of Jan Lubrański, Bishop of Poznań; of the Płock Bishops Erazm Ciołek and Samuel Maciejowski; and Jan Dantyszek, the Bishop of Warmia. Secular magnates, and also some wealthy burghers, competed with the dignitaries of the church.

In the first half of the century, the Cracow patricians — the Boner and Decius families — achieved a great deal in this field. During meetings organized in the houses of the burghers, the ideas for new and important works were sometimes born. In such an atmosphere, *A History of Poland* by Maciej of Miechów was written. Among the most famous and best known courts were the following: that of the Szydłowiecki family in Szydłowiec, which attracted many artists; that of Piotr Kmita, Rej's patron at Wiśnicz; the mansion owned by the Tęczyński family at Tęczyn; by the Tarnowski family near Tarnów; by the Black Radziwiłł; and finally Jan Zamoyski's residence, which was the most active at the end of the century.

THE SOCIAL ROOTS OF ART

Intellectual activities and art were connected in various ways to the aspirations and needs of the entire society. Art was inspired, as it had been in the Middle Ages, by the greatness of the country and the magnificence of its great families. This can best be discerned in the renovation and reconstruction of the royal residence in Cracow. The beauty and richness of the architecture, the unusual decorations of its coffered ceilings in the Deputies' Hall, with its 194 sculptured heads, the beautiful set of 356 Arrases made in Brussels, the wonderful furniture and carpets — all of these expressed the greatness of the country and its ruling dynasty. The large friezes represented knightly contests and troops marching in front of Sigismund the Old; another frieze showed the progress of human life from childhood to death beginning with an allegorical representation of misfortunes and adversity and finally ending in happiness and virtue.

Other newly constructed or reconstructed royal residences performed a similar function: the enormous castle at Kamieniec Podolski dating from the beginning of the century; the castle at Piotrkow, constructed during the years 1511—18; the castles at Niepołomice, built during the period 1550—71, and at Nowy Korczyn, Sandomierz and Warsaw; and in Lithuania, at Vilna.

The greatness of the country and its ruling dynasty was inseparable from the greatness of the wealthy families, which sought the same means of expression. Wawel served as a model for the Piast castle at Brzeg, decorated with busts of the Piasts, sculptured according to the illustrations included in the chronicles of Maciej of Miechów. It also was the model for another, smaller but equally charming residence for the Leszczyński family at Baranów, Mikołaj

Szydłowiecki constructed a castle in Szydłowiec, his brother Krzysztof in Ćmielów and Stanisław Szafraniec at Pieskowa Skała. Various other magnates constructed residences throughout Poland. Exceptionally magnificent were the castles in Tęczyn near Cracow and in Janowiec near Puławy (compared by contemporaries to the Wawel castle). Throughout the Renaissance and the Baroque periods, magnificent castles with arcaded courtyards were built in Baranów and Krasiczyn. The castle built by the Myszkowski family at Książ at the end of the sixteenth century was in a completely different architectural style.

The greatness of the dynasty and the magnate families also found expression in the need to ensure themselves a lasting place in the memory and in the hearts of those who would succeed them. Renaissance culture in Poland, as in other countries, did not dwell exclusively on happiness in life and life's charms; it sought also to overcome death by commemorating fame — in historiography, in poetry, and in sculpture.

For this reason, Jodok Ludwik Decius wrote glowingly about Sigismund the Old, his life and achievements; Maciej Drzewicki continued the work of Jan Długosz, presenting the history of the bishops of Wrocław; Łukasz Górnicki described the reign of Sigismund Augustus; Reinhold Heidenstein wrote of Stephen Báthory and Jan Zamoyski in order that the generations to follow would never forget them; Stanisław Orzechowski wrote about Jan Tarnowski.

The poets registered the great moments in the lives of the kings and wealthy magnates, anxious to commemorate their fame. Among these poets were Andrzej Krzycki and Paweł of Krosno, who worked at the royal court of Sigismund the Old. Stanisław Kleryka also specialized in writing such poetry. At the end of the century, Andrzej Zbylitowski portrayed the death of King Stephen, the victory of Jan Zamoyski, and various events from the times of Sigismund III. Bartosz Paprocki dedicated his whole artistic life to these commemorative works, including in them also portrayals of the gentry.

The same role was played by architecture and sculpture. The royal court also set an example in this field. The sepulchral chapel at Wawel, a great Renaissance work of art, built and designed under the personal supervision of Sigismund the Old, became an example for many secular and ecclesiastical magnates, who started building richly decorated mausoleums in their own churches. Those less wealthy ordered monuments or memorial tablets. The Primate, Jan Łaski, ordered marble memorial tablets for the bishops of Gniezno and located them in the cathedral; Jan Tarnowski financed the building of three such tombstones. In the second half of the sixteenth century hundreds of tombs and memorial tablets were erected which reveal the rich and varied history of family feeling, both private and patriotic: sorrow, pride, homage and praise. Some of these memorials provided almost a chronicle of greatness — for example the memorial to Hetman Tarnowski, sculpted by Padovano.

Tombs were often designed and made during the lifetime of those whose memory was to be preserved in this way for posterity. Chancellor Krzysztof Szydłowiecki adopted this method, putting up a tombstone with a bronze plaque, showing a marvellous scene of mourning for the deceased, in the collegiate church at Opatów.

Painters had less work in this field, although they were also involved to a certain extent in the commemorative process. This is indicated, for example, by the great family album *Liber geneseos* made for the Szydłowiecki family, illustrated with portraits of members of the family.

The majority of the gentry could not compete with the artistic activities of the royal court and the great magnates. Monumental Renaissance architecture was limited to the very richest groups of society. Over most of the country the same old manor houses of the gentry were still standing, although they were often modernized according to the latest fashion. The design was basically a rectangular block, with defensive towers at the four corners. The manor-house built at Szymbark in 1550 is an example of this style. Various modifications were later introduced to this basic plan, as can be seen in the construction of Wawrzyniec Lorek's manor-house in Pabianice in the 1560's.

These manor-houses were usually built by local craftsmen and artists whose role was also significant in the area of sacral architecture. The Gothic churches remained as a standard model, though new architectural elements were frequently added by the craftsmen. The range of this type of architecture can be illustrated by the fact that at the end of the fifteenth century and in the first half of the sixteenth century, 130 new churches were built by the gentry in Great Poland alone. These new constructions reflected both the tastes of the community and the skill of the local master-craftsmen.

Of particular significance was the construction of wooden churches, some of which were built on the orders of local peasants and village administrators. A sixteenth century chronicle remarks that "the carpenter, Jan Joachim Kukla of Grybów, received an order from the *sołtys* and peasants to build a church in Ptaszkowa". These small churches kept the traditional style of country architecture; some of them were decorated by wall paintings, executed by local artists. The native Polish character of these church paintings, as well as the wooden churches themselves, rarely survived; most were destroyed by fires and wars. Those that have survived — in Dębno Podhalańskie, in Krużlowa, Libusza, Krosno, Grębień, and Grybów — represent a Polish art that was both Renaissance and folk art, a trend similar to that produced in literature.

The architectural "face" of the Polish Renaissance was also shaped in the cities, in Gdańsk and Cracow and scores of poorer ones. Here, the activities of the famous foreign architects — especially the Italian and the Dutch — were always supplemented by master-builders of Polish origin. Under these circumstances, many new stylistic variations appeared, and the work often bore a marked local stamp.

Urban architecture consisted mainly of city halls, which, in the sixteenth century, were constructed or reconstructed in, for example, Cracow, Poznań, Tarnów, Sandomierz, Chełmno, Gdańsk, Biecz, Łowicz and Przemyśl; and in many towns in Silesia like Dzierżoniów and

Oleśnica. The wealthy families could afford to build houses, usually around the main market-square, not only in such cities as Gdańsk, Cracow or Lvov, but also in Tarnów, Krosno or Biecz. The facades of these houses and their interiors became one of the elements in the new life-style, in which, in contrast to the magnate mansions, the Renaissance joy of life went side by side with the work that was the source of their wealth.

Zamość was an outstanding example in the history of Polish towns. It was built by the chancellor, Jan Zamoyski, during the years 1580—1600. Another town of an equally exceptional character was Żółkiew, built a little later by Hetman Stanisław Żółkiewski.

Both were designed as fortified trading centers, as well as family seats, and both were built according to carefully drawn up plans. Jan Zamoyski possessed particular artistic and social ambitions. His town, constructed within a period of twenty years, constituted a perfect example of an architectural complex, which served people's day to day comforts, their intellectual aspirations (the Zamość Academy is an example of his ideas), commercial needs and defensive purposes.

Religious experiences were a great source of inspiration for artistic activities. Despite the fact that this was a continuation of the trend started during the Middle Ages, new forms and new elements were added. Religious experiences became a matter of personal and emotional needs; these were variously expressed by different artists. Philosophical meditations, concerning scholastic, metaphysical, and political problems, almost completely disappeared during the Polish Renaissance.

Moral problems remained important but arguments were expressed through different means, that is, Humanism. For the majority of society, religious needs and experiences were expressed through music, painting, and poetry. The integration of these three was one of the characteristics of the epoch.

At a more popular level, this integration took place in liturgical ceremonies and drama. Few historical documents provide evidence of this: a sixteenth century text of *The Story of the Glorious Resurrection of Our Lord*, written by Mikołaj of Wilkowiecko, who was prior of the monastery in Częstochowa, has survived, but there must have been many more such mystery plays. All the texts of the Polish morality plays were lost, but we know that the demand for this type of literature was enormous. Some attempts to appease the hunger for these plays were made by Marcin Bielski, in his *Comedy of Justyn and Konstancja*, and by Mikołaj Rej in his *Merchant*.

At the turn of the Middle Ages, a new symbiosis of word and image was reflected in such illuminated works as *The Gradual of King John Albert* and *The Pontifical of Erazm Ciołek*. The social demand for such masterpieces, all of them executed with painstaking care, was still significant. Many artists specialized in this area and the Cracow workshop of Stanisław Samostrzelnik of Mogiła, which prepared these illuminations, gained a national reputation.

During the reign of Sigismund the Old, this workshop produced magnificent prayer-books for Sigismund the Old and Queen Bona, and a beautiful missal for Bishop Piotr Tomicki. The bishop highly appreciated Stanisław of Mogiła and his work, stating that "there was no other painter who could better or more beautifully paint".

While expensive illuminated painting had a limited range of influence, music was accessible to almost everyone. The Reformation movement made wide use of music. The changes in the character of divine services and the involvement of believers in religious ceremonies led to a dynamic growth in the role of religious songs. Many hymn-books were printed, in which the music, together with the poetry, became a way of expressing the religious needs of the people. These needs were not only of a devotional character; they were frequently connected with the ordinary life-style. In Jan Seklucjan's hymn-book, *Christian Songs, New and Old,* published in Królewiec in 1559, we also find a patriotic hymn in honor of Sigismund Augustus which invokes the Lord to safeguard the happiness and greatness of Poland.

The favorite topic for musical composition among the Protestants (especially due to the creative work of Wacław of Szamotuły and Cyprian Bazylik) were the Psalms, based on the texts translated by Jan Kochanowski.

Catholic hymns were also set to music: Mikołaj Gomółka composed music to Kochanowski's *Psalms of David,* which became a book appropriate for individual reading and for personal meditations.

At the same time, music gained greater opportunities for independent development. Many orchestras and choirs were established, the most popular of which was the College of the Roratistes at the Sigismund Chapel at Wawel Cathedral. The Roratistes performed classical pieces composed by domestic and foreign composers. Among Polish composers were Mikołaj of Cracow, Wacław of Szamotuły, Cyprian Bazylik (who was at the same time a writer and translator of the Latin masterpiece by Andrzej Frycz Modrzewski, *On the Reform of the Commonwealth),* and Mikołaj Gomółka. Their musical compositions expressed the entire richness of the constantly changing feelings and moods of religious experiences.

The greatest possibility of expression was however given those that used words in bombastic and moralizing prose or lyric poetry. *The Polish Domestic Postils* by Grzegorz Orszak, published by Seklucjan in Królewiec in 1556, and Mikołaj Rej's *The Postils Written in Simple Polish Language, for Ordinary People,* published in Cracow in 1557, were not meant to be used in church services but rather for private reading and meditations among simple people. These books were meant to reveal the Holy Word in ordinary day-to-day life.

The poetry written by Kochanowski opened a direct way to God on which the church did not have exclusive rights, according to the words of the hymn, "What Do You Want, Lord, for Your Generous Gifts?" — lines indelibly etched in the consciousness of the nation throughout the centuries. His poetry was a dramatic and moving conversation between a man and the Creator, a conversation in which all of nature, sharing the same creator and protector, participated.

THE PERFECTION
OF LANGUAGE EXPRESSION

The process by which art became rooted in society and enriched its means of expression could be seen primarily in the main sphere of the cultural life of the nation — in literature. In the sixteenth century the Polish language not only gained significance in literature, poetry, religious and political writings, and in science and philosophy, but also reached a high level in artistic expression. People at the time were conscious of this development. Jan Rybiński, a teacher from Gdańsk and Toruń and also a secretary of the Toruń town council, described, in a dissertation published in Gdańsk in 1589, the values and the development of the Polish language. Rybiński's observations were correct: in the sixteenth century, scientific and literary Polish was fast developing.

This process had its roots in Poland itself, under the influence of the forces of social development that were replacing the *Regnum* of the Middle Ages by a modern Commonwealth. These progressive social forces abolished the élite monopoly on "scholarliness" which had been originally the preserve of the clergy and later of those connected with the university, and brought in the entire society, which was to abandon the "barbarian and simple life" and become a society of educated people.

Polish writing, beginning with the first books published by the Cracow printers and the various books by writers such as Bielski and Rej and ending with the Reformation and the political movement during the second half of the sixteenth century, was meant to serve the "simple people". This was the statement most frequently found in the forewords and dedications which explained the reason for publishing a particular book.

The dialogue form, so characteristic of the Polish Renaissance, was derived from a realization of these social tasks. It was not, of course, a Polish discovery, but its universal usage in Poland for various purposes was characteristic of this period. The dialogue form indicated that literature should be a "conversation" between the author and the reader; or also between a group of readers who all have different opinions, and the author, who tries to reconcile them, or to decide who is right. Everything became a subject for "conversation". Conversation removed the barriers between literature and life by introducing life into the written and printed text, while at the same time allowing the text to take part in life.

The second basic artistic category of contemporary writing, speech, played a similar role. The roots of this also stretched back to the Middle Ages, but again the sixteenth century provided a major turning point. Speech became a universal form for intellectual expression and for social agreement on all questions and in various social situations: at court and in the Seym, at celebrations of various kinds, in church and at synods, in local diets and during rebellions. But speech did not only consist in words that were actually pronounced, but was also a prepared text for a speech or a text prepared in this way and then simply printed. The art of oratory developed from the first great Seym speeches of Mikołaj Sienicki to the later speeches of Hetman Jan Zamoyski at the end of the century; this also influenced written literature, as can be seen in the books of Stanisław Orzechowski or the sermons of Piotr Skarga.

THE INTELLECTUAL AND POETIC
ACCEPTANCE
OF THE WORLD

The links between Poland and other European countries were already close during this period. The knowledge of new artistic and intellectual trends was fairly deep, particularly among certain social groups. Italian Renaissance art and the humanist canons of beauty were also gaining ever-increasing significance. Direct contact, frequent visits of foreigners to Poland and numerous visits of Poles abroad, deepened the knowledge of the new trends, and initiated the desire and ability to work in this new style.

However, a sharp borderline between the art of the late medieval period and the art of the Renaissance did not exist in Poland during this period, especially in painting and sculpture. The crowning achievements in these areas in the second half of the fifteenth century were witness to a growing trend towards realism in the depiction of reality, an increasing interest in the psychological meaning of the experiences and feelings of the people taking part in the events shown, and the acceptance of the role and force of expression. All these elements opened the doors to the art of the new epoch.

This was both varied and monolithic. It was, in essence, the expression of the order existing in the universe, described both in categories of truth and of good and beauty. There was a deep harmony in convictions and aims among the most outstanding figures of the Polish Renaissance: Nicolaus Copernicus, who sought the laws governing the motion of the planets and the order of the universe; Andrzej Frycz Modrzewski, who sought moral laws, which were to be the basis for a new social order and for the peaceful coexistence of peoples of different nationalities, different social classes and different religions; and Jan Kochanowski, whose poetry recreated the visual world and its moral order.

Such creativity went beyond common interests and needs. Copernicus realized this fact. In a letter dedicating *De Revolutionibus* to the Pope, he insisted that only mathematicians had the right to judge his heliocentric theory and bravely stated that he was not concerned with the noisy opinions of laymen.

Modrzewski similarly realized his isolation: he was attacked from all sides, abandoned by his friends, and persecuted by the church's censors. He could rely on the acceptance of only a handful of the most outstanding humanists of Europe, who alone understood the magnitude of the ideals that he propounded.

Jan Kochanowski expressed these same experiences in the words of a poem entitled *The Muse*. He wrote with sorrow: "I sing but to myself and to the Muses. For who else is there on earth/who would like to lighten his heart by listening to my songs?" But he was also full of pride that "above envy, I shall despise the well-populated city". Declaring his loyalty to the Muses, regardless of "how the common folk accept it," he understood that he was "reaching for a different way from that of the herd".

This strong opposition to the idea of a dialogue with the "commoners" gave rise to a different and new artistic style. It contributed to and shaped the scientific prose of the era as, for example, in the works of Copernicus, written in a language of debate and argumentation. Other examples are the works of Frycz Modrzewski and Marycki, the author of a marvelous book, *De Scholis seu academiis libri duo* (1551), so basically different from the composition and the style of works by Orzechowski or Solikowski, concentrated and intellectually disciplined, always subordinating descriptive analysis to necessary abstractions. This new style was dominant especially in the poetry of Kochanowski and Sęp Szarzyński. It was they who, aside from creating a literature that described life, rich in the lasting contemplation of the attributes and foibles of people, developed a poetry emphasizing the secluded individual kingdom of man. It was not in the sense of confronting life or escaping from it, but in the sense of "laying down justice to the visual world", the raising of man to heights from which the beauty of the world could be seen and appreciated, together with its order, to be observed even in catastrophies and misfortunes. Kochanowski believed that it was possible to fly to Heaven on the wings of poetry.

This outlook on human life was also conveyed by Mikołaj Sęp Szarzyński. In the more dramatic experiences of the era which was drawing to a close, on the borderline of the Baroque period, he placed himself somewhere between attachment to the passing pleasures of life and the desire to experience steady spiritual happiness. "Struggle" was to be the crux of our "earthly existence."

The greatest achievement of these poetic visions of the world was the *Threnodies*. A tragic occurrence in the life of Jan Kochanowski, the death of his daughter, was transformed by poetic expression into a symbol of man's lot on earth dealing with the common human problems of sorrow and comfort.

Poetry not only presented the human condition but also the entire world. Both Kochanowski and Sęp Szarzyński were fascinated with the magnitude of nature, the changing of light and darkness, the sun and the storm, but particularly with the beauty of the starlit sky.

Kochanowski's most beautiful poetry in fact represents the relation of nature to its creator, a fervent prayer for the sustaining of life, offered up in both sunshine and rain.

But in these poetic visions of existence a particular beauty remained in the sky filled with a multitude of stars. The great architect of the world, wrote Kochanowski, "built the sky and embroidered it with golden stars." Sęp Szarzyński described the sky in similar words.

This was the same starlit sky that Copernicus observed from his tower in Frombork, seeking the great *harmonia mundi*. Its mysteries were to be unveiled through mathematics; and mathematics was a sister of poetry, which itself explained this harmony in its own way.

The poetic view of the universe, the high dome that covers us all, where the sun and the stars rule in turn during the brightness of day and the darkness of night, was strongly related to the view of space and to the attitude towards shaping it that had been offered by Renaissance art from the beginning of the sixteenth century.

Renaissance architecture in Poland began with the reconstruction of Wawel, where the unusual proportions of the arcades, with three levels of galleries encircling the interior courtyard, created a completely new spatial lay-out. It began also with the sepulchral chapel at Wawel Cathedral, called the Sigismund Chapel, the dome of which suggested the arch of man's destiny, the triumphal and mortal arch of the sky.

The reconstruction of Wawel, initiated by Sigismund III Vasa, concluded the history of Renaissance architecture in Poland and initiated a new era. In this reconstruction, the king ordered the sole use of the whites and blacks of polished marble and the dazzling glow of gold. This dramatic and almost mournful monumentality was directly related to the imagination of Sęp Szarzyński and to the Baroque period which was beginning, just as the poetry of Kochanowski was associated with the colorful and cheerful Wawel of the Jagiellonians, the period of the Renaissance.

Culture in Society

DEVELOPMENT
OF PRINTING AND MASS CULTURE

In Renaissance Poland, as throughout the world, it was the invention of the printing press which proved the turning point in the process of dissemination of culture. In the place of expensive manuscripts, at times absolutely unique and difficult to obtain access to, books began to appear. Still expensive but infinitely less costly than the old richly decorated manuscripts, these books were becoming readily available, thanks to increased editions. Circulated from hand to hand, even though they may not have been bought for personal use, they were read over and over again until completely worn out.

The first printing shop was set up in Cracow in 1473. In the following year, the first printed calendar was published. From this time, printing began to develop rapidly in Poland. The wealthy burghers of Cracow helped establish the printing shops of Jan Haller (who also had his own paper mill), Florian Ungler, Hieronim Wietor and Marek and Maciej Scharffenberg. Printers, of course, did not merely print books; they were also publishers liable for any losses that might be incurred in publishing a book. They were therefore interested in the potential circulation of books and which books would turn out to be most profitable. It was because of this that they often published books on their own initiative, and often cooperated with Polish religious and scientific organizations, especially with the University of Cracow and the Cracow Episcopal Curia. They also sought aid from the schoolteachers of the towns.

The social significance of their activities was even greater since a considerable portion of the printed works appeared in Polish, whereas in official life and schools, the only accepted language was Latin. The printers of Cracow were becoming pioneers in the struggle for the rights of the native language, and they were well aware of society's demand for this. It was of almost symbolic significance that one of the first books was Łaski's monumental *Statutes,* published in Cracow in 1506 by Haller. It was prefaced by the hymn *Bogurodzica,* printed for the first time ever. And indeed the Cracow printers made it clear in many declarations in their books that they had formulated a conscious program of polonization.

In the second quarter of the sixteenth century the development of printing was able to meet to an ever greater extent the demand of readers, by offering an increasing number of religious and secular, scientific and practical, literary or poetic books. At the same time, printing was better able to serve the interests of contemporary writers, ensuring that all new works could be published, from the works of Rej onwards.

In the second half of the century the social role of printing took a great step forward. Printing houses became the chief tools in the hands of the Reformation, a weapon in the ideological battle being waged among the followers of the various creeds. For a certain period of time the Królewiec (Königsberg) printing house was of primary significance. In 1553 a printing house was opened at Brześć under the patronage of the Calvinist Mikołaj Radziwiłł, which was later to become famous for its 1563 edition of the Bible, known as the Brześć (Brest) Bible. There was also a Calvinist printing house at Vilna and many Arian printing houses: at Pińczów, Lusławice, Nieśwież and Łosk, where a Polish edition of the works of Modrzewski was published; the main Arian printing house was at Raków. By the end of the century Jesuit printing houses were spreading, especially at Vilna, Poznań and Braniewo. The Jesuits often took over Protestant printing houses. Printing houses working directly for schools were also of importance: a printing house attached to the Toruń gymnasium was set up in 1580; and in Zamość in 1594, a printing house was opened for the requirements of the Zamość Academy. There were also also many printing houses operating in Gdańsk.

Polish printing houses worked together with those abroad. Many Polish books — the works of Copernicus, Modrzewski, Kromer, and Mączyński — were published in Basel, Zurich, Antwerp, Nuremberg, and Cologne. Thus they were becoming more readily available to the world.

Publishing, especially in the first half of the sixteenth century, created a type of Polish mass culture during the Renaissance.

Jan of Koszyczki, a teacher from Cracow, translated a book entitled *Conversations between King Solomon the Wise and Marchołt the Chubby and Obscene,* published in Cracow in 1521. He insisted that readers should "buy it and read it avidly." He argued further: "This you must understand, that quickness of mind comes from these writings and simple writing brings knowledge to the people." Jan of Koszyczki was not an isolated case: a large group of graduates of Cracow University, burghers by origin, and teachers by profession, cooperated with him.

They published translations and edited works which they hoped would attract readers. Their judgment was sound: their books were often worn out by reading. Although published in large editions, only a handful have survived, mostly in single copies, and many are known to us only from later editions. This literature satisfied the tastes of a vast majority of the public, who preferred to read in Polish rather than in Latin and who were interested in the world and the people in this world. These books were an arsenal of knowledge of all kinds, fictitious and fantastic, but always fascinating. A true gold-mine of all kinds of knowledge were the so-called "histories", such as, *The Histories of Many Kinds Selected from Roman and Other Times, The History of Apollonius, the King of Tyre, The Beautiful History of Pontianus, The History of the Life of Alexander, The Sad and Frightening History of Franciszek Spierza,* and many others. The line of demarcation between historiography, adventure and fiction was never observed here.

But even "serious" literature, which sought simple means of reaching the "simple" reader, began to acquire a multifunctional character: it was to provide teaching and recreation, aiming at presenting important problems in a direct yet picturesque way, a way more in line with people's experiences.

Such literature, which depicted the colorful and changing chronicles of life, into which contemplation and advice, condemnation and praise were interwoven, was addressed directly to the reader.

Related to this literature were religious tales of various kinds. A majority of these books were both religious and secular, combining authentic biblical stories with fairy tales and legends of various peoples and eras.

But in line with the interests and needs of their readers, the authors of this type of literature went far beyond translation or adaptation of popular literature from all over the world, or the exploitation of classical or biblical stories. As they knew many curiosities and stories which were handed down by word of mouth, they introduced these to literature, in this way recording local "histories" and introducing them to a much wider readership.

However, the interests of many of the readers were much wider than these extraordinary classical and biblical stories or funny tales of human wit. The main works of the literature of reflection and moralization, satire and denunciation, the bitter but at the same time optimistic literature of the common sense of ordinary people, were the *Conversations between King Solomon the Wise and Marchołt the Chubby and Obscene,* as well as *The Life of Aesop the Phrygian, the Decent Wise Man, Together with his Tales,* published approximately during the same period and written by Biernat of Lublin.

There was also interest in philosphical speculation. This did not, of course, involve the great theoretical problems that were taken on by the Cracow Academy, but rather those aspects which focused on the world and man, the unique "experiences of this world." Andrzej Glaber of Kobylin, the author of *Problemata Aristotelis,* published in Cracow in 1535, explained to his readers that, although he elaborated greatly upon the text which had been widely circulated in the medieval period and although he had gone back to the original, he had to retain the traditional title, because "many people insisted to the printer that the treatise be published completely in our language."

This characteristic "social demand" referred to elemental knowledge about man, "the order of human structure" and, according to the author's intent, was "as playful as it was useful." Most likely the book by Marcin Bielski, *The Life of Philosophers, that is The Sages of Natural Science,* published in the same year, was also intended to satisfy popular interest in philosophy. The book contained many fictitious tales, but it also brought forth a great many "golden ideas", chosen from the writings of individual philosophers, not always authentic, but always inspiring deep reflection about the world and life.

Other authors translated these philosophical concepts into a language of practical advice. These included essays on "economics" understood as a "domestic science indispensable to all classes of Christians" or teachings "of how all Christians ought to behave in business".

The culminating achievements in this area were the works of Mikołaj Rej. The writings of Rej were full of local tales and polemics, anecdotes, real happenings, interwoven with political and moral lessons. Rej particularly liked to bring together themes and moods of this kind, for example *Bestiary,* in which the various estates, people, animals, and birds, and their shapes, happenings and customs were depicted, similar to his *Trifles or Various Court Adventures.*

In this way, wide social circles, the gentry and the burghers, had their own literary and scientific world, a world of strange stories and important maxims, a world which inspired reflection and where imagination became the "meat" of the cultural participation of simple people.

THE DEVELOPMENT OF SCHOOLING

In the sixteenth century, science and learning became the theme of systematic contemplation and philosophical reflection, due to which entirely new elements were added to constitutional theory, and education gained political significance.

Frycz Modrzewski was the main participant in this area. In his great work, *On the Reform of the Commonwealth,* next to a volume dealing with the church, he devoted an entire volume to the problems of education. In his view, education was not only important because it prepared the young for life in society, but also because it supplied the older generation with the knowledge necessary to govern. The ruling of a nation should be based on justice, and the understanding of what justice is based on required a philosophical background.

In the writings of Maurycjusz of Pilzno, Sebastian Petrycy and many others, one heard the argument that science and learning were not only the mainstream of personal, cultural development, but a basic aspect of social life and state organization.

This social function of education was not easy to realize in practice. The political system, in which class privilege was gaining in importance, was the main force opposed to the development of education and the understanding of its significance in regard to the needs of the state.

Despite this, the importance of educational tasks was understood by many of the leaders of the gentry and also the king's court. Educational matters often won the attention of deputies and were often debated on the floor of the Seym. They were also a matter of concern to the social groups involved with the ideas of humanism and the Reformation.

Due to this, many humanist and Protestant schools were formed in cities and towns, on the estates of magnates, and even in small Protestant communities.

Although attempts at setting up new universities at the beginning of the sixteenth century (in Wrocław in 1505, in Elbląg in 1508, in Chełm between 1473 and 1506) did not succeed, other more modest but equally important attempts were becoming a reality. The first such action to succeed was the formation of the Lubrański Humanist College in Poznań in 1519, which was to flourish later and was given the name of Academy, thanks to the work of Krzysztof Hegendorfer, professor of humanist studies and a reformer of the institution. For a short time the University in Królewiec, founded in 1544, was in operation. But large schools of a new type were of greater significance: for example, in Gdańsk, the Academic Gymnasium, founded in 1558, and the Gymnasium in Toruń, founded in 1568, based on the concepts of John Sturm.

Calvinist schools were also founded: in Cracow, Dubiecko, Secymin and Łańcut. In 1551 the Gymnasium in Pińczów was founded in which Piotr Statorius worked for many years and which contributed largely to the translation of the Calvinist Brześć Bible. The Bohemian Brethren also ran many schools. The best known of these was founded in Leszno under the auspices of the Leszczyński family. They set up important schools in Poznań and Koźminek. In the seventeenth century, the headmaster of the school in Leszno was Jan Amos Komensky (Comenius). Lutherans founded their own schools as well (in Rawicz, Elbląg, Wschowa and Bojanowo), mainly in Great Poland and Pomerania. The Arian school in Raków, founded in 1602, gained a European reputation. Many foreign scholars lectured there. The school maintained a very high standard in such areas as biology and mathematics, as well as modern philosophy and ethics.

The heightened activity of non-Catholics was a challenge to the Catholics themselves. In Cracow, for example, in 1559, a new school was founded by Benedykt Herbest at the Church of the Virgin Mary. The Jesuits were very active in this field. Jesuit gymnasiums were formed in Pułtusk (1567), Poznań (1573), Jarosław (1577), Płock (1580), and also in Lublin, Riga, Nieśwież, Dorpat, Gdańsk, Lvov, and Kalisz. After prolonged efforts, a

66. Castle gate in Brzeg, 1551—53, designed by Francesco Parro and with sculptures by Andreas Walther I

67. Andreas Walther I, Piast images, detail of the castle gate in Brzeg, 1551—53

69. High Gate in Gdańsk, 1586—88, designed by Johannes
Kramer and with sculptures by Wilhelm van dem Blocke

70. Interior of the Grand Debating Chamber
in the Townhall of the Main City
in Gdańsk, 1593—1611

68. Georg of Amberg, Castle gate in Legnica,
completed in 1533

71. Kasper Fotyga, Townhall in Szydłowiec, 16th cent.,
with parapet dating from 1601

72. Giovanni Battista Quadro,
Townhall in Poznań, 1550—60

73. Orsetti house in Jarosław,
1580 and 1640

74. Bernardo Morando
(from 1591)
and Jan Jaroszewicz
(from 1622),
City hall in Zamość

75. Cloth hall in Cracow,
with parapet dating from 1556—60

76. General view of the Wawel Castle
in Cracow

77. Francesco Fiorentino and Bartholommeo Berrecci,
Arcaded loggias at Wawel Castle, 1507—36

78. Deputies' Chamber in the Wawel Castle, 1530's

80. Bartholommeo Berrecci, Sigismund Chapel
at Wawel cathedral, 1519—33

79. Southern view of the royal cathedral at Wawel

81. Courtyard of the royal castle
in Niepołomice, 1550—71

82. Santi Gucci (?), Courtyard
of the castle in Baranów, 1591—1606

83. Galeazzo Appiani,
Castle in Krasiczyn, 1598—1633

84. Wawrzyniec Lorek, Manor-house in Pabianice, 1565—70   85. Fortified mansion in Szymbark, 1585—90

86. Silver altarpiece
in the Sigismund Chapel at Wawel cathedral, 1535—38. Bas reliefs
by Melchior Baier modelled on Peter Flötner and partly
on Albrecht Dürer's woodcuts

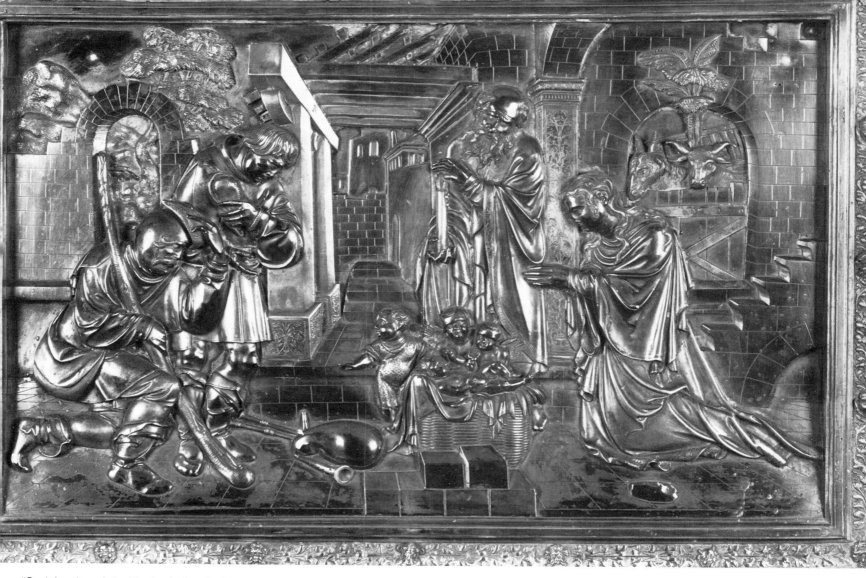

87. *Adoration of the Shepherds*. Panel of the silver altarpiece in the Sigismund Chapel at Wawel cathedral, 1535—38

88. *Adoration of the Magi*. Panel of the silver altarpiece in the Sigismund Chapel at Wawel cathedral, 1535—38

89. Jan Michałowicz of Urzędów,
    Gravestone of Filip Padniewski
    in Wawel cathedral, 1572—73

90. Gravestone of Jan Grot (d. 1579) and his son (d. 1580)
    in the Dominican church in Cracow

91. Bernardino de Gianotis and Giovanni Cini, *Opatów Lament*. Bas relief
    on the sarcophagus of Krzysztof Szydłowiecki in the collegiate church in Opatów. 1533—41

92. Wilhelm van dem Blocke. Cartouche with the emblem of Poland. Detail of the sculpted decoration
on the western front of the High Gate in Gdańsk, 1586—88

93. Bell-founder's workshop.
Miniature from Balthasar Behem's *Codex*, early 16th cent.

Das ist das gesetze der Goltschmide wy sy sich vnd ire tzeche halden sollen vnd ist von den hern rothmad vnder rem Insel gegeben zw des rouis willen welchs buff also lawtet ·

Jr Rothmann der Stad Crakow bekennen offentlich mit disem buffe vor alln vnd itzluchen dy yn zehn ader horen lezen das wir mit vnsern eldstn Rothe willen vnd wissen den goltschmiden vnsir Stad

94. Goldsmith's workshop.
   Miniature from *Balthasar Behem's Codex*, early 16th cent.

95. Stanisław Samostrzelnik,
Miniature from *Liber geneseos illustris familiae Schidloviciae*, before 1532

96. Unknown painter, *Battle of Orsza* (detail), c. 1515—20

97. *Portrait of Sigismund the Old* from Pawłowice, c. 1540

98. *Portrait of Sigismund Augustus,* 1547

99. Late 16th cent. Polish painter, *Portrait of Stephen Báthory*

100. Unknown 16th cent. Polish painter,
    Portrait of Benedykt of Koźmin, c. 1550

101. *Portrait of Sebastian Petrycy of Pilzno*, 1626

102. *Musician*, detail of a polychrome, c. 1530

103. Hans Dürer after *Tabula Cebestis*
by the moralist Cebes, *Youth.*
Detail of the frieze *History of Man's Life*
in the Deputies' Chamber of Wawel Castle, 1532

104. Hans Dürer after *Tabula Cebestis*
by the moralist Cebes,
Dances. Detail of the frieze
History of Man's Life in the Deputies'
Chamber of Wawel Castle, 1532

105. Antoni of Wrocław,
Infantry Parading before King Sigismund the Old.
Detail of the frieze in the Troops Review Hall
of Wawel Castle, 1535

106. Hans Dürer and Antoni of Wrocław,
Before a Fight.
Detail of the frieze
in the Tournament Hall
of Wawel Castle, 1534—35

107. Hans Dürer and Antoni of Wrocław,
Sword Fight. Detail
of the frieze in the Tournament
Hall of Wawel Castle, 1534—35

108. Izaak van dem Blocke,
Allegory of Gdańsk Commerce, 1608

109. Antoni Möller,
    Building the Temple of Solomon (detail).
    1601 (?)

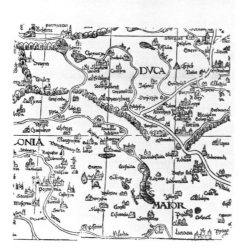

110. Bernard Wapowski, *Mappa . . .*
    Poloniae ac Magni D[ucatus] Lithuaniae (detail), 1526

111. View of Cracow in the late 16th cent.
Illustration from G. Braun and A. Hoggenberg's,
Civitates orbis terrarum, Cologne 1597—1618

112. View of Warsaw in the late 16th cent.
Illustration from G. Braun and A. Hoggenberg's
Civitates orbis terrarum, Cologne 1597—1618

113. *Holy words
and lordly matters . . . ,*
title page of Mikołaj Rej's
Kronika albo Postilla,
Cracow 1556

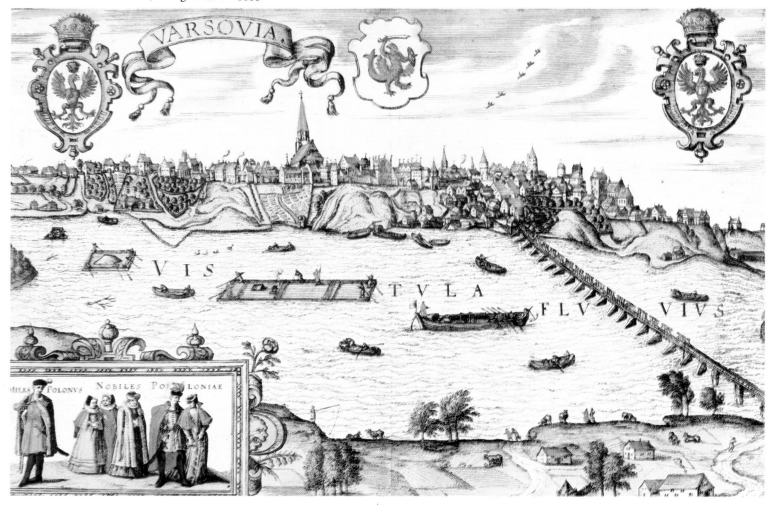

Tu ná żiemi będżie sie kocháło/
Muśim z niego ná ine roſkoßy/
Gdy precz z ćiáła śmierć duße wyploßy.

Famam extendere factis est uirtutis opus.

Przećiw prawdżie rozumu nie.

114. *Never against the truth
of reason . . .*, woodcut from the title page
of Marcin Bielski's *Chronicle*, Cracow 1564

Biblia swieta/
Tho ieſt/
Kſięgi Stárego y
Nowego Zakonu/ własnie z
Zydowſkiego/ Greckiego/ y
Láćińſkiego/ nowo ná
Polſki ięzyk z pil-
nośćią y wiernie
wploßone.

115. Title page of the *Radziwiłł Bible*,
also known as the *Brest Bible*, 1563

116. Jan Herburt's *Crown Statutes and Privileges*, Cracow 1570

SPRAWIE DLIWOSC

CZWARTA POWIN-
NOSC KROLEWSKA.

Spráwiedliwość czynić ſam : y in-
nych od vkrzywdzenia powśćiągáć.

SPRAWIEDLIWOSC
zacność Królewſka.

556.   ABowiém zacność Królewſka / prze grzéch nieſpráwiedli-   Olbrácht
2.   wośći bywa zelżoná.   w Piotrk
                                                                1 4 9 6
                                                                Liſt 50.

117. *Justice.* Woodcut from Stanisław Sarnicki's *Statutes and List of Crown Privileges,* Cracow 1594

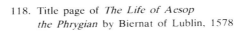

118. Title page of *The Life of Aesop the Phrygian* by Biernat of Lublin, 1578

119. *Prisoner in Stocks.* Illustration from *The Life of Aesop the Phrygian* by Biernat of Lublin, 1578

Spytaymy go co za rzecz miał,   Lepak Xántowi vczniowie,
Iż sie táko roskoßnie śmiał: Mowili ták sámi k sobie:
Powiedzże nam miły bráchu,   Smießnoć temuto żádnemu,

120. *Aesop surrounded by peasants conversing*
with scholars. Illustration
from *The Life of Aesop the Phrygian* by Biernat
of Lublin, 1578

DIALOGVS LV
CIANI NVPER E GRECO IN LA
TINVM VERSVS. INTER
LOQVVTORES POE
TA ET ASTRO,
LOGVS.

AD LECTOREM.
Cum legis auctorem lector mi credere ſphingem
Noli, materiam quo teris inuenies.

121. *Conversation of a poet with an astrologer.*
Title page Lucian Samosata of
Dialogus poetae et astrologi by

PEREGRINATIO STVDIOR CAVSA SVSCEPTA
13

Defiderium Profitiandi

Admiratio Illustrifiee

122. *Departure for studies abroad.*
Illustration from Tomasz Treter's
Theatrum virtutum Cardinalis Hosii, 1588

BACCALAVREATVS.
12

ACADEMIA CRACOVIEN
CELEBERR

FELIX
PRÆSA
GIVM.

Rhetorica

Dialectica

123. *Baccalaureatus, pupil*
of the celebrated Cracow Academy.
Allegorical etching from Tomasz Treter's
Theatrum virtutum Cardinalis Hosii, 1588

Spráwy świete á pámięci wiecżney godne thego Krolá
Włádysłáwá Jágełá Wielkiego X. Litewſkiego/ á naprzod
záłozenie Akádemijey Krákowſkiey: ſkąd káżdey cno
ty dobrey pocżątek wychodżi/ Roku
1 4 0 1.

V maſz mátkę cnot świetych od cżáſu dawnego/
     Wárownie záłozona przez Krolá sławnego /
Przypátrzże ſię iey ſynom ktore wychowáłá/
     Jáki przez nie pożytek oycżyznie dżiáłáłá:
Przypátrz ſię kleynotowi mieyſcá ták zacnego/
     Rozmyſlnie nádánemu od Krolá bácżnego:
Przetoć ſceptrá Krolewſkie dał im bárwy złoty /
     Jż ie bacżył Kſiążety być/y Krolmi Cnoty.

124. *Examination taken by students
of the Cracow Academy.* Illustration
from Bartosz Paprocki's *Nest of Virtue,* 1578

125. ·*Chess playing*. Title page
of Jan Kochanowski's *Chess*, c. 1567

126. *Dice playing in an inn.*
Woodcut from J. Muczkowski's
Collection of Woodcuts, 1849

127. *Singers in a Bay Window.*
Woodcut from Stephanus Monetarius'
Epitoma uriusque musices, 1515

128. *Farmstead.* Illustration
from Hieronim Spiczyński's *Herbs,* 1542

129. Arras with the coats-of-arms
of Poland and Lithuania
and "cherub" personifying Victory,
after 1553

130. Medallion with the silver Polish Eagle
from the royal pew in Wawel cathedral

university was founded in Vilna in 1579, thanks to the continued help of Stephen Báthory. The Jagiellonian University attempted to challenge the Jesuit educational system by setting up its own branches. In 1588 the first such branch was founded, the Nowodworski Gymnasium in Cracow. It was conceived as a type of introductory college and concentrated on the teaching of young people coming in from parish schools. The large attendance suggested that this type of schooling was socially necessary, particularly for the plebeian masses. In subsequent years, other branches were formed; thus general secondary education was made more readily available to the masses.

The importance of such activity can be evaluated in the light of the development of parish schools. The sixteenth century witnessed great growth in this field. Although the process of limiting the rights of the burghers and the peasants was an ongoing one, still, along with a nationwide rise of interest in scientific and artistic activities, the general standard of education was also improved in the small parish schools in cities, towns and villages.

This rich and varied development and changes in schooling indicated both the growing significance attached to education by public opinion and the wide participation of various social groups — city councils, religious congregations, wealthy patrons, and also scores of teachers — in the educational process within different social spheres and at various levels. Under such circumstances, schools were becoming "public property," related to the many aspects of life and to the aspirations of the public. This was a characteristic feature of the Polish Renaissance.

STUDY ABROAD

An education in Poland was often completed by study abroad. Popular even during the medieval period, during the Renaissance this became a true educational institution. It was brought about either by participation in missions and delegations, at times allowing for a prolonged stay abroad, or by trips especially undertaken for the purpose of studies.

The country most often visited was Italy, especially by church officials. From the fifteenth century, wealthy noblemen would also travel to Italy. The deputations of Jan Ostroróg, Jan Łaski, and Erazm Ciołek made possible longer and closer relations with the Italian humanist movement. It was in Italy that church dignitaries, writers and poets sought their education, including Jan Lubrański, Mikołaj and Krzysztof Szydłowiecki, Piotr Tomicki, Jan Dantyszek, Andrzej Krzycki, Jan Hussowski, Klemens Janicki, Bernard Wapowski, Samuel Maciejowski and Mikołaj Czepiel.

Hosius, sketching the life of Piotr Tomicki, wrote the following: "His eyes were constantly turned toward Italy; nights and days his mind would venture there, Italy is what he most missed: he knew that the sciences of Greece had been transferred there, that the center of all studies was there." He did, in fact, study for four years in

Bologna, and for the following two years worked in the Roman Curia. After returning to Poland, he initiated a Renaissance style of life at his court; he gathered around him scholars and artists; he funded a number of stipends and scholarships for study abroad; he aided the Cracow University with his donations; he managed his episcopal estates in an exemplary fashion; he helped organize the king's chancery, and hired qualified scribes and translators. He was a very demanding individual: he required that all letters and documents be prepared with the highest degree of perfection and paid great attention to the proper treatment of foreign guests. Cardinal Stanisław Hosius further stated that "when he dismissed them in the king's name, people could only wonder which to admire more: the wise and elegant contents of his speech, the beauty of the word, or the gracefulness of his conduct."

Tomicki was not alone. Many other secular and church dignitaries, after studies in Italy, changed their life-styles, built magnificent mansions, brought scholars and artists to their courts, and aided talented youth.

In the second half of the sixteenth century, a permanent Polish mission was formed in Italy. There were more Polish centers connected with the Roman Curia. In 1569, Hosius created the hospice of St. Stanislaus in Rome, established to help less wealthy young men live and study in Italy.

Foreign excursions were not limited to the rich. The children of various burghers and gentry also traveled to Italy. At universities, particularly in Bologna and Padua, hundreds of Poles came to study. "Polish nationals" were gaining importance at Italian universities. Poles often occupied distinguished positions in academic life. The popularity of such studies can be attested to by the fact that in the sixteenth century more students came to study in Padua than were enrolled at the University in Cracow.

These journeys to Italy aided in developing wide contacts and private relations between Italian and Polish humanists, which later surfaced in correspondence and the exchange of views on scientific and literary matters.

The period of the Reformation opened new horizons for foreign study, especially in Germany and Switzerland. This was of a different character than study in Italy. It was no longer merely the universities which attracted students but the main centers of Reformation thought which were becoming interesting to both young and older people who were seeking the truth of the Holy Word. Sons of the gentry and more particularly the sons of the burghers would travel to Wittenberg, the city of Luther and Melanchthon. They undertook studies in Leipzig and Frankfurt. The Calvinist gentry preferred the south, such cities as Altdorf, Marburg, Heidelberg and Strasbourg. Many were taught by John Sturm, the creator of the modern, humanist school, which advocated a mixture of piety with wisdom and rhetoric.

Basel gained importance as the main center of humanist and Reformation thought. It was also a major printing and publishing center in Europe. The most outstanding individuals held close relations with the Basel publisher Oporinus (Johannes Herbster). From his publishing house came the works of Modrzewski, along with the works of outstanding leaders of the Reformation such as, for example, Calvin, Castellio, Servetus and Socinus. Jan Osmólski, originally from Lublin, created a Polish scientific and literary institution in Basel. He supervised many Polish students.

The Counter-Reformation led young Poles to yet other destinations. Vienna and Graz, Freiburg and Mainz, Ingolstadt and Wurzburg were cities in which many young Catholics from Poland, particularly Jesuits, came to study.

Although during the Middle Ages some scholars had already traveled to France, it was relatively late in the Renaissance that these journeys began again. By now, Paris was the main center of attraction. The Łaski family enjoyed close relations with the court of Francis I. Andrzej Zebrzydowski, Andrzej Frycz Modrzewski and Jan Kochanowski visited Paris. In the second half of the century these relations developed greatly. The newly opened Collège de France and the Valois court attracted many Poles. French Calvinist centers maintained lively relations with Poland: for example, the Polish Gymnasium in Pińczów was modeled along French lines and employed French teachers.

Voyages to England also had some significance, but only a few traveled there, and usually not for academic purposes. In the mid-sixteenth century, Jan Łaski organized a church in London and the Tęczyńskis and Tarnowskis stayed at the royal court.

In the first quarter of the sixteenth century, Jan Tarnowski battled with the Moors in Spain and Jan Dantyszek, as an experienced Polish envoy, developed many contacts in Madrid, which were later strengthened. Thanks to these relations, an abridged version of Kromer's *History of Poland* was published in Madrid.

This short overview of the travels of Poles abroad, whether for educational or diplomatic purposes, depicts the wide social range of this form of education in the sixteenth century; it had its own unique significance. Education abroad was not simply a matter of formal schooling: it was multilateral, direct and alive. It enabled one to overcome the cramped and enclosed circles of local experience, to see other countries, other peoples and traditions, to learn new ideas and values.

THE SOCIAL SOURCES
OF INTELLECTUAL EDUCATION

Schools and trips abroad were important educational tools. But the most important factor was the life-style of people of the Renaissance — varied, filled with a multitude of concepts and inspirations. The political movement of the gentry drew in an ever wider part of society and demanded a certain knowledge and specific oratorical talents. The Reformation had become a great school of theological disputes, in which an increasing body of people participated. The resolutions of the regional diet in Środa in 1534 related to these very needs of education growing out of life itself: "We ask that our priests not forbid us to print our history, our chronicles, our laws, and other things, particularly the Bible, in Polish. They demand that various materials be printed; why then should they not be printed in our language? It is here where we see great injustice thrust upon us by the priests since each language has writings of its own; yet our priests ask that we remain dumb."

The gentry, which was becoming the dominant estate in the country, undertook new and difficult political duties. And although the gentry did not always resolve all problems faced at various seyms and diets, they were forced to have deep historical knowledge and familiarity with the law. Because of this, the sixteenth century was a period devoted to work on various editions of Statutes. In 1506, on the initiative of Jan Łaski, the grand chancellor of the crown and archbishop of Gniezno, a volume of laws was published as an official document, accepted by the king, often read by the gentry and cited in senate debates. The need for knowledge of law was so great that the *Łaski Statutes*, which were fairly difficult to use, proved inadequate. Many authors, including Jakub Przyłuski, Jan Szczęsny Herburt, Stanisław Sarnicki, and Jan Januszowski, wrote their legal commentaries collating existing laws. Bartłomiej Groicki, and later Paweł Szczerbic, prepared a version of existing laws for use by the burghers.

The gentry's political activities also required oratorial abilities. At regional diets and congresses, and later, at elections and confederacies, the art of oratory was developed, demanding an in-depth erudite training, especially in the fields of ancient history, which was often referred to. In this way, political life was becoming a unique "school" for the gentry.

This education was greatly enhanced by active and universal participation in the Reformation movement. Religious discussions were held not only by pastors, writers or publishers: in Protestant parishes, the gentry were active, expostulating their views concerning the complicated issues of the exegesis of the Holy Scriptures, the dogmas of faith, the organization of the church and religious communities, and the social and political consequences of one or another "confession of faith." At synods, particularly Arian synods, lively discussions were held, prepared beforehand, engaging those for and those opposing various issues. Equally extensively disputed and attacked were the rulings of the episcopal courts in matters of faith, even when these were no longer enforced by the secular authorities. The concept of holding a national convention excited wide enthusiasm among the gentry, and the idea of a unified confession of faith for all Protestant groups drawn up by Stanisław Lutomirski, an Arian, the superintendent of the congregations in Little Poland, presented to the senate in 1555, was indicative of how deeply engaged were the gentry in the process of resolving subtle theological and dogmatic questions and of what level of education this required.

The political movement of the gentry and the Reformation enlarged the circles of people participating in intellectual life and gave it a new character. It was becoming obvious that education was a necessity if one wished to participate in political activities and religious disputes. In this way, education was becoming an element of public life. The program of educational and intellectual development, under these conditions, was fast becoming widely accepted though formulated from various standpoints.

This meant the realization of the programs of Szymon Marycki and Andrzej Frycz Modrzewski, and also the programs of Mikołaj Rej, Stanisław Orzechowski, Łukasz Górnicki and several other writers, many of them unkown, both from among the gentry and the burghers.

THE SPREAD OF ELITE CULTURE

In Renaissance Poland, culture was widely disseminated among various social classes and groups. Whereas during the fifteenth century, culture was still concentrated around large towns, centers of both state and ecclesiastical authorities, during the sixteenth century, culture left the narrow circle of the élite, the wealthy and the foreign-educated, and spread throughout the country, often adapting itself to local conditions and needs. This new form of cultural life developed spontaneously, but it was also the product of conscious actions of various ambitious educated individuals. The intellectual élite of the Polish Renaissance was recruited from the entire country. Young men from small towns and villages, not only from the great cities, came to study, found sponsors, went abroad and succeeded in many areas of intellectual endeavor.

One need only be reminded of the most outstanding: Janicki came from the village of Januszkowo near Gniezno; Rej was born in the village of Żórawno near Halicz; Kochanowski in the village of Sycyn outside of Zwoleń; Andrzej Frycz Modrzewski came from Wolborz; Stanisław Orzechowski from Przemyśl; Łukasz Górnicki from Oświęcim; and Piotr Skarga from Grójec. Hundreds of others came from similar small towns and villages.

This territorial dispersion does not only indicate that the intellectual and artistic élite came from all over Poland, but also that there were lasting and active centers of culture dispersed throughout Poland. And it was this which characterized Renaissance Poland. Cultural life in the larger cities was, of course, more intensive — in Cracow, Wrocław, Gdańsk, and by the end of the century in Vilna and Lvov; but it also developed in the smaller cities, such as Poznań, Lublin, Warsaw, and Toruń. In addition, it encountered good conditions for growth, quite unexpectedly, in places hitherto entirely unknown. Pińczów and Raków became centers of the Reformation movement: they led the country in publishing and discussion, in creating exemplary schools, and attracting many foreigners. Raków became famous in Europe. Printing shops were set up not only in large cities but also in Brześć, Lusławice, Łosk, Pułtusk, Szamotuły, Grodzisk, and Zamość. The formation of a printing house was equivalent to the establishment of an intellectual center. The royal court exerted wide influence in Lithuania. Mikołaj Radziwiłł (the Black) created a great center for Reformation thought, attracting many activists to Brześć. It was there that the great translation of the Bible was prepared, which was to fulfill the dream that the Holy Word "be offered to all in this world in their own tongue." It was also there that the excellent writer, Cyprian Bazylik, worked, translating, among other things, Modrzewski's work *On the Reform of the Commonwealth* (1577). Szymon Budny also worked in Lithuania, in Łosk; he was an outstanding writer, publisher and translator. Dissenting schools were founded in Birże, Iwie, Słuck, and Kleck.

The literary and intellectual movement was very active in the Lublin region. It was here that what was known as the "Commonwealth of Babin" was created, a quite uncommon institution, combining the force of satire with jaunty anecdote, related in a friendly atmosphere. In this region, especially in Lublin and Lewartów, the most intense polemics between the Arians and the adherents of other religious views were being carried on. The schools in Kock and particularly in Lewartów gained wide recognition. It was here that Wojciech of Kalisz, a student of John Sturm, worked. At the end of the century, almost instantaneously, a new center of intellectual thought sprang up in Zamość.

Similar centers were taking shape in other parts of Poland. In the northern region of Poland, apart from the cities of Gdańsk and Elbląg, Warmia became a center of art, culture and science, due to the work of Copernicus and Dantyszek. In the western part of the country, Silesia played a similar role.

This social and geographical distribution of cultural activity became possible due to increasingly widespread knowledge of Latin, the main tool of cultural exchange, and also due to the fact that an increasing number of books were being translated into Polish.

In Poland not only the very rich noblemen, such as Łaski, and wealthy burghers like Decius, who knew Latin, were interested in the works and activities of Erasmus of Rotterdam; it must be emphasized that his works were also translated into Polish for the general public. An unknown writer translated the *Colloquia* in 1543, and explained in beautiful Polish that "words have their wings" and that when allowed to fly, "they multiply and expand," gaining independence.

The choice of this particular work of Erasmus was not accidental. Language was a powerful tool of Renaissance culture. The native language restricted cultural participation to national borders; Latin made it possible to cross these borders. This crossing over was characteristic of the culture of sixteenth century Polish society. In 1521, Decius wrote the following: "A unique case would be one in which a well-bred Pole were not able to speak the languages of three or four nations; the knowledge of Latin is common to all." Kromer, in the middle of the century, extended this diagnosis, remarking that everyone was learning Latin — the gentry and the burghers, the wealthy and the poor, and even the common folk. Girolamo Lippomano confirmed this observation, emphasizing in his report about Poland, that "Latin is so common in everyday usage, that not many can be found amongst the gentry, or among the burghers and the craftsmen, who could not understand it or speak it fluently." The papal nuncio Fulvio Ruggieri confirmed this view in 1566 indicating the reasons for the phonomenon: "It is not difficult to learn this language, since in every city, in almost every village, there is a public school."

Marcin Kromer, commenting upon the social processes and educational aspirations of the gentry and the burghers, wrote the following: "Now that they have become aware that a linguistic education is priceless, as is the ability to speak beautifully, they have taken it up with alacrity but do not seek fame through its use, but rather usefulness in political and everyday life."

In such an atmosphere over the vast territories of the country, a new style of life was being shaped. Beginning with living conditions and the splendor of clothing, to a knowledge of the world and social customs — all these were influenced by increasing financial satisfaction and the level of education of the society, by more lively trade and political relations, by scientific and artistic contacts with various European countries, by a greater intensity in public life, both in the towns and in the country as a whole, and by the functioning of its political institutions.

Szymon Marycki described the culture of Polish society in the sixteenth century as follows: "The minds of our countrymen acquired a certain force and their activity has intensified more than anywhere else. It is manifested in the architecture of the cities, in the accumulation of luxuries and in the increasing of wealth, in both men and women being always elegantly dressed and, finally, in enchantment with the beauty of thought processes and customs. If one is to compare our Poland of the past with that of today, and the people of our age with those of yesteryear, one comes to believe that on the one hand is barbarism and the lack of all culture, and on the other, a fully civilized life-style."

THE CULTURE OF THE ROYAL COURT AND OF THE COUNTRYSIDE

In the process of cultural integration of Polish society, which took place in response to its participation in the humanist and Reformation currents of the epoch, tensions and opposing forces were also present.

Artists and scholars, although supported by wealthy sponsors, as they were throughout Europe, could not always find understanding among them. The royal court showed a great deal of concern for the splendor of the state and of the dynasty, but its cultural activity, apart from the care accorded Wawel, was more or less of a symbolic nature. Sigismund the Old did not display any intellectual interests; Sigismund Augustus' passion was the collecting of precious stones and gold products, and his love for books was superficial; Stephen Báthory was more interested in politics and war. The royal court was able to impress, but it could not inspire or act as a partner in creative thought and the arts.

Stanisław Orzechowski rightly argued that "tremendous gifts of nature and talent are hidden in our countrymen," but due to lack of interest "they are as if covered by fungus." Jakub Przyłuski, in trying to influence Sigismund Augustus to take grater cultural initiative, enumerated a number of poets, writers and scholars who were living in Poland and who were not being utilized for "the pride of the state and the fame of the nation." He further argued that "the interest in talent" and "the sponsorship of the sciences" would open entirely new prospects for Polish culture. The momentum of scientific and artistic activities would "come upon us as the wave of a powerful mountain stream covering all obstacles."

This, however, did not happen. The activities of spiritual and secular lords often had a similar character. Influenced by the royal court, they attempted rather to enhance their family residences, than to inspire cultural creativity. The Wawel galleries were often imitated, not only in Baranów, but also in the homes of wealthy urban patricians. Often architecture was modeled on the Sigismund Chapel. Such ambitions were not foreign to the wealthy burghers. Seweryn Boner built a monumental, extremely picturesquely situated, medieval-style castle in Ogrodzieniec; Jost Decius built a Renaissance villa in Wola Justowska, of which he was extremely proud, since one could see Cracow from its arcades. Łukasz Górnicki adapted Castiglione's *Il Cortegiano* to Polish, dipicting the character of the court life-style, its social attributes, its grace of conversation and "mind games", its subtle humor and its untainted cheerfulness. Górnicki's *The Courtier* presented the limits of such a style of life. The great contributors to Polish culture had noticed these limits for some time.

Mikołaj Rej, although well-respected and presented with gifts at numerous courts, valued life at home in the country above all, obedient to the rhythms of nature and not to royal conventions, which made possible the "free thought" that the malicious and gaudy atmosphere of courts destroyed. Jan Kochanowski also gave up court life to settle down in Czarnolas, since he believed that "good ideas" would not visit him "even though his walls were richly decorated in silk."

The conflict between artists and writers and life of the courts was accompanied by a widely growing conflict between the model of country and family-based life-style and the worldly model of life presented by the courts. Rej and Kochanowski were not alone in returning to the countryside where they might find a peaceful, truly "human" life-style. Such beliefs were becoming more and more common. They were proclaimed most often as a protest against the materialization of life which was taking place in the "great world". The satirists and moralists of the epoch fought this threat. Starting with Biernat of Lublin, through Rej and Bielski, and finally to Kochanowski and Skarga, all participated in the attack against the materialization of life-styles.

The changes that took place in Poland in the fifteenth and sixteenth centuries led the gentry to greater awareness of its role in the country, which brought important privileges, but also responsibility for the entire Commonwealth. They, nonetheless, continued to seek the luxuries and comfort of a wealthy life-style. Many elements contributed to these complex events: pride in the Commonwealth's "constitution", supposedly the best in the world, with fear of what the future would bring. The praise of a country life-style was combined with moral and patriotic condemnation of the decline of the spirit of chivalry; the respect for books and intellectual culture was in opposition to their love of feasts and hunting.

An impressive number of works praised both national greatness and the charm of country life, including a dramatic vision of its future. All of these feelings were present in the poetry of Jan Kochanowski: the beauty and peacefulness of country life and dramatic predictions on the future of Poland. "This complicated world is not worth serving and worrying about," he wrote. "One must live modestly and happily." And once again Kochanowski's poetry was winning a permanent place in the Polish national consciousness, largely due to his famous apostrophe: "Peaceful countryside, happy countryside. What voice does you justice?"

In the early seventeenth century, the idylls of Szymon Szymonowic were becoming particularly popular because they presented the cheerful, joyous and, in spite of everything, sunny rhythms of village life.

But at the same time opposing views were present. Shutting oneself up at home in the countryside meant a resignation from one's civic duties and responsibilities. And these were of utmost importance for the country and the people. The famous monologue of Ulysses from Kochanowski's *The Dismissal of the Greek Envoys* was repeated quite often: "O, unruly kingdom, close to doom", or the Chorus's appeal: "You, who rule Poland and hold human justice in your hand"; or the prophetic words of Cassandra on the imminent fall of the state.

Towards the end of the Renaissance, Piotr Skarga wrote in his *Seym Sermons:* "The lands and grand duchies which united with the Polish crown, and grew together into one body, must fall apart and disintegrate because of your discord. . . And you, who have ruled other nations, will be like a bereaved widow. And your enemies will revile you."

The problem of dualism in Polish cultural life — a problem that some writers of the period perceived very acutely — was becoming an ever more worrying one. This could be seen on the one hand in a more profound attitude toward intellectual and artistic values, in contacts with the intellectual élite of Europe, creativity in various fields of life, and on the other hand in the superficial acceptance of foreign patterns and in the slavish following of fashion. A conflict therefore developed between "the civilized life" and the egoism of existence in the countryside, which brought with it material greed and a deterioration in the standard of civic life.

Foreign Culture in Poland and Polish Culture in the World

FOREIGN INFLUENCES

"The muses traveled to Sarmatia, attracted by the genius of its inhabitants," wrote the Flemish mathematician Gemma Frisius, who was interested in the work of Copernicus. And indeed, during the Renaissance era, western culture penetrated Poland abruptly and through various channels. Many foreigners came to Poland; Poles traveled abroad more frequently; a lively correspondence took place between humanist and Reformation centers in Italy, Switzerland, France, Germany and Polish institutions; the latest publications were brought into the country. The most outstanding individuals of the epoch were known in Poland not only through their works but through personal contacts. Jan Dantyszek kept in touch with the entire contemporary scholarly world, with Thomas More, Melanchthon, Erasmus of Rotterdam (who was also in close contact with Decius, a Cracow burgher, with Krzysztof Szydłowiecki, Piotr Tomicki and the Łaski family. Many works by Erasmus were dedicated to Poles.

Waves of novel ideas repeatedly reached Poland. First of all, there was humanism. Ever since Kallimach and Grzegorz of Sanok, Italy had become the great school of humanist thought and styles for Poles. Although the most radical works of the Italian humanists did not reach Poland, the more moderate forms that did provided a turning point in the Polish view of the world and in means of artistic expression. Humanism also opened up wide perspectives of classical culture. Not only were Polish poets raised on classical culture, but Polish politicians and even a wide spectrum of the gentry were also affected by it. Roman political phraseology came into popular usage and Poland was called, according to the humanist traditions, *Respublica*, although it was a kingdom, and it was referred to as *Patria*, although the word homeland was already in use.

The "execution" movement of the gentry and its Seym leaders constantly returned to the Roman models, and their speeches sounded as if they were being delivered by Roman senators. Jan Zamoyski, as a student of twenty-one, published a book in Venice, *De Senatu Romano,* and as chancellor of Poland preached Roman political models and subsequently built an "Italian" city — Zamość.

The humanism introduced to Poland by Erasmus of Rotterdam was different as was his concept of classical culture. Well known in both Latin editions and Polish translations, the works of Erasmus stressed criticism of established traditions and put forward the view that truth and the principles of morality should be sought in a common effort of the mind and in mutual tolerance. Frycz Modrzewski, in his courageous mediating activities, was a loyal follower of Erasmus. From this perspective, the philosophical views of Cicero and Seneca seemed quite close. Many works of these authors were also translated.

Italian artists, brought to Poland by the royal court, were engaged in architectural and sculptural work at Wawel Castle, in the city of Cracow, and at the courts of feudal lords. They brought a new artistic style into Poland and they taught the first generation of Poland's artists and craftsmen. A second great wave of ideas was introduced into Poland by the Reformation. Not only the teachings of Luther and Calvin became popular in Poland, but also those of other factions of the Protestant movement. Germany and Switzerland, particularly Basel, were becoming the centers from which these ideas radiated. The religious tolerance found in Poland attracted many radical philosophers, especially those persecuted in other parts of Europe. A religious fanatic, Józef Wereszczyński, wrote that "all the monsters and rascals cast out of Italy, Spain, France and Germany" came to Poland. In reality, the influx of these fugitives gave birth to a lively intellectual movement, which attracted both the gentry and the burghers. Never before — nor again — would the matter of faith and Christian life be so openly and vigorously discussed.

As humanism opened the doors to classical culture, so did the Reformation pave the way for Biblical traditions. Five centuries earlier, Christianity had been introduced into Poland, but not until the sixteenth century did the Bible become a widely read book. In fact it was only in the sixteenth century that the Bible was widely read. Each denomination provided its own translations of the Holy Scriptures. *The Psalms of David* were also translated many times. In 1532 Wietor published *The Psalms* based on old manuscripts; and in 1539, a translation by Walenty Wróbel, edited by Andrzej Glaber of Kobylin, was published; Rej also worked on a translation of *The Psalms of David,* which many consider to be the "foundation of all Christian writings"; the translation by Jan Kochanowski was famous; later, in 1594, the Rev. Wujek translated *The Psalms,* as did the Calvinist Maciej Rybiński in 1605.

Biblical stories and personages were coming to life in dramas written by everyone from Rej to Szymonowic. They appeared in other literary forms, such as religious postils, prose and poetic paraphrases and stories, and in abundant parables, which were intended to provide models for living.

OPINIONS OF POLISH CULTURE

The opinions of foreigners concerning Poland changed significantly in the fifteenth and sixteenth centuries. The increasing international prestige of the Jagiellonian state, the growing diplomatic and trade relations, the journeys by foreigners through or to Poland for prolonged visits, made possible a better understanding of the country, its people, and its culture. Poland was no longer an exotic and unknown country; it was also no longer barbarian.

There were three basic reasons for the increased interest in Poland. One of them had political connotations. In the face of the increasing Turkish threat to Europe, the victories of Poland in battles against the Turks — the relief of Sofia and the Peace in Szeged in 1444 and later the heroic death of King Ladislaus in the battle of Varna in the same year — turned the attention of many European politicians toward Poland, as "the bulwark of Christendom", as first Kallimach, and later Machiavelli put it.

A second reason was the increasing significance of Poland in cultural matters. The fame of the University in Cracow, and particularly its faculty of mathematics and astronomy, the strength of the humanist movement at the turn of the fifteenth and sixteenth centuries in Silesia, Toruń, and especially in Cracow, its international relations, and its religious tolerance which allowed many persecuted Protestant leaders to find shelter in Poland — all these created a new image of Poland in the minds of the other peoples of Europe.

Praise of Poland — in gallant words — was given by many humanists who were familiar with the country directly or through correspondence. For example, the Swiss historian and geographer Joachim Vadianus, after visiting Cracow in 1519, stated that "this nation, although with Scythian roots, was illustrious and in culture very different from the simple-mindedness of the old Sarmatians." The patronage of Piotr Tomicki, the royal vice-chancellor, enabled Jan Campen of Louvain to complete his scientific work. But most important, of course, was the opinion of Erasmus of Rotterdam.

In a letter to Decius, a Cracow banker and humanist, Erasmus wrote the following in 1523: "I compliment this nation, which in the past was scorned due to its barbaric nature, on the fact that now in both the sciences and legislation, in customs and religion, and in everything, it has separated itself from the blame of barbarism, that it blooms so beautifully, that it can compete with the leading and most outstanding nations."

The development of the Reformation was the third reason for changes in opinions about Poland. The religious tolerance existing in Poland was an object of wonder in Europe and was held up by radical intellectuals as a model to be followed. Orthodox worshippers of various creeds — both Catholic and Protestant — criticized this tolerance. Théodore de Bèze, one of the leading French Calvinists, wrote that there existed in Poland a "devilish freedom of conscience"; similarly the Jesuits wrote with grief about the protection that heretics received in Poland. The burning of Michael Servetus in Geneva on the orders of Calvin, who defended the sentence in *Defensio Orthodoxae Fidei,* mobilized the proponents of tolerance to fight for freedom of religious views and for peace between the creeds. Sébastien Castellio, Laelius Socinus, Bernardino Ochino and many others participated in this struggle. In this respect, Poland seemed to be free from "Satan's traps", which, according to the views of the defenders of tolerance, created tensions and hatred among worshippers of different creeds. The Huguenot writer, Hubert Languet, struggling for such tolerance in France, affirmed that in Poland people of different religious beliefs could coexist in peace, and the state did not suffer because "it is ruled by people of different religions, and offices are parceled out among them without any prejudice." Many other French writers held similar views. Much was written in England about Poland, in which "no one's conscience is tormented"; George Abbot, later Archbishop of Canterbury, indicated with pride that "in Poland the freedom of all religions is guaranteed." In the Netherlands, Dirck Volkertszoon Coornhert argued that tolerance did not lead to unrest in the state, as Poland itself could prove. Celio Secondo Curione dedicated his treatise, *About the Broadness of the Kingdom of God (De Amplitudine Regni Dei)* to Sigismund Augustus. He tried to illustrate that a good life and not fanaticism in the defense of a particular creed led to Salvation.

And although many attempted to explain away this tolerance in Poland as religious indifference among Poles, a large majority saw in it the confirmation of the privileges of the gentry; some saw in it the humanist attitude of one human being toward another and political wisdom, guaranteeing the solidarity of all citizens in national matters through religious tolerance.

Opinions about Polish culture were also being shaped in the West by observing Poles living abroad. Polish students were usually ranked high among other nationalities and were considered trustworthy; often they occupied important positions in university centers. Many professors maintained warm and close relations with Poles who arrived there to study. Polish missions had, however, an even more spectacular significance, particularly those in Italy and in France. Polish envoys were envied for the wealth and originality of their costume as well as their high standard of education. Certain comments have survived concerning the fabulous entourage of Jan Ostroróg, and about his son Stanisław, who set off for Rome in 1513, about his audience with the Pope, during which he was "bathed in gold, with a double chain and a multitude of gems, especially at the hat." The Polish envoys who came to Naples to fetch Bona in 1517 amazed everyone with their wealth of costume and horses' livery. A French historian, describing the arrival of a Polish mission in Paris in 1573, wrote the following: "The gentlemen and courtiers were aflame with shame when to the beautiful speeches of the Poles, delivered in Latin, they could only murmur back, since they were not familiar with this language."

CULTURAL COOPERATION

As early as the Middle Ages, a feeling of independence and pride in the greatness of the state were taking shape in the Polish national consciousness, as evidenced by the conduct of Spytek of Melsztyn before Charles IV in 1357. But the age of the Renaissance deepened this feeling and widened its influence. Jan Ostroróg, as a Polish envoy, represented the greatness of his country to Pope Paul II and extolled the magnificence of the Jagiellonian dynasty. The all-around education of Jan Ostroróg in Erfurt and Bologna enabled him to present such a stylistically beautiful speech, which made an enormous impression on the listeners, in spite of the fact that they were told a fantastic piece of news: that it was the Poles who had defeated Julius Caesar. This national pride was present in Ostroróg's *Memorial,* dealing with the reform of the country and with the strengthening of its sovereignty.

Stanisław Orzechowski, describing the increasingly widespread knowledge of Greek and Italian in Poland, wrote that "recently wild Sarmatia has become a second Italy or Greece."

Many writers stressed Polish intellectual and artistic talents and Polish achievements. Szymon Marycki of Pilzno stated that "Poles do not lack talent, acumen of intellect, or seriousness in treating matters." Jakub

Przyłuski wrote about "talents which grow so abundantly." Andrzej Patrycy Nidecki felt that "our abilities are by no means any less than the talents of any other cultured nations." But at the same time they were forming critical judgments according to which, as Adam Lubelczyk noted, "the talents of Poles, endowed with unbelievable ingenuity, were rotting and turning sour under the dust and rust of the schoolmen." Others stressed the fact that these studies were not very systematic and that "a multitude of sciences were merely touched upon" rather than allowing for a more detailed understanding. Still others complained about the lack of sufficient care given studies and incentives for scholars and artists.

All this — criticism by others as well as self-criticism — produced a balanced awareness that Poles were on an equal footing with the rest of the civilized world, and that they were taking full part in its development.

And in fact, the contribution of Poland to the overall culture of Europe in the sixteenth century was very large. This was based mainly on the fact that Poland was becoming an active center of cultural development for lands under its own jurisdiction and for bordering countries as well.

One of the factors contributing to this situation in the fifteenth and sixteenth centuries was the University in Cracow. The number of foreign students in attendance rose constantly. Among the entire 17,263 matriculated students between 1433 and 1509, 7,611 came from outside Poland, an impressive 44 percent. A majority of foreign students were from Hungary; a large proportion were from Silesia. In the beginning of the sixteenth century, Cracow was the main center for mathematics and astronomy. Pope Leo X requested the University to prepare a new reformed Julian calendar, which was accomplished by Marcin Biem of Olkusz. Many students came to the University because it was here that Copernicus had once studied. The high level of scholastic philosophy continued, represented by Jan of Głogów, Michał Twaróg of Bystrzyków, Michał of Wrocław and many others. The University was fast becoming a center for humanist studies. After Latin, Greek was also taught, and the needs of the Reformation were satisfied by studies of Hebrew. Both Poles and foreigners were creating a lively center of learning and poetry of a new type. A large number of students came from more distant countries, such as Germany, Switzerland, and Austria. Particularly active was the group from Silesia, widening and strengthening close cultural ties with Poland. Many German humanists, beginning with Celtis, studied and worked in Cracow.

In the northern part of the country, Gdańsk was a lively center of intellectual life; although within the borders of the Commonwealth, as an important port it was open to the world. The Vistula was a trade route which connected Gdańsk with Cracow. The gymnasium of Gdańsk, although not a university, maintained a high standard and its relations with central Poland were very active.

The situation was similar in East Prussia, also known as Ducal Prussia, especially during the Reformation.

Królewiec became a center of religious activity in Latin, German and Polish. In Królewiec, Reformation texts were published — catechisms, hymnals, treatises and creeds — as well as dictionaries, grammars and Polish readers. Writings of Polish Protestants — Marcin Krowicki and Jakub Niemojewski — were translated into German, as later were the writings of Stanisław Hosius and Marcin Kromer from Latin. The publisher and writer Seklucjan worked mainly in Królewiec. During the Counter-Reformation, as early as 1564, a Jesuit college was founded at Braniewo, at the instigation of Hosius.

Polish-Bohemian and Polish-Hungarian relations were of a different character. The Reformation enlivened relations with Bohemia in both directions: the Bohemian Brethren persecuted in their homeland found refuge in Poland; the Polish Protestant Postils reached Bohemia and Rej and other authors were translated. In the era of the Counter-Reformation, such works as the Postils of the Rev. Wujek, the works of Hosius, Piotr Skarga, and other Catholic writers were readily translated. Bartłomiej Paprocki, the temperamental author of the armorial of the gentry, spent over a dozen years in Bohemia, translated Kochanowski, and also published his own works in Czech. Relations with Hungary had long political traditions. In the sixteenth century the Reformation played an important role; it gave rise to new ties between Polish and Hungarian Protestants, especially Arians. Grzegorz of Brzeziny and Blandrata were very close; many Hungarians attended Arian schools, particularly in Raków and Lusławice. During the Counter-Reformation, the Jesuits also gained significance in this respect. It was they who organized schools in Poland and Hungary. Rev. Wujek lectured in Kolozsvár (modern Cluj in Romania).

The significance of Poland and its contribution to European culture increased a great deal due to the Reformation. During the second half of the sixteenth century, all Protestant sects which were persecuted in other countries found an opportunity to live and teach in Poland. While the followers of Luther and Calvin met with constant opposition in France, Germany and Switzerland, the entire radical left-wing Protestant movement found refuge in Poland; among these were the Bohemian Brethren, given protection, particularly in Great Poland, by the wealthy Górka and Leszczyński families; the Mennonites of the Netherlands settled mainly in the Żuławy region; Anabaptists from various countries were usually attracted to Royal Prussia, the Lublin region and Volhynia; from Italy and Germany came those professing an anti-trinitarian view. From the British Isles came the Scots and Irish who settled mainly in the northern provinces of the country; the Jews, persecuted in other countries, also settled in Poland. Many outstanding radical Reformation leaders came to Poland, including Giorgio Blandrata, Laelius Socinus, Faustus Socinus, Bernardino Ochino, Gianbattista Bovio, Christian Francken, and Jacob Paleolog. Sébastien Castellio was also to come, but sudden death terminated his plans.

An Italian emigrant living in Poland, Bernardino Bonifacio d'Oria, attempting to influence Castellio to come to Poland, wrote the following to him: "You would find here a great freedom, to live according to your ideals and views, to write and be published."

Under such conditions, a battle of importance to all Europe could be fought in Poland, a great debate concerning the principles of religion and behavior.

Religious tolerance in Poland was not accidental. It was not merely due to the good will of the monarch. It was the consequence of social relations, the current political system, the intellectual biases of church and secular dignitaries, as well as the attitudes of the majority of the gentry and the burghers. In this way, Poland was not only showing Europe of the sixteenth century possibilities for religious tolerance but also possibilities for organizing a nation around a system of mutual cooperation between its citizens and its ruler, a wide representation of the majority, that is the Seym, and the Senate, composed of church and secular dignitaries. Such an organization of the state guaranteed individual freedom to everyone who in this system of estates had civil rights.

The system of absolute monarchy that was taking shape in Europe put forward the principle of *cuius regio eius religio* against the idea of tolerance, and was opposed also to democratic-parliamentary organization of the state on the Polish model. But with hindsight and regardless of the later evolution of Poland's gentry democracy, the Polish model was an important contribution to the development of modern institutions of state and government. A very controversial and almost symbolic opposition of these two systems was the famous conversation between the Polish mission and Henri de Valois in Paris, before he was crowned King of Poland. When Henri opposed the tolerance outlined in the Warsaw Confederacy, which required that the king maintain peace among worshippers of different faiths, Jan Zborowski sharply replied: *"Nisi id feceris, Rex in Polonia non eris"* ("If you won't do this, you won't be King of Poland").

POLISH CONTRIBUTION TO EUROPEAN CULTURE

The ideals that Poland presented to Europe in the sixteenth century, a unique and important contribution to modern culture, found expression in the works of outstanding writers and scholars, which gained respect far outside the borders of their native land.

Klemens Janicki was celebrated as a poet in Italy, given honors, according to tradition, in the name of the Emperor Charles V. Jan Kochanowski, at the end of his career, evaluating his own work, wrote: "And I ventured upon the beautiful heights of Calliope/Where Polish traces had yet left no mark."

His poetry, both in Polish and in Latin, did indeed gain great recognition in the world. The number of translations into other languages attests to his popularity. Szymon Szymonowic, who used the name Simon Simonides to suggest the Greek poet, also gained noteworthy fame. His poems, entitled *Poemata Aurea*, were published in Leiden in 1619.

In philology, Andrzej Patrycy Nidecki shone as a

publisher and editor of fragments of the writings of Cicero. His four volume work, published in 1565 in Venice, was reprinted many times in the sixteenth century and widely appreciated by humanists in other countries. Maciej of Miechów opened new horizons for Eastern European geography; in his *Tractatus de Duabus Sarmatiis, Asiana et Europiana,* he took a position against current views concerning this part of the world, stressing in his introduction that only by experiment and not by reference to authorities will "the truth appear in concise words." This work was reprinted many times and translated into various languages. Józef Struś also gained worldwide recognition in the field of medicine; he was the author of a basic work about the pulse, which appeared in Basel in 1555 and was reprinted several times in the sixteenth century.

The Cracow school of mathematics and astronomy, however, was the most renowned throughout all Europe. Marcin Bylica, a friend and associate of Regiomontanus, did his research here; as did Jan of Głogów, an outstanding observer of the motion of the planets; and Wojciech of Brudzew, an astronomer and humanist, a friend of Celtis. In 1493, Hartmann Schedel, in his famous *Weltchronik,* stated that there was no equal to this school in all Germany. It was from here that Nicolaus Copernicus emerged, the most outstanding Polish scientist of the epoch. His scientific methodology, which overcame not only the limitations of Aristotelian scholastic philosophy, but also the generalizations of empiricism, opened the way leading, through Galileo and Newton, to the modern natural sciences. His heliocentric theory, which raised such a controversy in Protestant Germany and which was strongly crticized by Luther and Melanchthon, found defenders and proponents in Poland, even in the later period, when Rome also came out against it, as evidenced by two great mathematicians from the beginning of the seventeenth century, Jan Brożek and Stanisław Pudłowski. Copernicus was also the author of a pioneering work in the area of economics, explaining the process by which a weaker monetary unit is driven out by a stronger one. This discovery preceded Gresham's law. The courage of criticism in such varied disciplines is evidence of the greatness not only of Copernicus but perhaps also, as noted by Nietzsche, of the Polish scientific environment, in which a feeling of the usefulness of the individual was able to grow and creativity to blossom.

Another example of this is Modrzewski. His great work *On the Reform of the Commonwealth* was not only a courageous proposition for reforms which should take place in Poland, but also a treatise in the area of political science. This treatise, published in Basel in 1554 and in 1559, attracted worldwide attention. In fact, it truly was an exceptional book. His constitutional theory related in a unique way elements of ancient traditions to the needs of contemporary times, as well as strict legal arguments to moral postulates, and, finally, a bright realism to utopian foresight, presaging an ideal Poland. Nothing in the political literature of the sixteenth century could compare with it. The work of Wawrzyniec Goślicki, *De Optimo Senatore Libri Duo,* published in Venice in 1568, and in

Basel in 1593, was also of significance although to a much smaller degree than the above. It was translated into English and published twice in England (1598 and 1607) and confiscated twice, since it proposed limitations on the absolute power of the king.

Some Polish Catholic and Reformation leaders also gained European recognition. Jan Łaski, after his studies in Padua and Paris, spent time in Basel, where he studied under Erasmus of Rotterdam. He purchased the latter's magnificent library, allowing Erasmus to use it for the rest of his life. Later, after a period in Poland, he left for Frisia, and then for England. There he was coorganizer of the Anglican Church. Persecuted by Catholics and followers of Luther, he returned to Poland toward the end of his life. His theological treatises, translated into many languages, brought him world renown.

No less well known in Catholic circles was Stanisław Hosius. His book containing the Catholic creed, published in 1558 in Latin and a few years later in Polish, *Books Concerning the Enlightening and Honest Words of God,* was translated into English, French, German and Czech; it was reprinted on numerous occasions. It was the most popular Catholic "catechism" of the Counter-Reformation.

Conclusions

While it is difficult to define clearly the points of time at which the Renaissance began and ended — where it emerged from the Middle Ages, where it faded into the Baroque — there can be no doubt that it was short-lived. While medieval culture developed over a period of five centuries, the Renaissance lasted only one-fifth as long. The High Renaissance lasted an even shorter time: it was only during the third decade of the sixteenth century that the first Polish books were published; the Renaissance reconstruction of Wawel Castle took place from 1507 to 1536; and in 1564 the first Jesuits were brought to Poland by Hosius, and immediately began their educational activities; the first Jesuit college was formed in that year in Braniewo; and propaganda was begun against the Reformation and humanism. Describing the duration of the Renaissance in terms of generations, we can note that in fact it encompassed the activities of only a few: the first, at the beginning of the sixteenth century, represented by Biernat of Lublin (b. 1465), Copernicus (b. 1473), Krzycki (b. 1482), and Dantyszek (b. 1485); the second, those born at the beginning of the sixteenth century, like Rej (b. 1505), Modrzewski (b. 1503), and Orzechowski (b. 1513); and the third, the generation of Kochanowski (b. 1530) and Górnicki (b. 1527), active in the second half of the century. The fourth generation, that of Skarga (b. 1536), Klonowic (b. 1545), Sęp Szarzyński (b. 1551), and Szymonowic (b. 1558), was active in the years just prior to the end of the Renaissance.

And yet, this short period was a great one in Poland's history. It was during this epoch that the process of shaping the national consciousness, begun in the Middle Ages, was completed. This was shown in awareness of the greatness and power of the state, strengthened in its victorious battles with the Teutonic Knights and able to cope with the threat of the Turkish invasions; in the winning and consolidation of sovereignty in the face of the pretensions of the Roman curia; in the prospects for the future development of the state and its international significance under the rule of the Jagiellonians. The victory of the Polish language as a normal means of communication and a medium for creative writers was both cause and result of this national consciousness. After 1543, all the constitutions of the Seym were in Polish and at the Seym in 1563 Mikołaj Sienicki thanked the king for allowing him to give his speeches in Polish and for permitting all proceedings to be conducted in Polish. This national role of the Polish language was further confirmed in the many decisions made by craftsmen and burghers who began to use Polish in places where up to that time only Latin or German had been used. The Polish language was also becoming an obedient tool of journalism and literature, due to which the social range of influence of intellectual concepts and emotional ideas — an important factor of national integration — increased considerably.

This process mingled with another, also begun in the Middle Ages, concerning social responsibility for the state. The state was still a kingdom but in the opinion of its inhabitants it was becoming a common wealth, and they themselves, although still subjects of the king, were slowly becoming citizens. Under the Jagiellonian dynasty Poland was an hereditary monarchy but in practice the king was elected. After the dynasty came to an end, elections became an institution; the royal candidate had to agree to certain conditions of rule, but once in power he was a sovereign ruler. In spite of various conflicts, there was a clear tendency to form a political system which reconciled citizens' rights with the necessity of central authority.

The proportion of society entitled to participate in government was not clearly established. This was a society of estates and political privileges were not granted to all estates. But the borders between the different estates were not yet fixed and impassable. They were open for the burghers fairly widely and were not completely closed for the peasants. The participation of both of these estates in culture — including cultural creativity — was relatively significant. Royal and church chanceries opened still other possibilities for work and advancement. Poland was not yet exclusively a Commonwealth of the Gentry. The national consciousness, exemplified in the feeling of responsibility for the fate of the state, was not yet the monopoly of any one class. It was shared by vernacular writers and printers, burgher and peasant artists and humanists, like Janicki, and particularly Reformation leaders.

It was not until the succeeding epoch that a permanent hardening and closing of the class structure took place, together with the destruction of the balance existing between the king, the senate and the house of deputies, and a growth and strengthening of the privileges of both the magnates and gentry.

In the sixteenth century all the roads leading into the future still offered a variety of possible outcomes and solutions. And even if poets and writers warned against the dangers which threatened the country, they were creating with full optimism a great program for citizenship. This program encompassed the shaping of everyday life of all people and of their social obligations. In the first instance models of feudal and court life were presented, contrasting, yet still mutually complementary. Criticism of the very narrow intellectual horizons which threatened life in the countryside, and criticism of the superficial and hypocritical life of the court, were intended to show the positive sides of both of these styles of life, attainable either concurrently or alternatively. In the second instance similarly contradictory but at the same time mutually complementary models of life were presented: as public military and political service, and as private existence. In this context self-serving tendencies were also to be done away with and although public service was never in conflict with the charm and beauty of private life, it was supposed to be based on individually attained attributes of virtue and education. It was Rej, as Andrzej Trzecieski pointed out, who "although choosing to exist freely," still "when occasion demanded, never denied his services to the Commonwealth or his friends."

This program of social education, which was to shape the consciousness and the development of the citizens, was a unique ideological reality, built upon political reality, which when changed, became either a challenge to all the citizens of the country and strengthened their patriotism, or a threat, requiring struggle and strength in the overcoming of obstacles.

The greatness and importance of this program can perhaps be measured not only in terms of its influence on sixteenth century society, but also in terms of the lasting significance which it gained in the social consciousness. Even today, certain formulae which politicians and writers of the sixteenth century proposed are still vivid and alive. Is there anyone through the centuries that has not heard the phrase: "The stairway to heaven is open for those that serve their native land"?

Something more was also encompassed in this great program of national education. It contained not only proposals for shaping the social and individual sense of obligation, but also the recognition of culture as an individual and important attribute of human existence. Over the growing material well-being of the masses, a world of desirable intellectual values was constructed: learning and education, art, music and poetry. In the Middle Ages these values were accessible to only very few and always intertwined with the reality that the church was forming through its ideology and liturgy. During the Renaissance in Poland, as well as in other countries, an independent attitude toward these values was being formed. It was becoming important not only to build churches but also to fund the building of castles and residences, the reconstruction of old ones, and to ensure the material beauty of life. Education was becoming something desired; intellectual discussions were highly praised; as was practically applicable knowledge. 74

Modrzewski wrote the following about a reception at the home of Trzecieski: "Before we sat down to dine, we went to the host's library, which was full of volumes of all sorts. Each one of us — and we were not few — according to his desires, perused books of his preference." The monopoly of the church in the area of learning was broken: secular man became aware that he could know more or know better, even in the area of religion. Catholics and non-Catholics alike questioned the dogma that "the common people should seek the Will of God in the mouths of priests". Poetry and art gained importance. In public life, great royal ceremonies, like the wedding of Sigismund I and Bona, the wedding of Sigismund Augustus and Elizabeth of Austria, the great festival in 1583 at the wedding of Jan Zamoyski, and in 1592 the wedding of Sigismund III — all were presented theatrically, a great integration of music, dance, poetry and sculpture. Due to *The Dismissal of the Greek Envoys,* a tragedy "presented at the theater to His Majesty and Her Majesty in Jazdów outside of Warsaw," the higher artistic and intellectual level of the role of poetry became evident. Poetry in private life may have had an even greater significance. The proud declaration of Kochanowski: "I sing but to myself and the Muses" was contradicted by the popularity of his works. Not only *The Psalms* but also *The Songs, Epigrams,* and *Threnodies,* seemed to be a vital source for the people. Polish life during the age of the Renaissance required poetry. In this we see the greatness of the period.

BAROQUE

Introduction

We accept the term Baroque to define the period between the Renaissance and the Enlightenment, from the end of the sixteenth century to the middle of the eighteenth century. It is a long and varied period. To portray the variations characteristic of each stage of development, we could, at times, use two other terms — Mannerism, to describe the early phase, and Rococo, to describe the last phase. These terms, although they have a definite meaning in the history of art, cannot, however, be applied to other disciplines. Baroque culture, in spite of the differences between its various phases, was a relatively monolithic unity.

This was a period when humanism was fading and the Counter-Reformation was winning, a time when wars and disasters swept over the whole country like a flood. It was also a period of spectacular victories for the Polish army; a time which witnessed an increase in the might of the magnate oligarchy but also of the local diets in which the democracy of the gentry was expressed; a time during which life in the manor-houses of the gentry delineated the absolute limits of culture, which gave shape to literature and to both individual and mass art; and a time when all foreign fashions seemed increasingly deserving of criticism.

Succeeding generations also viewed this period as a unified whole. Those who criticized it, for example during the Enlightenment, believed that the development of Polish culture ended with the Renaissance and everything that followed, up to the middle of the eighteenth century, represented a decline. Those who recalled this epoch with understanding and feeling — as did the Romantics — found in it a precise synthesis of what was Polish in the past.

Place in Europe and Historical Consciousness

THE DEFENSE OF POLAND'S BORDERS

The Commonwealth, with an area of about one million square kilometers, the largest state in contemporary Europe after Russia, had uncommonly long borders which required constant defense. Only in the western part of the country was there any reasonable peace. All other directions — Sweden from the north, Russia from the east, Turkey from the south — posed constant threats. The changing political situation in Europe allowed for the formation of short-term and unreliable alliances — with Turkey or Sweden against Russia, or with Russia against Turkey or Sweden — but the outcome of these alliances usually was settled on the battlefield. And bloody and destructive wars filled this entire period of Polish history.

The war with Russia, which had overrun Livonia, a prosperous and productive region, was begun by Báthory, who convinced the gentry that "not only are we fighting for Livonia but for everything." Three great military expeditions restored Livonia to Poland but did not destroy growing Russian power. Báthory's policy was continued by Sigismund III. In 1609 a new war was begun, in which the Poles, under the leadership of Stanisław Żółkiewski, took Moscow and forced the recognition of Ladislaus, the son of Sigismund, as the Czar of Russia. However, the further course of the war brought success to the Russians. The war finally ended in 1619 with guarantees that Poland was to acquire the Smolensk, Chernikhov and Seversk districts.

But in 1632, war broke out again. It ended with a new truce in 1654, but Russia, in supporting a Cossack uprising, renewed martial activities, which continued for many years. They were ended finally with the peace treaty in 1686, according to which part of the Ukraine, which included Kiev, was to come under Russian rule.

During this period a new conflict, between Sweden and Poland, was developing. In 1598, at the beginning of Sigismund III's reign, a war began on Swedish territory, and in 1600 in Livonia. In the area of Riga, Karol Chodkiewicz won a great victory; the Polish fleet, under the command of Jan Wejher, was also successful in battles around the Hel peninsula. Battles continued intermittently for many years. Between 1626 and 1629, they were transferred to Royal Prussia and the Vistula delta. The Swedish army then took control of the towns of Braniewo, Elbląg, Tczew, Oliwa and Puck. The Truce of Altmark (1629) was a compromise. In 1655 Sweden began a major offensive against Poland which met with great success. Almost the entire country was conquered. Charles Gustavus advocated the partitioning of Poland. According to a secret agreement of 1656, Poland was to be partitioned among Sweden, Brandenburg, the Ukraine and Transylvania. In the aftermath of this agreement, the army of Transylvania under the command of György Rákóczy, began its own powerful offensive in southern Poland. But the increasing resistance of the people — particularly the peasants — and the activities of the army under the command of Stefan Czarniecki, together with changes in the international scene unfavorable to Sweden, defeated the plans of Charles Gustavus. The Treaty of Oliwa (1660) ended the conflict which had lasted for many decades, and basically restored the territorial *status quo*.

Intermittently, during this same period, Poland was fighting yet another war, with Turkey. The Turkish threat had been present for centuries and the Polish people remembered well the defeat at Varna. In the sixteenth century, the Poles became more aware of the need for vigilance against the Turkish threat.

The south-eastern regions were for a long time the scenes of battles. The Cossacks organized raids to the shores of the Black Sea; the Tartars reached far into the heart of the Commonwealth. The politics of the Polish magnates encouraged various interventions in Moldavia. This was the direct reason for the Turko-Polish war. It began with a tremendous defeat at Tutora (Cecora) in

1620, where Hetman Stanisław Żółkiewski died. But in the following year, at Chocim (Khotin), the Turkish offensive was overcome. A treaty was signed but battles — particularly with the Cossacks and the Tartars — continued long afterwards. The Tartar and Turkish legions at times penetrated the Polish borders. The plans of Ladislaus IV for initiating a new war with Turkey did not find support among the gentry.

During the second half of the century, the Turkish attacks once again gained in strength. Although Poland did win the great battle of Chocim in 1673, the war was not terminated and continued for another thirty years. The war came to an end, however, after the treaty of Karlovci in 1699, which returned Podolia to Poland, along with the city of Kamieniec, and the vast areas of the Kiev and Bratslav regions.

In the chronicle of these wars the battles between Poles and Cossacks were particularly dramatic. The Cossack uprising, begun in the eastern border regions, gained in strength largely due to the support of the people of the Ukraine. The raids into Poland organized by Bohdan Khmielnitski in 1648, brought him many victories: at Żółte Wody, at Korsun, and later at Pilavtse. The army of the Commonwealth of Poland ceased to exist. Admittedly in 1651 the Cossack army was defeated at Beresteczko but three years later, the Ukraine was united with Russia. From 1654 the Russian army fought on the territory of Poland, aiding the Cossacks. In 1655, a Cossack division took the city of Lublin and reached the River Vistula. Battles continued for a few more years and finally ended with a truce at Andrussovo in 1667, followed by a peace treaty in 1686. Russia — now linked with the Ukraine — took over the regions of Smolensk and Chernikhov-Seversk, together with a part of the Ukraine which included Kiev.

This century of continuous wars, which destroyed the country and disorganized it politically, did not, however, result in major territorial losses. Certain areas were given away in the north and east, in Livonia, Smolensk, and on the River Dnieper. What mattered much more was the abandoning of plans and attempts to develop and strengthen Polish rule on the Baltic seacoast, and to regain lost lands in the west, particularly Silesia, which during the Thirty Years' War was the scene of hard fought battles, during which an exiled prince of the Piast dynasty. John Christian, asked Ladislaus IV for help and protection.

The outcome in Western Pomerania was similar. During the Thirty Years' War, the Swedish and Brandenburg armies controlled these lands. After the death of the last of the princes of Pomerania, Boguslaus XIV, this region was turned over to Swedish rule. Only the areas of Lębork and Bytów were partly returned to Poland, while Słupsk and Szczecin were lost completely.

But, in the last analysis, at the beginning of the eighteenth century Poland's borders did not differ greatly from those at the end of the sixteenth century. The effect of this century of wars was the maintenance of the *status quo*; the retention of the country's independence, almost lost due to the Swedish invasion of 1655, commonly called "the Deluge"; the settling of centuries-long disputes with

Turkey and Sweden; and the establishment of new relations with Russia. The multinational, magnate-gentry Commonwealth still had enough strength to defend its existence. But its policies turned out to be ineffective and its borders became open to its neighbors — supposedly friends, but in fact, enemies.

THE FATE AND RESPONSIBILITIES OF ORDINARY PEOPLE

These war chronicles had particular significance for the social consciousness. Wars were fought not only on the borderlands of the country, but penetrated deep within. The destruction and devastation reached almost everywhere.

As early as the Seym of 1597, deputies stated anxiously that the Turkish threat was not far away, and that "the time has come when not from across the ocean, not from the other side of the Danube, not from behind the walls of impenetrable fortresses do we hear of them, but as if from the other side of the door." In the seventeenth century, Turkish as well as other threats had become a fact of everyday life for millions of citizens. The Cossack uprising, which spread across vast territories and mobilized the Ukrainian people, reached as far as central Poland. The Swedish "Deluge" covered the entire country, reaching almost to the Carpathian mountains. The Swedes took control of both the old and the new capital and forced the king to flee. No quiet corner existed in Poland. War ceased to be merely a public, patriotic duty; it became the personal lot of millions of people, who were murdered and stripped of their possessions, and who sought ways of saving their own lives, or simply of revenging themselves.

This was particularly true of the first few years of the eighteenth century. In 1701, after his victory over Russia and the armies of Saxony, Charles XII invaded neutral Poland, allegedly in pursuit of his enemies. In the following years the Swedes again conquered the capital as well as Cracow. The armies of Saxony opposed them and Poland remained virtually non-partisan. Only later agreements with Russia, which ensured Russian assistance in the struggle with Sweden, mobilized the gentry. Still for a number of years, until Charles XII's defeat at Poltava in 1709, the Polish lands provided a site for the maneuvers and battles of three armies: Saxon, Swedish and Russian — all of which destroyed the country.

These wars, virtually waged at the front doors of manor-houses and cottages, were accompanied by strong internal political disagreements and battles between bitterly opposed forces. In the beginning of this epoch, the long-waged rebellion of Mikołaj Zebrzydowski unveiled the conflicts which existed between the magnates and the royal court on the one hand and the middling gentry on the other. By the middle of the century, Poland was divided into pro- and anti-Swedish factions; fratricidal war had begun. These conflicts did not cease after the victory over the Swedes. Some detachments of the army formed a "Holy Union", antagonistic towards the royal court. Other military groups opposed this union, forming their own "Blessed Union." The rebellion of Jerzy Sebastian Lubomirski continued for two years (1665—66). After the abdication of John Casimir (1668), his successor, Michael Korybut Wiśniowiecki, had the far from easy assignment of calming the country; to defend the crown, the Gołąb Confederacy (1672) was set up, which conducted a bloody war against the Sapiehas in Lithuania.

In the beginning of the eighteenth century, a deep schism split society; the supporters of Augustus II and the supporters of Stanislaus Leszczyński fought long and hard-won battles for a number of years. One side was aided by the Saxon and Russian armies; the other by the Swedes. Which side should be supported? Which represented "true" patriotism? And which was treason? No one at the time could answer these questions with complete assurance; even today one can find arguments in support of both sides, but at the time everyone had to choose between them simply by the way he behaved. This perplexing situation shaped dilemmas and conflicts in the national conscience; in the future they would always play a dramatic part in the history of the country, and would become one of the characteristic features of Polish culture in the modern era.

HISTORIOGRAPHY

The dramatic conditions created in Poland by these wars which affected everyone changed the vision of the fate of the Commonwealth in the social consciousness into a vision of the individual experience of its citizens.

This process was reflected in the historical interests and historical visions of society. The period of the Baroque was incapable of synthesizing its own history, nor did it have outstanding historians. In the beginning of the seventeenth century, attempts were still made to refer to the old historiography, which presented the development and might of the country and was intended to effect major political goals and to shape the national consciousness. But the king's order to stop the printing of Długosz's *History of Poland;* the confiscation of many historical works, such as, for example, *A History of Sigismund I,* edited by Szymon Starowolski; the demands of the Moscow deputies that Samuel Twardowski's great work entitled *Ladislaus IV* should be publicly burnt — all of these worked against the development of a monumental historiography. Many works, like, for example, the various studies by Łukasz Opaliński, remained in manuscript.

Under such conditions, historiography was becoming more a science dealing with the life of people in a community rather than a history of the state. This was confirmed in a characteristic move away from Livy, who stressed the might of ancient Rome and praised the greatness of the *populus romanus* as the foundation of the nation, towards Tacitus, who presented the era of the downfall of the Caesars and the decline of the morality of the citizens, an era of decadence, and who analyzed the mechanisms governing human passions.

The only real achievement was a small historical synthesis by Joachim Pastorius, born in Silesia, a professor at the gymnasiums in Elbląg and Gdańsk, the secretary of King Ladislaus IV. His work, *Florus Polonicus seu Polonicae Historiae* first appeared in Leiden in 1641, and later was published several times abroad and in Poland. In 1645 in Cracow and in 1649 in Amsterdam, Paweł Piasecki published his *Chronica Gestorum in Europa Singularium* in which he presented Polish history within the context of European history.

The synthesis of Polish history collated by the Arian Andrzej Lubieniecki in his work *Poloneutychia or the Good Fortune of the Polish Kingdom* (1616), showing religious tolerance as a particular Polish feature, was never published.

The history of contemporary local events developed much more intensively than the history of the nation: such history was presented in memoirs and running chronicles, in accounts of military expeditions, and in reports on important private and national occurrences. This literature was written by almost all church and secular dignitaries, hetmans and army commanders, magnates and gentry, and burghers. At times, it reached the level of studies of current political events; at other times, a record of information about individuals, interwoven with history. These works, seldom published, were circulated in manuscript copies to relatives and friends among the gentry.

Jan Chryzostom Pasek was unsurpassed, so far as narrative style was concerned. His memoirs showed how the history of Poland was "shrunk" into household gossip regarding the gentry manor, and great national events were seen from the viewpoint of individual participation in wars, elections and tribunals. History ceased to be a serious record of events and became a tale, an anecdote, "a fantasy"; the objective world became an individual adventure; status and political views turned into a play of imagination and passions; the dramatic fate of the country was an inspiration for a unique introverted journey to the gentry's country life and pastimes.

Man and the Forces of Production

SERF EXPLOITATION

In the first half of the seventeenth century, Poland's population was approximately ten million, a small figure compared to the enormous area of the country. The population distribution was uneven. In Silesia, on average there were thirty people per square kilometer; in Great Poland about nineteen; in Little Poland approximately twenty-three; and in Mazovia about twenty-four. In the Grand Duchy of Lithuania, on the other hand, there were only six, slightly less than in the Ukraine.

Production was equally unevenly spread. The coal-mining and metallurgical industry was concentrated mainly in the Cracow region, in what is called the Old Polish Basin, and in Silesia. Craft production was developing mainly in the cities, particularly in Cracow, Poznań, Toruń and Gdańsk.

But still the most important commodity produced was

grain, cultivated throughout the entire country. Its export from various regions depended primarily on transportation possibilities. The lands along the Vistula were in a favorable position since they made use of the seaport in Gdańsk. The exporting of grain from the Ukraine was greatly hindered, mainly because of the barrier represented by the Tartars and Turks.

In the social organization of production the gentry manor became the predominant unit, and the land owned by the gentry increased at the expense of peasant holdings; ever greater use was made of corvée, that is compulsory and unpaid peasant labor. In many instances the serf was required to work continuously for six days a week. The work-day lasted, in general, from sunrise to sunset. Various other types of service for the manor were exceptionally exhausting, for example, the transporting of grain.

In the eastern lands, the situation was different. While in central Poland at least eighty percent of all arable land belonged to the gentry, in Lithuania and the Ukraine great landed estates owned by the magnates were developing, accounting for over sixty percent of the land area. The old Polish magnate families acquired enormous estates as, for example, the Zamoyski, Potocki and Koniecpolski families; and, in particular, the landowners of Ukrainian (Ostrogski, Zasławski, Wiśniowiecki) and Lithuanian (Radziwiłł, Sapieha) descent. These enormous estates were administered by the landless gentry; as on lands of the gentry, the local peasants were the labor force, similarly exploited.

This property-owning and legal system shaped the unique mentality of the gentry regarding socio-economic matters. It was formulated as early as 1588 by Anzelm Gostomski, who was not above acting unscrupulously in order to obtain maximum profits.

The wars of the seventeenth century increased these economic conflicts and strengthened the mentality of exploitation.

The Cossack uprising and the Swedish "Deluge" destroyed almost all of Poland in material terms; military activity and plundering left derelict tens of cities and hundreds of villages; the population was drastically reduced. Starvation and the plague, a post-war epidemic, killed many. Vast territories of the country became uninhabited.

The level of losses was extremely high. The population of the Commonwealth decreased by one third. In some areas this decline was even sharper: in Mazovia it reached 40 percent in the villages, and 70 in the cities; in Royal Prussia it reached 60 percent. The population density, which before the "Deluge" was 26.3 people per square kilometer, decreased to below 20. By the end of the century natural growth somewhat compensated for these losses; but during the Great Northern War, Poland lost about half a million people.

Many towns were destroyed. Over half of the villages were burned down; in some areas destruction of agricultural properties was even greater. According to records kept on royal estates in Great Poland, over 70 percent of peasant land was uncultivated. In all areas of Poland there were some villages not even destroyed, where all of the

inhabitants had been either murdered, had fled or died of disease. While at the end of the sixteenth century only five percent of the land was uncultivated, by the end of the seventeenth century this had risen to 40 percent.

It is estimated that agricultural production on peasant holdings during the 1660's amounted to only 30 percent of that at the end of the sixteenth century; and that on the gentry manors, to about 45 percent. Livestock was reduced by about half.

At the same time, there was technological regression: the centers of steel and iron production were destroyed; many coal mines were flooded; almost half of the flour mills were burned down. The peasants returned to using primitive milling devices and had no plows.

All of this contributed to a hardening of the corvée system. The serfs were to be exploited to the ultimate limits. Tied peasants were sought everywhere; peasants fleeing from other manors were always welcome; people were bought; sometimes a man would be paid for in horses; people were handed over as security, and what was termed voluntary acceptance of serfdom provided absolution from punishment, even from the death penalty for committing murder.

Under such conditions the serf manor system was not only an economic institution, but shaped unique concepts and attitudes regarding inter-personal relations. Wacław Potocki was aware of these internal changes, which more and more contradicted pure Christian morality. After all, he wrote, the peasants are our brothers, since they are human beings "according to the Apostle"; why, then do "Catholics dare to trade in their brothers?"

THE PROSPECTS
FOR A NEW ECONOMIC MENTALITY

During these most difficult years, whenever there was peace even for only short periods of time, attempts were made to rebuild the economy. During the final decades of the seventeenth century, before the Great Northern War added to overall destruction, there had been tangible achievements. The population increased; the export of goods produced in the country grew; the economy of certain towns was being reconstructed. The once depopulated and almost completely destroyed city of Warsaw by the year 1676 already had 18,000 citizens. Due to the grain and cattle trade, such cities as Kazimierz and Sandomierz developed. But in other cities of Mazovia, the situation did not appear so sanguine. Cracow also still remained in ruins. The financial crisis continued, although fiscal reforms were attempted. In 1662, the Seym ratified a new universal capitation tax. Although not very popular among the gentry, it was, nonetheless, a new duty for the citizen.

The reconstruction of the country also raised new problems. The unfavorable prices of grain, cattle and timber limited the profits which could be made from the trade in these goods everywhere in Europe, and particularly in Poland. Was it to remain a country of agricultural export, the so-called "granary of Europe?" Or were there other ways of economic development at hand? Such questions were examined with anxiety and reluctance in a society which for so many years had been connected inextricably with the agricultural style of life. The gentry were blinkered by the bounds of this life-style.

The first who dared cross these bounds was Andrzej Maksymilian Fredro, a defender of the freedoms of the gentry, but also the author of a modern program of economic recovery for Poland. This program presented in *Monita Politico-Moralia* (1664) encompassed five main points, since, according to Fredro, "there are five factors in ensuring the wealth of nations." These were the following: stock breeding and land cultivation, the production of raw materials, industry, trade, and transportation. Valuing highly farming as a source of wealth, Fredro nonetheless emphasized the importance of handicrafts — that is, the development of that aspect of human activity which is art and which provides wealth of a different type from that offered by farming.

To put this program into effect, Fredro called for a change in policy toward the towns and especially toward crafts and manufacturing, as well as changes in social and educational policies. He called for the employment of "free people" and for the forcing of towns to send their most talented young people to France or the Netherlands to study the "more subtle and distinguished crafts."

As a part of his program, Fredro also formulated a great project regarding the development of roads in Poland to facilitate transportation; the waterways were also to have particular significance. A network of canals was to enliven trading activities between not only east and west, but also among the Baltic, the Black, and the Mediterranean Seas.

Fredro's ideas were not readily accepted. During the years 1716—20, based on the proposals of the chancellor, Jan Szembek, and on King Augustus II's instructions, discussions were undertaken concerning the reconstruction of the country, the development of industry and handicraft, the laws of the towns, and the building of land and water routes. But this program of reconstruction of the economy was dependent in large part on the changing and modernizing of the mentality of society which was still tied to the magnate residence and the gentry manor. However these problems went beyond the purview of this particular epoch.

Social Unrest

THE PEASANT QUESTION

The increasing exploitation of serfs on the gentry manors brought about various outbreaks of opposition and aggression. Many peasants left their own holdings and their lord's estate to seek better living conditions elsewhere; the number of "empty fields" was increasing. The runaways at times formed, particularly in the mountainous regions, marauding bands. Strikes were fairly common, especially during the harvest, and usually ended with harsh reprisals. In the Nowy Targ region a peasant uprising took place during the years 1624—33; it took four army divisions to put it down. These various forms of protest and rebellion reached full strength in the middle of the seventeenth century and encompassed almost all parts of the Commonwealth.

Such robber leaders as Janosik, Ondraszek and Proćpak, became legends among the people and were depicted with sympathy by writers and poets of both the burghers and the gentry. The peasant uprising in the sub-Carpathian region in 1651 under the leadership of Kostka-Napierski gained similar fame.

The increase in anti-feudal resistance among the peasants, combined with their patriotic fight against the Swedish invasion, led to reflections on Poland's social system and possibilities for its improvement. John Casimir solemnly pledged in 1656 that "because we feel a great pain in our heart, that all the disasters that we have endured during the last seven years — epidemics, wars and other misfortunes — were sent by the Almighty as punishment for the oppression and suffering of the peasant, we hereby pledge, that after regaining peace, we together with all the estates, shall use all the means at our disposal in order to free our people from all unfairness and oppression."

This pledge was never kept.

Peasant unrest was indicative of the basic contradictions in the social system. Under such circumstances, the peasant problem was of much greater significance than simply the question of the feudal serf economy. It was becoming a political matter, and a matter for the conscience of Christians and citizens in general.

Literature often and variously depicted these ideological contradiction and pangs of conscience, creating and rooting new and important values in the national consciousness.

Arian poets and writers reached deeper into the moral aspects surrounding these social problems. Jan Stoiński, in his *Prayers of the Pious* (1633), included "prayers of lords for their vassals," which exemplified Christian brotherhood and Christian responsibility for the fate of others.

The works of Wacław Potocki constituted a harsh criticism of current social conditions. In strong, almost brutal words, he described the slavery of peasants in Poland. A serf lives solely with the hope of freedom and "never ceases to search for a hole in the cage through which to escape." Everywhere he sees enemies and tyrants; "in his heart he sharpens a knife aimed at them."

In this way the peasant problem was becoming one of the most fundamental characteristics of the Polish culture of the Baroque — criticism of reality, the questioning of conformistic acceptance of facts, and a leaning toward the mind and the conscience. And while the politics of the state of the gentry — the king and his court, the senate and the seym, and the local elders — defended class privileges, almost all literature, irrespective of the ideology or artistic preferences of the writers and poets and regardless of their social background, voiced strong criticism of existing conditions, unmasked their false and dangerous foundations, and attempted to appeal to the mind and to the conscience.

This was accomplished mainly through writings patterned on Til Eulenspiegel. But alongside this literature, which was created by peasant schoolteachers and traveling minstrels, a number of wealthy burghers and members of the gentry composed similar works. Sebastian Klonowic, Szymon Szymonowic, Szymon Zimorowic and Bartłomiej Zimorowic depicted the situation of the peasant, the cruelty of exploitation, and the lawlessness of the lords.

THE CONFLICT BETWEEN THE GENTRY AND THE BURGHERS

The conflict between the gentry and the burghers did not use protest and battles to shape Polish culture. It was of a different social character: the burghers — as opposed to the peasants — were not directly dependent on the lords; in spite of everything, they formed a separate estate in the Commonwealth, had their own organization, held certain privileges, and had large fortunes in their possession.

The wealth of the burghers was often envied by the gentry, which in turn left its impact on economic policies aimed at limiting the economic privileges of the burghers, the taking over by the gentry of all the more profitable privileges, the subordination of town administration to the feudal lords, and the creation of areas within the cities which were outwith the municipal jurisdiction etc.

The policies of the gentry engendered actions of self-defense on the part of the burghers. However sporadic and ineffective these actions were, the sheer number of towns involved indicates the scale of the conflict.

At the end of the sixteenth century there were over one thousand towns in Poland. Among them the largest were: Cracow (28,000 population), Poznań (20,000) Warsaw (20,000), Gdańsk (40,000) and Elbląg, Toruń, Bydgoszcz, Lublin, Riga, Królewiec, Lvov, Vilna and Mohilev. More than one hundred cities had over three thousand inhabitants. Urban dwellers formed 23 percent of the country's population.

In the first half of the seventeenth century, the people were losing much of their previous wealth and many of their privileges. The opportunities for international trade were decreasing; the national market was restricted; competition from the gentry was on the rise, particularly in the trade with Gdańsk and through Gdańsk.

The rebuilding of the economy in the towns after the Swedish "Deluge" was very difficult and slow. Under these conditions, only limited possibilities were available for the reconstruction of urban crafts, since the traditional guild and trade system had disintegrated. Conditions of international trade both by land and sea were becoming less and less favorable. The monetary crisis struck the towns in particular.

A new wave of military destruction, fires, looting, and contributions swept through the towns in the beginning of the eighteenth century. The largest towns fell to the level of ruined settlements with a population of only a few

thousand. The capital, though severely damaged, was still able to maintain its size, as did Gdańsk, despite the fact that during a six months' siege in 1734 by the Saxon and Russian armies, it lost as many as two thousand houses.

The economic downfall of the cities was viewed with alarm by the more educated members of the ruling sector, but literature and journalism often looked upon it from an entirely different point of view from that which gave a clear picture of the peasant question.

Literature patterned on Til Eulenspiegel and the literature of the burghers presented microcosms of the everyday life of merchants, craftsmen, students, and traveling jugglers, as well as of the city's everyday life, holidays, and festivals. This literature had the appeal of a smile; it was an epigram, a joke. Many critical observations were hidden in these jokes, but it was still far from the predominant tone found in works depicting the life of peasants and their defense.

The literature of the gentry also did not deal with this matter. For many of the gentry, life in the cities was worthy of envy: it was varied and happy. Journeys by noblemen to Gdańsk with the grain crop were becoming more and more an encounter with the beauties of the life-style of the city. Under these conditions, it was difficult to estimate the true life of the cities and particularly their importance in the national economy and culture.

Neither were the satirists, who stressed the faults of the gentry, able to see this. They considered the life-style of the town from the point of view of patriotic morality, which was to reincarnate traditional virtues. In this old Polish model, the most important place was given to the fighting spirit and after this the quiet life in the country. The town seemed to be synonymous with all vices: greed, waste, and cheating were rife there.

They admired the myth of the rebirth of knighthood and attacked viciously the contemporary mentality; neither the economic values accumulated in the towns, nor the style of life, so advantageous to the growth of artistic and scientific culture, were given their due.

Under such conditions, Polish culture was confined within the walls of magnate palaces and the manor-houses of the gentry, where the grey reality of serf exploitation and class egoism were evened out by the bombastic praise accorded the life-style in the country. Modernity, exemplified in seventeenth century Europe by the development of the urban economy and trade, the blossoming of science, and the shaping of a new mentality, remained out of reach for contemporary Poland.

THE CATHOLIC NATION

A wave of intolerance rose up in Poland in the seventeenth century causing the intensification of religious differences. Although it did not cause religious wars, still a deep wound in the national consciousness was created. The answer to the question — Who is Polish? — was becoming more difficult since *dissidentes de religione* were often refused citizenship by new Counter-Reformation ideology or violence or even by new laws.

The Arians were affected first, since they were spoken of as people "who ought not to be called Christians." In 1638, the Arians of the town of Raków were brought to court, charged with the destruction of a roadside cross; in 1647 the Seym ratified an agreement to close down all Arian schools and printing works. Although this was never widely put into effect, still various town and local diets contemplated even stricter measures.

The situation existing in Ruthenia was even more complicated. The Reformation of the sixteenth century reached far into the east. The Ruthenian gentry and magnates were quick to change their religion to Calvinism, Lutheranism and Arianism. But the Jesuits took on the battle, which — after the defeat of the Reformation — was to bring the Ruthenians back to Catholicism. At the same time, the Russian Orthodox church — particularly in Lvov and Vilna — began the fight for souls. New Orthodox schools were formed — in Lvov, Ostrog, Łuck, and later the Mohyła College in Kiev, which were to help people of Orthodox belief to assimilate. Although Ladislaus IV was not in favor of the Jesuit postulates concerning a return to Catholicism, he did not develop the Mohyła College. This was indicative of the Polish gentry's distrust of people of different ethnic backgrounds and religions. They were less opposed to accepting the Uniate gentry within the circle of the Polish national community. In any case, the Uniate group abandoned the Greek rite in favor of the Latin.

Only after the Swedish "Deluge" did it become clear that there was a direct relationship between internal religious differences and the problem of patriotic obligations and national unity. It is true that large numbers of Catholic gentry supported Charles Gustavus but his main supporters were Polish Protestants; however, in Royal Prussia it was this group which remained loyal to the king.

After the victory over the Swedes, attempts were made to bring the traitors to justice. But under such circumstances, who was not a traitor? The Seym of 1658 had to make these difficult decisions. Again the blame was placed on the weakest groups of non-Catholics: the Bohemian Brethren abandoned the devastated town of Leszno and went abroad. The decisions of the Seym of 1658 threatened the death penalty for Arians who did not either change their religion or leave the country. Although such sentences were never carried out, and a number of Arians still remained in the country worshipping in secret, the majority left Poland.

In contrast, the Lutherans and Calvinists, protected by certain towns and by wealthy patrons, were allowed to retain their rights as citizens, but, in the opinion of the gentry, remained on the outskirts of the national community.

Due to these processes, the nation of the gentry was increasingly becoming a nation of the Catholic gentry. This was officially confirmed when in 1673 it was agreed that only Catholics would be accepted into the ranks of the gentry. In 1717 all dissenters were banned from holding government office.

This religious exclusiveness was in contrast to the fact that Poland still remained a multinational and multireligious state with many Protestants, Orthodox and Uniates still living within its frontiers. The problem of Catholicism and the Polish heritage was, therefore, becoming quite important. But its political significance in the national consciousness did not become evident until the second half of the eighteenth century.

The Commonwealth

MILITARY FORCES

In the first half of the seventeenth century, Poland had a population of about ten million. But of this figure only 40 percent were Poles, who lived in a compact society on lands which covered slightly less than one fifth of the entire territory of the country and were quite densely populated, around twenty people per square kilometer (while in Lithuania there were only six people per square kilometer). The social structure of the ethnically Polish population was 67 percent peasant, 23 percent burgher, and 10 percent gentry.

But, after all, the strength of Poland was not determined by population nor by its social structure, although both of these factors were of significance. The determining factor was the organization of the army. And this, compared to other countries, was becoming increasingly outdated.

Very many and varied formations of the army were organized by the state, such as mercenary divisions, by individual voivodeships, by the magnates, by the towns, and directly by the king. But the size of these divisions was not great; coordination was difficult; and the short time spent by each soldier in the ranks did not allow for good training. In the view of the gentry, the main military force was what was termed the mass levy, which would mobilize the entire gentry in defense of the country. It was called up many times in the seventeenth century — in 1621, 1649, 1651, 1655—57, and 1672. Its military strength was different at various times. The mass levy was trained mostly on the battlefield, where the price paid for this belated education was at times very high.

Its neighbors outranked Poland both in the size of their military forces and in their military training. The Turkish army, which attacked Poland in 1621, fought with about 100,000 soldiers against only about 45,000 Poles. In the middle of the seventeenth century, Poland's standing army was never bigger than 15,000 soldiers; during the same period, the Holy Roman Empire had 40,000 soldiers at its disposal, as did Sweden; the Russian army had a strength of about 133,000 soldiers. Mobilization did at various times increase the number of soldiers, but still there were generally not more than 40,000 on hand; nor could they be very rapidly deployed. By the end of the century, this disproportion between the size of the Polish army and that of its neighbors increased even more: the Russian army reached 200,000; Turkey, in 1683, fought with an army of about 150,000; and even Brandenburg had an army of over 30,000 soldiers. It was with such military force that Poland conducted its defensive wars, which lasted through two thirds of the seventeenth century.

The battle with Turkey at Cecora in 1620, during which Hetman Stanisław Żółkiewski, a symbol of heroism for Polish soldiers and leaders, lost his life, signalled the beginning of a series of defeats for the Polish army. In 1648 Bohdan Khmielnitski, the leader of the Cossack uprising, destroyed the main forces of Poland at Żółte Wody and at Korsun, taking captive both hetmans leading the army. During the fall of the same year, the Polish army fled in panic from the battlefield when attacked at Pilavtse by Khmielnitski. This event was often recalled with grief by the gentry.

But at the same time Poland still possessed enough power to win great, at times spectacular, victories, which often were related as legends not only in the country but also abroad. Such was the victory of Karol Chodkiewicz at Kirkholm in 1605 over a Swedish army that was several times greater in size. Stefan Czarniecki led his expeditions into Denmark in much the same way, in particular, the landing on the islands of Als and Funen in 1658—59. In the war with Turkey, John Sobieski, then still a hetman, effected a fabulous victory at Chocim in 1673. Ten years later, the expedition of Sobieski, now king, to Vienna against the Turks, gained him European fame when he overcame the Turkish army, thereby freeing Western Europe from the threat of Turkish occupation. Sobieski later wrote the following about these battles: "Our Lord and God, blessed for all time, gave victory and fame to our nation, such as the past centuries had never heard of."

The Swedish-Polish War — a great test of the national will to survive and of national strength — had particular significance in the chronicles of defeats and victories of Poland. It was truly a "patriotic" war, a war carried on, in spite of the treasonable behavior of many wealthy magnates, by the gentry, by the burghers, and by the peasants. When victory seemed inevitable for Sweden, an irregular war began in Great Poland, Podlasie and the sub-Carpathian region. The peasants and the highlanders answered the pleas of John Casimir, who was in hiding in Opole in Silesia, to participate in partisan warfare and in this way won many battles. In this same region, the inhabitants of Pilzno, Biecz, Krosno and Nowy Targ defended their towns. The defense of the Jasna Góra monastery at Częstochowa became a symbol of courage and the will for victory, an appeal to all patriots. By the end of 1655 John Casimir returned to the country. In the decisive battle in the fork between the Rivers Vistula and San, the Polish army commanded by Czarniecki was victorious. From then on, the momentum was on the side of the Poles. The basis of this success was not only the gentry's fear of losing their privileges in the event of a Swedish victory, but rather the patriotic unity of all sectors of Polish society. In the face of a tragedy, all disputes and social conflicts ceased; all mistreatment and exploitation was forgotten; it became evident that Poland was a true motherland even for those for whom she was a stepmother.

The significance of this century of wars was that in the national consciousness feelings of "knightly duty" toward the country were strengthened. In hundreds of memoirs and dozens of literary works, the triumphs of the Polish army were extolled, heroism and acts of courage were presented, and the model of knighthood was held up as an example.

At the beginning of this epoch, Piotr Kochanowski translated the *Gerusalemme liberata* by Torquato Tasso (1618). But the history of this century formed a truly native and heroic epic. Among the populace "soldiers songs" about heroes and great hetmans — Chodkiewicz, Żółkiewski and Czarniecki — circulated, as did songs about the victories and the defeats, about the conquering of Smolensk and Moscow, and about the defense of Jasna Góra and the victory at Vienna. Samuel Twardowski, Wacław Potocki, and many other great poets wrote epics on these themes.

In all of these works one could sense the feeling of history, the interweaving of the history of the country with the heroic deeds of individuals, visions of greatness as a measure of events and of people. All of these works brought the past closer to contemporary times; they treated the memories of "knightly advantages" as an element of everyday life; the tolling of the bell for past victories and defeats was aimed at the hearts of contemporary people, particularly those who were becoming "tired of war", and goaded them to action.

THE ROYAL POWER
AND THE FREEDOMS OF THE GENTRY

The political mentality of the Baroque era was shaped by controversies concerning the royal power and the liberties of the gentry. This epoch, beginning with the rebellion of Mikołaj Zebrzydowski, was filled with various confederacies and rebellions, like that of Sebastian Lubomirski, and was terminated by the long-lasting civil war between the supporters of Augustus II and Stanislaus Leszczyński.

The ideology of Zebrzydowski's rebellion, expressed in hundreds of leaflets, various discourses, scripts, replies, responses and speeches, reflected the commitment of the gentry to traditional freedoms, and its watchful and distrustful attitude towards the policies of Sigismund III. One broadsheet made the following assertion: "His Majesty, due to his nature, cannot govern the Polish Kingdom and rule over free people."

The attempts of Sigismund III to strengthen his royal power by associating with the Counter-Reformation and the policies of the Habsburgs met with opposition among the Polish magnates as well as among the dissenters, who remained a significant group. Mikołaj Zebrzydowski, the voivode of Cracow, led the opposition, assembling the gentry at Stężyca, Lublin and Sandomierz. As a result a civil war broke out and although the rebels lost the battle, the king gave up his previous plans.

Ladislaus IV's attempts to strengthen his royal power failed in much the same manner.

During the reign of John Casimir, another trial of strength took place. After the Swedish Wars, the devastated country was in need of fiscal and administrative reform, with a strengthening of central government and executive authority. But the magnates and gentry were sceptical of the need for such changes. A number of Seym sessions was broken off. The magnate, Jerzy Sebastian Lubomirski, Field Hetman and Grand Marshal of the Crown, organized a rebellion and in a decisive battle at Mątwy in 1666 won a victory over the king's army. Although it led to a compromise settlement, the political situation in the country remained tense until John Casimir abdicated in 1668.

The situation did not change during the rule of John III (Sobieski), when most Seym sessions were also broken off, as also were local diets. New military confederacies were again repeatedly formed, while the hetmans conducted their own policies. The death of Sobieski in 1696 ignited the spark for new bitter struggles, and for internal and international intrigues. The election of Augustus II, the Elector of Saxony, was opposed by supporters of the candidate of Charles XII, Stanislaus Leszczyński, whom the gentry — infuriated by the arrest of the sons of John Sobieski, also candidates for the Polish crown, in Saxony — chose as king in 1704. This event became the reason for a civil war in which the Russian and Saxon armies also participated, since they were at war with Sweden.

The gentry's political mentality was shaped during this period under the influence of many varied and contradictory tendencies. The obsession with freedom was evident in the oratory which imitated that of the Roman Republic, and also in a unique traditionalism expressed in admiration for forbears. The pride displayed when speaking of the unique system of the Commonwealth, where the gentleman was subordinate to no one, was associated with fears of "conspiracies" that would eventually lead to the limiting of these liberties. Freedom was a call for loyalty towards the motherland "by one's own free will" and without any pressures other than moral duty; it was also the root of responsibility for the fate of the whole, the fate of the state.

Within this concept of society, there was still room for egoism, individualism, particularism, and political shortsightedness. A very narrow borderline existed between this world — of slightly utopian hopes that service to the Commonwealth and responsibility for its future could be based on a system of freedom, which brought government down to the gentry's manor-houses — and the real world, in which material interests played a determining role, as did private and group ambitions and animosities, family aspirations and mercenariness, and the determination to maintain present privileges.

This duality — which in future centuries would be interpreted by optimistic admirers of the former Commonwealth and by pessimistic critics of it — was already noted by some of the more discerning contemporary observers of public life.

THE POLITICS OF THE MAGNATE FAMILIES

The politics of the magnates, the great "princes", was aimed at helping mainly their own family interests. The history of the seventeenth and eighteenth centuries proved that to be true more than once. The great magnates — Zbaraski, Wiśniowiecki, Koniecpolski, Potocki — had at their disposal not only great riches, but also powerful armies. Every magnate in the border regions retained a few thousand soldiers. Private armies were not much smaller than the national Polish army during periods of peace.

But the main evil confronting the political life of the country was not that some magnate families took advantage of their military strength under favorable circumstances — as during the "Deluge" — and that by so doing, committed treason against the king and, therefore, against the state, but that their actions, based on covering up their private interests under a semblance of legality and patriotism, disorganized the activities of public institutions, particularly the Seym, local diets, tribunals, and thereby disorganized the political consciousness of the majority of the gentry.

The latter strongly defended the principle, even if fictitious, that everyone who had a coat-of-arms belonged to a community of equals. When in the Seym Constitution of 1690 the phrase "lesser gentry" was used to refer to the less wealthy gentry, a great uproar arose, which led to an amendment in the statute during the Seym of 1699, stating that an error had been made and that "with the consent of all estates this word would be scratched out *in perpetuum;* all agreed that *in aequalitate* you have neither lesser not greater."

The policies of the magnate families undermined not only the basis of equality of the gentry, but also central rule and the efficiency of the state government. It had a particularly destructive effect on the Seym. The activities of the Seym were in fact for a long time cramped by instructions that deputies received from the gentry when they were being chosen. These rules were not strictly enforced, however, and the Seym's resolutions were usually ratified or discarded by majority vote. At the end of the sixteenth century a proposal was discussed at one of the local diets, to treat as an enemy of the state anyone "who would dare to rupture the agreement of all." However although the controlling of the proceedings of the Seym was not so easy for the magnates, on the level of regional diets it was accomplished without major difficulties. Enforcing the requirement that all members must observe all the voted instructions led to influence over the Seym's proceedings, or even to preventing them. Thus, during the seventeenth century, the hands of Seym deputies were tied more and more by the decisions of the regional diets — at times it was even demanded that deputies be fined for not following the rules — and it became more and more difficult to agree on resolutions. Many Seyms ended without any final resolutions, for example, during the reign of Báthory in 1576, 1582, 1585; during the reign of Sigismund III in 1597, 1600, 1605, 1606, 1615; and during the reign of Ladislaus IV in

1637, 1639, 1645. But from the middle of the seventeenth century it became more common to break off the Seym's meetings, at times even at the instance of individual deputies. This *liberum veto* had become freedom's tool for the gentry. Between 1736 and 1736 all Seyms were broken off.

These actions blocked the undertaking of fundamental decisions regarding state policy and almost fully paralyzed the activities of the central government.

The degeneration of the Polish Seym led not only to the deterioration of authority in the country, but also became a factor in the disintegration of the political consciousness. To conceal the true motives of these actions, a well-structured patriotic rhetoric was used, relating to great ideas deeply rooted in tradition. In this way, a fundamental split was established between reality and the rhetorical mystification of reality; henceforth this was to be one of the negative aspects of the Polish political consciousness.

How deep this demoralization reached can be seen not only in the statements of deputies and gentry leaders made during Seym sessions and at regional diets, but also in the political literature which expressed the views of the contemporary intellectual élite.

ON INEFFECTIVE COUNCILS

In sixteenth century Poland, the political consciousness was shaped by both reality and political literature and poetry. In the seventeenth century the importance of the written word diminished considerably. Its contact with reality was related basically to moral problems, expounded mainly by Arian poets, as well as by Catholic writers, who propagated — as, for example, did Szymon Starowolski — a program of "reformation of Polish customs." The literature written by common townspeople and the burghers only presented pictures from life, stressing — at times, very harshly — existing injustice; it did not form a political program. The satirists did much the same. Only Łukasz Opaliński was different in this respect. His *Satires,* described in the subtitle as "warnings aimed at improving the government and customs in Poland," in fact contained suggestions for the improvement of the Commonwealth in the area of moral issues, the raising of the young, the system of the state and its administration, the organizing of the army, and the situation in the towns. The *Satires* became quite popular, and the volume was published three times during the author's lifetime (1650, 1652, 1654) and several times at the end of the seventeenth century after his death. But it was read as a literary work rather than as a political program, especially since such a program was not formulated — as it was during the Renaissance — by political literature.

The most important publication in the area of political literature was Aron Olizarowski's *De Politica Hominum Societate* (1651). It was a theoretical and erudite work, written in a spirit of rationalism and tolerance, with undertones of social criticism, especially when referring to the peasant question.

Perhaps one of the reasons for this moderation in political literature and its minor social significance was touched upon by Stanisław Herakliusz Lubomirski at the end of the century in his treatise entitled *De vanitate consiliorum* (On Ineffective Councils). His pessimistic views must have well described general feelings — and not only the personal experiences of the author — since this booklet, in spite of prohibition by the censorship, was published fifteen times in Latin and five times in Polish, both in Poland and abroad.

This scepticism voiced the experiences of a society which could no longer control its own destiny — inundated by the wave of defeats and chaos, whose institutions had ceased to function effectively and purposefully, whose king had no voice, and where the Seym, as Lubomirski wrote, seemed to be "a gilded cage," which held within "the most powerful eagle." This society could hardly attain political consciousness, whereby it might actually perceive reality and not accept mystified visions of reality, understand the mechanism behind what was happening, and foresee ways of salvation. Thus, the period of the Baroque was coming to an end in Poland without political consciousness, and with the defeat of the reason needed to deal boldly with the problems of political life. It was characteristic that a new era in the development of Polish culture should commence with the optimistic rationalism of Stanisław Konarski, who by adumbrating a view at variance with the scepticism of Stanisław Herakliusz Lubomirski, would formulate a program of reforms called "Effective Councils", which would eventually release the eagle from its gilded Seym cage.

View of the World

THE ANTAGONISM
OF PLEASURE AND HEROISM

The *joie de vivre* of the Renaissance took on a different complexion during the Baroque. The horizons of the Renaissance which depicted variety and richness of experience were losing their dynamism and internal tensions. In the model of life the accent was shifted in some circles to what would now be called a consumer approach. To describe this phenomenon in sociological categories, one might say that this model stressed country life rather than court life; the activity of the landowner rather than the creativity of the artist or intellectual; love of adventure was not part of it, for example the lives of reckless travelers and brave knights; peace and mediocrity were becoming more appealing.

One concept of life was rhetorically well developed and widespread: man's indifference to metaphysical problems and their consequences was treated more or less decoratively, and escape from troublesome moral and social problems strengthened simple everyday optimism and the search for pleasure.

Hieronim Morsztyn, in his collection of poems entitled *Worldly Pleasures* (1606), frequently re-issued in the seventeenth century, presented the world as being created for the "pleasures of man" which he sought in "the life of the landowner". Such were the beliefs of many poets and writers. Andrzej Zbylitowski, for example, in his work *Life of a Gentleman in the Country* (1597) contrasted this peaceful life with the dangers associated with knightly duty.

This country life had to be "closed" in order to gain protection and peace. The nobleman's manor-house became a fortress in which "freedom, leisure, pleasure, peace and relaxation dwelled."

Such a concept of the world and such a model of life-style were constantly criticized from different viewpoints, but always with the same intention of presenting and popularizing a model of existence opposed to the search for pleasure.

The spearhead of this attack was formed by defenders of traditional, patriotic and religious values, most often idealized. These were the protagonists of the Counter-Reformation, particularly the Jesuits — who initiated a program of social enlightenment, in the past "poisoned" by humanists and non-Catholics — and writers concerned with the new intellectual tendencies, sensitive to the anxious problems of metaphysics.

Piotr Skarga, the furious preacher, violently attacked the "cupidity of domestic greed" from which "the antipathy toward the Commonwealth" was growing. It was Skarga who formulated the famous words: "Do not cramp or diminish your love for your country in your houses and individual advantages. Do not close it within your chambers and vaults." Skarga was accompanied by other writers, by Szymon Starowolski and Fabian Birkowski in particular.

The most significant fact concerning the national consciousness, however, and one that was particularly characteristic of contemporary attitudes, was the inclusion in the model of life of both religious and patriotic values. This is illustrated in the works of a poet who was neither a preacher nor a champion of the gentry's ideology — in the poetry of Mikołaj Sęp Szarzyński, whose creative life blossomed at the turn of two epochs — the Renaissance and the Baroque. His words, "peace is happiness but fighting is our earthly lot," described both his sad reflection on the impossibility of reaching happiness on earth and heroic pride in man's spiritual struggle. This battle was a war with Satan, who is described as a "cruel hetman of darkness," and at the same time a battle with the pagans, the enemies of the country.

This concept of life depicted in sixteenth century poetry (Sęp Szarzyński died young in 1581) was also dominant in the seventeenth century. Writers and poets alike were developing and popularizing it. But as the years progressed, during which the Counter-Reformation was becoming victorious and the history of the nation produced bitter experience for everyone, religious visions of the world descended from philosophical heights and individual experiences to simple and everyday matters, to the picturesque liturgy of masses and processions.

THE ARIAN VIEW OF THE WORLD

Arians also criticized the materialistic model of life, its principles and consequences. Within this community also the chief values which should guide man's conduct were religious.

But the Arians reached far deeper. They took into consideration the problem of Christian life on earth; hence not only the matter of piety and salvation, but also, and perhaps primarily, secular matters. The great debate begun in the sixteenth century about the "right of the sword" — that is, about war and justice and "holding office" — was not yet over. What was the life of a "true Christian" supposed to be like in this country of the gentry?

In the early seventeenth century Ludwik Wolzogen actively advocated radical concepts. According to him, "there is no place for secular rulers in Christ's Kingdom: kings and magnates who rule by force over property and estate, as well as over the lives of their subjects, utilize the services of others not only because there is a need for these services, but mainly for ostentation and worldly pride." Wolzogen's attack was directed against the state and the system of social exploitation. The Arians believed that the small group of righteous Christians following the will of God, was surrounded by a crowd of people serving the political and social order as well as the world's riches and wisdom. Therefore this handful of people was persecuted and condemned.

But was it really possible to remove from the life of a righteous Christian and nobleman the entire issue of his social duties in such a radical way? Jonasz Szlichtyng and Samuel Przypkowski opposed Wolzogen's theory. "I would be afraid," wrote Szlichtyng, "to confine Christianity only to private individuals, plebeians, and the common horde. That is how things stand today because of man's mistakes and faults; in my opinion, however, the Christian religion may take in kings and emperors equally, for it brings God's mercy to all estates and professions of men. It makes all people live piously and moderately and kings wield power well." In this light a Christian's participation in a war — but only when defending his country — was not a sin so long as "his conduct as a soldier is decent and righteous."

Marcin Ruar, an outspoken Arian leader who came to Raków in 1614, expressed the same opinion. When he was asked whether it was right for a nobleman to join the French army which was fighting against Spain, he answered: "I cannot blame someone who takes up arms because he has to defend himself and his kin. But a soldier who volunteers to go to war to gain fame and money acts against the rules of life prescribed for all of us by the Saviour and His Apostles."

Samuel Przypkowski, the author of a splendid work, *Animadversiones,* dealing with the relations between church and state, religion and public life, became deeply involved in these polemics. He believed in the principle that "within a Christian society a dual system can and actually does exist, based on apparently antagonistic principles: one system is based on the equality of people and the absence of coercive authority; the other on differences among persons and the existence of certain constraints. One is represented by the church, the other by the state." Mutual relations are sometimes difficult but can be harmonious, since "spiritual authority unconstrainedly leads the mind, conscience and man's soul to the perfection of virtues. State authority, on the other hand, equipped with force, leads an externally muzzled man not to a virtuous life, which in no way can be achieved by the use of force, but to respect the political order and to restrain him from wrongdoing."

This division of man into an internal and external creature, striving either for "the most perfect virtues" or "obeying the rules," was later expounded by David Hume, who divided all virtues into natural virtues which arise from sympathy, and artificial virtues which arise from justice. Eventually, Hugo Kołłątaj used similar categories as a basis for establishing the ethics of justice, charity and heroism.

A common program of all Polish Arians was aimed at deepening mutual friendship and tolerance among people. It was explicitly formulated by Jan Crell in his treatise on freedom of conscience entitled *Vindiciae pro religionis Libertate* that was published in Amsterdam in 1637, and later translated into French and Dutch. Crell recommended more liberal tactics in religious activity through inspiration and models, through devotion, but never through violence. "The greater virtue," he wrote, "is connected with perfect faith. Therefore, those who, while enduring atrocities for the sake of religion give irrefutable evidence of their own virtue, will attract all other people who cherish virtue. Those, on the other hand, who propose violence, discourage others and undermine confidence in their own religion, which induced such hostility towards innocent people." Religious peace, according to Crell, also had political value, "since those who peacefully coexist with others in a secular society and do not endanger anyone's peace and security cannot possibly be excluded from within such a secular society, let alone be denied their own right to peace."

Crell believed that it was "possible to maintain peace within the country in spite of incompatible religious beliefs." Only where there is no room for the rights of peace, there is room for the rights of war, which are equally cruel for both sides. War "does not bring salvation;" therefore praying for peace is of greatest importance to people: "We beseech you for peace, O Lord."

This attitude of the Polish Arians was deeply rooted in their concepts of religion and human understanding. Andrzej Wiszowaty went furthest along this road when he strongly defied scholastic rationalism and mystical theories that combined religion with the human mind: "If the human mind," wrote Wiszowaty in *Religio Rationalis* (1685), "is not needed to understand matters of faith, then the principles, or what are called confessions of a faith, could have been presented to irrational creatures to believe in." This cannot hold true, however; therefore "our religion and our confession of faith must actually reflect a righteous conscience, in such a way that a man

fully cognizant of these truths and convictions, might profess his faith with equal awareness and lead his life accordingly. On the contrary, if there is no knowledge understood in a broader sense, that is awareness of things acquired by the mind or reason, then there is no conscience, and consequently no faith."

From this point of view Wiszowaty criticized restrictions placed on the rights of reason by Catholicism and some Protestant sects. He demanded that irrespective of the Christian sect they belong to, "people, if they truly want to remain people, that is rational creatures, should open up the eyes of their minds and use reason, and not allow their eyes to be closed or veiled." This reasoning led Wiszowaty to establish the fundamental principles of his philosophy, including the axiom: "Every real man is a human being."

CLASSICAL TRADITIONS
IN ATTITUDES TOWARD LIFE

The Arian concept of life was the creed of a small group of well-educated and intelligent people. All shared the same fate, experiences, and aspirations, and they lived mainly in Raków. After the city's downfall, they dispersed all over Poland and Europe. In the first half of the seventeenth century this intellectual élite ceased to play an important role in the mass culture of the gentry, and by the end of the same century its influence had disappeared altogether. The dispute concerning the view of the world and life was not limited solely to controversies between those who believed in "worldly pleasures," and religious moralists who called on men to serve God and country or, more radically, to create God's Kingdom here on earth. Another trend existed, leading from the concepts of Renaissance humanism towards the humanitarian ideals of the Enlightenment. This trend was less concerned with matters of religion and devoid of radicalism in social issues. It followed a much more moderate line and, by the same token, became more permanent and less vulnerable to various attacks from the outside.

The movement was initiated by vernacular literature, which flourished among poor scholars, and also by the philosophy of the schools, taken up by the more affluent philosophers such as Sebastian Petrycy in Cracow and Adam Burski in Zamość.

A vernacular poet, a teacher from Pilzno, Jan Jurkowski, illustrated this heroic (Hercules) and hedonistic (Paris) attitude toward life in *The Tragedy of a Polish Scilurus and the Three Crowned Sons of the Polish Country* (1604). He agreed with Diogenes who criticized "the bizarre world" and "weird people with their silly minds." Similarly, the strangeness of the world, "the weird human minds and their weird characteristics were depicted in picaresque literature which sought a vague and difficult way to improve the world.

Sebastian Petrycy developed his brilliant and intelligent lecture on ethics (1618) in a long preface to the works of Aristotle. He claimed that ethics instructed everyone "how to govern his life in this world" and "how to achieve the holiest blessing in the world." "Men," wrote Petrycy, "impose obligations on themselves, to be wise and to be good." While considering a variety of virtues, Petrycy chose wisdom as "the hetman of human affairs." It was wisdom that ruled over valor and justice and led men rationally through life. According to him, "wisdom without justice is no longer wisdom but cunning, while valor without justice is not valor but simply a joke or cruelty." Justice "concerns two things: first, that we should not bring damage and harm to anyone; and second, that we should help other people." In the first case, justice is laid down by law and protected by the courts; while in the other, it goes beyond the requirements of common and everyday kindheartedness and expresses the direct attitude of one man toward another.

Adam Burski encouraged people to follow Stoic rationalism rather than Aristotelianism. His *Ciceronian Dialectics*, published in Latin in 1604 in Zamość, is an original discourse on Stoic logic, which was understood as both an instrument and a component in a new outlook upon the world. According to Burski, philosophy is divided into three fields: logic, ethics (his treatise on Aristotelian ethics still remains in manuscript) and finally, physics (his commentary on Aristotelian physics was also unpublished). Logic then was the basis of all other philosophical considerations. Burski deserves credit for reviving the Stoic traditions and formulating the principle of empiricism even before Bacon. This method was to be "the first way and justification of discoveries, sciences and the art."

This movement in Stoic philosophy remained lively, thanks to contacts between Poles and Justus Lipsius. Krzysztof Opaliński wrote in one of his satires that "he who is wise enjoys common things as his own and his own things as common."

From this point of view, and it was repeated dozens of times, "virtue in itself is the best and the most real good," and this good "exists inherently in reason" and makes man "a human being". It follows that "virtue, together with wisdom, constitute our life."

However, what are people really like? Do they live in this way? A story about Diogenes, in which Opaliński continued the plebeian cult of the Greek philosopher, gives us a rather pessimistic answer to these questions. Taking Diogenes as a model, Opaliński decided to look "with a lentern" for human beings, in particular among the gentry.

Stanisław Herakliusz Lubomirski remained faithful to neo-Stoic concepts. In a comedy, *Ermida, or a Shepherd's Queen* (1664) he criticized the myth of Arcadian happiness in nature, outside society; man must live within civilization, and he ought to know that "he is happy who is content with what he has." Lubomirski paid tribute to Seneca in his work written in Latin, *Adverbiorum Moralium ... Libellus* (1688), which was illustrated by Tylman van Gameren. In this work he presented the truths of human life that had already been adumbrated in the Old Testament. His other work, entitled *Ecclesiastes*, represented an analysis and criticism of the wisdom of Solomon.

Lubomirski believed that one must live an honest life since "honesty itself makes man what he is — a man." These ideas found full expression in the *Conversations Between Artaxes and Evander* (1683) which referred both to Seneca and Montaigne.

CATHOLIC INSTRUCTIONS

This bitter Stoic wisdom was not of course the generally professed outlook upon life during the Renaissance or post-Renaissance eras. A large number of the gentry proclaimed themselves in favor of a less severe and less pessimistic outlook upon life, based on objective laws, rather than on their own rational choices. Such an outlook guaranteed supernatural help and support for people, and also convinced them of the righteousness of the conduct that they were ordered to follow. In short, they were in favor of Catholicism.

In the second half of the seventeenth century Catholicism had no longer any internal "enemies" that it had to fight against. The Church and Jesuit order were generally triumphant. Thus literature that dealt with moral improvement and devotion was produced freely and in large quantities. It met the needs of a vast number of the gentry and, at the same time, formed their vision of the world and the human condition.

Klemens Bolesławiusz's famous work, *An Awesome Echo of the Last Trump* (1670), published several times as late as the nineteenth and twentieth centuries, was evidence of these religious moods. It portrayed the terror of the last judgment and was a condemnation of evil people, including lords and the clergy, who were living on "greed and treason" and made "the poor weep."

Adam Kempski's great poem on the human condition turned out to surpass all other works at the turn of the century. His *Thoughts about God and Man*, published in Warsaw in 1756, was a dramatic description of the misfortunes of a man defeated by the hostile world and nature, and at the same time was an expression of man's faith in Providence. "In short, the whole book," wrote the author, "is a consolation," but its main content is the "miseries and imperfections of earthly happiness," which disclose man's perpetual longing and his despair. This "universal longing" of the common people and philosophers, rich and poor, hard-working and lazy, defines the human condition in this world, in which "everything works contrariwise." This happens because "the world, the flesh and the Devil," all work together against man.

The Arts

THE IMPORTANCE OF POETRY

Literature, and poetry in particular, remained the main area of artistic creativity; architecture and theater, although very important, were not equal to literature, so far as impact on the public was concerned; music and painting took part in creating cultural values on a smaller scale than before but they contributed considerably in spreading Baroque elements in the every day life of the gentry.

Literature reached a wider circle of people, thanks to the development of printing. Many works were published several times. Some texts were used until they were no longer readable. When printing did not suffice, the traditional method of copying out by hand prevailed. *Silva rerum*, containing handwritten documentation on political events, private affairs and also the hobbies and tastes of the squire, began to be written in the manor-houses of the gentry.

Poetry took the lead in the area of literature. Political opinions, great historical events, recollections, and descriptions of family splendors were all presented in poetic language.

The greatness of poetry and its peculiar calling were noticed and explained by Maciej Sarbiewski. In his Latin discourses, and in particular, in a study entitled *On Perfect Poetry,* Sarbiewski, consciously departing from Aristotle, pointed out that the essence of poetry, in contrast to the other arts, is creation. The poet does not imitate the objects that he writes about, since he does not depict them "the way they are but rather shows them the way they could or should be, and by the same token gives them new existence, by creating them for the second time." No other artist, according to Sarbiewski, behaves in this manner, "because neither a sculptor creates wood or stone, nor does a blacksmith his iron or bronze . . . nor does a representative of any other realm of art create that which he is dealing with . . . Only the poet creates, in a sense, that which he is being absorbed with", he is a creator "in the image of God".

This is where the special greatness of poetry lies in respect to other arts, and also in relation to history, which in turn seems to be restricted, since it has to deal with detailed facts and relate what has actually happened; the poet, on the other hand, ought to — and may — treat his subject matter in more general terms by showing what his subject might be and was in its essence, even though the details of realization are of a different nature. In this way, poetry delves deeper into the nature of men and their deeds than do history and rhetoric, which are entangled in empirical reality. Thus poetry shows truth and therefore is of great significance to people. The discovery of this significance — exceptional in Europe at this time — was especially characteristic of the early Polish Baroque.

Like poetry, music was becoming more popular. It was being played in churches, monasteries, schools, manors and even the houses of the poorer gentry and burghers. Neither religious nor secular ceremonies took place without music. Numerous professional music ensembles were to be found in the mansions of bishops and magnates. Choir schools were founded at churches. The gentry were also very fond of having their own bands.

A benefaction founding a permanent music center attached to St. Barbara's Church in Cracow in 1638 read: "Every one has to approve of such a project since no church nor any brotherhood can function without music." Thanks to this benefaction a music chapel was formed. It

lasted for over a century and became as well known as the royal College of the Roratistes. Maciej Łubieński, bishop of Włocławek and Pomerania, organized another permanent chapel and choir school in the middle of the seventeenth century.

Music was not only listened to; it was also widely composed and played by amateur performers. Foreigners were delighted with the advanced level of musical performances and the widespread popularity of music in the religious and secular life of the country.

The social demand for music was also expressed in the production of various musical instruments. The Polish violin, made of spruce and maple wood and produced by such violin makers as Marcin Groblicz and Jan and Baltazar Dankwart, was a popular item all over Europe. Large workshops producing various musical instruments were located in Cracow. They were run by Bartłomiej Kiejcher from the second half of the sixteenth century, and by Jan Homol who specialized in constructing organs at the beginning of the seventeenth century. The largest Polish organ was built by Jan Głowiński in 1682 in Leżajsk.

Architecture became another privileged art, alongside literature and music. All of Poland was being rebuilt, and war damage became an important factor in both construction and reconstruction. Castles and residences, mansions and small manor-houses, churches and monasteries, colleges of various orders, townhalls and granaries were being built. Architects were in demand and well-respected. They were provided with good salaries and excellent working conditions. Many foreigners were offered jobs in Poland. Some architects of burgher origin were knighted. John III established a special award for outstanding artists — the title of the Knight of the Golden Spur.

The social significance of architecture was also expressed in studies devoted to theoretical and applied engineering. Adam Freytag's book, *Architectura Militaris*, published in 1631 in Leiden, became an acclaimed success in Europe. It was translated into French and reissued many times. In the middle of the seventeenth century an anonymous treatise was published, on Łukasz Opaliński's initiative, intended especially for the Polish public. In this *Short Treatise on Building Mansions, Castles, Palaces according to the Heavens and the Polish Tradition* the author considered a great range of problems in architecture, such as durability, comfort, and shape, and looked for the best solutions, so far as the Polish climate and building traditions were concerned. The book was not intended for specialists. It was supposed to serve the magnates and the gentry, and all those who were either building or reconstructing their households.

Painting and sculpture, however, were in a rather lamentable shape. It was the harshness of religiosity that did such serious harm to the development of painting. The Cracow synod of 1621 defined the canons of religious painting. It condemned all deviations from these as "wanton painting" and specified in great detail the way religious scenes were to be represented by painters. Religious censorship also reached beyond the church itself and interfered with the secular arts. By the end of the sixteenth century Dymitr Solikowski demanded that paintings depicting mythological scenes, "the vanities of Jove, Mars with Venus," be burned. He felt that this was "pagan and sin-inducing" art. Fabian Birkowski, in the beginning of the seventeenth century, condemned with indignation the fact that "a great many filthy paintings can be found in bedchambers, rooms, dining-chambers, in gardens, by fountains, above portals, and all over the roadside."

Such attitudes of censorship forced Marshal Mikołaj Wolski to order on his death-bed the destruction of his large private collection of Italian paintings, which he had accumulated throughout his entire life.

Sacral painting, restricted by regulations, depicted schematic religious scenes. Its main function was moralizing, to represent "the art of a good death," the vanities of secular pleasures, and the dreadful infernal punishment for sins committed.

The creative accomplishments of Dolabella, Venantius of Subiaco and several other foreigners exceeded the average contemporary level in both religious and portrait painting. In the middle of the seventeenth century Herman Han of Pelplin, Bartłomiej Strobel of Wrocław, who was active mostly in Kujavia and Pomerania, Franciszek Lekszycki, a self-taught artist from the Benedictine Order in Cracow, and finally the most famous of all, Daniel Schultz of Gdańsk, formed a group, which while differing in style remained homogeneous in its religious inspiration.

Painting and sculpture did not attain in Poland the high level reached in the rest of Europe; the seventeenth century was after all the age of magnificent art produced in the Netherlands, France, Italy and Spain. Polish crafts, however, could match anything in the world. Craftsmanship was an art form that was real and close to life, connected with the everyday life of the people. It provided ornaments for their attire and trappings for their favorite horses. It decorated households and furnished churches with splendor and magnificence, which through richness of decorations isolated the Baroque mass from the external world and from intensely intimate experiences associated with that world.

Churches and monasteries provided craftsmen with orders for liturgical vessels, chasubles, equipment to furnish the interiors of monasteries and chapels, and other objects of worship necessary in liturgical rites. The development of church architecture called for sculptors and painters who could make richly ornamented altar-pieces in Baroque places of worship. Marble altars, portals, and other architectural elements were produced in Dębnik near Cracow. Numerous workshops, situated at the foot of the Carpathian mountains, specialized in wooden sculptures, and in particular, in the production of multi-tiered wooden altarpieces, stalls and pulpits.

This decorative art, like poetry, developed its own style, which arose from the junction of the artistic tendencies of the West, especially of Italian and Flemish art, with the art of the East, in particular of Turkey, whose influence became even greater due to the wars and subsequent peaceful relations between Poland and the East. This fusion was actually carried out within Polish frontiers and produced original results. Even though foreign influences were predominant in some works of art, in the majority of cases the indigenous Polish artistic output remained distinctly native. The native character of the arts prevailed, thanks to Polish artists and craftsmen of burgher or peasant origin who remained faithful to local traditions and tastes. Many original, national works that were created turned out to possess universal values; this was true in particular of the Polish Baroque churches, the interiors of the manor-houses of the gentry, carpets and rugs.

ARCHITECTURE:
THE ART OF THE POLISH BAROQUE

Members of the ruling social stratum provided great demand for the arts, since they had material resources at their disposal. During the Baroque period, the artistic demands of this group focused mainly on building and architecture. They wanted to possess great residences; they wanted them furnished in keeping with their family position. Both the gentry and the burghers demanded rich and magnificent mansions that would reflect the splendors of both their ancestors and themselves.

The royal court led the way in this area. Sigismund III had Wawel reconstructed after the fire of 1595. Italian architects, sculptors, and painters were hired for this purpose; the most famous of these were Giovanni Trevano and Tommaso Dolabella.

The transfer of Poland's capital to Warsaw brought the reconstruction of the Warsaw Royal Castle in 1597—1619. It replaced the former old Gothic castle and put an end to the Gothic style in architecture which had hitherto prevailed in Mazovia; it thus became a proof of a new era, during which Cracow's Renaissance influence steadily declined.

Ujazdów, situated near Warsaw, was the king's suburban residence. These royal residences, the Warsaw castle and Ujazdów, were models of architecture for magnates and clergy who willingly imitated the life-style of the court. In Warsaw palaces fashioned after the royal style were erected for Crown Treasurer Mikołaj Daniłowicz in 1621, Jerzy Ossoliński in 1641 and Stanisław Koniecpolski in 1643. A particularly magnificent palace was built by Adam Kazanowski.

Suburban and country mansions also followed the royal style. In 1630 the Denhoffs' residence at Kruszyna was completed, and in 1641 the Lubomirskis' castle was built at Łańcut. In Kielce, Bishop Jakub Zadzik built a splendid residence for the bishops of Cracow during the years 1637—42. At the same time, the famous Krzyżtopór castle near Opatów was was begun and finally completed by Krzysztof Opaliński. Stanisław Koniecpolski erected a beautiful residence in Podhorce, designed by Andrea dell' Aqua, a theoretician in the field of artillery and a fine architect. The castle of Krzyżtopór was an imposing edifice. Its dimensions exceeded all previously known: each of its storeys was ten meters in height with the windows seven meters high; it had a huge inner courtyard, and the entire architectural layout was extremely original. During this period, a good number of fortified castles were either built or reconstructed, like the castles of the Ligęzas in Rzeszów and the Lubomirskis at Wiśnicz. Various fortifications were erected in the south-eastern border region: the fortresses at Bar, Brody, Zbaraż, Trembowla, and Kamieniec Podolski.

During this time architectural styles changed fairly often. The original Baroque style began to lose its purity when old Polish traditions began to reemerge. This Polish traditionalism, hostile to humanism and culture of the towns, harked back to past epochs of great kings and ancestors.

Baroque art, in opposition to Renaissance models, explored the Medieval Gothic and even Romanesque traditions, in which religion and the spirit of chivalry were expressed. Baroque churches were built with Romanesque spires; castles and residences were decorated with corner towers using medieval ideas in the ornamentation of facades and portals.

Restoration was begun shortly after the Swedish "Deluge", which caused tremendous war damage, had been repulsed. Architecture flourished anew during the reign of John III; in 1677 the construction of the palace of Wilanów was begun at his order. The Lubomirskis invited to Poland an outstanding Dutch architect, Tylman van Gameren, who by the end of the seventeenth century supervised the construction of the Krasińskis' palace in Warsaw, and Primate Radziejowski's palace at Nieborów.

The magnates' building craze continued throughout the entire period of Wettin rule. The Potockis competed with the Lubomirski and Pac families. Franciszek Salezy Potocki erected a large residence at Krystopol; Józef Potocki built at Stanisławów, Założce and Tarnopol; Mikołaj Potocki built a palace at Buczacz, but the famous monastery (Lavra) in Poczajów was his greatest pride. Jan Klemens Branicki, a distinguished military leader, owned as many as seventeen mansions, including the magnificent palace in Białystok, which contemporaries called the Polish Versailles. Around 1730, the Czartoryskis began to re-develop Puławy on a large scale.

The further development of palatial and sacral architecture, already rococo in style, was not halted despite the difficult political situation. Jakub Fontana, a widely acclaimed architect, built a great number of churches and palaces in the new rococo style. Many churches were erected in Cracow, Lvov (the Dominican Church and St. George's Cathedral), Vilna, as well as in numerous small towns, which were being restored after war damage.

All the residences constructed during this period were magnificent, both in architectural style and form, as well as in interior furnishings. Many magnate mansions were built in Warsaw under the Wettins, for example, the palaces of the Mniszechs (1714), the Lubomirskis (the Tin-Roof Palace), the Przebendowskis (1728), the Sapiehas and Czapskis (1730). Residential architecture developed rapidly during Augustus III's reign.

These mansions changed Warsaw's profile, in terms of architecture and even in its social structure, since burghers now constituted only one part of the population. The city ceased to be the province of burghers only and became a center where the ruling class had rich and imposing mansions built. The latter represented the beginning of new social patterns in which court intrigues intermingled with glamorous parties given by rival houses. During periods of important political events, when the Seym was in session or foreign envoys arrived in Warsaw, the city boiled over with an animation which was incomparable with the traditional pace of work and leisure.

Under the Wettins residential mansions cropped up all over the country; for instance, the Lvov Archbishops' in Obroszyn near Lvov, the Sanguszkos' in Lubartów, the Poznań Archbishops' in Ciążeń, the Potockis' in Radzyń, Castellan Stanisław Rupniewski's in Grabki Duże, Stanisław Lubomirski's in Równe, Bishop Antoni Ostrowski's in Wolborz, and many others.

The church and monasteries were the second major source of patronage of the arts, after the royal family and the magnates.

Jesuit churches were founded as early as the sixteenth century. One of the first was constructed in Nieśwież in 1582, at a time when the Roman prototype for Jesuit churches — Il Gesú — had not yet been completed. Soon afterwards, Jesuit churches sprang up in Lublin, Kalisz, and Jarosław. The most opulent of them all were the St. Peter and St. Paul Church in Cracow, built at the beginning of the seventeenth century, and St. Casimir's Church in Vilna.

Great complexes of sacral constructions were characteristic evidence of Baroque religiosity. These were erected to commemorate the Stations of the Cross and were made up of several dozen chapels: for example at Kalwaria Zebrzydowska, Wejherowo and Góra Kalwaria.

Another variation of the Baroque style was presented by the collegiate church of Zamość, built by Bernardo Morando to the order of Chancellor Jan Zamoyski, and the Cameldolese Church at Bielany, near Cracow, built by an Italian architect, Andrea Spezza, to the order of Crown Marshal Mikołaj Wolski, as well as two churches in Wiśnicz, also built by an Italian, Matteo Trapola, on the initiative of Stanisław Herakliusz Lubomirski.

Later, larger complexes of churches and monasteries were founded by the Tęczyńskis at Rytwiany, the Firlejs at Czarna, and the Ossolińskis at Klimontów.

A considerable number of churches was built throughout the entire period in small towns. Some were constructed by local craftsmen and artists, while others were built in collaboration with foreigners. As time passed, the names of the builders were no longer remembered and many of their works were destroyed during subsequent wars. The late seventeenth century church at Tarłów may serve as one of the few remaining architectural documents of the epoch. Its facade is adorned with two huge statues of Polish saints, Stanislaus and Adalbert; the interiors, and especially the decoration of the sepulchral chapel of the Oleśnicki family, demonstrate the interrelation that existed between the religious vision of life and death and the everyday experiences of the gentry.

Although brick building was widespread, a great deal of

construction was still in timber. Carpenters' guilds developed and produced famous masters who gained national recognition, and then passed into oblivion.

Small wooden churches were built in many parts of the country; several Orthodox churches were built in the southern and eastern regions. Wooden synagogues, often beautifully ornamented, were also constructed.

The gentry, however modest its contribution, was the most universal advocate of the building craze. The manor-houses of the gentry were a peculiar architectural and social phenomenon of the Baroque epoch. They were kept as hermetic kingdoms isolated from the world. Jan Kochanowski's brother, Mikołaj, wrote: "Don't let the world in, but close the door against it."

Especially popular were wooden manor-houses built in a style recalling peasant cottages. Some of these residences of the gentry, although made of wood, were finished with magnificent splendor. They had more than one storey and were ornamented with wings and galleries. But "the houses of less affluent noblemen looked like peasants' cottages and were often covered with thatch"; these humble manor-houses "had two rooms on either side of a hallway"; they were "surrounded by a wattle fence" and had "a tall gate."

Architecture was also the main artistic concern in the cities. Gdańsk, a great center of trade and culture, was the leader in this important art from, having close and strong ties with the Netherlands and Venice. A Dutch architect, Anton van Opbergen, built a magnificent arsenal in the Mannerist style between 1602 and 1605, while another Dutch artist, Abraham van dem Blocke, constructed the Golden Gate (1612—14). Painting, mostly historical and allegorical, in praise of the Hanseatic city of Gdańsk, also flourished. The city employed many immigrant artists from the Netherlands who did decorative work on municipal buildings that had been constructed; these included Anton Möller, Izaak van dem Blocke (the creator of *The Allegory of Trade,* an oval ceiling painting made in the Red Chamber of the City Hall), and Herman Han, who painted religious scenes. Burghers built luxurious houses in many cities on the coast and also in central Poland, for example, in Lublin and Kazimierz.

Urban building boasted elaborate ornamentation. This was also true of wooden houses in which the motifs used in brick building, such as arcades and columns, were applied. In some cities wooden, two-storey buildings surrounded market squares; various towns built wooden richly ornamented town halls and granaries.

THE DECORATIONS OF LIFE AND DEATH

Architecture created the environment for everyday life, leisure, and devotion. Beauty, thanks to this art, penetrated into everyone's life and was intensified by this decorative richness. Baroque culture was a decorative culture, created to enhance the beauty of life and the horror of death. The abundant decoration of interiors and facades of places, mansions, churches and monasteries combined those motifs which, although contradictory, depicted the inevitable fate of man. Thus art was an expression of this fate.

Black marble was introduced in Wawel by Sigismund III and was used later in the Warsaw Castle. This austere and mournful material created quite a different architectural atmosphere and produced different feelings from the colored marbles of the Renaissance. Black marble was also successfully used in decorating magnates' mansions, sepulchral chapels, and churches, especially the Vasa Chapel at Wawel, the Zbaraskis' Chapel in the Dominican Church in Cracow and St. Casimir's Church in Vilna. Dębnik, a small town near Cracow which produced black marble, now overtook Chęciny, which had been famous up to that time for brown marble.

Moderation and geometrical proportion were abandoned during the Baroque period. The famous burgher houses of the Celej and Przybyła families at Kazimierz on the Vistula represented a style which Jan Andrzej Morsztyn was applying in his poetry. The latter's poems had a peculiar style of expression, seemingly artificial and mannered, yet communicative enough to define this odd and delightful world: "Like a sailor who had traversed impassable seas" he registered the world's sensory appeal by means of poetic images in order to enhance beauty and savagery.

This exaltation served the dramatic concept of man. In his *Tales,* the author brooded over the contradictions of a human being who cherished red, the color of love and blood, and who, at the same time, brought everyone around him the black color of death.

Many other poets of the epoch, whether Arians or Catholics, adumbrated the Baroque vision of life as a life of contradictions. Such poetry was written by Sebastian Grabowiecki, Stanisław Grochowski, Kasper Miaskowski, and later, by Stanisław Herakliusz Lubomirski. In a clever style of similes and contrasts they expressed the greatness and meanness of man's life, the contradictions of body and soul, the brightness of days and the darkness of nights which assail man, and God's mercy and wrath. This complex and ingenious form of expression reflected the intense moments of the life of man who, although lost in this world, remained entirely absorbed by its beauty.

Literature was indeed a huge mirror reflecting heaven and earth, depicting man's experiences and teaching him how to live. Religious and historical stories were always didactic. Meditative lyric poetry was meant to stir emotions and purify the heart. Light-hearted pictures of life, gay songs, bawdy love poems, satires and parody were one extreme of literature. The other extreme included poems depicting the vanity of man and his world, and a terrifying vision of the Last Judgment. In a manner characteristic of the Polish Baroque, these two extremes were linked by the motif of love and death, the two main motifs of contemporary poetry. Love and death were opposing forces, like day and night, and these symbols were often employed. On the other hand, love and death constituted a peculiar whole, since in the Christian religion love led to a happy death. Philosophical and stylistic allegories expressed the dialectical unity of love and death.

The fine arts, like poetry, frequently expressed human

experiences of this type. It is true that painting and sculpture were sometimes used to serve the purpose of representing and glorifying the splendor of noble families in showing their prosperity and passion for art collecting. However, on a greater scale and in a broader social context, the fine arts expressed religious, patriotic, and personal experiences and reminiscences, as well as a desire to commemorate individuals and their families. In this sense, it was not "art for art's sake"; like poetry it was engaged in man's personal vicissitudes: an art of family portraits and church tombstones.

Death was an occasion to manifest both pride and humility. Funerals were glorious events, and the mourning rituals lasted for a long time. The bereaved family hired musicians, poets, painters, and sculptors. Times of war became an additional source of emotional response. Poems of recollection and threnodies, poems of glory and didacticism, were written in great numbers along with poetry of "lamentable celebrations", "of knights' catafalques" and "unhappy separations." Mikołaj Sęp Szarzyński wrote such threnodies to commemorate heroic deeds; Szymon Szymonowic was the author of several "elegies" and a collection of poems under the title *Epitaphs of a Chosen Retinue.* However, this type of poetry flourished in earnest in later years. Wacław Potocki wrote over a hundred poems, entitled *Epitaphs of People of Different Stations and Conditions.* In his numerous poems Zbigniew Morsztyn paid tribute to love and commemorated the dead — those close and dear, and also outstanding public figures.

The fine arts served the same cause. Sculptors worked on tombs, ordered by both magnates and the gentry to commemorate the deeds of their ancestors. Santi Gucci, an architect and a sculptor, arrived in Poland in the mid-sixteenth century. His art, especially during the reign of Stephen Báthory, attracted many Polish sculptors and stone-masons to the town of Pińczów. Gucci himself sculpted ornate sepulchral monuments and tombstones, including those of Stephen Báthory and Anne the Jagiellon. His pupils worked all over Poland, serving affluent families, and sculpted tombstones, altarpieces and portals for their palaces.

The Pińczów center competed with the Gdańsk workshop of Wilhelm van dem Blocke and his son Abraham. The latter workshop radiated its influence to the whole country from the end of the sixteenth century. Sebastian Sala worked in the same field in Cracow to orders from Krzysztof Opaliński. Other centers of this kind were in Wrocław and Lvov. In the early seventeenth century Jerzy Boim founded the famous Chapel of Gethsemane in Lvov. It was partly built by a citizen of Wrocław, Jan Pfister, who executed various monumental tombstones. His major work was the magnificent tomb of the Ostrogskis in Tarnów. This was a huge multi-tier structure its central scene depicting the donors kneeling at the foot of the Cross in attitudes of humble prayer.

This rich art work, mainly Mannerist and early Baroque, expressed both the dynamic family ambitions and the pride of magnates and the gentry. It also provided evidence of religious experiences in which man's humble

attitude towards God was linked together with the old-Polish concept of *miles christianus.* The countless monuments in memory of knights, particularly tombstones, marked Poland's exceptional position in Europe during the age of the Counter-Reformation.

Mourning portraits were another exceptional reflection of Polish culture and tradition. Some of them were epitaph portraits, painted on oval metal plates, often during the deceased's lifetime; others were painted on polygonal metal plates, usually after a person's death. The latter were affixed to coffins and served both as a record and a family token of remembrance. These were usually head and shoulders portraits, rendered very realistically, and were generally made by local artists who had been in direct contact with the persons they portrayed. Their artistic merit usually left much to be desired, but they represented a characteristic phenomenon of the Polish Baroque. They appeared at the end of the sixteenth century and they began to decline during the Age of the Enlightenment. They constituted an outward demonstration of the contemporary life-style and attitudes toward death. They expressed the unity between the living and the dead and were a funeral manifestation of family continuity. Devoid of panegyric fervor and pomposity, they depicted, in a simple manner, solemn faces which were free of the sorrow and pleasure that earthly life provided. They were firmly fixed in family memory and evoked reflections on the human condition.

Religious painting remained faithful to Polish religious traditions. That this trend continued can be seen in the works of Szymon Czechowicz of Cracow, who was faithful to the tradition of Polish piety.

The art of sculpture, which provided decorations for facades and especially the interiors of churches and palaces, also developed rapidly. Sepulchral sculpture became more and more elaborate thanks to the works of Andreas Schlüter of Gdańsk and an Italian, Baltasare Fontana. Schlüter's works depicted the greatness of man's heroism and, at the same time, his nothingness. In addition to creating the monumental tympana of the Krasiński Palace in Warsaw, he sculpted the ornate decorations of various churches, including the Royal Chapel in Gdańsk, the altarpieces of the church at Czerniaków in Warsaw and, especially, the four tombstones ordered by King John III in Żółkiew. A wooden crucifix made for the church of Węgrów, startling in its dramatic expression, was evidence of Schlüter's great talent, which proved he was capable not only of linking the lightness of the rococo style with classical traditions but also of expressing deep religious experiences.

Polish sculptors also became famous. One of them was Antoni Frąckiewicz of Cracow, who made a pulpit framed with a circle of angels in flight in the church of St. Anne in Cracow. The work of these sculptors, already tinged with the rococo style, provided many remarkable pieces in both churches and palaces, as well as gardens in many Polish towns, such as Lvov, Lublin and Warsaw.

The sharp baroque contrasts were appeased at the turn of the seventeenth and eighteenth centuries. In the atmosphere of the rococo, the joy and the lightness of life seemed to provide shelter from earthly sufferings and misfortunes. The architecture of Wilanów Palace, including its interiors, was an example of such a tendency.

The Palace of Wilanów, built at the order of King John III Sobieski, was to be a representative royal residence. It was located near the capital, as was customary in other countries. The palace was designed by Agostino Locci and construction was begun in 1677. It was extended and reconstructed several times. Numerous painters and sculptors, in particular Jerzy Siemiginowski and Andreas Schlüter, worked on its construction and its decorations. Employing mythological themes and heroic ideology, they managed to create an atmosphere of *joie de vivre,* which was generally rare in the arts of contemporary Poland. Their work opened up a new era in which the rococo culture was accepted by the rich and was successfully utilized in their palaces and chambers.

THE ART OF THE THEATER

The art of the theater belonged to the culture of the Polish Baroque. The royal court and magnates' families, churches, monasteries and schools — especially Jesuit — as well as groups of wandering actors, both foreign and Polish, made up of students and minstrels who organized "live theater" — all took part in different ways. There were different plays for different audiences but they all had one common bond, that is, a demand for theatrical events that would incorporate action, movement, gesture and words that would move or perhaps even horrify the public.

The royal theater, for which Sigismund III had magnificent facilities built in the Warsaw Castle, ranked highest among these theatrical institutions. The auditorium was impressively large — "enjoying an abundance of guests" — and could accommodate over one thousand people. Its repertoire was quite varied.

Ladislaus IV supported the royal theater in a more systematic way than did his father. A permanent theater was formed and an outstanding Italian troupe was hired. Italian operas and musical comedies were presented along with foreign comedies in Polish and adaptations. Original works were also staged, based most frequently on the motifs of the *commedia dell'arte.*

John Casimir was also interested in drama. His theater staged a production of Corneille's *Le Cid* in Jan Andrzej Morsztyn's translation. The Polish première took place in Zamość, in 1660; two years later it was presented at the Warsaw Castle. During the reign of John III Sobieski, a number of plays were produced not only in his theater in Warsaw, but also in other royal residences in Jaworowa and Żółkiew.

The royal court influenced the magnates and the affluent gentry. Krzysztof Opaliński organized theatrical performances in his Sieraków residence. Albert Łubieński staged a comedy by Piotr Baryka, *Peasant into King,* in his residence. At the end of the seventeenth century the theater founded in Ujazdów by Stanisław Herakliusz Lubomirski became famous.

Theaters at schools, both Jesuit and Protestant, as well as those run by the Piarist Order, had an uncommonly great social impact. The Gymnasia of Gdańsk, Toruń, Elbląg and Leszno maintained permanent theaters. They had varied repertoires, with not only religious and morality plays but also mythological productions. Sometimes historical and contemporary themes were also explored.

Participation in theater was also possible in a different way, through the widespread religious spectacles that were produced and associated with churches and monasteries. These usually coincided with the greatest liturgical celebrations. The audience at these events became actors participating in the play. This was true, for example, of the great Easter Week masses which in the beginning of the seventeenth century were transformed at Kalwaria Zebrzydowska into great religious events. They were organized as processions which traveled from one chapel to another, following the Stations of the Cross of Jesus Christ in Jerusalem.

These events attracted crowds of spectators from near and far, even pilgrims from all over the country.

Nativity plays, depicting Christ's birth, were performed around churches and schools and served the same religious purpose. As a rule, these plays had a local character.

Folk theater also developed rapidly. It was for sacral, satirical and entertainment purposes. Fairs provided an opportunity for wandering minstrels to perform. They had their own repertoire and depicted typical situations with varied characters and conflicts. All kinds of musical and non-musical plays were popular. They were organized on such occasions as private and public meetings in the towns, the manor-houses, and even the villages.

The intensity and variety of theatrical life provided a real contribution to the culture of the Polish Baroque. This culture, in terms of contemporary phraseology, could be called integrated visual culture, a culture of image, gesture, word and music.

Culture in Society

CULTURE AND EDUCATION

Schools provided the main form of cultural initiation. The seventeenth century began not only with full awareness of this principle, but also with numerous and diversified attempts to develop education. A number of excellent schools were founded during this period which achieved wide acclaim both at home and abroad. Among them were such colleges as the Zamość Academy, organized between 1594 and 1600, or the Jesuit Vilna Academy, founded as early as 1579 but which began to flourish only in the mid-seventeenth century; there were also gymnasia, which at one time were institutions of higher education, like, for example, the famous Raków Academy, organized between 1600 and 1603, where many foreigners lectured, or the Toruń Gymnasium, founded in 1568, but expanded and

131. Giovanni Trevano,
SS. Peter and Paul's
church in Cracow, 1619

132. Cistercian convent
in Trzebnica, 1697—1726

133. Jesuit church and monastery
in Święta Lipka. 1687—1730

134. General view of the monastery in Lubiąż.
Etching dating from the mid-18th cent.

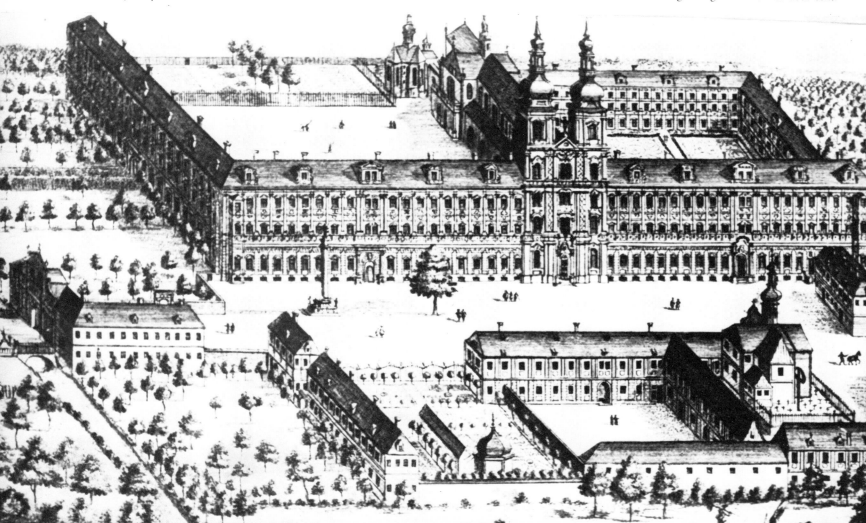

135. Timber church in Powroźnik, 1643

136. Andrea dell'Aqua, Mansion of Stanisław Koniecpolski in Podhorce, 1635—40. Etching by E. Gorazdowski

137. Wawrzyniec Senes, Krzyżtopór castle of Krzysztof Ossoliński, 1631—44

138. Castle of the Lubomirski
     family in Łańcut,
     1st half of the 17th cent.

39. Tylman van Gameren,
    Gniński-Ostrogski
    mansion in Warsaw, 1681—84 (?)

140. Tylman van Gameren,
Palace of the Krasiński
family in Warsaw, 1689—95

141. Andreas Schlüter,
Triumph of Marcus Corvinus,
tympanon of the Krasiński
palace in Warsaw, 1692

142. Constantino Tencalla, Clemente Molli,
     and Balthasar Tym, Column
     of Sigismund (III) Vasa in Warsaw, 1644

143. Houses of the Przybyła family
     (St. Nicholas, c. 1615, and St. Christopher,
     before 1635) in Kazimierz Dolny

144. Celej house in Kazimierz Dolny,
     before 1635

145. Detail of the parapet
of the Celej house in Kazimierz Dolny,
before 1635

147. Statues personifying the faculties
of Cracow University in
the altarpiece of St. John Cantius
in St. Anne's church in Cracow, 1695—1703

146. Conversation of a nobleman with Death.
Detail of the stucco decoration in the church
in Tarłów, c. 1650

148. Herman Han, Adoration
of the Shepherds. Detail of the picture *Nativity*, 1618

149. Krzysztof Boguszewski, *St. Martin of Tours* (detail), 1628

150. Tommaso Dolabella, *Battle of Lepanto*
(detail), after 1620—25

ARIANISMVS PROSCRIPTVS

151. Studio of Tommaso Dolabella, *Trial of the Polish Brethren.*
Two details of the plafond in the bishops' palace in Kielce,
1st half of the 17th cent.

152. Kazimierz Tomasz Muszyński,
Last Judgement. Two details
of a plafond in the Dominican church
in Lublin, 1654—55

153. 17th cent. Polish painter,
Jan Karol Chodkiewicz

154. Painter active in Poland
in the 1st half of the 17th cent.,
Sigismund (III) Vasa

155. Unknown painter active in the 1st half of the 17th cent., *Ladislaus IV*

157. Bartłomiej Strobel,
Portrait of a Young Magnate, 1635

158. Bartłomiej Strobel,
Jerzy Ossoliński (1595—1650)

156. Follower of Rubens,
Equestrian Portrait of Ladislaus IV, after 1634

159. Unknown painter active
in the 2nd half of the 17th cent., *John Casimir*

160. Daniel Schultz,
Portrait of Stanisław Krasiński

161. Brodero Matthisen,
Portrait of Stefan Czarniecki.
1659

162. Jan Tretko (Tritius),
Portrait of John III. 1677

163. Jerzy Eleuter Szymonowicz-Siemiginowski,
Portrait of John III, 1683

164. Court painter to John III active
at the turn of the 17th cent., *Sobieski Family*

165. Claude Callot (?), *Aurora*,
Ceiling painting in the Queen's Cabinet
in the Wilanów Palace, 1682

166. Claude Callot, *Allegory of Learning*.
Ceiling painting in the King's Library
in the Wilanów Palace, 1682

167. Bernardo Bellotto called Canaletto,
North-Eastern View of the Wilanów Palace

168. Jerzy Eleuter Szymonowicz-Siemiginowski,
*Painting Commending
the Artist to the King's Care*, c. 1682

169. Coffin portrait of Stanisław Woysza, 1677

170. Coffin portrait of Barbara Domiceła,
     née Szczawińska, Lubomirska Grudzińska,
     before 1676

171. *Danse macabre*, late 17th cent.

172. Szymon Czechowicz, *Ecstasy of Mary Magdalene*

173. B. Gebhard (?),
Sebastian Sobieski, royal
standard-bearer, carrying
the banner of Sigismund III.
Detail of the so-called
Stockholm Roll, 1605

174. *Session of the Polish Senate.*
Woodcut from Aleksander Gwagnin's
*Chronicle of European
Sarmatia*, 1611

CONSTITVCIE
SEYMV WALNEGO
Koronnego Warſzawskie°
M. DC. I.

W KRAKOWIE,
W Drukarniey Królá Ie° M. Łázá-
rzowéy, M. DC. I.

175. Coat-of-arms of Poland surrounded by the emblems of the Polish regions and voivodships.
Title page of the *Constitution of the General Crown Seym in Warsaw*. 1601

176. Mateusz Merian (1595—1650),
Polish Kings from Lech to Sigismund (III) Vasa

177. Stefano della Bella,
*Jerzy Ossoliński, Envoy
of Ladislaus IV, Entering Rome*, 1633

179. Romeyn de Hoogh, *King John III in the Victorious
Battle Fought against the Turks at Chocim*, 1675

180. Erecting the Column of Sigismund III in Warsaw.
Detail of a copperplate by Wilhelm Hondius
after a drawing by Agostino Locci the Elder, 1646

178. Adolf Boy (?), *Swedes Besieging
the Jasna Góra Monastery in 1655*, 1659

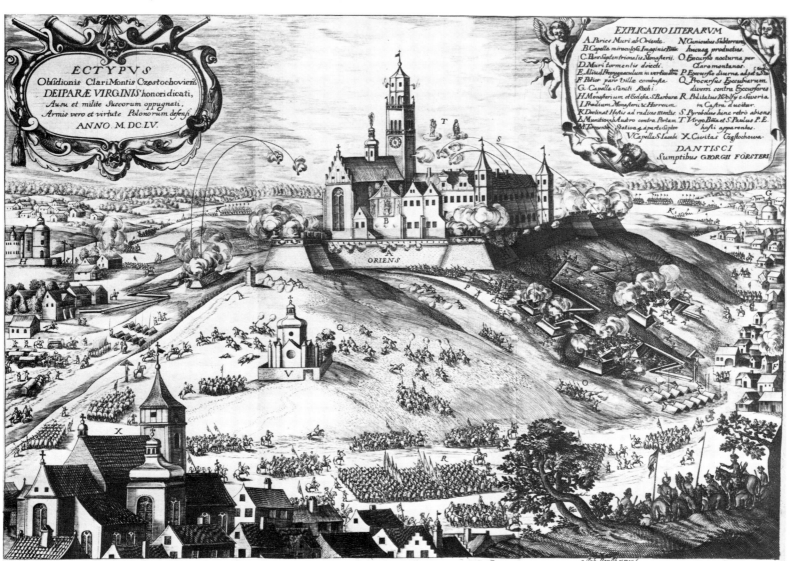

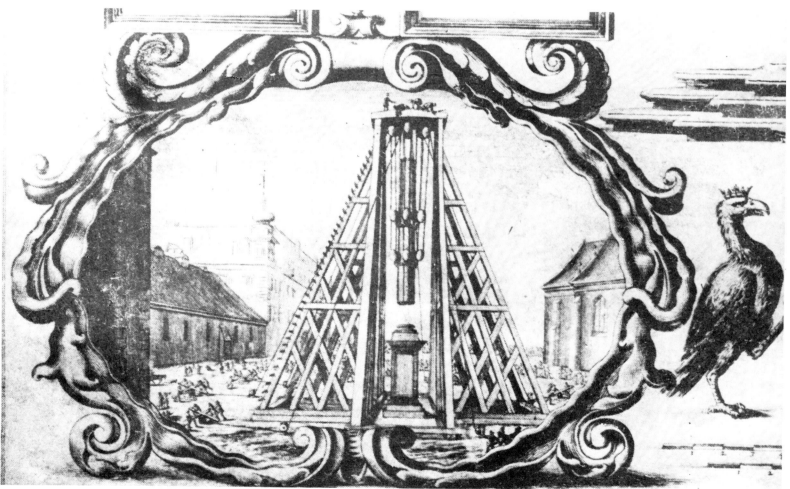

181. Title page of *Peristromata regum seu Memoriale principis menitorum symbolisexpressum* in: Andrzej Maksymilian Fredro's *Scriptorum seu Togae et Belli notationum fragmenta*, Gdańsk 1660

308 ANDREÆ MAX. FREDRO
PERISTROMA PRIMUM.

182. Copperplate from *Peristromata regum seu Memoriale principis
menitorum symbolisexpressum* in: Andrzej Maksymilian Fredro's
Scriptorum seu Togae et Belli notationum fragmenta. Gdańsk 1660

SECRETO
VIDET

183. Copperplate from *Peristromata regum seu Memoriale principis*
menitorum symbolisexpressum in: Andrzej Maksymilian Fredro's
Scriptorum seu Togae et Belli notationum fragmenta. Gdańsk 1660

184. Copperplate from *Peristromata regum seu Memoriale principis
monitorum symbolisexpressum* in: Andrzej Maksymilian Fredro's
Scriptorum seu Togae et Belli notationum fragmenta, Gdańsk 1660

185. View of Warsaw from the Vistula. Etching by N. Perelle after
     a drawing by E.J. Dahlberg, 1656

OVIA
Regum
ila qua con
amiço prafe
a etä S R M
occupata
56

Monsahum   Ars Regia   Templum   Temp. S. Iohannis   Templum et Colleg   Curta   Turris Mareschall   Templum et Canobium   I.S Georgi   S Bennen Temp   Templ. S Maria   Suberbium denartatum
Angusten   Josuitarum   Domaisterorum   Gornanorum

Mons Fr

FLU   VIUS

PORTA
TEMPORE REGIARUM
NUPTIARUM IUXTA
PRÆTORIUM IN FORO
CIVITATIS GEDANENSIS
EXTRUCTA.
ANNO SALUTIS
M.DC.XLVI.

186. Triumphal arch erected in Gdańsk on the occasion
of the wedding of Ladislaus IV and Marie-Louise Gonzaga in 1646.
Copperplate by Wilhelm Hondius

MATHIÆ
CASIMIRI
SARBIEVII
E SOC. IESV
LYRICORVM
LIBRI IV.
EPODON LIB. VNVS
ALTERQ.
EPIGRAMMATVM.

Pet. Paul. Rubens pinxit.   Corn. Galle sculpsit.

ANTVERPIÆ, EX OFFICINA PLANTINIANA BALTHASARIS MORETI, M.DC.XXXII.
CVM PRIVILEGIIS CÆSAREO ET REGIO.

187. Title page of Maciej Sarbiewski's
Latin works, designed by Rubens, 1637

Vela tument Zephyris, niueis te protegit alis
CYGNVS, tranquillum præstat Apollo salum.
Ad fortunatum Nauis Pagaseia portum
Ritè BONIS AVIBVS diceris ire celer.

188. Jan Aleksander Gorczyn,
Sarmatian Ship. 1664

189. Johann Hevelius, *Machina Coelestis*,
Gdańsk 1673. Title page with a copperplate
by Jeremias Falck

190. *Peasants stating their grievances
against the lords*. Drawing from the mid-17th cent.

191. Horse-driven windlass from
the salt-mine in Wieliczka.
Detail of an etching
by J. Nilson·after a drawing
by J.G. Borlach, dating from 1719

192. Transport of salt in the salt-mine
in Wieliczka. Detail of an etching by J. Nilson after
a drawing by J.G. Borlach,
dating from 1719

193. Tapestry with the Topór
coat-of-arms, c. 1650

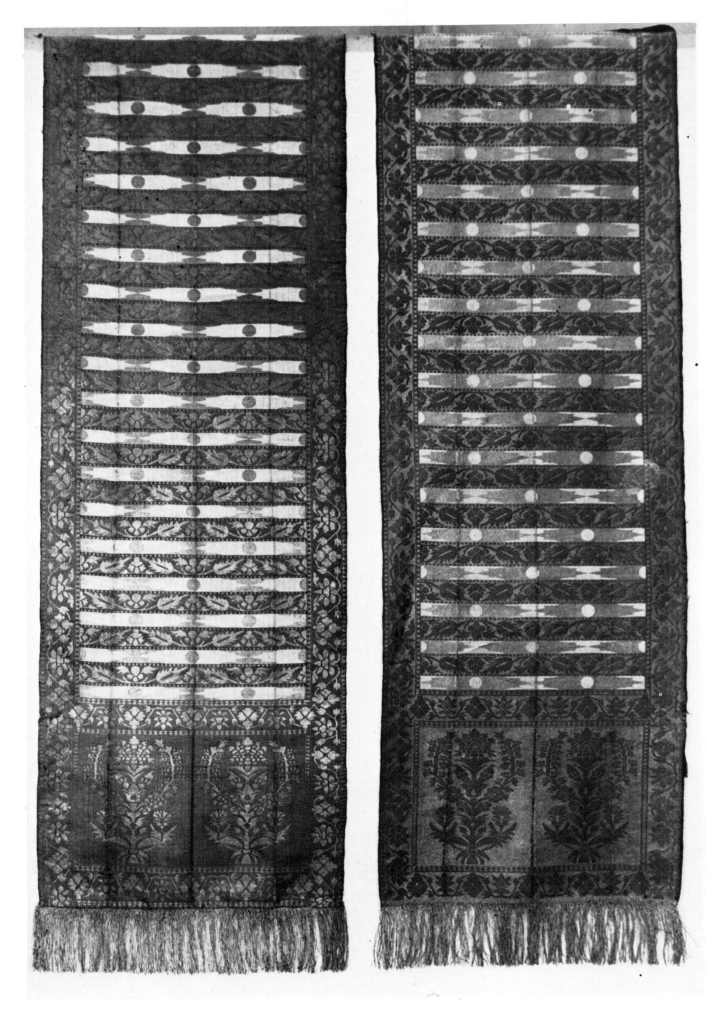

194. Sash with the trade mark of Iwon Markonowicz, 1st half of the 17th cent.

reorganized in 1594—1600. An important role was also played by the gymnasia which Keckermann reformed in 1603, in Gdańsk, Elbląg, and Leszno, especially from 1626 under the direction of Jan Rybiński and Andrzej Węgierski, and later under the supervision of Johann Amos Comenius; and finally the gymnasium in Sieraków, directed by Jan Misalski.

These schools were sometimes developed on the initiative and under the protection of municipal authorities, as for example, in Gdańsk, Toruń and Elbląg; or as a result of sponsorship of various magnates: Jan Zamoyski was the founder of the Zamość Academy; the Leszczyński family sponsored gymnasia at Leszno and Sieraków; or finally, due to the efforts of communities which were unified by creed and needs, like the gymnasium at Raków, maintained and developed by the Arians.

The variety of principles and programs of these diverse schools did not however destroy a certain community of basic aims. The idea was perfectly defined by Johann Amos Comenius in the first statute of the Leszno gymnasium: "Let everyone consider the school a workshop of humanity and for that reason not only agree to it, but also strive to take shape in it, as is common in a workshop."

This program was first implemented at the famous Arian school at Raków.

Raków was founded by Jan Sieniński, who in 1567 issued a charter promising universal toleration to all who would like to settle there. This spirit of liberty attracted to Raków Poles and foreigners alike, who were eager to share a common life, for the sake of learning and study. Inhabitants of Raków, in the words of Stanisław Lubieniecki, were to be "a new and separate people, set free".

In the school, as in Raków itself, a spirit of freedom of conscience and thought prevailed. A Silesian, Joachim Pastorius, who was associated with the school, stated: "A much more certain and clearer truth emerges ... as though from harmonious discord, than would be the case if everybody thought the same without any variety".

The school's objectives were served by books specially prepared for this type of education, which constituted the first series of school textbooks in Poland, namely: Joachim Stegmann's textbook of mathematics (1630) and Jan Crell's ethics (1635). The school existed until 1638, and was called the Athens of Sarmatia. It brought together and educated both Poles and foreigners. In Raków, in addition to its founder, Jan Sieniński, the following were active: Hieronim Moskorzowski, Walenty Smalc, Piotr and Jan Stoiński, Andrzej and Stanisław Lubieniecki, the Morsztyn and Wiszowaty families, Szymon Pistorius, Jonasz Szlichtyng, Paweł Krokier, Jan Crell, Marcin Ruar, and many others, arriving in Raków from all over Poland and from several countries of Europe. The school was indeed a great intellectual center, one of the most important in contemporary Europe.

The school's activity was supplemented by the Raków printing shops, which made possible international circulation of Arian thought. The Raków printing complex, like the school, was an exceptional institution. Continuing the activity of its forerunner, the Arian printing shops of Aleksy Rodecki, it published over 300 books between 1600 and 1638, thanks to the efforts of Sebastian Sternacki, and later of his son Paweł. Thus, it was one of the most important in the country, and also had a wider range of influence than other Polish printing shops. Raków publications circulated all over Europe. They were known in the Netherlands, France, and Germany; they reached Kiev and were secretly sent to Transylvania. Evidence of the popularity of this printing house can be found in the fact that a number of books were published abroad using a forged Raków imprint.

Despite the great contribution of some of these schools, the general state of education, especially the parish school system, increasingly worried enlightened people and produced disillusionment among the teachers and professors; satirical literature accurately presented prevailing conditions. An anonymously published comedy patterned on Til Eulenspiegel had the title of *School Misery Arranged in Dialogues* (1633).

Inspections of parish schools corroborated this state of affairs: the pitiable material conditions of the schools; the crumbling buildings, the ruined classrooms, the poor income of the teachers; the unwillingness of the church authorities, especially parish priests, who treated schoolmasters rather as sextons or organists, and the lukewarm sponsorship of the town authorities.

On the level of secondary and higher education the situation was slightly better. The development of the Jesuit schools came relatively slowly; the first was admittedly founded by the Jesuits in 1564 at Braniewo, but only a few were organized by the end of the sixteenth century. It was not until the seventeenth century that they began to spread rapidly. The Jesuit school system had a number of assets: education was free of charge; the school buildings were new and well-equipped; and the teachers were well-trained. But this educational system, implementing the ideals of the Counter-Reformation, was of a cosmopolitan and religious character; learning was abstract and rhetorical. The system was criticized from the beginning. Jan Ostroróg, Voivode of Poznań, in his dissertation published in 1615, mentioned the main reason why he did not want his sons to be educated at the Jesuit colleges: "The aim and objective of the order is to redeem souls" and training "in theological virtues" is of primary importance, and yet he who "has to participate in public life" and will not wear "the monk's cowl" should be instructed in a different manner.

In 1625 sharp criticism of the Jesuits was launched by an outstanding mathematician, a professor at Cracow University, Jan Brożek. His work, *Gratis,* became the point of departure for numerous polemics. In 1632 Kasper Siemek published a study, *Civis bonus,* in which he analyzed the problem of the education of a citizen. He attacked the school system because it did not include in its program what was most important for the education of citizens: "It fails to address itself to the glory of freedom, the shaming of slavery, the unmasking of tyrants, the love of native land, and to the duties of honorable men and citizens."

A struggle with the Jesuits was waged from the end of

the sixteenth century by Cracow University which organized secondary schools on its own. These schools, mainly in the city itself, were to provide preparation "for a virtuous life on earth and to administer the Commonwealth". Similar schools were founded in other towns: Poznań, Gniezno, Tuchola, Biecz, Pińczów, and Stanisławów — a whole network of schools, sponsored by the University. However, the decline of learning at the University itself, and the strengthening of reactionary forces in the country, made a complete victory in this undertaking impossible.

The numerous projects for reform and improvement of the educational system, sometimes farsighted and rational, but rarely implemented, were symptomatic of the way in which the social conscience was troubled by "the school problem".

As early as the sixteenth century Jan Łaski put forward a plan for the organization of a Protestant university. Efforts were made to implement his ideas at the end of the century in Royal Prussia. The strife within the Reformation camp, and its gradual enfeeblement, made the implementation of the plan impossible. Attempts to found a university in the Eastern regions also failed: this was intended to be a Polish-Ruthenian academy; the Archbishop of Kiev, Piotr Mohyła, creator of the Kiev Mohyła College, made numerous attempts to implement these plans. Counteraction by the Jesuits stopped much of the preparatory work; but the university in Lvov, founded by John Casimir and subordinated to the Jesuit Order, failed to be approved by the Pope.

Although this public system of education embraced almost the entire country and served the children of the gentry and burghers, the education it provided was not considered suitable for the sons of the magnates and the wealthy gentry. The latter sought education abroad and at the great courts. Yet the implementation of this program of education through voyages abroad and direct participation in life, a program which was formulated many times during the era, was increasingly difficult, not only because the constant wars made study abroad impossible, but mainly because social and political reality was increasingly losing its educational value.

In the sixteenth century the great intellectual current connected with the Protestant debate and with the political program of the gentry, had embraced a fairly wide circle of the community. In the seventeenth century, the movement subsided. The Counter-Reformation advocated a subservient religious attitude, demanded devotion close to bigotry, and warned against the dangers of "being too clever". Political life went astray toward internal strife, motivated by the ambitions of wealthy families and material interests; political education at the seyms and local diets taught quarrels and vain rhetoric rather than intellectual skills and civic responsibility.

Under these conditions, the significance of the homes of the wealthy as institutions of cultural development of the country also decreased. Many great houses became merely centers of political intrigue; the gentry were considered as clientele at these courts, important during the regional diets and Seym debates; and also as the number of swords that could be counted upon to support the family ambitions of the magnates. Only a few courts — of the Leszczyński, Opaliński and the Koniecpolski families — remained centers of learning and the arts, undertaking the responsibility of patronage and assistance to scholars and artists.

Although it was in this field that the role of the royal court greatly increased, particularly during the reigns of Ladislaus IV, John Casimir and John III Sobieski, the social range of its cultural influence was not significant. Many foreign scholars and artists were usually active at the royal court; for this very reason the gentry was unable to find a common language within these circles. An additional hindrance were political fears and common resentments, especially towards the so-called French faction. Opposed to the ever-increasing foreign influence, they tended to emphasize the merits of native culture, blocking still further any possibility of worthwhile contacts with the world of contemporary civilization.

There were, however, a number of rather important, although isolated, attempts to search for new solutions in the areas of cultural development. These emerged mainly in the towns, particularly in Gdańsk: a town library was opened in 1596, followed by a gymnasium, bringing together many eminent scholars. A publishing movement developed; a number of institutions dedicated to scientific research in such fields as astronomy (Hevelius), cartography (Hondius), technical workshops in the fields of precision instruments, and mechanics, and private botanical gardens were also founded. The first attempts to establish scientific organizations, especially among physicians and natural scientists, were made in Gdańsk. These efforts, partially implemented, led at last in 1720 to the foundation in Gdańsk of a learned association — Societas Literaria — devoted to the development of "learning and virtues."

In the seventeenth century, books more than ever before provided both the expression and the source of intellectual needs. Publications increased, although many works, poetry and diaries, still remained in manuscript form. Some of these circulated in hand-made copies, but their range was rather small. A number of works, however, went through several printings which indicated the cultural needs of the community.

The kings possessed great libraries; the magnates matched them, especially Rafał Leszczyński at Baranów, and the Opaliński family at Rytwiany and Sieraków. The wealthy gentry also began to collect books, as evidenced by the Słupecki library. As could be expected, many Cracow professors and physicians had large and well-stocked libraries. The private libraries of the burghers, for whom books constituted not a professional tool but a personal choice, bore witness to the intellectual climate of the country. The Baryczka family in Warsaw and the Alembek family in Lvov collected books, which was indicative of the care and thriftiness of numerous generations. Even some master craftsmen collected books: in the library of a certain Cracow embroiderer, all the most outstanding works of the sixteenth century were found. In Gdańsk, burghers, tradesmen and craftsmen possessed books. Works of a religious nature predominated, but one could also find medical, historical and natural-science books in these libraries. They were becoming, as it were, one of the daily needs of the people.

Some of the great magnates undertook large-scale initiatives in this field; for example, Łukasz and Krzysztof Opaliński began to create a great family library at Sieraków, systematically buying books in Amsterdam. Noblemen's libraries were also well-stocked.

The significance of libraries to the intellectual life of the country was more and more clearly appreciated. Some of these libraries were indeed becoming public libraries. The Gdańsk library had not only to serve the Gdańsk gymnasium, "but also the rest of the schools for embellishment, the city for its glory, and the students for encouragement and advantage". Andrzej Maksymilian Fredro called for establishing public libraries in the cities.

Printing aided both intellectual culture and the libraries. Despite the difficult war years, despite the defeats and ruins, printing developed in various regions of the country. It was most lively in dissenter centers, such as Raków (the printing complex was closed by a Seym resolution of 1638), Toruń, Gdańsk, and Leszno which distributed books throughout Europe. Catholic printing works operated in Cracow, Zamość and Vilna. There were active printing works in Wrocław, Brzeg, Wschowa, Królewiec and Supraśl; printing houses were also founded in Warsaw. Under the sponsorship of the magnate Jan Szczęsny Herburt, a printing works operated by Jan Szeliga at Dobromil in the Eastern marcher region was also established. Its publishing activity, which implemented the principle that there was in Poland "no room for the slavery of the Spanish inquisition", was the target of bitter attacks by the gentry and church authorities, as well as the royal court.

These various attempts, undertaken in the spirit of modernity, subsided at the turn of the seventeenth and eighteenth centuries. Within the community of the gentry, a superficial presumptuousness about the merits of native, homely, daily culture established itself, on guard against culture-promoting institutions which spread foreign and harmful ideas and patterns. Rationalist and secular urban culture had no way of approaching this gentry-landowner society. Sarmatian culture was self-generated, spontaneous and direct, local and original. Only Jesuit schools were able to serve it, teaching piety and rhetoric.

CULTURE AND LIFE

During the Baroque period culture in Polish society evolved and flourished in distinct and separate social circles: among the magnates, the gentry, the burghers and the peasants.

The frontiers between these cultural circles were not hermetically sealed. The palaces of the magnates stood open to the gentry, and the larch-wood manors of the gentry took many ideas from these costly marble residences. At the same time, within the magnates' luxurious halls, a sentiment for the simplicity of the landowners' life was born. It was connected with the peasant background by the landscape and by farming. The bitterness of social strife became sometimes less sharp due to the community of religious rites, homely pastimes, and musical and dancing entertainments. Folk art often reached upward on the social ladder, especially in architecture, in music and in decorative art. Yet the peasant culture as a whole remained within the bounds of the social misery caused by the rule of the gentry.

The court of Sigismund III employed many artists, mostly of foreign descent. The king himself engaged in painting, music and goldsmithery. He employed outstanding architects and sculptors, for example, Santi Gucci and Giovanni Trevano, the painter Tommaso Dolabella, and commissioned Rubens to paint his equestrian portrait in ceremonial dress; while in Italy he visited the workshops of Guercino and Guido Reni. He also bought pictures abroad.

The king was a devotee of music; the court orchestra of Sigismund III achieved European fame. It was directed by outstanding musicians, mostly of Italian origin. Some of them were also composers. Later, an increasing number of Poles played in the orchestra, especially during the reign of Ladislaus IV. In connection with this musical life of the court, Polish music also developed; Adam Jarzębski, who was at the same time a poet, Piotr Elert, Marcin Mielczewski and Bartłomiej Pękiel, all achieved acclaim and popularity.

Due to the initiative of Sigismund III a rich suburban residence was erected at Ujazdów in a garden with a view of the Vistula, richly furnished with works of art. The king bought paintings, particularly by Italian masters, and appointed Tommaso Dolabella as his court painter. He also enjoyed the theater, and often invited foreign troupes of actors to his court: an English company provided a resident theater at the king's court for a number of years.

This cultural and artistic tradition was continued and enriched by Ladislaus IV. The king's orchestra became famous in Europe, and there were more opera performances organized at the court during the period 1635—48 than in the Paris opera. The king, like his father, bought paintings and works of art and continued his contacts with Rubens, who painted his portraits. For future generations, he remained the founder of the famous column of Sigismund III on the Castle Square in Warsaw. Many Polish and foreign painters and sculptors worked at his court. They decorated the interiors of the Castle and created "the marble room" in which were collected portraits of the Jagiellonian family; the Ujazdów palace was also similarly embellished.

The culture of the court was very closely connected with the culture of the leading countries of Europe. News of the artistic currents and developments emerging in Italy, France, the Netherlands, and England quickly reached Warsaw. In the royal theater of King Sigismund III, Shakespeare's plays were produced, something which, outside of England, was a rare thing in Europe. Corneille's *Le Cid* was produced at the Castle in 1662 in Jan Andrzej Morsztyn's translation with a prologue in which the Vistula paid tribute to the royal couple after the victorious ending of the wars with Sweden and Muscovy.

The royal theater also flourished during the reign of John III, when a number of French plays were performed. The royal residences in Warsaw and at Wilanów were widely admired. Foreign visitors compared Wilanów to Versailles, writing that "it is rich and beautiful; royal performances are magnificent, the whole court loves luxurious dress and is fond of the latest French fashions. Whenever a lady has to go to church, even a dozen yards away, she would always take a carriage drawn by six horses. Gentlemen do the same."

Contacts with foreign countries did not, however, destroy the Polish character of this environment.

The reception rooms of the castle were decorated, on the king's order by Dolabella, with scenes of victories over Muscovy and the Emperor Maximilian, and a great genealogy of the Jagiellonians. Paintings by Polish artists, depicting battle scenes, especially the triumphs of Polish hetmans on battlefields, were often commissioned. The Lvov guild of painters specialized in such works.

John Casimir, who was king during a period of wars and disasters, was less successful as a patron of the arts than his predecessors, but John III Sobieski again continued the lively tradition. His residence at Wilanów was used as the official residence of the monarch; Żółkiew held the family relics; and the manor-house at Jaworów was a quiet private residence. The king greatly increased the number of painters and sculptors who worked for him.

Under the influence of the royal court, the magnates began to sponsor various projects, for example, Zamość built by Jan Zamoyski, and Żółkiew, founded by Hetman Żółkiewski. How art was esteemed in these circles can be evidenced by the fact that Jerzy Mniszech, setting off for Moscow to attend the coronation of the False Dimitri, took with him the painter, Szymon Boguszowicz, in order that the great event be commemorated in painting. Dymitr Solikowski, a devout Catholic, sponsored a great deal of artistic activity, as did Hetman Stanisław Koniecpolski, patron of the Protestants, and of the most radical wing at that. Łukasz and Stanisław Opaliński were also active in the arts. The Kazanowski and Ossoliński palaces in Warsaw were filled with first class masterpieces; Aleksander Lubomirski's gallery consisted of over 200 paintings; and the Radziwiłł collections were even larger.

The contents and style of this court and magnate culture descended, in a sense, down the social hierarchy, and were assumed by the more wealthy gentry and rich burghers, especially of Gdańsk and other Pomeranian towns. That downward movement was affected by various means, mostly through theater, music, and social life. However, it was not attained without resistance. The culture of the gentry fought for its separateness.

The Baroque period in Poland was, to employ a modern expression, one of mass culture. It was, of course, socially limited to one segment of the nation, but that segment was able to experience it fully. Literature and art rarely reached beyond that particular level of the readers and the audience to whom they were addressed. But because of this, art and literature were close to them; they were their own.

Hundreds of *Silva rerum,* the gentry's private home anthologies, were witness to the generalization of culture. They were, in the words of one nobleman, "good thoughts of the obliging landlord." They contained everything that seemed important and interesting. Quite often in these domestic archives and anthologies, they collected their own original work: diaries and poetry. They were collections of texts, constantly supplemented, read for pleasure and reminiscence, perhaps at times from sentiment, handed down to their descendants who continued and added to them. Some, like the famous *Poetic Garden* by two generations of the Trembecki family, Jan and his son Jakub, preserved highly important poetic texts, especially Arian ones. Culture was becoming a living and familiar thing, private and home-made, and participation in it became active.

The landowner's style of life paid particular attention to furnishing living quarters. Under these conditions artistic craftsmanship flourished. The production of gobelins, rugs, kilims, embroideries, belts, arms, furniture, earthenware, silver and golden ornaments, tableware, candlesticks, and decorative playing cards served the needs of the royal court and the magnates, the churches, and also wide masses of the gentry.

Goldsmiths were concentrated in the towns, especially in Gdańsk, Toruń, Lvov, and Żółkiew. In 1643, Hetman Stanisław Koniecpolski founded in Brody a center for the production of gobelins and carpets and especially cloth of gold; at the beginning of the eighteenth century, the workshops of the Olizar family in Volhynia, the Radziwiłłs in Biała Podlaska, in Mir, Nieśwież and Korelicze became famous; richly embellished Polish sashes were produced mostly in Stanisławów, Brody and Słuck. Beautiful earthenware, especially tiles, were produced at Glińsk and Żółkiew. Saddles and harnesses were also in demand, as were embellished arms, partly imported from the East, partly produced in the country, particularly in Lvov. Cabinet-making flourished in Gdańsk and in Pomerania, the famous Gdańsk furniture; furniture made in Kolbuszowa was also immensely popular.

Graphics were also produced on a mass scale, and were more easily accessible to the gentry as a whole than were paintings, murals and sculptures. A Lvov inhabitant, Jan Ziarnko, achieved great fame. He emigrated to France, where he spent the rest of his life, but always emphasized his Polish origins. Marcin Morawa also went abroad. In Poland, Wilhelm Hondius, a Dutchman living in Gdańsk, enjoyed great popularity. He was commissioned by the king to paint townscapes and maps, as well as portraits. Jeremias Falck from Gdańsk, a painter of many portraits and allegorical scenes, was his pupil.

Devotional and panegyric graphics, produced on a massive scale, were sold at the fairs in front of churches and in market-places. They were sometimes published in book form, with didactic commentaries, for example, *Speculum vitae* and *Tractatum theologicum.* Graphic art attained a high standard in Gdańsk and Wrocław. The Eastern provinces were unusually active in graphics, especially artists employed at the courts of the Radziwiłłs at Nieśwież and in Vilna. There was also a center in operation at Częstochowa. Other centers of graphic 100 production were: Grodno, Pociejów, Kamieniec Podolski, Humań, Mohilev, Lvov, Berdyczów and Kiev.

On the other hand, the demand from the gentry in the field of painting was mostly limited to portraiture. Portrait painting triumphed from the sixteenth century at the royal and magnate courts, providing evidence of the greatness and brilliance of individuals, and of their wealth and power. Magnificent portraits of Báthory and Anne the Jagiellon, painted by Marcin Kober, which linked the Mannerist style with Polish artistic traditions, occupied a peculiarly significant place in this great gallery of powerful families. But the seventeenth century became the age when the gentleman's portrait spread throughout the Commonwealth. These portraits, which figured significantly in the daily life of the gentry manors, were a tangible connection between the dead and their descendants, with lasting and common values of dignity and pride, solemnity and a chivalrous spirit. A portrait displayed the physical and psychological traits of the gentry, their robust joy of life, ambition and licence, their temperament and social culture, as well as their devout religious attitudes.

Remarkable evidence of this character of Polish culture, and not only during the Baroque period, were the numerous women's portraits, usually in ceremonial dress, which was evidence of the sitters' wealth and social position. The faces looking out of the portraits are full of expression, sometimes of lyrical warmth, at other times musing, or projecting family pride.

Under these circumstances portraiture became a most popular art form. It was cultivated by hundreds of artists. In most cases the portraits were painted by local artists, sometimes even by amateurs who lived in the near vicinity of those being painted. Only very rich people could afford the choice of a really talented portrait painter. Bartłomiej Strobel of Wrocław, Daniel Schultz of Gdańsk, who for some time operated at the court of John Casimir, and Jerzy Siemiginowski of Lvov, the favorite painter of John Sobieski, achieved great fame as portrait painters.

THE BURDEN OF EXISTENCE

At the beginning of the Baroque period in Poland, religious conflicts still prevailed; later, history was to bring defeats in war. In both areas the human plight appeared ever more complicated.

The Protestant movement subsided. But conflicts of conscience became more acute: whether to abide by the new or return to the old creed.

Hundreds of believers remained true to the new creed. Poetic songs and ditties, prayers, elegies, hymns, and tales, diaries and short verses, pleas and thanksgivings, all these made up a whole great subterranean literature which accompanied the people throughout their hard lives. Not all the names of the authors have been preserved. Unknown, they were writing morning and evening songs, prayers to God for the opportunity to listen to His word, and prayers to God for relief in times of conflict, in times of fears, and in times of trouble. Some names and titles of

Arian authors and their works have been preserved: Zbigniew Morsztyn, Erazm Otwinowski, Jan Stoiński, Olbrycht Karmanowski, and Wacław Potocki. These were passionate and melancholy verses, full of restlessness, especially when it came to choosing between being true to one's creed and to one's fatherland.

Arian poetry was an expression of personal experiences, profound, disquieting, involved in the dramatic fate of the times. And so was that of Catholic poets, who, while finding support in the church, failed to find it themselves.

Sebastian Grabowiecki, a long-forgotten poet, author of *A Hundred Spiritual Rhymes* (1590), expressed this atmosphere of restlessness and loneliness. In metaphors of "a mermaid", "wind" and "flying clouds", typical of Baroque poetry, he dealt with life, in which sadness was human destiny.

Another poet, Stanisław Grochowski, asked: "What is man?" and replied: "Only shadow and vain steam", and his real home was where "the brightness of the everlasting sun shines". In the same way, Kasper Miaskowski, and many other poets, envisioned man.

Art cooperated with religious poetry. Religious painting and church sculpture produced a characteristic Baroque atmosphere of public piety: paintings, illustrating the Holy Bible, as for example, the great canvases by Dolabella, *The Wedding at Cana* and *The Last Supper; Baptism in the River Jordan* by Venantius of Subiaco; *The Fall Under the Cross* by Franciszek Lekszycki; and scenes form the lives of saints Ladislaus, Hyacinthus, Ursula, and Anne by Bartłomiej Strobel; and Louis Gonzaga by Daniel Schultz. Paintings presented "the art of dying" and "the dance of death". To influence the viewer more strongly, artists used details from actual life. The well-known *Art of Dying* from the Sochaczew church (1635) depicted a scene of the death of a wealthy nobleman, surrounded by his family and servants. In the church at Tarłów an artist realistically and suggestively presented a Polish version of the *danse macabre*.

Later, religious poetry became softer; peace reigned in the human conscience; trust in the protection by the Church increased. People were becoming more openly pious; the forms of religious worship were more externalized. Cross and sword, humility and pride, subservience and "ambitious phantasy" molded the daily life of the magnates and gentry.

Life was full of contrasts, manifesting itself, for example, in the unusual last will and testament of the Grand Lithuanian Hetman Michał Pac, who wished to be interred under the entrance to the Church of St. Peter and St. Paul at Antokol in Vilna; the people entering the church would then have to walk over the dust and ashes of its founder.

SARMATISM

The Confederacy of the Cracow Voivodeship in the year 1733, expressing curtly and austerely the decades-long conviction of the gentry, demanded that "Polish customs be observed". In this program of defense of the national way of life against foreign influence, various trends were focused: from fanaticism and obscurantism, hostile to the progress of science and to the new style of life determined by economic advancement, to the defense and strengthening of national, specifically cultural and moral, values. This program was formulated under the banner of Sarmatism. Although as early as the tenth century a French chronicler described Poles as Sarmatians, it was only links with the tradition of Roman historiography during the Renaissance period that extended the use of that name. Sixteenth century historians and geographers, particularly Maciej of Miechów and Kromer, promulgated among the gentry the conviction that the Polish nation descended from the brave Sarmatian people.

From that time on, elements of greatness and the ancient history of the Polish nation were underscored in the concept of Sarmatism. Towards the end of the sixteenth century this concept was enlarged in the work of the historians Aleksander Gwagnin (1578), Maciej Stryjkowski (1582), and Stanisław Sarnicki (1587).

In the seventeenth century the name of Sarmatia became common property, and its derivatives — Sarmatism and Sarmatian — became synonymous with meritorious behavior, especially of a chivalrous spirit, morality, patriotism, and piety, qualities which were valued among the gentry and defended by them against other nations, as well as against other social classes within the Commonwealth. Sarmatism was also becoming a political program, in which the necessity for limiting royal power, especially that of foreign kings, and of defending common privileges and tradition was being formulated. Jan Żabczyc stated: "There is no greater failure in the Commonwealth than the invention of new laws, and the transgression against good old customs."

Jerzy Ossoliński made the following remark to Pope Urban VIII in 1633: "Young people are spending their early years not with lutes and dances, but in the war camps; the gentry are not ashamed to cultivate land and shun urban pleasures, which enfeeble the warring spirit. In low huts dwell people with lofty hearts; they know nothing of fortified castles and draw-bridges; for they feel safe with their native laws and the innocence of life ... Religion and the Latin Muses have soothed the savageness of the Sarmatians."

In the second half of the seventeenth century the Sarmatian ideology was strengthened. The battered Commonwealth proved its strength and ultimately victoriously concluded the war with Sweden, Muscovy, and the Cossacks. It seemed to be evidence of the greatness of the nation of the gentry and of the wisdom of the political system of the Commonwealth, perhaps even of the special grace of God who protected the country.

The gentry's demand for works based on the knightly legend provided a source of rich heroic literature: recollections of the great Polish warriors — Chodkiewicz, Żółkiewski, and Czarniecki — of the great victories and defeats. In this spirit Piotr Kochanowski translated *Orlando furioso* by Ariosto and the *Gerusalemme liberata* by Tasso (1618). The Polish counterpart to these heroic epics were the poems by Samuel Twardowski, the anonymus author of *The Siege of Jasna Góra* (1673), and *Chocim Naumachia* by Jan Bojanowski (1622). But the most interesting work of this kind was an epic by Wacław Potocki, *The Transaction of the Chocim War,* not published until 1850.

Art, especially painting, satisfied the same social demand. The greatness of the kings, the splendor of the magnate families, the brilliance of the hetmans commanding the armies, the glorious Polish victories — all of these constituted the subject matter of patriotic paintings, in which panegyric elements commemorated the fame of families which had served their native land. Such painting was in demand by the royal court, by the magnates, and even by the monasteries. Wawel and Warsaw Castle were hung with such paintings. The high point of this type of art came during the reign of John III. Martin Altomonte, on the orders of the king, painted several canvases commemorating the monarch's war deeds, especially the Vienna victory. How deeply these patriotic needs were rooted in the community can be witnessed by the fact that historical and war paintings developed not only under the sponsorship of the king and magnates, but also on the initiative of the church hierarchy. Such paintings appeared in monasteries and churches. In 1743 at the Opatów collegiate church, the walls of the presbytery and the transept were decorated with a great cycle depicting the Polish victories at Psie Pole, Grunwald and Vienna.

In this religious and patriotic philosophy of history, the national soul-searching to find justification for the punishment inflicted on the country was linked with the hope of regaining the protection of God, and with an almost provocative appeal to His justice and mercy.

An expression of this concept of religious life was the development of the cult of saints. While in the sixteenth century there were 36 saints-day fairs, in the seventeenth century their number had increased to 103.

This political myth of the exceptional values of the Commonwealth embraced other elements. There was pride that Poland was "a bulwark of Christendom" and each war with Turkey strengthened that conviction. There was also pride that Polish grain fed all of Europe.

An important element of Sarmatian culture was the worship of rural life, conceived as a particularly valuable type of human existence. Discernible already in the sixteenth century, the apotheosis of rural life achieved greater intensity during the Baroque period. But life in the country — the nobleman's manor — was a kind of mini-republic, defending jealously its rights, independent because of the privileges it possessed, ambitious and proud. A nobleman "on his estate" was "his own court, speaker of the House, and his own lord."

It was commonly repeated that "a nobleman in his abode is equal to the voivode"; they were proud of their freedom and independence in regard to the king and the authorities of the Commonwealth; they conducted a self-sufficient, closed life, with complete jurisdiction over their peasants and servants.

Under these conditions, as a supplement to the political myth, a particular Arcadian myth was being shaped: that of the free and happy life.

102

From the viewpoint of the nobleman's manor, everything that was alien, remote, and incomprehensible was worthy of condemnation: voyages to the West, luxurious dress, elaborate dishes, as well as arguments used to undermine traditional, simple, bigoted religious views and the principles of "the golden freedom" of the gentry.

While court life, full of splendor and wealth, was subject to foreign patterns and customs, rural life, true to tradition, was molded on the Sarmatian model. Diarists have left minute descriptions of the daily and holiday life of the gentry and peasantry, underscoring its diverse and opposing characteristics: piety close to fanaticism, curiosity about the world and prejudices, hospitality and violence, readiness to serve the public cause and egoism, countenance and common sense, primitive existence and the exquisite elegance of living quarters and dress, extravagance and thriftiness, revelling in festivities, gluttony and drunkenness, but also ascetic and religious pilgrimages, "an attachment to the lord's doorknob" and a defiant independence.

This style of life was an expression of the feeling of freedom and independence that resulted from the privileges of the gentry estate. In effect there was no higher authority which it had to obey. A nobleman had ultimately to obey the will of God, but that did not mean that he should be a subject of the church, particularly of the clergy. Still less did he consider himself subject of the king, whom he elected to the throne, the state administration, the will of the country magistrates, the order of the hetman, the verdict of the tribunal — all of these had no mandatory power. Rebellion against the king, like an assault on a neighbor, launched against the ruling of a court, only served to prove the independence of a nobleman. In the final analysis it was the saber and the conscience of each nobleman that decided the cause of service to the Commonwealth, his relations with his neighbors, and care for his personal interest.

Foreign Culture in Poland and Polish Culture in the World

FOREIGN CONTACTS

During the first half of the seventeenth century, contacts with foreign countries continued, due both to the numerous voyages abroad by Poles and to the visits of many foreigners to Poland. The first place among these contacts was occupied by Italy, the country most frequently visited by Poles. Traditionally, monks and clergymen went to Rome, but also scholars, particularly lawyers and physicians; contacts with Padua were kept alive, and Florence was discovered as a center of research in the natural sciences.

Trips to Germany became increasingly frequent. Altdorf drew radical young Protestants; a representative of the Polish student group, Adam Sienieński, was appointed

rector of the university in that city. Many Poles studied at Heidelberg. Young Catholics were taught in Vienna and Ingolstadt. The university in Louvain attracted students because of the fame of Justus Lipsius. Krzysztof Opaliński on his way through Louvain wrote that he felt as if he were in Poland. France attracted Catholics as well as Calvinists, and especially Unitarians, and also scholars and politicians. Paris was enthusiastically accepted by everybody. Very lively contacts were also kept with the Netherlands; the university at Leiden educated lawyers, naturalists, theologians, and promoted a rationalistic culture. Grotius was held in particular esteem, and several times was invited to Poland. At the end of the sixteenth century, Jan Zamoyski directed the attention of the Poles to England. Mutual relations became more lively at the beginning of the seventeenth century. The activity of John Dury, a minister of a Protestant church in Elbląg between 1630 and 1652, was of wide significance, as was the work of Samuel Hartlib, who after studying in Silesia and Królewiec went to England, but kept close contacts with Poland, especially with Johann Amos Comenius. Johann Hevelius, an astronomer from Gdańsk, established links with the Royal Society in London, which was founded in 1660.

Maciej Sarbiewski was correct when, in his magnificent characterization of the Poles, he declared that they "are journeying to all countries and similarly allow others to visit their country. No nation knows the entire world better and no one is better known throughout the entire world."

However, the Thirty Years' War significantly hindered journeys to the West, and the wars in Poland in the middle of the seventeenth century and later limited them even more. Only very few individuals could go to study abroad. But in the course of this period, lively and diversified scientific, religious, and artistic contacts with foreign countries were widened due to the numerous journeys of foreigners to Poland. In this field a great role was played by the policy of the royal court, during the reign of three monarchs: Ladislaus IV, John Casimir and John III Sobieski. Though plans to extend protection to and attract to Poland famous celebrities like Lipsius, Galileo, and Grotius failed, they were evidence of the scale of cultural ambitions in the seventeenth century. Ladislaus IV, especially, made great efforts to invite foreign scholars and artists to Poland. His court provided favorable conditions for work to Valeriano Magni, famous for his experiments on the vacuum; the physician Vorbeck-Lettow; the astronomer Livius Burattini; the poet Martin Opitz; and to many other people who dealt with history and military science.

After the death of Ladislaus IV, court sponsorship was continued and even widened by his widow, Marie-Louise, later wife of John Casimir. Her court became a center of diverse and lively contacts with France and Italy. At the Ujazdów Castle an astronomical observatory for Burattini was set up; contacts with Accademia del Cimento were established; several outstanding Italian and French physicians and naturalists were invited.

John III was personally interested in many branches of

science. Leibniz, who heard of the king's interests, wrote about them enthusiastically to Adam Adamandy Kochański, an outstanding mathematician active at the court. The king urged systematic scientific contacts with Italy.

While in the sixteenth century foreign contacts opened ways for humanism as well as for the Reformation, which became intellectual movements with a wide range of social impact, during the seventeenth century, Polish trips abroad and journeys of foreigners to Poland were rather of an educational and social character. They did not lead to the dissemination of ideas in wider circles of the community, which remained on the whole indifferent to them, or even hostile, shutting themselves off within their own particularism, especially during the second half of the century. Jan Chryzostom Pasek, fearful lest "a French good-for-nothing be introduced to the kingdom", acclaimed the violent reaction of the gentry *"in teatro publico"* in Warsaw when they shot at the French actors with bows and arrows.

Under these conditions, foreign contacts could only minimally open the way to a dissemination of ideas, and particularly for those currents which in the seventeenth century were taking shape in Western Europe. The names of Bacon and Descartes were almost unknown in contemporary Poland. Only Comenius was an enthusiastic supporter of Bacon, yet a bitter opponent of Descartes and of the modern natural sciences; he also was opposed to the heliocentric theory of Copernicus, which, defended at the beginning of the seventeenth century by the professors of the University in Cracow, later became a target for many attacks. The conditions for literature and art were slightly better. Morsztyn was a representative of the European tradition in poetry, but the great majority of the poets of the period remained enclosed within a Sarmatian framework.

Interest in the world was increasingly directed toward local curiosities and the pleasures of journeying, toward criticism of foreign customs and equally superficial enthusiasm for foreign ways. How popular was this sensation-hungry interest in the world is evidenced by two editions, in the middle of the eighteenth century, of Benedykt Chmielowski's encyclopedia, *The New Athens,* in which the author compiled details of minor curiosities from all over the world and from various nations. And yet, uttering his judgment of the world, he particularly esteemed European civilization: "Europe leads in arms, in the fame of its sciences, in the collection of great kings and lords, in the state of policy, in all kinds of glorious governments, in its choice of habits . . .".

POLISH CONTRIBUTION
TO EUROPEAN CULTURE

What was the relation of Poland, during the Baroque era, to the world? What was her contribution to its culture?

The political system of Poland was the subject of fairly universal interest. Europe, which was heading toward absolutism, looked, depending on the standpoint of the viewers, with the approbation or condemnation at the country which, although nominally a kingdom, called itself a *res publica,* because it elected its king and restricted his prerogatives. In times of increasing religious conflict, the tolerance reigning in Poland was condemned, although the oppressed in various countries considered Poland a model worthy of imitation.

One of the French Huguenots wrote from Vienna to his friend: "The habits of that nation you will like a great deal, and perhaps you will experience more culture there than here." The famous political writings *Vindiciae Contra Tyrannos* (1579) were produced within these circles. They defended the principle that all power comes from the people who make a contract with their monarch. Poland was often cited as an example of a country which possessed safeguards against tyrants.

A fundamentally different stand was taken by Jean Bodin, theoretician of monarchy. John Barclay, a Scotsman, sharply attacked Poland's system, but it was hotly defended by an outstanding lawyer, Althusius. Campanella, in his poem about Poland, praised free elections: "O, Poland! thou art higher than those other kingdoms/Where scepter is achieved by heritage."

As chaos grew in the country and the Counter-Reformation gathered force, judgments about Poland became more bitter. Comenius appealed to Charles Gustavus: "Restore freedom to the Poles, but widen it to include everybody, to all and under every aspect. To everybody — and in so doing, you order freedom to all and each one individually, to the magnates, to the lesser gentry, to the cities and towns and to the peasant people . . . Everything should be free — bodies, minds, conscience . . . Every aspect of peace and liberty should be arranged, not in name only!".

In these words was disclosed the main charge made against Poland: the unjust social system, based on privilege.

Poland was criticized more sharply by Hermann Conring of Helmstedt, with whom Jan Sachs from Toruń debated victoriously. Leibniz spoke very cautiously, though approvingly; whereas Ulrich Huber of the Netherlands, who was active in the last quarter of the seventeenth century, was an enthusiastic supporter of Poland.

But as political chaos, together with intolerance, deepened in Poland, opinions concerning the values of the state system were changing. An outstanding French politician and political theorist, René d'Argenson, stated, in analyzing the situation in Poland in the first half of the eighteenth century, that there existed in it neither authority, nor freedom, since laxity, egoism and injustice reigned. Montesquieu voiced a similar opinion: "The worst of all aristocracies is one in which that part of the people which obeys is in civil subjugation to that part which rules, like the Polish aristocracy, where the peasants are slaves to the gentry." Similar critical remarks were made in the middle of the eighteenth century by David Hume, Adam Smith, and Voltaire. But this was not a universal opinion. Although the declining state could not win approval for its organization and institutions, its "liberal" system, considered anachronistic in Europe, which was then building centralized absolutist monarchies, began to gain some popularity in the eighteenth century within that camp which inaugurated the struggle for human and civic rights and for government reforms, aimed at the removal or limitation of royal power. Rousseau perceived these values when he wrote to the Poles: "You love freedom; you are worthy of it." And the Polish gentry welcomed enthusiastically the American Revolution as a kind of rebellion against foreign and absolutist power. For these reasons, Poland's best sons took part in the war for the freedom of this far-off nation.

But the most significant contribution of the Polish Baroque to European culture was the achievement of several generations of Arians, both Poles and foreigners who had found their second fatherland in Poland. In the *Encyclopédie* Naigeon wrote the following: "Du socinianisme au déisme il n'y a qu'une nuance très imperceptible, et un pas à faire". Indeed, the participation by Polish Brethren — both those from the earliest times, those from Raków, and those from the later decades of the seventeenth century — in the radical intellectual movements in Europe was significant. Contacts were inaugurated by Marcin Ruar during his journey to the Netherlands when he established links with Jacobus Arminius and the Remonstrant Brotherhood and with the leader of the irenic movement, Grotius; later, a large group of Raków youth established contacts with various eminent French scholars, including Martin Mersenne, Pierre Gassendi and S. Sorbière.

The Polish Brethren — and in fact only they — were becoming partners of the philosophers who were creating in the West of Europe foundations for a new world view and a new organization of social life. Spinoza discussed the views of the Polish Brethren which were circulating in the Netherlands among the collegians, and owed much to them in shaping his concept of philosophy as *meditatio vitae.* Grotius copied the Raków catechism in his own handwriting and drew on the Arians' opinions in defense of the ideas of liberty and tolerance and in defense of peace; he also kept up direct contacts with Ruar, Szlichtyng, and Crell. Leibniz studied Stegmann and Wiszowaty. Wolzogen began a thorough disputation with Descartes. The links of the Arians to radical circles in Paris, where they presented the "Raków truth" directly and by means of correspondence, were very close. This ideology also reached England by various routes. The printing of the Raków Catechism in London in 1651 became a subject for legal investigation; Milton was among those examined and the matter ended with an order to burn the work.

The ideological inspiration present in that work and in other works by the Polish Brethren, gained great importance and became a part of the culture of the Enlightenment, especially due to the importance of Socinianism for Pierre Bayle and for the English philosophers, from Locke with his views on tolerance, to the deists, particularly Toland and Tindal. The ideology of the Polish Brethren was also continued in America in Unitarian circles, which later prepared the ideology of the American Revolution, especially its principles of human and civil rights.

The collected works of Polish Arians, *Bibliotheca Fratrum Polonorum,* edited in Amsterdam in ten volumes, from the year 1666, played an important role in the processes of shaping the early Enlightenment and of the new style of thinking.

Voltaire in his *Lettres anglaises* declared: "The sect of Arius begins to revive in England, to say nothing about the Netherlands and Poland. The great Newton honored that denomination with his willing attention. According to the philosopher, "Unitarians argue more geometrically than we do."

Alongside the great ideas which radiated from Poland to the world came a few individual scholars and artists who achieved European significance. They were not numerous. A small group of professors, sometimes at home, sometimes abroad, was a part of the intellecutal élite of the age. Marcin Chmielecki twice held the position of rector of the university in Basel, where he was a lecturer in logic, the natural sciences, and medicine. Bartłomiej Keckermann of Gdańsk taught philosophy in Heidelberg for a time; his pupil Jan Makowski became an outstanding professor of philosophy in the Netherlands. At Frankfurt on Oder Jan Kołaczek of Gdańsk, a pioneer supporter of Cartesian philosophy, was twice rector of the university. Yet the greatest fame was attained by Stanisław Pudłowski, by the Gdańsk astronomer Johann Hevelius, an associate of Galileo, an excellent scanner of the sky and in particular the creator of selenology, as well as by Adam Kochański, who worked in mathematics and mechanics, in collaboration with Leibniz and with many other scholars.

Also well known in Europe were Jan Jonston, and especially two military engineers, Adam Freytag and Kazimierz Siemieniowicz, precursors of rocket technology.

In the field of the humanities, a study of Ciceronian dialectics by Adam Bursius of Zamość was significant, as were many philosophical works by Keckermann of Gdańsk, and philosophical Arian studies by Przypkowski, Wiszowaty and Crell.

Maciej Sarbiewski, made poet laureate in 1623 by Pope Urban VIII and who was read throughout Europe, achieved world fame. His Latin works, published in Cologne in 1625, *Lyricorum Libri Tres,* were reprinted in Antwerp in 1630, in Leipzig in 1804, and 1840, in Strasbourg in 1805, Dresden in 1814, and Graz in 1831; another edition of Sarbiewski's poems, which appeared in Leiden in 1631, was re-edited and enlarged in Antwerp in 1632, 1634 and 1646, under the significant title *Horatius Sarmaticus* and was reprinted in Cologne in 1721 and 1781, and in Paris in 1759. Numerous editions appeared in the nineteenth and even in the twentieth century: for example, in Los Angeles, a photo-offset reproduction of the edition of 1646.

Andrzej Maksymilian Fredro was also known abroad. His *Monita politico-moralia,* published in Gdańsk in 1664, had numerous foreign editions. As many as nine editions appeared in Frankfurt. They were also translated into German and published twice at the end of the seventeenth century, and into French, published in Potsdam in 1700. Up to the end of the eighteenth century, there were a total of 25 editions of the work.

Conclusions

What did the Baroque bring to the history of Polish culture: the Baroque, often attacked, although sometimes praised as being most Polish?

The long decades of the period abounded in contradictions, in which progress and retrogression were intertwined, as were tolerance and fanaticism, ardent religious feeling and bigotry, the struggle for the rights of reason and the obscurantism of the gentry, the sacrifice for the Commonwealth and private interests, patriotism and national megalomania, a vision of a quiet life based on social injustice, and the luxury of the life of the magnate families, the egoism of which endangered the country.

The list of contradictions demonstrated certain lasting and significant trends.

The consciousness of the greatness of the Polish nation and of the importance of its state was shaped during this period. Although this consciousness sometimes bordered on national megalomania, generally it had a patriotic character. It was appreciated that the Commonwealth embraced a wide territory, that it was one of the largest states in Europe, that it governed millions of inhabitants, that it provided possibilities for economic and cultural eastward expansion, and that it defended Western countries from Turkish aggression. However, from the middle of the seventeenth century, military and political defeats exposed the weakness of the great Commonwealth and the increasing danger to it: "The homeland blazes with war. It is half burned. Its fame and borders have shrunk," wailed Wacław Potocki. This meant that then and for ages to come, a tradition of dramatically alternative experiences took shape: of greatness and decline, of victories and defeats, of power and danger.

The culmination of these dual experiences came with the Swedish assault. An almost unbelievable, almost total, disaster followed. There remained only a few bastions of defense already condemned to defeat. Unexpectedly, the strong patriotism of the oppressed masses of people who organized a "resistance movement" appeared. Victory was won from the very depths of national defeat. The great tasks of reconstruction of the ruined country were undertaken. That was the historical experience of Polish patriotism: unknown in such proportions to preceding ages, but recurring over and over during later periods.

In addition to widening the range of the national consciousness and of patriotism, the seventeenth century strengthened and developed the Polish version of Catholicism. In the sixteenth century the scales of traditional and Reformation faith were still in the balance; Polish society was only a step away from the great change that would bind it to the Protestant countries. The seventeenth century became the age of triumphant Catholicism, which became increasingly more intolerant and severe toward dissenters.

During the Swedish wars the dissenters were accused of high treason; thus, the identification of Catholicism with Polish citizenship was effected.

Concurrently, a Polish version of Catholicism was established. It was the work of the Jesuits, who conducted their religious mission in the community which, after a time of dissenting passions and ardor, proved incapable of grand-scale rational or mystical religious experience, so characteristic of seventeenth century Europe, and which manifested its piety rather superficially.

The social structure became rigid. In the sixteenth century the barriers dividing one estate from the other were not yet entirely unsurmountable; the ways of social advancement were still half-open to the peasants, and the role of the burghers was still of some significance to the economy and to culture. In the seventeenth century the Commonwealth became a Commonwealth of one single estate, the gentry. This class jealously guarded its privileges. This class also, identifying itself with the state, tried to implement its economic and political plans in the East, where the inhabitants were neither Polish nor Catholic. In this manner, national and denominational contradictions were superimposed upon the feudal hierarchy of "lords" and "peasants" and, in social reality as well as in the national consciousness, basic conflicts emerged between Polish culture, based on a numerically weak group of Polish magnates and Polish gentry, and the native culture of wide masses of the people, especially Ukrainian. This was the problem of the eastern marcher regions, which would be of exceptional importance during more than two centuries of Polish history.

In this society of sharp class differences, maintained within the closed ranks of the peasant, burgher, gentry and magnate communities, a still weak and unclear group of intellectuals was forming. In contrast to the medieval and Renaissance periods, it was not linked solely to the university, and now became more democratic. It consisted of schoolmasters, depicted sympathetically in plebeian literature, especially in the *Synod of the Subcarpathian Clergy* (1607), a group of university and gymnasia professors who were gradually losing their importance.

The seventeenth century also strengthened the basic polarity of Polish socio-cultural life: the luxury of the magnates' residences linked with foreign fads and the rich simplicity of noblemen's manor-houses, which cultivated the national style of life. Curiosity and loathing regarding foreign patterns, sentiment for, but also criticism of, Sarmatian traditions — this medley of confirmation and doubt, of hope and denial was to shape the attitude of the Poles toward native and foreign things.

But the Baroque period was not only an ephemeral link in the development of Polish culture to be registered in the historical consciousness, but simultaneously, it was one which is in a way still with us. While previous periods, the Middle Ages and the Renaissance, are remembered because of the existence of a few remnants, albeit quite famous, the repercussions of the Baroque period are much more extensive and diversified. It was then that the architectural landscape of the country was established — of churches and chapels, providing protection for village cottages, or embellishing towns and cities. Religious ceremonies at the Baroque altars, even in the churches which had been built in the previous epochs, were important and colorful social manifestations, complete with singing and banners. Perhaps the natural environment of the country favored the Baroque mentality. Maciej Sarbiewski, the poet of the early Baroque period, remarked that "our fields and plains symbolize the sincerity and simplicity of our hearts and our trustworthy habits" even if we were considered crude. Sarbiewski's comment could be enlarged in relation to the changes that came later. There has always been some Baroque character in the irregular and whimsical lines drawn through the fields by the roads and balks — and in the dramatic expression (how very Polish!) of the arms of old willows, stretching to the sky, or in the branches of the birches weeping perhaps over life or over the destiny of man?

During this period numerous buildings were constructed for various religious orders, especially for the Jesuits. Magnate residences, scattered all over Poland, were erected, particularly in Warsaw before and after the Swedish invasion.

And lastly, as a link in the development of Polish culture, the period of the Baroque had (and still has) a very special meaning, different from all other epochs. This was a period of great events, which shook the power of the state and which have become a point of departure for an unending national soul-searching.

In the great argument about the causes of the downfall of the state and the partitions, the attention of the accusers was focused on this period, drawing up a list of guilt and errors; and also the attention of the defenders, who were trying, against the background of Europe, to show the worth of the old structure of the Commonwealth and the greatness of the ancient Poles.

THE ENLIGHTENMENT

Introduction

This period of Poland's history abounded in contradictions. Reforms were effected in many fields of public life, but the State of the Gentry declined. Civic virtues and heroic sacrifices were expressions of patriotism, against which private interests, bribery, and high treason stood out the more strongly. For progress to take place in the areas of reason, tolerance and public enlightenment, forces of obscurantism and fanaticism had to be overcome. The re-opened window onto intellectual Europe was being stubbornly closed by defenders of the Sarmatian way of life. The sophisticated culture of the royal court and magnate centers was opposed by the traditional gentry culture, which, for the most part, was reactionary and rarely more than a superficial fashion for things foreign.

Efforts to modernize the economy were treated with distrust and hostility by conservative magnates and the majority of the gentry. The modest degree of economic progress did not improve the standard of living of the basic class of society, the peasants. Vainly did the peasants present various appeals; in vain did they undertake efforts at self-defense and struggle, especially around Warsaw, Cracow, Sieradz, Bielsk, Lublin, Koło, and Garwolin; the peasant rebellions in the Ukraine ended in defeat. Only at the end of the century did possibilities, albeit modest, of lessening social inequalities appear.

But, even under these conditions, progressive forces were winning victories. Great improvements were brought about in the Commonwealth, from educational and political reforms in mid-century to the reforms of the Four Year Seym and the plans presented by Kosciuszko. Both achievements and proposals contributed to the modern national identity. They were kept alive during the long period of servitude, because they were proof that the neighboring powers had annihilated a state undergoing a process of renewal, and not a state in decline.

Place in Europe and Historical Consciousness

THE FIRST PARTITION OF POLAND

In 1772, the first partition of Poland took place; Prussia annexed Warmia, Pomerania, and part of Kujavia; Austria, almost all of Little Poland, Red Ruthenia and part of Podolia; Russia, Livonia, the Polotsk and Vitebsk voivodeships, as well as Mstislav and Mohilev, embracing the territory East of the Dnieper. Poland lost 30 percent of its territory and 35 percent of its population. The new boundary with Russia deprived Poland of the remote and ethnically alien marcher regions, especially in the North and North-East, in the Dnieper region. But the new frontiers with Austria and Prussia were an incursion of those states into central Poland and its native lands. The entire area South of the Vistula, Wieliczka and Tarnów, Rzeszów, and Przemyśl, and also further East, Zamość, Lvov and Zbarazh, passed under Austrian domination. Cracow and Sandomierz became border cities. Prussia, too, reached into the depth of the Commonwealth's territory, taking away Warmia with Olsztyn and Lidzbark, and also Pomerania and Kujavia as far as Inowrocław and Kruszwica. Toruń and Gdańsk remained within the Commonwealth, as islands within the territory of the Kingdom of Prussia.

The first partition of Poland and the threat to its sovereignty that followed became a basic new element shaping the national identity. It was a time of opposing political views; support for defense at all costs or hope in the success of diplomatic activity; and the adherents of these factions indulged in mutual recrimination. Heroism and sacrifice coexisted with treason and bribery; despair with balls and dances, during which people tried to forget about national defeats or simply thought of saving their own riches. Adam Poniński, the Speaker of the Seym which approved the first partition of Poland, and Tadeusz Rejtan, a deputy who had the courage to protest against the pending law, became symbols of national treason and sacrifice, symbols which were kept alive for decades and were consolidated in the national consciousness during the second half of the nineteenth century by Jan Matejko in his famous painting, *Rejtan at the Seym of 1773*.

In this way, the first partition of Poland became a source of new ideas and trends in the national consciousness. The question of the historical legality of the act of violence committed by neighboring countries and its moral justification became sharply focused. Stanislaus Augustus tried to defend the interests of the country by means of erudition and an appeal to justice. On the king's initiative, various studies were undertaken; of particular significance was the work of Feliks Franciszek Łoyko, author of numerous works in Polish and French, in which he exposed the wrongful claims of the three partitioning powers to the lands of the Commonwealth.

Questions emerged, which from then on greatly agonized the national consciousness, as to whether history was a tribunal of justice and truth, or an area where power and violence prevailed? Were there any institutions to whom weak nations might appeal when they were subjugated by powerful states? Was there "a world conscience" or a reasonable and moral "meaning of history", or was the history of mankind merely a chronicle of "accomplished facts"?

These problems would be raised for a second time by writers and philosophers of the Romantic period, enthusiasts and critics of Hegel's philosophy of history.

Yet the main consequences of the first partition appeared in the internal life of the country. Society was mobilizing its resources for defense. Of symbolic significance was the fact that the year 1773 was not only a time of the ratification of the partition by the Seym, but also the year of the foundation of the Commission for National Education. In the course of the next few years after the national defeat, the process of the remodeling of the feudal society and the gentry state was effected.

The development of science and culture radiated 110

throughout the country from Warsaw, the crystalization of modern political ideology and success in the work of reform of the gentry and magnate state — all these processes continued after the first partition of Poland against a background of defeat, and under the increasing threat that the Polish state would entirely cease to exist.

This duality characterized the Polish culture of the period. Its artistic and literary brilliance, its intellectual and social hopes, its optimistic view of the future, were being destroyed by an underground voice of despair, by the fear of something worse to come, and by the restlessness and shame felt in a country robbed by foreign armies and governed by foreign ambassadors.

Under these conditions, patriotism began to mean a defense of the homeland menaced by collapse, and a limitless sacrifice for its safety. An expression of this patriotism was the famous poem written in 1774 by Ignacy Krasicki — something of a national anthem for contemporary Poland — which the officer cadets learned by heart and sang during school ceremonies: "O, sacred love of the beloved motherland, Thou art felt only by honest minds."

Patriotism during the Enlightenment manifested itself mostly in awareness of the significance of the native land. Sympathy with the country's plight was becoming a new and meaningful element of patriotism.

The poetry of the period, which honestly expressed the sentiments of the nation, returned over and over again to the experience of joy and sadness, evoked by the free and the subjugated land. Franciszek Karpiński in his numerous verses expressed these feelings of sorrow and devotion; for example, in his famous "Laments of a Sarmatian," in "Songs of a Beggar from Sokal," and in many lyrical poems, like "Yearning for a Homeland."

The "handful of native soil" would become a symbol of the link with the motherland, the most cherished memory of exiles, the consolation to those dying far from their country, and a holy relic for those emigrating in search of bread.

THE SECOND AND THE THIRD PARTITION OF POLAND

On 23 January 1793, Prussia and Russia signed an agreement regarding the further partitions of Poland to "prevent the Jacobin epidemic". Prussia took Gdańsk and Toruń, after some street fighting, and the lands West of the line Częstochowa—Sochaczew—Działdowo. Russia annexed the Byelorussian and Ukrainian territories East of the line Druya-Pinsk-Zbruch.

In this partition, the Commonwealth lost about 60 percent of its land, and kept only 200,000 square kilometers and little more than four million inhabitants. Half of Polish ethnic territory came under foreign rule.

The last Seym of the Commonwealth met in Grodno in 1793. It was almost symbolic, since Grodno was only a memorial of the old magnificence of the country of the times of the Polish-Lithuanian Union. The old Jagiellonian castle was in ruins; the second castle was rebuilt, but

without the necessary attention to detail. The great achievements of Antoni Tyzenhaus were also in ruins.

The Seym accepted the final declaration of the partition of Poland in silence. And although the Seym agreed under pressure to the changes, the patriotic part of society never acknowledged them.

Throughout the country, in both the lost and retained parts, especially in the towns and cities, turmoil continued and the will to resist increased. The cooperation of Turkey was expected, as was assistance from France, although, for ideological or sometimes for tactical reasons, revolutionary principles were denounced. On 24 March 1794, Thaddeus Kosciuszko announced in the Cracow market-place an act of insurrection. Its first victory, at Racławice, became a source of hope and, at the same time, an expression of the patriotism and strength of peasant soldiers who fought with scythes. On 17 April 1794, the victorious uprising in Warsaw began, followed slightly later in Vilna. Members of the Targowica Confederacy were attacked; in Warsaw traitors were hanged on 9 May and 28 June. But on the battlefields the scales of victory were tipping toward the Russian side. The help expected from France came to nothing. Saint-Just accused the insurgents of treason against "republican ideals". The insurrection subsided: Russian and Prussian armies seized Cracow and moved on Warsaw, which was attacked simultaneously from the West, North and East. Yet Warsaw managed to defend itself. The uprising in Great Poland at the end of August forced the Prussian army to retreat from Warsaw. It was a temporary victory, however. The strong army of Suvorov routed Kosciuszko's troops at Maciejowice; the wounded commander was imprisoned. Legend, which was in fact false, claimed that the wounded Kosciuszko uttered the words: "Finis Poloniae". In early November, the Russians took Praga and Warsaw. The final division of the lands of the Commonwealth amongst Russia, Prussia and Austria followed.

In October 1795, Russia, Austria and Prussia signed a final agreement. In November, Stanislaus Augustus abdicated. In July 1796, the delimitation of the frontiers was completed. Russia took the Ukrainian, Byelorussian and Lithuanian territories, leaving the ethnically Polish lands to Austria and Prussia. The Austrian border ran along the Rivers Vistula, Pilica, and Bug; Prussia annexed the rest including Warsaw, which meant that Poles formed 40 percent of the population of Prussia.

The Polish state ceased to exist. Yet, in a prolonged and uneven fight, the nation which remained on its native soil, defended itself.

A great chapter of Poland's history started with the defense against depolonization. Deprivation of nationality had been, up to that time, the plight of the population of previously ceded territories. Now it was to be the destiny of the entire nation.

For decades to come, Poland remained a dual reality: one, in which it was possible to a limited extent to live openly and legally, and another in which it was possible conspiratorially to carry out cultural and educational activity and to prepare for armed action.

It was becoming a dual reality in yet another meaning. The fall of the state compelled many citizens to leave their native land. Thus in addition to the Poland-at-home there was born a Poland-in-exile. Each was becoming a center for the continued development of a consistent, yet diversified, Polish culture.

THE NEW HISTORIOGRAPHY

When the ground was being pulled from under the foundations of the Polish home, the significance of history as an ideal world became all the stronger. In that ideal world, Poland was to keep its place on the map of Europe. The national identity gained a new orientation which would last through the whole period of bondage. Historical interest originated not only because of political needs to prove Poland's rights to its lost territories; but also to fulfill the needs of national self-awareness, a conviction that historical identity would strengthen an awareness of national virtue and strength. When mediocrity and weakness seemed universal, historical greatness appeared a source of truth about the nation and of faith in its future, built on the quicksands of actuality.

These goals explain the efforts aimed at the revival and modernization of historical culture. The former fictionalized and mythologized historiography was opposed by erudite historical studies, based on critical analysis of documents and the denunciation of popular fairy-tales and legends.

A historian of the era, Adam Naruszewicz, wrote studies along these lines. He was preceded by the Gdańsk historian, Gottfried Lengnich, whose Latin work, *De Polonorum Maioribus* (1732), inaugurated a discussion about the origin of the Poles and the birth of their state. Naruszewicz's *History of the Polish Nation* (1780—86), however, became the main historical work of the epoch, also owing to the fact that it was written in Polish. His work (he was also a poet) was a breakthrough in awakening the historical consciousness of the community. This work was supported by other writers and poets, including Krasicki.

Naruszewicz inaugurated the characteristic national soul-searching made up of a bitter criticism of mediocrity, which was egoistic and envious, hostile to any authority and to the dictates of patriotic duty.

From this point of view Naruszewicz promised, in his *Memorial on the Writing of National History,* to expose "the harmful internal turmoils", and especially the "willful freedom" and the "pride of private magnates", the consequences of the rebellions and confederacies, the religious struggles, and the "peasant wars". Understanding history as "education in the truth" that should "speak to the people", Naruszewicz rejected the naive, indiscriminate worship of the past. "The examples of our predecessors cannot teach us unless, prior to that, they will themselves be led to certain rules of virtue, justice and citizenship." And yet, unfortunately, the significant promises of the *Memorial* were not fully implemented in his laboriously prepared great *History of the Polish Nation,* published in

six volumes. Erudite and critical, revealing a new wealth of historical sources, it was, as Hugo Kołłątaj remarked, political history, formulated from the standpoint of the royal faction with its program to strengthen the authority of the monarch.

National history during this period was of interest not only to professional historians and politicians; it also proved to be a characteristic need of the enlightened community, a challenge which, sometimes quite unexpectedly, was taken up by writers and poets whose basic approach was quite different.

History was also an important area for the prince of poets from the period of Stanislaus Augustus, Ignacy Krasicki. In 1779 he published *A History,* in which he presented enlightened critical views on the history of the world.

He returned to historical subjects in his other works, especially in his free translation of Plutarch's *Lives,* in *Lives of Illustrious Men in Plutarch's Manner,* and in *Dialogues of the Dead.* In these works he expressed his belief in the significance of private virtues in public life and formulated a program of rational action by means of historical examples. Characteristic of his method was the dialogue between Boleslaus the Brave and Casimir the Great, included in *Dialogues of the Dead,* in which Boleslaus complains that the later generations did not appreciate his merits, bestowing the epithet "Great" only on Casimir. But Krasicki merely confirms the universal opinion because the king who "is busy with the internal government, multiplies agriculture, builds up trade, promotes learning and constructs" is better than the king "who topples and destroys with sound and fury." And when Boleslaus proudly talks of the frontier posts he placed "in the rivers", Casimir replies that he "would immediately order them to be taken out of the rivers, lest they prevent the flow of crops and goods."

Franciszek Bohomolec, by no means a historian by profession or vocation, also obeyed the historical appeal. He prepared and edited, in four volumes, *A Collection of Polish Chroniclers* (1764—68), consisting of chronicles by Marcin Bielski, Maciej Stryjkowski, Marcin Kromer, and Aleksander Gwagnin; he also re-edited Stanisław Orzechowski's *The Life and Death of Jan Tarnowski* (1773), and wrote two biographies, *The Life of Jan Zamoyski* (1775) and *The Life of Jerzy Ossoliński* (1777).

Literary fiction, the historical novel, and epic poems were also subordinated to the new historical consciousness. The epic, *Casimir the Great* by Julian Ursyn Niemcewicz, staged in 1792 to commemorate the anniversary of the Constitution of the Third of May, enjoyed great popularity. Earlier still, in 1777, Michał Mniszech dedicated a biography to Casimir the Great, who was considered a model of the just thrifty monarch. The production of Naruszewicz's *Casimir the Great* at the National Theatre became a patriotic manifestation, especially because of the scene in which Casimir the Great promises to defend the country and to implement reforms. Stanislaus Augustus was said to utter from the Royal Box the famous promise to fight for the independence of the state: "I'll stand up and take the risk."

Art went hand in hand with literature during this entire period. On the king's initiative, Marcello Bacciarelli embellished the Knights' Hall in the Royal Castle in Warsaw with huge paintings, depicting the military and political power, as well as the cultural brilliance of ancient Poland: *Granting Privileges to the Cracow Academy, The Union of Lublin,* and *Sobieski at Vienna.* For the same hall, Andreas Le Brun prepared bronze busts of eminent Poles. The Marble Room was embellished with a cycle of portraits of Polish kings.

HISTORICAL CULTURE

There were three features which were characteristic of historical culture during the Enlightenment in Poland: first, that the fate of individuals was linked with historical events; secondly, the great judgment passed on the national past; and thirdly, the frontiers of the past were transcended, opening up perspectives for the future.

Although during the Baroque period wars and defeats embraced the entire territory of the country and revealed to its inhabitants that the history of a nation determines the fate of individuals, during the Enlightenment this truth became an even more painful experience.

In the lyrical poetry of that epoch, the borderline between the personal and national fate disappeared. Joyfully and cynically, Kajetan Węgierski in the 1770's mused on his own life in *The Sad Remnants of the Fatherland.* Not only poets of "the heart", such as Franciszek Karpiński and Franciszek Dionizy Kniaźnin, but also representatives of the rationalistic current of the Enlightenment, like Ignacy Krasicki or Hugo Kołłątaj, expressed similar experiences. Even Stanisław Trembecki, courtier, and poet of the Targowica Confederacy, described "how the speedy news of sadness used to fly"; for the last years of his life he withdrew from the world, and lived alone and estranged from society.

The works of Ossian and Young, which were avidly read and commented on, made up the climate of the times. Ignacy Krasicki, the prince of the "enlightened" poets, master of the charm of life, translated Ossian's ballads. Franciszek Ksawery Dmochowski, the champion of classical poetry, author of *The Art of Writing Rhyme,* translated Young for, as he declared, "it's pleasant to cry with the crying Young."

The poetry of Young and Ossian was close to everyone who in their lyrics and patriotic elegies tried to express individual and national suffering. But these events did more than generate poetry of sadness and mourning. The cruelty of real fate would not submit itself to poetic effort. Above the world of poetry, in life itself, the linking of the nation's destiny to the fate of the individual was effected. It was to become a basic motif in the further development of Polish culture. The verdict of history, which destroyed the Polish state, also destroyed its best citizens. According to contemporary evidence, Adam Naruszewicz died because of the sorrow he felt for the country's misfortunes. Franciszek Karpiński retired from life and cleared the woods in the Białowieża wilderness together with the peasants. Franciszek Kniaźnin spent the last years of his life in madness; Franciszek Zabłocki withdrew from life and entered a monastery.

Trembecki also left the life of the court, dedicated himself to meditation, and finally lost all contact with the world: he was not even able to recognize his own verses when they were read to him.

The second feature of the historical consciousness of the Enlightenment was the steadily increasing conviction of the limitations of traditional historiography. The wisest people of the period perceived the painful and harmful limitations of that vision of the past. Thanks to them, the historical consciousness, which was maturing during this period, was a split one. A critical question was being raised: what, in fact, are we taught by history? Whose is this history which we generally regard as the only history of Poland?

Staszic tried to convince the gentry that they were not "the whole nation" but only one of its estates. From this point of view he differentiated between "noblemen's history", which told of triumphs of individual families, and the history still unwritten, the true history, which would expose the destiny of the entire nation and the road leading to the liberation of the oppressed groups. Such a history would prove the thesis that "the ruin of Poland came through the lords themselves."

Kołłątaj treated the historian's objectives in shaping the national consciousness in a similar way. He clearly recognized the two different concepts of history. The great program of historical research evolved by Kołłątaj after the partitions was to lead to a real history of the nation, which would show its intellectual, cultural, social, and economic development, and in particular the role played in the history of the nation by the peasantry, in whom, most profoundly and most lastingly, the national character was preserved. Kołłątaj promised to write "a second" history, that is, about the Poles who "pushed Poland into anarchy."

In this way, the historical culture of the Polish Enlightenment reached a level of development in which the knowledge of the national past was becoming a living and austere trial of its merits and errors; it compelled the nation to painful reflection. This dualism, which has survived until today, became a basic characteristic of the nation's consciousness.

The third particular characteristic of the historical consciousness of the period was the vision of Poland in the future. When reality was too small or too cruel, looking at the beautiful past did not encourage or provide the strength which was necessary to live in defeat. The dramatic nature of current events, however, opened horizons of the future as a field of hope. A new dimension of historical consciousness was shaped, which would be a great and important orientation of the nation, sometimes consistent with traditionalism as the foundation of a future victory of Poland, sometimes running against the past, with its faults and guilt.

This was the nature of *The Polish Bard,* written by Adam Jerzy Czartoryski in 1795, but published much later. The work presents a young poet, who is wandering about the devastated Polish land, meeting people who are crushed by the national tragedy. The Polish cause becomes a human cause, but above all, it is an affair between humanity and God, the ruler of the world. It may be resolved only in terms of faith and hope.

Faith in the future was not, however, the monopoly of religious people in this period. It was also expressed and explained by secular and radically-minded writers, for example, Franciszek Zabłocki.

The question of the future was most eloquently described by Jakub Jasiński, poet and Jacobin. Linking the fight for independence with that for social liberation, in his poems "To the Nation" and "To Polish Exultants on Constancy", he preached like a prophet "to listen to the bard's unerring admonition", to him who "reveals the destiny of humankind". That destiny will bring an end to fanaticism and despotism, and then "the golden age of freedom" will begin, when people will learn to honor their own dignity and will "topple thrones"; and "the family of men will be one of brothers".

Deliberations by scholars on the philosophy of history ran parallel with these poetic visions of the future. *Human Kind* by Staszic, a great work intended to answer the question of why Poland had perished, was written during this period. A major analysis in terms of the philosophy of history was required to answer this question — which would attempt to explain why humanity abandoned the road of universal bliss and how it would be able to return to it, making amends for the wrongs done to people by people and to nations by nations.

During this period, Hugo Kołłątaj also applied himself to the great problems of the historical development of mankind. This interest was shaped by the long years of his work to reform the state and its educational system, in disputes with conservatives who did not see historical differences between nations, especially with Seweryn Rzewuski, on the notion of liberty, and in reflections on methods of understanding man and society, which he occupied himself with after the downfall of the state.

But the main source of these considerations was in the Polish reality. The defeat of the state and the future of the nation were becoming an issue of universal history, the course and false turnings of which were to be discovered by science, revealing, as Staszic planned, the causes of mankind's deviation from the path of reason. Kołłątaj linked it with the great disaster of the "deluge", which "changed not only the surface of the earth, but man himself."

Man and the Forces of Production

REVIVAL OF THE ECONOMY
AND THE NEW ECONOMIC MENTALITY

The process of rebirth and reform which characterized the era of the Polish Enlightenment also affected the economy. The latter was in a state of decline, although under the Saxon dynasty attempts were often made to reform it. But it was not until the reign of Stanislaus Augustus that effective and consistent economic policies were pursued.

During this period there was a remarkable increase in the population, amounting to about 17 percent. Cities developed. In mid-century Warsaw had about 23,000 inhabitants; by 1792, its population had increased five-fold to about 110,000. The population in other cities also increased, but not so dramatically. Cracow, which in mid-century consisted of a few thousand inhabitants, increased to over 10,000; after the incorporation of the suburbs, the number reached about 30,000. Many cities and towns were just arising from the ruins wrought by the Northern War. Although in 1775/6, there were 858 towns in the Crown territories, of these 781 were really only large villages. But even the few dozen "real" cities was quite a large number. Great Poland was the most heavily urbanized; and the smallest number of towns was to be found in Kujavia, Mazovia, and the Białystok region. The growth of the cities was linked to the development of manufacturing, crafts, trade, and services. Despite various constraints, the cities were entering a period of development. Their increasing political consciousness was evidence of that. Staszic declared: "The burgher estate in Poland has already enlightened themselves to such a degree, that they feel that they are men."

Agriculture also developed considerably. The rural economy improved; crops increased. In fact, this was partly due to the greater rigors of corvée, but mostly to better methods of husbandry and to the policy of substituting money rents for the duties of serfdom. The acreage under cultivation also increased, in some regions of the country by up to 20 percent.

The growth in agricultural production was accompanied by that of industry. In Great Poland, by making use of old traditions, the textile and foodstuffs industries developed on a large scale. In Little Poland, the iron industry developed rapidly. The latter supplied 80 percent of the country's output of iron, while Great Poland provided 70 percent of the country's textile production.

Silesia, which remained outside the country's boundaries, but was linked by many economic bonds with the motherland, was also developing very quickly. In the late eighteenth century Silesia possessed 43 blast furnaces, more than in the entire Commonwealth. Iron and zinc mills were founded in Kluczbork and Tarnowskie Góry. In Wrocław, a sugar industry developed.

However, there were many obstacles which inhibited the development of industrialization. The social structure remained virtually feudal. Investment was scarce. The foreign trade balance was unfavorable. The trade agreements imposed by Prussia in 1775 were unfavorable to Poland and, to a great degree, limited the independence of her economic policy.

Despite these difficult conditions, Polish trade increased. Great quantities of corn and timber were exported through Gdańsk and other Baltic ports, and directly to Austria. The export trade through Królewiec and Szczecin also increased.

However, economic success was not the only factor of importance for the national consciousness. Of greater significance was the growing understanding of the economy as a national enterprise, and not only as a field of individual activity. This idea was new. Traditionally the gentry treated their economic activity as a private enterprise, for the sake of which they had to strive in order to gain adequate privileges. Of course, the period of the Enlightenment did not put an end to such convictions and claims, but created the foundations for an understanding that the economy also had social and national aims, that it had to serve "to make the nation happy."

This new view of the economy was close to the new concept of education. Education, considered traditionally as an individual good, shaped according to the private plans of parents for their children, was slowly becoming a public affair from the time of Stanisław Konarski and due to the reforms effected by the Commission for National Education. Education, serving individuals, had to implement national goals, had to serve the interests of the state by shaping young people into good citizens. Like the economy, it had to unify general and individual interests.

An exponent of these new economic concepts was the Lithuanian Treasurer, Antoni Tyzenhaus, who with unusual energy founded several dozen factories in the Grodno region. They employed about 3,000 people. Acclaimed by some, criticized by others, Tyzenhaus' initiative ended in bankruptcy; yet it constituted a characteristic example of the new mentality: production ceased to be solely a matter of physical effort but was becoming a matter of skill, technology, and organization. In the struggle against nature man stood armed with the weapons of his reason and of his mechanical tools.

The awareness of the significance of such power over nature also increased. Józef Osiński, in his book *The Description of Polish Iron Works* (1782), formulated the notion of conducting a minute study of these works, and at the same time, of further possibilities of their development, based on knowledge of the country's natural resources. Although this notion did not mean much for the backward economy of the country and although the process of utilizing technology in production was haphazardly being employed, it was nonetheless important for the national economic consciousness.

It opened up new perspectives in the field of formulation of goals for the national economy, in particular, of linking it with the advancement of science and technology, and concurrently created the basis for a new method of evaluating the merits of people from socio-economic points of view. In economic studies and political writings of the period, more and more often demands were voiced to break with the traditional scale of values, in which chivalry was placed first, followed by the traditional virtues of the landowners.

In this manner, the fight for a new model of life and activity was undertaken, though it proceeded with difficulty and embraced only a small section of society. Within the range of the existing and strong feudal system, based mainly on the work of the serfs, the seeds of a new attitude toward the economy were planted, championing

initiative, enterprise, hard work, investment risk-taking, and rational calculation. Next to the tradition of the nobleman-knight and nobleman-landowner a completely different model emerged, committed to industrial and commercial activity, which the Sarmatian tradition had condemned as disgraceful for a nobleman.

MEDICAL CARE AND PROTECTION OF THE WORKING MAN

With the change in views on the role of the economy in the process of "making the nation happy" and with changing attitudes toward work, Polish society discovered and developed respect for the biological value of man and understanding of how technological progress could improve and lighten his work. This was of fundamental consequence for the character of the culture of the Polish Enlightenment.

The medical sciences, which in former periods played only a small part in the organization of health services and in shaping more humanitarian notions about the condition of life and work of the oppressed classes, were now embarking on that social mission.

Cracow was becoming the main center for the theory and practice of medicine. Jędrzej Badurski, Kołłątaj's collaborator in the work of reforming the University, was one of the first physicians to direct his attention to the social tasks of medicine.

Similar ideas were propounded by his university colleague, the founder of Polish surgery, Rafał Józef Czerwiakowski. In his *Dissertation Concerning the Noble-mindedness, Necessity and Use of Surgery* (1791), he pointed out the social tasks of the surgeon during war and peace; he particularly underscored his duties in regard to the people.

In these various medical dissertations, an absolutely new problem was examined: the adaptation of the working man to machines and the protection of his health.

Wacław Sierakowski's book, *On Motors* (1799), was devoted to "preserving the health of those working with heavy loads", which bore witness to the close relations existing in the contemporary mind between technological progress and protection of the health and life of working men.

The rudiments of the modern problem of work safety were thus developing at this time: in awareness of the links between the health, strength, and skills of people on the one hand and their work, influenced to an ever greater degree by machines, on the other. The significance of technical training was perceived from this point of view. Hugo Kołłątaj, when reforming Cracow University, recommended that in towns where there were schools, lectures on mechanics should be organized for craftsmen. Kołłątaj's ideas found their way into the curriculum with difficulty, winning wider recognition only at the end of the century.

The usefulness of the medical sciences in technology was perceived, and also appreciated disinterestedly as proof of the greatness of man. The enlightened public displayed a passionate interest in electricity and its significance regarding health. Andrzej Trzciński, a professor at Cracow University, published a study on the subject, *Dissertation Concerning the Use of Electricity in Medicine* (1787). Air balloons were also fashionable. Stanisław Okraszewski, a year after the Montgolfier experiment, inaugurated similar experiments in Warsaw, several times launching an "aerostatic ball". In that same year several Cracow scholars, Jan Śniadecki among them, constructed a large balloon, which flew fairly high. Similar attempts were undertaken in smaller towns: Kamieniec, Pińczów, and Puławy, which Kniaźnin described in a special poem. The greatest sensation, however, was elicited by the balloon flight in Warsaw in 1788 by Jean Pierre Blanchard. The poetry of the period treated this event as a great triumph of human reason.

Social Unrest and National Integration

SITUATION OF THE PEASANTS AND ATTEMPTS AT REFORM

The peasantry constituted more than three quarters of the population of the Commonwealth. Although their material position was diverse, depending on local conditions, they were all deprived of basic civil and human rights. They were simply and solely "subjects", enslaved people, who could dispose neither of their own persons, nor their work, nor the earth they cultivated, nor their dwellings.

During the Enlightenment, some prospects for the improvement of the material standard of the peasantry were inherent in the policy of commutation, which substituted money rents for feudal dues and serfdom. The process of transformation of the traditional economy based on serfdom into a more modern one, based on money rents, moved slowly. In Great Poland about 30 percent of the peasants paid rents, but the rate was far less in other territories; for the entire country it amounted to barely 10 percent. Significantly, the mere fact of paying rent did not alter the material situation and social position of the peasant. It sometimes offered an opportunity for additional exploitation, wherever the rents were high. The increased demand for agricultural products encouraged the gentry to increase the amount of work and made discipline more rigorous.

The broad masses of the peasantry were thus living under the pressure of injustice and exploitation. This gloomy situation can be seen in the numerous peasant petitions, and is also confirmed, by the end of the century, in literature, and in documentary painting and drawings, especially by Norblin.

In peasant petitions, lamentations about wrongs and lawlessness, poverty and cruel penalties, recurred again and again. They pleaded: "In our troubles and afflictions, in which we groan as if in the yoke of slavery, deign to look into our matter with charity."

However, complaints were not the only weapon of the oppressed. Despair and anger were growing. Rebellions broke out time after time. They took different forms: from refusal to work, or a work slow-down, to escape, or even to organized resistance and rebellion. The most popular form was a partial or a complete refusal to carry out feudal duties. But in various parts of the Commonwealth, especially in Kurpie, Podlasie and the Cracow region, numerous demonstrations and armed fights occurred. In 1768 a great, bloody popular uprising began in the Ukraine. The Ukrainian peasant uprising of 1768 embraced the eastern marcher territories and its echo reverberated even into central Poland, especially into the region of the Carpathian foothills. The watchwords of the uprising included many themes: defense of the Orthodox religion, which had been supplanted by the Uniates and Catholics; defense of language and nationality; a social struggle for "breaking out of slavery and liberation from our yoke and burden."

The Polish peasants did not join in this revolutionary action. The Ukrainian uprising was suppressed after heavy fighting, but complete peace never returned to these lands. The events in the Ukraine were never erased from the national memory.

Hollow echoes of these events and sporadic acts of rebellion lasted uninterruptedly, especially in the marcher regions, manifesting themselves in restlessness and fear among the gentry, and mobilization of forces for revenge among the peasantry. These warnings reached the capital time and again, introducing an unexpected and harsh note in the atmosphere of the "enlightened society."

The peasant cause had, for a long time, been perceived in all its sharpness by politicians and political writers among the gentry. During the first half of the century, the author of *Free Voice* (probably not Leszczyński, but Mateusz Białłozor), and Stefan Garczyński in *Anatomy of the Polish Commonwealth*, spoke in defense of the peasant, as did the *Monitor*, the same periodical in which Ignacy Krasicki published his famous article, "They Cannot Love the Commonwealth Who Possess in It Nothing of Their Own". The *Monitor*, in 1767, published an article recalling Diderot's article in the *Encyclopédie*, asserting that "the mob has more sense than men of noble descent." In the following years, all progressive political writing in Poland remarked on the poverty of the peasants and the injustice which existed in varying measure throughout the different territories of the Commonwealth. There was scarcely a political article which did not criticize existing conditions and did not suggest reform. The greatest public acclaim was won by Józef Wybicki, who in his *Patriotic Letters* (1777—78) demanded an end to serfdom; and by Stanisław Staszic, who in his *Warnings to Poland* (1790), presented a shocking picture of the plight that was destroying "five parts of the Polish nation."

The general trend of the Enlightenment was humanitarian and from this point of view, the inhuman plight of the people was a source of unending qualms of conscience. But the proposal to educate the peasantry while retaining serfdom seemed to many writers, Staszic in particular, to suggest a special cruelty. The proposal to enfranchise them prior to educating them seemed dangerously revolutionary to the conservative gentry. An antinomy in the culture of the Enlightenment was emerging between the unlimited progress of reason and the limited possibility of educating the general public. Krasicki perceived it with unusual sharpness: "It is bliss to the nation when sciences flourish and scholars are venerated," but at the same time he felt that the "felicity and virtue" of the wide masses should be the overall objective; and that was still very far off.

A great dispute over the peasant question was going on in the press. A fundamental reform was suggested, which would bestow civil rights on the peasants, but on the other hand the feudal hierarchy of the community was also zealously defended. The creators of the Constitution of the Third of May were looking for a difficult compromise.

The Constitution of the Third of May did not use the word "serfdom", and declared that the peasantry should be taken "under the protection of the law and the government of the country" and encouraged a system of contracts with the peasants; yet personal freedom, as well as freedom to settle and to choose one's form of work, was reserved only for immigrants from abroad.

The Constitution did not put an end to serfdom, although contemporaries interpreted it in this way, thus stimulating hopes among the peasantry and vehement protests among the conservative gentry.

Boldly overstepping the limits of compromise in the Constitution of the Third of May, and despite the universal fears concerning peasant rebellion, Kosciuszko believed it was possible to win over the peasants to participate in the fight for independence, if only "the people feel that their estate will be happier in a Poland saved from bondage than if aliens were to rule over her."

These hopes were not in vain. On 4 April 1794, at Racławice, the attack of the scythebearers decided the victory. Racławice had since become a symbol of peasant patriotism and strength in the fight for the freedom of a country which had yet to become their real homeland.

Kosciuszko understood this perfectly and in his many messages he repeated the thought: "Let the peasants willingly take to arms not from compulsion but with a true feeling of improving their condition and with love for their common fatherland."

The Połaniec Proclamation, announced on 7 May 1794, declared that "the arms of their foes would never be fearsome to the Poles" if they would only "unify their hearts and minds," and, particularly, "abandon their inhuman treatment of the people." In this way only, according to Kosciuszko, would it be possible to "oppose a gang of scared slaves with a potent mass of free people, who fighting for their own happiness cannot fail to win."

It was for this reason that the Połaniec Proclamation guaranteed people "the protection of the government of the country", personal freedom, a reduced burden of feudal labor, and "ownership of the land in their possession", in the sense of protected occupation.

For the national consciousness, the most important element in the Proclamation was the proposition that "humanity, justice and the good of the homeland" ought to counteract "the ruse of domestic anger". That meant that "the oppressor and persecutor of the defenders of the country, would be punished as a foe and traitor to the homeland."

In this way, the traditional consciousness which divided people into gentry-lords and peasant-subjects was overcome. The line of division was to distinguish between those who defended the Commonwealth and belonged either to the gentry or people, and those who were indifferent or traitors to the country.

THE STRUGGLE OF THE CITIES FOR THEIR RIGHTS

From mid-century, despite the resistance of the conservative gentry, efforts were made to revive the towns. Mostly on the initiative of Warsaw, the towns decided to act together to bring about new conditions for the urban economy and a new position for burghers in society. They understood the political nature of such a collective manifestation (Cracow refused to participate), but they explained that it was reasonable and cautious, emphasizing that they were united by "a gentle link, far from being rebellious." The manifestation was important, and the black dress of the delegation who handed a written Memorial to the king, served to underscore its dramatic significance: "The slave tears violently at his bonds, wherever his sovereign stifles all rights of the citizen and man."

Political writing supported the demands of the burghers. In papers, books, and pamphlets, arguments were presented, and the most urgent tasks were discussed. The slogan of Stanisław Staszic became a battle-cry: "Make one nation of the gentry and city youth."

However, the implementation of the program of improvement was difficult, not only because it was necessary to infringe upon the rights and privileges of the gentry and hit at the ambition and pride of the class which autocratically ruled in Poland, but also because the program presumed new concepts of life and culture, demanded the acceptance of the new values and ideals, which went contrary to the landowner-knight tradition and thus endangered the very foundations of the Commonwealth of the Gentry.

The struggle for these ideals was only beginning.

THE SITUATION OF THE GENTRY

The gentry as a whole, although to a great extent dependent on the magnates, steadily emphasized their significance in the state, through their political power and their historical mission. In words full of exaltation, these watchwords and principles were on every occasion reiterated. The Constitution of the Third of May ceremoniously confirmed them, by acknowledging "all freedoms, liberties, prerogatives, and priorities in public and private life due to the estate of the gentry." The priciple of the "equality of all gentry" was also emphasized.

Reality, however, was fairly remote from the ideological image. After the first partition, fewer than half (i.e., 300,000) of the gentry owned landed estates which could provide them with a livelihood. About 400,000 belonged to the minor or landless gentry; they possessed the remnants of previously large estates or lived at the magnate courts, allowing themselves to be employed by the aristocracy or wealthier gentry.

Under these circumstances, the declaration of equality which was widely disseminated, particularly in the Seym or local diets, masked the true situation. In this way, tendencies to blindness and delusions, characteristic of the national consciousness, were generated in order to facilitate the acceptance of meaningless words which were considered unusually important.

These ambivalent feelings of the poor gentry against the magnates were taken advantage of on various occasions and for various reasons.

This line of opposition to the upper class was not singular. The threat from the peasants and burghers was increasing, though it carried varied dangers for different groups of the gentry. The landed gentry was directly threatened; to the gentry who had lost their land but retained only their coats-of-arms, the danger of peasant revolt was not so terrible, although it always remained menacing and censurable.

Relations with the burghers were different. The wealthy gentry did not hesitate to enter into commercial contacts with the burghers. But the poor gentry, having no possibilities in this field, stubbornly defended the ancient order, according to which the trading professions were not allowed social intercourse with the élite. When the good of the country demanded the development of industry, trade, and crafts, it was considered a barrier which while honorable, was out of date and difficult to overcome. The conservative gentry stubbornly defended the principle that a nobleman should not dabble in industry and trade, nor burghers achieve the status of noblemen.

Numerous and passionate discussions were conducted on this topic. The progressive gentry actively tried to overcome the traditional dogmas and to create a modern consciousness for which work and the fruits of work, not descent or coats-of-arms, ought to decide the model of life and human relations. An entire century was to pass before the noblemen's concept of life would lose its influence: only the positivist attack would victoriously end the conflict in the last quarter of the nineteenth century.

Within the burgher-gentry conflicts, a special place was reserved for the Jewish population. Jews sometimes constituted a high percentage of city dwellers and were among the city's poor inhabitants, but they were also among the wealthy urban patricians. Both groups — rich and poor — had a common religion, which marked them as a closed community from the Christians, both Catholics and dissenters.

During the eighteenth century, the problem of the integration of the Jewish population with the rest of society appeared more sharply than at any time before.

Assimilation was not difficult for the wealthy class, although these processes were not willingly accepted by the conservative gentry, who opposed the political and social emancipation of the burghers in general. Yet it was almost impossible for the poor Jewry, who were fanatically attached to their religion, language, and customs. Progressive political writers welcomed the possibility of overcoming the isolation of that part of the population, and of creating for them conditions of equal civic rights. Their action brought favorable results, although, among the orthodox Jews and among the conservative gentry, unwillingness to accept the program of integration lasted for a long time.

The tradition, enhanced especially during the Baroque period, which identified being Polish with Catholicism also became an obstacle in the efforts to resolve the political problems of the dissenters who inhabited Poland. A fairly large group of Protestants lived in Poland, particularly in the northern parts of the country; and in the East, there were even more numerous groups of adherents of the Eastern Orthodox Church. Prussia and Russia willingly undertook the protection of these inhabitants of Poland which aroused additional resentment from the gentry toward them. It seemed that national interests were endangered by this foreign intervention and that it was necessary, despite the existence in many circles of the idea of tolerance and religious good-will, to oppose granting political equality to the dissenters. This resistance was successfully broken and a compromise was effected; the political coexistence of Catholics with non-Catholics was implemented in stages, although in the social consciousness of some groups of the gentry, there still remained the conviction that only a Catholic could be a "real" Pole. Some residue of distress and distrust still remained in these groups and would only subside, together with many other similar social attitudes, during the nineteenth century.

A MENACING REVOLUTION BUT DESIRED

Class conflicts and social struggles in Poland during the Enlightenment were not factors contributing to the disintegration of the nation, but a source of a new understanding. The point of departure for this difficult and meandering evolution consisted of a defense of the existing feudal system in which the gentry estate had all the political power, and enjoyed all the rights which guaranteed individual freedom and property ownership, together with many economic privileges. The conservative faction which sanctioned this state of affairs, always spoke of the military merits of their ancestors and the contemporary duties of the gentry in the defense of the state.

But these arguments were losing ground under the blows which the neighboring powers were applying to the Commonwealth of the Gentry. The growth of social tension which was going on simultaneously and the ever more visible manifestation of the strength of the peasantry and the burghers made critical reflection all the more necessary. Progressive political writing repeatedly stressed the need for a breakthrough within the unbending feudal system of concepts, principles and reality.

Staszic, with his characteristic powers of persuasion, turned to the "most honest estate of the gentry with an appeal that they at last understand that they are not the whole nation, but only one of its estates."

Kołłątaj agreed with this judgment. Treating ownership as "a primary precondition to influence the government", he felt that "only two estates, that is, the landed gentry and the wealthy burghers, should constitute the majesty of the government". He also foresaw the participation of the contemporary intelligentsia — teachers, civil servants, and the clergy. The peasants were not to possess political rights, but were to gain human rights. But this moderate and compromising social solidarity did not satisfy adherents of radical views and those growing more radical in the course of political developments. Franciszek Salezy Jezierski drew the following radical conclusion based on his observations: "What was above will be below, what was below will be above." Further, he stated: "Common people should be called the first estate in the nation, or speaking more clearly, the complete nation," for they not only give the whole community their work, but also "maintain the national character," which members of the upper classes often betray.

This revolutionary radicalism, which was the declaration of political faith by a small but active group of Polish Jacobins, did not become a program of political action, but very strongly influenced the new image of the nation at the decline of the Poland of Stanislaus Augustus.

During the Kosciuszko Insurrection, the Department of Education, which continued in a more radical way the work of the Commission for National Education, described the nature of the insurrection in the following way: "This is not an uprising of merely one class, seeking by these means to increase its prerogatives and privileges at the expense of other classes; but this is a holy uprising of the entire mass of Polish people."

The idea of a "holy uprising", of an insurrection of "the people and the nation" would soon become the great historical watchword, and at the same time, the great political problem of a nation descending into bondage.

Reform of the State

FIRST REFORMS AND THE MENTALITY OF THE BAR CONFEDERACY

The problem of reforming the Commonwealth, first raised in the sixteenth century by Modrzewski, remained constantly in the social consciousness of the nation, always distressing and unresolved, always disputed.

Only on the accession to the throne of Stanislaus Augustus did the possibility of implementing the various programs of reform open up. For the first time since the Renaissance, the problem of reforming the Commonwealth was becoming not only a subject for satirical writers and moralists, but also a task for

politicians who dealt with it with varying degrees of success. The Age of Enlightenment was an age of political reforms, and therefore, constituted a profound breakthrough in the national consciousness. It proved that society was not only capable of critically evaluating the reality it was living in, but also of remodeling it.

The first steps of the new king were watched with distrust by the conservative camp, especially the old aristocracy, who grew anxious of their position in a state which was to be reformed by a monarch who enthusiastically endorsed the English model of government. Gossip was circulating that the king not only wanted to "free the peasants" but to create "a confederation of the peasantry." These fears seem to have lasted a long time, since, as late as 1789, Seweryn Rzewuski cautioned that the king might "stir rebellion among the subjects in order to defeat the gentry, subjugate that estate with the help of the peasant estate," and then put "the yoke on the shoulders of both."

The plans of the king were far from a revolution in society or absolutism. He aimed at the improvement of the Commonwealth to the degree which he considered possible under prevailing political conditions and in a country hostile to all reform. Thus, he was striving for the improvement of public administration and for the re-education of society.

This, however, was by no means clear to everyone. On the contrary, the reforms inaugurated became a challenge to the traditionalists, who were opposed to all change and hostile to foreign influence at the royal court. An expression of this protest was the Bar Confederacy.

The Bar Confederacy was not only an event in Polish political history, but became an important and characteristic element of the national consciousness at the end of the eighteenth century, and even later, during the period of the partitions.

Organized at Bar, on the Turkish border, it appealed in its manifesto, published on 20 February 1768, "to save the homeland, faith and freedom, rights and liberties of the nation, which were deteriorating." The manifesto was written in a traditionally exalted style, which became a model for the future.

It expressed attachment to the Catholic faith, and the Church, and especially to "the Częstochowa fortress, famed for its miracles", and for the recognition of traditional liberties and old laws of the Commonwealth.

The manifesto called for armed action, bold and self-sacrificing, conducted under the watchword "Jesus-Mary."

In the name of these principles, the confederates launched a war against Russian troops in Poland, attempted to abduct the king, and established many contacts with foreign powers. They also tried to appeal to Slav solidarity and gain the support of the Russians in a common fight. At the same time, they sought understanding with Krim Girej, leader of the Tartars, and with Turkey. The program of the Confederacy was never precisely defined. Within the Confederacy many quite different elements had come together; patriotic resistance to czarist intervention, an attachment to gentry liberties, an open hostility to the program of progressive reforms sponsored by the king, and a zealous piety and Catholic fanaticism. This religious element was particularly strongly emphasized.

The political ideology of the confederates was conservative, in the sense that they wanted to defend the political privileges of the gentry and appealed to the "wisdom of their ancestors." But at the same time, their criticism of absolutism gave them an apparently modern character and elicited the sympathetic cooperation of eminent political writers in the West, known for their critical attitude to absolutist power. Appealing to this group, they expected support for their system of Polish political liberties. Their expectations were satisfied. The ancient Polish system seemed, especially to Rousseau, laudatory, since liberties were based on virtue and on the patriotic community of the citizens. The Confederacy was also acclaimed in Poland because it inaugurated an armed struggle for the integrity and independence of the endangered country. Because of this, within the ranks of the Confederacy, there were a great number of young people; Casimir Pulaski, one of the chief leaders of the Confederacy, was only thirty. In connection with the Confederacy, young people in Cracow organized the first Polish student conspiracy.

Despite patriotic zeal, the Confederacy had little military success. The hope of enlisting foreign aid proved futile. The confederate action ended in defeat.

The Bar Confederacy lost both on the battlefield and in diplomacy, but its defeats did not give rise to accusations or oblivion. On the contrary, the Bar Confederacy came to be thought of in Poland as the first legion of desperados in Polish history whose bravery and recklessness were considered patriotic virtues. In the national consciousness this defeat was worthy of the highest acclaim. Rousseau was one of the first writers and politicians who created the foundations for the legend that "the Bar Confederacy, in dying, rescued the homeland."

After the defeat, the confederates dispersed. Some left the country. This was the first compulsory emigration in Poland's history. And for the first time, members of this emigration claimed for themselves the exclusive right to represent the nation and pronounce verdicts on the community inside Poland.

Some of the confederates in foreign lands, for example, Casimir Pulaski, inaugurated the struggle for the liberation of other nations. It was the first struggle in Polish history for the as yet unknown slogan — "For your freedom and ours."

NEW POLITICAL CONSCIOUSNESS: THE CONSTITUTION OF THE THIRD OF MAY

The protest of the Bar Confederacy did not impede the process of reforms conducted by the royal camp, or the projects formulated in intensive political discussions. In 1773, the Commission for National Education was appointed by an act of the Seym and endowed with various estates formerly belonging to the Jesuits; it was instructed to conduct a basic reform of the educational system. The activity of the Commission, as well as lively polemics concerning curricula and textbooks, constituted an important factor contributing to change in the field of national consciousness in both general philosophy of life and the manner of understanding the duties of the citizen. In 1775, a Perpetual Council was formed, composed of 18 senators and 18 deputies, which was to act as the highest instance of political and administrative power between sessions of the Seym. The Council was presided over by the king. In this way, significant continuity of authority was established and the operation of the state apparatus was strengthened. To the public at large, the Council was proof of the "presence" of the state in the everyday life of the community. Bacause of this, it was treated with distrust by the conservative camp who saw in it a veiled form of absolutism.

The next stage of these reforms was to be the codification of laws valid in Poland and an end to the chaos which existed in this field, the main source of injustice and lawlessness. The act of the Seym of 1776 entrusted this task to Andrzej Zamoyski.

The following collaborated in this codification: Józef Wybicki, Joachim Chreptowicz, and Michał Węgrzecki. Józef Wybicki explained the principles of the new legislation in his *Patriotic Letters*. Zamoyski and his team however moved noticeably farther. The draft codex introduced a variety of progressive changes, although for tactical reasons it referred to the legislation of Casimir the Great and John Albert. The conservative gentry violently attacked the project. The Seym of 1780 rejected it almost unanimously. In spite of the defeat, work on the project and its editing became an important link in the crystallization of modern concepts in the field of general civil rights and of a general critique of the ruling magnate and gentry customs.

The anti-magnate and patriotic program of action, despite the difficulties that were encountered in its implementation, made headway during the 1880's. A new generation began to enter the arena of public life, a generation brought up in a school system reformed by Stanisław Konarski, better educated, aware of new movements and ideas. Within the ranks of the gentry, a camp began to form in which attachment to ancient Polish traditions, as well as hostility to foreign fashions remained, but which differed more and more from conservative Sarmatism. Simultaneously, the burghers, fighting for economic and political rights, not only exposed the dark sides of prevailing conditions, but also suggested methods of amending them, which could have been implemented if the gentry had understood the new situation of the state and their new tasks.

The Seym convened in Warsaw in 1788: it was later to be called the Four Year Seym, because it sat for this period of time. The Seym instigated a basic review of the state of affairs in the country and enacted fundamental directives for its improvement. Polish reality, for the first time, became exposed in public debate, and not only in satires and political writing, as had been the case earlier. The penury of the state treasury was exposed, and 120 efforts to repair the situation were made. Indeed, the tax burdens in Poland were up to twenty times lighter than in other European countries, and thirty times lighter than in England and the Netherlands. The financial reconstruction of the state was not an easy task, the more so because the fundamental obstacle was the egoism and life-style of the wealthiest sector of society.

The military weakness of Poland was perceived, particularly in comparison with Poland's neighbors. The Prussian army was some ten times the size of the Polish army. People consoled themselves, it is true, with the fact that the mass levy could raise around 200,000 men, but this was a myth rather than reality. A Seym act of 1788 prescribed an army of 100,000, which constituted one percent of the population. But even between the years 1788 and 1790, Polish military expenditure amounted to less than half of Prussian expenditure, one sixth of Austrian and one eighth of Russian expenditure.

All the ideological prejudices inherent in the general consciousness, which inhibited implementation of political reforms, were brought into relief: superficial traditionalism, the megalomania of the gentry which pointed to the feudal system as a model for the society of the future, the egoism and private interests identified with freedom, the treatment of the power of the state in categories of absolutism, or even despotism, and the Commonwealth as a collection of feudal landed estates.

Kołłątaj was perfectly aware of this obstacle, when he defined the goal of political writing as "the abolition in the human psyche of the view of the Commonwealth as the private property of the gentry."

At last, on 5 August 1790, the Seym was presented with an outline of the new constitution. It aroused vehement opposition. But the patriotic party acted consistently and systematically. On 24 March 1791, a law on local diets was enacted, which abolished the political rights of the landless gentry and thus limited the influence of the magnates on which the masses of the landless gentry were dependent. On 18 April 1791, the law on royal boroughs was passed. Two weeks later, owing to their use of the element of surprise, the Seym adopted the Constitution of the Third of May. Only one third of the deputies participated in the session; armed troops secured order; the Warsaw mob was mobilized. The Constitution was adopted by acclamation.

It was a great triumph for the patriotic and progressive forces, a great success for the king, a great achievement, as we would say today, of "pressure groups", which manifested their will in the streets of Warsaw and in front of the Royal Castle. It was a great day for Polish history, because the Constitution, despite all the compromises it contained, constituted a magnificent expression of new principles for political order. It was the second progressive and modern act of legislation ever to be enacted after the American Constitution; and on the European continent it was the first. To the national consciousness it became evidence of the force of revival, which the community of a state systematically being destroyed by its neighbors was able to produce. Accepted by the Seym by way of a kind of *coup d'état*, it was not so alien to the community as one would assume from the method of its enactment. This was evidenced by the fact that in February 1792, a majority of the local diets accepted the Constitution.

Under the protection of Russia, the magnates and gentry who were opposed to the program of reform organized a confederacy in St. Petersburg on 27 April 1792, the manifesto of which was then announced at Targowica, a small border town. The Targowica Confederacy annulled the laws of the Four Year Seym which "broke cardinal laws, swept away all the liberties of the gentry . . . established a new form of government with the help of burghers, soldiers, and lancers." The Manifesto attacked everyone who "was spreading democratic projects far and wide" and following "the example of unfortunate Paris." The leaders of the Confederacy applied for armed assistance to the Empress of Russia, Catherine II.

The intervention of Targowica and Russia met with resistance. War broke out. In his Message to the Troops of Both Nations of 25 May 1792, Stanislaus Augustus wrote: "Your common father, king and commander, gives you the signal to fight forever. Children, either we live independent and esteemed, or let us all die with honor."

The Polish troops, fighting in defense of the Constitution and the country, were a young, modern army. There was a good officers corps, trained in the Knights' School; their command rested with young generals, Prince Joseph Poniatowski, Szymon Zabiełło, and Thaddeus Kosciuszko. The cooperation of arms, especially between the artillery and the cavalry, and their patriotic zeal, allowed them to win local victories, at Zieleńce, Chełm, Dubienka, and Zelwa. During these difficult and heroic battles, the Virtuti Militari order, which to the present day remains the highest military decoration, was instituted.

PATRIOTISM AND REVOLUTION

In this struggle for the defense of the Constitution and independence of the country, one more ideological current crystallized, characteristic of the Polish Enlightenment and significant for the future. It was linked with the radical faction of the patriotic camp, with the "Polish Jacobins". They had a social base among the intelligentsia — writers, poets, journalists, and actors — as well as among a certain part of the city dwellers, especially in Warsaw.

On the day that the Constitution of the Third of May was passed, the "mob" demonstrated in the market-place and streets of the Old Town in Warsaw, as well as in the gallery of the Seym. In July 1792, the news spread that the king had joined the Targowica Confederacy, which aroused the mob who manifested, "in the Parisian manner", against the king. On the second anniversary of the Constitution, in 1793, a great manifestation again took place. In the spring of 1794, at the end of April and at the beginning of May, "free people gathered" and "orators" uttered revolutionary slogans. Jan Kiliński, as "leader of the people", organized the masses and drew up petitions. They were curt and harsh: "The people ask and demand

and command" that weapons be distributed and that armed action be taken, and that the "punishment of the traitors to the homeland be begun." News arriving from Vilna confirmed that "a mob was arming" and encouraged increased action. On 8 and 9 May, manifestations gained in strength; there were shouts of "Vivat revolution!." Under pressure of the people, the criminal court pronounced a death sentence on the Targowica confederates. On 27 and 28 June, the people started to punish the conspirators, hanging without trial those considered villains and traitors.

This action aroused numerous protests and perturbed even many a radical activist, Kosciuszko included. Yet Franciszek Ksawery Dmochowski justified the events: "In the history of every nation one can find examples where the people themselves meted out justice to the guilty." In numerous occasional verses, the wisdom and courage of the people was praised and traitors were attacked.

The events were characteristic evidence of not only the ripening of the class struggle between gentry and burghers, but also of the awakening among the radical sectors of the city inhabitants of a feeling of responsibility for the plight of the nation as a whole. Dramatic scenes of judgment in which the "traitors" were duly tried, occurred in the name of the interests of the homeland; and in the market-place of the Old Town in Warsaw, according to an eyewitness, "throngs, referred to as patriotic, gathered day after day, to debate the destiny of the country and to make plans."

Under these conditions there emerged an absolutely new, plebeian and revolutionary national consciousness. The subsequent course of political events put an end to it at the very moment of its birth. But later generations would return to these sources.

PATRIOTISM OF THE ENTIRE NATION: THE KOSCIUSZKO INSURRECTION

However, it was not the action of Polish Jacobins, but the Kosciuszko Insurrection that became the most important act of courage and hope for the whole nation in the years when the Commonwealth of the Gentry, but not Poland, was dying.

The term, "the entire nation", has a geographic as well as a social connotation. The insurrection started with the oath of Kosciuszko in the Cracow market-place on 24 March 1794, and stretched to all of the Commonwealth, to Vilna and Warsaw, Great Poland, and the Lublin region. It also aroused enthusiasm in former Polish lands, in Silesia and the Opole region, as well as in the territories lost during the first partition, in Warmia and Mazuria.

In a social sense, the insurrection was an act encompassing all segments of the nation.

Poland proved itself able to take organized armed action; the army was winning victories. The battle of Racławice and the charge of the scythebearers aroused hopes throughout the country. At the same time, the Kosciuszko Insurrection marked a great program of social reform: it pointed out to the peasants that the

armed struggle for independence could lead to "the improvement of their plight," that they would be "incomparably happier in a Poland rescued from captivity than under foreign rule."

How important and urgent was the matter of a modern definition of the concept of patriotism can be discerned in a pamphlet published in 1794 under the title, *What Does It Mean to Be a True Patriot?* Its author, probably one of Kołłątaj's collaborators, made the distinction between a "true" and a "false" patriot, stressing the necessity to oppose traitors and "indifferent" people, people making bombastic statements about the homeland, and chastising people who masked their treachery with lofty slogans. In contrast to these, "a spirit of true patriotism links people to people, does not differentiate between the estates," and acts disinterestedly "for the sake of the homeland, for the sake of the people." This description drew a line between the newly defined patriotism and the patriotism of the gentry, even when the latter was understood as traditional chivalrous service for the benefit of the Commonwealth, and gave it a progressive and revolutionary character as opposed to the feudal system. The Kosciuszko Insurrection carried into effect this new type of patriotism.

And although it suffered a defeat on the battlefield, this patriotism — for the sake of the homeland, for the sake of the people — proved to be a lasting victory of the Kosciuszko Insurrection. It was also a great contribution by Poland to the struggles for freedom in Europe, because it held up the Prussian army and thus prevented the latter's attack against revolutionary France.

View of the World

FREEDOM AND THE WORLD

Philosophy did not constitute the most important page in the history of the Polish Enlightenment. It so happened that the most significant, and virtually unique, philosophical works of the men of the period — Staszic, Kołłątaj, and the Śniadeckis — appeared only at the beginning of the nineteenth century, long after the chronological end of the Enlightenment, although a remarkable portion of their scientific and journalistic activity coincided with the period of the Commonwealth. However, in view of their origins and nature, these works belong to the culture of the Enlightenment. They were a significant element, sometimes even a great achievement, of Polish philosophical thinking.

Yet the fact that they appeared in print so late meant that they were unable to play a part in shaping the intellectual culture of the last decades of the Commonwealth. This fact had a negative influence on the period, which, for the most part, was marked by bitter and superficial polemics between the defenders of traditional religious concepts and the pioneers of a new science and a new philosophy. In these polemics, however, there appeared, slowly and not always consciously, a series of views regarding the world and life, which was characteristic of the Polish Enlightenment.

They expressed the view that all reality, natural and social, is bound by uniform laws, that these laws might be learned by men. Due to the knowledge of these laws, rational and useful activity becomes possible, which in turn leads to social progress and happiness of mankind. This rational and empirical method was to lead to knowledge and understanding, the main value of which was utilitarian; optimistic trust in the ever-increasing success in the future was a characteristic feature of these concepts.

In reference to Locke, whose *Essay Concerning Human Understanding* had been translated in 1784, and thanks to Condillac's logic, already introduced to the schools, and to the growing knowledge of modern natural sciences (*Epoques de la Nature* by Buffon was translated and praised in the introduction by Staszic in 1786) and to the mathematical and physical sciences, a new vision of the world was emerging. It was believed to be so strict that it was suggested that it be called science, rather than philosophy. One of the professors of Cracow University, Andrzej Trzciński, in his study, *A Dissertation on the Increase of Lights Through the Spirit of Observation and Experience* (1791) wrote: "The eighteenth century has already moved to the point of enlightenment and skills where it has freed philosophers from being philosophers and turned them into physicists."

Staszic was especially fascinated by the thesis of a monistic system of the universe and the uniform character of the laws governing all phenomena. He wanted to include in one chain of evolution all the transformations of the earth, the development of living creatures and the changes in human societies, although he was aware of how difficult it was "to comprehend" such a theory. This theory, however, was the basis of his socio-political directives propounded in *Warnings to Poland,* which were the "consequences of the laws of nature", and of his great historiosophical concepts, developed in his *Human Kind;* he returned to them again in his great study *On the Geology of the Carpathian Mountains.*

So did Kołłątaj. He was assured that "all beings are bound by general laws, as if by a chain which connects all things into one order." This "chain of beings" is divided into three great groups: inorganic bodies, vegetables, and animals (man is also included among animals). Yet man belongs, to a certain extent, to the remaining two links of existence as well: his body is composed of the elements of "earth", and the "living organization" of that body is similar to vegetables. Because of this, man, subject to laws proper to his being, is also subject to those biological and physical laws to which all living creatures and the entire material world are subject. These "laws common to all beings" and the "particular laws" are "the steady, unchangeable and necessary rules, according to which every being supports itself according to its existence."

On this basis, Kołłątaj erected his theory of a "physical and moral order", as well as his great historical and philosophical concept, in which the deluge was treated as a turning point in the evolution of mankind.

These problems concerning the uniformity of existence were also of interest to Jędrzej Śniadecki. In his well-known *Theory of Organic Beings* (volume I, published in 1804; volume II, as late as 1811), he occupied himself with the organization of living creatures at various levels of their evolution. He also analyzed the possibilities of the birth of life from inorganic matter.

These monistic and deterministic views constituted a novelty in the development of Polish culture, which in the social mind, shaped throughout centuries by religious education, created distressing and difficult issues. The concept of God as creator and protector of the world was adumbrated.

In the light of these new scientific concepts, belief in Providence was unacceptable. All that occurred on earth had to be explained by earthly causes: good as well as evil. "Men are the sole cause of their misfortune," preached Staszic. It was human reason, according to Kołłątaj, that achieved success in the fight with despotism and fanaticism. Political writing and poetry taught the same truth about independence and responsibility.

More complex was the issue of God as creator. Although deistic concepts, both English and French, were fairly well known in Poland, their interpretation was always a delicate and vague matter.

Nobody dared to cross the line between deism and atheism, although Catholic polemicists defining the steps leading to atheism often mentioned deism as the most dangerous doctrine of all. Not even Staszic or Kołłątaj, most advanced in their critical studies on religion, dared to go further. They were both more involved in the issue of the social role of religion in history. And both wanted to arouse in people the courage to act independently and rationally.

Within these perspectives, the metaphysical issue, whether God exists or not and how the First Cause should be interpreted, that is transcendentally or immanently, did not seem particularly important.

To Polish thinkers of the era "the hypothesis of God" — to use the classical term — was not necessary for analysis of and reconstruction of the social world. This switch of the focal point of philosophical considerations from metaphysics to the theory of human social activity — rational, just, responsible — was the most important feature of the view of the world taking shape in Poland during the period of the Enlightenment.

THE PHILOSOPHY OF HISTORY

The drive to move universal problems from a metaphysical plane to a historical perspective became ever more pronounced in the course of the development of political events which were increasingly endangering the safety of the Commonwealth. Staszic explicitly stated: "Man is not born to metaphysics." And he felt adamantly that the improvement of the social life of all nations and of mankind was the main task of the people who should understand that "men are the sole cause of their misfortune." These considerations and theses were brought to fruition in his *Human Kind,* the most distinguished philosophical work of the period.

This work belonged to the great family of historiosophical studies which appeared in Europe during the Enlightenment. It expressed the same belief in progress: but the "injustices", which were the point of departure in Staszic's reflections, directed it along different and peculiar lines. More clearly than anyone else during the Enlightenment, Staszic perceived the class structure of society, based on the unequal possession of property. And more sharply than other writers, he presented the fight of the oppressed with their oppressors. In this fight, the churches stood on the side of those who had power and wealth. Science on the other hand was made use of in various ways: it sometimes served oppression; sometimes it became the weapon of those who fought for their own rights. Staszic understood progress in categories of struggle and the "revolt of the people", in the perspective of hope that "the mob", liberated from oppression, would open the way to the advancement of science and the dissemination of education. In such terms, progress was a result rather than a cause of social change. Staszic did not share the illusion, prevalent during the Enlightenment, that the advancement of science and education would bring, by itself, justice and universal happiness to all. Staszic's philosophy was much more realistic and dramatic; he thought that the struggle of the oppressed had been and would be a driving force in history, a source of progress.

In this victorious fight, a moral renaissance of the people would be effected. In feudal societies, according to Staszic, and in those which had emerged from feudalism but had not overcome it, conditions were unfavorable for the "moralization of the People." Where violence and oppression reign, where injustice rules, and the wealth of one class is paid for by the poverty of others, envy and anger, greed and hatred, indifference and hypocrisy will emerge. But under a just social system, the sources of immorality will be eradicated; the people, freed from the bonds of poverty and degradation, will acquire a "moral sensitivity". Education then will be able to realize its aims.

The concept of "natural laws", to which Kołłątaj together with the entire age of the Enlightenment adhered, did not supply adequate answers. It permitted the construction of an ideal model of society and radical criticism of relations contrary to such a model, rather than an understanding of the concrete socio-political situation, of necessary and possible programs of action, and the mechanisms of progressive and reactionary forces. Kołłątaj, who all his life was engulfed in "political works", sought a philosophy that would permit the interpretation of concrete situations. History, according to Kołłątaj, ought to become the tool of such a philosophy.

"History cannot uncover the first principles of the laws of nature; but the stages by which the human community has been perfected, the causes of the errors by which men have arrived at such a state of society — these can be discovered nowhere else than in properly understood history." Such a history, according to Kołłątaj, would show the development of human needs, both "natural, on which the preservation of our existence depends" and those which men acquire through social development. Such a history will teach how an inevitable course of events can be linked with human liberty and responsibility. Such a history will also be able to show "why some nations have grown to be giants, while others remain dwarfs, although their growth began at the same time."

In this way, Kołłątaj was forming a synthesis of a rationalistic concept of the law of nature, which had been preached by many philosophers and writers of the Enlightenment, especially by the physiocrats, and of historicism as a method of anthropological and social research, as a philosophy of self-knowledge among men resulting from their historical action, which as a whole constituted their "human" reality. It opened up perspectives for subsequent romantic historicism, and for materialistic interpretations of the "sum of human actions," which made possible satisfaction of growing human needs.

THE ETHICS OF JUSTICE AND HUMANITY

The philosophical concept of society and of history found its last outlet in pedagogical theory and practice, in which, incidentally, experience was attained regarding what man is and what the philosophy of man and society should be. This link developed with the passing of time: the foundation of the Commission for National Education and its program were the result of the "new philosophy"; while at the turn of the century, pedagogical experiences were becoming a point of departure for philosophical deliberations, as witnessed by Staszic's activity.

In the great debate in the Seym of 1773 concerning the aims of education, Feliks Oraczewski, rector of the Main School, asserted that "we need to make Poles of the people, and citizens of the Poles." This formula constituted a program of patriotic and, at the same time, humanitarian education. The program was implemented by the Commission for National Education, in its attempt to modernize civic education. In reference to Konarski's reform, to practices applied in the Knights' School, the Commission developed new curricula for education and prepared new textbooks of "moral science", which was to be simultaneously the science of civics: "It is impossible," the Commission argued, "to exclude political duties from moral science. Because we are all sons of our homeland and members of the social union, everyone should know what duty is expected of him." Acting in this manner (the Commission's textbooks were hotly disputed and attacked by the conservative camp), the Commission inspired a more profound, a more theoretical reflection on the issue of man and his conduct in society.

These ideas had earlier been inaugurated by Stanisław Konarski in his study, *De Viro Honeste et Bone Cive* (1754), in his collection, *Dialogues Interesting and Useful,* in *Philosophical and Political Matters* (in three volumes, 1760—62), but particularly in his widely disputed dissertation, *On the Religion of Decent People* (1769). In whatever way Konarski's views concerning the relation of morality to religion might be interpreted, it is certain that during the Enlightenment Konarski introduced the category of "decent people" as one more deserving of theoretical and practical application.

Traditionalists defended the thesis that morality must be based in religion; the progressive camp focused attention on the ideal of "decent people". The cadet officers' Moral Catechism, drawn up in 1769 by Adam Czartoryski and often reprinted, had such a secular character. The juxtaposition of the word "Catechism" in its title with the definition "Cadet Officers" was provocative. In the contents of the questions and replies, social and political issues prevailed. Knowledge and honor were to characterize the cadet officers, who were called upon to serve their homeland, to "liberate her from those two horrible tyrants — ignorance and superstition" — and "to populate her with citizens anxious about her fame, about the enlargement of her inner might and outside esteem, and about the improvement of her administration, the worst of its kind."

Similar ideology was evolved in the textbooks for schools by Antoni Popławski and Franciszek Ksawery Dmochowski. The latter in particular, in his book under the significant title, *On Social Virtues and Offenses Contrary to Them* (1787), attempted to base the principles of moral and political conduct on the natural attitudes of man and the advantages resulting from life in a community. This conduct, in turn, was founded on two main principles — justice and humanity.

The most significant achievement of Polish ethical thought during the Enlightenment was Kołłątaj's great study, *The Physico-Moral Order.* Unfortunately it was published very late (1810) and did not play a part in the educational system; but it did have significance in the history of philosophical thought. A point of departure for Kołłątaj's considerations was his theory of the order of the universe as a whole, in which physical and moral laws constituted an unbroken unity, and his concept of human needs, which developed in history and molded the character of men. This point of departure enabled Kołłątaj to give an incisive sociological interpretation of morality and to free ethics from its abstract and purely fanciful character. The concept of a "physico-moral" order enabled Kołłątaj to root ethics in reality, and his concept of increasing human needs opened up new horizons and objectives. In his analysis of the concept of "duty", Kołłątaj made an important point, asserting that our duties are to a certain limit defined by common laws and habits, but outside these limits lies an area of action which we are not obliged to undertake, but which constitutes an exceptionally valued sacrifice to society. In the former area, human behavior is ruled by justice; in the latter, by charity and heroism.

This differentiation, similar to the opposition between justice and humanity, about which Dmochowski had theorized, was an expression of the social and national situation. Under conditions, when ruling laws remained inhuman for the major part of the community, the appeal for just and humanitarian behavior beyond what the laws demanded, was becoming of great importance; under conditions in which political defeats were destroying the state, the duty of its defense opened a field of action from which destiny would surely demand heroism.

HEDONISM AND THE PHILOSOPHY OF LOVE

"Social virtues" and responsibility to history, fulfilling one's duties regarding charity and heroism — these were directives for a difficult life of self-denial. But the age of the Enlightenment, even in Poland, was an age of hope for a happy life. There existed an opposition, sometimes an open one, sometimes veiled, against the ideology of social tasks and obligations. For although it included the rights of the individual, and although it embraced not only the "duties" but also the "privileges" of man, not everyone considered this approach satisfactory. Equally unsatisfactory seemed Kołłątaj's thesis, formulated during the later period of his life, which distinguished between elementary and "artificial" needs, with the latter growing "through complete development of social life". Within this concept the individual remained an element of a greater whole and was subordinated to it. The individual's right to happiness was limited.

"Was it impossible to think otherwise?" was a question posed by many people to whom the culture of the Enlightenment was an encouragement to live in joy. This period knew the taste of life and made the category of "play" or "entertainment" (understood, incidentally, more broadly than today), an important element in it. They wanted to teach — it certainly was an age of Enlightenment — but to teach by play. A significant contemporary periodical was called *Zabawy Przyjemne i Pożyteczne* (Pleasant and Useful Games). Social games, or parties, were organized in the drawing-rooms, in parks, and in gardens. In this approach to life, a more profound philosophy was inherent.

Hedonistic accents found expression in Ignacy Krasicki's poetry. Although his great works had a didactic character and encouraged readers to be good citizens, in his short lyrical verses and in his "letters", sometimes intimate and private, and also in some of his fables, there appeared an apology for a life directed toward joy and felicity, defined by personal interests and desires.

Almost all of the poetry written by Stanisław Trembecki was pervaded by an atmosphere, which, incidentally, reigned in contemporary Parisian drawing-rooms where Trembecki spent many years, and in the aristocratic residences in Poland, especially at the homes of the Czartoryskis and Potockis: "I consider pleasure the highest good of man," he wrote in "Sofiówka," a poem dedicated to the magnificent residence of the Potocki family.

The concept of life as pleasure constituted a rather feeble opposition to the rational-utilitarian directives of good citizenship. It was treated as some sort of escape from serious obligations, as the egoistic retirement of the individual from society. It could be tolerated as a requirement of the moment, but not as a basic aim in life. Another current constituted a deeper opposition. It was connected with sentimentalism, especially with the protest voiced by Rousseau against the superficial aristocratic civilization in the name of authentic values of the heart and of real communion between people. From this viewpoint, various questions were posed: What is the nature of social ties? What are the motives which entice people to coexistence? On what does man's real happiness depend? Criticism was applied to rationalistic concepts, to unsatisfactory utilitarian motives, and to ineffectual moralization based on the idea of duty.

Franciszek Karpiński' study, *On the Felicity of Man: A Letter to Rosina* (1783), became a manifesto of that movement. Never before in Polish literature had love been treated in such an extensive and differentiated manner as in this dissertation by Karpiński, which showed love as a basic force governing all nature, and thus, all of society.

Karpiński thought that love, not the will, was the source of virtue. He worked out an entire program of education, thanks to which man would be able to understand his fellow man and coexist with him.

A similar philosophy was proclaimed by other writers of the period. Unusually popular was the novel by Dymitr Michał Krajewski, *A Podolian Girl Educated in the State of Nature*. The novel, an adaptation of a French novel, went through seven printings in the year of its publication (1784), and aroused great polemics, the first extensive literary dispute in Poland.

Similar convictions were expressed by the well-known poet and political writer, Józef Wybicki. In his *My Happy Hours,* published after the partitions, he made the distinction between a private and a public man. The latter is devoted to society, holds various posts, exercises various functions, but becomes more and more alien to himself, and less and less "a man". The private man, although living within the community, remains, however, "a man in nature". His life flows quietly on in the bosom of his family, the existence of which is his daily care. In such a life, Wybicki emphasized, morality is a direct expression of the heart, and not a fulfillment of the rigid rules of law and tradition.

The concept of life as love, formulated in various ways, constituted an important element of the contemporary philosophy of life. Together with other cultural aspects of the Enlightenment, it was opposed to Sarmatism and its Baroque decorativeness which prohibited direct and authentic, "simple and tender," experiences. This concept in the culture of the Enlightenment was in opposition both to the rationalist current and to sentimentalism.

From this standpoint, a new view was unveiled concerning the national past and "plain, Polish souls," and on Polish literature, from whose ranks only Janicki, Kochanowski, Sarbiewski and Krasicki were acceptable. In the nineteenth century, Romanticism would refer to these concepts, which manifested themselves so clearly during the Enlightenment, although, unfortunately, they did not attain philosophical expression. They remained only a voice of the heart, protesting against the "artificiality" of the life of enlightened people and courtiers.

RELIGION OF THE ENLIGHTENED

The opposition between the law of God and the law of nature, as well as between the state of nature and culture, which pervaded views on the world and on life during the Polish Enlightenment, was accompanied during the entire period by a movement of general and lively religiousness. This enlightened age, in trying to define precisely the secular vocation of man, in attacking passionately and viciously the obscurantism and fanaticism of the clergy and monks and the bigotry of the masses, was more than seemed likely an age of faith, which constituted the center of everyday life for the people.

Polemicists, especially the Jesuits, particularly active even after the dissolution of the order, provided no evidence of this state of affairs. In hundreds of books, pamphlets, leaflets, in numerous articles printed in periodicals, in thousands of homilies, they concentrated attacks against the new intellectual currents arriving from the West, against all efforts at modernization. This attack was of a political character, linked most frequently with a reactionary program of defense of the ancient "freedoms and privileges" of the gentry.

Nor were philosophers witness to the intensity of religious life of the epoch. In this age, as before, there were no great religious thinkers. Jesuit and Piarist professors never reached intellectual heights. They mainly worked on compiling books, for the most part polemical.

The intensity of religious life was, however, witnessed by literature, especially poetry. A collection of Józef Baka's verses, *Remarks on the Inevitable Death Common to Everybody* (1766), was often scorned, but his *Remarks on Ultimate Things and on Sinful Vice,* discovered only in 1936, so mutilated through zealous reading by contemporaries that only one copy was saved, has changed the commonly held view. This was a poetry of unusual religious ardor, passionate and pathetic in the Baroque manner, connected with mystical and ascetic traditions.

Religious sentiments were also present in the works of Konstancja Benisławska. Her *Songs Sung to Myself* (1776) had, as indicated in the title, an intimate character. Her poetry was not meant to be accusatory, or to christianize, or to educate. It sprang from a heartfelt need to express free-flowing emotions or as a meditation on the Lord's Prayer.

To this traditional religiousness, writers of the Enlightenment often juxtaposed another, more profound concept of life, connected with the emotions, sometimes sentimental.

This type of religious feeling was represented by Karpiński. He endeavored to express his own experience in poetry. His ambition was to create religious poetry "for the people." Such a motivation induced Karpiński to undertake, two centuries after Kochanowski, work on a translation of the Psalms of David. Similar motives guided him when he wrote *Pious Songs* (1792), destined for a wide circle of the community, and for the peasantry in particular. The author managed to give them an unusual simplicity, and, at the same time, connect them with the peasant religious tradition, expressed in fealty to the Holy

Mother and Child and to the Sorrowing Christ. They achieved a great popularity. His poems were used as prayers. Such hymns as "When the Morning Glory Rises" and "All the Cares of Our Daily Life", such Christmas carols as "God Is Born, Power Dies" — all these works have become the common property of every Pole.

Kniaźnin, the poet of love, whose *Love Poems* enjoyed great popularity among the courtiers, also dedicated a remarkable portion of his poetry, especially during his mature years, to the religious experience. He accepted the challenge constituted for the Age of Enlightenment by the fact that the Renaissance Psalms of David, in Kochanowski's translation, had not been revised and re-published. Thus, he undertook to make a new translation of these psalms, so deeply felt by men lost in the world.

In Kniaźnin's religious lyrics new sentiments appeared, which emerged from the dramatic plight of the country. Although the connection between religious and patriotic sentiment had for ages been a characteristic feature of Polish intellectual and emotional life, and although the poetry of the Bar confederates made from this a program of knightly renewal and political action, the national disaster taking place at the turn of the century produced a feeling that there was a contradiction between Providence and the plight of Poland. Kniaźnin perceived that contradiction, and in one of his odes to God he exclaimed: "Give perseverance, and also faith!"

In the consciousness of the generation of defeat, the matter could not be resolved in such a simple way as by the words of a prayer-like request. It was becoming a subject for philosophical and religious divagations regarding divine justice or theodicy.

Theodicy was a frequent topic of reflection during the Enlightenment. Voltaire's poem on the earthquake in Lisbon was commented upon throughout all of Europe, as it was in Poland. His poem was translated, published several times and disputed. But Lisbon was far away. Disputes over the earthquake which destroyed the entire city could only be academic. Poland, however, was close, and a political earthquake here threatened the national existence. In the hearts of Polish patriots a concrete and painful question emerged: how was it possible to reconcile the real and impending disasters with divine mercy and justice? The Bar confederates still believed that the wrath of God was temporary and that He would restore His favors upon the Catholic nation, which had been faithful to Him for ages.

This traditional vicious circle of despair and faith was broken by Jakub Jasiński, poet-soldier, poet-Jacobin. His criticism of the cloistered life, undertaken in his *Arguments* which continued Krasicki's satire, went on to attack the whole basis of the Christian religion. He applied his criticism from the standpoint of a man, who could not reconcile evil with Divine Providence. Providence might embrace the world in its entirety, but Providence did not care about the fate of individuals and nations. God and nature are indifferent and blind. And he stated: "Either Thou art powerless, or Thou art a cruel tyrant."

But if God is "powerless" or "a cruel tyrant," how are

people supposed to live? Questions like this appeared more and more frequently under the influence of national defeats at the end of the century. It is a significant reference to the great dispute concerning "decent people", inaugurated by Konarski, which was being conducted at the beginning of the Polish Enlightenment. Jasiński, asserting that it was not important to what denomination someone belonged, provided he was a "virtuous man", referred to Konarski, whose dissertations regarding morality and religion were given the title *On the Religion of Decent People,* suggesting by that a conviction, although not clearly defined, that, in a way, morality is the foundation of religion and not vice versa.

But this reference was being made at a different level of ideological development. By discarding the concept of Providence, one placed man face to face with evil. When the cause of evil could no longer be explained, neither theologically in terms of God's wrath and mercy and of men's guilt and merits, nor in any other system of theodicy which allegedly excused evil and exposed the imperfection of human reason, there remained only one way for reflection and practice, the secular way. Its watchword was formulated by Staszic when he declared that men themselves were the cause of their misfortune.

The Arts

SCIENCE AND POETRY

It was a particular feature of the Enlightenment that science became a subject of great public interest. People expressed their needs and goals through and thanks to science. Previously, science and learning had been the exclusive domain of a small group of men — apart from such areas as historiography, and during the Reformation, biblical studies. During the Enlightenment, however, science became a public matter. It assumed first place at school and in the drawing-rooms. The press devoted a great deal of attention to it. Numerous textbooks and books popularizing science appeared. Although it was not high-caliber science, it was useful to the community in many areas. Such fields as farming and the economy, medical care, construction, and education ceased to be merely the practice and the continuation of a tradition; they were attaining a scientific basis, and while new ideas were still frequently considered offensive, they were greatly appreciated by the enlightened public.

Although science was a new and important medium of expression for the social consciousness, literature, and poetry in particular, held a privileged position. Universal attention was turned to it; theoreticians occupied themselves with it, and criticism was focused on it. Numerous studies were devoted to literature, to the art of poetry, to oratorical skills. These studies ranged from the works of Konarski, devoted to the reform of rhetoric in the schools, to *The History of Liberal Sciences* by Carlancas, translated from the French, with Polish supplements for use in the Knights' School.

In these studies, the social meaning of literature was defined. With reference to the old Polish and Roman traditions, the significance of "oratory" was stressed as an expression of thought, thus as a weapon in the struggle for a better knowledge of reality. Filip Golański continued Konarski's program. In his textbook, *On Rhetoric and Poetry,* he sharpened his criticism of rhetoric in the Saxon period, pointing to the great political goals standing before all citizens who were called to the "diet" and to social responsibility in an epoch which he referred to as one "of good taste and light." Within these perspectives the specific place of poetry was clarified.

One of the first to define the place of poetry was Joachim Chreptowicz in a study on poetry, included in his *Collection of More Useful Information.* The very fact that it was deemed appropriate to include in "useful" information an item on poetry was significant evidence of the appreciation of its role in society. Even more interesting was what Chreptowicz said. While accepting poetry that teaches, he ascribed great significance to poetry that entertains. But the entertainment was to rely on the fact that "poetry flows into man's heart and once inside it, heats, caresses, and lifts it up", because "poetry is in the very nature of man" and is born "of the abundance of thought, of passions, boiling and violent" within him.

Franciszek Kniaźnin most profoundly felt and expressed the mission of poetry. In his *Love Poems,* he showed what was "the aim of singing" and what songs could be played on the lute, an instrument close to nature and birds. Convinced of the force of poetry, Kniaźnin referred to Orpheus, dedicating to him a beautiful poem, "Orpheus' Lament for Euridice". In later years, he expressed this belief with greater strength in his ode, "To the Lute". The various defeats which the nation suffered made Kniaźnin abandon the Orphean territory and to treat poetry as a peculiar message of the Just God who with His wrath was to purge "the hearts that clung to crime."

Art did not attain the position as a means of expression and an instrument of cultural communication that was accorded to literature, partly because it did not reach as easily to the mass of the gentry as did literature; partly because it was produced by foreign artists who did not always manage to establish contacts with the citizenry, although some of the artists were quickly Polonized.

In the great family of the arts, architecture assumed a privileged place. The king's initiative and building projects became a model and an inspiration. Wealthy aristocratic families built or reconstructed their residences. Great churches were still built in the Baroque style, because the traditionally-minded gentry wanted it that way. In Warsaw, the wealthy burghers erected banks and residences. Architecture was given a theoretical basis only during the following century, through the books of Sebastian Sierakowski and Piotr Aigner. However, during the Enlightenment, the great distance dividing the architecture of the well-to-do from the "building" of the poor was easily perceived. Piotr Świtkowski dedicated a book to this problem, *Village Construction, for the Consideration of* *Heirs and Owners of Estates* (1782). It found a ready audience and was reprinted by Michał Gröll in 1793. It was evidence of the fact that the dual nature of architecture, as the art of construction which guaranteed a "roof over one's head" and as monumental and representative art, had a particular position in the social consciousness of the period.

THE SOURCES OF ART

The manifold contents of the culture of the Enlightenment were an expression of different social situations, attitudes and strivings of men. They also fulfilled various functions; they were not always fully integrated with one another, remaining frequently parallel as manifestations of different, sometimes even opposing existential orientations. Owing to this, the culture of the Polish Enlightenment was much richer and more varied than is usually thought.

The royal court was a center of artists, scholars, and politicians, who created a program which included the reform of the state and the re-education of society. The philosophy and science that they cultivated and inspired were not an expression of an individual and disinterested curiosity, of an intellectual need for the construction of a worldview, but an expression of the need for rational and useful action in every field of the life of society: in the fight with obscurantism and fanaticism, in the modernization of the economy, in structural and legislative reform, in the remodeling of the system of training and education. The socio-political magazine, *Monitor,* published in Warsaw uninterruptedly for twenty years from 1765, was the literary mouthpiece of the program. It opened up a window onto the world, bringing to its readers the most recent news of scientific and philosophical research, promoting the significance of the development of "experimental physics" and of the education of "men versed in all branches of mathematics." At the same time, *Monitor* promoted knowledge of historical and legal studies which were to serve to "the advantage of the homeland."

Literature, painting and architecture, in languages of their own, expressed the same aspirations. The Royal Castle, renovated and rebuilt, became a symbol of this new public life; its reception rooms were embellished with portraits of Poland's great kings and great paintings on historical subjects by Marcello Bacciarelli, which depicted the cultural, political, and military triumphs of Poland: *Ladislaus Jagiello Granting Privileges to the Cracow Academy, The Union of Lublin, Sobieski at Vienna,* and others. The majesty of the Commonwealth was displayed in a magnificent portrait of the king in coronation robes. Merlini built a library wing onto the Castle, which was to serve Polish science and culture; Marcin Knackfuss built an Astronomical Observatory in Vilna; as did Feliks Radwański in Cracow. The Kazimierzowski Palace was converted into a Knights' School, and the Collegium Nobilium was rebuilt by Stanisław Zawadzki. The Vilna Cathedral, rebuilt by Wawrzyniec Gucewicz, received a monumental classical facade, as did the city hall in Vilna. Stanisław Zawadzki

195. Efraim Schröger,
Carmelite church in Warsaw, 1781

196. Piotr Aigner and Stanisław Kostka Potocki,
St. Anne's church in Warsaw, 1788

197. Domenico Merlini,
Królikarnia palace in Warsaw, 1786—89

198. Palace in Natolin

199. Throne Chamber
in the Royal Castle in Warsaw

200. Canaletto Room
in the Royal Castle in Warsaw

201. Jakub Fontana, Design
of the Marble Cabinet
in the Royal Castle
in Warsaw, 1771

202. Marble Cabinet
in the Royal Castle in Warsaw

203. Domenico Merlini, Jakub Kubicki and Jan C. Kammsetzer, Library in the Royal Castle in Warsaw, 1780—84

204. Domenico Merlini, Palace-on-the-Lake in the Royal Łazienki Park in Warsaw, 1784—88

205. Garden view
of the mansion in Rogalin, 1768—73

206. Manor-house in Woyszyce, 18th cent.

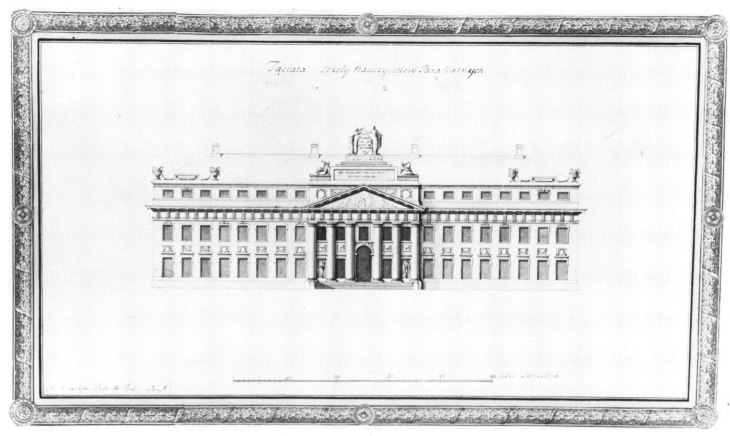

207. Jan Chrzciciel Knackfuss, Design
of the building of a seminary
for teachers of parish schools, 1776

208. Giacomo Monaldi, *Chronos*.
Sculpture in the Knights' Hall
of the Royal Castle in Warsaw.
1784—86

209. Tadeusz Kuntze-Konicz
Fortune, 1754

210. Marcello Bacciarelli, *Apotheosis of Stanislaus Augustus Supporting Sciences and Fine Arts*

211. Jan Bogumił Plersch, *Kosciuszko Taken Prisoner at Maciejowice*, c. 1795

212. Marcello Bacciarelli,
*Portrait of King Stanislaus Augustus
in Coronation Robes.* 1768—71

213. Marcello Bacciarelli,
Solomon's Offering. Painted decoration
in the Solomon Room of the Łazienki Palace, 1789—90

214. Marcello Bacciarelli,
Union of Lublin. c. 1785—86

215. Marcello Bacciarelli,
*Ladislaus Jagiello Granting Privileges
to the Cracow Academy,* 1784

216. Marcello Bacciarelli,
Prussian Homage. 1785—86

217. Jan Chrzciciel Lampi,
Portrait of Stanislaus Augustus Poniatowski. c. 1791

218. Bernardo Bellotto called Canaletto.
Election of Stanislaus Augustus at Wola. 1778

219. Bernardo Bellotto called Canaletto,
View of Warsaw from Pleaga, 1770

220. Bernardo Bellotto called Canaletto,
*View of Warsaw from the
Terrace of the Royal Castle* (detail), 1773—74

221. Kazimierz Wojniakowski,
    Society Gathering in a Garden, 1797

222. Jean Piere Norblin,
    Trip to the Lake. [1785]

223. Jean Pierre Norblin, *Bathing in a Park*, [1785]

224. Franciszek Smuglewicz,
*Ratification of the Agrarian Law Granted
to the Peasants in Pawłów
by Paweł Ksawery Brzostewski in 1769*

225. Jean Pierre Norblin,
*Proclamation of the Third
of May Constitution of 1791*

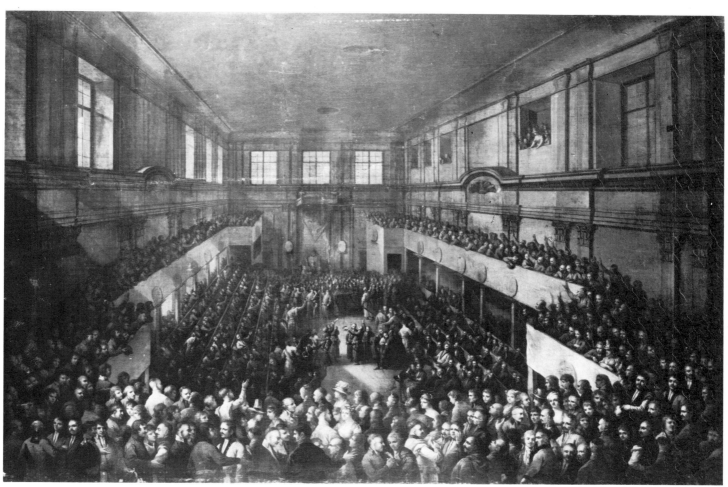

226. Kazimierz Wojniakowski,
Passing of the Third of May Constitution. [1806]

227. Kazimierz Wojniakowski,
Portrait of Thaddeus Kosciuszko, after 1794

228. Krzysztof Lubieniecki,
School Teacher, 1727

229. Stanisław Staszic,
Warnings to Poland, 1790. Title page

230. Daniel Chodowiecki,
*Stanislaus Augustus Extending
His Protection to all Estates*

Die neue Polnische Constitution
La nouvelle Constitution Polonnoise

231. Jean Pierre Norblin, *Diet in Church*. [1808]

232. Jean Pierre Norblin,
Fighting in Miodowa Street in Warsaw

233. Jean Pierre Norblin,
Market in the Slaughterers' Gate in Warsaw

234. Jean Pierre Norblin,
*Distribution of Meals at the Sigismund Column
at Castle Square in Warsaw*

235. Jean Pierre Norblin,
Design of stage sets for a play on peasant
themes produced in the court theater in Puławy, 1802

236. Józef Richter. View of the Sibyl Temple in Puławy. c. 1830

237. Józef Richter.
    View of the Palace in Puławy. 1830

238. François Boucher.
    Coat-of-arms of Stanislaus Augustus surrounded
    by personifications of Peace and Justice.
    Design for the coping of the throne

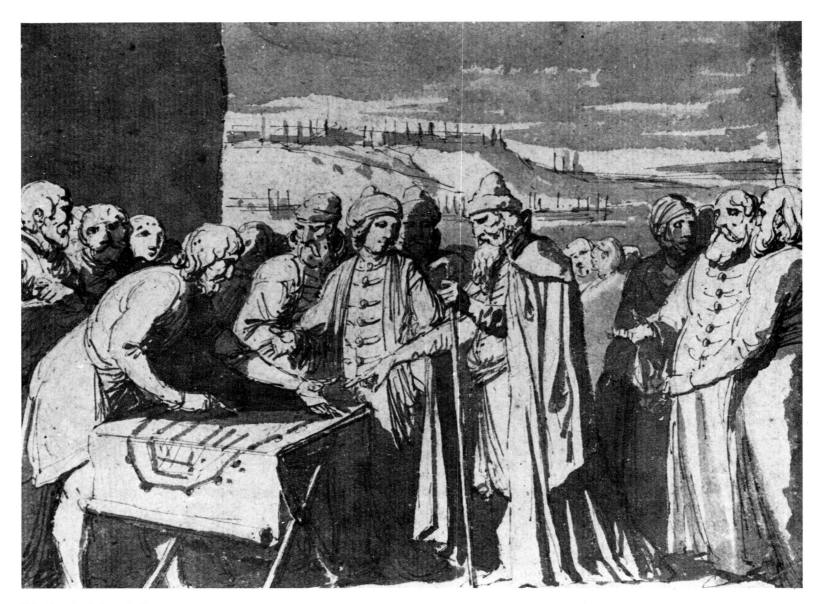

239. Franciszek Smuglewicz,
*Ladislaus Jagiello and the Elders Debating
on Plans of a New Town*

240. Zygmunt Vogel, *Palace-
on-the-Lake in the Royal Łazienki Park*

241. Zygmunt Vogel, *View of the Palace
in Puławy from the River*. 1796

244. Jan Wahl, *Warsaw Councillors Taking an Oath of Loyalty to the King*

242. Zygmunt Vogel,
*View of the Officer Cadets' Palace,
also known as the Kazimierzowski Palace*

243. Zygmunt Vogel, *Załuski Library*

245. Michał Stachowicz,
*General Thaddeus Kosciuszko Taking
an Oath in Cracow on 24 March 1794*
Colour drawing, 1797

246. Aleksander Orłowski,
Design of the statue
of Prince Joseph Poniatowski
in general's uniform, 1818

Monument projeté, à la mémoire de Poniatowski
par Orłowski

247. Aleksander Orłowski, *Battle of Racławice*, *[1797]*

248. Aleksander Orłowski,
     On the Ramparts, [1798]

249. Philibert Debucourt
     after Horace Vernet,
     *Death of Prince
     Joseph Poniatowski
     in the Elster*

250. Vase produced in the Belvedere
manufactory

251. Soup toureen with a cover
from the manufactory in Korzec

also reconstructed and built huge army barracks, especially in Warsaw.

This new vision of the state and public life was also expressed in numerous designs for monumental buildings, unfortunately never carried out; for example, the seat of the Academy of Sciences (by Domenico Merlini), the college for parish school teachers (by Jan Chrzciciel Knackfuss), the complex of buildings for the museum and the great church in Vilna, monumental in classical form, reminiscent of the Roman Pantheon, similar to the Church of the Divine Providence in Warsaw, treated as a temple of National Fame.

The poetry and prose of Naruszewicz also served to build the monumental image of Poland. Bacciarelli paid tribute to him, according to contemporary fashion, by including the figure of Naruszewicz in his painting, *The Prussian Homage.*

Satire also played a part in the program of national re-education. It was the favorite genre in literature during the Enlightenment, permitting writers to attack vices and faults, expose hypocrisy and falsehood, and condemn obscurantism and fanaticism. Leaders in this field were Naruszewicz and Krasicki; other poets assisted them. The didactic novel was an ideal vehicle for satire, as were the royal, school and the public national theaters in which bitter, satirical comedies were produced, like for example, Franciszek Zabłocki's *Zabobonnik* and *Sarmatism,* and plays were staged containing "positive heroes", who wisely served their homeland, as for example, *The Return of the Deputy,* by Julian Ursyn Niemcewicz.

However, not all artistic and intellectual activity helped in the improvement of the Commonwealth and in the education of a new people; neither was it always a testing ground for those contemporaries who did not live up to the image of Poland's greatness.

This creative work was also an expression of a new style of life and its joy. Architecture especially gave proof of love of the beauty of life; this quality could be discerned in the palaces and villas erected by the king and his family, by the aristocrats and wealthy bourgeoisie, at Natolin, Jabłonna, Królikarnia, Powązki, and most of all Łazienki, reconstructed and built for Stanislaus Augustus in the 1780's as his favorite private residence. Their example influenced the entire country. For joy of life, parks and gardens were laid out, temples of contemplation built, and sentimental country cottages erected.

In this way, a new style of individual and social life was created. Music, painting and poetry expressed and produced the atmosphere of sophisticated entertainment, of the specific charm of *fêtes champêtres,* of the glamors of evening walks among the trees in the park, of tender gestures and the sentimental experiences of love, ruled by the laws of courtly gallantry. These were the themes of Kniaźnin's *Love Poems* and Trembecki's verses describing the charms of the magnate residences and gardens. The works of painters expressed similar experiences: particularly the paintings of Norblin, the author of the joyful *Dawn,* painted on a ceiling of the temple of Diana at Arkadia near Łowicz and of the paintings of court parties, visionary and unreal, like *Bathing in the Park* or *The Dance of the Greek Nymphs.* It was also served by music: songs were admired, opera loved passionately, especially the heroic works of Pietro Metastasio, based on Greek motifs, yet lyrical and sentimental, providing a variety of experiences. Court poets, particularly Kniaźnin at Puławy, prepared texts for theatrical productions, taking into account local color and introducing serfs and village maids into the action.

There was no clear line between the two kinds of life: seriousness intertwined with joy, science with entertainment, monumentality with intimacy. In the halls of the Royal Castle various paintings glorified the charms of life, its allure and pleasures. At the same time, four figures of Polish kings were mounted in the rotunda at Łazienki: Casimir the Great, Sigismund I, Stephen Báthory and John III Sobieski, and on the bridge a statue of John III, the last king of Polish knightly triumphs. In the paintings by Kazimierz Wojniakowski, which extolled the charms of the landscape and the joy of sentimental games in the forest and in the park, there appeared an ominous sign of catastrophe — Poland in fetters.

But other subjects were also dealt with in the creative works of the Enlightenment. These were universal human experiences and longings, which reached beyond action for the sake of current social and political reform. The culture of the period, especially literature and art, was connected with the needs of man, with his individual experiences and anxieties, and with his image of the world and of life.

Poetry, more than anything else, gave expression to these feelings, and helped fulfill man's needs. It found its way to "the tender heart", as Karpiński defined it. Similarly, Józef Szymanowski wrote that "it is the effect of tenderness that we try to catch in writing all the beauties that can delight the sensitive soul." This opinion of poetry was also held by Kniaźnin, when in thwarting the reigning didactical-satirical style he turned to Orpheus, when he created a new version of the *Threnodies* — an elegiac cycle entitled *Orpheus' Lament for Euridice,* in which he expressed the despair caused by the death of the wife of his friend, Franciszek Zabłocki. The love lyrics, in which various poets in different ways broke with court conventions to speak directly of love, were examples of the new wave in poetry. Pastoral poetry too, despite the sometimes artificial sentimentality, reached for real experiences. Some of these verses, like "Laura and Filon" by Franciszek Karpiński, remained popular for a long time.

Fables were especially favored during this period. A critical and sceptical point of view, alien to philosophical treatises which were rare in Poland during the Enlightenment, found its way into the fables. In these curt stories — Krasicki and Trembecki excelled in them — all the bitterness of life in a world full of folly, outrage, fanaticism, pride and envy was exposed. And yet the fables taught that one might find some happiness in this world, humble and lasting, all one's own; and one could attain an aloofness in the face of reigning evil, a wise peace amidst chosen, true friends.

In opposition to this secular program of consolation and equilibrium was religious poetry. It entered forever into the consciousness and imagination of the nation — after all, carols and songs produced then are still sung today — as did fables whose echoes can be found in proverbial phrases and maxims containing the mature wisdom of life.

The expression of patriotic sentiments also attained universal significance. Although it was not a new element in Polish culture, since it was present in all previous epochs, at the time of the Enlightenment there appeared a new emphasis. Even during the Enlightenment itself, although the period was quite short, it underwent important changes. At the end of the century, social conflicts emerged more strongly than ever before, and at the same time the need for national integration in struggle and defense; the apparently clear traditional concept of patriotism required revision and restructuring. Even the enlightened model of a "good citizen" was insufficient, since it often led to opportunism, perhaps even to national treason, in circumstances which required revolutionary action. What, then, was to be true patriotism, and did it require revolutionary action? The personal destinies of men were more and more dramatically caught in the plight of the nation. Religious faith and trust placed in Providence in times of national defeat were also complex issues, filled with contradictions.

Under these circumstances, poets and artists expressed and shaped new experiences, new intellectual subjects, a new style of action and a new sensitivity.

Remarkable evidence of the attractiveness of Polish culture was the fact that a number of foreign painters were capable of expressing in art the Polish patriotic experience and emotions connected with the Polish situation. With minute precision, Bernardo Bellotto called Canaletto painted sights of Warsaw and the figures of its inhabitants, the majesty of Wilanów Palace, and suburban landscapes. Josef Grassi, against the background of various landscapes, portrayed the leaders of fighting Poland — Poniatowski and Kosciuszko; he participated in various campaigns in Polish uniform. The painter most involved with Polish life was Jean Pierre Norblin. In his paintings and drawings, he dramatized contemporary Polish history, as for example, *The Proclamation of the Third of May Constitution,* and portrayed representatives of the various estates. His art also served the uprising: the upheaval of the people of Warsaw, the hanging of the traitors, Kosciuszko's encampment and the scythebearers; and lastly, the fall of the insurrection, *The Assault on Praga* and *The Slaughter of Praga.*

THE VARIETY OF STYLES

New subjects and themes were searching for new forms of expression. The Enlightenment gave birth to a new style in expression of intellectual and emotional experience, in the principles of communication among people, and in the treatment and remodeling of reality.

This style was, above all, one of rational lecturing, with clearness and effectiveness being the main consideration. Progress in this field was distinctly apparent when one compared, for example, the logical and abstract method of

Kołłątaj's argumentation with the characteristic traits of political treatises dating from the first half of the eighteenth century. Konarski inaugurated this great movement for the renewal of the art "of proper speech and proper thinking", and the schools, reformed by the Commission for National Education, tried to implement it. How great was the attention attached to logic is seen by the fact that Condillac was asked to write a textbook on logic, which was successfully completed.

A basic condition for the implementation of this program of intellectual education was the creation of a flexible and universally accessible tool of information and communication, that is, a language. On the threshold of the Enlightenment, Poland was still, so far as the ruling class was concerned, a bilingual, Polish-Latin country. Yet Latin was deteriorating more and more, and the native language, interspersed oddly with Latin phrases, was far from clarity and perfection. The fight for the clarity, functionalism, and beauty of the Polish language had been inaugurated by Konarski. It was, by the same token, a fight to end an elitist language of social privilege, and to create one national language, common to all the citizens of the country. This was not an easy fight.

Latin was more deeply rooted in the consciousness of the gentry than in other nations. Despite fundamental differences, which, in contrast to the situation in Romance language-speaking countries, divided Latin from the Polish language, it was still the language of politics and administration.

A systematic campaign for the right to have a native tongue was begun by Franciszek Bohomolec in his Latin study, *De lingua Polonica colloquium* (1752), translated a few years later into Polish. Ignacy Krasicki took up the struggle in several articles published in *Monitor* in 1765 and 1766; than by Stefan Kleczewski, author of a book entitled *On the Beginnings, Duration, Varieties and the Perfection of the Polish Language* (1767); and by several other writers. It produced the proper atmosphere owing to which the Commission for National Education was able, especially thanks to Onufry Kopczyński, author of *A Grammar of the Polish and Latin Languages,* the first formal textbook on the subject, to promote action in the field of popularization of the native language among wide circles of society. Wincenty Skrzetuski even suggested setting up an Academy of Language, declaring that "there could be nothing more useful to our nation."

The struggle for clarity and skill of linguistic expression was won. Its success also made possible the development of poetry.

For a number of years during the development of the culture of the Enlightenment the aesthetic awareness of poetical styles was formed in different ways. There was a common front against the bad traditions of the Saxon period and distortions of the Baroque style, but as to a positive program there were differing approaches: Filip N. Golański, professor of rhetoric in the Piarist schools, in his work *On Rhetoric and Poetry* (1786) and Franciszek K. Dmochowski in his *Art of Writing Rhyme,* presented a classical concept, true to rationalism and didacticism, although with a tendency to reach beyond its stiff   130 limitations. A theoretician of Rococo poetry, Józef Szymanowski, was considered to lay down the canons of good taste; whereas Karpiński, in his work entitled, *On Oratory in Prose or in Verse* (1782), advocated poetry of the heart.

While there were many studies devoted to rhetoric and poetry during the Enlightenment, no theoretical study appeared in the field of art. But although artists did not comment on their work, as did poets and writers, in practice there emerged tendencies similar to those which characterized the fight for literary styles.

Architecture was a branch of art in which a characteristic variety of styles manifested itself. The classical style, one of equilibrium, regularity, clarity, and yet of grandeur, solemnity and simplicity, prevailed in palaces, residences, and churches. It appeared in many variants, of which the most important was the personally sponsored one by King Stanislaus Augustus. He did not like drawing-room Rococo art; he appreciated great, majestic solutions, although not devoid of the tradition of wealth and color. This style was called the classicism of Stanislaus Augustus.

The ancient type of classicism was more austere, and developed mostly in Vilna, thanks to the activity of Wawrzyniec Gucewicz. This style, so close to the majestic odes of Naruszewicz, had from its very beginning, like its counterpart in classical poetry, an opposite pole. The latter was even earlier in origin than classicism itself and derived not so much from architectural practice, as the practice of laying out English gardens. In the mid-eighteenth century many such romantic and sentimental gardens were designed. They became fashionable especially after 1774, when Izabela Czartoryska had such a park laid out at Powązki, and Helena Radziwiłł at Arkadia near Łowicz. Bogumił Zug was among the architects most sensitive to the charms of that sentimental atmosphere. He erected buildings later termed "neo-Gothic" reaching back to the Polish medieval tradition, to the epoch of Casimir the Great, the king most esteemed by the Enlightenment.

This sentimental art, abandoning the enthusiasm for antiquity, eagerly turned toward Chinese, Turkish, and Egyptian patterns, as well as toward the art and culture of primitive peoples. Although this art, usually limited to various park follies, including artificial ruins, did not have the same significance as classical art, it constituted a characteristic romantic and sentimental counterweight to grand rational architecture.

Painting also displayed a variety of styles during this period. Artists were called upon to execute paintings which were to provide evidence of the greatness of Poland's past. The classical style was most suitable for the task. Yet at the same time, they had to fulfill decorative tasks, in which Baroque traditions and Rococo colors became more pronounced. Jan Bogumił Plersch and Marcello Bacciarelli painted the castle rooms, the rooms in Łazienki Palace, and interiors of some of the aristocratic residences in this style. Jean Pierre Norblin rendered the majestic atmosphere of court life in imitation of Watteau; Gianbattista Lampi and Josef Grassi employed a similar romantic and sentimental Rococo style. Grassi

also painted lyrical portraits depicted against the background of sentimental park landscapes.

These various styles were also intertwined in sculpture. Andreas Le Brun created great allegorical, classical figures, which decorated the rooms of the Royal Castle and Łazienki Palace. He also sculpted statues of Polish kings and made two cycles of busts of famous Poles, destined for the Knights' Hall of the Castle. Tommaso Righi embellished the theater in Łazienki, which was on the lake and among the trees, with allegorical figures representing comedy and tragedy, as well as with several statues of famous playwrights beginning with antiquity, and ending with Niemcewicz and Trembecki. Jan Obrocki and Maciej Polejowski were active outside of Warsaw: their sculptures had a lyrical Rococo character, unlike the classical style.

But the most important development was not so much the conflict between these stylistic movements as the birth of a realistic style, registering the drama of Polish life, both social and political. The first step in this direction was made by Bernardo Bellotto, called Canaletto, still classical in the treatment of his views of Warsaw; but even in these paintings he showed scenes of the daily and holiday life of the various social classes, including peasants and beggars. In his townscapes appeared both the real charm of Warsaw, and the character of Polish dress and customs, depicted as carefully as in the historical paintings which he also produced with realistic, documentary zeal.

The highest achievement of this style, however, was reached by Jean Pierre Norblin, who in the course of passing years and changing historical situations departed more and more from the aristocratic world. An unusual shrewdness of observation permitted him to draw Polish types — magnates, noblemen and peasants — and to expose the poverty and denigration of the peasants, to depict mindless and drunken scenes from the local diets and markets, showing the anarchy of the wealthy and the cruelty of exploitation, and scenes from the life of the masses — bazaars, horse fairs, etc. Not since the days of Naruszewicz and Krasicki had anyone presented such a comprehensive panorama of Polish life; no one had evaluated it so shrewdly and severely.

In Norblin's art the atmosphere of the Polish landscape and local color manifested itself. These tendencies found an outlet in the works connected with revolutionary events in Warsaw and with the Kosciuszko Insurrection — in paintings and drawings, representing the trial of the traitors, street fighting, the defense and defeat of Praga, etc. What was expressed fragmentarily by the short-lived poetry of the revolution and the war years Norblin presented in all its richness of detail, and at the same time with unusual expressiveness. His work marked the birth of a new style, in which the contrasts between monumental classicism and sentimental rococo were less important, a national style of painting, which would be the dominant style throughout the nineteenth century, not only during the Romantic period. In this way art, which for a long time had been outdistanced by literature so far as the portrayal of Polish life and Polish national consciousness was concerned, was attaining a very important place at the end of the century.

Culture in Society

THE SOCIAL DISTRIBUTION OF CULTURE

What exactly was the culture of the Enlightenment expressing? By what social forces was it organized? To whom did it speak? Who followed its directives?

The social distribution of intellectual and artistic culture was clearer during the Enlightenment than during any other period.

The most important center was the royal court. Never in Poland's history had there been a king so personally committed to cultural matters as was Stanislaus Augustus. Never had the role of previous kings been so long lasting, systematic and comprehensive as the initiatives and activities of that last ruler of Poland, who by his contemporaries and later generations was often accused of displaying much more interest in matters of art than he was in the destiny of the state.

All intellectual and artistic culture remained under the constant care and protection of Stanislaus Augustus. On his initiative the Knights' School was founded; thanks to his personal supervision, the Commission for National Education developed its activity; he inspired the development of science and learning, especially historical studies, and made efforts to create an Academy of Sciences in Warsaw, the building of which was designed by one of his architects; he promoted the foundation of a theater, the first permanent theater in Poland. On his orders, architects, painters, and sculptors from all over Europe erected palaces and richly embellished residences. Because of his personal interest in knowledge of literature — he himself was a writer — the most outstanding writers and poets of the period were gathered around him.

The famous Thursday Dinners, a combination of a traditional and modern scientific and literary society, provided a breeding-ground for new ideas and arbitration on matters of good taste. The guests were varied: poets, writers, scholars and teachers, painters and architects, lawyers and statesmen. New literary works were read, as were new theater plays, fragments of scholarly dissertations, including studies on astronomy. Economic and political topics were not avoided; projects of legislative and constitutional reforms were debated. Treated with derision by those not invited, the Thursday Dinners played an important part in the shaping of literary and artistic opinions, and in the undertaking and implementing of various research projects. The rich correspondence of the king with scholars and artists extended the range of influence of the Thursday Dinners and permitted the participation of such persons who, owing to the remoteness of their residences, for example, Krasicki, rarely visited the capital.

The great aristocratic families followed the king's example. But the many Warsaw salons were not able to play such an important role. It was only rarely that anything more than purely social functions were arranged. The Czartoryskis provided an exception to this rule. Adam Czartoryski gathered together numerous writers and artists at the Blue Palace in Warsaw. Izabela Czartoryska created a new type of residence at Powązki between 1774 and 1783, situated in a garden, favorable to the sentimental outpourings of the Rococo gallantry. Poems were dedicated to this residence by Naruszewicz, Krasicki, and Trembecki.

The significance of Powązki was outweighed by that of Puławy, the second great residence of the Czartoryski family, who in 1783 left Warsaw to create a center of culture in opposition to the king's policies and to court classicism. Puławy was to remain a harbor of national traditions, as opposed to foreign fashions, and was meant to produce a new attitude toward the past and a new type of intellectual and emotional life.

The significance of Puławy increased at the end of the century, in the face of national disaster. Jan Paweł Woronicz, in *The Temple of Sibyl*, written after the downfall of the state, described the mementoes gathered there, making of them a visionary image of Poland's history, and putting in the mouth of Izabela Czartoryska a prophecy regarding the plight of the homeland.

The royal court and the courts of the Czartoryskis, and to a lesser degree other magnate residences, as for instance, that of the Ogińskis at Słonim, a center for music, were instrumental in developing the culture of the Polish Enlightenment.

The gentry did not play a significant part in the social inspiration of culture. In contrast to the sixteenth century, during which the gentry created a national literature, together with political writing and Reformation polemics, and even in contrast to the seventeenth century, during which almost all culture, especially literature and art, was a "gentry" culture, during the Enlightenment the gentry remained, almost exclusively, the villains of satires and comedies.

Political literature of the conservative movement was most frequently connected with the magnate centers, and the progressive program was worked out by individuals, who, like Kołłątaj, were not among the leaders of the gentry, or, like Staszic, did not belong to the gentry estate. The significance of the gentry as an estate in preparing and implementing state reforms, particularly of the Commission for National Education and the Constitution of the Third of May, was negligible. The Jesuits and the aristocratic families who continued to conduct a policy of self-interest were the inspiration behind opposition to these movements.

The intellectual and emotional attitudes inherent in the culture of the masses of gentry, were almost completely absent from the creation of culture, whether in philosophy, or in literature and art. A remarkable feature of the period was that all cultural activity was connected with the ideology of the Enlightenment. Apart from the occasional poetry of the Bar confederates, all poetry was "enlightened". Within a certain sector of the gentry, diaries, at best, were popular, but even in this genre, only Jędrzej Kitowicz attained a high standard. Of more lasting value were the diaries of Karol Lubicz Chojecki, who described the fate of those Bar confederates who were banished to Siberia. The memoirs of Maurycy

August Beniowski (a confederate and Hungarian by descent), written in French, published in English, and translated later into Polish, can hardly be included among the works of the Polish gentry Enlightenment.

The main current of art was flowing outside the gentry group. Great architecture flourished in Warsaw and radiated throughout Poland by way of magnate residences. The small manor-houses of the gentry were situated on the fringe of the current, even when some of the trends were intercepted and adapted. By the same token, painting, developed by foreign artists, was by no means an affair of the gentry. Native painting, portraiture and religious scenes, true to the traditions of Baroque realism and so distant from "fashionable" art, was dying. Science was comparatively new. The intellectual life of the Sarmatian world could only be found in calendars and prophecies, religious and ascetic studies, tales relating unusual events, in polemics with the "seeders of offense", and the news, in manifestos, in speeches at the Seyms and in resolutions passed by the local diets. The attachment to religion and to the church, bordering of fanaticism and bigotry, the attachment to national traditions, which was expressed in this sort of writing were also manifested in their allegiance to Polish dress and customs. The Sarmatians, who masked their rhetoric in patriotic zeal in order to serve the cause of their reactionary political programs regarding the defense of "liberties" of the gentry, expressed violent feelings of hatred toward anything new, and a mental sluggishness toward the natural and political reality, with the egoism and fanaticism of the one who finds himself in an endangered position.

The Polish Enlightenment was not the culture of the masses of the gentry. However it was, to a great degree, the work of the people, individuals and groups, who were emancipated from the traditional bonds of the estates and were winning an even greater margin of freedom in their activity. They were writers, especially political writers, editors of daily newspapers and periodicals, publishers and booksellers, professors of the University of Cracow, teachers in colleges, officials on the Commission for National Education, and organizers of theatrical life. To describe this group of people, one could use, though perhaps rather prematurely, the term intelligentsia; this consisted of people with varied educational backgrounds, from various professions, closely linked to the life of the large cities, particularly with Warsaw.

Within certain parts of this group there slowly ripened a feeling of their own separateness and the mission they were called to perform in society as a whole. In this way, an "academic estate" began to form, the character and vocation of which was, for decades to come, defined by Piramowicz in his famous *Duties of a Teacher*. A similar, but much more free, feeling of singularity was formed within the group of "literati". Franciszek Salezy Jezierski introduced the word in his encyclopedia entitled *Some Words Gathered in Alphabetical Order*.

Journalists, active in the progressive press, were also gaining a consciousness of their vocation in consequence of the attacks led by the conservatives.

In other circles of the "intelligentsia", the feeling of a cultural and social mission also ripened. From the time of Mitzler de Kolof, who opened a printing house in 1756, printers, who were often also publishers, attained in their work a feeling of a social role. A publisher from Cracow, Jan Maj, in 1791 opened up a reading room in his shop because he thought that "the growth and improvement of our cities is helped by enlightenment of people, and this enlightenment mostly stems from the reading of books and useful writings." The Warsaw printer, Piotr Dufour, in 1789, wrote in defense of the freedom of speech: "It seems an equally useful thing in this kingdom, as in England and in the Netherlands, to establish the freedom of the press" and he demanded that "the tribunal to try such matters be not composed of persons belonging to one estate, whose interest it is to keep people stupid."

Similarly, actors were also developing a professional and cultural consciousness. Wojciech Bogusławski, the founder of the national theater, bore witness to this process in his memoirs.

The relative autonomy enjoyed by members of these various groups became most evident during the debates of the Four Year Seym, and particularly, during the period of the Kosciuszko Insurrection. The social antecedents of the writers, publicists, poets and scholars were no longer important. With few exceptions, these people offered their talents to the patriotic program of reform and national insurrection. Of such a universally national character was the group of activists gathered around Hugo Kołłątaj, his so-called Forge; later, it was augmented by the Jacobin Club, which, like the Kołłątaj group, included revolutionaries, for example Kiliński, together with more "sober-minded" citizens of foreign origin, like the scholar Samuel Bogumił Linde. During the turbulent days of the patriotic revolutionary struggle in Warsaw, men of the theater, poets, philosophers and political writers, took massive part in the battle for liberation, assisting it with the weapons of words and thoughts. In Bogusławski's theater, the atmosphere of the street was perfectly gauged; songs were sung which later found their way back to the streets, welcomed by the demonstrating masses with enthusiasm.

REFORM OF NATIONAL EDUCATION: THE FIRST MINISTRY OF EDUCATION IN EUROPE

In the mid-eighteenth century, simultaneously with the action to promote a new worldview and a program of socio-economic and political reform, work was underway to remodel the educational system with the aim of rearing "a new generation of Poles."

Education in Poland had a long and glorious tradition. But, apart from the Reformation, when dissenters attempted to set up schools of their own, never before had it been so much a social task, a matter of implementing national objectives, as it was during the Enlightenment. Existing schools run by religious orders, although appreciated by the gentry, were for their children only and, as such, served definite objectives of this estate. Stanisław Konarski broke up the system when he opened in 1740 the Collegium Nobilium, which had as its aim the education of a new type of citizen. Konarski's school, so bitterly criticized by the conservative gentry, was meant for the whole state, and was to serve the state.

The reform of the educational system during the reign of Stanislaus Augustus followed along the same lines. Its first, almost exemplary, project was the Knights' School organized by Adam Czartoryski by order of Stanislaus Augustus.

The king, referring to seventeenth century Seym resolutions, undertook to set up this school at the Seym of 1764. The Knights' School was duly opened in 1765. Organized as a military school, it was supposed to cultivate the Polish knightly tradition, stimulate a patriotic spirit, a sense of honor, self-denial, and a civic attitude. Czartoryski composed the textbooks and formulated the regulations for the school. A Moral Catechism, in question and answer form, defined the virtues of a good citizen and soldier; it recommended "the repayment of a citizen's debt to the homeland", care for one's honor, a critical attitude toward Sarmatian vices, and solidarity with all "enlightened, honest and rational persons". The cadets were to "change the obsolete shape of their country", as Czartoryski wrote in a preface to one of his books, to disseminate the "light that they generated by their hard work" at scholl, and to liberate their homeland "from those two horrible tyrants — ignorance and superstition."

During the thirty years of its existence, over a thousand young men from all over Poland experienced this patriotic, civic education. Among the pupils of the school were: Thaddeus Kosciuszko, Józef Sowiński, Karol Kniaziewicz, as well as many later prominent leaders in the field of education, administration, science and literature, like Niemcewicz and Jasiński. At the time of the partitions, graduates of the school refused to take the oath of allegiance to the Targowica Confederacy, they joined the insurrection of Kosciuszko, an "old graduate of the Knights' School".

Konarski's reforms and the plans of the Knights' School were later taken over by the activities of the Commission for National Education, established by an act of the Seym in 1773. It was the time of the first partition of Poland, and, incidentally, of the dissolution of the Jesuit Order. The first fact led to efforts to rescue the country by fundamental means, that is, by reshaping the community through educating its youth. The latter allowed the use of the Jesuit landed estates, school buildings and, to a certain degree, their teaching staff. These opportunities were taken advantage of, and the post-Jesuit estates were used to reform education.

The Commission for National Education was organized as an administrative authority, responsible for education to the Seym. It was to reform the schools on all levels, starting with the university, to introduce new curricula, textbooks and teaching methods, to prepare the lay teaching staff and train competent inspectors of education. Its activity reached beyond the education for the gentry and included schools for the people. The Society for Elementary Books, created by the Commission, was to prepare textbooks, mostly for the early years of schooling.

The Commission was thus a virtual Ministry of Education, the first of its kind in Europe.

The Commission, which had its headquarters at the Palace of the Republic, but held sessions most frequently at the Castle, often in the king's presence, was led by a group of prominent personalities, who although holding various political views were able to work together successfully: Andrzej Zamoyski, Michał Poniatowski, Joachim Chreptowicz, Ignacy Potocki, Adam Kazimierz Czartoryski, and Grzegorz Piramowicz. This cooperative spirit excited admiration and respect, and was responsible for the remarkable success of their work, which lasted twenty years, and only ended with the downfall of the state.

From the very beginning the Commission was well aware of the great tasks awaiting education in a country which required profound reform. The oft-quoted statement made by Chancellor Jan Zamoyski, founder of the Academy at Zamość, that "Republics will always be such as is the upbringing of their youth" was highly significant. All the activity of the Commission was directed to the implementation of this principle. One of its members accurately defined the basic aim of their activity: "to create a nation by public education". To create a nation meant to awaken the awareness that "all the citizens in the country are the limbs of one body, parts of one head, sons of one mother". To create a nation meant to overcome private interest and the feudal traditions of local particularism and privilege, and to shape a patriotic attitude in its citizens. To create a nation also meant to develop a modern, scientific consciousness in the people.

Out of this spirit originated the famous words of Thaddeus Kosciuszko: "I will not fight for the gentry only; I want freedom for the whole nation."

The directives included in the Commission's program modernized traditional curricula by limiting Latin, introducing the natural sciences, and taking into account moral and civic responsibilities from the very first years of education. At the same time, verbal and abstract teaching methods were criticized and discarded in favor of cultivating the ability to think and to act rationally.

The schools run by the Commission did not restrict themselves to educating the country's children. Annual public speech days provided a kind of intellectual salon for the community. Even the king sometimes honored such occasions with his presence. New discoveries in the fields of science and technology were presented here; philosophical problems were discussed; the traditions of Konarski's college were upheld, when pupils debated the question of the welfare of the Commonwealth. Disputes were often introduced regarding the resolution of urgent social and economic issues.

The activity of the Commission was the object of numerous attacks by conservative circles. One of the first decisions of the Targowica Confederacy, established toward the end of the existence of the Commonwealth, was to dissolve the Commission for National Education. The manifesto of the Confederacy declared: "The homeland will profit more from virtuous citizens than it will from mathematicians, astronomers and the like."

INSTRUMENTS OF THE CULTURAL OFFENSIVE: THE PRESS, BOOKS, THE SALONS, AND THE THEATER

Apart from the schools, the main links in the system of the promotion of culture were the printing shops, publishing houses, the press and books, libraries and reading-rooms, theaters, salons and clubs. The press, almost unknown in previous epochs, was gaining a dominant influence in this system. Although the first periodicals appeared as early as the seventeenth century, they were ephemeral and contained only selected, concise information about the world. The Enlightenment was the first era in the history of Polish culture, when cultural developments were inspired and publicized by periodicals. The variety of periodicals and the commitment of a majority of them to the defense of the new philosophy made them the main tools of progress. And the existence of conservative magazines increased the intensity of the polemics, bringing greater bitterness into the fight.

In the second quarter of the century, daily papers with information on domestic and foreign politics began to appear regularly. The privilege to publish was first granted to the Piarist Order; later, the Jesuits received permission. In the second half of the century a number of foreign language periodicals appeared in Warsaw. Undoubtedly, the greatest social and political influence was wielded by the "scholarly" press. It too had a long genealogy. The pioneering periodical was the *Polnische Bibliothek,* edited in Gdańsk by Gottfried Lengnich in 1718—19, which bore on its title page a reminder of the Polish victory at Grunwald. Numerous publications devoted to scientific developments in Poland and in the world appeared in Toruń. In Warsaw, Mitzler de Kolof began in 1753 to publish the *Warschauer Bibliothek;* two years later *Acta Litteraria Regni Poloniae et Magni Ducatus Lithuaniae* appeared; and from 1758, a non-periodical magazine beautifully and characteristically called *Nowe Wiadomości Ekonomiczne i Uczone albo Magazyn Wszystkich Nauk do Szczęśliwego Życia Ludzkiego Potrzebnych* (The New Economic and Scientific News, or a Magazine of All the Sciences Needed for a Happy Human Life) began publication.

Various periodicals on the natural sciences and economics were a continuation of these efforts, aimed at "universal advantage" or the "enlargement of practical skills". During the 1760's, "moral" periodicals began to appear. One of them was named *Patriota Polski* (The Polish Patriot), promoting the rarely used term "patriot". The leading publication became the *Monitor,* published regularly from 1765 for twenty years. It presented the royal court's program of the renewal of the state and society, attacking Sarmatian habits, obscurantism and fanaticism, economic backwardness, and the exploitation of the peasantry. Krasicki and Bohomolec were editors of the *Monitor* during its early period, and virtually, in most cases, the only contributors creating various forms of modern political journalism.

While the *Monitor* dealt with a wide range of modern problems concerning political philosophy, state organiza-

tion, and the reconstruction of the community, another periodical *Zabawy Przyjemne i Pożyteczne* (Pleasant and Useful Games) edited by Jan Chrzciciel Albertrandi from 1770, followed by Adam Naruszewicz, dealt with literature, stressing the traditions of Polish Renaissance poetry, classical poetry, especially Horace, and formed, in this way, the concept of a new poetic style.

In the 1880's, Piotr Świtkowski, editor for over ten years of the *Pomiętnik Polityczny i Historyczny* (Political and Historical Diary), the *Magazyn Warszawski* (Warsaw Magazine), which was devoted to the "fine arts and sciences", and the *Wybór Wiadomości Gospodarczych* (Selections of Economic News), greatly developed the art of publishing. Other editors undertook similar initiatives; numerous political and economic and scientific-literary periodicals were published.

The number of publications increased with the passage of time and with the intensification of political struggle in the country. Characteristically enough, a handwritten press was also in circulation, especially outside Warsaw, bringing news as well as political and cultural gossip, and attacking or defending the program of reform. The ideological orientation of the press was becoming more and more polarized. The *Gazeta Warszawska* (Warsaw Gazette), published from 1774 by Stefan Łuskina, consistently and violently attacked the ideology of the Enlightenment. The *Gazeta Narodowa i Obca* (National and Foreign Gazette), and *Korespondencja Obywatelska* (Civic Correspondence) supported the program of the patriotic party. The Targowica Confederacy founded several publications in order to influence public opinion. During the Kosciuszko Insurrection, the press was almost exclusively patriotic, but it was radical to varying degrees. It was becoming the true brains and conscience of the revolution and the insurrection.

Periodicals that molded society were accompanied faithfully by books, which Franciszek Salezy Jezierski called the "promissory notes" of truth and lies to be paid for in "later times". The intensified publishing trade in the country, foreign contacts, an increased supply of foreign books, and an enlarged reading market — all these were reasons why traditional forms of making use of books were insufficient and the necessity to look for new forms emerged. In earlier times Poland had possessed great private collections of books — royal, magnate, episcopal, professorial, and burgher libraries — only rarely accessible to the public. Yet the Enlightenment was a period of increasing educational needs, and demand from readers was too great to be met by private collections and libraries.

The brothers Józef and Andrzej Załuski met this demand, founding the first public library in Poland in Warsaw in 1747. Skillfully and with great care, they accumulated over 180,000 items, precisely catalogued. The library slowly gained readers. In 1773, it came under state ownership and developed under the protection of the Commission for National Education. From 1781, every printer was obligated to donate one copy of a book printed by him to the library.

Periodicals and books were produced in printing works

which were a vital instrument in the development of intellectual culture and its social scope. Remarkable quantitative and qualitative progress in this field was effected during the Enlightenment. Printing shops not only executed standing orders; but in many cases they were also publishing houses and, at the same time, book-shops. Because of this, the network of printing complexes was instrumental in determining the geographical distribution of culture, and the center where it was produced and disseminated.

The majority of printing houses were situated in Warsaw. Besides the printing houses located in monasteries, which from the beginning of the century also operated in the area of secular publications, the first private printing shops were opened up in 1756; during the same year, Mitzler de Kolof founded a printing house, which he subsequently gave to the Cadets' Corps. In 1759, Michał Gröll began his extensive activity in this field. In 1775, Piotr Dufour founded a printing house; two years later Piotr Zawadzki set up one of his own.

Numerous printing houses were opened in Cracow, Poznań, Gdańsk, Vilna, Lvov and in many smaller towns, sometimes exerting a nationwide influence: for example, the printing house at Berdyczów in 1767, published one of the most beautiful illustrated Polish books, *The Beauties of the Ukrainian Lands,* by G. Trześniewski. The printing house at Supraśl published not only religious books but also a number of scientific and literary works; the printing house in Grodno specialized in publishing political writings.

These printing houses were often owned by wealthy magnate families, as for example, the houses at Nieśwież, Puławy and Tulczyn. Many of them belonged to the monasteries. Sometimes, as in Toruń or Krzemieniec, they were owned by the schools.

Although the amount published by these numerous printing houses differed, their network, covering almost the entire country, defined to a significant degree the possible range of cultural influence. The institution of literary and scientific salons was highly characteristic of the Enlightenment culture. As in Western Europe, they also flourished in Poland, particularly in Warsaw.

The receptions given by the king's sister, Elżbieta Branicka, and at the home of the primate, Michał Poniatowski, were widely renowned. Stanisław Małachowski, the Speaker of the Seym, provided his guests with fine concerts and exquisite dinners. Various aristocratic homes received guests on different days of the week: the Sapiehas, Mniszechs, and Ogińskis. The well-to-do bourgeoisie followed the same pattern, especially the rich bankers, for example, Tepper.

But the character of the salons slowly changed. Not everyone was satisfied with these meager exchanges of ideas; some desired to use the power of thought to act in the community. The traditional salons were transformed into centers of thought which soon became a weapon.

The Forge (Kuźnica), founded by Hugo Kołłątaj, was described "as a new sect interested in man's freedom and equality". It was a singular institution. At the entrance to Kołłątaj's house was placed a locked box — a Polish version of the Roman *bocca della veritá* — destined for letters, requests, memoranda, and various complaints. Kołłątaj handled the correspondence personally. It provided him with information as to public opinion, wrongs done to the people, and the need for reform.

In Kołłątaj's salon, journalists, literary men, and politicians gathered together. Memoranda and legislative projects were prepared, manifestoes and leaflets written. The following were permanent associates of the Forge: Franciszek Salezy Jezierski, an erudite and lively political writer; men of science, like Jan Śniadecki; representatives of the bourgeoisie, like Jan Dekert and Franciszek Barss; numerous poets and writers, like Franciszek Ksawery Dmochowski, author of the *Art of Writing Rhyme* but also an astute satirist, and Franciszek Zabłocki, author of several comedies and very bitter and successful satires, published mostly as ephemeral letters, which circulated in Warsaw; and also a number of radicals.

The ideological and artistic climate of the salons also found expression in the theater. The court theater was the most characteristic phenomenon of the era. Almost in every magnate residence and in many rich manor-houses, theater productions were held; permanent theaters were opened; touring companies of artists were welcomed; repertory actors were engaged; and young apprentices were educated. In harmony with the tone of the era, these actors were often looked for among the children of the serfs, clerks, and overseers. Sometimes, special acting schools were founded for them, where drama, ballet, and music were taught. In many residences special theaters were built; sometimes other premises were adapted for this use, and often open-air summer auditoria were built in parks.

Information about more than fifty such theaters has been preserved, which, even allowing for the ephemeral life of some of them, is still evidence of the intensity of the theater life and theater culture of the Polish community during the eighteenth century.

Warsaw's theater life was especially rich and varied. Numerous theaters sponsored by the magnate palaces operated there, called *théâtres de société,* since usually the owners and their guests performed there. The theaters of Princess Sanguszko, Alojzy Fryderyk Brühl, and the Primate Gabriel Podoski, in which representatives of the most distinguished magnate families performed, were well known, as were many others.

Plays were systematically produced at the Royal Castle: from 1782, the court theater at Łazienki was in operation, at first in a separate building, which in time was razed, later on a stage built on the island, and finally, in the orangery.

The theater movement slowly embraced the entire country. In Lvov, productions began in 1780, rivalling the German theater; in Cracow a permanent stage was opened in 1781. In Vilna, efforts to organize a permanent theater were made as early as 1777, but it was only in 1785 that Bogusławski succeeded in establishing a permanent theater. At about the same time, theaters were opened in Lublin, Grodno, and in Poznań.

However, the center of theater life was the public theater in Warsaw, founded by order of the king in 1765, with three stages at its disposal: French, Italian and Polish. Many original plays by Polish authors, Bohomolec in particular, were produced. In March 1779, a cornerstone was laid for the erection of a new theater building; in September an auditorium for an audience of 800 was ready. From 1782, Bogusławski became director of the theater, and he administered it, with several breaks, up to the massacre of Praga by Suvorov's army in 1794, and later, after the failure of the Kosciuszko Insurrection, he again assumed the duties of director. During the Four Year Seym, the theater became a great political and patriotic platform. Such plays as *The Return of the Deputy,* and *Casimir the Great* by Niemcewicz, *Proof of the Nation's Gratitude* by Bogusławski, and *The Bourgeois Gentleman* by Wybicki, were produced in the theater. On 1 March 1794, *The Cracovians and Highlanders* by Bogusławski was produced, a harbinger of the uprising which would begin six weeks later.

Wojciech Bogusławski (1757—1829) was a phenomenon of the theater. An actor who performed various parts, a director and producer at many theaters, the founder of a drama school, he was also a prolific playwright. His collected works, published in Warsaw between 1820 and 1823, amounted to twelve volumes and did not include all of his plays. He wrote comedies and operas, adapted works by other authors for theater, translated and adapted Shakespeare, Lessing, Molière, Voltaire and many others.

As organizer and manager of theaters, Bogusławski was active in Warsaw, Poznań, Grodno, Dubno, Vilna, and Lvov; year after year he visited Łowicz, Kalisz, Białystok, Cracow, and Gdańsk. He was an indefatigable organizer of theater life in the country during all the varying periods of its history. The downfall of the state did not put an end to his activity. When he had to leave Warsaw, he organized a theater in Lvov; then again in Warsaw. He also performed in Poznań, Kalisz, and Łowicz, and was given permission to perform in towns of so-called Southern Prussia. During the period of the Duchy of Warsaw and the Kingdom of Poland, he operated mainly in Warsaw. In this way, Bogusławski's theater became an institution of cultural life and, at the same time, a school of patriotism during a difficult period of Poland's history.

SARMATISM, FOREIGN FASHIONS AND NATIONAL CULTURE

The great magnate courts no longer had the significance that they had once possessed in the sixteenth century, when they were centers of learning and culture. During the Enlightenment, they were rather consumers than creators of culture, distinguished rather by their life-style than by their artistic and intellectual contributions. Scattered fairly densely over the wide territories of the Commonwealth, they provided centers of contemporary fashion and continued the Sarmatian predilection for sophisticated entertainment and banquets.

In the comedies of Bohomolec and Zabłocki, in the satires by Naruszewicz and Krasicki, the new world was exposed, at first in a positive light, then more critically, but in both cases, as life diametrically different from that in the old gentry tradition. In this life, the young people appeared fashionably dressed, returning home from abroad, usually from Paris, distinguished by their society polish and conversational skills, but sometimes also by their accurate appraisal of Polish prodigality, negligence, deterioration, autocracy, and vulgarity. In this life there was room for music and poetry, and for amateur theatricals, with plays written by the lady or the master of the house.

In this contradiction between the Sarmatian and the fashionable world, the attitudes of the defenders of both ways of life became even more obvious. But, simultaneously, conditions were born to formulate a program in which both elements of modernity and of tradition were emphasized: modernity that would not superficially imitate foreign fashion, and tradition that would not preserve bad Sarmatian habits. This program, later called Enlightened Sarmatism, had many variations because it was implemented by various social circles.

In the higher reaches of society, it was carried out by the Czartoryskis. Their residence at Puławy was a counterpart of a metropolitan and foreign style of life. At Puławy the Sarmatian poet Kniaźnin faithfully expressed the moods reigning there: the attachment to Polish traditions and mementoes, the love of rural life and chivalrous sentiments.

It was not an empty gesture. Large numbers of the middle gentry, who were attached to ancient Polish patterns of life, were fascinated by the myth of the return of the Golden Age of Sigismund. During the Seym debates, followers of the reform program, not only conservatives, more and more frequently underscored the merits of the old political system and the need to respect particular national traits. Even prominent politicians like Kołłątaj and Staszic supported the idea of a unique Polish political system that would preserve valuable elements of Polish political traditions.

An expression of the alliance forming between followers of the reform program and the defenders of the national tradition was the call to return home, directed by the Seym to Bishop Adam Krasiński, one of the leaders of the Bar Confederacy. After returning, he joined in the preparation of the Constitution, which was being carried out by the patriotic camp.

The composition of the Seym testified to the social scope of this alliance. In the 1788 and 1790 elections, many candidates, followers of the old Sarmatian conservative ideology, were defeated, whereas deputies who understood the need for reform were elected. Manifesting their national traditionalism in their dress, they enacted laws that fundamentally changed the political system of the country. Niemcewicz's play *The Return of the Deputy,* which was performed during the Seym session and was enthusiastically acclaimed by the public and frequently commented upon, was proof of this new movement. The patriot-deputy was portrayed as a rational, modern Pole, who was true to Polish tradition. His opponents were both a fashionable cavalier, and an old-fashioned, conservative Sarmatian.

This ideology of Enlightened Sarmatism, a concept of

life which was equally modern and traditional, appealed to the wide masses of the gentry: the theater, press, and calendars were evidence of, and agents for, this new movement.

The variety of cultural life, its wealth and contradictions, appearing with varied force throughout the country, was centered in Warsaw. Warsaw held the foremost position in the Commonwealth. No other city could match it. Cracow was only just rising from its prolonged lethargy; Gdańsk stood on the threshold of economic catastrophe; and Poznań remained a small provincial city. Warsaw was a metropolis. Its population was fast increasing. The aristocracy and rich bourgeoisie had magnificent residences in Warsaw. The royal court was flourishing. Numerous foreigners visited the city.

Warsaw provided the visitor with all possibilities to participate in cultural life. In Warsaw, one could also enjoy every pleasure. Balls and parties were often held; numerous theatrical touring companies, both Polish and foreign, entertained audiences; there were many fashionable coffee-houses; various fêtes were organized; and the newest inventions were demonstrated, for example, balloon flights.

Warsaw was a magnet which attracted many people from the provinces, in quest of a way of life different from that they had to lead at home.

However, Warsaw was not only a city which promised fashionable and old-fashioned fun and pleasure, a city both desired and condemned; it was also a center of cultural life. The intellectual and literary life of the country was centered in Warsaw; discussions and polemics were waged; projects of reforms were drawn up; leaflets written; and opinion was molded. The style of life was not attractive to everybody; yet it had its charms for the select few. A new category of people was just then appearing called "literati", who kept abreast of social life and influenced important public matters. It was they, called by their opponents "scribblers and idlers", who fired up the masses in "gardens, promenades, and coffee-shops". In this atmosphere emerged the prototype of the political leader. Even priests, like Józef Mejer, Florian Jelski, and Michał Karpowicz, were attracted to the movement.

Under these circumstances, still another model of cultural life was taking shape, different from that defended by both conservative Sarmatians and enthusiasts of foreign lands, different even from that represented by enlightened patriots. It was a model of life which involved participation in the social and patriotic movements of the nation, and which, while opening up prospects for the future, brought with it intellectual values and opportunities for artistic expansion. This style of life was a legacy left by the Enlightenment to the generations born in bondage.

FOLK CULTURE

The peasantry remained outside the reaches of the culture of the Enlightenment. It constituted a social group isolated from that cultural life in which the gentry and the bourgeoisie participated. Although parish schools belonged to the national educational system and the Commission for National Education exercised some guardianship over them, they provided for only an elementary education and did not open up opportunities for advancement. The possibilities of reaching any higher levels of education were almost non-existent. A way out of this isolation could only be a career in the church, which was also hardly accessible to the sons of the peasantry. Both these ways, provided one succeeded, meant social advancement at the cost of relinquishing one's peasant background.

The peasant class thus lived in a tightly closed world of its own. Its material existence was generally hard; its social position was insignificant; and its everyday life was one of toil and hardship. Literature and art, especially Norblin's paintings, recorded this tragic state of affairs. Political writers attacked the egoism and shortsightedness of the gentry. Staszic described graphically a great march of peasants bearing signs with the slogan of social demands: "Human beings with a request for human treatment for human beings."

Under such unfavorable conditions, the peasantry lived with a culture of their own. As in previous eras, it was still rather the culture of work and everyday things, customs and rites, than that of the written and printed word. This type of culture did not leave lasting evidence behind, apart from various material objects, which would enable later generations to reconstruct its roots. The social discrimination and prejudice of the "higher" estate nonchalantly expressed scorn for these relics and did not allow them to be collected and preserved.

However, a characteristic trait of the Polish Enlightenment was the struggle against this prejudice, expressed in the care to register and preserve relics of peasant culture. The physiocratic movement aided these efforts. The conviction that the soil was the only source of wealth led to a positive assessment of the peasantry as the main producers of commodities, and, consequently, to an interest in its life and culture. Such was also the aim of sentimentalism, which, though at first it emphasized fictional values of the people and of the "complete man of nature", later opened up possibilities for a more realistic view of peasant culture.

Various projects in the area of research on the culture of the peasantry were recapitulated perfectly by Kołłątaj, with his usual acuteness. His concept of folk culture exposed the peculiar characteristics of the routine of everyday work and ceremonial feasts, relationships inside the village community, and the artistic and intellectual values, which maintained old beliefs and equally old prejudices.

At the same time, he showed that the peasant culture went beyond local interests and needs, that also oppressed and wronged people had an image of the world as an entirety, except that from their viewpoint different perspectives were opened up and an appreciation was made which differed from that accepted by the ruling classes.

Wojciech Bogusławski, with great artistic and political intuition, discovered the human values of the peasant outlook which were expressed in village songs. To universal human reflections in *The Cracovians and Highlanders* were added national ones. But they were not only a literary motif in a theater play; the Cracovians and Highlanders had often in Polish history really taken up arms for their homeland; not merely on the stage but also on the battlefields of Racławice, Szczekociny, and Warsaw. They participated in the fight with a "perverse" world for a free life and a just state. Peasant participation in the Kosciuszko Insurrection was evidence of the intensity of the patriotic feelings alive in folk culture, although the social and material position of the peasantry did not encourage them to defend the state, which still remained the sole domain of the gentry. Thus Krasicki was wrong when he wrote in the *Monitor* in 1765 that "they cannot love the Commonwealth who possess in it nothing of their own."

In this way folk culture, almost untouched by the culture of the Enlightenment, yet wholly opposed to the gentry's style of life, especially to conservative Sarmatism, entered into the composition of a new national culture. The specific values of the peasant culture — common sense, diligence, self-denying action for the universal good, and a sense of justice — were becoming the elements of patriotism which defended the state, and after the state's downfall, would guard the very existence of the nation.

Foreign Culture in Poland and Polish Culture in the World

FOREIGNERS IN POLAND

The Enlightenment in Poland was an age of lively contacts with the other countries of Europe. Although Poland had always had close contacts with the culture of Southern and Western countries, during the reign of Stanislaus Augustus these increased.

The first signs of this animation date from the reigns of the Saxon kings, when Stanisław Konarski in his Collegium Nobilium, and later in the reformed Piarist schools, opened up the window onto Europe, taking into account news of scientific progress, of modern philosophy, and of economic and political changes in Western countries. During this time, the brothers Andrzej Stanisław and Józef Andrzej Załuski began their acivity. In 1747 in Warsaw, a great public library was founded, mathematical and astronomical laboratories were set up, and contacts with foreign scholars were established, particularly in Germany. At the same time, Laurentius Mitzler de Kolof from Saxony began to publish occasional periodicals in German, Latin, and Polish. Mitzler's activity was supported by Józef Aleksander Jabłonowski, who established a scientific foundation in Gdańsk in 1761 (he later transferred this organization to Leipzig as Societas Jablonoviana), and Jan Małachowski who was especially interested in a new magazine entitled *Nowe Wiadomości Ekonomiczne i Uczone albo Magazyn Wszystkich Nauk do Szczrśliwego Życia Ludzkiego Potrzebnych* (New Economic and Scientific News, or a Magazine of All the Sciences Needed for a Happy Human Life). With Mitzler's assistance, in 1761 T. Bauch from Toruń inaugurated the publication of a periodical called *Patriota Polski kartki tygodniowe zawierający* (The Polish Patriot with News of the Week). It contained news about science and philosophy in Germany. The *Monitor* directed society's attention to England. Published from the year 1763 in Gdańsk by Adam Kazimierz Czartoryski, it appeared as an occasional periodical with a wealth of information conveyed in excellent literary form.

Other contacts were made possible due largely to Augustus III's court theater and the magnate theaters. Augustus III had seven theaters in his residences; in addition, he built a huge edifice called the Operalnia in the Saxon Garden. In these theaters French plays were produced, as well as Italian comedies. The operas of Pietro Metastasio were exceedingly popular and thirteen of them were staged in all. The magnate theaters, of which there were at least ten, had a very rich and varied repertoire. French seventeenth century classics in Polish translations were also staged, as were plays by Voltaire, for example, *Rome sauvée*. Mystery plays were also produced, such as the *Lord's Passion* by Pietro Metastasio, translated by Załuski.

Stanislaus Augustus' accession to the throne signalled an increase in foreign contacts, and, at the same time, gave direction to the Enlightenment. Owing to the activity of special agents, especially M. F. Grimm in Paris, the king had ample information about the artists, scholars and philosophers of all Europe. Royal initiatives covered a wide range. Although his personal interest directed the policy of the court toward the problems of art, the king, nonetheless, understood perfectly the significance of learning to a modern state and dedicated to it a good deal of attention. His action was appreciated abroad, as evidenced by the nomination of Stanislaus Augustus as a member to the Academies of Sciences in Berlin and St. Petersburg.

On the king's initiative, lively contacts were maintained with German scientific centers, especially with the German Academy of Sciences in Berlin. Charles de Perthées was active in Poland from 1764 on as a cartographer preparing maps of the whole country on the king's orders. In his work he cooperated with the Petersburg Academy of Sciences and with the outstanding mathematician, Leonhard Euler. Closer contacts with France were also made, greatly augmented by the fact that a great deal of information about France was included in the papers and that lively contacts were established by Poles going to Paris.

Tyzenhaus invited to Poland the French physician and naturalist, Jean Emmanuel Gilibert, who later described the Lithuanian flora. Adam Czartoryski invited the French physicist, J. B. Dubois, who, in 1777, founded the Society of Physical Sciences in Warsaw.

Characteristic evidence of the scope and intensity of these various scientific contacts was the participation of many foreigners in the works of the Commisssion for National Education. Pierre Samuel Du Pont de Nemours was a secretary to the Commission; Christian Pfleiderer was active in the Society for the Preparation of Elementary Books. The Swiss Simon L'Huiller prepared textbooks in mathematics. In 1777, Ignacy Potocki visited Condillac and asked him, on behalf of the Commission, to write a textbook on logic. Condillac agreed, and his book appeared in Paris in 1780. Unfortunately, the Polish translation was published only in 1802. The usefulness of this book is attested to by the fact that it was reprinted in 1808, and again in 1819.

However the largest group of foreigners in Poland was made up of artists: architects, painters, and sculptors. They were employed, for the most part, by the royal court, but also by the aristocratic families. After his death the royal architect Jakub Fontana was succeeded in 1773 by an Italian, Domenico Merlini, who designed the reconstruction of the Royal Castle and Łazienki Palace. Jan Kamsetzer, of German origin, worked with Merlini. Bonawentura Solari was active in Poznań, Józef Sacco of Verona in Grodno, Jan Chrzciciel Knackfuss and Carlo Spampani in Vilna. Efraim Schröger of Toruń worked for the Warsaw bourgeoisie and numerous buildings were erected by Szymon Bogumił Zug, both of German descent. Joachim Hempel and Piotr Aigner worked for the Czartoryskis at Puławy. Stanisław Kostka Potocki brought Vincenzo Brenna to Poland. When Stanisław Zamoyski decided to reconstruct his residence at Zamość, he invited, besides architects working in Poland, like Hempel and Aigner, the most outstanding architects of Europe, like Percier and Fontaine, to design the project.

The same was true of painting. There were painters from Italy: Bernardo Bellotto called Canaletto, Marcello Bacciarelli, Gianbattista Lampi, and Josef Grassi; from France: Louis Marteau, Jean Pierre Norblin, Jean Piliment, and Charles Bechon; from Germany: Josef Pitschman and Anton Friedrich Lohrman. Sculptors, too, arrived from various countries. The greatest renown was attained by Andreas Le Brun of France, who worked mostly for the royal court; several Italian sculptors worked with him, including Giacomo Monaldi, who embellished the Łazienki Palace, Tommaso Righi and Giovachino Staggi. Numerous groups of foreign artists worked in craft production, especially in the manufacture of china at Belweder and Korzec.

To the list of these foreigners must be added numerous artists who, although of foreign descent, lived in Poland for a long time and considered themselves Polish in spirit: among the most prominent were Jan Bogumił Plersch, born in Warsaw; Dominik Estreicher of Moravian descent; and Daniel Chodowiecki from Gdańsk, who always emphasized his Polish roots.

Other artists, working in Poland as first generation immigrants, were subject to a process of Polonization which was evidence of the great attractiveness of the culture. Some accepted posts in the civil and military services. Sacco was a major; Knackfuss, a captain of artillery; others, like Norblin and Grassi, were personally committed to Polish patriotic movements, as for example, the Kosciuszko Insurrection.

Finally, it is worth mentioning that Poland was visited by adventurers and mountebanks, who were often notorious in contemporary Europe. Giovanni Casanova, who amidst his many love affairs aspired also to various high posts at the royal court, stayed in Warsaw during the years 1765—66; a dozen years later, in 1780, Alessandro Cagliostro, who combined mysterious alchemy and magic with his Masonic activities, arrived in Warsaw. L. Harrsch, an Austrian working in Poland from 1779, proposed many spectacular but highly dubious technical ideas.

DIALOGUE WITH WESTERN CULTURE

Contacts with foreign culture were of course not limited to the activity of foreigners in Poland. A growing number of Polish visitors abroad — of young people from wealthy families, artists, poets, writers, and political leaders — were a source of knowledge concerning the social and cultural life of other nations. Many people traveled in order to study various fields of science abroad, as, for instance, was the case with Staszic and Śniadecki; in other cases, these trips served as a means for gaining new experiences and new artistic skills. Politicians and economists, deputies and senators of various political views also made such trips. From the days of the Bar Confederacy, it became almost obligatory to establish such contacts.

At the same time, hundreds of translations of works by the most outstanding foreign authors began to appear. After years of relative isolation, every new movement of European intellectual and artistic life became a source of interest. Several seventeenth century writers, especially French, were finally translated. But translations of Bacon and Descartes were still not published; their Latin translations were considered adequate. Pascal was also ignored. On the other hand, prominent eighteenth century writers were translated *en masse*, in their entirety or in abridged form, sometimes in adaptations. Polish readers had direct access to the works of Locke, Montesquieu, Pope, Fontenelle, Voltaire, Rousseau, Young, Ossian, Buffon, and Diderot. Of course, Catholic apologetics was translated, as, for instance, the works of Caracciolli, Pable, and others. It was also customary to prepare more or less precise synopses of the opinions of various foreign authors, especially the more difficult authors, like mathematicians and philosophers, whose theories had been referred to in Polish books; this was the background of two physics textbooks, by Samuel Chróścikowski (1764) and Józef Rogaliński (1765—76).

At the same time, booksellers, taking advantage of the wide knowledge of French among the richer classes of society, imported the latest Parisian publications to Poland. The conservatives, highly upset by these activities, asserted that in Poland one might buy books "which on pain of harsh punishment were not allowed to be sold in any other European state."

Under these circumstances, the intellectual and artistic culture of Poland was interwoven in various ways with all movements of the era. In the salons and in the press in Warsaw, as in other capitals of the world, discussions were conducted on the paradoxical thesis of Rousseau, concerning the progress of civilization and the happiness of man. Voltaire stimulated bitter disputes in Poland as he did elsewhere. His philosophical writings, tales, and dramas had their defenders and opponents. The information and criticism which was included in the *Encyclopédie* aroused interest. Numerous works by the most outstanding French and Italian lawyers were utilized in improving the country's legal system. Montesquieu was a favorite writer from the days of Konarski to the Four Year Seym. At the same time, Ossian's "melancholy" poems were winning popularity beyond Puławy: Krasicki, the rational poet, translated this somber and sentimental poetry. Similarly, Dmochowski, the arbiter of classical style and a follower of Boileau-Despréaux, was fascinated with Young's poetry and translated some of his works. The novel, especially the French novel, had its admirers and imitators. Dramas and comedies, especially Italian, were translated and adapted. The classical writers also experienced a renaissance in the Poland of Stanislaus Augustus. Their texts were read in a way different from former times when the gentry's political movement was alive and the later rhetorics of the Baroque were in style. Moralists and poets were appreciated: for example, Virgil, who was avidly imitated. Lucian of Samosata was translated by Minasowicz and later by Krasicki. Krasicki was influenced by Lucian, to whom he devoted one of his studies, in writing his "conversations of dead Poles". On the other hand, Karpiński wrote his *Dialogues of Plato with His Pupils* under the influence of Plato.

This influx of foreign literature was a source of numerous and complex controversies. The author of an article which appeared in the *Monitor* in 1767, complained: "Who, particularly among respectable people, reads books written in their native language? There is now more attention given to foreign deceits, than to more useful works born in Poland . . . Ultimate scorn of Polish wits and blind love for things foreign never achieved such a high level as it has now."

However, it cannot be denied that these same translated books brought new and important knowledge to Poland, knowledge which was also useful in practical matters. Even the Jesuits appreciated this fact. In the preface to *A History of Custom and Reason* (1762), translated by Andrzej Bromirski, the following statement appeared: "One who does not think about science in the terms Descartes applied to physical matters is not worthy of living in the present age." In *Zabawy Przyjemne i Pożyteczne,* edited by Adam Naruszewicz, we find the following comment: "Look at Descartes, mocking the obsolete peripatetic philosophy . . . Look at Bacon, who leaves the dark remnants of ignorance." Another periodical stated the following: "Copernicus had the courage to follow the light of his own reason; Galileo followed Copernicus' opinion . . . Gassendi discovered the easiest and most perfect way of dealing with philosophy . . . Much of its light and perfection philosophy owes to Newton, Leibniz, and Locke."

Under these conditions the line separating Polish and foreign scientific literature was similar to that which divided old-fashioned scholastic philosophy and the underdeveloped natural sciences from modern scientific progress and rationalist empirical philosophy which made possible technical progress.

The fight in defense of the old positions could only be led from a metaphysical and religious standpoint. Much polemical literature, for the most part Polish, attacked the "philosophy of *recentorium*", accusing it of leading to atheism through the intermediate step of deism, and consequently, to universal demoralization. However, despite the opposition, new movements were not only winning appreciation but, during the last two decades of the eighteenth century, also became a source of modern and socially significant Polish scientific thought and popular science studies.

It was not so simple in other fields, especially in the field of socio-political issues: it was not always clear where the demarcation line between progress and backwardness was. Konarski, in his desire to reform the Polish Seym, referred to the models of Venice, England, and the Netherlands and attacked the upstart Sarmatian concepts concerning the superiority of Polish structural forms. His argumentation, however, did not convince everybody. Followers of conservative ideology contrasted the "liberties" prevailing in Poland with the "bondage" that reigned in other countries.

This dispute between partisans of foreign constitutional structures and their opponents, which in effect was a dispute between people of the reform movement and the Sarmatian gentry, became more complicated in the last quarter of the century, when an unexpected compatibility between the free institutions of the Commonwealth and the ideals of the French Enlightenment and its struggle against absolutism was discerned. Rousseau, who was to produce a draft of reform for the Polish constitution, did not find a great deal to improve in the existing law.

It appeared that the recognition of native Polish traditions ceased to be a sign of backwardness and could be reconciled with modern thought.

It required considerable intellectual maturity to formulate a program for the modernization of Poland on the line of the developed Western states and in accordance with the ideas of the Enlightenment, since it might well seem that the radical libertarian ideology of pre-revolutionary Europe and America could only be embodied in a country ruled by the people, and not by an absolute monarch.

The falseness of such suggestions was clearly perceived by the most outstanding leaders of the reform camp, especially by Staszic and Kołłątaj. Kołłątaj stressed the dependence of the political system on local conditions, from which it ensued that no model could be transplanted from one country to another and no model could "provide a pattern of wisdom and perfection". In his comparison between Poland and other countries, and not only in relation to royal power, Staszic stated: "Here stands Poland! And how far have other countries gone! . . . Poland is still in the fifteenth century. The whole of Europe is approaching the end of the eighteenth century."

The growth of radical ideology in Europe and finally the French revolution convinced many that social change was the measure of modernity and progress and that in this respect Poland was far behind other nations which in various ways had overcome the feudal system. This meant that Poland could learn something from these examples.

But it was experience of revolution that for many became a warning signal and again strengthened the conviction about the wisdom of the "Poles of yore" and the old order. Only the small group of Polish Jacobins stressed the significance of French developments for the whole world. The majority of public opinion, frightened by these events accepted the declarations of the conservative camp and their program for the restitution of Sarmatism.

Under these circumstances the policy of the patriotic camp was becoming increasingly more difficult. Its leaders were aware, however, that they were preparing and conducting reforms that would "change the old shape of the country", while not necessarily being an imitation of any European model. The creators of the Constitution of the Third of May in a book published after the downfall of the state, *On the Making and Fall of the Third of May Constitution,* asserted the following: "Poland, until recently condemned as a nest of barbarism and feudalism which trampled upon human rights, showed in the acts of the Constitutional Seym that it was a match for the most eminent nations in Europe in its true enlightenment, reasonable legislation, sentiment and esteem for human rights."

On this note the great controversy between Sarmatian megalomania and subservience to foreign lands, between native and foreign influence — a controversy also known during other periods of Poland's culture, though never in such a sharp form — was finally ended during the period of the Enlightenment. Kołłątaj's diagnosis accurately assessed the results of the controversy. A possibility opened up for a third way which would saddle the two extremes: original, and yet European, rooted in tradition and yet modern, a way in which "homeliness" was not identical with conservative blindness and foreign influence did not necessarily mean national resignation or national renegation.

This experience became the most significant achievement of the social consciousness of the Enlightenment and was carried over into later periods. Henceforth, it would be more obvious than ever before that the issue of Poland and the world could not be dealt with within the dual categories of things native and foreign, but rather as seeking and finding, by new means and under new conditions, a third road, the road of dialogue and responsibility.

POLAND IN THE EYES OF THE WORLD

Of what significance was the Poland of the Enlightenment to the world?

The system of the Commonwealth, so unusual in the context of the modern development of European countries, and the partitions, which by stages annihilated the great state, were subjects of reflection for many philosophers, politicians, historians, and writers, especially in France, England, Germany and Switzerland. Even the most outstanding of them — Montesquieu, Rousseau, Mably, and Hume — were interested in Poland.

Montesquieu in his *Defense de L'Esprit des lois* sharply criticized the Polish political system, pointing out that "out of the liberty of every nobleman comes universal oppression". Similar views were expressed by an outstanding lawyer, Gaspar de Réal, in 1762, who criticized the free elections, the *liberum veto,* the confederacies, the economic weakness, and the oppression of the peasantry. Pierre Solignac, secretary to Stanislaus Leszczyński, in his *History of Poland* which he published in 1761, stated the following: "Unmoved in the corner of Europe, they did not go through any of the revolutions which occurred elsewhere; everything around them has changed, and they have remained unaltered, just what they were four centuries ago." In establishing the image of Poland in European opinion, a study in three volumes by Father Gabriel Coyer, *A Story of John Sobieski* (1761), had great significance. Although dealing with the reign of only one king, it contained a great deal of information about Poland and reflections upon its system and on the Polish national character. Coyer emphasized both the good and the bad sides of Polish life: love of liberty, heroism, hospitality, and at the same time, licence, anarchy, exploitation of the peasants, economic backwardness, anachronistic administration, and a political system full of contradictions. The author of the article on Poland included in the *Encyclopédie,* who characterized the Polish way of life as "a natural love of freedom and wild instinct which superseded the laws and the authority of the king", relied heavily on Coyer's study.

A renewed interest in Poland came with the Bar Confederacy. The confederates' envoy, Michał Wielhorski, visited Rousseau and Mably, who both commented extensively upon the situation in Poland and its internal conditions.

Rousseau, in his *Considérations sur le gouvernement de la Pologne* (1771), stated that "while reading the history of the Polish government, it is difficult to understand how a state so oddly organized could have lasted so long". Rousseau, however, did not form a negative conclusion about the country's fundamental political institutions. On the contrary, free elections, the confederacies, and the *liberum veto,* were, according to Rousseau, an expression of the intensity of social life, of the greatness of patriotism and communal feeling. It was the ceaseless "fire of youth" which had so many times saved Poland in times of danger. In a country where "souls still preserved their great bravery", asserted Rousseau, it was possible to keep even "the beautiful right of *liberum veto*". Unable to wage an aggressive war, Poland appeared to be a country of liberty to those under despotic rule. And even if she were to succumb to the despots, a reduction in the size of her territories would be of advantage to the nation.

Voltaire, too, although he occupied a position different from that of Rousseau, expressed a similar view. Although with his usual sharpness he criticized the chaos and poverty in Poland and the laziness of its inhabitants who in his opinion, "do not shine in diligence", he appreciated the powerful force of "the love of freedom" in Poland and a stubbornness in resisting misfortune and danger. "The Poles," wrote Voltaire, "compare themselves to reeds bent towards the earth by a storm, but which right themselves immediately after the wind passes."

Mably, although he too appreciated the liberal institutions in Poland, was more severe in his appraisal of their merits within the contemporary political situation. He perceived the anarchy that was growing in Poland, yet believed in the possibility of renewal, based on patriotism and the wisdom of the gentry. Later, after his visit to Poland, his prognosis about the future of the state became more pessimistic. But the eventual defeat of Poland would be the defeat of a free country, though monarchical, a defeat inflicted by despots. This thought was elaborated upon by Claude Rulhière in a great three-volume work, published later in 1807, in which he compared the situation of Poland vis-à-vis Russia to that of Greece in the face of Persia, and praised the great merits of Poland which had been destroyed by military might.

Similar opinions, although without these analogies, were expressed by various English writers, who were concerned with the growth of despotism in Europe. Criticizing anarchy and the oppression of the peasantry, they asserted, however, that the true danger to Poland was, as John Lind had remarked earlier, "the tyranny and ambition of the three powers".

Stephen Jones confirmed this view in his study. While criticizing Polish anarchy and social injustice, he appreciated the efforts to reform the state and exposed the intrigues of foreign powers, especially those of the King of Prussia, Frederick II, who proved to be "more tyrannical than could be imagined". Writers in America, who remembered Polish participation in their fight for independence, watched with anxiety the increase of despotism and reaction in Europe, one manifestation of which was the annihilation of Poland.

This anxiety grew with the growth of danger to Poland. Under the impact of these new developments, many writers altered their old views. For example, Hume, who in 1754 had severely criticized the backward and unjust system which existed in Poland, expressed regret that "barbaric Vandals" had gained in power at the cost of a civilized nation. Diderot, an admirer of the intelligence and merits of Catherine II, called the partition of Poland "an offense to humanity". Many other liberal writers reiterated their critical opinions regarding the partitions of Poland, sensing the danger to the European community and to smaller nations, faced with the greed of the larger nations. Conservative writers in England, however critical of the Polish system, greeted the partition of Poland with uneasiness, comparing it to the Tartar invasion. The most outstanding of these, Edmund Burke, in a speech delivered in Parliament, called the Constitution of the Third of May a model of moderate and gradual solution for serious social and political problems.

Opinions of philosophers and historians, formulated from afar, found confirmation in records based on direct contacts with the country and its inhabitants. In the eighteenth century, as in previous eras, Poland was an object of interest to travelers — trade agents, diplomats, and artists. In their accounts, critical judgments of Polish reality — the roads, the inns, the material conditions of life, the decline of the towns, the poverty of the peasants, the despotism of the gentry — interlocked with enthusiastic praise for the people, their openness and conviviality, their love of a free life, and their patriotism. Johann Kausch, in his book *News About Poland,* published in Graz in 1793, declared: "I honor that nation with all my heart."

The Prince de Ligne, doted upon in all the courts of Europe, wrote the following about Poland: "Who would not prefer of all cities to stay in Warsaw, where the best French tone rules, combined with a certain Eastern feature, European taste married to the Asiatic, the elegance of manners of the most civilized countries and a hospitality that one can nowadays find only among the untutored? Who would not adore a nation, in which he finds figures most noble and most kind, customs gentle and simple, politeness and frankness or good-natured rudeness in the villages, an easy understanding, a volatility and grace in conversation, good manners, all the talents . . . taste for the arts . . . delights in luxury . . . a carefree life, kindness, tenderness and gratitude?"

All these opinions of Poland, of its history and present day status, treated Poland as a subject deserving of interest, especially since its plight was, in the words of Stephen Jones, "becoming an important issue to all of Europe." The Swiss historian Johannes Müller defined it more precisely, writing that the first partition was "a harbinger of the annihilation of European freedom" by despots. Müller also expressed the hope that even the loss of statehood would not destroy the great nation and that "we will still witness the renewal of the Piasts, Jagiellonians and Sobieskis."

Yet taken as a whole, Poland's share in European culture during the Enlightenment was not great. When Latin ceased to be a universal language, the language barrier began to operate mercilessly in all those fields which used the word as a means of expression: in science, philosophy, literature and theater. Certainly, Staszic's and Kołłątaj's philosophy of history were a definite step forward, compared with contemporary philosophical systems in France or England, in the formulation of new problems and providing a broad vision of the development of Humanity. These reflections, however, never entered Europe's intellectual life because of the language in which they were written. Certainly, Krasicki's or Trembecki's fables deserved to take their place among the best eighteenth century literature. Europe never took notice of them, although some of Krasicki's works were translated into German and French. The great political literature linked with the reform of the state during the Four Year Seym deserved to be placed alongside the political writings of revolutionary France; these works not only included a program of local action, but formulated general, universally significant principles. Only a later translation into German of the work *On the Making and Fall of the Third of May Constitution* made by Samuel Bogumił Linde, directed the attention of philosophers and politicians to that issue.

Only those who wrote in foreign languages were known abroad. The memoirs of Maurycy Beniowski, published in English in 1790 and in French in 1791, as well as Jan Potocki's novel *The Saragossa Manuscript,* published in French in 1813, were popular abroad. These books represented Poland only indirectly, as a starting point for adventure, for the exotic, or for oriental reflections.

No linguistic barrier existed in art. But in this field, Poland had nothing worthy of great attention: neither in painting, and sculpture, nor in music. Only in architecture, although for the most part created by foreigners, were there more significant achievements. "The style of Stanislaus Augustus" had an individual eloquence: it was European, but, at the same time, Polish.

There was one more field in which language did not constitute a barrier because it was governed by a universal tongue: that of arms. In this area, Poland during the Enlightenment made her most notable contribution to international solidarity in the struggle for freedom. It is astonishing that Kosciuszko and Pulaski were motivated in the direction of a far-off country to participate in a fight for its freedom. What was it that led the young Kosciuszko into the ranks of Washington's army? What led the commander of the Bar confederates and defender of Częstochowa to the field of battle in America, where he won a victory in March 1779, at Charleston, and died a soldier's death in the fall of that year? The motivation can be found in the idea, formulated so often in the political writings of the Polish Enlightenment, that the cause of liberty is indivisible and that the struggle for it anywhere is a fight of all nations for the sake of each nation, and of each nation for all nations. This thought was reiterated in one of the speeches after Kosciuszko's death: "Defending with his life the liberty and independence of his nation, he saved, by that action, the right of all nations, proving again by his example that the instincts of free people are unerring."

With this brave and self-denying participation in the struggle for American independence, the Poland of the Enlightenment inaugurated a great road, which was to be taken "For your freedom and ours".

Conclusions

A remarkable feature of the Polish Enlightenment was that it progressed much more rapidly than the evolution of society. During the entire period Poland remained a feudal state in which, as was the case in previous centuries, all political power and economic privileges rested in the hands of the gentry. Only at the turn of the century, and in a limited measure, did the Constitution of the Third of May alter the situation. This contemporary class structure was reflected in the mentality and in the traditional, thoroughly feudal, morals of the period.

Despite this contradiction, the Polish Enlightenment taught how to perceive and appreciate and also transform the social world from the viewpoint of man and humanity.

Both concepts were new; both aroused uneasiness; both were targets of attacks. Franciszek Salezy Jezierski wrote the following: "The paragons of nobility had to stand under the Parisian street-lamps in order that their light might show them what actually is the name 'man'." Kołłątaj moved outside the boundaries of European thought, stating that "everybody, both white and black slave, is a man". The solidarity of all peoples in the struggle for progress constituted Staszic's main proposition. He often explained that "the rights of man violated in one country become an injury and danger to all mankind". The title of his most important work was *Human Kind.* Jakub Jasiński expressed the idea of universal solidarity in the words, "the human family". An anonymous poet wrote: "The number of clergy, nobles and lords in a country is the number of tyrants conspiring against humanity."

There was increasingly bitter opposition to the view that divided society into gentry and non-gentry: that is well-born people and all others who did not deserve the name of man. And even when that classification was not made overtly, discrimination was applied in practice, in appraising people and their privileges.

The Polish Enlightenment created other criteria for evaluating people — the idea of natural equality, accepting only disparities arising in consequence of their education, abilities, and diligence. It presented a vision of society in which people would not rule people, entering instead into mutual relationships in a direct way, not defined by class criteria. It also established new principles of evaluating man and his activities. Kosciuszko proclaimed: "From now on when promoting someone, I shall consider ability more than tradition."

The Polish Enlightenment effected an unusual emancipation of thought from the bonds of feudal society in a dual meaning, individual and social.

Individually, the creative activity of the men of the Enlightenment broke with the limitations it was subjected to by the social structure. First of all, it freed itself from the ties of the church hierarchy. The most outstanding writers of the Enlightenment belonged to the clergy: Staszic, Kołłątaj, even Jezierski. Some, like Krasicki or Naruszewicz, were bishops. But their intellect was not bound by this. Similarly they were not bound by class limitations. Kołłątaj was a nobleman; Staszic a member of the bourgeoisie, but their scientific and political activity was independent of their origin, very much alike, and attained a universal, national character. They were not exceptions. During the Enlightenment a group of people emerged from various sectors of society, tied by a common idea of action.

The Polish Enlightenment established the foundations for a truly modern method in knowledge of nature and society, and the discovery of the laws governing them. Scientific knowledge was utilized in the economy, education, health services, and military art. Efforts were undertaken to combine theory with practice, requiring scholars to make their discoveries useful. Others were encouraged to take advantage of science. Staszic felt that "the sciences were but a vain discovery, idle conclusions of reason or futile entertainment, unless they are applied for the profit of nations". Simultaneously, the Enlightenment, not restricting learning within purely utilitarian limits, made it interesting for wider circles of society, since for the first time in the history of Polish culture, learning was not only to be cultivated, but also disseminated, thanks to schools, periodicals, salons and even church pulpits. The meaning of learning for society was also apparent in the social and political spheres. Scholars were included in public life; efforts were made to raise politics to the level of scientific observation and scientific predictions. Very rarely before, and infrequently later, was there such an alliance between the social sciences, in the contemporary meaning of the word, and political action, as was the case during the Enlightenment.

In the history of Polish culture, it was the first epoch in which rational thought and useful action were taught. During the short era from the accession to the throne of Stanislaus Augustus to the downfall of the state, many serious reforms were planned and carried out. They did not constitute social revolution (sometimes the Enlightenment was accused of compromise and fearfulness) but formed a remarkable step forward on the way of progress. And they demonstrated to society that rational planning and wise, self-denying people were able to change reality.

Poland, which in the opinion of conservatives had "fallen into anarchy", tried to save its own existence by means of reform of the state organization and of the social consciousness. Transforming the feudal mentality, opening up prospects for public activity and economic calculation, the Enlightenment did not cancel out all traditional values. The Polish chivalrous tradition was interpreted in a specific way, endowing it with the modern form of *virtuti militari*. Although the Knights' School taught this new "catechism", the program of the Commission for National Education was only a "civic" one. Kołłątaj criticized this in the face of the menace to the country, and Staszic also had reservations asserting that "these schools were educating rational people, but not diligent and valiant ones".

And concurrently, the Enlightenment, in emphasizing the laws of reason, defended the rights of the heart more than is usually believed. This is evident not only in poetry, represented by Karpiński and Kniaźnin, but also in the discussions about "men of nature", who "had no education", but had "tenderness". It was also apparent in the widespread current of sentimentalism and the attachment to national mementoes and to national history; it could moreover be seen in the conception of morality, where charity and heroism were placed above the level of utilitarian accounts. It was evident in the concept of love of homeland, which Krasicki asserted could only be felt "by honest hearts". Staszic, in 1786, stated: "In education, above all, the heart should be shaped... It seems to me that we have neglected the heart altogether."

The course of historical events, which shaped the plight of the nation, became a great school for the education of the heart, diametrically opposed to the fashionable sentimental education of the salons; the partitions, and the danger of complete annihilation of the state, the difficult victories and painful defeats on the battlefields during the armed struggle for freedom and independence, the awareness of the great injustice and wrongs which undermined the "natural" order of the life of the nation; the protest and appeal addressed to mankind and to the Creator of the world as well, the search for salvation by means of the nation's own forces in acts of heroism and self-denial — this was the education of the heart, which during the Enlightenment allied itself with the education of reason, attempting to define the best strategy for action, a program of social revolution, which would give new meaning to the concepts of patriotism on the streets and squares of Warsaw, Cracow and Vilna.

Absorbed by concrete tasks within the sphere of politics in the broadest meaning of the term, the Polish Enlightenment rarely reached great heights in areas of philosophy and metaphysics, although it searched for the ultimate, universal laws of the world. The majority of thinkers of the Polish Enlightenment accepted, with some reservations, deism, but never crossed the borderline which divided it from atheism. Perhaps because of this no enlightened criticism of the church, or of religion, took root in Polish society. Some of the criticism, poetic rather than scientific, directly attacked the Pope.

But this period of freethinking and criticism resulted in some religious verses that became a living and lasting national heritage to this very day, like for example, Karpiński's Christmas carols, and especially his morning and evening hymns.

The variety of ideological currents during the Polish Enlightenment was the legacy forwarded to future generations, after the fall of the state; this legacy consisted of the integration of political and cultural movements, as well as moral patterns and models for life, which later would appear separately, sometimes even in contradiction. In the culture of the Enlightenment, even when contradictions did appear, the various directives for action were generally coherently associated. The program of education was combined with the prospects and tasks for reorganizing the state and reshaping the social consciousness, combined in such a manner that the implementation of the program was to precede political reform. Political reform was combined with economic change, and economic renewal with the restructuring of the social system. This restructuring in turn was to be a condition for the success of the armed struggle for the preservation of the state's independence, and success in the fight was to be a precondition for implementing social reform.

In the work and activity of the most outstanding people of the Enlightenment, this integration, filled with tensions and contradictions, and yet significant and creative, was implemented. The Kosciuszko Insurrection can be evaluated in this light, although future generations would offer contradictory interpretations. And while in the future a division would be made between educational and political action, between a program of armed struggle and of social revolution, between economic growth and ideals of social justice, the Polish Enlightenment would remain an example of the reconciliation of contradictions, completed sometimes at the cost of compromise, yet nevertheless always true to the real value of life.

THE PERIOD OF BONDAGE

Introduction

There was no Polish state from 1795 to 1918. However, the Polish nation existed and struggled for its existence within the borders of Russia, Prussia, and Austria. And, consequently, Polish culture also existed. The fate of culture during this era has particular significance in the thousand years of Poland's history.

The period of political bondage was long. Many things changed in Europe during this period and therefore many things changed for the partitioning powers and on Polish soil. The international situation was in flux, processes of social and economic change were going on, intellectual and artistic ideas were emerging and passing. The nineteenth century was witness to many changes everywhere. These changes may be divided in many ways into various periods in order to show different stages of development. Poland could not escape these changes. The country participated in these European processes in fuller measure than ever before and with no major delays. It is possible to speak of Poland's cultural history according to European standards of the age and in several different periods, sometimes even mutually contradictory. One contradiction in particular established itself in the social consciousness, that between Romanticism and Positivism.

We shall, however, present cultural history during the period of captivity as one comprehensive unit. For, despite the great differentiation, the basic situation concerning the threat to the nation's existence remained unchanged throughout, as did the same overall task of defending that existence by means of a daily battle against the policy of the partitioning powers, and through diplomatic channels and an armed struggle for the restoration of the state's independence. Various phases of Polish culture of the period, while connected with various forms of European culture as a whole, were at the same time an expression of changing conditions of life, as well as of changing strategies of action. Polish Romanticism and Polish Positivism were merely variations expressed within the limits of the same fundamental basic experiences of national existence and within the framework of the same overall objectives.

While stressing the overall unity, we do not mean, of course, to overlook the differences. The nation's bondage began when the period of the Polish Enlightenment was still in full swing. But the catastrophe that befell the state left a distinct mark on Polish culture, that later was characteristic of all other great cultural currents of the nineteenth century in Poland. The 1820's witnessed the birth of Romanticism, and the plight of the nation weighed heavier on the development of this movement than it did on other artistic and intellectual currents. The romantic style of life in Poland, as in no other country, had to undergo a great ordeal, that of the 1830 Insurrection. Romanticism, the most deeply national art, reached its peak not on home soil but in exile, under circumstances alien to the development of the trend elsewhere around the world. The greatest works of Polish Romanticism were created abroad, mostly in France, where all the most outstanding poets — Adam Mickiewicz, Juliusz Słowacki and Zygmunt Krasiński — lived for years on end. Concurrently in their native country, until as late as the 1850's, other non-romantic styles of art developed, always hampered by censorship.

From 1850 on, developing in different ways in the different partition zones, another current was born in Warsaw circles named Positivism. Its development, too, although closely linked with European philosophy and learning, was taking place within the orbit of social and national needs and actions, differently organized under changing conditions of economic and political life, under new structures of class relationships which took shape only after the abolition of serfdom and the beginnings of the labor movement.

Even this trend in Polish culture changed at the turn of the nineteenth and twentieth centuries, the period commonly called the era of the Young Poland, or Neo-Romanticism, or Modernism. Not one of these names was sufficiently comprehensive, but all of them applied to that movement in art which developed particularly in Cracow, because political conditions there permitted a relatively freer development of Polish culture than was possible in other parts of the country. However, within the Kingdom of Poland during the era of the growing forces of social revolution and the events of 1905, combined with the omens of the forthcoming armed conflict between antagonistic blocs in Europe, new experiences and new hopes were also emerging. They left a distinctive mark on the culture of the era which ended with World War I and with the regaining, after 123 years of foreign rule, of Polish independence.

Place in Europe and Historical Consciousness

BEAUTY OF THE NATIVE LAND

At the end of the nineteenth century the Polish state disappeared from the map of Europe and Polish lands were incorporated into the territories of Russia, Prussia and Austria. But those lands remained the home of the Polish people and that home, as expressed in the Polish national anthem, "shall not perish so long as we are alive". These circumstances produced a particular attachment of the people to the soil which, albeit unprotected by state organization, remained the basic element of the homeland and was present within the social consciousness in a greater and more profound way than ever before. Science and philosophy, poetry and painting, all contributed to the expressing and the shaping of this relationship to the native soil. By a common effort a great page in the history of Polish culture was written forever, remaining at the same time true to the experiences and needs of a stateless nation.

The first steps in the new direction were taken by the pseudo-classicists, especially Franciszek Wężyk and Kajetan Koźmian. The Romantics, who followed suit, managed to render the particular atmosphere of Polish nature which took under its protection men who tried to find refuge from a hostile world. *The Song of Our Land,* written by Wincenty Pol in 1835 and published in 1843, became exceedingly popular. It was an appeal to youth, repeated many times, to take interest in their native land in order that they might embrace their patriotism and gain strength that would allow them not to fall "under the heaviest blows."

The Song of Our Land was a model of its kind. However, almost all literature of the period spoke of the native land in much the same way, and the same was true of philosophy. In his well-known dissertation, *On the Love of the Homeland,* the philosopher, Karol Libelt, turned his attention to the significance of the native soil as a fundamental component of patriotism, whereas his system of aesthetics included, to a large degree, the beauty of nature as an important element of spiritual life. The poet, Teofil Lenartowicz, uttered these same truths in his poetry.

The image of the homeland and the emotional ties binding the people to it gained new perspectives from the viewpoint of émigrés and refugees. After the abortive November Insurrection, thousands of Poles had to leave their country, but their hearts remained at home. Their far off country was to them an ever-present reality.

Mickiewicz's *Pan Tadeusz* presented an image of the homeland created by the longing heart, an image of "woody hills and green meadows", of the Lithuanian wilderness, the "homely trees", of sunrise and sunset, of evening concerts of noisy birds and choirs of frogs in the ponds, "speaking to each other across the fields".

This longing for their homeland also molded the experiences of thousands of Poles, mostly of peasant descent, who were forced, under the pressure of social conditions, to leave their country "in search of bread" as described by Henryk Sienkiewicz in his short story of the same title. In this work, as well as in his well-known *The Light House Keeper,* the yearning for a lost and remote homeland, which constituted the basic element of the life of the emigrants, was exposed. The same sentiment was most forcefully expressed by Maria Konopnicka in her epic poem, *Mr. Balcer* (1910), a dramatic epic of wandering Polish peasants in Brazil.

This depth of love for their native land did not abate during the whole period of the partitions. It even increased on the threshold of the events that brought freedom to Poland in 1918, as evidenced by the work of Stefan Żeromski, a writer who restored the memory of the Baltic coast to the national consciousness.

Painting supported literature in molding and strengthening this image of the native land in the social consciousness. Whereas during the Enlightenment the Polish landscape appeared rather rarely and only as a secondary element in the canvases, the period of bondage became an era of exceptional and unique flowering of landscape painting. It was inaugurated during the first half of the nineteenth century by Jan Nepomucen Głowacki. In the second half of the century an entire group of landscape painters was already active, the most outstanding of them being Wojciech Gerson (1831—1901), Józef Szermentowski (1833—76), Aleksander Kotsis (1836—77) and Władysław Aleksander Malecki (1836—1900). With ever greater intimacy they presented the Polish rural landscape, the vast expanses of the fields and meadows with peasant huts crouching among them, huge trees with wide forked boughs, flowers, or gloomy mountain views with highland villages and churchyards under dark, dramatic skies.

This trend in art gained a new character at the turn of the nineteenth century, with the work of Józef Chełmoński (1849—1914), Maksymilian Gierymski (1846—74), Jan Stanisławski (1860—1907), Ferdynand Ruszczyc (1870—1936), Włodzimierz Tetmajer (1861—1923), Julian Fałat (1853—1929), and many others. Each of the above painters had a creative individuality of his own. All were fascinated by the Polish landscape, though each of them viewed it in a different way. In their works the native landscape acquired new, diversified aspects; sometimes it was a sentimental manifestation of peace, or of dramatic skies, laden with clouds, hanging over the men seemingly lost in the world of nature; sometimes it was the theme of peasant toil and peasant poverty, but also of their weddings and dances. This native land was displayed as a self-enclosed landscape, serene and homely. A wide range of colors displayed its daybreaks and dusks, the charm of flowering meadows, the darkness of the nights, the shimmering streams and gloomy forest wilderness, the silvery firs, the lonely churches, and mills standing above dammed mill-ponds.

Hundreds of such pictures created a world of imagination which, easily accessible to a wide segment of society by means of exhibitions and prints, contributed to the patriotic feelings which attached Poles to their homeland.

THE PEOPLE DRAW
THE FRONTIERS OF POLAND

The homeland, however, was not only the soil; it was also the people by whom it was inhabited. Already during the Enlightenment a new interest in ordinary people, the peasantry, emerged. Franciszek Salezy Jezierski suggested that only the common man, and not the rich and educated, remained true to the language, the national tradition, the customs and character; while Hugo Kołłątaj in 1802, in an Austrian prison, worked out a great project of research concerning the life of the common people. Tadeusz Czacki prepared a similar plan in 1805. The Society of Friends of Learning in Warsaw tried to organize a collective study in this field.

Yet, only when the rule of the oppressors began to be felt more acutely did the truth of Jezierski's and Kołłątaj's observations appear in its full light. The growth of Romanticism increased interest in the peasantry. A large group of enthusiasts started work, compiling an inventory of Polish and Slavic monuments of folk culture, both ancient and contemporary. The group included Wawrzyniec Surowiecki, Walenty Skorochód-Majewski, Benedykt

Rakowiecki, and the best known among them, Zorian Dołęga Chodakowski, an indefatigable wanderer who crossed huge territories in Poland and in Russia, collecting samples and exhibits of folklore. His work, *On the Slavic World in the Times Prior to Christianity,* gave birth to numerous disputes, especially regarding his concept of "the northern soul" and his idea that the introduction of Christianity had enfeebled or even obliterated national feeling.

Chodakowski's followers rarely expressed such radical opinions, although they followed his lead in industriously registering the relics of old folklore: artifacts, religious rites, habits, legends and songs. Among these scholars were Łukasz Gołębiowski, a librarian at Puławy, author of several books on folklore; and Kazimierz Władysław Wójcicki, whose *Tales, Ancient Legends and Stories of the Polish People* (1837) ran into many editions and was translated into German and Russian. Other authors conducted similar activity. However the greatest of them all was Oskar Kolberg, who traveled throughout Poland collecting material between the years 1846 and 1857. The results of his research were published in a huge, thirty-four volume work entitled *The People: Their Customs, Way of Life, Language, Legends, Proverbs, Rites, Sorceries, Pastimes, Songs, Music and Dances.* The work is considered of such lasting value that it has been reprinted (together with supplements) many times.

The writers and poets of the period worked together with scholars and collectors. The subject matter they took up disclosed the creative cultural force of the people and assisted the program, expressed by Edward Dembowski in these laconic words: "The essential part of a nation, its real heart, is the peasantry."

Native soil seen as the land of the Polish people was thus gaining a wide geographical meaning. Each region had its enthusiasts, poets and collectors of its own. And virtually in each region the inhabitants manifested their own national identity. From the second half of the nineteenth century, the national revival was in full swing in the ancient Polish lands of Pomerania and Silesia. In Warmia and Mazuria, many young writers were also engaged in renewed activity. This renaissance also embraced the Kashubian area due, in particular, to the activity of Florian Ceynowa and Hieronim Derdowski.

The process was particularly visible in Silesia. In the Cieszyn region, in Upper Silesia and in the Opole region a number of writers of peasant and worker backgrounds stressed the Polish character of that land. They included Paweł Stalmach in Cieszyn, Jakub Kania in the Opole region, and Karol Miarka, Józef Lompa, Juliusz Ligoń and Jan Kupiec in Upper Silesia.

The ties connecting these regions to the homeland through the people inhabiting them became an element which helped strengthen and develop a feeling of patriotism during the period of the partitions. The overall consciousness of the community acquired a source of ever-increasing wealth from the regional differentiation of the Polish nation; whereas local identity gained a feeling of its own singularity and of the membership of the greater, national community called Poland.

It was an amazing historical process. Under conditions of political subjugation, in a country severed by three frontiers which allotted parts to three different states, an awareness of national community which spread over these political divisions not only remained, but even increased in intensity. Simultaneously, in various regions of the Polish lands, even in those lost a long time before, an awareness of allegiance to the homeland and to the nation was awakening, an awareness produced in a specific, regional manner. The Polish soil, which legally belonged to foreign states, seemed more Polish than could have been anticipated on the basis of eighteenth century experience. And, although it did not exist on the political map of Europe, it expanded its frontiers as it did during the Piast and Jagiellonian eras.

SPECIAL ROLE OF THE TATRA MOUNTAINS IN POLISH CULTURE

Within these manifold ties binding the social consciousness to the native land, an exceptional place belonged to the Vistula River and the Tatra Mountains.

The Vistula, as the largest of Polish rivers, had from times immemorial attracted the attention of geographers, historians and poets, but from the end of the eighteenth century, it became purely and simply the symbol of Poland. During the period between the uprisings, that is between 1830 and 1863, there was scarcely a poet who did not utter on the banks of this river, as *super flumina Babilonis,* his lament, or look for a glimpse of hope, or else give vent to melancholy and emotion. Almost all the poets of later times paid their homage to this river so much a part of Polish history.

But of more significance than the Vistula to national culture were the Tatra Mountains. People had walked and explored the Tatras for many years. The pioneer in this was Staszic, but he was responsible for impassioned observations and research concerning the geological structure of the mountains and of some particularities of the life of the highlanders. It was only Seweryn Goszczyński who, with the eye of a Romantic, perceived the beauty of the Tatras and the significance that they might have for the poetic vision of the world.

During the second half of the century the Tatras became one of the sources of emotion and creative work for artists and thinkers, as well as of experience for wider circles of the society. For poetry the Tatras were discovered by Adam Asnyk, who in a cycle of poems written in 1880, painted their menacing beauty which evoked metaphysical emotions.

Soon the limits of purely poetical emotions were transcended. The Tatras and their highland people were introduced to the life of the community, while at the same time patriotic feelings were directed towards the Tatras, revealing their real and symbolic greatness. This came to pass by means of the activity of a group of people of different beliefs, origins and professions, bound by a similar enthusiasm for the Tatras, the same prophetic feeling of the exceptional values that could be found in their midst and among their inhabitants. This group included Tytus Chałubiński, a physician; Józef Stolarczyk, a priest; Władysław Matlakowski, a physician, literary critic and expert in folk culture; Stanisław Witkiewicz, a painter, writer and art critic; and Franciszek Nowicki, a teacher and socialist leader. A cycle of sonnets, *The Tatras* (1887) by the last of these revealed for the first time a wide range of social and patriotic experiences that one felt among the mountains: "I look to the Tatras," wrote the poet, seeing a parallel to the Polish knightly tradition and a vision of freedom not attainable anywhere else in Poland.

The Tatras also became a favorite subject of painters and composers. In painting the theme of the Tatras was first used in the first half of the nineteenth century by Jan Nepomucen Głowacki. Others followed, especially Wojciech Gerson, who painted numerous beautiful landscapes, for example, *Cemetery in the Mountains,* where realism of presentation was combined with a romantic concept of the human plight, set against the background of a village churchyard in the mountains, under a somber cloudy sky.

A real outburst of work in painting of the Tatra Mountains occurred toward the end of the century. Paintings by Stanisław Witkiewicz (*Foehn*) and by Leon Wyczółkowski (the series *The Eye of the Sea),* not only introduced the Tatra theme forever to Polish art, but succeeded in making of it a lasting element of the national imagination. Concurrently, from the turn of the century, these most Polish of all mountains together with their inhabitants, began to attract the attention of ethnographers, historians, philosophers, and musicians.

The Tatra Mountains and the Podhale (Tatra foothills) highland region were the subject of studies by Władysław Matlakowski and Stanisław Witkiewicz. In literature they were extolled by Kazimierz Przerwa-Tetmajer, Władysław Orkan, Tadeusz Miciński, Jan Kasprowicz and a great many others. The work of the painters and poets coincided with that of composers. The Tatras were the subject of songs composed to the words of poets, and of independent compositions, like the overture *The Tatras* by Władysław Żeleński, or the overture *The Eye of the Sea* by Zygmunt Noskowski. Mieczysław Karłowicz's whole life, and even his death (he died under an avalanche on the slopes of Kościelec above Czarny Staw Lake) was connected with the Tatras. His works, especially his great symphonic poems, rendered the metaphysical aspect of experiences in the Tatras. The original music of the highlanders was slowly becoming for the composer what the highland fables were for the writer — raw material for artistic transformation. The work of the outstanding composer, Karol Szymanowski, followed along these lines.

Thus the Tatra and Podhale regions, together with their people, became a source of creative inspiration, a source of patriotic sentiment for the enslaved nation, and an image of freedom attainable only during the trips through the rocky peaks and passes, a source of reflection about the vagaries and greatness of human life, incorporated into the infinite grandeur of the mountain landscape.

Zakopane, the capital of Podhale, was for a very long time to become the "spiritual capital" of Poland.

HISTORIANS DELIVER THEIR VERDICT ON THE NATION

From the very beginning of the period of bondage to its very end, there was an awareness that, although the Polish state could be erased from the map of Europe, it was impossible to eradicate it from the history of the world, that is, from the old but unforgotten reality, so long as there was a living nation to preserve and remember its history.

Research on national history was conducted by the Society of Friends of Learning in Warsaw. This was inaugurated by Tadeusz Czacki and Hugo Kołłątaj. Despite the close friendship between the two men, their views on history were different and formed two starting points for two different roads of development for Polish historiography of the whole period of the partitions.

In Czacki we find a severe judge of Polish history, which he evaluated in terms of the efficiency of the state administration and the wisdom of the rulers. "States fall," he wrote, "through lack of government, through the fault of their rulers, the weakness of their defenses, and contempt of their laws." These were the causes of Poland's downfall. Czacki severely criticized free elections, the weakening of the royal power, the *liberum veto,* anarchy and lawlessness, and a mistaken Eastern policy. He critically appraised Polish military victories, as well as the Polish-Lithuanian union which led to the "mutual attrition" of the two nations.

Kołłątaj's attitude was different. His was the vision of Polish history as a history of a nation and not of the ruling classes, perhaps even as a history of the people, revealed in their work, customs, attachment to their native language and their distinctive culture.

In a sense Joachim Lelewel who undertook historical research in the spirit of democratic ideals was Kołłątaj's disciple. His judgment of national history, although harsh, expressed his belief in the strength of the Polish nation, the history of which had always been, according to Lelewel, that of struggle against despotism for liberty's sake. *A History of Poland Told Colloquially,* which Lelewel published in Warsaw in 1829, disappeared from bookshops with lightning speed. Often reprinted, sometimes altered without the knowledge and assent of the author, it was decade after decade the most popular textbook on national history, and went through about twenty editions.

In the middle of the nineteenth century a particularly strong trend developed of going back to the past, and there were various efforts, based on documentary sources, at its reconstruction.

Only during the second half of the century, however, was there a marked development of historical research, particularly in Cracow. It was then that important works were published synthesizing results. Passionate polemics followed on both the causes of the downfall of Poland and an assessment of the political and cultural values of ancient Poland. This period of dispute was inaugurated by Józef Szujski in his pamphlet entitled *A Few Truths from Our History to be Considered During Present Times*

(1867) and in larger works regarding the Renaissance in Poland and, finally, in his book *Polish History Concisely Told in Twelve Books* (1880). Simultaneously, there appeared Michał Bobrzyński's popular and often reprinted *History of Poland* (1879), and Walerian Kalinka's great work, *The Four Year Seym* (1880).

Despite the differences that divided these authors belonging to the "Cracow school" of history, in these and in many other publications, they proposed a new image of the Polish past. Counteracting Lelewel's views, they underscored the Polish "sins" which allegedly consisted of deviations from Catholicism, both during the Renaissance and during the Enlightenment, of the weakness of the kings and of the governments, combined with the lawlessness of the masses of gentry which was safeguarded by pernicious laws and institutions dangerous to public life. Among these sins they also included a misconceived Eastern policy of expansion and senseless waves of knightly zeal, as well as cultural retardation which, according to Szujski, proved that Poland was still in "the early stages of the development of civilization."

The criticism levelled by the Cracow historians was continued by the Warsaw school, especially by Tadeusz Korzon and Władysław Smoleński. In numerous studies, mainly in those dealing with the period of the partitions, they demonstrated the process of the nation's revival during the second half of the eighteenth century and opposed the pessimistic judgments of Kalinka and Szujski. Korzon's great study, *The Internal History of Poland under Stanislaus Augustus* (1882—86) and Smoleński's often reprinted monograph, *The Spiritual Revolution in Eighteenth Century Poland,* shed new light on the nation's efforts during the most dramatic periods of its history. Smoleński was also the author of a synthesis, *History of the Polish Nation* (1897), the very title of which pointed to a new standpoint: its main theme was not so much the Commonwealth of the Gentry as the Polish nation and its historical evolution.

This viewpoint not only permitted an altogether new evaluation of specific events, but also allowed the drawing of optimistic conclusions concerning the political values of the Polish community, as well as of the national character, seen as the source of the social revival, even under most unfavorable conditions. The studies of a number of Warsaw scholars, together with the works of Oswald Balzer in Lvov and Stanisław Kutrzeba in Cracow, pointed in the same direction. Their opinions about the form of government in the old Commonwealth and also about the process of rebirth expressed through the eighteenth century reforms, and in the Third of May Constitution in particular, formed historical premises for an optimistic appraisal of the nation.

WORSHIP OF THE PAST AND FAITH IN THE FUTURE

Writers and poets supported the historians. Never before was literature so deeply involved in forming the historic image of national life as during the period of bondage. That involvement proved more profound than the various, often opposing aesthetic concepts of the consecutive intellectual and literary currents. Artistic slogans and canons continued to change, but interest in the past remained the same, though expressed in different ways. So also, though differently expressed in various political circumstances, did the will to revive the past in all its beauty, its victories and defeats, its greatness and decline, and its conflicts between patriotism and egoism, told for the sake of emotional reassurance, sometimes for the sake of sentimental experience, or else for the sake of severe judgment. However thanks to literature, the national past was always present in the social consciousness.

The period of partition began with *The Temple of Sibyl* by Jan Paweł Woronicz, written in 1800, published in Lvov in 1818, the poem presenting the greatness of the Poland of old, from Casimir the Great to the Kosciuszko Insurrection. It began also with *Historical Songs* (1816), by Julian Ursyn Niemcewicz. This volume of poems was enormously popular, displaying the greatness and the glory of Polish kings from the legendary first Piast to John (III) Sobieski, and the heroism of the Polish commanders, Zawisza the Black, Hetman Stanisław Żółkiewski, and Stefan Czarniecki. From that time on, there was scarcely a writer who did not draw inspiration for his works from national history. Classicists and romantics, positivists and neo-romantics, historians and poets, even political writers, in hundreds of works — dramas, poems, lyrical verses alike — reverted over and over again to the national past, with its great chivalrous exploits, social conflicts, and emotional tragedies.

The most spectacular successes belonged, however, to the historical novel. Though initially it too reached back to the tradition of the Enlightenment, by the middle of the nineteenth century it truly became an important element of the national consciousness. At first these novels glorified the traditions of the gentry in recent times, like Henryk Rzewuski's *Memoirs of Soplica* (1839) and *November* (1845—46), or Ignacy Chodźko's *Memoirs of a Bursar* (1844) which went through ten editions. But soon the range of historical vision extended further. This occurred during the second half of the nineteenth century and was due to the work of Józef Ignacy Kraszewski whose historical novels provided a vast panoramic view of Polish history. Kraszewski had a clear sense of his vocation. "The times have passed," he wrote, "when authors wrote for literary circles only; today they have to become the leaders and the moral guides of their age." In accordance with this precept, Kraszewski undertook the gigantic task of acquainting his generation with the entire Polish history. Starting with *The Ancient Tale* (1876), which portrayed pre-Christian times, Kraszewski presented the history of the country up to the downfall of the Commonwealth and the struggles waged in the nineteenth century. In these series of novels he displayed an unusually colorful panorama of history, depicting both the great national events and ordinary human conflicts. Thanks to his work, the past appeared as something familiar to everybody.

Henryk Sienkiewicz understood his literary vocation in a different way. His great historical novels, *The Trilogy* (1884—88) and *The Teutonic Knights* (1900) were, in the writer's words, "written to lift up the people's hearts" and concentrated not so much on important problems of the state and the nation as on the indomitability, in spite of all defeats, of the great Polish knights. These novels did not pronounce a verdict on the past; their aim was not to stir the conscience. They were meant to awaken faith in the effectiveness of such virtues as courage and self-sacrifice for the homeland in difficult situations, which called for heroism. At the time of their publication, and later, Sienkiewicz's novels met with harsh criticism from radical circles. The author was accused of creating an image of Poland which instead of teaching political sense, encouraged uncritical enthusiasm for the past of the gentry and knightly tradition. But this was the very effect that Sienkiewicz wanted to achieve: to make the old, simple-minded warriors, and even converted adventurers, live again in the imagination of their descendants. And he succeeded to an inordinate degree in making them come alive. When *With Fire and Sword* was issued, one of the readers wanted to pay for a Mass to be said for the soul of the late Podbipięta. Even to today's audiences, readers and movie-goers, the heroes of his novels, Jagienka and Zbyszko, Kmicic and Oleńka, Podbipięta and Skrzetuski, and Zagłoba, are real, live people. Other contemporary writers of historical novels were not equal to Sienkiewicz's talent. Only Walery Przyborowski, because of his novels for young readers, gained some significance. Next to didactic novels for young people, in which positivist ideas were promulgated, the most widely read books were the historical novels of Przyborowski, and his contemporary, Wołody Skiba's *Higher Levels* (1887).

Equal to the social impact of the historical novel during the period was that of painting, which too became the common property of the entire nation, at first due to illustration of the words of writers and poets. In 1805, *The Polish Bard* by Adam Czartoryski was thus illustrated; in 1816 an illustrated edition of Julian Ursyn Niemcewicz's *Historical Songs* appeared. Characteristically, in both cases the illustrations were not the works of professional painters, but were done by "society ladies".

As time passed, however, painting became independent of literature and rendered its own vision of Polish history. This art form, particularly in the paintings of Franciszek Smuglewicz and Aleksander Orłowski, broke with the documentary functions and with didactic ideology and, liberated from the sponsorship of kings and magnates, turned into a national image of Polish history, intended for the entire nation.

Yet only in the middle of the nineteenth century was great historical painting born through the work of Piotr Michałowski. His superb paintings, executed in a romantic manner, had for their themes Boleslaus the Brave, the Polish hetmans, and the Polish struggles under Napoleon. Thanks to Michałowski, Somosierra became the best known example of Polish heroism.

During the second half of the century two painters turned the course of historical painting in different directions. Their artistic approaches coincided with the two different modes of the historical novel of the era: the first, which tried to save from oblivion the chivalrous history of the gentry; and the second, which aimed at teaching the nation to understand its historical destiny. Those painters were Juliusz Kossak and Jan Matejko.

From the 1870's onward, Juliusz Kossak proposed a characteristic model for presenting the traditional image of Poland in general, and of knighthood in particular. In this spirit, he illustrated the works of Wincenty Pol, Władysław Syrokomla and, above all, Henryk Sienkiewicz's *Trilogy*. This symbiosis of literature and painting won for him a huge circle of admirers and strengthened by visual means what the writer's imagination had created in words.

While Juliusz Kossak's paintings, above all his watercolors, were executed on a rather small scale, his slightly younger contemporary, Józef Brandt, painted large canvases that occupied entire walls and were devoted to the glorious pages of Polish chivalrous history, mostly from the eighteenth century. A direct successor to Juliusz Kossak was his son Wojciech. The latter painted hundreds of canvases depicting the Napoleonic wars and the battles waged during the insurrections, but also picturesque and sentimental scenes showing uhlans and girls, manor-houses and village cottages, hunts and parties, the whole traditionally Polish world. They enjoyed very high esteem and are still appreciated to the present day.

However, the greatest significance was ascribed to Jan Matejko as creator of a wide panorama of historical events.

Beginning in the 1860's, Matejko for thirty years continued to offer to the Polish community canvases exposing all the glories and all the tragedies of Poland's history. His inexhaustible industry combined with unusual intensity of historical imagination permitted him to make familiar to his contemporaries the great personalities and the great events of the past from every epoch of Polish history, and to reveal merits and disclose errors.

Bitter reflection of the past was seen in *Court Jester* (1863), a portrait of the royal jester who, according to historical legends, had been better able to foresee the imminent dangers to the state than the members of the Jagiellonian court responsible for its destiny. *Skarga's Sermon Before Sigismund III* (1864) presented a picture of the patriotic wrath of a great preacher denouncing the sins and weaknesses of the magnates and the court of Sigismund III, as well as those of the gentry and the deputies. *Rejtan* (1866) commemorated the futile protest of one of the deputies against the passing of the law which was to approve the first partition of Poland.

At the opposite end of that great searching of the national conscience stood paintings which portrayed the political wisdom of the community and its rulers, the grand uplifting events of its community life and culture. Such canvases included *The Union of Lublin* (1869), which recreated the great act of joining the destiny of two nations, Poland and Lithuania, in 1569; *The Prussian Homage* (1882), which portrayed Albrecht

Hohenzollern with his entourage, swearing allegiance to King Sigismund I in Cracow in 1525; *The Constitution of the Third of May* (1892), which was donated by the painter as a gift to the Seym of Galicia, to be delivered at a later date when the hope of restored independence was attained, to the Royal Castle in Warsaw, where the Constitution had been proclaimed in 1791.

Yet, the most singular place in Matejko's work — and in the social consciousness — was reserved for the paintings which presented the great battles fought by warriors in defense of their country and of Christianity, the glorious victories and defeats of the Polish army.

Such was the aim of *The Battle of Varna,* portraying King Ladislaus' death in the battle with the Turks; *Sobieski at Vienna* (1883) presented the great Polish victory over the Turks, more than two centuries later, and was given by the artist to the Pope; *Báthory at Pskov* (1872) was dedicated to an important episode in Poland's wars with Muscovy. The most significant painting in this group, perhaps even in all the works of Matejko, was his *Battle at Grunwald* (1878). This commemoration of the great victory over the Teutonic Knights in 1410 became an important part of the education of hundreds of thousands of Poles, to whom it was shown in Cracow, Warsaw and Lvov. It also became a manifestation of Polish identity for the foreign public in St. Petersburg, Budapest and Berlin, where it was exhibited. This painting, considered nationally sacrosanct, was hidden and defended at danger to life during the Nazi occupation. The public in Vienna and Paris had an opportunity to see another of Matejko's paintings, *Kościuszko at Racławice* (1888), which portrayed the Polish victory in the struggle for independence in 1794. The Polish community bought the painting through private subscription.

Mention should also be made of two more series, created by the greatest Polish historical painter: *The History of Civilization in Poland* and *The Procession of Polish Kings and Princes,* displayed Polish history in its great variety and complexity and thanks to numerous prints were accessible to the masses; in this way society saw its entire history through the eyes of Matejko.

After 1863 a very special position in the development of historical painting was held by Artur Grottger. He was a painter of the January Insurrection; thus he touched upon contemporary events which were only beginning to fade into the past. In several large series, foremost of which was *Polonia* (1863) and *Lithuania* (1864—66), he presented recent events, but profoundly tied in with the entire history of Poland's struggle and Poland's heroism. His pictorial vision revealed the January Insurrection as a link in the long chain of the history of Polish mourning. The moving melancholy of these scenes blended with the atmosphere of sorrow and hopelessness which followed the defeat of the uprising. The same events were also the subject of Maksymilian Gierymski's pictures, but he saw in them an act of courage and strength. However, the artist who had the strongest appeal to the Polish soul was Grottger who commemorated scenes of violence, death, annihilation, prayers, lamentations and mourning.

While Matejko concentrated on the greatness of Polish history regarded as the work of the whole nation, Grottger's paintings recreated the times of national defeat, when calamity entered Polish homes. The defense of Poland became, in this way, a defense of the manor-house. This was a tragic and futile act, it was fire which brought in its aftermath ruins and ashes, leaving behind only famine and poverty. It was useless to ask whether it was brought about by men or jackals, or whether human beings were really descended from Cain. The angelic image in his paintings beckoned to the unhappy to follow him through this vale of tears, in quest of signs of terror and perhaps also of hope.

Continuing this Grottgerian climate in the 1880's, Jacek Malczewski painted his history of Polish martyrdom in *The Staging Post, The Siberians, Christmas Eve of the Exiles,* and many other works. From his paintings emerged a symbol of the Polish pilgrimage, which often recurred in Malczewski's later works: that of a soldier in his long coat, with a stick in his hand and a bag on his shoulders. Malczewski several times returned to Słowacki's vision presented in *Anhelli,* portraying *The Death of Ellenai* in various versions at different times.

Music, too, continued to focus its attention on Polish history. The most characteristic was the work of Stanisław Moniuszko, especially his numerous patriotic songs, as well as *The Haunted Manor,* an opera composed in 1865, and closed down by the censor after only a few performances because it aroused patriotic sentiment. The program of music deeply involved with national history was continued by many composers. The Lvov production in 1885 of Władysław Żeleński's opera, *Konrad Wallenrod,* aroused patriotic reflection throughout Poland. Żeleński composed two more operas: *Goplana* (based on Słowacki's drama *Balladyna)* and *The Ancient Tale,* adapted from Kraszewski's novel. During the Young Poland period, Ludomir Różycki drew on historical subjects in his symphonic poems, *Boleslaus the Brave, Anhelli* and *La Varsoviénne.* His ballet *Pan Twardowski,* often performed today, became his most popular work.

Architecture also displayed a similar inclination toward history. Although, particularly in Warsaw, the peak of classical architecture coincided with the first decades of the nineteenth century, the style was still alive, mostly in Galicia, even in later years. After 1830, neo-gothic and neo-renaissance architecture prevailed. Palaces, like the Kórnik Chateau, erected in the middle of the nineteenth century, and country mansions and churches were built in neo-gothic style. It was then that the facade of the Warsaw Cathedral was reshaped in the English mock-gothic style, and plans were underway to rebuild the Royal Castle in the same manner.

In public buildings the neo-renaissance style prevailed. Several houses in Warsaw were built in this fashion, including the Europejski Hotel, the Land Credit Society, a huge grain elevator in Modlin, and several industrial plants. The same monumental style triumphed in Lvov during the 1870's, in such buildings as the Governor's residence, the Seym, the University, and the Polytechnic. The style was also in vogue in Cracow, one example being the building of the Society of Friends of Learning, later occupied by the Academy of Learning. The neo-renaissance style was also popular in the construction of huge apartment houses and in country residences of the villa-type.

All the styles — classical, neo-gothic and neo-renaissance — were connected with Polish history, but at the same time they possessed the obvious traits of European architecture of the nineteenth century; and, as such, they were criticized by those architects and artists who were trying to develop a style with a more pronounced national character. The latter turned toward the tradition of Polish Gothic, the so-called Vistula Gothic, and toward the Cracow renaissance tradition.

A new element in this search was the discovery of the values of the architecture and the decorative arts of the highlanders. During the 1890's Stanisław Witkiewicz, an eminent painter and literary and art critic, author and moralist, inaugurated the construction of highland-style villas in Zakopane, which to this very day remain models of a great architectural tradition, inspired by Tatra regional art. From the year 1904, he published a periodical, entitled *Styl Zakopiański.*

Stanisław Wyspiański chose different ways for reaching a Polish style. This poet, painter, and stage designer united, as did no other artist, the classical and the folk, particularly the Podhale traditions and recreated them, thanks to the unusual strength of his artistic vision, inspired by the visions of the era of the Piasts.

He first became famous in Cracow for his murals and stained-glass windows in the Franciscan church and also as the designer of the interiors of the buildings belonging to the Fine Arts Association and the Medical Society in Cracow. Dissatisfied with these "petty forms," he created, as part of a conservation and reconstruction program, a monumental project involving the transformation of the entire Wawel complex into a "Polish Acropolis."

The historical motif in writing, painting, music and architecture took on new characteristics at the turn of the nineteenth and twentieth centuries. No longer a matter of uplifting tales concerning historical events, it was now an effort to find in events the hidden "mystery" of the Polish soul. This new movement was given momentum in the painting of Jacek Malczewski, in the poetry and drama of Stanisław Wyspiański, and in the novels of Stefan Żeromski and Tadeusz Miciński. History was a code to be deciphered, and art, which undertook the task, became symbolic in a very special meaning of the word, because it was meant to disclose the hidden significance of the events, to reach into the soul of the nation.

In the area of sculpture, the expression of these ideological and artistic tendencies was best exemplified in the monumental work of Wacław Szymanowski, *Procession to Wawel* (1912), presenting several dozen figures from Polish history on their way up the hill leading to the "Polish Acropolis."

In Malczewski's paintings Polish history appeared both mystical and real as, for example, in his triptych, *The Homeland* (1903), and especially in his canvas entitled *Melancholy* (1894), which, according to the artist, was meant to show the "last century of Poland" and expressed the atmosphere of a generation of defeat, sorrow and pain shown against a background of the charge of the scythe-bearers which recalled, with resentment or with hope, a peasant version of the Polish chivalrous tradition. During World War I, Malczewski painted several versions of *Polonia,* canvases which symbolized Poland in the form of a female figure, either elated and joyful among huge flowers, or walking against a background of fields and trees, adored by a tired workman on his knees.

Man and the Forces of Production

DEMOGRAPHIC AND ECONOMIC DEVELOPMENT

Like the rest of Europe, Poland experienced accelerated demographic growth. This acceleration was considerable during some periods, but was unevenly spread across the three partition zones. On the threshold of World War I, the country was much more heavily populated than at the moment of the downfall of the Commonwealth of the Gentry. At that time the population of Poland had amounted to roughly ten million, including more than four million non-Polish inhabitants.

The period of wars at the beginning of the nineteenth century diminished the population, which, however, started to increase again shortly thereafter. This process took place most swiftly in Upper Silesia, where the population doubled between 1816 and 1856, while during the same period in the Kingdom of Poland it increased only by 30 percent, and in Galicia by 20 percent. By and large, during the first half of the century the overall increase was 45 percent, and during the second half (to 1913) over 100 percent. Particularly rapid growth was registered between 1870 and 1910, when the number of Poles more than doubled, increasing from ten to twenty-two million.

The pattern of population movement was similar in the various parts of the country: the peasant regions were steadily becoming overpopulated, and the number of city inhabitants increased rapidly. During the period 1870—1910 the city population in the Poznań region doubled, as it did in the Kingdom and in Galicia, while in Silesia it quadrupled. Some centers registered even faster growth. Łódź, for example, in 1864 numbered only 40,000 inhabitants, and a half a century later almost 700,000.

Various factors contributed to demographic growth. Although the general living standard was still very low, especially among the peasants in Galicia, there was nonetheless a steady improvement. The disastrous famines and mass epidemics which had decimated the rural population at the beginning of the nineteenth century were disappearing. The state of hygiene in towns and cities also improved. The death rate decreased; by the middle of the nineteenth century in the Poznań region it fell from 34 to 24 per thousand, in Galicia from 37 to 25, and in the Kingdom of Poland from 38 to 20 per thousand.

A great service was rendered here by the medical profession. Especially during the second half of the nineteenth century Polish medicine not only achieved major scientific successes, but also succeeded in defining and undertaking social duties. One of the characteristic features of the culture of this period was, in fact, the voluntary social activity of outstanding physicians who were concerned not only with the health of their individual patients, but also accepted the responsibility for the health of the general public by organizing a network of hospitals and medical centers. This was the basis of the concept of "Offices of Health," the plans for which were prepared by J. M. Brodowicz. The most respected figure was "Doctor Marcin", Jan Karol Marcinkowski, organizer of economic self-help in the community, founder of the Association for Scientific Help, first and foremost a devoted physician who, walking untiringly along "paths unknown to others that led to the darkest corners of poverty," saved the lives and the health of the poorest. Similarly Józef Dietl in Galicia and Tytus Chałubiński in Warsaw and Zakopane combined medical service with social activity.

Similar motives spurred on social and medical initiatives which found expression in the great Exhibitions of Hygiene in Warsaw in 1887 and again in 1896, as well as in the foundation in 1898 of the Warsaw Association for Hygiene, which under the dynamic leadership of Doctor Józef Tchórznicki launched projects, vigorously conceived and executed, for the benefit of the poor urban and rural population.

The demographic development formed the basis for a new and more dynamic concept of national life, with its needs, possibilities and prospects. The population of the country, considered by politicians in previous eras, with the exception of Staszic, solely in terms of a labor force for the estates of the gentry, now was seen as the object of patriotic and humanitarian care. A new style of thinking was born and in keeping with it the population was considered essential to the size and strength of the nation.

At the same time, a development was taking place in the forces of production in agriculture and industry accompanied by a fundamental change in the economic consciousness of the community.

Farming was increasingly becoming an activity requiring scientific qualifications. Agrotechnical education, a professional press and popular books on agricultural science, were supposed to provide the necessary instruction. The first school for foresters was founded in Warsaw in 1818. The first agricultural school, at Marymont on the outskirts of Warsaw, was founded in 1820. Reorganized in 1835 by Michał Oczapowski, it became a significant research center. This center published a huge ten-volume encyclopedia of agricultural science. In 1856 a Higher School of Agriculture was opened at Dublany, and a similar one, in 1858, at Czernihów. An important influence was also exerted by various agricultural societies. As early as 1811 an Economic and Agricultural Association was founded in the Duchy of Warsaw. But the full development of these societies came during the second half of the century. Prominent among these institutions

were the Economic Society in Lvov, the Central Economic Society in Poznań, and the Agricultural Society in Warsaw. Numerous agricultural exhibitions were organized to promote progress in modern farming. In 1874, the Museum of Industry and Agriculture was opened in Warsaw.

This activity precipitated the birth of a new, professional attitude in the field of agriculture, influencing, at the same time, a modern outlook on the organization and utilization of resources for the sake of economic and social progress. In the national consciousness, up to that time burdened with feudal traditions of a "carefree landowner existence," a deep transformation was thus being effected.

Similarly, but with rather more intensity, industrial development made an impact on the community.

Despite many obstacles created by the investment and tariff policies of the partitioning powers, fundamental changes were coming about in the national economy, which was not so far behind the general progress of the world economy. Although Poland participated sporadically in the area of technical and industrial progress so characteristic of nineteenth century Europe, and although this participation was different in measure during various periods and in different parts of the country, yet, all in all, between the two crucial dates — the beginning and the end of the years of partition — the overall development was enormous. Whereas in the declining days of the Poland of the gentry, only the very beginnings of industrial technology existed in manufacturing, and in the coal and iron basins, by World War I, significant regions of the country possessed highly developed industry, and its technological progress managed to keep abreast of other countries of the world. True, the global industrial product of the Polish lands remained substantially below the level of the highly industrialized Western countries, yet the Kingdom of Poland was the most highly industrialized region of the Russian Empire, while Silesia under Prussian rule was second only to the Ruhr. The economic success was all the greater in that the economic policy of both these hostile countries tried at various times to inhibit the development of their marcher provinces in the interests of the central ones.

The increase in coal production during the period 1870—1907 provides an indicator of global industrialization at the turn of the century: in the Kingdom of Poland it had risen from 312,000 tons to 4,624,000 tons; in Upper Silesia from 5,854,000 to 34,641,000; in Galicia from 197,000 to 1,367,000; and in Cieszyn Silesia from 2,612,000 in 1882 to 7,121,000 tons in 1907. Similarly, production of pig iron increased during the four decades between 1870 and 1913, in the Kingdom of Poland from 27,000 to 409,000 tons and in Upper Silesia from 230,000 to 613,000 tons.

The industrial development in the three occupied areas brought changes in the map of the country. The coal- and iron-processing regions took on final shape: the Old Polish area and the Silesian and Dąbrowa regions, where traditions in fact reached back to the times of the Commonwealth of the Gentry, became during the period of bondage densely populated industrial agglomerations. 156

The textile industry was concentrated around Łódź, Białystok, Tomaszów and Bielsko. Warsaw, and several other large cities of the country, became industrial centers, attracting from their vicinity and even from more remote regions a large percentage of the population who were looking for work. The main communication routes took on final shape, especially railroads, which ran North-South and East-West, as well as between the more important centers of the country. Many new towns emerged on the sites of ancient villages or of old, ruined small towns. Hamlets, like Sosnowiec or Łódź, which at the beginning of the nineteenth century numbered merely a few hundred inhabitants, grew into large industrial cities.

In the midst of these new industrialized and urbanized centers, the ancient, agrarian character of Poland was not lost. Almost all the land under Austrian rule, that is, in Galicia, remained rural, as also did the Mazovia and Lublin areas, Great Poland and Pomerania. Communications and trade consolidated these territories within a modern economic organism, created during the period of foreign rule. The consolidating forces were so strong that sometimes they even crossed state frontiers. Population migration was often not only for political, but also for economic reasons. The abolition of the divisions between partition zones after World War I, immediately revealed the economic unity developed during the period of bondage, between some of the neighboring regions of the country, which were artificially divided by foreign state boundaries.

These changes, bringing new elements into the Polish environment and landscape, opened the national imagination to new forms of material existence. For century after century Poland had been identified with forests and fields, cottages and manor-houses, churches and abbeys, palaces and city halls, fortified towns and castles. It had been a landscape of rural and chivalrous folk, a landscape of a Christian community of noblemen. Love of the native land manifested itself in attachment to this "land of woody hills and green meadows," "of fields painted with variegated corn," a land of huge, overgrown willows under skies filled with sun and clouds. Poetry and painting had impressed that image in the national consciousness during the whole period of subjugation: from Mickiewicz to Żeromski, from Szermentowski to Chełmoński and to Ruszczyc.

And then abruptly, industry created a new image of Poland. A landscape of mines and steel mills, of factories and railroads, was being born. Nothing but smokestacks rose into the skies, and the smoke from them hid the sun and the clouds. The human role was also changing in this new, technological habitat: the conditions of life, of work, and of machines. Poetry and art seldom turned to this new world. They denounced the grey, hopeless life under these conditions, the symbol of which was the "broken pine tree", growing on the edge of a mine. But the creator of this symbol, Stefan Żeromski, was able to perceive the sinister beauty of the new, industrial life and of the new pattern of human work. And giving vent to the hopes of millions, he painted the future of Poland as that of "glass houses" — a country of equity and happiness, created by the people and for the people.

Thus, these two Polish landscapes became at the end of the period of bondage lasting elements of the national imagination, providing by the same token a starting point for future intellectual and artistic contemplation of their mutual interconnections.

INDUSTRIAL RE-EDUCATION OF THE COMMUNITY

From the very beginning the process which resulted in the emergence of a new, industrialized and urbanized civilization, generated significant and difficult problems which demanded solution. To a good many writers and activists in the Duchy of Warsaw and in Congress Poland, it was obvious that the era of Polish feudalism, of aristocratic and gentry families with their privileges of descent and of wealth, based on the ruthless exploitation of peasant labor, was at an end, together with the carefree attitude, the idle life, the conformism and egoism of the landowner class. In this new epoch, there appeared a strong demand for a new type of economy, consisting of skill and discipline, vigorous and bold enterprise, opened up by the prospects of advancement in industry and trade. This meant that a new way of life and new people were needed.

The first front espousing the education of the community was formed by writers and activists from the Duchy of Warsaw and from Congress Poland: Stanisław Staszic, Wawrzyniec Surowiecki, Fryderyk Skarbek, and Feliks and Henryk Łubieński. Staszic, as organizer of the school system, emphasized specialized professional instruction at all levels, from the lowest to the highest, extending in this way the limited horizons drawn up by the Commission for National Education. In his numerous speeches, he appeared as an advocate of a new style of life, based on work and learning. During this period, largely through Staszic's activities, the first Polish technical schools were founded: the Mining School in Kielce and the Polytechnic School in Warsaw, both dissolved after the November Insurrection.

Wawrzyniec Surowiecki, who together with Staszic administered the schools in the Duchy and in the Kingdom, wrote in the preface to his book, *On the Decline of Industry and Cities in Poland* (1810), which he dedicated to Łubieński, the following words: "With the decline of industry fell the power of the nation."

The second act in this struggle for a re-education of society came during the period between the uprisings, 1830—63. Along with the development of great Romantic poetry in emigration and the widespread conspiratorial activity at home, culminating in the armed struggle, the battle with the remnants of the gentry culture was gaining strength. The center of this struggle was Poznań, where economic activity was linked with a campaign to increase the amount of property owned by Poles. Karol Marcinkowski provided a model for such activity: he organized many Polish associations and in 1841, founded the Bazaar, a huge center for Polish trade and crafts in Poznań. Concurrently, in the Kingdom of Poland Andrzej

Zamoyski at Klemensów was involved in activity almost entirely aimed at the modernization of farming.

The third act of the struggle for re-education came during the 1860's and culminated in the period immediately after the abortive January Insurrection.

The press, particularly in the Kingdom of Poland, led the attack on the traditional concepts. It popularized the cult of work and industrial enterprise and of the organization of economic activities. A conviction was slowly ripening that technological advancement was not only a source of industry, bringing advantages to the entire community and profit to enterprising individuals, but was also an agent of direct education of the people, and of the proper development of their minds.

The positivist ideology of "working at the roots" and of "organic work" was by no means the last stage in the struggle for the re-education of the community, where feudal and gentry traditions remained very strong. The next stage of this fight came with the activity of the Polish oil industry pioneer Stanisław Szczepanowski, who tried in his numerous speeches to provide modern economic meaning for romantic enthusiasm and heroism. Collections of his speeches and writings, published after his death, *Thoughts on the National Revival* (1903) and *Of Polish Traditions in Education* (1912), proclaimed a new version of the old program of economic education. His interpretation of Romanticism permitted the amalgamation of this concept, considered as the most deeply characteristic feature of the Polish mind, with modern economic goals. Industrial enterprise, despite the positivists' common sense, was seen as peculiarly Promethean, and the romantic hero, Farys, was to undergo a transformation into a bold industrialist.

The problems of technology were not limited to the horizons of industrial development and to the shaping of a new attitude toward life, opposed to the landowner and gentry tradition. The sheer size and range of technology was fascinating and opened formerly unknown vistas of civilization, created by the Promethean talents of man. This attitude was shared by Aleksander Świętochowski and Bolesław Prus, particularly in the latter's novel, *The Doll*, in which he promised a quicker rate of social progress, due to inventions; whereas Żeromski linked technology with the hopes for victory in the fight for independence.

Thus, in this attitude toward technology all the ideological trends of various origins were concentrated: the rather naive, half-superstitious belief of an agrarian nation in the almost magical power of those who could control and subdue the elementary forces of nature; a Utopian vision of the triumph which technology guaranteed to good and wise people in their hitherto hopeless struggle for freedom and justice; a desire to catch up with highly developed western communities for whom science and technology were utilized as tools of success and the sources of a new outlook on life; and finally the conviction that Polish genius could do just as well. In the midst of these diverse ideological currents, the process of absorbing technology by the community during the era of bondage took shape, before the working class was to put it on a new track.

Social Unrest

THE STRUGGLE FOR INDEPENDENCE AND THE PEASANT QUESTION

The peasant issue, unresolved during the times of the Commonwealth of the Gentry, remained the basic question during the whole period of servitude; it was constantly present in the national consciousness, an ever-living task, which was dealt with both theoretically and in terms of political action. As a point of departure for these deliberations and activities a question was formulated by a Jacobin political writer, Józef Pawlikowski: "Can the Poles fight their way to independence?" *(Czy Polacy mogą się wybić na niepodległość?).* His booklet under this title, published in Paris in 1800, thanks to the initiative and cooperation of Kosciuszko, gave a clear answer, that this would be possible only when the entire nation resorted to arms. It meant that the peasant had to be freed and to become a full-fledged citizen.

The Kosciuszkian ideology of solving the peasant question from the point of view of the needs of an armed struggle for independence was the main trend of thought and action in the Kingdom of Poland and during the November Insurrection, in the period immediately following the Insurrection, and during the "Springtime of Nations" (the 1848 revolutions) up to the January Insurrection.

The November Insurrection did not effect the Kosciuszkian idea of calling to arms the entire nation. No decision of the sort was made in the course of the fight itself.

The émigrés understood their errors. The Polish Democratic Society, founded in Paris in 1832, pronounced an indictment against the insurgent leaders and defined a wide platform for socio-political action which was to link any future armed struggle with the final solution of the peasant problem.

Dealing with the issue from the viewpoint of a strategy to win the peasantry for the cause of armed struggle, however, limited the horizons of the problem, and postponed its solution to a later date. This point of view was unacceptable and insubstantial to those who considered the resolution of the peasant problem not so much a clever way of recruiting soldiers but as a question of social and moral justice.

Because of this, the radical activists of the Democratic Society formulated the principles of their organization in the following manner: "All for the people by the people: that is a most general principle of democracy, embracing both the objective and the form. All for the people, for everybody — that is the aim; all by the people, by everybody — that is its form."

Father Piotr Ściegienny tried to implement this vision of a revolutionary movement, when in 1843—44, he organized a peasant uprising. Henryk Kamieński also worked toward this goal, when he prepared a strategy for a popular war. Edward Dembowski whose *Manifesto to the Polish Nation* contained promises to bring freedom, "the like of which had never before existed anywhere", died for this cause in 1846 in the Cracow uprising.

158

The prolonged democratic propaganda and experiences during the years 1846 and 1848, were not futile. During the January Insurrection, the resistance of the conservative faction was finally broken and fundamental decisions were made in regard to the peasant problem. In 1861, the Agrarian Society passed a resolution, outlining the path that would lead the peasants to "full ownership of the land they worked." The Manifesto, proclaiming the insurrection in January 1863, also insisted that all peasants participating in the uprising would receive a grant of the land that they had cultivated, and also promised land to landless peasants. The land-grant decrees were proclaimed throughout all the villages to induce the peasants to join the insurrection. In many detachments the peasants made up more than half, often a majority, of the soldiers. But the policy of granting land was not implemented everywhere. Conservative aversion to reform sometimes manifested itself through repressive measures; and the ancient aversion of the serfs to their lords often ended in acts of violence. And yet, among those sentenced by the czarist government for their part in the uprising, one third or perhaps even one half, were peasants. This was a measure of the success achieved by the strategy of Kosciuszko and of the Democratic Society.

After the land reforms carried out in the Prussian zone between 1811 and 1823, and in the Austrian zone in 1848, the granting of land to the peasants in the Russian zone in 1864 finally concluded the feudal chapter in Polish history. Concurrently, it opened a new and difficult chapter, amounting to a real reshaping of society, to the integration of the peasants with the rest of the nation. Under these circumstances, duality of action, so characteristic of the first half of the nineteenth century, occurred once again: one campaign conducted and organized by the ruling classes, motivated by very diversified political intention; and another, originating within the peasant community, organized by its leaders. No clear-cut divisions existed between them. On the contrary, one of the characteristic features of the situation which existed at the turn of the century in all parts of the country was the intertwining of both kinds of action. Representatives of the intelligentsia often worked among the peasants; and peasant leaders equally often entered the circles of the ruling class. Sometimes however sharp divisions appeared between the political, cultural and educational actions undertaken from below and from above.

THE PEOPLE AND THE NATIONAL LIFE

The peasant movement, which emerged in the three parts of the country under different conditions, achieved various measures of political consciousness, and in taking up the fight for material well-being, with wider cultural and social aspects, applied diverse strategies in different periods and in different regions. At one time, the movement stressed the advancement of cooperative institutions; at other times strikes and radical propaganda were intensified. Under these circumstances, no consolidation of the entire peasant movement was ever achieved in

Poland, nor was a clear political program ever drawn up. This was to come only after the restoration of independence.

On the other hand, an unusual feature, a characteristic of Polish culture of the period, was the introduction of the peasantry to the national consciousness by means of art, first and foremost through literature, but also through music and painting.

Romantic poetry, at first at home, and later both among emigrés and in Poland, added new meanings to this current; but it was only during the second half of the nineteenth century that art and literature seriously took up the cause of the peasantry.

The breakthrough was anticipated in the works of Cyprian Kamil Norwid. Already in his youthful works, written in Warsaw, he understood the peasant better than did other poets, his contemporaries. He showed the peasants in terms of the prospects that they opened up for both the nation and all of humanity; he revealed their love for simple, unfalsified truth, their solemn attitude toward life, manifested in work. These views obtained mature presentation in *Promethidion* (1851). Considering art, Norwid concluded that "a national artist organizes imagination" just as a politician organizes the nation's strength. Completion of the task is possible only through contact with the peasantry, because in its life, truth combines with work, "song", with "practical life."

This metaphysical and historiosophical concept of the peasantry, conceived by Norwid, did not generate direct followers. But the poets and writers of Positivism agreed with Norwid in their conviction that the peasantry was more than simply an ethnographic category, producers of songs and dances, fables and tales. Maria Konopnicka, reaching beyond the horizons of the folk-style poetry of Teofil Lenartowicz or Władysław Syrokomla, directed her attention to the realities of peasant existence.

In a similar manner, Eliza Orzeszkowa expressed her interest: a forerunner of this trend can be seen in one of her first stories, *A Sketch from the Years of Hunger*, in which she defended the human values of the peasant. But only in her later works did she show deep concern for the peasant problem and managed to create works of lasting values: *Dziurdziowie* (1885), *Winter Night, The Yokel* (1888) and, to a certain degree, *On the Niemen*. Fascinated by the contrast between the true and the false civilization, by the antinomy of natural village life and the unnatural bourgeois culture of the big cities, with their "high society," Orzeszkowa looked for moral values and human dignity among the peasants, always fully aware, however, of their fanaticism and obscurantism.

A symbol of the period was Bolesław Prus' *The Outpost* (1885), a story of a blind, but successful, resistance put up by a Polish peasant, in defense of the land of his fathers. Of that novel Żeromski once wrote: "*The Outpost* may serve as an oracle in all reflections on our national psychology."

The peasant issue also attracted the attention of a writer who otherwise kept aloof from the social program of democracy, Henryk Sienkiewicz. His short stories, in particular *Janko the Musician, Bartek the Conqueror* and

In Search of Bread, proved a lasting element of the national consciousness and expressed a certain view toward the peasant problem.

The next stage of literary development, labeled Neo-romanticism or Young Poland, not only preserved but extended the positivist trend of including the peasantry in the national consciousness.

Jan Kasprowicz, Kazimierz Przerwa-Tetmajer, Stanisław Wyspiański and Władysław Reymont, created unusually suggestive, if discordant, images of the peasantry which to this day are regarded by society as lasting elements of Polish culture and of the national community at large. Kasprowicz, himself of peasant origin, in his poems and dramas, as well as in his historical plays, such as *The Rebellion of Napierski,* stressed his belief that "in the peasant dwells unbreakable strength," while reflecting the mood of "the dying world" in his peasant-like religious litany, entitled *The Hymns. Marchołt* — a result of several years' work — was an effort to get to the roots of peasant wisdom. Kasprowicz's last poems, *My World,* were closely linked with the poetical and pictorial folk imagination. Not so broad were the aspirations of Tetmajer, yet his tales, *In the Rocky Podhale,* established the highlanders in Polish culture with all the wealth of their artistic imagery and their unusual folk vision of the world. But perhaps most exceptional in his grasp of the issue was Stanisław Witkiewicz. In his studies, *On the Mountain Pass* (1890), and *From the Tatras* (1907), and in his many newspaper articles, he insisted that "peasant cultures had everywhere remained the only sanctuaries of relatively pure primeval forms of existence of any nation", and that a future moral and social revival, a future national integration, would receive its impetus from the peasants' dignity and solemn attitude. Władysław Orkan, born at Poręba Wielka in the Gorce Mountains, portrayed the conditions of life of his fellow countrymen in his lyrical verse, *From This Land of Sorrow* (1903), and in his novels, *In Roztoki* (1903). Stefan Żeromski viewed the problem of the peasantry in a broader, historical perspective of the culpability of the gentry, and denounced the ensuing age-old serfdom of the villagers, their shame and suffering, their desire for revenge, accompanied by their hopes for a better future, based on work. *Ashes, The Faithful River* and *A Word about a Farm Hand,* interpreted the destiny of the peasants in historical and contemporary terms, as a pilgrimage along roads of disaster toward a new Poland, a Poland of peasants and workers, as a civilian version of the story of the Polish wandering soldier.

In contrast to this presentation of the peasant in national life was the position taken by Władysław Reymont. In his great epic, *The Peasants* (1904—09), he portrayed peasant life in connection with the cycle of the seasons which govern the work, and the rites of the people; and yet he managed to reveal all the wealth inherent in individual and social experiences, the conflicts and the hopes always present in that world, seemingly self-contained and isolated from the rest of national life, and yet constituting a lasting basis for it.

By far the greatest influence in this field was exerted by Stanisław Wyspiański, especially his drama *The Wedding.* No other literary work could match the force with which that theatrical travesty of a marriage ceremony between Lucjan Rydel and the sister of Tetmajer's wife (Tetmajer for years had been a member of the village community at Bronowice near Cracow) overwhelmed the nation's imagination and its political thinking. The symbols of this work — the Strawman, the golden horn, ghosts appearing at the wedding (Stańczyk, Szela, Zawisza, Wernyhora) — and dozens of laconic, brilliant and bitter aphorisms picked out of the dialogue of the play were made part of everyday speech. The probing of the national conscience was often carried on in these terms as was analysis of the false or true merits of the belief in the power of the peasantry as alleged guarantors of national liberation. The possibility of different interpretations of *The Wedding* never diminished its influence on contemporaries or on later generations; on the contrary, new modes of deciphering the true meaning of the drama of Polish history and the Polish soul have been uncovered and today, the play has triumphed both on stage and in films.

A characteristic feature of the culture of the period was the way that painters worked together with poets and writers. Although villagers had been an interesting subject for painters since the eighteenth century, yet — as in literature — it was only during the second half of the nineteenth century that folk themes in art acquired new traits, which extended far beyond the horizons of those realistic documents cultivated by Jean Pierre Norblin or Jan Feliks Piwarski. The painters of the positivist period traveled about Poland in order to get sufficient knowledge of the countryside and its population. Franciszek Kostrzewski exposed the abuse of peasantry; Józef Szermentowski painted melancholy scenes from the life of the villagers. In a similar fashion Aleksander Kotsis, a painter from Cracow, portrayed the life of the peasant, the plight of orphans, and the sorrows of death and destitution. These pictures, like Konopnicka's poems, expressed emotions generated by a close, but unknown, reality.

Włodzimierz Tetmajer produced paintings at Bronowice with themes of village life viewed in a broad historical perspective, from *The Angels Visiting Piast* to *The Battle of Racławice.* That final triumph of the peasants' courage and patriotic zeal was a popular subject of many works: Władysław Anczyc's play *Kosciuszko at Racławice* enjoyed great popularity, while a huge panorama of the battle painted by Jan Styka and Wojciech Kossak, unveiled during the centennial of the actual event (1894) in Lvov, aroused a wave of enthusiasm.

In contrast to this heroic art, Wyspiański painted simple and touching heads of peasant children while Malczewski pointed to the place of the peasantry in a symbolic, allegorical vision of the world, as well as in Polish history. Somewhat similar in nature was the work of Vlastimil Hofman and Jan Rembowski who settled in Zakopane. Religious and ethnographic values in village life fascinated many contemporary artists, including Władysław Jarocki (*The Return from Golgotha*), Kazimierz Sichulski (triptych *Springtime*), Leon Wyczółkowski (*Beetroot Digging*), and Ferdynand Ruszczyc (*The Soil*).

Evidence of the force with which art introduced the peasantry to the national consciousness may also be found in music, which, like painting and literature, turned to the peasantry from the beginnings of the period of bondage. The work of Karol Kurpiński, for example, was in this spirit. However this new movement had begun in music earlier, with Frédéric Chopin. His mazurkas were called "musical epics of the Polish people, unique in their originality." Far from producing village music, or imitating it, Chopin transformed his material in such a manner that it projected both national and international values without losing its exceptionally individualistic character.

Almost symbolic of the role music played in establishing the peasantry in the national consciousness during the period of servitude was Stanisław Moniuszko's opera *Halka.* On the opening night, 1 January 1858, in Warsaw, it was highly acclaimed, provoking, however, some severe criticism because more conservative critics did not like its melancholy story about a country-maid. It is remarkable how this work became later, and still is, accepted as a model of Polish national opera, despite the obvious lack of great national events in its story, which is, as the author of the book wanted it to be, a simple tale of a poor highland girl. Her plight became a symbol of all the wrongs done to the peasants and of the uneasy qualms of the national conscience.

THE WORKERS' MOVEMENT AND THE PROLETARIAN REVOLUTION

The Manifesto of the Social Democratic Party of the Kingdom of Poland and Lithuania (SDKPiL) proclaimed in January 1905, stated the following: "We the toilworn, we with our rough hands, we the expropriated, have come out in the forefront of society, we the working class are today the leaders of the nation in Poland." A long and difficult road had led Polish workers to this state of political consciousness, to this awareness of their role in the nation and of their responsibility for its destiny.

The beginnings of the workers' movement extend back to the first decade of the nineteenth century; yet only in the second half of the century, concurrently with the development of industry in Upper Silesia, in the Dąbrowa Basin, in Warsaw and Łódź, did the movement gain force and consciousness. The organization of the movement was a difficult and dangerous task. The authorities in the three partitioning powers collaborated in persecuting and imprisoning the leaders; attempts at extending the movement in Poznań and Galicia brought only limited effects. In Warsaw, Ludwik Waryński founded a workers' organization, Proletariat (1882), which was to cooperate with the Russian Narodnaya Vola. It had an illegal publication of its own, *Proletariat,* which advocated a program of international proletarian revolution, maintaining that the core of the matter was not as much to win Polish independence as to liberate the working masses, putting an end to social and, consequently, to national oppression. In 1884, the czarist police destroyed the organization; its

leaders were executed; Waryński was confined into the Schliesselburg prison where he died in 1889.

The revolutionary movement started again a few years later. Julian Marchlewski and Adolf Warski founded the Union of Polish Workers in Warsaw in 1889, while in Galicia, the Social Democratic Party was first organized in 1892, as a branch of the Austrian Social Democracy, with which it later broke, achieving full independence. However, the most important event was the establishment, after prolonged disputes, of two workers' parties: the Polish Socialist Party (PPS; 1892), which linked the cause of the revolutionary struggle with that of the fight for national independence; and the Social Democratic Party of the Kingdom of Poland (1893), later, from 1900, called the Social Democratic Party of the Kingdom of Poland and Lithuania, which proclaimed a revolutionary program, aimed directly at an international upheaval according to the views of Rosa Luxemburg.

In the years 1904—05, both platforms took part in practical revolutionary action. This proved that huge masses of workers, the urban proletariat, radical intelligentsia, and students had spontaneously developed a desire to fight for social justice, a better future for everybody, and national freedom. Peasant strikes were also spreading, especially among the farmhands on the big estates.

Revolutionary activity was mainly focused in the big cities. Soldiers in Warsaw attacked the May Day demonstration; in Łódź workers fought at a hundred barricades; in the Dąbrowa Basin a workers' militia took over power; in the Sandomierz region the czarist administration was ousted and the so-called Republic of Ostrowiec was created, including the areas of Ostrowiec, Ćmielów and Iłża. The czarist army and police struck back at the revolutionaries with increasing ruthlessness; the revolutionary movement could not derive direct advantages from the fight of the masses of Russian workers, although the ever-increasing advance of the revolutionary wave compelled the czarist administration to make some concessions which applied also in the Kingdom. These concessions included, above all, education as well as the right to form associations, namely trade unions, but were all on a rather small scale. As late as 1906, revolutionary actions were still breaking out in various areas, mostly in Łódź. Rural strikes were also breaking out. But the lack of a united leadership was sharply evident in the revolutionary movement. The two-year struggle of the Polish workers ended amidst wave after wave of terror exerted by the czarist army and police, in an atmosphere of hostility and disgust on the part of the propertied class towards its own society, in an atmosphere of hopelessness generated by the defeat of the revolutionary movement in Russia; it was the first struggle in Polish history undertaken and conducted by the proletariat, and the first one connected with the revolutionary movement in Russia.

Polish art, so deeply committed to the peasant cause, showed remarkable restraint in the face of the workers' cause and sometimes even manifested obvious antipathy to the revolutionary workers' movement.

Prus treated revolution as a politically irresponsible

game, as a tragic farce of false hopes, and ineffective action. Sienkiewicz perceived in the revolution dangers which threatened the national identity which in itself was searching for new roads to the future. Wacław Berent's novel, *Winter Seed,* was to some degree an act of faith in the revolution; for in it the workers went out onto the streets as a test of their professed ideas; their ordeal, however, as the title of the novel indicates, would not bring immediate fruit, not until the long winter was over. Similarly equivocal in its meanings was Żeromski's drama, *The Rose.*

While art remained, on the whole, indifferent to or censorious of the workers' movement, philosophical thought supported it from the very outset. It was a remarkable feature of the period. The young Warsaw intelligentsia, headed by Jan Karol Potocki, Ludwik Krzywicki, Wacław Nałkowski and Jan Władysław Dawid, sympathized with the movement. Art and literary critics, like Bronisław Białobłocki, Józef Tokarzewicz and, finally, Stanisław Brzozowski, even launched an offensive against writers for their unwillingness to understand the significance and impact of the revolutionary events. Sociologists, including Stanisław Krusiński and later Edward Abramowski, were linked with the experience of the movement; and others like Julian Marchlewski and Kazimierz Kelles-Krauz, were constructing a theoretical basis for it. Virtually everything that was new and significant in the history of Polish thought of the era was linked with the workers' movement and with the intellectual interpretation of its historic mission. The wealth and the diversity of these reflections extended beyond the limits of the socialist party platforms and the principles of political strategies. They also did not fit into the then predominant concept of Marxism. But these ideas went their own way, in quest of solutions to problems important to the country; they made bold use of national experiences and national needs, contributing in a creative manner to the development of modern Marxism.

THE INTELLIGENTSIA AT THE CROSSROADS

The development of Polish culture during the era of bondage was defined not solely by social conflicts between peasants and landowners, or between workers and industrialists; nor was it defined solely by disputes and alliances between the gentry and bourgeoisie.

During the period of foreign rule a very special social group called the "intelligentsia" arose. Its history reaches as far back as the end of the eighteenth century with the remarkable increase in the number of people who were involved in science, education, literature, politics, journalism and also with civil service and diverse professional activities requiring special instruction. The group had already gained some social significance and a certain measure of influence on public opinion. However, the determining factor was still the system of estates; and all basic political decisions were made by the ruling estate, distinguished by its coats-of-arms and privileges.

Basic changes were not made until the Duchy of Warsaw, at a time when life was being organized on the French model.

In the Russian part of the country, in Congress Poland, the process developed with ever greater intensity.

Apart from the cadres of intelligentsia employed in different levels of the civil service, another group of people was emerging, connected with creative work in literature, the arts, theater, and the press. University students were also linked with this group. Within this group a conspiracy was initiated which led to the November Insurrection in 1830 in opposition to the official representation of the country and its higher functionaries.

The failure of the insurrection made conditions for the development of this group more difficult. The administration was, for the most part, taken over by Russians; higher educational institutions were closed; political journalism was prohibited.

In these circumstances different groups of intelligentsia developed in different ways. The strongest numerically were civil servants employed in the offices still accessible to Poles, and as private office staff. A smaller group was composed of teachers (the state secondary schools employed only 500 teachers), together with physicians and representatives of technical professions. A relatively large group was made up of musicians and painters. And despite all limitations, a group comprising scholars, writers and journalists, was also active. The Warsaw scientific and literary world was based on this group, on the Warsaw Boheme and the Women Enthusiasts, and on the popular science and social press (e.g. *Przegląd Naukowy* and *Biblioteka Warszawska).* When Samuel Orgelbrand inaugurated the publication of his *Popular Encyclopedia* in 1859, he easily mustered up 115 experts from various branches of learning. In a country where development was systematically inhibited, and where Polish higher education was virtually nonexistent, it was unusual to see such an intensity of intellectual life.

Similarly unfavorable conditions prevailed throughout the two remaining partition zones. In Galicia, the civil service remained in German hands up to the 1860's and neither a feebly developed industry nor a primitive agrarian economy could offer any alternative employment. The situation was a little better in the Poznań region, that is, in the Prussian sector. Although the state administration was also German, the economic development of the country offered new possibilities, while the intensity of political life, especially during the "Springtime of Nations" in 1846—48, opened up a field of action for the intelligentsia. On the basis of these experiences, Karol Libelt propounded his ideas about the social role of the intelligentsia as a group destined to guide the entire nation.

This specific and practically important mission of the intelligentsia was to be referred to more and more often throughout all three parts of occupied Poland.

However, during the positivist period, other aspects of this issue also appeared. Could the creative intelligentsia really become the leading group of a community in an epoch when the organization of material progress and the general appeal for "organic work" seemed of foremost significance? The answer to this question was shadowed in doubt.

Stanisław Wyspiański directed his criticism of the intelligentsia from another angle. In *The Wedding* and *Deliverance* he exposed the falsehood of the life of the intelligentsia, its intellectual irresponsibility, its sentimental delusions and its vain traditionalism, its false poetization and complete lack of will and ability to act. A much sharper criticism was formulated by Stanisław Brzozowski. His censure of the delusions of consciousness, of belief in autonomy of thought, of inclination towards the free, irresponsible play of imagination was, in essence, criticism of the creative intelligentsia in general, and writers and poets in particular. Thus Brzozowski was among the first who tried to bridge the gap which, according to general opinion, divided the intelligentsia from the world of labor: "Our culture today," he wrote, "is based on an intelligent proletariat."

Stefan Żeromski dealt with this idea in numerous studies, above all in *The Beginnings of the Labor World,* in which he expressed hope that the intelligentsia and the proletariat, "supplementing each other, might form an absolutely dominant force in Poland which would lead steadily along the road of continuous progress."

Battle for the State

GRAND STRATEGIES

At the end of the eighteenth century the Polish state ceased to exist. But during the whole period of bondage it was not forgotten, nor did the will to regain it ever vanish.

Two conflicting strategies of action clashed throughout the era: on the one hand, clandestine preparation for an armed struggle with the enemy, which sought a solution on the battlefield; on the other hand, organic work, which was supposed to win national autonomy, perhaps even independence, by means of economic development.

These two ideas alternated throughout the period of bondage: the Legions of Dąbrowski and Congress Poland, the November Insurrecton and the subsequent period of repression; the "Springtime of Nations" followed by defeat; the January Insurrection and the time of organic work; and the 1905 Revolution and its disastrous aftermath. However, these recurring rhythms did not fully characterize the culture of the era. The two opposing ideologies not only alternated but they also coexisted and this simultaneous existence of both currents was characteristic of the period.

The dualism of views appeared immediately after the downfall of the state. It was at this time, after the victory of the Targowica Confederacy in 1792 and later, after the defeat of the Kosciuszko Insurrection in 1794, that the first wave of exiles in Polish history had to leave the country. It was then that for the first time on foreign soil efforts were made to transform the Polish cause into the cause of all Europe. In Paris, the first severe accusations against the gentry were formulated by Józef Sułkowski, and the first plans for radical agrarian reform, based on land grants to the peasants without compensation, were prepared by Piotr Maleszewski. Thanks to the efforts on the part of Henryk Dąbrowski, the Polish Legions, organized in Italy in 1797, were incorporated into Napoleon's army. Their battle song, "Poland Shall Not Perish So Long As We Are Alive," was later to become the Polish national anthem.

During this time an image of an uninterrupted armed fight for independence was established in the national consciousness. Dąbrowski's Legions linked the Polish cause with the policies of Napoleon, who appeared to the Poles not only as a "god of war" but also as a source of hope in the fight against tyranny and despotism. His defeat did nothing to diminish his reputation. From the day Prince Joseph Poniatowski, ever faithful to Napoleon, perished in the River Elster at Leipzig, up to the time of Mickiewicz's lectures at the Collège de France in the 1840's, Bonaparte's name remained a banner and a symbol of freedom and heroism.

The antithesis of this heroic concept of life was the activity of Adam Jerzy Czartoryski, undertaken at the end of the eighteenth century, with the consent of Czar Alexander I, which championed the cultural development of the country in alliance with Russian policy. The same antithesis could be discerned in the activities of the leaders of economic and cultural life in the Duchy of Warsaw, and later in Congress Poland: Stanisław Kostka Potocki, Stanisław Staszic, Tadeusz Mostowski and, above all, Ksawery Drucki-Lubecki. The latter's program of economic expansion was implemented at the expense of the working masses. The dual meaning of organic work now became evident: as a means, first, of strengthening the nation, second, of increasing the profits of the propertied classes.

The heroic concept of life was supported by conspiratorial societies and Walerian Łukasiński represented a challenge to people of Lubecki's kind. Young conspirators, organizers of the November Night, when they took up arms against Russia, opposed at the same time those segments of their own community who were partisans of a peaceful development of the country. Their cause lost, and under conditions of increased oppression, all that remained for them was to focus attention on the simplest conditions of national life, the difficulties of everyday existence. Then, visions of heroic life began to prevail among the emigration and found their way back to Poland. Father Ściegienny remained faithful to the idea when he mobilized the peasants; so did Edward Dembowski, leader of the Cracow Insurrection of 1846, as well as various leaders of the Poznań Uprising in 1848.

At the same time, Karol Marcinkowski developed his economic activity, and Karol Libelt analyzed the idea of love for one's native land in terms of work and civil courage. August Cieszkowski maintained that "the era of the spirit" would come to life through the everyday, economic and social toil of the people. In the Kingdom this pattern of economic life was contrasted with the prodigality of the gentry and speculation by the nouveaux riches: what Józef Korzeniowski was doing in literature,

Andrzej Zamoyski tried to implement on his estate at Klemensów, where he assembled a group of landowners, partisans of the new agrarian policy. This theory of economic and social work found expression in Józef Supiński's book entitled, *The Polish School of Social Economy* (1862).

The strategy of armed struggle was also gaining ground. The opportunism of organic work was criticized; the path of conspiracy and manifestations was chosen again; and, finally, armed fight and alliance with Russian revolutionaries. Wielopolski's activity, limited to the polonization of the civil service and to the founding of a national educational system, seemed like high treason. The fate of Poland was to be decided in war. But the power of the Russian armies proved overwhelming. In cruel and tragic guerilla warfare, waged through partisan forays and forest fights, the bulk of the Polish forces was broken, but the heroic readiness to fight remained to the end within small detachments, even in individuals. Symbolic of this spirit of resistance was Father Brzóska, who with a small band of insurgents, mostly peasants, persevered at a forlorn outpost for a number of months after the defeat of the uprising.

The failure of the January Insurrection initially strengthened the hand of the adherents of the program of organic work. Aleksander Świętochowski in his *Political Recommendations* (1882) argued that "the independence of the state is, in a way, a title, an office one can lose without losing the essential features of one's personality." Therefore "the existence of nations is not founded on the external forms of political self-government" but "on all that is generally called the thought of the nation." In his numerous writings, he advocated a modern and intensive program of peaceful work, which would lead to economic victories. His views, however, aroused vehement protest both in the Kingdom and in Galicia.

Growing conflicts among the partitioning powers in the early twentieth century, and the possibility of war, again activated the younger generation. In numerous sports associations, in radical political parties, both peasant and proletarian, clandestine action was revived to prepare the cadre in case of an armed conflict in Europe.

Chief among the organizers preparing for armed action was Józef Piłsudski. Scion of a wealthy family of gentry of the Vilna region, he preserved, from that landowning and romantic home, painful reminiscences of the 1863 defeat. His program envisioned a "fight between a popular army and the czarist troops". His dream was to wipe out the guilt of his predecessors who were defeated in 1863. True to his ideals, on 6 August 1914, a few days after the outbreak of war between Austria and Russia, Piłsudski entered Congress Poland at the head of a small detachment of riflemen.

THE VISION
OF A FUTURE DEMOCRATIC POLAND

Prior to the November Insurrection, the question of readiness for the armed fight and the link between this and future democratic reforms was brought up time and again. Maurycy Mochnacki gave his reply to the question in mid-1831. In émigré circles his program was adopted by the conservative wing and was disputed among the democrats. Mochnacki wrote the following: "Let us first become a nation, and only then make appropriate changes in the internal structure of our community."

This ideology was opposed by the democrats. Seweryn Goszczyński spoke for the Polish Democratic Society in 1840: "Some people think that the base of the Polish cause is the independence of the nation. We consider that view wrong. Independence with regard to a nation must, of necessity, be somehow qualified; it must have one main feature with which to define its nature."

Another activist declared the following: "The goal of a future insurrection in Poland would not be solely to achieve independence" but would include the simultaneous implementation of "a social revolution." In this way, "the nation would have an external enemy to fight, and an internal one to overpower at the same time."

On the basis of these premises diverse visions of a democratic future were created; this democratic future had to form part of all preparatory actions prior to the emergence of a Polish state.

The official platform of the Democratic Society, advocating liberty for each and every citizen, equal rights for all, and universal political responsibility, was subjected to strong criticism by various radical groups, including Stanisław Worcell, Zenon Świętosławski and Ludwik Królikowski, who propounded a program of wide revolutionary changes aimed at creating a completely new society, based on a true community of interests. These various visions of the future — moderate and radical, realistic and utopian — induced constant polemics and led to factions and secessions, to manifestoes and protests.

The second phase of the great dispute concerning the future shape of Poland took place during the latter half of the nineteenth century, mostly among the socialists, and had for its subject the choice of the supreme goal of the future war: either the independence of Poland or proletarian revolution. The pioneers of the movement solved the dilemma on principle by choosing revolution.

Ludwik Waryński declared the following: "The universality of revolution emerges solely from the fact that not political but also economic upheaval is our aim." He prophesied that the coming of the uprising would not be greeted with "Long live Poland!" but with "Long live the social revolution!"

An opponent of this ideology was Bolesław Limanowski, who emphasized the social values of patriotism and its significance in implementing the program of the liberation of the proletariat. At the beginning of 1889 a group of Limanowski's supporters inaugurated the publication of *Pobudka,* a "national-socialist" periodical which proclaimed adherence to the principle that "the independence issue and the social issue are inseparable."

The Polish Socialist Party, formed in Paris in 1892, formulated its platform for action which was to liberate Poland as an "independent democratic republic."

At the beginning of the twentieth century, the number of political parties greatly increased, as did the number of political programs defining the strategy of action, which depended on the different visions of a future Poland. The intensity of disputes concerning these visions also increased. This continued to cause anxiety among those parts of the general public who were not directly involved in the struggles of the political parties and who recalled the remark made a century earlier by Cyprian Godebski, who criticized those who designed "a house built out of hope" in too great detail, and who instead of steering the ship of state into port were quarelling over "the new helm of government" while still far out at sea in the midst of storms.

INDIVIDUAL RESPONSIBILITY AND SOCIAL COMMUNITY

In these various controversies pertaining to the strategy and the objectives of political action, the idea of individual and collective commitment as well as of collective and individual responsibility of the people for the life of the community constantly recurred. The existence of a nation without a state meant that it could not develop in a regular way through public institutions It often seemed obvious that the nation had to defend its existence despite the existing institutions. Under such conditions a safeguard to national survival was the spontaneous activity of individuals associated in groups and conducting overt, and sometimes covert, activity in different areas of life. When the state was not a guarantee of national development, being, on the contrary, a menace to it, all matters relating to the future had to be resolved within the community itself.

The men of the Polish Enlightenment had already perceived and understood this obligation, when historic destiny compelled them to act under conditions of foreign domination. And they, Staszic and Kołłątaj in particular, had passed that obligation to others and continued hopefully to anticipate the future, because they believed in the strength of the nation. Staszic's words "a great nation may fall, but only a base one will perish" and Kołłątaj's maxim *"nil desperandum"* were important messages during the entire period of bondage, and they called for social, spontaneous and self-governing action.

This austere and imperative truth was also taught by Mickiewicz in his *Books of the Polish Nation and the Polish Pilgrimage,* in his famous appeal and promise, venerated decade after decade: "Inasmuch as you extend and improve your souls, you will improve your laws and extend your frontiers." This axiom formed the source of the success of Andrzej Towiański, who preached to the exiles who were denied any possibility of action on behalf of their homeland, the good news that they could serve it in a humble, and yet most effective way, that of freeing their inner life from all sins and transgressions.

This idea about the life of a stateless nation lasted even longer in the social consciousness, although during the post-Romantic era, under another form. Liberated from metaphysical, even mystical connotations, it acquired a new type of explanation through sociological considera-

tions. The peculiarity and originality of Polish sociological thought was defined by the very fact that it expressed the social situation of a nation which had to live without a state of its own.

Stanisław Witkiewicz explained it in the following way in 1905: "It is obvious that the existence of a subjugated nation relies exclusively on the quality of each individual."

This situation served as point of departure for the then famous, but now forgotten, book by Jan Brzoza, *An Issue of the Policy of Independence.* Published in Cracow in 1911, it contained an unusual theory regarding an invisible Polish state which allegedly was "the helmsman of the daily will" of its citizens, who lived within the organism of foreign states.

Even if paradoxical, the fundamentals of this concept, expressed in viewing state reality as one of the attitudes, strivings and consciousness of its people and not solely in terms of institutions, organizations and power, was a characteristic feature of Polish sociological theories of the era. The conviction that the people themselves were the main agents of any historical change was shared by all writers of the religious camp, both orthodox and those, who, like Wincenty Lutosławski, preferred metaphysical systems of their own. The strategy of social action, advocated and implemented by Lutosławski was effected through the Association Eleusis: small groups formed on the basis of moral rebirth, based on the experience of the Philomates, that is, the union of Vilna students during the second decade of the nineteenth century.

More characteristic of Polish culture at the turn of the century, however, was that the principle of moral revival was formulated by writers who suggested a program based on the economic modernization of the community.

Stanislaw Szczepanowski was a part of this movement. His philosophy aimed at the intensification of economic activity of the Poles along West-European lines, with the difference that he put strong emphasis on moral values. Mickiewicz's concepts concerning the deficiency of the civilization of material well-being, frugality and order, recurred time after time in the deliberations of this author who willingly assumed the pen-name "Piast", and demanded spiritual rebirth from and through practical activity: "There can be no economic revival without moral revival."

An even more characteristic feature of Polish culture was that the principle of moral revival as the basis for revolution was proclaimed by those writers who belonged to radical circles or who were linked with them by profound sympathy for the cause of social progress.

In diverse ways, but for the most part unanimously, sociologists who followed a Marxist line also emphasized the significance of such subjective factors as the consciousness and will of the masses, and protested against objectivist and determinist concepts which tended to eliminate the role of man.

Kazimierz Kelles-Krauz wrote the following: "In a community everything happens in the people and by the people, only through the people's activity can economic forces find expression in the law, state and other social institutions." Julian Marchlewski maintained that "people make history; so the future lies in our hands." An image of that future as described by Polish Marxists bore the particular features of a community of brothers, individual freedom and wealth of cultural life.

This vision of the future gained still other values of creative freedom and community in the writings of Ludwik Krzywicki and Edward Abramowski. According to Krzywicki, the fight with the unjust and exploitative capitalist system and with degenerate urban culture was carried out in the name of a future where social life would have creative and communal features.

In this vision, human work was to be freed of all bonds of compulsion and monotony. "The society of the future," maintained Krzywicki, "instead of cultivating senseless work from which all elements of attraction have evaporated will build workshops in which not only motors but the live impulse of inner vocation will be used." Productive, vocationally and professionally motivated work will be shaped according to the rules of artistic and intellectual activity in which to the fullest degree "the liberation of the spirit from the bonds of anonymity and inhuman numbers" will take place.

The greatest achievement in this field was attained by Abramowski. In his fundamental studies, *The Issue of Socialism* (1899), *Individual Elements in Sociology* (1899), and *Socialism and the State* (1904), he presented a concept of man "as parent of the social world." In his analysis of the processes of social development, he demonstrated the role of individual counterparts and explained how "out of the small human changes, the moral changes in man and in his everyday life, out of the remnants of the new conscience, originates the mighty spirit of death and of social rebirth. . . The collective will be such as is the most common type of individual, and social institutions are of such quality as is the conscience of the average man."

On these foundations Abramowski based his concept of "moral revolution as the practical principle of socialism"; and his strategy of cooperative action and his ideal of "socialism without a state," which was to emerge and last in the form of "free associations."

In his essay, *Ethics and Revolution* (1899), Abramowski formulated the principles of "moral revolution," stating that the ideas of socialism should become existentially concrete motivations for the masses, and that only a permanent revolution, continually alive in man's behavior and deeply rooted in his conscience, his daily beliefs, could become a really revolutionary force and achieve the social and humanitarian ideals of the proletariat; the strategy of revolutionary action could safeguard the political victory of the proletariat.

Abramowski's ideas, an extension of the romantic traditions of "enlargement and improvement" of the soul, won over many adherents, among whom was Stanisław Witkiewicz. In his study *Years After* (1906) Witkiewicz opposed the various political movements which reduced social issues to matters of material well-being and division of wealth. Witkiewicz declared the following: "Too little attention was paid in social accounts to the poverty of souls."

THE INCREASING STRENGTH OF THE NATION

The sum total of the battles for restoration of the state registered nothing but defeats. None of the Polish insurrections was successful. The downfall of each was followed by bloodshed and prolonged repressive measures. All diplomatic calculations, memoranda submitted and interventions undertaken proved futile. The wars waged by the partitioning powers were of no avail to the Polish cause, and parliamentary actions or statements of loyalty to the reigning monarchs brought little fruit. Political parties appeared and disappeared in all of the three partition zones under pressure of changing circumstances, and, deprived of any real possibility of action, both in the country and abroad, were prone to the typical ailments brought on by too much discussion, bitter polemics, theoretical projects and visions.

And yet the balance did not show only loss. On the contrary, during the 123 years of bondage, unusual progress was made in the field of modernization and integration of the Polish political consciousness. Although unable to manifest itself in organizations and public institutions within a state of its own, it was assuming new shape and new strength.

Whereas immediately after the partitions Poland was, in fact, divided by the boundaries set up by the invaders, during the long years of bondage a process was effected in which the frontiers were ignored in both the political and cultural life of the country. The November Insurrection was fought by the community of the Kingdom of Poland, but the post-insurrection émigrés became spokesmen for political thought and action on an all-Poland scale. Their ideology exerted influence in all Polish lands, stretching its conspiratorial arm from the Duchy of Poznań to Lithuania. Similarly, the January Insurrection was fought solely in the Russian partition zone; yet its downfall generated attempts to create a political organization embracing all Poland. The first such organization was the Polish League, at least during the first period of its existence, when it was founded in Switzerland in 1897. All subsequent strong political movements — nationalist, peasant, and socialist — aimed at the same objective and made ever more contacts among the partition zones. The feeling of national unity, of a great Polish program, prevailed over the particular differences between pro-Russian and anti-Russian, pro-German and anti-German, pro-Austrian and anti-Austrian orientations.

However, the most characteristic process during the period of bondage was the rise and development of national awareness among the masses in the lands lost long before: in Silesia, Pomerania, in Warmia and Mazuria. These changes proceeded with elemental force at the very roots of society, where neither Polish schools nor political parties could openly function, nor conspiratorial action be inflamed. In essence local and self-generated movements, they developed in harmony with the changes in the national consciousness, under the influence of the general conditions of Polish political life and various journalistic campaigns.

This process could be discerned first in Silesia, where Józef Lompa, a teacher at a popular school in Lubsza, published a number of pamphlets intended for the peasants: a farming almanac, collections of stories and a first popular outline of the history of Silesia. The intensity of activity increased during the "Springtime of Nations." It also extended into the Wrocław and Opole regions, and to Cieszyn Silesia. In the second half of the nineteenth century, Karol Miarka was active in this area, together with the already large group of young peasant Silesian intellectuals, poets and writers.

The peasants in Kashubia, Pomerania, Warmia and Mazuria fought against the extinction of the Polish spirit in the mid-nineteenth century. Krzysztof Mrongowiusz, Herman Gizewiusz and, later, Florian Ceynowa were pioneers in this field. Many others soon joined the movement: writers and journalists, who sometimes wrote in the vernacular. Periodicals, novels and poetry continued to strengthen the patriotic sentiment, to express affection for the homeland and its history.

A similar process was going on within the working class. During the first half of the century, it was closely connected with the peasant section of society, especially in the former agricultural areas, where an accelerated process of industrialization was taking place as, for example, in Silesia. When, during the second half of the century, the working class started to take shape, its road to an independent Poland and to responsibility for the country began to differ from the road it had formerly shared with the peasantry. Capitalist forms of exploitation, almost identical throughout all three partition zones, were stimulating working class solidarity and the will to act collectively.

The program of social liberation proclaimed a struggle against capitalism and for national sovereignty. Although certain political parties sometimes omitted this idea of a social and national liberation struggle from their platforms, the link always remained alive in the working class consciousness. And, together with the peasant movements, this was one of the great achievements of the period of bondage, one on which the future was to be built.

View of the World

THE PHILOSOPHY
OF HISTORICAL MATURITY

During the long period of bondage social conflicts and the struggle for independence went on under different guises both at home and abroad, among the émigrés. Various intellectual and artistic currents continued to appear and vanish, connected in various ways with the transformation of national life. And yet, through all the diversity and instability, the same or similar issues, the same agonizing questions, expectations, and disillusionments always recurred. The returning waves were never simply repetitions, but under different conditions they assumed new shapes.

Dramatic alternatives of doubt and hope manifested themselves, above all, in those philosophic and poetic arguments which concerned the factors determining the development of the world: that is, god and history. God and History — linked or opposed — provided the main theme for national reflection during the period of foreign rule.

This reflection opened up vistas to rich and complicated metaphysical and historical issues: whether history is the only and the highest plane on which situations and events occur in human societies and in their interrelations, or whether there are supra-historical planes rooted in the very nature of the world.

Arguments concerning Polish historical reality reached beyond the limits of empirical historical events, in an attempt to appraise boldly the world of accomplished facts from the point of view of other higher values.

In this respect, Polish culture during the period of bondage drew on the heritage of the Enlightenment, because the latter assumed the existence of a dual order in the world: natural and historical. An order based on the laws of nature guaranteed liberty and equality for the people. Within the historical order this guarantee was to be implemented through historical development, and this in fact constituted progress. It could happen within historical reality that, in a given time and place, the natural order would be subject to temporary violation. Polish writers, Staszic and Kołłątaj in particular, paid a great deal of attention to this issue and formulated a basic question: Was there any justification for hope that the violated laws of nature could be reinstituted? The question reached deep, to the very metaphysical roots of social existence.

The question was raised again during the romantic era in an effort to find a reply different in kind, and yet basically the same. This was founded on the spiritual concept of the world. Characteristic of this concept was the acceptance, drawn from Christian inspiration, of an inner dualism, of the fight between good and evil, which only in the future, after sustained defeats, would end with the triumph of good. From that point of view, liberty, value, and community, which made up the real contents of social life, might even undergo annihilation by hostile forces — satanical forces as some said — but they did not lose their power to resist and to regenerate.

A form of this type of reflection on national history was Polish Messianism. Harbingers of this religious concept of national destiny can be already discerned in the age of the disasters which almost destroyed the independence of the state in the seventeenth century. But only the state's downfall at the end of the eighteenth century freed the whole intensity of despair and the need of hope, founded on the exceptional grace of God, which was to lead the Polish nation for ages along the road of its destiny and to subject it to various tests of suffering. In his writings Jan Paweł Woronicz expressed the growing conviction in society that turning attention to the past does not merely satisfy the needs of sentimental traditionalism, but also bolsters faith in the future; it is not only a desire to strengthen the nation through linking it with tradition, but also a search for a basis and strategy to guide patriotic actions under foreign rule. His was a very remarkable augury of Polish Romantic Messianism.

This concept was developed by Kazimierz Brodziński in numerous articles published during the November Insurrection, particularly in his famous speech, *About the Nationality of the Poles,* delivered at a session of the Society of Friends of Learning in Warsaw in 1831, on the anniversary of the enactment of the Third of May Constitution, an event that was to be often recalled by later generations. In Brodziński's opinion, the mission of the Polish nation was "to grow the tree of freedom and brotherhood under the sun of religion" and overcoming the natural egoism of the nation, to teach other nationalities that none of them should be an object in itself, but all should concentrate like planets around the unique sun, meaning "the cooperation of all mankind." By this token the Polish nation "appeared like the Copernicus of the moral world."

Brodziński's ideas were taken up and developed by writers in exile, headed by Adam Mickiewicz. His *Books of the Polish Nation and the Polish Pilgrimage,* published anonymously in Paris in 1832, translated twice into French, as well as into English and German, became a true national gospel for the Poles. Fragments of the book were read and memorized during the whole era of servitude. In particular his "Pilgrim's Prayer" and "Pilgrim's Litany" took on — like the old hymn "O God, Who Hath Protected Poland" — the character of patriotic prayers and were perhaps read communally. In them the evidence of Polish martyrdom was linked to the readiness to fight and a plea for "a universal war for the liberty of the peoples," a request which seemed to have been granted in 1914.

The Books justified the political and moral mission of the émigrés, but first and foremost gave a vision of Polish history in which the simile, "Poland, the Christ of Nations," constituted a source of trust in the future. In that analogy, Christ appeared not as a savior of individual souls, but as Overlord of the world; his sacrifice, his death and resurrection, were harbingers of God's kingdom on earth; Poland's plight and her future destiny was to be a repetition of Christ's way. The history of Poland seen from this standpoint changed into a "holy" history in contrast to the "pagan" world, a history of freedom opposed to despotism, the history of a simple agrarian people counterpoised against "the peddlars and traders," promoters of materialized science.

The further development of Messianism and its influence on Polish culture were linked, for the most part, with the activities of Andrzej Towiański. On his arrival in Paris from Lithuania for a lengthy period in 1841, he acquired an unusual influence over the émigrés. His followers included Adam Mickiewicz, Juliusz Słowacki and Seweryn Goszczyński. The future of Poland allegedly depended on the moral quality of the people belonging to the circle of followers of Towiański; they had the task to "turn the scales of Poland's fate," since Poland was called upon to relive in modern times the acts and fate of ancient Israel, which had inaugurated the first epoch of history.

Of a more social and historical nature was the branch of Messianism which tried to inspire hope for the future of Poland with an analysis of her past history. Especially in the studies and poetry of Zygmunt Krasiński, Messianism appeared in the form of a theocratic notion of history, justifying the hope for a "dawn," which supposedly was to initiate a new stage in the history of mankind.

Polish national philosophy approached the philosophy of history differently, beginning with a fundamental critique of Hegel. Great differences divided August Cieszkowski, Karol Libelt, and Bronisław Trentowski, but all of them shared a commom conviction that history, far from being finished, had just entered a new phase thanks to bold, conscious and creative human activity.

The polemics with Hegel was inaugurated by August Cieszkowski in his book, *Prolegomena to the Philosophy of History,* which appeared in German in 1838, and aroused great interest in intellectual circles. It was highly praised in Germany by Moses Hess and Karl Ludwig Michelet. Instead of the Hegelian division of history into four epochs, Cieszkowski introduced a three-fold structure: ancient times, present times (that is, Christianity) and the future, or the era of deeds. This philosophy, opposed to the concepts of "finite history," opened a source of hope for a country, which in its present state could only look to the future.

Yet the vision of the future, a steady undercurrent of the Polish community during the period of bondage, acquired quite a different meaning, due to the treatment of this issue from the vantage point of the oppressed classes, especially the peasants. In the early decades of the nineteenth century this issue was not yet defined directly; but the radical gentry defined from this standpoint certain attitudes toward Poland's past, and Poland's future prospects. The following question was then formulated: Should the history of Poland remain what it always had been, a history of the gentry, hostile or neutral to the mass of the peasantry, or could it be acceptable, at least in part, as a truly national history? Concurrently with that question there emerged a fundamental doubt: Might the history of Poland in any way be looked upon as a safeguard for a happy and free future, or on the contrary, would the future require the complete abolition of previous history, in order to create a new reality, free of all ancient errors? While the conservative Messianists believed that the values of Poland's history justified trust in a Polish future, radical writers and leaders were of a different opinion: the future, in their eyes, depended on the ability to overcome the errors of the past.

The issues of a Polish future and Polish history with all their dramatic force faced the founders of the Democratic Society in Paris. The first declaration of principles drew on the revolutionary tradition of the French Enlightenment and, from the viewpoint of human and civil rights, applied fundamental criticism to Polish history.

In the final version of the *Manifesto* of the Democratic Society the judgment on Polish history was modified. The notion of ancient practice of rule by the communes, and an accusation against the gentry for their monopolization of privileges and for the oppression of the peasants was introduced. At the same time there was also an appreciation of the democracy within the gentry estate and of their defense and development of the national culture.

The most radical transgression of the limits of traditional historical thought was attempted by the philosophy of creationism evolved by Henryk Kamieński.

In his debate with Hegel, he followed a path different from that of Cieszkowski; and in his definition of creationism, he tried to take into account the conditions of material reality. His main philosophical work was the *Philosophy of Material Economy of Human Society* (1843—45). He propounded a thesis that "matter is an object that must be overpowered by the existence of man who ought to impress on it the mark of his creation." Man is not pure spirit but, on the other hand, he is not condemned to mere passivity. The essence of man is creation, in the full meaning of the word. From this standpoint, Kamieński opposed not only the intellectual philosophy of Hegel but also the rationalism of Descartes whose statement, "I think, therefore I am," he counterposed with another one: "I create, therefore I am" in an article published in 1843.

This principle, which abolished the idea of history as dead tradition and welcomed history as the product of the people was also professed by Edward Dembowski. According to him, creativity, originated by popular sources, was the main trend of life and progress which also shaped the new reality.

But, whereas the notion that history formed a final instance of justice and value was discarded by modern Polish consciousness under the influence of the disaster of the partitions, the various attempts to rise above history included in the concepts of the law of nature, the religious theory of history, and Polish Messianism, or in the national philosophy and the philosophy of creationism, could not retain their validity either, particularly during a period when science was beginning to exert an increasingly strong influence on philosophy.

Under these conditions a need appeared for views of history which did not oppose historical development to human understanding of value and equity and would not construct supra-historical, theological and abstract instances which were fruitless from the viewpoint of history. How could one respect the reality of the historical world, and at the same time maintain understanding and a desire for effective action against all that ought to be fought against and changed in it.

This question formed a steady current of the Polish national consciousness during the second half of the nineteenth century.

The existence of objective laws of development, which could be discovered by science, became one of the truths universally acknowledged in the positivist camp. Comte, Spencer, and Buckle were their favorite authors. In their writings, evidence could be found in favor of this concept. One could also interpret Darwin's theory along these lines and indeed this was often done in the analysis of social processes.

Philosophy, presupposing the existence of objective laws which were discoverable by science, could not, however, fully guarantee the values esteemed by the people.

A deeper methodological reflection on the nature and basis of scientific study led to the conclusion that it was, of necessity, hypothetical and limited in range. A characteristic manifestation of these neo-positivist tendencies was interest in the critical theory of cognition. In this atmosphere, Polish readers encountered the most important treatises by Henri Poincaré: *Science et Méthode* and *Le Science et l'hypothèse*.

A different kind of battle against historical determinism was carried on by Polish Marxists at the turn of the century. While accepting the basic premise of historical materialism, as well as a determinist concept of social development, ruled by the development of the means of production and a corresponding class struggle, they still strongly emphasized the role of conscious human activity. From this point of view they opposed the concept of evolutionism, interpreted as a theory freeing people of all action and responsibility. They also opposed the treatment of ideas as secondary manifestations of social life. On the contrary, while appreciating the social origin of ideas, they were of the opinion that their role in social development was significant. Such views were represented by Bronisław Białobłocki, Stanisław Krusiński and, later by Kazimierz Kelles-Krauz.

Foremost in the development of these ideas stood Stanisław Brzozowski who, while accepting the theory of historical materialism, launched a most vehement attack against the inertia of Polish society and called for heroic deeds. The theories of Sorel, and above all, of Labriola, were a significant intellectual inspiration in the theoretical works of Brzozowski; he undertook to formulate a program of active, creative Marxism opposed to various vulgar interpretations of determinism. In this fashion, Brzozowski created a "philosophy of historical maturity," (the sub-title of one of his main works) and introduced this idea into the consciousness of the Polish intelligentsia which still sought either to escape history or to escape into history.

This "philosophy of historical maturity" contained both a modern faith in the future, won and built by the hands of workmen, and a continuation of all the heroic, Promethean strivings of the Polish romantics.

VARIOUS CONCEPTS OF SOCIO-POLITICAL ACTIVITY

The struggle to overcome historical fatalism and the entire philosophy based on the worth and significance of "accomplished facts" was a point of departure for all deliberations concerning the possibilities of social action and the tasks that it could achieve in the historical development of the nation. During the entire period of bondage, these deliberations remained the main philosophy, oriented toward life and practice.

The downfall of the state had, from the very beginning,

become a source of conflicting, though often complimentary, approaches: one aimed at saving the menaced existence of the nation by preserving all that could be preserved from the past — language, customs, tradition and also the social structure; the other saw the way of salvation in the restructuring of life, removing the faults which had caused the downfall of the state, through a great national revival.

The conservative point of view was founded on the notion of society as some organic entity, possessing its own rhythm of development which could not, and should not, be impaired by arbitrary action of groups or individuals. Under these conditions, human activity was significant and necessary, but the character and objectives of that activity had to be limited by an inviolate social reality, with respect for its stability and slow rate of progress.

The conservative social philosophy was primarily intended to serve the tradition and actual state of affairs, defend achievements and existing interests, while respecting the "organic" requirements of national growth.

A broader horizon of action was opened by the evolutionary social point of view, which had its roots in the eighteenth century theory of progress, professed by the writers of the Polish Enlightenment. But evolutionism seemed to develop a lasting basis for rational and useful national action only during the second half of the nineteenth century. The political writers of the positivist era vigorously attacked all "options" in the programs of action: romantic enthusiasm and "folly," the revolutionary acceleration of the rate of development, and conservative indecision.

In the center of this philosophy of action stood the notion of work as a human activity which could shape nature and generate well-being. Józef Supiński propounded this view, as did Jan Hempel in his *Place of Work in Social Development* (1868), in which he explained how work had produced civilization, helped to overcome feudalism and contributed to the strength of society. Thus, the ideology of work stood in opposition to the romantic tradition of sentiment and exaltation.

The political writings of the positivist era consistently defended the program of reconstruction of Polish society and of the Polish psyche by means of work.

However, in all its variations, the program of organic work was an expression of an acceptance, in some measure, of previous historical developments and of given conditions. Although the program had taken the future into account, it recommended actions that would respect existing circumstances — which would perhaps be changed in the distant future.

This attitude was assailed from the very first years of bondage, especially within the circles oriented toward the future, which strove to change it by revolutionary means, as opposed to evolutionary ones. Arguments in this field, as in so many others, began during the first days of bondage and with the first attempts at rebellion against reality.

The conspirators of the November Night attempted to work out a philosophy of the revolutionary attitude. Tradition, though of highest significance to the national mind, had inevitably to "pass through the volcano of revolution."

These ideas were developed by writers who, after the failure of the insurrection, were active in the country. Edward Dembowski evolved a thesis linking thought and emotion, as elements of the creative act that constantly changed existence. This creative act was understood in terms of the creative activity of people but also, apart from this, as "an infinite chain of actions." From this standpoint Dembowski discerned intellectual and artistic creation; the revolutionary action of the masses, he called "social creation."

Similarly Henryk Kamieński, considering the Polish cause from the point of view of an émigré, underscored the significance of inherent social forces which originated in the wide masses of society. This type of "common wisdom" was to provide a defense against a doctrinaire approach and against utopianism. To find and develop these forces was a principal directive of political action. He evolved this idea in his book *Essential Truths about the Polish Nation* (Brussels, 1844), which included a summons to "a popular war."

In poetic language this revolutionary principle was expressed by Juliusz Słowacki in a number of poems and in his philosophical treatise, *Genesis of the Spirit,* which in conservative circles aroused disgust and condemnation, yet, particularly among the radical intelligentsia, was enthusiastically received.

At the source of the concept of genesis lay the will of the spirits, demanding "forms" and working out ever more perfect ones through their own efforts, by sacrifice or suffering, but also, when creation required, by an act of violence. According to the concept, the greatest sin consisted of "laziness," manifested by satisfaction with the achieved forms; while the highest virtue was that of a brave fight for a new form. Although no attempt was made to translate this poetically philosphical vision into the language of concrete political action, it was established in the social consciousness as a set of ideas and ideals, which inspired the fight with all varieties of conservatism and conformism and stimulated the quest for a great reform.

The concepts of the Polish Marxists, formulated from a different point of view, were a continuation of the theories of revolutionary action. During the early years, only a few thinkers, like Stanisław Krusiński, emphasized the fact that economic development was of a revolutionary character by itself, and that it had to be realized through upheavals. Others, however, relying on the premise that the socialist future was "a necessary consequence of the historical development of society," were of the opinion that "the most important social upheavals necessarily take place by means of peaceful regular development, that is, through evolution."

Only later, during the 1880's, did it become obvious that the objective and compulsory character of the laws of social development did not exclude the possibility or need of a conscious struggle of the oppressed classes and did not eliminate revolution as a method of removing obstacles from the road which led to new forms of social life. 170

At this time Ludwik Krzywicki analyzed the circumstances of the birth of these new ideas, the mechanisms of their circulation, and the social effects achieved. He felt that "the range of influence by an individual person" always increased when he implemented objectively mature trends of development. In this manner, "spontaneous acts" transformed themselves into conscious action.

EXISTENTIAL PROBLEMS

The plight of the nation molded the individual lives of its people. During the periods of struggle for independence, for social change, for economic and cultural development, the pressure of historical situations and tasks increased; in the more peaceful periods and during times of inhibited progress, this pressure subsided, but it was always present in the consciousness of the people.

Of course, not all Poles considered themselves involved in equal measure with the course of historical events and obligations. Yet circumstances themselves generated conditions compelling participation. After all, the great political events of the years 1806, 1830/31, 1846—48, 1863 and 1905 influenced the lives of each generation and usually twice: the memory of one disaster had not yet subsided when new action was already in preparation. The situation was not different even during the longest period of peace which occurred between the January Insurrection and the proletarian revolution of 1905.

The policy of the occupying powers in addition reached deep into the private life of every Polish home. Active patriots were persecuted more routinely and cruelly, but hostile hands touched others as well. Fundamental human rights were denied: the native language, all levels of education, church and religion; decrees, concerning, for example, compulsory service in foreign armies, and obedience to foreign administration — all these injured everybody. In many families memories of the struggle were still alive: someone's grandfather or father, someone's fiancé or brother had been killed in battle, had gone into exile, or had come back home after years of imprisonment or transportation. Family photographs and carefully guarded keepsakes preserved history in the intimate surroundings of private homes.

Characteristic evidence of how history invaded the everyday life of the Poles may be seen in the reactions of young people: the period of bondage began with the protest of the Philomates in Vilna, and it ended with the school strikes of the children at Września and in Warsaw.

Thus concurrently with a daily, intimate, home-oriented life of tranquility and happiness ran a foreign and cruel reality; yet, in this difficult reality, character was tested and people stood up for the truths in which they believed. This dual existence was a remarkable feature of Polish culture to the very end of the period of bondage.

Thus apart from problems involving God and history, fundamental philosophical issues, sometimes of a metaphysical character, touched upon man in the world and, particularly, man and his homeland.

Polish romantics tried stubbornly to solve this great issue. When unable to find the truth in printed books, they opened up "the great book of life:" "My hand has opened in vain a thousand books," wails Wacław, the hero of Stefan Garczyński's poem. "I shunned books and entered the world of the living," confessed Ryszard Berwiński. Polish national philosophy, in diverse variations, built a theory of action. It was a singular philosophy of practical life. The biographies of countless contemporary personalities offered the test of life as its greatest proof. Mickiewicz was acknowledged a symbol of such an existence: "A doctrine," he said in one of his Paris lectures, "becomes dead as soon as it is formulated. What cannot be shaped, what exists, what lasts, is man himself, the world incarnate."

Within this patriotic life, special significance was attached to moral problems of revenge, treason, and hatred. When historical destiny summoned a Pole to leave his quiet home, he had to descend underground into the kingdom of conspiracy and duplicity. It was necessary for him to seek asylum in the forests against an enemy more powerful than any forces that could be mustered against it. It was necessary to follow a path on which not only defeat but also treason crouched. It was necessary to recognize who were friends, who were foes, and who might be spies: "The country of one's childhood" became either a land of exile or "a land of tombstones and crosses."

During the period of servitude, Polish thought revolved incessantly around these topics: "What have we been looking at in our childhood," wrote Niemcewicz, "but treason, insult, scorn and most painful wrongs. How happy the people of the world are who never experienced, as the Poles did, the terrible wrongs perpetrated on their native country; they are free of a passion most unpleasant to a noble heart, the feeling of hatred."

For decades Mickiewicz's hero, Konrad Wallenrod, impressed upon the Polish consciousness the tragic link between patriotism and subterfuge; the poem, "To a Polish Mother" remained, throughout the entire period of bondage, an expression of a conflict between simple maternal sentiment and the national demand for a heroic life, ensnared by cheating and treason.

That dramatic conflict was present throughout this entire period in Polish culture. Its particular characteristic was that a man in quest of the meaning of his life had to be entangled in historical situations involving fear. National destiny burdened the existential fate of an individual. Consequently, a disquieting question had to be raised, different from Hamlet's: How was it possible to lead the life of a worthy man, and, at the same time, of a patriot?

Romantic poetry showed particular sensitivity to this issue. The fate of man in the world was in this poetry a fundamental moral and artistic topic. The experiences encountered in such an existence were dramatic indeed: the world was trying to annihilate the individual, whose "heart, like crystal, was covered with hundreds of flaws and would so remain forever," according to Słowacki. Yet, it was important not to depart from this world, though suicide often seemed an easy way of settling accounts. Was it possible to change the world while being a part of it? Many tried but found that it was necessary to renounce all personal happiness. And it was necessary to enter the road of action, where sceptics and rationalists predicted little hope of success. And it was necessary to accept methods of action which were in many instances morally doubtful. And, lastly, it was necessary to conquer one's own doubts and loneliness.

Thus a basic problem emerged under these conditions: man versus himself. It manifested itself in the agonizing questions: Who am I? What am I? Do I remain true to myself when I change? Do I become all that I have within myself, while still remaining the same? Am I able to remain the same, while not being what I used to be?

Romantic poetry explored all these questions, and looked for answers in lyrical verse and in drama, in declarations of faith and in irony, in deep involvement and in scorn. In seeking answers to such questions, people were led to explore complex philosophical issues which, in explaining the meaning of life, contained an element of hope and consolation, namely, the deepest foundations of the development of personality and community.

Polish traditional Catholicism provided such a philosophy. The strength of this faith, which was weakened in the era of Stanislaus Augustus, increased steadily from the early years of bondage, as witnessed in particular by the poetry of the era.

Poets turned to God, the guardian of Poland, and also the guardian of individual people. Some of these works, like "O God, Who Hath Protected Poland" or "With the Smoke of the Fires," won a lasting place in the national consciousness; others, more personal, had a more intimate meaning as, for example, a conversation of a hapless man with his God, Creator and Guardian. In these experiences poets returned to biblical traditions, as did Stefan Witwicki, author of *Biblical Poems* (1830) and, first and foremost, Kornel Ujejski, in his *Lamentations of Jeremiah* (1847) and *Biblical Melodies* (1852). Like the earlier *Psalms of David*, this was poetry of grievances and pleas, prayers and humility, faith and hope.

During the positivist era, Catholic philosophy directed its interest to the new issues, connected with scientific progress. This was particularly true of Father Stefan Pawlicki, author of a number of studies on the history of ancient and modern philosophy, critical monographs on Ernest Renan, on Darwinism and materialism; and of Father Marian Morawski, who devoted his work to the definition of the tasks of philosophy, to the problems of the purpose in nature, and to the foundations of ethics and law. His *Evenings on the Lake of Geneva* (1896), a dialogue concerning a religious approach to science and life, won a wide circle of readers.

All these concepts of religious consolation had been within the limits of Catholic orthodoxy. But a characteristic feature of Polish culture of the period were the currents extending beyond these limits. Sometimes condemned as heretical, they nonetheless achieved remarkable significance.

This trend was represented by many writers, from Andrzej Towiański to Wincenty Lutosławski.

Mickiewicz, too, conducted his political activity in defiance of the church; his religious experience manifested itself in poetry related to the great mystical tradition, always in close affinity to "heresy."

Słowacki, in his famous prayer in *Beniowski,* attacked those who believed they could find God in "tears shed on the threshold of a church" and who tried to find Him "in fashionable and good deeds." To such people of "small heart and mean faith," he proposed an image of God visible "in the blue fields of the Ukraine," above the "steppe tombs of the ancient knights," but also "in daffodils and forget-me-nots," a God who "likes the stormy flight of giant birds" and does not bridle the raging stallions."

This current of evangelical, but not churchlike, religiosity, mystical and non-dogmatic, a religion of love and sacrifice, not of sin and repentance, was opposed, at least from the mid-nineteenth century on, by those who considered science the basic approach to any philosophy.

A program based on science flourished during the era of Positivism. Support was sought in knowledge and not in religion or the church, nor in spiritual philosophy. This world of ideas was ruthlessly scoffed at as a heap of illusions, as a harmful figment of the imagination, which, instead of enriching and strengthening human life, rather, disorganized it. A new and effective therapy was expected from science.

Yet the value of science, esteemed so highly in the fields of economic and social progress, of education and the modern style of life, quickly turned out to be rather doubtful, when applied to the existential needs of an individual. That rigid "envoy of the truth," Aleksander Świętochowski, who struggled consistently for the promotion of scientific culture in the community, for organization and progress of scientific research in Poland, and for the exploitation of scientific results in production and administration, in his famous *Reflections of a Pessimist,* published in 1876, at the peak of the triumph of positivist thought, gave vent to disillusionment and anxiety so far as science was concerned.

Bolesław Prus felt the same way. He cherished a belief in science, verging almost on utopianism, and yet always held that the main cause of evil in people and in society was "ignorance of the laws which govern daily life," laws not discernible by science but by simple human emotion. In line with this idea was Prus' belief that when real personal misfortune led man to the brink of the abyss, the only consolation and only source of strength — as experienced by the hero in his novel, *The Doll* — was "the soil, ordinary man, and God."

This multiformity of feelings of being lost in the world and of man lost in himself recurred with greater force at the turn of the century. The *fin de siècle* became an era of existential restlessness. According to the philosophical reflections of Maria Komornicka and, later, of Maria Grossek-Korycka, Satan ruled the world. Felicjan Faleński entitled fragments of his poem *The Dances of Death* (1899). Writers of the era of positivism dealt with the issues of anxiety and pessimism, for example Sienkiewicz, in *Without Dogma* (1891), and Eliza Orzeszkowa in *The Melancholics* (1896). During the era of Young Poland, Hamlet fascinated such diverse writers as Stanisław

Wyspiański and Władysław Matlakowski. Berent, in his novels *The Rot* (1903) and *Winter Seed* (1911), exposed, concurrently with Freud, the subconscious roots of personality. Stefan Żeromski, often called "The Last of the Bards," led a fight against Satan, in accordance with the romantic concepts of evil in the world and the inner struggles of individuals.

Yet this great wave of pessimism brought on by the defeats which affected everyone's personal life was accompanied by an equally strong wave of belief in the force and greatness of individuals, even the most lonely, who viewed the world as "a threshing floor for the independent thinking of all free spirits," and who, in Berent's words uttered in 1906, were to regenerate the Polish revolutionary movement in ways unknown to the rest of the world. In this belief all previous ideas recurred, which joined inseparably individualistic, existential problems with situations and perspectives of social and national life.

This road which led toward existential truth, not toward systems — religious, scientific or otherwise — was not reserved solely for pessimists, neurasthenics, sceptics or the like, who were lost in the modern world. Another branch of the same road were the analyses and reflection of those writers, who in their everyday struggle for progress, acknowledged how difficult were victories, even when won with the arms supplied by science. This issue was dealt with in a most profound manner by Ludwik Krzywicki in his work bearing the characteristic title *From the Abyss* (1909), in which he collected his reflections over a dozen years. This was criticism of capitalist and urban culture, which had extinguished human values and stemmed individual development and cooperation between individuals. Within such a community "there exist only dummies and short moments of public feeling"; this community is filled with a vegetating "anonymous throng of social atoms"; and the rebellious intelligentsia is helpless. Inimical to abstract deliberations, Krzywicki presented "a concrete man" who, tied by the bonds of bourgeois society, ought to look for roads which "lead to the liberation of the spirit from the shackles of anonymity and being addressed by numbers." Positive recommendations and models of such a life were included in his book for young people *Sic itur ad virtutem*.

Wacław Nałkowski was moving in a similar direction. Opposing Nietzschean and Tolstoian concepts, he advocated attitudes toward life which manifested themselves in love capable of sacrifice and action.

In the same manner Edward Abramowski created a vision of life founded on feelings of brotherhood and the need for freedom, manifested in morality "devoid of compulsion or sanction," without religious safeguards or scientific foundations; it was the morality of the human heart freed from the "barren pits" of capitalist civilization and bourgeois mentality.

The last traveler on this road was Stefan Żeromski, whose works met with great social acclaim. Żeromski linked ethics to the inner voice in man, to the Socratic tradition of *daimónion*, which obligated man to live in a certain way; that inner voice, not scientific ethics, expressed itself in the principle that man is a sacred being and must not be wronged by anyone. This inner voice called for sacrifice, even for resignation from personal happiness, for an uncompromising gift of love and caring for suffering people.

Almost all the ideological values, all the moods and symbols of the life of the Poles during the period of bondage, the patriotic activities and the conflicts of individual existence were expressed in the paintings of Jacek Malczewski. In his paintings, imbued with symbolic expression, he revealed the truths of human life and death. Life assumed various forms — of Fauns, Mermaids, Chimeras; but also of Christ, John the Baptist, and sometimes of Eros. The image of Death became Thanatos, the angel of consolation, placing his fingers on the eyes of tired man. Similar contradictions were expressed in various versions of Tobias' struggle with the angel, and several versions of *The Poisoned Wells*. They exposed the contradictions of "live and dead water," of the water of Christ, which revivifies during the long road of life both man and the nation.

Toward the end of his life Malczewski painted diverse images of life and life's end. Such paintings as *My Life, Consolation,* and *The Homecoming* were a backward look on the road of life already traversed. Through typically Polish landscapes of meadows and fields, trees and clouds, angels, so often invoked and adored by Polish poets, were leading people along narrow paths amid village hedges, or keeping watch over small shepherd boys whom they shielded with their wings against the chaos of life, teaching all to accept destiny.

Through all of these rich and complex creations, from the first to the last painting, a personal motif appeared: a self-portrait. Exposing his own life with its victories and defeats, entangled in the net of patriotic and metaphysical experiences, Malczewski once more confirmed the dramatic identity of individual fate with the plight of the nation, perhaps even of the world, which was so often expressed by Polish authors.

The Arts

CREATIVE WORK FOR THE SAKE OF THE HOMELAND

A characteristic feature of the period of bondage was the great development of literature, the arts, and science, indicators of the social and national consciousness.

Literature still occupied a leading place in the life of the community. During the first half of the nineteenth century, poetry achieved special significance. In the second half of the century the novel became more important, particularly the works of Józef Ignacy Kraszewski, Bolesław Prus, Eliza Orzeszkowa and Henryk Sienkiewicz. Poetry gave way, but regained its primacy at the beginning of the twentieth century when, side by side with novels by Stefan Żeromski, Władysław Reymont, and Andrzej Strug, which still had social purpose, the works of

Jan Kasprowicz, Kazimierz Tetmajer, Leopold Staff and many other poets, flourished. During this period, for the first time in our history, drama also won social triumphs, especially the plays of Stanisław Wyspiański.

All the most significant experiences, hopes and aspirations of society were reflected in literature, both in prose and poetry. Literature became an open, or veiled, platform for discussions and appeals; and, at the same time, a voice of the national conscience.

Art, too, became a manifestation of national life. Whereas during the age of Enlightenment it was an object of interest to and supported by a few wealthy social groups — the royal court and aristocratic households — during the period of bondage art became the property of wide circles of the community and attained nationwide significance. Painting especially, as well as music, became national arts. A characteristic tribute to the role of art could be seen in 1878 when Jan Matejko, standing before his *Battle of Grunwald* in the Cracow townhall, was given a symbolic scepter, which signified the power of art over souls. In a highly emotional speech, Matejko recalled Słowacki's vision of *The King Spirit* and held that during the times he defined as "the interregnum", Polish art was the king of the nation.

In the symbolic language of painting, Jacek Malczewski projected the idea of greatness and responsibility in such canvases as *The Small Painter, Melancholy* and *The Vicious Circle*, all painted in the last decade of the nineteenth century. The symbolic meaning of these paintings was properly deciphered by Stanisław Witkiewicz and Maria Konopnicka as "the dance of generations", striving for liberty, and as an image of the role of the artist who, in order to create life, rises above life. In *The Vicious Circle* (1897) Malczewski showed the painter sitting on top of a ladder, creating his vision of life and fate, high above the pageant of figures immersed in the chaos of existence. According to some sources, Malczewski, as professor at the Academy of Fine Arts, would "correct" his pupils' work by saying: "Paint to resurrect Poland.".

Stanisław Witkiewicz perceived the role of art in national life with greatest clarity. In his study on Matejko (1903), he introduced a concept of "the spirit of the nation" as the indestructible force of its existence, which was destined to last and win, in spite of the enemies' will.

Music, too, established itself deeper than ever before in the national consciousness. From the beginnings of the nineteenth century, national songs were turned almost into the common property of the community; historical operas by Józef Elsner and Karol Kurpiński introduced the royal figures of Ladislaus the Short, Ladislaus Jagiello and Jadwiga onto the stage. Yet here, as in the other branches of art, these themes were not the only elements which made music national. The music of Chopin achieved an unconquerable position in the spiritual life of the nation and has been thereafter synonymous with things Polish. The Polish spirit found refuge in his polonaises, ballads, mazurkas, even when — in fact particularly when — that music could be performed only in private homes and behind closed shutters.

A similar national role was played by Stanisław Moniuszko, especially his *Books of Home Songs* (censorship forbade the title, *The Books of National Songs)* and in his operas, *Halka* and *The Haunted Manor*.

Science also stood in the front line of social action. For the first time in Polish history, scientific activity extended beyond the limits of private interest and individual sponsorship, becoming — in the view of both scholars and the community — an activity which was highly important to the nation. Although the harbingers of such links were already discernible during the era of Enlightenment, they achieved greatest significance only during the period of bondage. The fact that only a few years after the downfall of the state the Warsaw Society of Friends of Learning was founded had almost symbolic meaning. Its president, Jan Albertrandi, proclaimed during the inaugural session: "There's only one way left for the love of one's homeland: science and skills."

Almost the entire history of bondage corroborated the truth of these forecasts. When science and learning were to assist "the salvation of the national spirit", the historical and philosophical branches played a major role; when they were to help improve work, more significance was attributed to agricultural and technological sciences; when it became necessary to conceive a philosophy, natural science was called upon; in teaching people how to think, mathematics gained priority.

During the period of Positivism enthusiasm for science and for its national role increased greatly. The foundation and operation of the Mianowski Fund, a scientific institution established in Warsaw in 1881 to make loans to researchers, was the best example of the social appreciation of the role of science. The Fund was set up on the initiative of Tytus Chałubiński, Filip Sulimierski and Henryk Sienkiewicz. It existed and developed thanks to private contributions, public charity, membership fees, gifts and legacies.

This awareness of the role of science in national culture was fully corroborated by the activities of the Academy of Learning in Cracow, and later of the Warsaw Learned Society.

ART AND NATIONAL INTEGRATION

A characteristic feature of the period of bondage was not only that all branches of creative work participated in the preservation and development of national life, but also that creativity, to an ever-increasing degree, was becoming an important element of consciousness in all sectors of the nation. The process of formation of a comprehensive national culture was inaugurated, like so many other processes of the nineteenth century, at the end of the eighteenth century, when the first breakthrough in the feudal structure of society was effected. Formerly, culture had been the possession of only one estate, guarded by a bulwark of class privileges, and class opposition to all efforts aimed at its universalization.

The process of abolition of feudal elitism during the first decades of the nineteenth century followed two paths. 174

Educational leaders, continuing the work of the Commission for National Education, went more boldly in the direction of making instruction universal, by organizing elementary and trade or vocational schools at various levels.

Parallel to the path by which education and culture descended to the masses, there was another path leading upward, paved by supporters of the peasant. The turning of attention to the peasantry, first inspired by the patriotic program of armed struggle, assumed new aspects after the fall of the state. Peasants were the rock on which to base the native tongue and national customs. The young romantics discovered in them something more: a religious interpretation of the world and a profound morality. This was the peasants' contribution to national culture, based on upward, rather than downward, mobility.

The making of these two paths leading to a popularization of culture was difficult. During the entire period of bondage diverse and conflicting trends interacted, particularly within artistic circles. Cyprian Norwid was the first to perceive most shrewdly the prospects and different objectives of national integration by means of art. His vision of the human world was based on the assumptions of the moral and historical community of the people, where there was no place for the elitist concept of artistic creation. In the historical vision of humanity's development Norwid turned toward the Greek myths, particularly of Prometheus and Orpheus, as well as to biblical tradition, especially to Moses, and pointed to "Adam's way" as a way to build civilization through the creative effort of those who formed "the forefront of the generation", and also of all who formed "the multitude". From this point of view, Norwid propounded the organization of a great working community.

The programs of Positivism, scientific activity and artistic creation were meant to serve everybody, and it was believed that this service would bring valid results for the entire community. The vocation of intellectuals and artists manifested itself through the wide range of popularizing activity which served as a measure of their social usefulness. And although the high rate of illiteracy in society greatly hampered the conclusion of alliances between the intelligentsia and the masses, the social scope of participation in culture was indeed widened.

A particularly characteristic pattern in this field appeared in the breaking of the illiteracy barrier, not only by means of education, but concurrently by the growing acceptance of the values of a non-written culture. To learn from the "ignorant" peasantry was part of the great romantic tradition, and this continued during the positivist era, when it became apparent that the peasantry would not only be the object of instructional activity by the educated circles, but also the subject of its own education, as well as a model for "literate" people in work, morality and art. Thus the link between scholars and artists and the community was transformed from a one-way relationship effecting the popularization of ideas into a two-way relationship effecting exchange of experiences. As a result of the exchange between the culture of writing and the word and that of life and custom, a new and integrated culture of the entire nation emerged. This end was served by a group of the intellectuals who, during the years 1886—1905, published the weekly *Głos* in Warsaw, which was devoted to socio-political issues and literature; similar work of reconciliation was undertaken by the "Zakopane group", headed by Chałubiński and Witkiewicz.

In the era of Young Poland an effort was made to liberate art from social duties. However this program, formulated by Zenon Przesmycki and Stanisław Przybyszewski, was often criticized.

Julian Marchlewski, censuring artists who escaped to the solitude of Parnassus, wrote about "a new, holy and glorious truth that art is not luxury, but the daily bread of the soul, not an ornament of life, but life itself."

THE SYMBOLIC EXPRESSION OF THE INVISIBLE WORLD

Complex and varied experiences were reflected in diversified means of expression. The period of bondage was one of a wealth of reigning styles, differentiated by the various conditions in the three partition zones. Those styles sometimes coexisted for prolonged periods, sometimes followed one another, contributing to the characteristic aspects of certain stages of cultural development.

During the first two decades of the nineteenth century classicism prevailed, faithfully representing the thoughts and emotions of the nation in the daily life of the landed gentry, as well as Napoleonic hopes and disillusionments, and patriotic dreams of the future. The style of those tragedies, odes, or poems did not seem, at the time, either artificial or bombastic. Its position in literature, particularly in poetry, appeared unquestionable; but in the 1830's, the young romantics achieved a final victory. From that time on, no one read classical works, except scholars.

Classicism, defeated in literature, triumphed in architecture and town planning. The new conditions of political life in Congress Poland, the development of a state administration, the economic revival, and the increasing significance of the cities — all these favored the development of architecture. The most important place was occupied by town planning, industrial architecture and public utilities. In Warsaw, huge squares were laid out, including Theater Square and Bank Square, both designed by the outstanding architect, Antonio Corazzi. The Theater (Teatralny) Square included the magnificent building of the Grand Theater (Opera) and on the other side stood the splendid new building of the city hall, converted from the old Jabłonowski Mansion. In Bank (Bankowy) Square, huge edifices were built in 1824—30: the Polish Bank, the Commission of Revenue and the Treasury, and the Palace of the Minister of the Treasury. Piotr Aigner rebuilt the Governors' Palace on Krakowskie Przedmieście Street in a late classical style, and designed St. Alexander's Church in the Square of the Three Crosses.

Classicism radiated from Warsaw to the provinces. This style was used in numerous public buildings in Płock, Kalisz, Siedlce, and Suwałki. City halls, courthouses, schools, and private residences were erected in this style. The first examples of industrial architecture in the Old Polish Basin and in the Łódź region, also had the classical stamp.

An outstanding proponent of this style was Jakub Kubicki, the designer of the new Belvedere palace in Warsaw, who favored in his work one-story manor-houses with porches, a style widely accepted by Polish architects of the era.

The triumph of classicism in its broadest social meaning was visible in the architecture of small towns and country residences: manor-houses and mansions were embellished with porches and columns, and the same style prevailed in church buildings, apartment houses, and public edifices. Sometimes entire small towns, for example, Krzemieniec, were built in this manner. This style of classical origin was thought by society at the time to be an arch-Polish style and was cherished with utmost patriotic sentiment.

Owing to the fact that the same style could be employed in a great public building and in the most humble rural manor-house, a singular feeling of national integration was fostered, in which the architectural manifestation of monumental greatness of the homeland was combined with private needs of intimate life. And while the works of Koźmian, Osiński, Feliński and other classicists of literature have been long forgotten under the dust in libraries, classical architecture has survived as a lasting element of the Polish landscape in town and country.

The failure of the November Insurrection brought a halt to the economic and administrative development of Congress Poland and ended the possibilities of further expansion of the classical style in architecture. The romantic style, which was winning proponents in literature as early as the 1830's, failed to produce any works of lasting value in the field of architecture.

The romantic style remained popular in poetry, painting and music, but even here it was not uniform. It was a mixture, as had been the case in the earlier classical architecture, which endeavored to reflect the world in all its greatness, together with personal, private aspects. This contradiction in romantic poetry was apparent in such works as *The King Spirit* and *Pan Tadeusz*.

This contradiction, however, was not so very distinct. In art, as in life, the dramatic image of the great world was interwoven with sentimental intimate and personal existence. The romantic elements in poetry included the motifs of departure from one's native home, leaving one's lover, wanderings through an alien and hostile world, exile, and death on foreign soil. Such a chain of events was not an invented plot for a literary tale, but a manifestation of a style of life, with which the style of writing agreed in all its variety of emotions and means of expression. *Forefathers' Eve* by Mickiewicz and *Kordian* by Słowacki excellently represented that process of interference of great historical events in the private, confined, sentimental life of an individual, which resulted in diverse conflicts, calamities, heroic deeds, feelings of guilt, spiritual defeats and victories.

Fancy and realism, irrationalism and rationalism, imagination and precise observation, pathos and satire, irony and humor mingled in the romantic style. These contradictory artistic methods were not divided from each other by any clear-cut boundaries. In Mickiewicz's *Forefathers' Eve,* as in *The Un-Divine Comedy* by Krasiński or in Słowacki's dramas, all the adverse elements of style were interlaced. A fantastic world penetrated reality, mundane life possessed tragic aspects, and lyrical emotion was countered by irony.

Probably the most important and lasting achievement of Romanticism, however, was the discovery that poetry constituted a specific category of human life, a specific style of man's finding himself in the world. Maurycy Mochnacki, the most distinguished literary critic of Romanticism, in his controversy with the classicists, defined the essence of poetry in a manner that was to be repeated many times, and in the era of Young Poland became a manifesto for the movement. When in science, in practice, and in our social life we are guided by calculation and experience, wrote Mochnacki, we ignore the other half of the nature of things. To overcome this limitation we need poetry, "the undeniable property of the human heart and mind," which by breaking through the barriers of "commonplace soberness of imagination and emotions," brings forth "a sensual, tangible color to inner, spiritual phenomena."

The romantic style was also found in painting and sculpture. The alliance between painting and poetry appeared in the portraits of Adam Mickiewicz and Alexander Pushkin, painted in a romantic melancholy mood by Walenty Wańkowicz. But only the work of Piotr Michałowski (1800—55) displayed all the dramatic wealth of the romantic style. His paintings portrayed great historical events, intertwined with the private fates of people, faithful to the grandeur of struggle and heroism, joined in a community of courage and suffering with their true comrades, their horses, that accompanied them to disasters and triumphs. In these paintings human life appeared like a road leading toward some end, with the speed of Farys, a heroic risk in a struggle with the obstacles presented by reality. But the same painter of Napoleon, "the god of war," of the great Hetman Stefan Czarniecki, of all the cuirassiers and lancers and uhlans, that painter of Somosierra, also rendered intimate interiors in which his children played with dogs and ponies, untouched by the cruel breath of history, in the midst of plain villagers, portrayed as they sadly and sternly mused about the world and social evil.

Yet while Michałowski's painting was barely known beyond the frontiers of his native country, the music of Chopin became, during his lifetime, what it remains to this very day: a great manifestation of the Polish romantic style throughout the world. Chopin expressed the entire diversity of human life, its personal and historical plight. In his work, especially in the polonaises, the chivalrous history of Poland manifested itself with such force that his music was considered "dangerous", on equal terms with insurgent political action; his mazurkas provided evidence that Polish culture had its roots in folk tradition; his preludes and nocturnes demonstrated his personal sentiments and impressions, his intimate world of feelings, shut

176

off from and endangered by reality; these contradictions revealed themselves with great lyrical and dramatic force in his ballads and scherzos, in melodies free of traditionalism, full of powerful dynamics or of the delicate cantilene manner.

The epitome of the romantic style was the work of two outstanding artists: Henryk Rodakowski (1823—94) and Artur Grottger (1837—67), the life span of whom extended beyond the historical frame of the romantic era, but whose art was strongly linked to it.

Rodakowski's patriotic interest in history manifested itself in such paintings as *The Envoys to Sobieski,* who asked King John III to assist Vienna in its war against the Turks (1861), or *The Hen War* (1872). But there was room for interest in human life, too, as perceived in many excellent portraits. A typically romantic link between both aspects of the world — historical and private — appeared in his portrait of General Henryk Dembiński, in his youth a captain in the Napoleonic army, later a general and commander-in-chief of the November Insurrection and, lastly, leader of the Hungarian Revolutionary Army in 1849. This painting, awarded the gold medal at the Paris salon in 1852, remained in the national consciousness as a symbol of tragic defeat and, at the same time, of invincible spirit. It was also an image of the chaos of life, over which towered a judicious will to survive.

The tragic failure of the Insurrection of 1863 was the theme of Grottger's work. In his rendering, military and political events changed into a romanticism of ruins and disaster, of heroism, and of human hearts gnawed and destroyed by fear, broken by the reprisals forced upon their loved ones. In Grottger's pictures these events appeared in the form of a cruel realism, above which the artist placed the symbolism of hope which might be achieved in some other dimension of life — in the romantic community of hearts that survived the ruins and ravages of the world.

Unlike romanticism, the positivist movement did not produce a style of its own. Aleksander Świętochowski felt that the main difference between the romantics and the positivists was that the former wanted to reform the world by means of poetry; the latter, by means of political writings. That is why positivist slogans were disseminated in hundreds of articles while there was no such thing as a positivist style. Positivism in Poland tended toward pragmatism, toward practical economic activity, and useful art. In the field of art, this led to naturalism and realism. In this way, the literature and painting of the positivist era were a continuation of the non-romantic trends of the former epoch, especially the realist movement.

The literature of the positivist era achieved various successes in this area. In the short stories and novels of Orzeszkowa, Sienkiewicz, Prus, Dygasiński and a host of other writers, and in the short stories and poetic "tableaux" of Konopnicka, the realistic trend continued to flourish, more artistically perfect than before and at the same time more critical of reality. Writers and poets exposed what was unjust and wrong or obscure and backward in life, but also showed what elements could guarantee a better future. This realism was accusatory, but also stimulated hope. It was always sympathetic to human suffering, but did not drop from view the prospects of a struggle, which would be led by science and education for the improvement of the world.

The most successful achievement of the realistic style in literature was *The Pharaoh* (1895—96) by Bolesław Prus. Criticized by contemporaries and later generations, who either preferred their art free of any social commitment or looked for romantic stories in historical novels, in *The Pharaoh,* Prus with penetrating insight created an image of society and state, of the fight for power and for progress, of conflicts between various segments of society, of prejudice and the significance of learning. The realism of this picture of ancient Egypt was based on sociological analysis which, in the events presented under historical Egyptian guise, could be clearly seen to be the lasting, even the everlasting mechanisms of social development and the techniques of power. Their actual connotations were so great that time and again efforts were made to find the key to identifying the figures of Rhamses or Herhor with contemporary rulers and politicians.

In the 1880's the program of realism was strongly defended by Stanisław Witkiewicz and Antoni Sygietyński in a series of articles which appeared in the Warsaw magazine *Wędrowiec,* published between 1884 and 1887. The forerunners of the program were the painters Maksymilian Gierymski, who in his paintings kept up the romantic and insurgent tradition; Józef Chełmoński, who was almost wholly preoccupied with the picturesque charms of the Polish landscape; and, lastly, Aleksander Gierymski, who more sharply than the others, revealed the social realities of his country, especially of the peasantry and Warsaw proletariat.

An uncertain line divided realism from naturalism, all the more so that the naturalist style played a very special role in Poland. An enthusiast of the latter, Antoni Sygietyński, defined clearly the particular social task of naturalism as a means of fighting the unjust social order. From this point of view, he was an admirer of Courbet and Zola, about whom he wrote that "they do not portra, the ideals of a happy humanity but the desperate conditions of broken individuals or of those condemned to poverty."

At the turn of the nineteenth and twentieth centuries an unusual and sudden outburst of poetry occurred, unknown to the Polish community since the times of Romanticism. In this era appeared poets like Kazimierz Przerwa-Tetmajer, Jan Kasprowicz, Stanisław Wyspiański, Tadeusz Miciński, Lucjan Rydel, Jerzy Żuławski, Leopold Staff, as well as Maryla Wolska, Bronisława Ostrowska, Kazimiera Zawistowska, Maria Grossek-Korycka, and an entire group of those less famous, but still significant in the history of Polish poetry, including Franciszek Nowicki, Antoni Lange, Stanisław and Wincenty Brzozowski, Edward Leszczyński, Jan Lemański, Artur Oppman, Edward Słoński, Franciszek Mirandola, Tadeusz Nalepiński and Bolesław Leśmian.

Each of these names represented an individual approach, both in the type of experience dealt with and the mode of expression, notwithstanding certain artistic tendencies, common to the majority, which differentiated this epoch of Polish poetry from that of the positivist era. This poetry was lyrical, at times very personal, often religious and full of metaphysical anxiety, exceedingly sensitive to the beauty of nature, to color and music; it expressed the changing moods and attempted to create the unity of personal experiences, sometimes exceptional, deeply rooted in spiritual life; the poetry of soft words, but also of pathos.

This poetry was like music. Poets, by means of rhythm, suggested musical moods, created various "autumn symphonies" or "melodies of evening mists"; some of the poets like Maryla Wolska, used musical pen-names (D-moll = d minor). Melodies were composed to the words of poetry. The outstanding composer of the era, Mieczysław Karłowicz, felt very strongly that there was an inner relationship between music and poetry; like many of the writers and poets of the era of Young Poland, he found in the Tatra Mountains greatness and silence, necessary requisites for reflections about human destiny.

Polish Romanticism was reborn in this poetic wave of emotions and moods. It was reborn not as a national program of action, however, but in the form of the poetic image of man in the world, man vis-à-vis himself; it was the return of "the other world," in the words of Maryla Wolska, who through her family recollections was close to Grottger and the year 1863.

The same poetic image of the world and of the human plight also manifested itself in the painting of the Young Poland period which was as rich and diversified as literature. The artists of the period were searching for moods and emotionally forceful expression: they were concerned with the themes of the nation and of the human soul, and they created symbols and allegories. Stanisław Wyspiański introduced folk and national features to art, depicting in his paintings, stage designs and stained-glass windows, the figures of great Piast rulers, ascetic saints, God the Father, Creator and Judge, and also the smiling faces of children. Władysław Podkowiński achieved fame within literary and artistic circles, due to his painting, *Ecstasy* (1884) and several other tragic compositions, for example, *The Skeleton Dance* (1892—93) and *The Funeral March* (1894). This pessimistic literary atmosphere was predominant in the paintings of Witold Wojtkiewicz, who in his surrealist and expressionistic visions denounced the cruel philistine bourgeois society which destroyed simple, human values, wreaked havoc even in the fairyland of the children's world, as portrayed in his tragic painting, *The Children's Crusade.*

Less involved in these metaphysical issues were other great painters of the era: Józef Pankiewicz, Jan Stanisławski, Leon Wyczółkowski, Włodzimierz Tetmajer, Ferdynand Ruszczyc, Olga Boznańska, Józef Mehoffer, Vlastimil Hofman, and a host of others. Yet they created art of unusual and diverse beauty, connected with Western movements but very Polish in their selection of themes and in modes of expression, as was also evident in the poetry and the novels of the period. Their landscapes, ranging from the Vilna region to the Tatras, represented

the Polish soil and, concurrently, expressed a Polish attitude toward nature. Human interest was discernible in the art of portraiture, cultivated by many artists; Olga Boznańska triumphed with her studies, filled with intimate charm, similar in mood to that which Maryla Wolska expressed in her verses.

The ideological and artistic bonds between the fine arts and poetry could also be seen in the sculpture of the period. Sculptors forgotten today, like Bolesław Biegas and Franciszek Flaum, a friend of Przybyszewski, to some extent illustrated the metaphysical aspirations of contemporary literature. Similarly, the work of Konstanty Laszczka was related to the philosophic and symbolic trends in literature, in such sculptures as *Infinity, Faith, Aquarius,* and in the folk current. The case was similar with Jan Szczepański, creator of a large sculpted group entitled *The Village Girls* (1903) and of the peasant figures decorating the front of the building of the Agricultural Society in Cracow. A philosophical restlessness was also displayed in the sculpture of Edward Wittig who was trying to liberate himself from Rodin's influence in such works as *Youth* (1907), *Awakening, Autumn* and *Eve* (1913—14), which later found an admirer in Guillaume Apollinaire. In his diversified and changing output Xawery Dunikowski, who was just beginning his work at the turn of the nineteenth and twentieth centuries, became engaged in the great issues of human fate, even in his early works, such as *Prometheus* (1898), *The Yoke* (1901), *Fatum* (1902), *Man* and *Breath* (1903). At the same time, Dunikowski also became involved with historical themes in Polish art, creating a giant composition, *Boleslaus the Bold* (1916).

The sculpture and painting of the era bore witness to its close relationship with literature and poetry, which never before in Polish culture was so deep and diversified.

In all the diversity of styles in the Polish art of the period of bondage there existed one stable trait, perceived at the beginning of the period by Maurycy Mochnacki and at the end by Zenon Przesmycki: the symbolic character of this art, not in the narrow sense which the term "symbolism" represented during the era of modernism, but in the wider sense, which pointed toward the immediately inaccessible, hidden, inner reality. That reality was the life of the nation flowing under the cover of external appearances; that reality was also the life of the soul disguised in socio-material forms of existence. The plight of the nation and the destiny of man formed that innermost reality, which was described by the characters and the events in novels and dramas, moods in poetry, colors and contours in painting and sculpture, and tones in music. An effort to reach into that reality was the common goal of that branch of art which was called realist and of that branch which displayed the world of its own imagination.

This characteristic of art was also underscored by those writers who, adhering to the idea of "art for art's sake," wanted to free themselves of any obligation to serve the nation. The theory and practice of art expressing the soul was developed at that time by Przesmycki and Przybyszewski. Przesmycki as early as 1891 launched an attack on contemporary art by stating the following: "Literature today is what you will: a toy, a means of killing time, an instrument to implement these or other trends, a weapon in factional struggles, science, philosophy, psychology, a 'document', journalism, and means of subsistence — but not what it necessarily and primarily ought to be." According to Przesmycki, it ought to be an expression of the soul, and a force that would "embrace the entire human being." From this viewpoint, "great art, essential art, immortal art, has always been symbolic; behind sensual analogies it hides the elements of infinity and reveals boundless, extra-sensory horizons."

In a similar way, Przybyszewski, in his famous manifesto called *Confiteor* (1899), proclaimed the following: "Art is a replica of what is everlasting, independent of all changes or incidentals, free of both time and space, and thus a reflection of essence, that is, the soul."

But even this soul-expressing art became, in the final analysis, national: "An artist," wrote Przybyszewski, "is anchored in the nation, but not in its politics, not in its external changes, only in what in a nation is everlasting." He remained personally true to that concept, when during World War I he wrote, in Polish and German, treatises concerning the Polish national soul.

Culture in Society

NEW MODELS OF LIFE

The eighteenth century was called, both throughout the world and in Poland, the age of Enlightenment. It is indeed impossible to overestimate its educational goals and achievements. But a real breakthrough in the cultural development of Polish society came in the nineteenth century, when, in spite of the unfavorable political conditions, the great process of reshaping the traditional, aristocratic-gentry, knight-landlord society into a modern, industrial-trading and bourgeois-intelligentsia community began.

In the course of this process new ways of propagating culture were found; new objectives appeared, as well as new horizons, new possibilities and new obstacles. Great intellectual and artistic movements of the period — the Enlightenment, Romanticism, Positivism, Modernism — functioned within the framework of these social changes.

The intellectual and artistic culture during the period of bondage truly expressed the experiences of the community in all its variety, its daily joys and sorrows, its great acts and tasks, as well as its hopes and frustrations. Science, education, literature and the arts, in the absence of Polish institutions in public life, were the main channels for accumulating and exchanging experiences.

One branch of the movement expressed the daily routine of "idyllic" village life. Many poets, during the early years of bondage, from Cyprian Godebski and Kazimierz Brodziński onward, tried to perpetuate the Polish traditions of the landowners. Kajetan Koźmian, a

dignitary in the Kingdom of Poland and a bitter adversary of the romantics and revolutionaries, worked on his grand poem, *The Landlords* (1839), for over thirty years. According to Koźmian, village life formed the most valuable part of the Polish tradition, abandoned by "the lost tribe" who preferred "luxury and love of money." Koźmian felt that the Poles had to return to that tradition and "returning to the thatch-eaves of home," oppose those who "waited day and night for the court's favors," and also those who "thronged the crowded cities, striving for office" instead of working in their villages.

When Koźmian's *Landlords* appeared, the readers were already familiar with *Pan Tadeusz,* a great tale about the days that were receding into the past which, however, reached far beyond the horizons of the landowner idyll. The moral problem of Jacek Soplica, the national cause of the Legions with the hope they implied, and the social cause of the peasants — all these were proof that the life of the gentry was not shut off from the great issues and great events of history. It was not Koźmian with his dream of a "happy village life", but Mickiewicz with his "poem of the gentry" which was yet so national, who impressed himself on the mind and imagination of future generations, who saw a symbol of the Polish way of life in that small manor-house on a "gentle hill, in a birch-grove." That manor ennobled hundreds of small manor-houses, in which national life was hidden and protected, and never came to an end.

Polish art portrayed a similar life, quiet and idyllic, but under a sky overcast with an impending storm. From Szermentowski to Chełmoński, Stanisławski and Wyczółkowski, Polish painting showed intimate village residences and small manor-houses, cottages lost amidst landscapes of mallows and sunflowers, farmers toiling in the fields, fishermen fishing in the ponds and lakes covered with morning mists, little shepherd boys in the meadows, plain and natural joys of life in close communion with nature, and the delights of an Indian summer. And the trees, like those Mickiewicz wrote about, the trees of Poland's landscape were grave and yet intimate, like one's family. Staff addressed himself to "a sister pine." Kasprowicz, listening to "the humming trees," felt metaphysical yearnings. And finally there were the skies, Polish skies filled with clouds, described already by Mickiewicz, arched over human life in pictures by Ruszczyc or Witkiewicz, dramatic and restless skies, portending an imminent storm.

Music, the significance of which steadily increased, gave vent to similar experiences. Chopin's manor-house at Żelazowa Wola has remained to this day a tangible relic of a world that has long passed away but is saved forever, because of his music: life within the Polish landscape, in the fields, and amidst the willow trees, in the joy of the sun and in the melancholy of the rain, so many times portrayed by the poets, in the mysterious rhythms of the heart and its feelings; life that enveloped men like the elements with its light, airy, but deep moods. But above that world of tranquility and emotions there continued to flow, as in poetry, reminiscences of the grand chivalrous past and expectations of great heroic events.

During the entire period of bondage neither the cottages nor the manors could provide a safe life on the side-lines of history. From the first years of the period a different kind of life was being developed, the main part of which was protest and struggle against prevailing conditions. Soldiers and conspirators bore witness to this revolutionary truth by their acts. And art was fast becoming a rich expression of that truth — in its entire tragic range, from the hope of victory to the fact of defeat.

Artists continued to express these complex, patriotic feelings at all times, from Norblin and his circle, who showed Kosciuszko taking the oath and his victory at Racławice, the slaughter of Praga and the death of Prince Joseph Poniatowski, through numerous versions of Piotr Michałowski's *Somosierra,* up to the great historical battle scenes painted by Jan Matejko, Józef Brandt, Juliusz and Wojciech Kossak and Maksymilian Gierymski. In the second half of the nineteenth century, some artists conveyed these patriotic moods by depicting great victories won by Polish arms; others by means of sentimental, intimate scenes, often painted variations of "the uhlan and the girl". Some portrayed the glorious successes won by great commanders at Grunwald, in Livonia, at Pskov, Vienna and elsewhere; and others preferred to show the bitterness of defeats suffered while persevering to the very end, in places like Cecora, Maciejowice or during the 1863 Insurrection.

Whereas painting expressed Polish military traditions and the yearnings of a chivalrous spirit, music pursued other roads. Historical operas by Józef Elsner and Karol Kurpiński lacked the force which could have established them in the national imagination, alongside the great paintings. Only battle and patriotic songs were universally popular, especially during the November Insurrection, although only one of them, *La Varsovienne,* with music by Kurpiński has endured: in the twentieth century, Wyspiański chose it for the theme of a drama.

Music was capable of expressing feelings of patriotic sorrow, which accumulated in certain eras, or the need of pious supplication during times of defeat. This accounts for the unusual popularity of the hymn, *O God, Who Hath Protected Poland.* Both the new version dating from 1861 and the new musical arrangement given to an old traditional song addressed to the Mother of God, were sung in the churches. Its refrain, "O God, deign to restore us the liberty of our Homeland," stimulated a particular, religious and hopeful mood. No less popular was the chorale *With the Smoke of the Fires,* written by Kornel Ujejski, with music composed by Józef Nikorowicz. Different in mood were the songs of Gustaw Ehrenberg, particularly *When the Nation Took to Arms,* and Włodzimierz Wolski's *Insurrectionary Songs,* among them, *The Song of the Zouaves* — all widely popular.

The music of Stanisław Moniuszko expressed a different feeling. It recalled the familiar tradition of the Polish manor-house and the Polish village, with its songs of the spinners, lyrical *dumki,* moving memories of childhood spent under a mother's care, the atmosphere of the entertainments of the gentry of old, of their hospitality, jokes and old chivalrous traditions.

Poetry was bolder. It reached deeper than did the painting and music of the period, becoming at once the national memory and the national conscience. Remaining free despite everything, it expressed the feelings of a nation that wanted to fight for its freedom anywhere in the world, wherever even a ray of hope appeared. It expressed the experiences of a nation which, remembering its former victories, enacted a ruthless soul-searching, accusing itself of responsibility for its defeats. It reflected the experience of a nation which was looking for hope and which changed defeats into victories, death into a harbinger of a new life, and sufferings into a proof of rebirth in the collective consciousness.

During the entire period of bondage a different pattern of communal life was beginning. Stanisław Staszic was among its first theoreticians. In his works, making full use of the contemporary achievements of social science, he defined the main directives for rational and useful action. It was a program of scientific, economic and social work, of organic work, as it was later called. This program embraced wide horizons and possessed historical and national significance. Its appeal to the younger generation was a *sui generis* "ode to youth," different from Mickiewicz's, but equally passionate. Its message was the need to learn about one's own land and to transform it by skillful work for the sake of the whole nation.

The model of economically useful activity suggested by Staszic found a number of followers, but more often than not, it was criticized by patriots who were eager to fight and committed themselves fully to insurrectional and revolutionary activities. Bitter polemics ensued.

On the eve of the January Insurrection, Norwid pronounced a severe verdict on the two forms of Polish patriotism. Highly praising all the struggle, heroism and sacrifice in our history he emphasized how neglected the field of social relationships was, how little progress had been made in that direction. "Poland is the hindmost society in the world, and the nation is first on this planet. A Pole is a giant," wrote Norwid, "but the man in a Pole is a dwarf."

During the positivist era there were great efforts to make amends for past negligence and deficiencies. Staszic's model of life was developed further. The ideal was defined as a man who could take advantage of the knowledge he had, organize his activity in a disciplined and effective way and keep his aspirations and hopes within the bounds of achievable things, esteem work and effort and not dreams. Such people would introduce progress into Poland, linking in an effective manner the material success of the national economy with a growth in education and social activity, with modernizing Poland, even if it came through revolution.

The young positivists lived their lives according to these principles. They attained an education and a profession, developed economic activity and built up the school system. They appreciated learning as an instrument of progress; they respected art insofar as it was socially useful. Life was becoming systematized and rationalized; activity was becoming orderly and purposeful. Man was looked upon as a link within the great social entity. This attitude was different from that which came before, a new way of life, a new character of culture and a new means of participating in its development. Whereas romantic art was cultivated by students and poets, within the manor-houses of the gentry and, particularly, the drawing-rooms and clubs of the émigrés, the new processes of propagating culture in society were connected with the activity of professional groups, particularly those of the engineer-type, in the life in the big cities and industrial centers.

However, this new model of life had its dangers. A thin line divided the work which was useful for the community from that aimed at individual enrichment. And although the political writings and the positivist novels by Świętochowski, of Prus and of Orzeszkowa, never limited the value of life and social goals to the narrow confines of advantage and austerity, yet only during the decline of the positivist era was there an awareness of the dangers and differences between organic work that was useful to the nation and that which brought profits to individuals, between the ideology of economic progress and the policy of the ruling classes.

Jan Ludwik Popławski inaugurated this type of criticism with a widely discussed article, "The Denigration of Ideals" (1887). He directed his attack against "the mean egoism of shopkeepers," which he considered the basis of "philistine dullness of thought and emotion." The watchwords of "organic work" were initially slogans of "the advance guard of the militant bourgeoisie," and then they made sense. But in the contemporary epoch, according to Popławski, "we are dealing with the triumphant bourgeoisie," which has accumulated wealth and has become even more ruthless and soulless. "In the market-place, there is no demand for such commodities as sentiments or ideals." We live today "in a terrible deterioration of spirit, self-inflicted denigration, in the gloomy darkness of apathy, when the stars of idealism, which once pointed the way, have been extinguished or dimmed."

Popławski's criticism created a great wave of controversy concerning the national values of the bourgeois system of cultural and political life. In the 1880's the novels and plays of Gabriela Zapolska denounced social relationships and social institutions, exposing bourgeois mentality and morality. The heroine of the title of the play *The Morality of Mrs. Dulska* became the symbol of the deceitful and cruel society of the "horrible bourgeoisie."

Criticism of the bourgeois model of life was evolved by Bronisław Białobłocki, a representative of the Marxist branch of radical thought. In his article "Decline of the Ideal" (1884), he critically observed that "our society is absolutely attuned to the bourgeois ideal"; it interpreted happiness egoistically as "a life in a nice little house" under the care "of a loving wife and solicitous mother," hoping to "bar its door against the street mob and to close the window shutters to remain undisturbed by the prolong-ed complaints of misfortune and poverty." According to Białobłocki, such a concept of happiness was not worthy of "an enlightened mind and tender heart"; it was also uncertain because social disaster and upheavals had and would spell destruction for the sanctuaries erected by the industriousness of ants and beavers. One must know that "the happiness of an individual depends, above all, on that of the community." This was Białobłocki's approach to the romantic tradition.

When at the turn of the nineteenth and twentieth centuries a great change in literature and art took place and again directed the nation's consciousness toward Romanticism, the new generation took the name of Young Poland, a term aptly used for the first time by Artur Górski. In the struggle with philistine and bourgeois mendacity, a new way of life was being discovered, often full of inherent contradictions, always varied. The radical political writings of Nałkowski and Brzozowski were intertwined with the elitist concepts of Przesmycki and the vagaries of Przybyszewski. The civil passion of Żeromski and Strug was accompanied by an invigorating vision of the nation presented in Wyspiański's dramas. Tetmajer's melancholy lyrics were contrasted sharply with Kasprowicz's dramatic protest. These names point to the diversity of the ideological and artistic concepts of Young Poland which was a basic reason for the popularity of the movement. And while for the older generation the banner of national culture still remained in the hands of Sienkiewicz, for the younger generation, Żeromski, widely read by the working intelligentsia and opposed by the conservative camp, formulated a new faith in Polish life. All the more important social experiences of Polish history, accumulated through the ages, and in particular during the period of bondage were emphasized in his works. He tirelessly listed the various models of duty: the patriotism of the "wandering soldier", who continued the knightly traditions; the desperate courage of the revolution-aries, fighting for democratic justice and equality; the self-sacrificing perseverance of the teacher or physician in their social service undertaken for the sake of the "homeless people."

EDUCATION OF THE HEART AND EDUCATION OF REASON

Throughout these diverse models of life, the great issues of education of the heart and education of reason recurred over and over again. The model of the romantic hero in all his diversity entered the manor-houses of the gentry, where young women memorized verses and songs along with sentimental feelings. Family albums changed into collections of selected intimate poetry, incomparably more personal than the books sold by the bookstores. Polish history, in the shape of numerous paintings, embellished the walls of many Polish homes. But history was on the alert that memories of the past should not be the only great events. The bugle-call sounded time and again, summoning all to battle. The forests reverberated with the news of cruel, unfortunate fights. National and personal mourning enveloped Polish homes time after time. Side by side with paintings depicting the triumphs of Polish troops, appeared the dramatic drawings of Grottger; behind closed shutters patriotic poems were recited and Chopin's music was played.

History and poetry turned into a great school of the heart: of love and compassion, of heroism and courage, of joy and mourning.

The post-romantic generation was also looking for such truths. Under new socio-political conditions, in an epoch of great programs for economization and usefulness, Sienkiewicz wrote his novels "to lift up the people's hearts"; Prus created the figure of old Rzecki, in order to edify the nation. Orzeszkowa returned frequently in her stories to the year 1863. Another bitter and dramatic version of this education of the heart could be found in Żeromski's novels on the history of Polish defeats: at Cecora, in the Napoleonic campaigns, in 1863, and in the 1905 revolution.

With the education of the heart, so often renewed during post-romantic times, was combined, sometimes in contradistinction, the education of reason. It was not as widely rooted in the old world of the gentry as was the education of the heart; but neither was it as separated from the tradition of the old Commonwealth as was sometimes suggested. Copernicus believed in reason. Modrzewski summoned "before the tribunal of reason" everybody concerned with the improvement of the state; and it was Konarski to whom the last Polish king gave a specially issued medal, "Sapere auso", and who helped to create a commission to reform "national education"; it was the people of the Polish Enlightenment who tried to erect on this earth under the sway of despots and fanatics a kingdom of reason.

The education of society was organized along these lines during the first decades of the nineteenth century. This was the goal of the educational system, set up in the spirit of the Commission for National Education, which, going beyond the old models, was also supposed to serve the national economy and vocational instruction. This was also the goal of the press, especially weekly and monthly journals which promulgated knowledge of the progress of the sciences and of crafts. This was also the goal of the Warsaw Society of Friends of Learning and of similar institutions in Cracow, Lublin and Płock.

The efforts of many people during the second half of the nineteenth century were focused on a program for the intellectual education of society. Periodicals formed the front line of battle. One of them bore the bold title of *Prawda* (Truth); Aleksander Świętochowski signed his articles as an "envoy of the truth." Towards the end of the century, on the initiative of Stanisław Michalski, the publication of a Self-Teaching Textbook was launched. Each of its volumes, in spite of the relatively high price, disappeared from the bookstores immediately.

These prolonged and diversified actions in the field of education of reason bore significant fruit. Polish culture during the period of bondage underwent a process of intellectualization, the best evidence of which was the activity of the democratic and radical camp who expected assistance from science in the organization of political activity and in the instruction of the oppressed classes. This would be seen particularly clearly during the "Springtime of Nations", when Dembowski and Kamieński cherished the hope that learning would lead to revolutionary practice. Such was also the objective of *Przegląd Naukowy* founded at that time. It appeared again during the positivist era, when followers of the program of organic work expected the help of learning in the economic progress of the country that had been instigated by the propertied class, and when the young Marxists demanded that learning expose bourgeois society and pave the way, in philosophical and political theory, for the proletarian revolution. These polemics bore witness to the progress made over a period of a few decades in the intellectual culture of the community thanks to science. While in the 1830's Father Ściegienny had based his system of utopian peasant socialism on peculiarly interpreted principles of faith and disguised his slogans in the alleged will of the pope, in the 1880's learning provided the main argument in favor of the justness and efficacy of the revolutionary program.

These ideas of education of the heart and education of reason, in which the culture of the times achieved its social significance, were opposed to each other only at their extremes. Both these instructional activities became intertwined in regard to basic matters more often than not. In education of the heart, an attempt was almost always made to overcome egotistic sentimentalism: in education of reason, there was usually opposition to scientism. Neither romantic poetry, nor romantic politics, nor Polish romantic philosophy was against reason, although each opposed some interpretations of it. Polish positivism, for the most part defined as an era of faith in reason, practically never neglected the rights of the heart. Of almost symbolic meaning is the fact that the inscription on Bolesław Prus' tombstone referred to him as "the heart of hearts." And a partisan of another camp, Józef Szujski, maintained that "the beginning and end of any education should be the education of hearts."

Culture, which spread rapidly into the daily reality of people's lives avoided unilateral development; it was to be a complete culture. Although a conciliation between these two main objectives was exceedingly hard to achieve, and although it was easy to accuse each of superficial compromise and sometimes even of altogether neglecting the other approach, the main current of Polish culture was determined by this uninterrupted conciliation of contradictions united into a rich variety of existence.

THE SCHOOLS OF THE PARTITIONING POWERS AND EDUCATION THROUGH PARTICIPATION IN NATIONAL LIFE

During the entire period of bondage, in all three partition zones similar conditions prevailed in the area of development and operation of institutions devoted to the promotion of culture; similar obstacles were put up by the three occupying powers to prevent the implementation of Polish goals. During this long period, the denationalization policy was at times either intensified or relaxed. Changes did not take place in all three partition zones at once. Thanks to this the areas where these conditions were more favorable exerted an influence over other parts of the country. At the beginning of the nineteenth century this role was played by Vilna, and later by Warsaw; after 1830, Cracow and Poznań took up leading roles; and after 1863, Warsaw and Cracow again gained ascendancy.

This instability characterized conditions for the promotion of culture in a fundamental area, that is, in the schools.

Immediately after the downfall of the state, Polish higher education developed only in the Russian zone. The university in Vilna was at the height of its powers. For years its rector was Jan Śniadecki, an eminent mathematician and philosopher. Among the teaching personnel were such outstanding personalities as Jędrzej Śniadecki, Joachim Lelewel and many foreign scholars who lectured in Latin. Political repression in 1823 brought to a close that illustrious period in the university's development. At the beginning of the nineteenth century Tadeusz Czacki, together with Hugo Kołłątaj, founded a model educational institution in Krzemieniec; it was conceived as a secondary school, and there were plans to turn it in the future into a university. It did not last long. The University in Cracow was subjected to Germanization after the partitions; its Polish character was restored only when Cracow was incorporated into the Duchy of Warsaw, and again when it became a Free City in 1815. But restrictions on the enrollment of students from outside Cracow undermined the significance of this institution. The University in Lvov remained under German influence. Better conditions prevailed in Warsaw during the era of the Duchy and later in Congress Poland: a university was founded, as were a number of technical and agricultural schools. But their activity was short-lived; the failure of the November Insurrection put an end to all such institutions.

By the middle of the nineteenth century no higher schools existed in either the Russian or the Prussian partition zones, while in the Austrian zone both universities in Lvov and Cracow were German. These conditions improved during the second half of the century. The Polish Main School in Warsaw was founded during this period, but after a few years, it was transformed into a Russian university. The universities in the Austrian zone regained a considerable measure of their Polish character, especially in Cracow. A Polytechnic School was opened in Lvov in 1877 and a Higher Agricultural School in Dublany. Poznań had no higher school.

Other stages of education developed along similar lines. Elementary and secondary education developed a Polish curriculum only in the Duchy of Warsaw, and later in Congress Poland; in the Austrian zone it remained backward; in the Prussian zone, the school system served Germanization policy from the beginning, although, after the "Springtime of Nations," some of the parish schools were granted, for a short time, the privilege of teaching in Polish. During the period between the uprisings, the number of secondary schools in the Russian zone decreased, and the development of primary education was limited. About 80 percent of the population was illiterate. Towards the turn of the century, the situation in elementary and secondary schools improved slightly.

Around 1900, illiteracy in the Prussian territories of Poland was eliminated, although the language used in reading and writing was German. In the Austrian sector 56 percent of the inhabitants were illiterate; and in the Russian sector, as many as 69 percent. These ratios improved during the period immediately preceding World War I. Also an increase in the development of secondary education occurred, especially in Congress Poland where, after the 1905 Revolution, private Polish secondary schools were allowed to open, and in Galicia, where the "gymnasia" possessed a generally Polish character and were accessible to a certain percentage of peasant children.

The history of education was one of uninterrupted defeats for Polish educational needs and initiatives. Not one of the higher schools developed in a normal way during this period, nor did it have a continuous history. The development of elementary and secondary education was constantly and in various ways inhibited. Numerous efforts to overcome these difficulties resulted in only short-lived success. The entire educational system in the Polish lands was a tool used to propagate an anti-national policy. Its forms and methods varied, but its aims remained the same.

The struggle for Polish education was conducted uninterruptedly during this entire period but the events at Września and in Warsaw received particularly wide publicity in the world. At Września in 1901, the Prussian authorities wanted to force Polish children to use German in their classes and in their prayers. The children refused and were punished by flogging. The children's resistance lasted for a whole year, and was joined by children from other towns in the Poznań district, stimulating protests by various Polish writers (for example, Sienkiewicz), as well as of outstanding representatives of West European culture. Of a different nature was the school strike organized during the 1905 revolutionary period by students from Warsaw. The young people, in solidarity with the workers' movement, demanded the opening of Polish schools, freedom of association, and the democratization of education. The first of these demands was fulfilled.

Thus, the struggle for Polish education, although extremely difficult, bore fruit. Germanizing and Russifying efforts failed; at times they even strengthened the national consciousness and the will to resist. Żeromski was right when he gave the title of *The Labors of Sisyphus* to his novel about a Russian school in Poland. The entire history of the period of bondage justified this analogy. These were the reasons why in Poland, during the period of foreign domination, factors other than the schools were of great consequence in national education.

In his Paris lectures Mickiewicz remarked: "National education emerges out of great national events and spreads by itself through living traditions." These words comprised an excellent synthesis of the advancement of national education in Poland during the first half of the century and provided important guidelines for subsequent decades. Indeed, more than in any other epoch of Poland's history, the great events of national life were constantly present in the social consciousness in the form of memories or models, remorse or subjects of agonizing disputes. Owing to their presence, attitudes and aspirations, understanding of the national character, a feeling of guilt, and a source of hope were shaped.

This was true from the beginning of the era of bondage to its very end. The increasing chain of "great events" during this period constantly enriched the historical resources of the social consciousness, constituting an ever more important factor in universal education. Hundreds of organizations appeared and vanished under the blows of the police and the courts, only to revive almost immediately in other shapes. Thousands of people followed their personal Stations of the Cross to Siberia, filled Russian, Prussian and Austrian jails, and were shot or hanged, sometimes publicly, under the eyes of their compatriots. Only a few managed to escape and led the lives of wanderers on the face of the earth.

The entire period of bondage is packed with the history of these organizations; they began to appear immediately after the fall of the state; they did not subside after the failures of the 1830 and the 1863 Insurrections, or after the failure of the revolution in 1905.

Owing to their operation, ideas circulated, attitudes became crystallized, and programs of action were formulated. The membership of these organization turned into a great school of national and social education, not only for those immediately concerned but for wider circles of the community, which were kept in contact with them by means of open or clandestine propaganda.

In all of the clandestine or semi-conspiratorial organizations, from the beginning of the period of bondage to its very end, the younger generations participated wholeheartedly, and, more often than not, formed the most radical element of these movements. It is true that Walerian Łukasiński, when he founded his National Freemasonry, was thirty-three, but the conspirators who instigated the November Insurrection were in their late twenties; Edward Dembowski was killed on the outskirts of Cracow at the age of twenty-four; Szymon Konarski was twenty-seven at the beginning of his conspiratorial activities, and Ludwik Waryński, when he started his work with the Warsaw proletariat, was only twenty.

Yet the role of the younger generation was not limited to participation in political organizations of the adult community. During the entire period of bondage, young people formed an active element of intellectual and artistic development, of patriotic and social action within its own groups, circles, and organizations.

This constituted an absolutely new factor in Polish history. It appeared for the first time in Vilna, with the Philomates' movement, and later commemorated by Mickiewicz, became a model and symbol for the entire period of bondage. The Philomates' Society was founded in 1817 by a small group of students from various departments of the university: Tomasz Zan, Józef Jeżowski, Jan Czeczot and Adam Mickiewicz. It influenced a wide circle of the university students and inspired various groups with different objectives. During the first phase of its existence, intellectual and artistic subjects prevailed in the society, followed by social and political issues. Plans

were also made to reach beyond the limits of the university to the entire community. In 1823, the activity of the Society was detected, the leaders were imprisoned, put on trial, and deported into the heart of Russia. The entire court procedure conducted by Novosiltsov, was reconstructed and established in the Polish national consciousness thanks to Mickiewicz's *Forefathers' Eve.*

The intensity of these juvenile movements during this period is corroborated by the fact that between 1817 and 1823 almost fifty illegal or semi-legal youth organizations were in existence. In Warsaw alone they numbered twenty.

In the period between the insurrections the activity of the unions of young people did not subside. It spread beyond the frontiers of central Poland, with branches in Wrocław and Kiev. Polish university students in St. Petersburg held that "without intellectual tasks life would be an unbearable burden to us."

Years later, in 1869, Walery Wróblewski, the future general of the Paris Commune, criticizing the peaceful ideals of organic work and advocating revolutionary fight as the only way, proclaimed: "I see only one path for the salvation of Poland: the steep path of martyrdom, covered with blood from bottom to top, the path of the apostleship of the word, writing, and deed, in the midst of ordinary people, through a conspiracy of youth."

LEARNING, ART AND THE THEATER AS EDUCATIONAL ACTIVITY

A very important place was held by various forms of voluntary educational activity during the period of bondage, implemented, according to variable conditions existing in the three partition zones, at different periods of time. These forms of activity were sometimes open and legal, sometimes of a distinctly conspiratorial nature, and at times the forbidden educational contents were skillfully hidden under the guise of forms permitted by the authorities. The levels and scope of these activities also varied, sometimes taking the character of organized instruction at a high and specialized level; at other times, aimed at the elementary education of wide segments of the population. The organization of these actions sometimes rested with experienced and educated people, who considered their educational activity as a singular civic mission; while at other times, the action was inaugurated by local leaders, tied by bonds of birth or custom with the regional population.

In the first half of the nineteenth century, an outstanding role in these educational activities was played by the Poznań region. At Gostyń in 1835, a so-called Casino for the well-to-do landowners was founded. Possessing the official character of a social center, in reality it was meant to educate people to improve the methods of soil cultivation and to better organize their agrarian economy. The Casino published its own periodical, *Przewodnik Rolniczo-Przemysłowy,* a professional publication, very popular with the landowners. In Poznań in 1841, Karol

Marcinkowski founded the Society for Scientific Help, which granted stipends to poor students.

A replica of this educational action could be found in Congress Poland in the activity of the Agrarian Institute at Marymont near Warsaw. Under the auspices of its director, an encyclopedia, *Husbandry*, also appeared. Andrzej Zamoyski went in much the same direction, by building on his estate at Klemensów, during the years 1843—47, a center for the dissemination of agricultural knowledge and progressive agrarian and social thought.

At the same time an ordinary rural teacher, Ewaryst Estkowski, appeared as a pioneer of popular education. He defined his aim in the following way: "The peasantry has to know, understand, accept and reveal its dignity; it has to achieve equality of rights and obligations with everyone else in the nation; it has to taste a higher life."

During the second half of the century the activity of Konrad Prószyński, widely known by his pen-name Promyk, acquired great significance. He was the creator of *The Primer* (first printed in 1876) from which thousands of peasant children studied; he also published many books for those who had already mastered the art of reading and promoted intellectual and artistic culture throughout the countryside.

At the turn of the century educational activity increased in all three partition zones. In the Poznań region resistance was organized against Bismarck's Germanizing policies which were conducted in the state civil service and in schools; his efforts to Germanize completely the lower levels of Church organization stimulated additional resistance. While the world watched with disgust this policy, conducted in the name of culture (the so-called *Kulturkampf)*, the Polish population adhered more closely to their national language and tradition, as well as to their Catholic faith. In Poznań in 1872 the Association for Popular Education was founded and set out to open village libraries. The Prussian authorities ordered the closure of the Association, but it was soon revived (1880) under the name of the Association for Popular Reading-Rooms.

In Galicia, during the second half of the nineteenth century, the populist movement became an increasingly important factor in political and social life; and, concurrently, it inspired educational activity. The first signs of it were Father Stanisław Stojałowski's periodicals *Wieniec* and *Pszczółka.* This activity acquired momentum when Bolesław Wysłouch, drawing on democratic traditions, organized a group of intelligentsia of peasant descent. Wysłouch's magazine, *Przyjaciel Ludu,* first published in 1889, won an increasing number of readers. He was also founder of the Society of Friends of Education in Lvov in 1890.

Simultaneously, and in agreement with the Poznań model, the peasant cooperative movement and savings bank were organized. This action, conducted mainly by Franciszek Stefczyk, also gave a stimulus to the educational aspirations of the village population. These aspirations were also served by the Association for Popular Schools founded in 1892, whose first president was Adam Asnyk. It operated in the spirit of national-conservative ideology.

The Mickiewicz Popular University, actively operating in the progressive spirit, organizing numerous lectures, was also opened in 1898.

This educational work was particularly intensive in Congress Poland. Dozens of societies and civic organizations emerged, the most popular being the Association for National Education, founded in 1875 in Warsaw with the aim of conducting educational activity in the countryside and, from 1899, known as the Association of Clandestine Instruction. The positivists paid special attention to the various levels of the dissemination of learning. On a higher level it was carried out through the so-called Flying University for women (1886—1905), so named because its operation was prohibited and lectures had to be held in different places; and through the publication, *Poradnik dla Samouków.* The 1905 Revolution intensified these activities. The Association for Learned Courses was instituted, conceived as the nucleus of a Polish university, as well as an Open University, which held lectures mostly for the working class in Warsaw. The Polish Alma Mater, which was founded to defend the native language, had a membership of one hundred thousand people; it sponsored about 800 elementary schools, many kindergartens and libraries. The czarist authorities dissolved it in 1907.

This campaign for education was backed up by academic institutions designed both for research and to raise the level of intellectual culture in society, by making available the results of their research and winning over the support of large groups of amateurs for their academic activities. The ability to organize voluntary bodies for purposes of this kind was in fact one of the benefits brought about by the partitions. Thus in a country where no national system of higher education was permitted to develop, and where there were no state-run academic institutions, a whole network of voluntary institutions and foundations was set up — sometimes making use of academic bodies already in existence in Russia, Austria or Prussia, but more frequently growing up alongside them or even in opposition to them.

The Warsaw Society of Friends of Learning was set up in 1800, with Jan Albertrandi as the first president, followed by Stanisław Staszic. In 1815 a Learned Society was founded in Cracow, linked with the university. This was intended not only to foster "progress in all sciences, skills and arts", but also — as was later stated explicitly — "to influence the development and popularization of education throughout the nation." Finally, after several unsuccessful attempts, the Poznań Society of Friends of Learning was set up in 1857, intended to "contribute to the dissemination of knowledge and science through the medium of the Polish language." In 1872, under the influence of the success of the Cracow Learned Society, the Academy of Learning was set up; this was to be the most important academic institution in partitioned Poland, fostering the development of academic study and the dissemination of learning. The Warsaw Learned Society was founded in 1907. Its organizers wrote: "An intellect without the stimulus of academic work slowly ceases to exist, vanishes... We need to set up our own fount of knowledge at home."

Voluntary initiatives — mainly undertaken by the aristocracy — gave rise to library, museum and historical foundations, intended to support the development and dissemination of academic learning. It was the Czartoryski family which first took the initiative in this field at Puławy, and their collections — badly damaged — were transferred first to Paris and then to Cracow where they formed the basis of the Museum of the Princes Czartoryski, which is still open to the public today. Józef Maksymilian Ossoliński set up a foundation in Lvov in 1817 which was known as the Ossoliński National Institution — Ossolineum — and which is still currently in operation, after moving from Lvov to Wrocław. Edward Raczyński established a great library in Poznań in 1829 which is also still in existence today, and Tytus Działyński did the same at Kórnik. In Warsaw the Zamoyski, Krasiński and Przeździecki families set up libraries; in Lvov the Baworowski and Dzieduszycki families did the same; and in Warsaw the Mianowski Foundation was established, building up within a period of two years a membership of 800 which provided contributions and donations. This was convincing evidence that science and learning had become a vehicle for national life.

The campaign to disseminate education throughout the nation passed through various stages. And at no time was it a totally unified campaign. In some periods it was intended almost exclusively to "save the national soul", and then historical research was given priority. At other times it was intended to improve the standard of work, and then the social, technical and agricultural sciences moved into first place. Yet again, sometimes the main aim was to inculcate a philosophy of life, and then the natural sciences were studied, and in particular the theory of evolution. Sometimes, the purpose was to develop the intellect, and then various disciplines were presented in a way intended to arouse curiosity, provoke intellectual effort and give rise to a desire to study and discover.

The social roots of these various campaigns were also varied. The most frequent basis was the ideology of national solidarity, with the promise of unifying the working and peasant classes behind the existing social order by suitable doses of education. It was believed possible to attain a "national concord" despite the social contrasts between manor-house and village, or between the great town houses of the aristocracy and the slum tenements of the workers. The democrats and radicals, on the other hand, expected academic education to help in raising the consciousness of the exploited classes and in organizing them for patriotic activity. These two contradictory intentions first became clearly apparent at the time of the 1848 revolutions — although indications of what was happening could be found earlier. But in 1848 people like Edward Dembowski and Henryk Kamieński, who wanted education to lead to practical revolutionary action, parted company with people like Bronisław Trentowski and Karol Libelt, who wanted to "bring up the peasantry" in peace and obedience to the law and historical evolution. The contradiction between the two approaches again came into the open at the end of the nineteenth century, when the program of education as part of the great pattern of evolution was put forward by young radicals and early Marxists, in opposition to the concept of solidarity through organic work. Many periodicals published both at home and abroad, like *Równość, Przedświt, Proletariat, Wiedza, Przegląd Socjaldemokratyczny,* or *Walka Klas,* took this new role in academic education, and outstanding writers and academics, like Krzywicki, Krusiński, Kelles-Krauz, or Abramowski, provided a suitable theoretical basis for the campaign.

These concepts were also reflected in educational theory. Jan Władysław Dawid's study, *Intelligence, Will and Fitness for Work* (1911) was an effort to demonstrate the links amongst these three elements in human life — something very rarely attempted in Europe, and at the same time a very Polish approach. "Ability, desire and power," wrote Dawid, "are the three things which reinforce human life ... These three factors in spiritual life correspond to intelligence, will and work." Dawid believed that thought was always linked with practical experience and was "an external implementation of goals and means".

Increasingly the social prestige of science and learning was equal to that accorded to art, and in particular painting. At the beginning of the era of the partitions, a new situation developed, which was to last longer than was expected: art, which had at one time been the exclusive preserve of royal and magnate patronage, now began to develop direct links with society. The education of artists reflected this new attitude. A Fine Arts Faculty was opened at the University of Warsaw: in Cracow the School of Fine Arts was amalgamated with the University; and at Vilna a Department of Painting and Sculpture was opened. Exhibitions and competitions were organized. The first major art collections were set up, as for example the Collections of Prints of Warsaw and Vilna Universities, with the help of institutions like the Warsaw Society of Friends of Learning.

The defeat of the November Insurrection put an end to activity of this kind, and later it could only slowly be reconstructed. Art education was gradually re-developed, large exhibitions were organized and museums were set up — in Warsaw in 1863, in Cracow the Czartoryski Museum in 1876 and National Museum in 1879, and also in Poznań and Lvov. The Cracow School of Fine Arts was made into an Academy of Fine Arts in 1900. The School of Fine Arts in Warsaw, which was founded in 1844 and closed down in 1864, was set up again in 1904. Private collections also grew during this period. Both members of the old magnate families — like the Zamoyskis, Raczyńskis or Przeździeckis — and gentlemen landowners and members of the intelligentsia — like Edward Rastawiecki, Dominik Witke-Jeżewski or Feliks Jasieński — collected works of art.

The various associations of friends of the arts played a major role in linking art to society. Societies of Friends of the Fine Arts were set up in Cracow in 1854, in Warsaw in 1860, in Lvov in 1866, and in Poznań in 1888. These societies organized contacts between the artists and their public, through numerous exhibitions, talks, publications and artistic premiums or gifts for members. The wide range of these activities, intended to "foster love for real and serious art", can be gauged from the number of members and attendance at exhibitions.

It was not however exhibitions, but the growth of the printing of reproductions, or albums of reproductions, which was of decisive importance in popularizing art, and therefore in increasing the role it played in society. Lithography began in the first decades of the nineteenth century; and it reached its peak in the middle of the century. It was through lithographs that large parts of society were able to see the whole of Poland: landscapes, cities and towns, the life of the peasants, great historical events, old architecture. Lithography made possible the construction of a great chronicle of things and events — both past and current. Lithography became a tool in patriotic propaganda, a weapon in political caricature, and a means of political agitation. Large and popular albums were published: *Portraits of Famous Poles* (ed. A. Chodkiewicz, 1920), *Zincographic Album,* by Jan Feliks Piwarski (1841) and *Picturesque Warsaw Stalls,* by the same author (1855—59), *Polish Portraits* by Maksymilian Fajans, *Album of Views* by Napoleon Orda, and many others. In the second half of the nineteenth century woodcut reproduction was popular, and widely published in illustrated periodicals at the time; it was also used for book illustrations. A few periodicals, for example *Chimera* or *Życie,* had exceptionally high standards in graphic art work.

This improved reproduction technology, particularly lithography, brought works of art down to a wider section of society. It was by this means that Grottger's series of mourning studies — showing the insurrection in Warsaw and Lithuania, the cruelty of the repression, and the miseries of war damage — became generally known. The originals were often far from Poland in private hands — in the collections of foreigners — but in the late 1860's the reproductions of them appeared in almost every Polish home, leaving society with a memory of that heroic and hopeless struggle that was at once realistic and allegorical. At the beginning of World War I, many art publishing houses issued beautiful albums, with the works of Polish painters, popularizing the "story in pictures" of Polish history, and the habits and customs of the Polish people, showing Polish historic monuments and great historical and contemporary figures. At the turn of the nineteenth and twentieth centuries the majority of households of the intelligentsia in Poland subscribed to publications of this type, thus setting up their own "museums of imagination" at home.

Throughout the whole period of bondage, the theater had considerable social and educational importance. The partitions brought to an end the splendid period in the history of Polish theater which had evolved under Stanislaus Augustus, with close ties to the hopes and desires of Polish society. When the Prussians took over Warsaw, theater life died out. Bogusławski attempted to rebuild it when he returned to Warsaw in 1799. The situation was similar in other Polish towns. There was some improvement at the time of the Duchy of Warsaw and the Kingdom of Poland. In 1814, Ludwik Osiński took over as director of the National Theater, and the group of aristocrats that met at the home of Count Tadeusz Antoni Mostowski formed a kind of advisory council on the repertoire and a theater critics' club. This national theater was inclined towards the pseudo-classical and did not suit the mood of Polish society after the defeat of Napoleon; nor did it appeal to young writers.

It was not until the second half of the nineteenth century that some sort of renaissance took place in the Warsaw theater. Although the management of the theaters still remained in Russian hands, since they were state theaters, nonetheless there was no attempt to introduce a campaign of Russification, as was the case in the schools. Plays by Russian authors were rarely performed on the Warsaw stage since they gave a satirical view of Russian life. Instead, works by the great playwrights of Western Europe, especially the French, were staged, along with the classics like Shakespeare, Schiller and Victor Hugo. Polish romantic plays were also performed, although without giving the names of the authors, and with changes in the text on occasions, as happened with Słowacki's plays, *Mazepa* and *Mary Stuart.* Comedies by Polish authors — Fredro, and younger playwrights like Józef Bliziński, Michał Bałucki and Józef Narzymski — were widely performed. Drama competitions were organized, although without great success. But the basis of the success of a theater were the actors. It was a period rich in acting talent, and there were also many people aware of the social and artistic mission of the theater. It was the period in which the following appeared on the stage: Helena Modrzejewska (Modjeska), Jan Królikowski, Bolesław Leszczyński, Wincenty Rapacki, and Alojzy Żółkowski. These were artists of the very highest rank whose names have become legends in the Polish theater; they cared deeply about the standard of the plays they acted in, sometimes developing considerable influence over what was included in the repertoire and sometimes writing plays themselves.

It was during this period that open-air, garden theater developed in Warsaw — a unique event in theatrical life, showing the exceptional demand for dramatic performances among large parts of society. Jan Russanowski first opened a theater of this kind in 1868, and from then on for almost forty years they entertained and educated the Warsaw public. They staged farces, but also good Polish comedies by Bliziński or Bałucki; they staged translations of foreign melodramas, but also Polish folk plays, based on legends or contemporary issues on which there was dispute. Sometimes they even staged classics by Shakespeare, Schiller or Molière. Plays in which the audience could see themselves were particularly popular: for example, Feliks Schober's *Journeys around Warsaw,* which was still being staged in different productions half a century later. The Warsaw garden theaters, reaching such a wide audience, exerted an influence elsewhere. In Cracow, Władysław Anczyc's play, *Kosciuszko at Racławice* (which could not be staged in Warsaw) became exceptionally popular when it was produced for the first time on Christmas 1881.

This wide repertoire of popular performances, making use of peasant and urban folklore, using humor attacking the shortcomings of the gentry, the historical pathos of patriotic plays, farcical or melodramatic effects — all mixed together in a unique way — produced a theater which did not have high aspirations, but was a live theater with its own devoted audience. And this was a new audience, which would only have entered an "official" theater with great reluctance. In the period when the court theater had ceased to exist, this was a new type of theatrical life, typical of the urban population from various social classes.

Outside Warsaw, the Cracow theater also developed notably during the second half of the nineteenth century, especially under the management of Stanisław Koźmian. Making use of the greater freedom of the Austrian zone, they produced many Polish plays — from Kochanowski to Słowacki, almost all the works of Fredro, and also popular plays, especially by Władysław Anczyc. They also staged many foreign, classical and modern plays. Many of the Russian plays that were banned in Warsaw were performed in Cracow: for example, Gogol's *The Inspector-General.*

The Lvov theater also enjoyed a renaissance. In 1872 the German theater there was closed, and many excellent actors and actresses were to be found in the Polish theater, for example Aniela Aszpergerowa who was immortalized in the poetry of Maryla Wolska, Roman Żelazowski, and Mieczysław Frenkiel. A permanent theater was not opened in Poznań until 1870; after it had constructed its own building over a period of two years, it began regular performances and also went on tour.

But the real turning point in the history of Polish theater, and the social role of the theater, came in Cracow at the turn of the nineteenth and twentieth centuries, under the theater management of Tadeusz Pawlikowski during the years 1893—99, and then after he had moved to Lvov, under Józef Kotarbiński, during the years 1899—1905. This came about primarily because of the atmosphere of renaissance in literature in general, and the work of outstanding foreign and Polish writers, in particular Stanisław Wyspiański. During this period the Cracow theater became an all-Polish theater: it was from Cracow that the dramatic Polish words of the great romantic plays spread throughout Poland: here for the first time Mickiewicz's *Forefathers' Eve* was performed, together with Krasiński's *Iridion* and *Un-Divine Comedy,* many of Słowacki's plays that had never previously been staged, and also plays by many well-known contemporary authors, like Ibsen, Hauptmann, or Maeterlinck. Plays by contemporary Polish writers like Przybyszewski, Kisielewski, Rydel, Zapolska, Rittner and Żuławski were also performed.

It was Wyspiański's plays, some of them produced by himself, that attained the highest degree of significance, indeed extending beyond purely theatrical success. The Cracow theater staged *La Varsovienne* in 1898; the much discussed première of *The Wedding* took place in 1901, and of *Deliverance* in 1903. It was not only the citizens of Cracow that saw these three plays. People made pilgrimages from the Prussian and Russian partition zones to the Cracow theater, as though visiting a national shrine. In fact the Cracow theater became the stage of the national conscience; it was here that bitter accounts were settled over the faults and drawbacks of the national tradition and Polish romantic poetry, and an attempt was made to discover the sources of the current strength and weaknesses of the society, checking its hopes and expectations. Never before and never afterwards had the Polish theater — probably theater in general — been to such an extent the true and dramatic voice of life.

In this whole great labyrinth of paths along which culture wandered during the period of bondage — educational organizations, the dissemination of science and art, the development of the theater — there was still one way more, which was exceptionally typical both of the period and of the Polish mentality. I am thinking here of the role of small and compact groups, the members of which were linked by opinions held in common, but above all by the links of friendship. The group that was called the Society of Philomates was by no means the first or only group of this kind, although it became the best known and has come down into history and Polish national legends.

In Warsaw, a new wave of associations of this kind swept through the city in the 1840's. Young poets and painters formed a group that was later known as the Warsaw Boheme; they opposed the hypocrisy of the drawing-room manners of the gentry, and wanted to create an authentic and sincere life-style based on democratic ideas and a return to links with the peasantry. The Bohemians included journalists, writers and poets, like Roman Zmorski, Włodzimierz Wolski — the author of the libretto for Moniuszko's *Halka* — and Józef Bohdan Dziekoński who wanted to direct "this handful of young people, working with the mind and spirit, going directionless into the future" towards activity to help the peasantry and "the poorest artisan class".

At the same time, a group known as the Women Enthusiasts was formed, led by Edward Dembowski and Narcyza Żmichowska. Żmichowska believed that meetings "around the hearth" with personal participation by all present, were the most valuable. She based her ideas about life and work in society on this experience. She thought that "love of humanity, hatred of evil cannot suffice; individual bonds are necessary" — that is individual commitment all the time and everywhere, and in even the smallest matter.

And these forms also remained at the end of the nineteenth and beginning of the twentieth centuries. Although political conditions permitted a certain degree of freedom in setting up cultural institutions and making use of them for national purposes, there still remained an enormous area where the process of propagating culture had to take on non-institutional forms. This was the case with a great deal of the educational campaigns, and with all campaigns to awaken the common people, and in particular the proletariat. There were, of course, forms of organization, but they had of necessity to be exceptionally elastic, and in many cases effects were achieved more through the self-sacrifice and devotion of individuals rather than efficient organization. This was how the first Polish revolutionaries operated among the Warsaw proletariat and the people. This was the way that those organizing the campaign for education and knowledge operated. Żeromski was right when he saw the activity of the self-sacrificing schoolmistress as "political" work to enlighten the peasantry.

Thus in this nation where the basic institutions of cultural life were in the hands of hostile, foreign powers, the conviction developed that it was possible to circulate ideas "non-institutionally", through direct contacts among individuals, and by means of inspiring and committed personal example.

The attention of the sociologists and psychologists was focused on these processes. The issue of the origin and circulation of ideas remained a subject of reflection for Krzywicki who, while underscoring the importance of material conditions of social life, perceived the pioneering role of individuals and groups, significant even if success was not yet achieved. He described the role played by these people in the words, "swallows of history." Jan Władysław Dawid analyzed that problem in his dissertation, *On the Moral Disease,* which showed how the patterns of life, implemented by individuals, radiated into their social environment.

The most profound conclusions from these Polish experiences was drawn by Edward Abramowski. His concept of the cooperative movement as a conscious commitment of individuals to mutual assistance, his vision of the future as a brotherhood created by means of "bonds of friendship" — constituted a collection of attitudes characteristic of the Polish community during the period of bondage, during which cultural development was connected to immediate relations between people, to their personal commitment to the community.

CULTURE OF THE PEASANT AND THE WORKER

The channels for the circulation of culture in the community, presented in the foregoing chapters, were limited to the so-called higher spheres: to the aristocracy, to the landed gentry, and lastly, to the new, nascent bourgeois and intelligentsia section. But the main problem of the era remained the crossing of the still-existing feudal barrier which prevented the masses of the nation from participating in citizenship and culture. The road to culture for the masses led, in words from the autobiography of the peasant writer Ferdynand Kuraś, through "the thorns of life." In his memoirs published under this title, with a foreword by Żeromski, in 1925, he described the conditions of life and education of the poor peasants at the end of the nineteenth century, based on his own experiences: "The entire property of my parents amounted to one fourth of an acre and nothing more. They were homeless." Kuraś' plight was not an exception. His way through "the thorns of life" was a universal peasant way, leading towards social liberation and education during the entire period of servitude.

And yet the path through "the thorns of life" led the masses to culture in an unusual way. Owing to this, Polish society underwent profound and multilateral evolution during this period of bondage. While at the beginning participation in culture was limited to a narrow segment of the nation and, while the magnate and gentry culture almost neglected all other sections of society, at the end of the era, on the eve of World War I, the national culture had taken shape, embracing the entire community. At the same time it acquired a new and specific form, which expressed the uniqueness of the peasant section.

This entire period was filled with rich educational and publishing activity, conducted by people descended from the ruling class, like Izabela Czartoryska, author of a popular history of Poland under the title *Pilgrim in Dobromil* (published in 1818), or by political emissaries such as Henryk Kamieński, or peasant leaders, like Jakub Bojko, or booksellers who initiated popular series of books.

At the same time, in the lands lost to the Commonwealth long ago, in Silesia, Pomerania, Warmia and Mazuria, a self-generated national revival was taking place, inspired by local leaders, regional writers and poets, local journalists, ordinary village farmers, devoted and zealous Catholic and Protestant priests. Cultural activity flourished on the wave of this revival. And, although rarely reaching beyond regional boundaries, it constituted a lively and authentic reality to the wide masses. Proof of this can be seen in the size of book editions, often many times greater than for books intended for the national market. The peasantry, now a part of non-feudal society, entered this new situation of equality with the awareness of its own separate character, of its own values which had to be preserved; concurrently, the progressive writers of the ruling class, who saw and accepted these values, attempted to promote them in society. They held, in contrast to conservative elements, that it was not the peasantry that ought to "nobilitate itself," as Zygmunt Krasiński had once dreamed, but that Poland should become the Poland of "transformed peasants," as Norwid once wrote.

These concepts were championed by Stanisław Witkiewicz. He pointed to the peculiar moral values of the peasantry and to the necessity of promoting modern education in the village community. He formulated the problem which for decades to come was to be the most difficult in educational and cultural activity among the peasants, very characteristic of the Polish mentality of the era. The issue, according to Witkiewicz, was related to him by a certain mountain dweller from the Podhale region, who asked his interlocutor: "How can one become a civilized man, yet remain a Polish peasant?"

The way to culture for the worker was different. This class of society was recruited from various social groups. Thus varied elements contributed to its culture: traditional peasant culture, the urban culture of the plebeians, the predilections and aspirations of the petite bourgeoisie, and also the gentry traditions which had national significance.

However, step by step, especially during the last quarter of the nineteenth century, these various and sometimes conflicting elements yielded before a new vision of the world, of the community, of man, which started to take shape under the influence of the experiences of work in a factory and in connection with the revolutionary aims of advanced groups of workers in Silesia, in Warsaw, in Łódź and, later, in the Dąbrowa Basin.

Socio-political literature, written or translated by young Polish socialists, began to appear and develop in the 1880's. Clandestine publications, sometimes only mimeographed, began to circulate among workers. Those who could read explained them to the illiterates. Those who could write in a simple and clear way took to writing, in order to further propagate socialist ideas. The twenty-two year old Szymon Diksztajn wrote his famous pamphlet: *Who Lives From What?* It appeared in Warsaw in 1881, and up to 1918 was published at least fifteen times. For the next forty years masses of Polish workers learned from this booklet about the first principles of socialism. It was translated into many languages in Europe and the world. Lenin mentioned it among the best "textbooks for the people."

Such socio-political literature was supplemented by poetry. A characteristic feature of the maturing proletarian consciousness was the need for poetic expression. This became a link with the Polish tradition, from the times of the Kosciuszko Insurrection, the battles of the Legions, the November Insurrection, the "Springtime of Nations," and the January Insurrection — all these events were accompanied by poetry and by revolutionary songs.

A new stage of this poetry was inaugurated by Bolesław Czerwieński in his famous *The Red Banner.* The leadership of the socialist movement, centered in Geneva, was aware of the revolutionary significance of poetry. In 1882, the periodical *Przedświt* published a small volume of verses, *What Do They Want?;* and in 1888, the Proletariat issued *A Selection of Poetry for Workers,* a subsequent volume from the Library of the Polish Worker. Most of the verses printed in the first book were, as the foreword indicated, "written by our comrades behind prison bars. They are some kind of testament handed down to our movement by these sacrificial lambs." A number of verses by Polish and Russian revolutionaries appeared in the second volume, which was also enriched by works of modern Polish poets. There was also a hint of Mickiewicz's poetry, in a travesty of his "To a Polish Mother," which was included in this volume.

Among the workers, the processes of the dissemination of culture extended across national boundaries. Socialism was an international movement and the Polish camp established strong links of solidarity with the world-wide proletariat. At the same time, for reasons of safety, many leaders had to leave the country, at least temporarily, and to direct the movement from abroad. Geneva was one of the centers which attracted Polish socialists; their organizational and educational activities were conducted from there. Contacts were established with revolutionaries of other countries, who also lived in exile. Many publications were printed there and later smuggled into the country.

The publications of Przedświt and Równość, of the Polish Workers' Society in Geneva and the Socialist Library, edited by Bolesław Limanowski, and the publications of Lud Polski, made up a rich library including theoretical studies by outstanding Marxist writers, and also popular texts, destined for a wide readership. How much attention was paid to this latter aspect may be judged by one of the Przedświt publications called *Janek Bruzda* (1882), a story written in the Mazurian dialect. At the same time, however, efforts at translations of basic works were not neglected. The first Polish translation of Marx's *Capital* was published in Leipzig in 1884. Russian-language literature was widely acclaimed among young people; both original works, and those translated from western languages. It was easily accessible and cheap. It was a sharp criticism of existing circumstances, and provided a compendium of revolutionary ideas and of new philosophical concepts. "Every young man anxious to broaden his horizons," wrote Ludwik Krzywicki, "tended towards these resources of thought."

Foreign Culture in Poland and Polish Culture in the World

CRITICISM OF EUROPEAN CIVILIZATION

Polish culture, retarded during the Baroque era, matched its Western intellectual and artistic counterpart during the Enlightenment. Throughout the entire period of bondage, it generally kept abreast of the changes going on in other European countries. Romanticism and the "Springtime of Nations" were experienced concurrently. Acceptance of the great wave of positivist ideology, as well as the beginnings of the workers' movement, was slightly delayed in Poland. Decadence appeared at the turn of the century, as did various currents of "art nouveau" which found adherents in Poland. On the other hand, the 1905 Revolution was a harbinger of the future, felt later in Western European countries.

These processes were reflected in various ways in the national consciousness. An inferiority complex in the face of the world and a conviction that the course of Poland's history was retarded mingled with a belief in the superiority of national values amounting almost to national megalomania.

During the decline of the Commonwealth of the Gentry, Staszic wrote with bitterness: "How far have other countries gone! Elsewhere despotism is already falling. In Poland there is still a gentry oligarchy. Poland is still in the fifteenth century. The whole of Europe is approaching the end of the eighteenth century."

Józef Szujski returned to the same diagnosis, when he formulated his well-known thesis concerning our national adolescence. "The Poles," wrote Szujski in 1871, "one of the youngest of European nations, never possessed a critical spirit. Everything was temporary, abrupt and passionate with them."

Such reflections on delays in Polish historical development appeared many times in the works of Norwid. But they acquired a slightly different character: they were enriched, owing to romantic hopes and romantic methods of evaluation.

Cyprian Kamil Norwid wrote: "We are still roaming between this non-traditional civilization whose great practicality is often very unkind, and our beloved traditional civilization, whose great kindness is very impractical." Norwid, however, believed in the future, and explained contemporary contradictions by the fact that "we have only just become a people of the nineteenth century."

Norwid's reflection reached to the root of the matter. It concerned Poland's place in Europe and the question of whether in being different from the rest of the world we really, or only seemingly, are worse than the world. In other words, whether being so different in our path of historical development, we are in fact "retarded", or rather, perhaps, ahead of the world.

These questions were raised and answered again and again.

Criticism of European civilization from this viewpoint was formulated by Mickiewicz in his *Books of the Polish Pilgrimage* and developed in his Paris lectures. While real civilization, according to Mickiewicz, depends on the virtue of devotion to the homeland and "to all people," the Western world "in idolatrous confusion of languages, regarded as civilization fashionable luxurious dress, tasteful dishes, comfortable inns, beautiful theaters and wide roads."

"We have arrived in the West," wrote Mickiewicz, "in a sad and queer epoch, in an epoch of societal dissolution; we are watching the Middle Ages, with all their hierarchy of kings and civil servants, on their deathbed."

"Christian Poland became a natural defense of Western civilization which originated from Christianity."

The romantic criticism of modern European civilization did not abate with Romanticism. Positivism, oriented towards scientific, technological and economic changes, continued the criticism in relation to many features and syndromes of that civilization. Not one outstanding writer or journalist promoted this model of life in its entirety. This can be explained by the delayed development of capitalism in Poland and by the resistance of the strong landowner tradition, but that does not alter the fact that critical and restrained evaluation of modern civilization was much more characteristic of the pioneers of progress than enthusiasm for the expected achievements.

The writings of Świętochowski and Prus, and even more so, of Orzeszkowa, were not only meant as propaganda for material and intellectual progress: for, at the same time, they pointed at various limitations to this. But during the positivist era, the contradiction between Poland and the world took on a new form. It was perceived, as defined by Świętochowski, as a conflict between particularism and cosmopolitanism. Between these two extremes, supposedly, the proper way could be found. Both the campaign against things foreign, and the cult of the foreign seemed to be symptoms of a disease.

Polish nationalism adhered to "familiarity," as Balicki

put it, and to the "national element." It was from this standpoint that Stanisław Szczepanowski inaugurated the great dispute on the national character of Polish culture, in his article under the significant title, "Disinfection of European Movements," published in 1898. In the same year, Marian Zdziechowski, in a lecture entitled "Dispute about Beauty," supported Szczepanowski's attack on young poets, writers, critics and artists. Artur Górski replied to these accusations in a series of articles entitled, "The Young Poland," as did Ludwik Szczepański, in an essay, "National Art." He perceived the national value of art in its being modern, and not in its serving old utilitarian political programs. Modern art fights for the future of the nation; the conservative concept of "tradition and the national spirit breaks us from our early years." Under difficult conditions of national life only individual art can form the source of great art for all; other kinds of art, according to Szczepański, are only "artistic industry."

This dispute extended beyond the limits of polemics about art to the field of civilization and its value. Criticism of the bourgeois civilization and defense of a different kind of civilization based on humanist values, became the main topic of disputes.

These disputes were permeated by the constant aspiration to modernity and originality and, at the same time, to faithfulness to tradition. The Young Poland movement brought up the old argument again about imitating foreign models which had recurred again and again from the time of the disputes between classicists and romantics. As always, it was a matter of overpowering the complex about backwardness, inferiority and imitation, intertwined with a superiority complex of exceptionalism: it was a matter of creative originality, both contemporary and future directed.

These disputes sharpened in the twentieth century. They were reflected in a new turn toward the Tatras, which symbolized choice of the civilization of nature and the common people, and not of the cosmopolitan city and industry. Concurrently they were also reflected in a swing toward social changes, showing the destiny and vocation of the working class, casting doubt on a capitalist civilization that produced "homeless people." And although remarkable differences existed between the critical vision presented by Witkiewicz on the one hand and Żeromski on the other, both of these images of the contemporary world expressed the conviction already voiced by the Polish Romantics: "We do not have to learn civilization from foreigners," but we must construct it by our own hands, according to the principle that "man is a sacred thing."

FOR YOUR FREEDOM AND OURS

The role in the world of Poland and of the Poles was during the period of bondage different from that which had existed before.

The first to emerge was the concept of Poland's role in the struggle for freedom, both her own and that of other nations. This idea originated from philosophy of the Enlightenment which, based on presupposed laws of nature, explained the indivisibility of freedom in the world and the menace to it from despotism. Kosciuszko's and Pulaski's participation in the war of American independence was external palpable confirmation of the idea of solidarity, formulated theoretically by the writers of the Polish Enlightenment, particularly by Staszic and Kołłątaj. The era of Napoleon brought further theoretical and practical enlargement of the idea but, at the same time, the first disillusionments. It became evident that not everywhere where they fought did the Polish Legions bring freedom to foreign countries. Cyprian Godebski acknowledged with bitterness that "we have left far behind the good, for the sake of which we went into exile. And those whom we had thought saviors of humankind have issued, God grant not for long, a decree for its condemnation." But participation in the struggles for liberty did not stop. In South America Poles took part in the insurrections against the Spaniards, organized by Francisco Miranda and Simón Bolivar, and also in the liberation of Mexico during the first quarter of the nineteenth century.

The November Insurrection revived hopes that the Polish cause would become a universal liberation movement. In January 1831, during the great manifestation organized in Warsaw in honor of the Decembrist Uprising, the following slogan appeared on the banners for the first time: "For your freedom and ours," coined either by Adam Gurowski or Joachim Lelewel. The former said during the manifestation: "Freedom not to one country or one people, but to all on earth, all humanity is one. Whoever wants his country to throw off the yoke will respect foreign freedom, too. Self-seeking interested parties divide and sow discord between one people and another."

The future course of the insurrection did not confirm these hopes. But the insurgents, on their way through Europe, found great sympathy among the common people: they were victims of the power of tyranny. Soldiers and commanders of the uprising engaged in battles for the independence of other nations: General Jan Zygmunt Skrzynecki was a commander in Belgium; Wojciech Chrzanowski built fortifications in Antwerp, and then led the Italian army in its fight against the Austrians. The émigrés took advantage of this atmosphere to propagate the ideals of freedom in the fight against despotic rulers and shortsightedness of diplomats; they appealed to other nations, over the heads of cabinets and diplomatic agreements. At the same time, the émigrés underscored the special role of Poland in this cause. Mickiewicz wrote with appreciation that the slogan, "For your freedom and ours", had appeared on Polish flags and that the word "your" was put before the word "ours" — in defiance of all previous diplomatic logic. This was the spirit of all progressive forces among the émigrés; such was the nature of Polish participation in the 1848 "Springtime of Nations" in Germany, Italy, and Hungary.

Józef Bem, after the battle of Vienna, was promoted to be Commander-in-Chief of the Hungarian Army in Transylvania and won many victories over the Austrians and Russians. After the failure of the Hungarian uprising of 1849, he reached Turkey and, under the name of Murad Pasha, was one of the leaders of the Turkish army. With Bem in Hungary was Henryk Dembiński, one of the leaders of the uprising, together with a number of Polish officers. Ludwik Mierosławski, freed in 1848 from a Prussian prison where he was waiting to be put to death, fought in Sicily and in Baden.

Many Polish volunteers participated in Garibaldi's Sicilian and Neapolitan campaigns in 1860.

All these experiences ended in failure. The Insurrection of 1863 also failed to corroborate the practical value of the slogan, "For your freedom and ours," although a solidarity between Poles and Russians and Poles and Italians could be detected in some of the events during this time. The meaning of this solidarity and the significance of Poland was appreciated in the Act of the General Council of the Communist International in 1864, which confirmed that "Poland waged war for independence in the interest of all peoples of Europe, and owing to its defeat, the cause of civilization and the progress of humanity experienced a great shock."

After the defeat of 1864 the will to fight for Poland's freedom and that of others did not subside. Hauke-Bosak contacted the Russian émigrés, especially Bakunin, and later Garibaldi, presenting a radical social and revolutionary program in his *Letters to the Commune about the Conspiracy of the People of Poland, Lithuania and Ruthenia* (1867). During the Franco-Prussian War, he commanded forces fighting against the Prussians in Burgundy, and died in the defense of Dijon.

Others also fought in the defense of France, including Jarosław Dąbrowski and Walery Wróblewski, who, later, as generals organized the revolutionary struggle of the Paris Commune. Jarosław Dąbrowski, the Commander-in-Chief of the Communards, died in Paris. Wróblewski escaped to London and for years played an important role as organizer of the international workers' movement.

This great chronicle of battles conducted all over the world shaped the national consciousness in a new way. The downfall of the state and the as yet futile hopes for the restoration of independence bred conflicting tendencies in the nation's self-image. Self-accusations and inferiority complexes intertwined with the conviction that the Polish nation possessed exceptional values which were underestimated by the world at large. These trends found expression in Europe's attitudes toward Poland, which demonstrated corresponding ambiguity: a critical stance toward a nation that had lost its independence was accompanied by expressions of sympathy and respect for those who were capable of defiantly fighting for freedom for themselves and for other nations of the world.

The unceasing soul-searching of the nation and the possibilities of alternative solutions to the eternally agonizing problem — Poland and the world — continued amidst all these contradictions. On the one hand, the Poles were victims of the violence of the despots, and the world accepted the victory of this violence. On the other hand, the Polish fight for liberty was not only a national

252. Jan Gładysz, *Portrait of Stanisław Staszic*, c. 1820

253. Walenty Wańkowicz, *Portrait of Mickiewicz*, 1828

254. Wincenty Kasprzycki,
Bankowy Square in Warsaw

255. Wincenty Kasprzycki,
*Fine Arts Exhibition in the Rooms
of Warsaw University*, 1828

256. Marcin Zaleski,
  Capture of the Arsenal. [1831]

257. *Kopernik Square in Warsaw
  with the Staszic Palace, headquarters
  of the Warsaw Learned Society,* after 1832

258. Piotr Michałowski, *Somosierra*. c. 1845—55

259. Piotr Michałowski,
Equestrian Portrait of Hetman Stefan Czarniecki, c. 1846

260. Józef Brodowski.
View of Wawel, 1825

261. Jan Nepomucen Głowacki,
Morskie Oko Lake

262. January Suchodolski,
*General Henryk Dąbrowski Entering Rome
at the Head of the Polish Legions,* c. 1850

263. Józef Simmler,
Death of Barbara Radziwiłłówna, 1860

264. Henryk Rodakowski,
Portrait of General Henryk Dembiński, 1852

265. Henryk Rodakowski,
Portrait of Leonia Blühdorn, 1871

266. Juliusz Kossak,
Mickiewicz and Sadyk Pasha. 1890

267. Leopold Loeffler,
Return from Captivity, 1863

268. Franciszek Kostrzewski,
Wharf for Steamships in Powiśle in Warsaw, c. 1853

269. Franciszek Kostrzewski,
Circus at Saska Kępa in Warsaw, 1852

270. Franciszek Kostrzewski,
Drawing-room of Wacław and Nina Łuszczewski in Warsaw, 1854

271. Józef Szermentowski,
Return from Pasture, 1876

272. Wojciech Gerson,
Cemetery in the Mountains, 1894

273. Władysław Malecki,
   Storks. c. 1874

274. Aleksander Kotsis,
    Homeless, c. 1870

275. Aleksander Kotsis,
    Last Chattel, 1870

276. Artur Grottger.
Evening Prayer. 1864—65

277. Jan Matejko,
Skarga's Sermon, 1864

278. Jan Matejko,
Prussian Homage (detail), 1882

279. Antoni Kozakiewicz, *Winter*

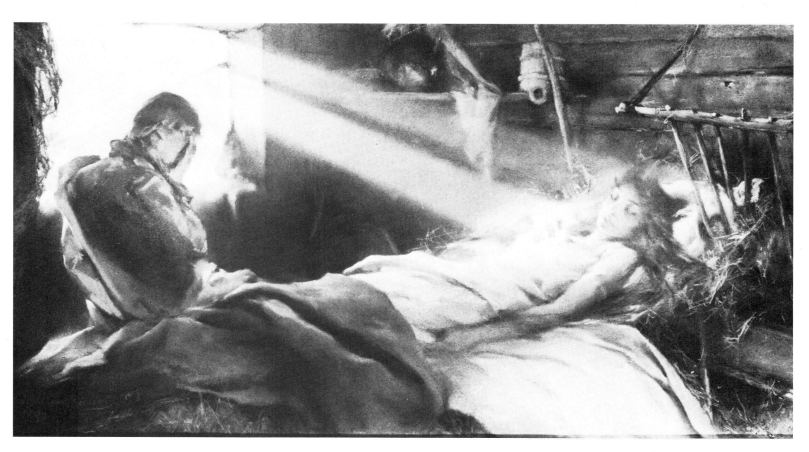

280. Tadeusz Pruszkowski,
Death of Ellenai, 1892

281. Maksymilian Gierymski,
Insurgent Guard in 1863, c. 1873

282. Aleksander Gierymski,
In the Summer-house, 1882

283. Aleksander Gierymski,
Peasant Coffin, 1894—95

284. Aleksander Gierymski,
Sand Diggers, 1887

285. Stanisław Witkiewicz,
Foehn, 1895

286. Józef Chełmoński,
Autumn, 1897

287. Stanisław Lentz,
Pay Day, 1885

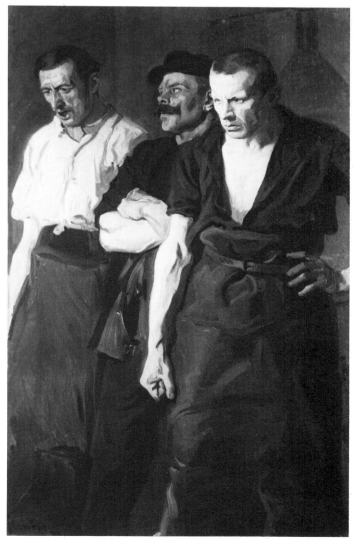

288. Stanisław Lentz,
Strike, 1910

289. Jacek Malczewski,
Death of Ellenai, 1883

290. Jacek Malczewski,
Melancholy, 1894

291. Jacek Malczewski,
Thanatos II, 1899

292. Jacek Malczewski,
*Workers on Their Way to
the Factory*

293. Stanisław Wyspiański,
Self-portrait with Wife, 1904

294. Stanisław Wyspiański,
Rhapsody, c. 1903

295. Leon Wyczółkowski,
Fishermen, 1891

296. Leon Wyczółkowski,
Beetroot Digging I, 1895

297. Władysław Podkowiński,
Ecstasy, 1894

298. Jan Stanisławski,
Cloud, c. 1903

299. Józef Mehoffer,
Strange Garden, 1903

300. Ferdynand Ruszczyc,
    Soil, 1898

301. Witold Wojtkiewicz,
Children's Crusade, 1905

302. Witold Wojtkiewicz,
Ash Wednesday, 1908

303. Józef Richter,
Palace in Tulczyn, 1836

304. Fryderyk Krzysztof Dietrich,
*Teatralny Square in Warsaw
with the Theater Building designed by Corazzi*

TEATR WIELKI w WARSZAWIE

305. Teofil Kwiatkowski,
*Chopin Polonaise or Ball
in Hotel Lambert*, 1849

306. Teofil Kwiatkowski,
After a Battle, 1869

307. Wojciech Gerson,
Jan Wilczek in Wilanów Asking John Sobieski
to Come to the Assistance
of Vienna against the Turks, 1889

308. Juliusz Kossak,
Cracow Wedding, 1895

309. Artur Grottger,
   Comet, from the series *War*, 1866—67

310. Artur Grottger,
   Polish Peasant and the Gentry, from
   the series *Warsaw*, 1861

311. Witold Wojtkiewicz,
Protest March, 1905

cause but, at the same time, the cause of all oppressed peoples. Thus, the Poles were better than the others, and yet were condemned to subservience to those "others."

THE POLITICAL AND SCIENTIFIC ACTIVITY OF THE EMIGRES

Concurrently, during this entire period, Poles participated in various revolutionary groups, in conspiratorial and underground political activities.

Marx and Engels, recollecting the plight of Poland on the 50th anniversary of the November Insurrection, stated: "The defeated Poles joined the ranks of the sans culottes army and assisted them in destroying feudal Europe."

Indeed, exiled Poles were active all over Europe. They were in Italy during the Napoleonic wars and as late as 1866; after the failure of the November Insurrection, German poets wrote that "together with the star of Polish freedom the light of hope" went out for other peoples. In Brussels, Stanisław Worcell and Joachim Lelewel, associated with the periodical *La Voix du Peuple,* created a center for democratic revolutionary thought. The Poles played an important role in the clandestine organization of the Carbonari; they organized this movement in Italy and, in particular, in Switzerland.

During the ceremony to mark the second anniversary of the Cracow Insurrection of 1846, organized in Brussels, Marx remarked: "Poland has taken the initiative again, but democratic Poland, and its liberation from now on becomes a question of honor to all European democrats." Engels formulated Poland's role even more precisely, stating that the uprising of 1846 aimed at creating "a new, modern, civilized democratic Poland, worthy of the nineteenth century; a Poland that would indeed be the vanguard of civilization". During the 1848 "Springtime of Nations" Polish activity increased, particularly in Germany and Italy.

The Paris émigrés developed lively long-term contacts with radical French groups. Paris became an international center of revolutionary movements, and the paper edited by Mickiewicz, *La Tribune des Peuples* was a medium of international solidarity in this struggle.

The range of Polish activity throughout the Slavic territories was also great. The watchword, "For your freedom and ours," originated in a conviction that there was a community of interests among the Polish and Russian peoples, as revealed by Mickiewicz's poetic image. This solidarity also grew in emigration. At a mourning ceremony in Brussels in 1848, to commemorate the shooting of Szymon Konarski, Bakunin evolved a program of cooperation between Polish and Russian revolutionaries; in 1855 Joachim Lelewel, recalling this ceremony, wrote the following to Alexander Herzen: "Poland cannot lift herself by herself, by her own national principle. Nothing but revolution can bring her the proper time. It will then be your task, our Russian friends, to join in our common cause, as it will be our task to rise in the common cause, when you raise the banner of freedom."

Polish activity in the Southern and Western Slavic lands had no direct revolutionary character, but was a factor in national liberation aspirations. The Austrian police often deported Polish patriots from Galicia to other parts of the monarchy. But there they stimulated the local national consciousness. This was true of Emil Korytko, condemned by the Austrian authorities to exile in Ljubljana; in Croatia Andrzej Kucharski, and, at the end of the century, Aleksander Jabłonowski, were active in the nationalist cause.

When in 1865 the 50th anniversary of the liberation of Serbia was celebrated in Paris, the participants went to Mickiewicz's tomb, demonstrating "by a live garland of interlaced arms," as Aleksander Chodźko described it, the indivisibility of the idea of the fight for liberation of the Slavic nations.

Evidence of solidarity was also seen in the Dąbrowski Mazurka, which in Slovenian, Czech and Serbian paraphrases, was one of the most frequently sung patriotic songs of the Southern and Western Slavs.

In Bulgaria, the Poles, despite their good relations with Turkey, assisted the patriotic cause, winning the respect of the Bulgarians for their chivalrous courage and technical skills. Evidence of this fellow-feeling was the mass participation of the Bulgarians in Mickiewicz's funeral in Constantinople.

The Poles participated in founding the first national schools in Bulgaria. The novels of Teodor Tomasz Jeż and Michał Czajkowski (Sadyk Pasha) were widely read, and the Bulgarian revolutionary poet, Khristo Botev, owed much to the one-time aide-de-camp of Sadyk Pasha, Ryszard Berwiński. At the end of the century, many Bulgarian students were studying in Poland, in Lvov and Cracow in particular.

Siberia had an exceptional place in this chronicle of the invincible spirit of the Poles. As early as the seventeenth century Poles arrived there as prisoners-of-war, but great waves of transported exiles started to flood the country from the end of the eighteenth century, as a result of the series of defeats in armed struggles (the Bar Confederacy, the Kosciuszko Insurrection, the Insurrections of 1831 and 1863), and also because of court sentences, almost continually condemning prisoners to hard labor and compulsory exile. Under these hard conditions, subsequent generation of exiles not only undertook to organize rebellions and escapes, but also found new meaning for their lives in social, and especially, medical and scientific activity.

Polish research work in such fields as geology, geography, ethnology and linguistics formed an important, sometimes even a pioneering contribution to the knowledge of Siberia. This long tradition was inaugurated by one of Kosciuszko's officers taken prisoner at Maciejowice, Józef Kopeć. His *Memoirs,* devoted to a description of Eastern Siberia, particularly Kamchatka, were published in Paris with a foreword by Adam Mickiewicz. A large group from the Philomates' Society (including Józef Kowalewski and Tomasz Zan) continued this research. After 1831, similar activities were carried out by a number of Poles, including Adolf Januszkiewicz, explorer of Kazakhstan, Bronisław Zaleski, Shevchenko's friend, Eugeniusz Żmijewski, and Leopold Niemirowski, the author of beautiful albums, containing landscapes and essays documenting the countryside and the people of Siberia. The most outstanding exiles after 1863 were the following: Benedykt Dybowski, because of his research in the fields of zoology and zoogeography, particularly of the Baikal region, and Wiktor Godlewski and Mikołaj Witkowski, who were the first archeologists to do research in Siberia. The pioneers of geological research, on the other hand, were Aleksander Czekanowski and Jan Czerski, both active in Northern Siberia. The last group of exiles sent to Siberia in the 1880's included the writers Adam Szymański and Wacław Sieroszewski, who explored Yakutia; as well as scholars, like Edward Piekarski, author of the first major Yakut language dictionary. The pioneering works of Bronisław Piłsudski described the language and culture of the Ainu, Gilyaks and the Goldi.

Siberia as an attractive area of research tempted a number of other Polish scholars, who of their own free will, and not as exiles, undertook numerous expeditions. These included Tomasz Augustynowicz, physician and naturalist; Bronisław Grąbczewski, geographer; Leon Barszczewski, explorer of the regions of Samarkand and Bukhara; Karol Bohdanowicz, a geographer and geologist who managed to explore almost the entire region of Siberia to the Pacific Ocean, and gained fame through his discoveries of numerous mineral resources in Southern Manchuria, in the Arctic Sea region, in the Khabarovsk Kray, on the Okhotsk Sea, and on the shores of Lake Baikal. Large-scale geological research was also carried on by Leonard Jaczewski.

This varied scientific activity was extremely difficult and required great strength of character and sacrifice. The hard Siberian conditions posed a threat to life at almost every step. Jan Czerski died in 1892 on a boat in the Indigirka and Kolyma estuary, leaving his wife to lead the expedition; Leon Hryniewiecki explored the Chukchi territory until his death: already seriously ill, he was returning to the post of which he was in charge, but when he felt his end approaching, he ordered the expedition to leave him on the riverbank and died in solitude, in a tent erected in the taiga, in 1891.

This chronicle of the manifold activity of exiles, prisoners and refugees was also, like the war chronicles, a great school of national consciousness. In this school, it was taught that life was to be a sacrifice, toil, a mission. It was taught that the "cause" was the highest value of the human world. These were the ethics of daily heroism for the sake of the "cause," so often formulated by philosophers and writers, presented in literature and art, instilled deeply into the consciousness of society, as a category for evaluating people and their activity. It was not opposed to the methods of armed struggle, but accepted it when necessary; it was oposed to a program of getting on in life, and making money, and to bourgeois virtues and to conformism of all kinds. Because of these ethics, it pronounced an austere verdict on the world which lived comfortably, in prosperity. For it gave expression to people who were "alien" in this world, people who, through perseverance, opposed its order and security, and contested the principles on which it was based.

PROBLEMS OF A "SECOND" HOMELAND

During the period of bondage, Poles wandered not only along roads leading to war and revolutions but also into exile. The plight of the émigrés was common to many thousands of patriots who had taken abroad with them the Polish tragedy, and also the Polish readiness to act under new, alien conditions. The geographical range and numerical strength of this compulsory movement was enormous: when Polish soil under foreign rule became too small or too dangerous for its own sons, the entire world opened up for the Poles. Thousands found a second homeland in North and South America, in Asia and Africa, sometimes even among the inhabitants of Siberia. Hundreds of Poles registered their names in the chronicles of scientific exploration and observations, in the history of the economic and social development of remote continents and foreign nations.

These diverse tasks manifested not only the will to secure for individuals a future and the desire to observe in a detached manner the new and alien reality of nature and society; but the background to the work organized by these exiles also led to particularly strong links of sympathy with the common people of foreign countries and a profound commitment to their affairs. Józef Kowalewski, condemned at the Philomates' trial to exile in Siberia, made such close contacts with the aborigines, Buryats and Tungus, that they called him "the living Buddha"; in his diary he described the close bonds which linked him with them: "Everywhere I have found equal and incessant favor . . . I share a piece of bread, a leg of lamb, a bowl of tea." Paweł E. Strzelecki, wandering through Brazil, wrote the following about the white colonists: "My hand cannot hold a pen; I hide my face from shame and dismay thinking of the calamities generated by the deeds of my fellow-creatures." In exploring Central Africa, Stefan Szolc-Rogoziński expressed similar views about "that civilization which was given to the black communities by Europe," and believed that their own civilization is of "much greater merit and offers unconditionally more hope." He also believed that "under the scepter of real light, the spiritual differences between the races will vanish in the remote dusk, together with other prejudices."

In the biographies of those engineers, technicians and scholars, the same pattern of events nearly always appeared: participation in patriotic actions at home; imprisonment and exile, or voluntary emigration; the finding of a "second homeland" — sometimes under the most difficult conditions of banishment; success in their new work, often beyond all expectations for an alien.

The life of Ignacy Domeyko exemplifies the vicissitudes of the exile. He was an active participant in the Philomates' group; jailed with the others; sentenced to exile in the 194 depths of Russia; after six years, he returned home, took part in the November Insurrection; as an émigré in Paris, he was a close friend of Mickiewicz and cooperated with him in much of his organizational work, at the same time studying at the Mining College, where in 1837 he was awarded an engineering degree. A year later, he left for Chile, taking up the post of professor of chemistry and organizing a Department of Mining. In this capacity Domeyko produced excellent results; in the course of a few years, he created a new educational system in Chile. For a dozen years he was rector of the Santiago University. He caried out a geological survey of almost all of the Cordillera. In his scientific work, he displayed the Polish sensitivity to social and national injustice. In his book, *Araucania and Its Dwellers,* published in Spanish in 1845 and well-known throughout the world in English, French and German translations, he undertook the defense of an oppressed tribe of aborigines, the Araucanians. When, after forty-six years, he left Chile to return home, the farewells were unusually ceremonious and warm. He wrote in his diary that one of the speakers asked him to return to the "second homeland that he had conquered with his heart."

Domeyko's Chilean accomplishments were equalled by the fame of Ernest Malinowski in Peru. A participant in the November Insurrection, he was an émigré in Paris, and later went to Peru. In 1866 he organized the fight against the Spanish invasion, winning the sympathy of Peruvian society. His greatest work was a railroad which crossed the Andes through a pass 4,769 meters above sea level. At that time such an enterprise required unusual boldness, and technological expertise. Many Poles worked with Malinowski, especially a number of exiles who had left Poland following the 1863 Insurrection. The organizational and technical talent of Władysław Kluger, the engineer of huge canals, roads and railways running through high mountain passes, was also widely acclaimed in Peru.

Bronisław Rymkiewicz, a participant in the January Insurrection, the engineer of railroads and ports, worked in a similar field in Brazil, as did Józef Siemiradzki, who was acknowledged as one of the most outstanding geologists of that country.

Many Poles found a second home in North America, in Canada and the United States.

Feliks P. Wierzbicki, after the failure of the November Insurrection, emigrated to America where he worked as a physician at the same time preparing the first monograph on California, which pointed to the prospects for development of this region. At the same time, Aleksander Edward Kierzkowski and Kazimierz Stanisław Gzowski distinguished themselves in Canada.

Kazimierz Gzowski, a participant in the November Insurrection, arrived in Canada and started a career as an engineer. He built ports, bridges and railroads. His greatest achievement was the construction of the great bridge over the Niagara in 1873. The breadth of his vision can be judged by the fact that he organized a great national park in this region, one of the first such ventures in the world.

In the United States, Ralph Modjeski, son of the great actress, became one of the century's most distinguished bridge designers, creator of many innovative methods in this field. His suspension bridge on the Delaware River, over 3 km in length, has remained to this day a magnificent technical achievement.

A number of Poles found their "second home" in Switzerland. Among the first was Joachim Lelewel's brother, Jan Paweł, an engineer, creator of grand scale improvement schemes for the canton of Bern; later they included other Poles, among them, Gabriel Narutowicz.

Exile trails also led to the Middle East, especially to Turkey where a number of Poles settled, especially those associated with the activity of Bem, Czajkowski (Sadyk Pasha) and Mickiewicz. One of the émigrés, a soldier in the November and Hungarian uprisings, Franciszek Sokulski, settled in Istanbul and built the first telegraph lines in Turkey; many Poles worked with him. A considerable number of exiles arrived after the failure of the January Insurrection in 1864. They built bridges, roads, factories and foundries.

Many Poles found favorable conditions for work in Russia and some of them remained in that country to the end of their lives. Stanisław Kierbedź, creator of the great bridge on the River Neva in St. Petersburg, and in other cities in Russia, distinguished himself as a result of his technical skills; as did Stefan Drzewiecki, who constructed submarines; Feliks Jasiński, builder of many bridges and railroads; as well as many scholars, particularly specialists in linguistics, headed by Jan Baudouin de Courtenay; and also the outstanding theoretical lawyer, Leon Petrażycki; and the classical historian, Tadeusz Zieliński.

To this list of outstanding people working abroad should be added the hundreds of thousands of emigrants, who at the end of the nineteenth century were going in "search of bread" to the West, as far away as the United States and Brazil. They formed the "Polish emigration," a coherent national community in the midst of an alien world and in their participation in the world, always preserved a feeling of national allegiance.

The entire, rich and diversified chronicle of Polish life in the world was a school of national consciousness. Its significance was, however, less than was that of the other two elements. The scientific, technological, and economic activity of the Poles in the world gave proof of the merits of the national character, but fairly often seemed like "treason", a shirking of national duties, or, sometimes, even a renunciation of national identity.

Under these conditions an agonizing question emerged: to what degree should a Pole, living and working abroad, remain a Pole, and to what degree was he allowed to belong to that "second homeland"? A great moral issue: let us call it a problem of the emigration of talents, which made it possible to understand nationality as something more profound than merly living and working in one's homeland, more than merely conducting revolutionary activity in a foreign land on behalf of Poland, more profound even than the language used to express one's thoughts and emotions.

Conclusions

What was the contribution of this long period of bondage to the history of Polish culture? After weighing in the balance political failures and successes, the final verdict pronounced by severe critics is negative. The restoration of independence in 1918 was due only in a small measure to Polish diplomacy and Polish arms. Polish uprisings, beginning with the Kosciuszko Insurrection, ended in failure. The chain of these failures did not make the Polish situation easier during World War I nor during the Versailles Conference when the new map of Europe was being drawn up. A century of efforts and plans by Polish diplomats both in emigration and at home — for Poles were sometimes ministers in the governments of the partitioning powers — led to nothing. No basis developed for diplomatic action, which at the end of the war had to be begun anew. The thousands of victims, shot and hanged, who died in prisons and in exile, proved of no avail. Even without that great martyrdom, the nation would have had its independence restored after World War I as a result of the new political situation, particularly of the Russian Revolution, the fall of the Habsburg monarchy, and the German defeat. This gift of freedom was bestowed on other nations, too, without having to pay for it with such sacrifice in the course of more than a century.

And yet such a view is unjust. Through the combined efforts of all segments of society, the nation was saved from the threat of annihilation during the period of bondage. Even if the restoration of independence in 1918 was not the direct consequence of Polish armed action but the singular gift of fortuitous political events, this gift was possible because a nation existed to accept it, demanding its own state and capable of organizing that state, a nation known all over Europe for it culture and patriotism.

That Polish society won the great and difficult battle for the salvation of a nation which had been divided among three foreign and hostile state organisms, not only constituted a fact of fundamental significance on the international arena, but, at the same time, formed the basic experience of Poland during that period. It proved that the national link was stronger than were class conflicts; although Poland was often a wicked stepmother to them, peasants and workmen proved more faithful to her than did some members of the aristocracy and the bourgeoisie. It was proved that the national bond provided the force which held the Polish community together over the frontiers of the three partition zones, and that it might grow among the populations which had been separated from the Commonwealth even before the partitions: in Silesia, Pomerania, Warmia and Mazuria. It proved that the struggle for national identity could be waged and won, in spite of the state mechanism of power and oppression, thanks to spontaneous and well-organized social action.

To treat the period of bondage merely in terms of saving the nation from the dangers which threatened it would be to underestimate its significance in the development of Polish culture. That age witnessed the deep process of remodeling the nation. The nation on whose lands World War I was waged was different from the one whose territory was partitioned at the end of the eighteenth century. And because of this, victory in the struggle for national deliverance was possible.

Poland, on entering the period of bondage, was a feudal country; the peasant masses remained within the bonds of serfdom; burghers were only beginning to demand their rights as citizens; the gentry, the only estate which possessed all privileges, together with the magnates who were formally on an equal footing with the gentry, remained the main factor in political life and in the conflicting programs of activity. On the threshold of independence Poland was a modern bourgeois society; all estate privileges were gone, although social inequality remained; the political consciousness of the peasantry was awakened; proletarian class consciousness had emerged; a distinct Polish intelligentsia had begun to develop; a group of wealthy bourgeoisie had taken shape among the urban population, and although partially of foreign descent, played a vital part in the economic development of the country; old aristocratic families retained their social and cultural prestige but lost their political significance; "new" people became leaders of the country — even if they were of gentry origin, nobody really cared: for example, Roman Dmowski, Ignacy Paderewski, Ignacy Daszyński, Józef Piłsudski and Wincenty Witos.

Concurrently, Poland changed from an exclusively agrarian country into a country with an agricultural and industrial economy. Large industrial centers emerged; the structure of employment changed radically; workers and engineers, formerly unknown in Poland, became dominant categories. For the first time the difference between the mentality of city dwellers and industrial employees, and that of the peasant population became distinct. A new model of life appeared, shaped according to the demands of modern work, based on good training, disciplined by the demands of the economy. Capitalist institutions such as banks and exchanges became, for the wealthy part of society, understandable and acceptable institutions, although earlier they had been neglected and denigrated.

Within these social and economic processes a modern nation was being shaped. Earlier, Staszic had to argue that the gentry was not the entire nation, but only one of its estates; he advocated forming one nation, but only from among the gentry and bourgeois youth. In the nineteenth century the common people were becoming a part of the nation, although the process was progressing slowly and at a different rate in the various partition zones. In the mid-nineteenth century literature and political programs anticipated this integration which was completed only at the turn of the century. Increasingly sharp conflicts were one more proof of the modernization of Poland according to the patterns of the capitalist societies of the era, and as elsewhere, were dialectically linked to the still increasingly widespread consciousness of the nation as a historically shaped unity.

Conscious cultural and educational action was aimed at strengthening the process. When the Commission for 196

National Education turned its attention to the instruction of the people, this attention remained within the framework of the feudal structure, which was to be reformed in the spirit of humanitarianism and according to the rules of physiocratic economics. The nineteenth century created the modern understanding of mass culture and universal education, despite the fact that schools remained in the hands of the partitioning powers, and existing technical means were limited. Education was to be the common language of national reconciliation and, at the same time, a personal asset of each citizen. These objectives guided those who had built the foundation for education, as well as those who led the action on higher levels of instruction. The limited possibilities of institutionalized activity made it imperative to look for other methods in educational work. Voluntary civic service in the field of education was created; self-teaching was organized at all levels, including the highest ones.

This activity was possible due to the development of the Polish language in the areas of literature and science. The Polish language had earlier witnessed periods of great progress, but only in the nineteenth century was it molded into a fully universal and modern language. The poetic language of the Romantics and Modernists became a language of expression, understandable and touching even to this day. Polish prose, shaped during the positivist era, has preserved its clear and suggestive idiom. A scientific and popular scientific language which we still use today also developed during this period. The shaping of the native language as a national language also made possible the growth and revival of the vernacular in Silesia, Kashubia, Podhale and in central Poland. Regional diversification became possible due to national integration, safeguarded by the national language.

A peculiar characteristic of the period of bondage was that this great process of emergence and development of a modern nation was effected without benefit of its own state, in an uninterrupted struggle against foreign governments in three divided partition zones. This was an unusual and amazing fact. Although no Polish central authority existed, a unity of national action throughout the partition zones emerged, which — stronger or weaker, implemented differently during different periods and areas of life — never completely subsided. And even if the rhythm of these changes followed different patterns in different partition zones and even if the differences between the Kingdom of Poland, Galicia or the Poznań region were sometimes great, the outcome of these processes appeared similar and, in the final analysis, converged in a coherent, common entity.

In this way common or analogous institutions and forms of public life evolved. They constituted as it were ready-made elements or organizational blocs, which at the time of the restoration of independence were at once included in the reconstructed state.

In this sense, the spiritual life of the nation — science, art and education — was quite mature and adequately prepared for national independence. During the period of bondage a number of basic institutions relating to scientific life were formed: Learned Societies in all partition zones; the Academy of Learning in Cracow; libraries and foundations; organization of group research work; universities and polytechnics; international contacts between scholars; scientific periodicals and bibliographical services, etc. Similarly, art was gaining a permanent base for development and social influence: museums emerged; a system of exhibitions and artistic salons was established; numerous artistic associations were founded, as well as societies of lovers of the fine arts, an art press, publications, and reproductions, etc. Theater became particularly significant in all the partition zones, even in the smaller cities: demanding and sensitive theater audiences grew up, the performance and promotion of music were expanded through the setting up of philharmonic orchestras and conservatoires; systematic listening to music and, to a certain extent, amateur performance of music, developed. In educational and instructional work, forms and methods of action were established, and the theory worked out; Polish education came about as a result of the period of bondage, as well as did implementing methods of education for adults.

The political life of the country was also ready for independence. During the period of servitude the main currents of political thought, as well as political parties, were shaped. The process of political ripening was unusual if we consider that only in Galicia and, what is more, only from the second half of the nineteenth century was it possible legally to organize political parties; in other partition zones it was much more difficult and political life always had to exist on two levels: legal and illegal. And yet, political awareness and political culture were developing in the community so intensely that the state which emerged in 1918 almost immediately achieved the political character typical of the bourgeois states of the epoch.

In the process of shaping political culture, under conditions of stateless existence, the ability to plan far ahead became a significant factor. In reality, the Polish state did not exist, but it existed as a future vision, which was worked out with minute precision and which was fiercely disputed. Political culture was only partly shaped by real circumstances or by political battles actually waged; in part, it was an outcome of reflections and projects, spiritual visions, and ideal models treated with great seriousness as if they actually existed. Since the testing of ideas through political practice was impossible, there was a danger of utopian or doctrinaire solutions, but this never negatively influenced the spontaneity of political discussions or the intensity of political involvement.

Under these abnormal political conditions, writers wielded a greater influence over the nation's consciousness than did political leaders. Prus maintained that "for us, poets replace politicians, philosophers, teachers, and even economists." It was true. Indeed, during no other period in Polish culture did art, even when closely linked to the political life of the country, have such significance as was achieved during the period of bondage, especially during the romantic period, and the positivist and modernist periods.

During the period of bondage, art became a main factor in shaping the national imagination and national consciousness. Romantic poetry played a major role here, and the cult of "the three bards" (Mickiewicz, Słowacki, and Krasiński) resulted not only from artistic experience, but also, and above all, from the conviction that their political visions were right. Wincenty Pol and Seweryn Goszczyński in the 1840's demanded that painting also assume tasks in the field of national education; in the second half of the century that request was fulfilled: paintings by Grottger, Matejko and Malczewski enhanced the national imagination with tales of dramatic contemporary events and of the great past and helped to produce and preserve national myths and allegories of patriotic life. Music, accompanying poetry, expressed the deepest emotions of the wronged nation from the song *O God, Who Hath Protected Poland* to the chorale *With the Smoke of the Fires* and *We Must Never Desert the Land of Our Forefathers.* The music of Chopin, particularly in the second half of the century, and of Moniuszko, were a manifestation of the Polish spirit, the Polish historical and popular traditions, the Polish way of life.

But simultaneously the period of bondage engendered in wide circles of the community a personal need to experience art. Political conditions, which limited the possibility of public life, contributed to the fact that family life and circles of friends, where hostile hands could not reach, were becoming centers of artistic experience. In thousands of Polish homes Chopin's polonaises and mazurkas, and Moniuszko's songs, were welcome daily guests; poetry was read and copied in private, intimate anthologies, prepared for personal use and according to personal tastes, and was also recited among friends and acquaintances, in keeping with the Philomates' traditions. Under these conditions habits of personal contacts with music and poetry were established and became one of the sources of the sensitivity of Polish society toward art, significant to the present day.

In this way Polish art during the period of bondage, in cooperation with socio-political strivings and with philosophical reflections regarding the plight of the nation and the destiny of the people, was becoming a national and personal value, a national and human philosophy of the world and of man. It was becoming a textbook of life. It was Polish art which provided the principal concepts of the life patterns that were taking shape: very characteristic, sometimes very Polish ones — the strength of these models has endured until today.

Previous ages produced chivalrous forms of patriotism, but the nineteenth century emphasized the patriotism of a nation in bonds, the patriotism of conspiracies and plots, the patriotism of an uneven struggle, the patriotism of defeat and death, and also the patriotism which resorted to treason and vengeance in order to reach its goals. These were new kinds of patriotism; while the pseudo-classicists presented models of ancient unblemished Polish knighthood (Stefan Czarniecki was a favorite hero), Mickiewicz acknowledged the greatness and efficacy of Konrad Wallenrod's treason, and Żeromski was fascinated by the heroic death of Żółkiewski at Cecora. A different model of life, stubbornly grafted onto the Polish consciousness, was based on work. Other periods could boast of achievement in this field, but they were limited to agrarian work, understood mostly as a noblemen's profession — and thus, one of overseers rather than producers — and of the work of craftsmen. In the nineteenth century the notion of work was extended; and attention was turned to work connected with technological progress and industrial development, which, after all, created the wealth of a modern nation. This work demanded instruction and discipline; new people had to be educated — persistent, systematic and enterprising. And lastly, the model of civic service had to be formed. There was no counterpart in old Poland, and it was very characteristic of the period of bondage. Civic service was understood in diverse ways: from self-denying educational activity to total involvement in the cause of social progress, through both legal and illegal activity; from absolutely voluntary social service, sometimes even heroic sacrifice, to service which was perhaps irrational and unnecessary. Prolonged discussion about the decision of Doctor Judym, the main character in *Homeless People,* was proof of the topicality of this issue.

INDEPENDENT POLAND

Introduction

In November 1918 Poland regained her independence. Thus an era of reconstruction began which lasted until September 1939. Hitler's invasion again deprived the country of its liberty. The occupation period repeated in a condensed form all that Poland had previously experienced under foreign rule: efforts to destroy the nation totally, everyday persecutions, prisons and concentration camps — and heroic resistance. Again, as of old, the liberation movement organized an underground structure to save the national culture and to create, in advance, a socio-political vision of the country's future, as well as a large-scale mobilization for the armed struggle. Again, as in former times, the forests turned into battlefields for a war against a powerful foe; and again, as before, the Polish Army fought on far-off fronts to come at last triumphantly back from foreign soil to its native country. And still another Polish uprising, as always heroic and tragic, defiant to its final defeat.

Victory over Nazism in 1944–45 brought liberty back to Poland, and opened a period of great reconstruction: of the social structure, of the national economy, of the administrative system, of education and culture, as well as of the ideals and attitudes of her citizens. This restructuring aimed at a new Poland, in sharp contrast to the Poland which had existed during the previous period of reconstruction between the wars.

Never before in Polish history was the immediately preceding link of its past as bitterly fought over as during the post-war era, the goal of which was a decisive severance of all ties with the pre-war period; and yet the whole course of national development never appeared as so coherent and consistent a continuum as during those controversial years. It confirmed the well-known truth that each national revolution is shaped according to the conditions and demands of the nation's history. The great social upheaval which took place in Poland in the wake of World War II, was both international and national in nature. Its course was set by the conflicts existing in the country, as well as by accumulated achievements — in material reality, in opinions, and in attitudes. For that reason the changes effected in People's Poland threw new light on the whole of Polish culture, especially on the two decades between the wars; and knowledge of that culture could explain much of the style and nature of the changes.

And although the leading ideas during these two epochs of revival and reconstruction of the state were different, both periods were closely connected not only by historical reality, but also by people. For it was the people from pre-war times who were building a new Poland after World War II, either by continuing along their old path of life or by abandoning their former ideologies for new ones, an alternative obviously more suited to the situation and the needs of the nation.

That period, full of inner contradictions and yet so coherent, is not yet closed. A clear date marks the beginning; the future completion date remains open. Each step along that way discloses a new face of People's Poland, allowing by the same token, a novel view of the past. The current and prospective socio-material reality are changing; the methods of evaluating the past and the choosing of a live tradition are also changing. The great historic process, that of shaping a socialist nation, a community of new human beings, is continuing. The eternal Poland grows richer, thanks to contemporary historical Poland; and the Poland of today and tomorrow draws on the values of the "eternal" Poland, accumulated through the nation's work during the past centuries.

The fact that this era of reconstruction and remodeling exists as a contemporary and future reality makes it even more necessary than in the previous periods of cultural history, to consider it carefully against the background of the developing tendencies, intentions and aspirations. The presentation of this period must above all reveal the inner forces which play a decisive part in its development; events and achievements belonging to a chronicle of passing culture are important only as manifestations of the forces that last and grow.

Poland Between the Wars

PLACE IN EUROPE
AND HISTORICAL CONSCIOUSNESS

The close of World War I brought liberty to a destroyed and ruined Poland. Demoralized units of the armies of the Central Powers were flowing through its as yet undefined territory; a destitute Polish population, on its way home from Germany and Russia, was pouring in, seeking a roof over its head and means of subsistence. Railway transportation was completely disorganized and devastated. Agriculture, destroyed in military operations and exploitation by the armies of the occupying powers, was unable to produce enough food; only half of the arable land of the country's huge territory was under cultivation and production per hectare was far below its pre-war level. Particularly catastrophic were the consequences of the loss in the number of horses, sequestrated through all the war years by the armies, because horses were the chief source of power in farming. In some regions one horse had to work two hundred acres of soil; and, often, plows were drawn by human beings.

Industry was almost completely destroyed. Steel and iron plants had ceased to exist; the textile industry was unable to renew production. Sugar production on the territory of former Congress Poland amounted to only a small percentage of its pre-war level. Coal-mines, on the verge of collapse, were working, but had been terribly exploited. The decline in employment — only 14 percent of the pre-war labor force could find work — was accompanied by a steady decrease of wages. As a result of the rising cost of living and of progressive devaluation, wages amounted to a mere 12 percent of their pre-war value. Housing conditions had badly deteriorated.

The population was severely undernourished; in the country bread was baked from heather flowers mixed with bark and chaff, with a little real flour added. Tuberculosis was becoming a national catastrophe; the death rate caused by this disease rose sixfold as compared with the pre-war level. There was a shortage of physicians, hospitals, medicines, dressings and disinfectants.

The state administration, in the process of organization, tried slowly and with great effort to overcome regional antagonisms. An effort to stabilize the currency (at least four different kinds of money were in circulation) was hindered not only by economic factors, but simply because there was neither a state mint, nor a printing press capable of issuing a national currency.

Under these very difficult conditions national feelings were intensified by the realization of the greatness and importance of the historic events through which Poland was regaining her independence. Above material and organizational difficulties towered an idealized vision of Poland as a generally unifying force, which would shape a strategy of further actions.

The idea of national independence and of a free national life stood foremost in everyone's mind. All that had been denied by foreign rulers was now becoming accessible to everyone: literature and theater, national celebrations, anniversaries and holidays. The white eagle became an emblem of the day, with white and red flags flying almost constantly. It was an unending everyday chain of festivities; the 1863 veterans in their dark blue uniforms were honored by children and young people.

Under these difficult and solemn conditions, processes of national integration were going on. Boundaries between former parts of the divided country — still missing from the map of Europe — were supposed to disappear with the nation's political existence, above all from the minds of its citizens.

Contradictions were being slowly overcome; the patriotic integration of the nation within its new frontiers was being slowly structured.

In mid-1919 the Treaty of Versailles delineated Poland's western boundary. The Poznań district was incorporated into Poland, together with Pomerania; and a solemn "reunion with the sea" gave Poland a strip of the Baltic shore, unfortunately very small, and without the city of Gdańsk. Henceforth, the integration of the Kashubian population was to become a serious task.

The Versailles decisions, however, did not satisfy the Polish community. The Silesian population rose against German rule. In that worker-dominated region, patriotic and social reasons went together, and the fight with German industrialists was aimed both at a new social order and national independence. Mass development of workers' councils on the Soviet model formed the main basis for revolutionary and liberating activity. German counteraction was twofold: on the one hand, it was a defense of the capitalist order in that region; on the other, a defense of the German *status quo*. Under these conditions armed conflicts broke out repeatedly, and by the middle of 1919 reached such proportions that they turned into a widespread uprising.

In August 1920 the Second Silesian Uprising, which was basically Polish self-defense movement, broke out and succeeded in removing the German police force from the region. Less than a year later, when the plebiscite to decide the future of the territory failed to bring about the anticipated results, the third and largest Silesian Uprising broke out to forestall the pending unfavorable decisions of the Allies. It started in the wake of a big wave of strikes on the morning of 3 May 1921, and soon embraced the whole region of Silesia, with some 60,000 armed men, backed by large numbers of the civilian population. It was a great national liberation movement in which for the first time volunteers from other Polish regions took part, manifesting by their presence on the battlefields the unanimous patriotic and social aspirations of the nation.

This Third Silesian Uprising, which lasted for almost two months, achieved not only military aims, preventing the Germans from annexing Silesia to their territory, nor merely diplomatic success, as a remarkable armed demonstration of strength on the international scene, but proved to be a manifestation — unexpected by many observers and enthusiastically welcomed by patriotic circles — of the lasting allegiance of the Silesian people to Poland and of its conscious working class identity.

A different and less favorable turn of events for Poland occurred in Warmia and Mazuria. These regions, under the name of East Prussia, remained within the boundaries of the Third Reich.

The issue of Poland's boundary in the East was an open one, remaining an exceptionally difficult problem since all decisions, political as well as military, stemmed from the basic view of the national identity created through the ages of Polish history. History had handed down the Piast idea, with its general westward direction, and the Jagiellonian idea, consisting of a great program of union and conquest in the East. To which part of this ideological heritage was the emerging Poland to remain true?

Polish society was influenced by the traditional concept of the Polish mission in Eastern Europe. Few people were ready to accept the eventual loss of Vilna and Lvov, cities which throughout centuries, and especially during the partition period, had remained centers of Polish culture. However, the incorporation of these cities, surrounded as they were by ethnically alien lands, was bound to open prospects, perhaps even the necessity, of a systematic, large scale political and military expansion in the East.

Józef Pilsudski, the Head of State, manipulated these hostile attitudes of the community to the proposed boundary along the river Bug, which followed the line dividing Polish from Byelorussian and Ukrainian ethnic territory, and would, in turn, imply the loss of Lvov and Vilna. Instead, he supported a vision of the Republic as a state embracing the Crown territories and Lithuania and also Ruthenia, that is the great territories in the East, extending as far as the rivers Dvina and Dnieper.

Such was the political aim of the war with the Soviet Union which, after the spectacular seizure of Kiev, brought immediate danger to Warsaw in the year 1920, and which finally ended with a compromise peace treaty at Riga in 1921, leaving the western parts of Byelorussia and the

Ukraine to Poland. Vilna was seized during a separate armed operation.

To many Poles such a boundary, although not satisfying the "great power" aspirations deeply rooted in the traditional eastbound expansion, remained to a certain degree true to that tradition. On independence, Poland seemed to have effected at least a partial realization of the vision of a multinational Republic, governing large territories in order to fulfill its "civilizing mission".

Radical circles took a stance against this traditional trend and determined to effect a fundamental remolding of the national mind in regard to Poland's place in the world and the understanding of her historic role. It was, above all, the question of her relationship to Russia, which ceased to be the czarist empire and became the first socialist revolutionary state in the world.

The change was not easy to achieve; equally difficult problems were emerging in domestic politics. Poland, having regained an independent existence, was within her new boundaries a multinational state. This created sharp political conflicts. For this reason, from the very first days of independence, the nation's patriotic integration involved more difficult and more dramatic efforts than did the task of practical unification of its various parts. The problem was the fact that regions populated by Ukrainians and Byelorussians fell within the new borders.

Almost from the first days of independence the attitudes of those politicians who tried to find inspiration in conservative and nationalist traditions (represented by such writers as Zygmunt Balicki or Ludwik Szczepański) diverged sharply from those of the radical leaders, who with deeper insight looked into the democratic tradition of the Great Emigration and the revolutionary hopes of Ludwik Waryński. The idea of a free nation was closely interwoven with that of freedom for other neighboring nations, and was in its deepest sense rooted in a program of social justice, of the liberation of the working masses — the workers and the peasants — and in the concepts of equality and brotherhood for all. National integration had, therefore, an altogether different meaning for them than for nationalist circles.

Comprehensive studies in Polish history written by contemporary historians represented the nationalist point of view and emphasized in particular the advantages of the eastern policy conducted by the old "Commonwealth of the Gentry". Ludwik Kolankowski, Oskar Halecki, and Henryk Paszkiewicz praised Jagiellonian Poland, outlined the history of the Grand Duchy of Lithuania, and analyzed the Polish-Lithuanian union. Politicians were anxious to take these historic issues as a motivation for diverse programs of action, varying from irresponsible concepts of creating a great federation of nations torn off from Russia and in some way united with Poland, through projects for the denationalization and assimilation of all minorities inhabiting Poland.

Polish nationalism sought to create a state for the Poles, and to make of all other sectors of the population second-class citizens.

It is true that their chauvinist program was never carried out; from time to time, however, right-wing elements would exert very strong pressure on the official policy of the government. A discriminatory policy was in operation especially in the eastern part of Poland, a policy which did not shrink even from shedding blood during pacification operations in certain regions.

These actions gave rise to protests in progressive circles.

The Declaration of Rights of the Young Generation in Poland, published by democratic youth organizations in 1936, demanded full equality for all nationalities living on Polish soil: "Brought up in the tradition of the struggle for liberation of our, as well as of other, nations and remembering 150 years of foreign rule, we consider it necessary to bestow the right of specific national culture and autonomy on all nations which inhabit the territory of Poland, because no nation which subjugates other nations can be free."

Thus, during the entire twenty year period the national consciousness was oppressed by feelings of doubt and uncertainty regarding the right direction of the chosen or imposed path of history. Whereas some were of the opinion that the Polish nation betrayed its highest ideals by neglecting its great civilizing mission in the East, others took to listing all the sins of nationalist policies in regard to neighboring nations. And whereas the progressive and radical camp formulated their program with the purpose of making Poland a home of liberty and justice for all citizens, the nationalist bloc continued to acquire new strength, aiming to transform Poland into a "great power" which would subordinate other nations and perhaps even reach out for new acquisitions.

This conflict in the national consciousness remained unsolved until the collapse of the state in 1939. The vision of the commonwealth of the landowning knights, of the gentry, a country extending from sea to sea, dominated the imagination of the upper classes, although the vision of a new Poland, enclosed in her national boundaries and arranging relations with her neighbors on a new basis, continued to gain followers among the ever-widening circles of progressive intelligentsia.

SOCIAL CONFLICTS AND NATIONAL GOALS

The process of regaining independence was not limited to the delineation of state boundaries only, since it was primarily the process of the reconstruction of a ruined country and its state organization.

The social consciousness of the era was a battlefield for two forces: an understanding that economic development was of foremost importance to the nation, and the conviction that economic progress would act for the benefit of the propertied classes.

This ambiguity of thought could be discerned from the very beginning of the state's existence and resulted in controversies between a basically uniform educational program aimed, among other things, at raising the level of the economy, and a program of education for a revolutionary social struggle.

Even under these conditions, however, new and valuable elements entered the national consciousness. For although economic activity was fundamentally considered as a source of individual gain, there were some signs of recognition that the economy was an omni-national problem. The construction of the port in Gdynia, which reopened a Polish way to the sea, shut off by the hostile policy of the Free City of Gdańsk, was generally recognized as a great national cause. Similar in nature was the reaction of the entire society to the construction of the Central Industrial Region in the fork of the Rivers Vistula and San. Here economic ambitions were closely connected with strategic motivations, which made the whole project all the more important to the nation. Evidence of the new elements emerging in the social mind was highlighted at the Universal National Exhibition organized in Poznań in 1929. The enthusiasm that its opening aroused was, on the one hand, a sign that the "Polish economic ineptitude" complex was being gradually eradicated and, on the other hand, an expression of hope that the young Polish state could and would act sensibly in the economic field.

Unfortunately, the reality of the national economic life did not confirm this hope. The economic indices for the inter-war period indicate that no spectacular progress was noted in the national economy as a whole.

Economic development fostered by the capitalist system tended to aggravate social conflicts. These stemmed from long-term, profound processes, in which the peasantry, the most populous class of society, resented more and more bitterly the rule of the landowners, and the working class, although weak and small, started their own conscious fight against capitalist exploitation. These conflicts not only did not show any sign of abating but, on the contrary, became the main areas of internal strife, which ripped asunder Poland.

From then on the contradiction between the revolutionary way of social upheaval, and the parliamentary tactics of building a bourgeois democratic state undertaking social reform, became the basic social controversy.

From the very first years of independence literature took an active part in the ideological struggle for the new shape of Poland. Stefan Żeromski, the most outstanding writer of the period, defended a democratic vision of Poland against attacks from the right, as well as against the program of the Polish communists. Marchlewski's polemics with Żeromski took on almost symbolic significance. Żeromski's vision of Poland, outlined in his political writings, was that of a home for the working masses which would make amends for all wrongs done throughout the ages to both peasants and workers. His vision of Poland as presented in his novel *Early Spring* was to be that of "glass houses."

But, on the other hand, in that same novel Żeromski declared himself against the revolutionary experience of the Soviet Union, and explained the Polish variation of the revolution in terms of cooperative and anarchist traditions.

This was the point of departure for Marchlewski's attack. Emphasizing Żeromski's sympathy with the "revolutionary robustness of the Polish worker and agricultural laborer," Marchlewski stated: "Not in the Tower of London, not in the Tuilleries, not in the Vienna Burg, but in the Kremlin of snow-white stone has the red banner flown for the first time, a symbol of liberation ... the sign of liberation not of the Russian proletariat only but of the proletariat in all countries; for there can be absolutely no doubt about it: the Russian revolution is a decisive factor in the history of mankind. A new era has begun with the Revolution, an era of socialism, an era of the liberation of the working masses, an era of a new culture."

Marchlewski's polemics with Żeromski developed from the socio-political program outlined by the Social Democratic Party of the Kingdom of Poland and Lithuania and the Left-Wing Polish Socialist Party. From their point of view Poland seemed increasingly often a country of oppression and proletarian poverty.

Aside from social conflicts a little later another conflict emerged slowly round the controversy between Piłsudski and his followers on the one hand and the remaining political groups, and to a certain degree, the rest of the community on the other. As the years passed, the direction of these attacks changed. Piłsudski began his rule in Poland as a representative of the left wing, and from almost his first days in office opposed everything really radical on the left. Despite this, the coup of May 1926 was accepted by the left-wing element as signifying at least some sign of social hope. The following years dispelled these illusions, notwithstanding the fact that Piłsudski's government proved as hostile to the right-wing parties as to the socialist and agrarian parties.

The coup carried out by Piłsudski represented an attempt to introduce into Polish political life new principles of state and government organization contrary to the former experience of bourgeois parliamentary democracy.

The widely publicized "state" education was to teach young people, as well as public opinion that the interest of the state should be treated as superior to that of the individual and to the "narrow" interests of the particular nationalities inhabiting the territory of Poland.

Piłsudski defined these *raisons d'état* many times in terms of the tradition of the gentry and the knights, and of the conservative brand of romanticism.

The chief ideologist of national education in the spirit of "service to the state" was Adam Skwarczyński. Brought up in the atmosphere of the socialist movement in Galicia and for years a contributor to the periodical *Przedświt*, thanks to his university studies he was associated with the ideological heritage of the Democratic Society, first and foremost with Stanisław Worcell, and also with the romantic concepts of the nation and labor which found expression in the writings of Stanisław Brzozowski. Skwarczyński, a blind follower of Piłsudski, was guided by the idea of "the socialization of the state" which was to be accompanied by the transformation of the "people of serfdom" into the "people of independence."

Drawing on the romantic tradition, he dreamed of a "new knighthood" which would drop from its vocabulary the words "we protest" and "we want", substituting for them the words "we aspire" and "we work", and in place of the word "interest" would introduce the word "service". He did not stop short of preaching an ideal of "austerity in life and manners" as opposed to the "bourgeois ideal of well-being."

Reality, however, would not yield to his visions and inspirations. "State" education in the hands of an educational administration turned into a tool of political jockeying and verbal manifestations.

The ideology of "state" education never became anything more than superficially accepted and was constantly overtly attacked or sabotaged. It was opposed, of course, by the whole nationalist camp for whom a "state" education for a Pole was synonymous with a "national" one. It was also opposed by the left-wing parties, though for completely different reasons. "State" education was meant to rally the entire community around the ruling camp and thus, in the eyes of public opinion, was an attempt at legitimizing the coup and aimed at consolidating anti-democratic methods of government.

The changes of the national attitude toward the state went much deeper. They appeared closely connected with the basic social processes which took place during the two decades, consisting mostly of the integration and unification of the social structure of the country, which had previously differed considerably in the three partition zones. At the same time they were directed toward the modernization of that generally traditional and backward structure, and toward its democratization. In this respect, the differences between the years 1918 and 1939 were significant and most remarkable.

The bourgeois society which emerged during the period was similar to that in other countries, with similar social stratification and typical class conflicts. The modernization of society owed very little to the conscious social policy of the government; of much greater significance were the socio-political aspirations of the oppressed classes. In actual fact, however, these processes proceeded spontaneously and inevitably, under the influence of such objective factors as a common market and a common state administration. They played a special role in crystallizing the social consciousness of the workers, peasants and intelligentsia. Whereas the landowner and bourgeois classes, already fairly well defined in the past, retained their traditional structure, the intelligentsia won new conditions for development in the newly emergent state, thanks to mass employment of its members in the civil service and education, that is, in fields where, during the era of partitions, they could only serve in inferior positions. Thus the intelligentsia, holding onto the prestige it had enjoyed under foreign rule as a group which created and nurtured intellectual and artistic values and thus concentrated in its hands the right to safeguard the Polish heritage, found new reasons for its privileges.

The intelligentsia was not a monolithic group. Because of its social background and of its functions, it was considerably diversified. Particularly sharp differences appeared between, on the one hand, the intelligentsia employed in industry and the civil service and, on the other hand, the creative intelligentsia and teaching personnel. The teachers, and primary school teachers in particular, formed a very numerous and strong group.

Differences notwithstanding, the group developed a feeling of community with the country as a whole, of participation in its history, and responsibility for its fate. Entering the period of war and occupation in 1939 Poland possessed twice the number of intelligentsia as compared with the period when Poland was regaining her independence, an intelligentsia characterized by a capability greater than ever before of thinking about national matters in real terms of the life of the state, especially in regard to areas of economic and educational activity.

Similar processes of growing self-awareness were going on within the worker and peasant sectors of society. Although industry developed slowly and remained mostly in the hands of foreign capital, and in spite of poverty and unemployment, a fairly fast process of integration of the working class was under way, particularly in regions with large concentrations of workers. In the course of this process proletarian class consciousness came to life and ripened, inspired and fired by the activity of the workers' parties and the trade unions. Particularly the city of Łódź and the Coal Basin appeared as centers of these processes which later spread to other regions. The struggle for improvement in living conditions and welfare achieved some success. Under the pressure of such demands, the administration was obliged to introduce a system of free medical care, provide certain forms of social insurance and make education, at least at the primary level, accessible to all. These successes gave the workers a feeling that their cause was just, and a concomitant awareness of strength which resulted in their victory. The situation also, however, brought increased awareness of the limited range of these successes, and opened prospects for a more fundamental fight, with targets reaching beyond the immediate improvement of living conditions and aiming at a revolutionary restructuring of the social system. This wide program of activity found growing expression in the numerous strikes and demonstrations of the workers, while, at the same time, economic stagnation and the increase in unemployment became mobilizing factors for the ever-widening labor circles to join in the struggle.

In this way the working class developed a sense of responsibility for the future of the whole nation. The two decades between the wars produced a similar integration among agricultural workers and the crystallization of the social identity of this class. Although this group was much diversified, consisting as it did of peasants with large and small holdings together with agricultural laborers and the poor landless population, and although it was politically organized in various parties, the struggle for an agrarian reform bill and its ensuing implementation, as well as a further fight to overcome stagnation in farming and to improve the unbelievably low standard of living, became integrating factors leading to common action. The fight acquired ever greater dimensions, culminating in the famous peasant demonstration at Nowosielce in 1936, and the big agrarian strike during the following year which opened a completely novel view on the coherence and social identity of this sector of the population. Its objectives were obviously defined as encompassing not only the improvement of living conditions but also as a

204

fundamental transformation of social relations in the country. The organization of their own educational system, independent of and even opposed to the state system, was characteristic proof that the peasants, like the workers, had ceased to be the exploited class fighting for the defense of their vital interests only, but had been transformed into a group fully aware of its national importance which, for the first time, tried to assume responsibility for the country's future.

The range of the changes occurring during the inter-war period within the workers and peasants groups may be properly evaluated in light of the events of the war and occupation. As early as September 1939 armed detachments of workers, commanded principally by political leaders whom the war had liberated from prisons, defended their native soil against Hitler's aggression. The Worker Brigade of the Defenders of Warsaw fought on the outskirts of the capital, whereas units of the Red Scythebearers, named after their predecessors of the Racławice tradition, took part in the defense of Gdynia. During the occupation, underground armies included many workers and peasants. The Peasant Battalions formed a separate military organization. At the same time, as a consequence of the aspirations and experiences of the working class, the Polish Workers' Party program emerged, a program to fight for a free People's Poland. Political organizations of the peasantry joined in the discussions regarding the future model of the state and its social reconstruction. Never before in Polish history did the peasants and workers so deeply and responsibly take part in considerations regarding the fate of the nation and the state, just as never before, from the times of Kosciuszko, had they so actively joined in the fight for the liberty and future of their country. And for the first time in her history, Poland, which had been a republic of the gentry and bourgeoisie, was to become People's Poland, the home of all her citizens, a dream envisioned by the best sons of the nation throughout the ages.

Because of the high level of maturity of the working masses, what the Lublin administration of 1918 failed to achieve during the few day of its rule, became a reality in Chełm and in Lublin, and later on in the whole country, in the years 1944 and 1945.

IDEOLOGICAL PLURALITY

The restoration of independence in 1918, important though it was in the reorientation of the socio-political programs, was not of great significance for general philosophy. Existing trends of thought continued to grow and develop, spreading in different degrees throughout the various sections and classes of society. They underwent, however, a significant process of modernization. New creative forces were born and began to operate.

This was characteristic especially of the Polish brand of Catholicism. Remaining a faith practiced mostly in Sunday church attendance and in liturgical rites by millions of citizens of the country, it began to acquire a new intellectual dimension among the élite of the period, a new intensity of experience, and new forms and methods of operation.

The Catholic University of Lublin, established in 1918, soon turned into a main national center for education not only for the higher clergy of the Church hierarchy but for the Catholic intelligentsia as well. The Renaissance association, founded in 1919, attracted young Catholics, mostly students from various colleges in the country. Compared to such former organizations as Iuventus Christiana, or Sodalitas Mariana, Renaissance adumbrated a wider program of activity with the objective of strengthening religious belief while taking into account contemporary issues and social and cultural tasks. At the same time the Jesuit *Przegląd Powszechny* published an editorial by Father J. Urban, inaugurating a serious discussion on the subject of a "Catholic intelligentsia", which according to the author was non-existent in Poland and should be developed.

This lively interest in philosophical subjects, so characteristic of the era, was amply manifested in books and periodicals. The philosophy of St. Thomas Aquinas attracted the attention both of the older generation, particularly the professors at the Department of Theology of the Jagiellonian University, and of the young Dominican scholars grouped in Lublin. Ever stronger ties were being established with Western centers of Catholic thought, particularly with Jacques Maritain who won a great number of readers in Poland as well as a following of intimate friends.

Even wider influence was wielded by studies in the life and doctrine of St. Francis of Assisi. That influence reached far beyond the strictly Catholic circles of the intelligentsia. An exquisite translation of the *Fioretti*, published by Leopold Staff as early as 1910, continued to exert an even more powerful influence in an era of worrying debate on "the decline of European civilization." St. Francis' ideal of life seemed to represent a symbol of the future to many lay writers and scholars. The celebrations of the 700th anniversary of the saint's death in 1926 added another factor in attracting popular attention to him, as evidenced by numerous studies and other works dedicated to St. Francis by various writers and poets. Stanisław Wędkiewicz's work, "Franciscan Ideals and the Crisis of What Is Termed Western Civilization" (1928), formulated an ideological attitude which was characteristic of all the circles of the lay Catholic intelligentsia.

But Franciscanism in Poland between the two wars was not merely an ideological or intellectual issue. First and foremost, it represented an ideal of zealous devotion to others. That attitude had already been displayed by the Albertinians — brothers and sisters — an order founded at the end of the nineteenth century by Adam Chmielowski (Brother Albert), a one-time participant in the January Insurrection and an outstanding painter, who even during his lifetime (he died in 1916) had enjoyed the fame of a saintly person. He was portrayed by Żeromski as someone searching for a means "to fight Satan." The same tradition was at the roots of the efforts of the blind Róża Czacka, who during the war founded at Laski near

Warsaw the Congregation of the Franciscan Sisters, Servants of the Cross. Later, through the work of Father Władysław Korniłowicz, Laski turned into a center of Christian thought put into practice through charity. It was an association of devout Catholics but was open to all who under the difficult conditions of modern civilization, were looking for ways to become personally involved. Laski, especially from the initial publication of its quarterly *Verbum,* which was devoted to problems of contemporary culture (1934—39), became a meeting-place for significant conferences in which outstanding writers, like Zofia Nałkowska and Karol Irzykowski, took part, together with naturalists, physicians, artists and philosophers absolutely alien to the Catholic philosophy.

The Lublin center focused its attention on social issues, and besides organizing an annual Social Work Week, turned its attention, with the help of the Union of the Polish Catholic Intelligentsia and its monthly *Prąd,* to frequent meetings called Catholic Days. Their theme in 1932 was "The Catholic Attitude in the Face of the Crisis." A growing influence was exerted on those circles by Teodor Kubina, the Bishop of Częstochowa. In his book *Catholic Action and Social Action* (1930) he advanced a thesis, controversial in those circles, that "man is the master and goal of economic life" and that "labor should never be considered as merchandise."

Literary activity assisted this Catholic movement only to a small degree. Among the poets only Jerzy Liebert expressed religious emotions in his verses, permeated with the atmosphere of approaching death. Historical novels by Zofia Kossak-Szczucka, like those of Sienkiewicz before her, met with severe criticism. In fact, the first novel touching deeper Catholic issues was *Peace of the Heart* (1938) by Jerzy Andrzejewski.

More concerned with these problems were the fine arts and music. The great talent of Xawery Dunikowski served a new vision of religious life. Between 1927 and 1929 he designed sculptures for the cathedral in Katowice. His bas-reliefs of the four Evangelists adorned the front of the Theological Seminary in Cracow. Several designs and fragments of statues of S.S. Barbara, Francis and Felix were intended for the Silesian Seminary in Cracow and for the portal of the church at Wawer.

Religious themes were also found in the paintings of Felicjan Kowarski who was fascinated by the Italian Renaissance and adapted religious topics to these interests. In the 1920's at the monastery at Jasna Góra, Kowarski designed a mural, *The Last Supper,* a variation of Leonardo's painting, to which he returned once more in later years in an oil version. In 1935 he designed a polychrome for the cathedral in Chełm Lubelski. During the war he was busy with planning a large basilica with a huge mosaic on the subject of Doomsday.

Religious fervor and yearnings were also expressed in music. Karol Szymanowski in his treatise, "On the Educational Role of Musical Culture" (1931), wrote: "The history of music is irrevocably linked with the greatest revolution in the world, that is, Christianity." He gave expression to this belief in a number of his works, particularly in his *Stabat Mater,* in the music composed to

Wyspiański's hymn *Veni Creator,* in his *Litany* composed to Liebert's poetry, and in *St. Francis.* Transgressing the lines of traditional liturgical music he looked for a new, modern means of expression. Commenting on his work on *Stabat Mater* he said: "For years I have been considering problems of Polish religious music, so different from stiff and frozen liturgical forms." He wanted to tie in more closely words with music in the manner "of country church chants like *The Holy God* or my favorite *Bitter Lamentations"* (Lent psalms). Szymanowski went beyond the limitations of Catholicism, seeking religious topics in Byzantine and Greek traditions, as in his opera, *King Roger* in 1926, or in religious Persian poetry, as in his *Third Symphony — The Song of the Night.*

The characteristic feature of the attitude in the face of life and death, which was popular in some circles of the intelligentsia, was a particular kind of non-confessional faith, the belief in metaphysical, sometimes mystical, aspects of nature and society. The quest for new "truths" of human life was going on in accordance with the Polish romantic tradition of religious experience liberated from any limitations of the established church.

Of remarkable importance for the whole trend was a book by Feliks Brodowski, *The Cedar House.* Brodowski thought that the Cartesian formula should be replaced by the following: "I love, therefore the thing I love is."

The same kaleidoscopic group included Wincenty Lutosławski, professor at Vilna University, and advocate of a new political and economic order based on the Polish Messianist philosophy, as well as a specific mental therapy for the individual.

Different social conditions gave birth to a so-called metaphysics of agrarianism, advocated by such writers and civic leaders of peasant background as Józef Niećko and Ignacy Solarz. According to Niećko, this metaphysics expressed the conviction that "we are all sons and daughters of the earth and the sun." He believed that the young people are marching toward the sun and "transform their souls in sunlight."

Artur Górski often presented the metaphysical vistas of life. "The cracked image of the human heart" supposedly expressed the fundamental dualism which "man's soul is composed of: exhilaration and dark terror, joy of existence and gloomy despair, certainty of immortality and inclination to nihilism."

In the 1930's less emphasis was placed on metaphysical speculation and perspectives and attention was turned to contemporary issues instead, to searching for righteous ways in the difficulties of modern civilization. This characteristic was developed in Górski's book, *The Anxiety of Our Times* (1938). He also undertook a great deal of organizational and editorial activity during this period, especially at the Literary Institute where, in collaboration with Stefan Kołaczkowski, he prepared an edition of the works of Stanisław Brzozowski. At the same institute Kołaczkowski was the editor of *Marcholt,* a periodical which directed thought and imagination toward fundamental values, to life enriched with reflections on heroism and on the tragic, toward defending culture and man in the face of advancing fascism.

This metaphysical and humanist philosophy embraced in an exceptionally characteristic way the issues of science and its impact, as a basic factor of existence, on the individual and on the community. Stanisław Michalski, Artur Górski's friend, inspired the intellectuals grouped around the Mianowski Foundation to work in this spirit. Such outstanding scholars of the era as Jan Rozwadowski, Florian Znaniecki, Czesław Białobrzeski, Antoni Bolesław Dobrowolski, and Franciszek Bujak examined problems of the relationship between science and philosophy, particularly between science and religion and science and the arts.

This development was accompanied by a steady growth, mostly among the intelligentsia, of a humanist and rational view of life. With its tradition rooted in the positivist era, this philosophy was almost as popular as during the Young Poland period among radical groups.

Like the approach discussed previously, this loosely defined attitude embraced a whole range of ideas. Some people, like Dobrowolski, believed in an oncoming new civilization which would emerge when the old and contemporary "ant-like communities", busy with material production and political activity would turn to creating "by common effort the greatest and most significant things on earth," that is, science and art.

Tadeusz Kotarbiński, for whom the special object of inquiry became the problems of ethics, viewed these prospects in an absolutely different light. At first his interest concentrated on a "philosophy of action" (1913) viewed in the light of his studies on the ethics of Mill and Spencer (1915). In his later activity, both scientific as well as literary, he espoused and advocated ethics free of any religious or metaphysical motivation: it was to be independent, exempt from maximalistic delusions, it was to be the ethics of practical realism, concentrating on "the defense of the people against adversity," and thus was called the "ethics of the reliable protector". This ethical scheme "implied values of constant behavior: courage, a kind heart, integrity, resolution in hardship, inner discipline."

Boy-Żeleński assumed a similar line in his attacks on the intellectual limitations of traditional views, bourgeois hypocrisy, patriotic falsehoods, and the tendency to mythicize reality.

Irzykowski, arguing with Boy, wrote that his arguments were somehow "narrow, unpleasant, mundane," limited to unveiling and exposing, which "please people because they excuse them from thinking." Irzykowski was of the opinion that it is possible to penetrate the depths of social reality and of the human psyche; he tried to develop his thesis in his novel, *Pałuba* (1903), with the help of a sharp intellect, which can reveal truths and enables communication and understanding between people.

A number of sociologists also joined the rationalist group, the most notable of these being Stefan Czarnowski. A follower of Durkheim's but linked closely with the workers' movement, Czarnowski, in his comprehensive studies on the history and theory of culture, disclosed the social mechanisms connected with the rise of "ruling ideas" and values, with the spread of intellectual currents, and the emergence of revolutionary situations and forces.

This rational sociological knowledge assisted the various socio-political activities, which during the 1930's were concentrated on fighting the fascist threat. With the sharp eye of a social scientist, he discerned in the ruling system the points which spelled the greatest danger to culture and man. Czarnowski placed greatest hope in the proletariat as a factor in the social struggle and a source of culture. In this way the rationalist philosophy gained a Marxist character. The left-wing civic leader and educator of teachers, Władysław Spasowski, in his work, *The Liberation of Man as Reflected in Philosophy, the Sociology of Labor and Education of Humanity* (1935), interpreted Marxism in a manner deeply rooted in Polish revolutionary and liberation tradition, as well as in the traditions of utopian radicalism. Spasowski argued that a social revolution of a socialist kind would open the possibility of creative life to everybody. "The meaning of man's life and true happiness lies in a feeling of comprehensive development, in an awareness of the great tension and widest expansion of individual life, in creative work on the social, scientific, philosophic, inventive and artistic levels."

Among the most characteristic features of this rationalist humanist philosophy was its emphasis on the merit of the "heart" — similar to that of the metaphysical and intuitive trends, although in a completely different way.

Defining the social ideal Leon Petrażycki wrote: "The highest good to which we should aspire in political life generally, and in legislative policy in particular, is the moral progress of man, the reign of high, rational ethics in humanity, in short, the ideal of love. A thesis that love is an ideal, the highest worth, is an axiom of practical reason and therefore needs no proof."

Not everyone, however, fitted into these three major philosophical trends, because one of the characteristics of the era was its reluctance to accept clearly-defined intellectual postures.

Very lively and inwardly diversified tendencies of fidelity to individual imagination and experiences, were characteristic of those segments of society which, while sometimes very few in numbers, preferred seeking to finding, and fighting and protesting to accepting already proven attitudes.

The works of Florian Znaniecki had wider social appeal. Contrary to the dominant trends in sociology in Poland, Znaniecki formulated an absolutely new, humanist and visionary science, a sociology of the arts, of the future world which would be shaped by leaders of "a youthful civilization and youthful society," consisting of people, "infinitely more creative and more active ethically than the people of today." Znaniecki's book which set out these prospects, *The People of Today and the Civilization of the Future*, became an intellectual manifesto of a world which found its poetic counterpart in the imagery of Bolesław Leśmian. There were also people in Poland who developed philosophical trends devoid of social content, which did not lead to ideological strife. Roman Ingarden, for example, espoused a phenomenology of the intellectual world separate from social reality. Władysław Tatarkiewicz, in his *History of*

Philosophy (1931), presented a panoramic view of the history of world thought, which did not encourage any definite ideological choice, but displayed in a masterly fashion the manifold faces of truth.

THE ART OF DISSENT AND EXPLORATION

The restoration of Polish independence gave birth to a host of avant-garde poetry and literary manifestos. As early as 1917 an avant-garde periodical, *Zdrój*, appeared in Poznań. In Cracow, in the same year, a group of "formist" writers and artists headed by Leon Chwistek and Tytus Czyżewski appeared. Another group, the futurists, including Stanisław Młodożeniec and Bruno Jasieński, also emerged.

In its introductory manifesto, *Zdrój* denounced naturalistic art for "seeing in man only a meager section of the human being, and in life only a poor fragment of the most trivial reality", and proclaimed a "return to the source of the Polish soul," that is, to the great romantic poetry, at the same time praising symbolism because "it represents the essence of genuine great art." Actually this program was traditional, and the futurists rebelled against it. The latter admired modernity and the poetic visions of revolution. One of them, Tadeusz Peiper, saw the future in terms of the three m's: the metropolis, the masses, and the machine.

But only Bruno Jasieński was fully aware of the prospects of social revolution. In 1921 he published a manifesto to the Polish nation, concerning the immediate futurization of life. This manifesto advertised "a sale of the old rubbish," appealed to poetry "to go on to the streets," and in contemporary life only respected "the machine, democracy and the mob."

The futurist offensive, launched during the years 1920—22, was of very short duration. Traditional poetry was against it, as were the young Warsaw poets, eager to sustain links with the classical traditon, rallying around Skamander; it was also opposed by the followers of national and popular poetry. However, the ideological ferment aroused by the avant-garde movement in artistic circles stayed alive for a long time afterwards, originating philosophic visions of the world and of human life. The evidence of its impact may be seen particularly in the activity of Leon Chwistek and Stanisław Ignacy Witkiewicz. Chwistek in his book, The *Multiplicity of Reality* (1921), propounded the thesis that "reality cannot be grasped by one consistent system for the simple reason that there is no complete reality, but rather, many realities." In his analysis of this multiplicity, Chwistek arrived at the conclusion that besides a reality of impressions there is one of notions, as well as reality of objects and physical reality. The reality in which a given individual lives shapes his attitude and activity. Unfortunately, according to Chwistek, restricted patterns were imposed on Polish social and political life which suppressed creativity each time that it appeared non-conformist.

That consciousness found its expression in the philosophy of Witkiewicz. In his book entitled *New Forms in Painting and Misunderstandings Originating Therefrom*, published in 1919, Witkiewicz wrote: "Artistic creation represents the direct confirmation of existence in its metaphysical horror, and is not any justification of that horror by means of a system of mollifying ideas ... The men of the future will need neither truth nor beauty; they will be happy — is that not enough?"

From that point of view the future meant the inevitable death of art because social progress was supposed to lead to a society of the contented masses.

Concurrently with the avant-garde trend in poetry a similar movement developed in the fine arts. It was just as aggressive and aimed at a revolutionary transformation of reality. In 1917 in Poznań an Association of Artists, called Bunt (The Revolt), was formed, under the leadership of the writer and painter Jerzy Hulewicz and the activist of the revolutionary left wing Stanisław Kubicki, who was also an artist and author. In his work, *The Dawn of an Epoch: A Struggle for New Art* (1920), the latter said that artists should not serve "citizens' pleasures" or aesthetic tastes, since the struggle that goes on "has for its aim the MAN, and the DAY which is to come"; it is a struggle for the liberation of the people from the bondage of trivia, a struggle against "the dread of today and its repulsive slogans."

It was on just such a novel concept of art that the artists represented by the Blok (Block, 1924—26) Group based their work.

They were adherents of art free from the obligation of reproduction, and favored a formally abstract but rigorously disciplined art, based on the principles of geometry and deeply committed socially. The leading representatives of Blok were Władysław Strzemiński, Katarzyna Kobro, Henryk Stażewski, and Mieczysław Szczuka who engaged chiefly in applied art and photomontage. They did not enjoy wide popularity in Poland, even in left-wing circles.

In a paper, "What Does Block Want?" (1925), Mieczysław Szczuka explained that the core of the matter is "the indivisibility of artistic and social issues which means that artists should look for practical applications of their creative urge," instead of yielding to a desire "to express their personal experiences or moods." The point is the "construction of things, consistent with the requirements of material, tool and purpose." Artists had to direct "their creative effort toward, in the first place, architecture, motion pictures, publishing, and the so-called world of fashion."

These tendencies in architecture and the arts aroused enthusiasm in Julian Marchlewski in 1900, and perhaps, under their influence Stefan Żeromski created his image of "glass houses".

But public opinion would not accept the new artistic fads subordinated to imaginative social visions, as evidenced by the tragic fate of the group's most outstanding artist, Władysław Strzemiński, originator of the avant-garde theory of art called Unism. His book *Unism in Painting* appeared in 1928.

Unism rejected all allusion in painting. The painted 208

canvas did not provoke associations with any existing thing; it was sheer painting. In collaboration with Katarzyna Kobro and Henryk Stażewski in 1930 he founded a separate group, AR (Revolutionary Artists). However, it did not exercise any great social influence.

A greater success in the social field accompanied the endeavors of more moderate artists, mostly architects, who left Blok and founded another group, called Praesens (1928).

Despite the indifference, sometimes even hostility, of society, this avant-garde and socially revolutionary trend continued and was several times revived in different places. Between 1931 and 1933 the so-called Group Cracow emerged, which united artists of radical, even communist, views — artists like Jonasz Stern and Henryk Wiciński. In the Żoliborz district of Warsaw, under the auspices of the "Glass Houses" Association, a group operated, which in 1936 assumed the name Phrygian Cap. They wanted to express visually "the ideals and aspirations of the world of labor"; they opposed "art for art's sake" as well as an art subservient to the requirements of the existing social system. But it, too, did not achieve great social significance.

On the other hand, the triumphs of Polish applied art, developing in the interest of serving the requirements of the upper classes of society, were significant. In the spirit of the Cracow and Zakopane tradition from the early 1920's, the artists began to create new avant-garde works. Jerzy Warchałowski, Wojciech Jastrzębowski and Karol Stryjeński originated a new style. They met with great success at the Exhibition of Decorative Arts in Paris in 1925, and the cooperative Ład (Order), founded in 1926, became an important way of popularizing this art in society. Among the propertied classes Ład enjoyed great popularity.

Stormy though the development of avant-garde poetry and art was during this era, particularly during the early years of independence, the main currents of art remained closely connected with the realities of Polish life, which was preoccupied with the analysis of social conflicts, with the exposing of painful problems and difficult objectives.

Toward the end of his life, Żeromski paved the way in his novel, *Early Spring*. The title itself implied the reign of harsh winter which still kept the social structure under its spell, expressing at the same time a belief that "spring" must come. Considered too radical, even revolutionary, in conservative circles, it was nonetheless attacked by left wingers for being too moderate and all-embracing.

During the entire period of Polish independence between the wars, *Early Spring* remained an object of many polemics and a touchstone of the typical attitude of the Polish intelligentsia, which, while championing social progress, maintained reservations about the communist experience.

To the same current belonged the work of Maria Dąbrowska, both in the literary and in the journalistic fields. She expressed hope that it was possible to mitigate the era's social conflicts through the application of a reasonable cooperative policy; at the same time she described the tragic lot of the peasantry in her novel

People from Over There (1925), calling for prompt and courageous action. Her novel, *The Crossroads* (1937) provoked vehement attacks.

Whereas Dąbrowska chiefly portrayed the social aspects of a program for action, Zofia Nałkowska introduced psychological issues into her works. Considering her experience during the war, she wrote: "Then I saw what another human being is; what other people are. I saw something which had previously been little known to me: the suffering of other people." The problem of pain was also that of wrong and evil and, therefore, of responsibility. In her stories *The Walls of the World* (1931) and in her novel *Frontier* (1935), she accused those groups of the intelligentsia which, by condoning violence, assisted in the rise of fascism.

Juliusz Kaden-Bandrowski wrote in a less radical mood, although with similar vehemence. He described Piłsudski's rule satirically, yet with some touches of apology, in his *General Barcz* (1923), or denounced Wincenty Witos' road to power in *Mateusz Bigda* (1933), and exposed the social problems of the Silesian region by means of a gloomy symbol in his *Black Wings*.

In the 1930's two outstanding novels appeared — *Kordian and the Yokel* (1932) by Leon Kruczkowski, and *The Homeland* (1935) by Wanda Wasilewska — both with the message that "the homeland of the peasantry" is incompatible with "the homeland of aristocratic conspiracy."

The theater for workers was yet another form of protest against social conditions. It was courageous and open in its criticism of capitalist and bourgeois civilization.

Revolutionary plays were staged at the Ateneum Theater under Stefan Jaracz, as well as in the Warsaw and Łódź theaters under the direction of Leon Schiller. Such productions as *Cyankali* by Friedrich Wolf, *Roar, China!* by Sergei Tretiakov and, especially, *Prince Potemkin* by Tadeusz Miciński. *The Un-Divine Comedy* by Zygmunt Krasiński in 1938 met with great success.

The most resounding voice of anger and hope was heard throughout these years from poetry, above all from Władysław Broniewski's collected poems, published under the titles *Smoke Over the City* (1927), *The Paris Commune* (1929), *The Sorrow and the Song* (1932) and *The Final Call* (1938). These honored the workers from Warsaw, Łódź and other industrial areas, the revolutionaries of all nations, the communards killed on the barricades of Paris, the patriots fighting in the mountain passes of Spain, the inmates of the Pawiak prison and the unemployed. They appealed to poets to join in the revolutionary fight, to lead "with iron steps" into the future.

Similar in its nature was the work of Bruno Jasieński, who at first collaborated with the futurists, and later began to call more and more emphatically for social revolution. His poem *The Song of Hunger* (1922), and collected verses *Earth on the Left,* published together with the works of Anatol Stern, were manifestations of this revolutionary ideology. His *A Word About Jakub Szela,* published in Paris, had a wide circulation in Poland. The image of the annihilation of Paris by a proletarian revolution presented in *I'm Burning Paris* (1929) brought Jasieński international fame.

At the end of the inter-war period, new, grotesque tones appeared, mostly in the works of Bruno Schulz, *The Cinnamon Shops* (1934), and *The Sandglass* (1937), and Witold Gombrowicz, *Memoirs from Adolescence* (1933) and *Ferdydurke* (1938). These works have had a "second life," both in Poland and elsewhere, after World War II, and have been admired both by readers and, in film and dramatic adaptations, by cinema and theater audiences.

The most extensive criticism of the reality of that era can be found in the numerous plays and novels of Stanisław Ignacy Witkiewicz. However, only a small portion of his work was published during his lifetime. The complete novelty of Witkiewicz's work was not understood until later; in People's Poland his surrealistic plays have conquered the stage, and some of his works which until recently remained only in manuscript, have also been published.

In the inter-war period, literature and art not only expressed the feelings of uncertainty aroused by the social situation of the country and the disappointment with reality which, contrary to previous dreams about "glass houses" was effected by the moneyed classes. They also expressed the desire to escape from the real world into the depths of inner life, or else along the path leading toward primitive art.

The poetry of Bolesław Leśmian was one of the manifestations of such a philosophy, seeking to reach beyond reality toward the shores of mystery, the unusual and happiness. His poetry was a great, fairy-tale ballet, a "dance of rebellion against the prose of life."

The poets of the Skamander group which was active in Warsaw during the 1920's, particularly Julian Tuwim and Kazimierz Wierzyński, created a different image of the world, the beauty of which was supposed to constitute a source of joy and awe and thus a means to escape the community of "the horrible bourgeoisie." Jan Lechoń had a place of his own among the Skamander poets; his main interest lay in the history of the nation perceived as a source of personal experience. Living within the sphere of such experience, he sought "salvation from one's own self" along roads "where poor human comedy might become divine."

The human condition and its dramatic moral and psychological conflicts formed the basic subject of the literature of the era. Ewa Szelburg-Zarembina exposed that world as a "river of lies" along which Joanna roamed, condemned to remain lonely amidst "the people of wax". Zofia Nałkowska described "the walls of the world," which imprisoned men and their "evil loves," and spoke about that "frontier" along which people lived their lives entangled in political reality, and, despite their entanglement, were responsible for the choice they made, or were compelled to make.

These existential experiences found their most profound expression in the works of Jarosław Iwaszkiewicz. His short stories and novels, *The Moon Rises* (1925), *The Maids of Wilko* (1932), *The Red Shields* (1934), *The Mill on the Utrata* (1937) and *The Błędomierz Passion*

(1938), were permeated with existentialism: with the solitude of man, his inevitable fate, the responsibility of choice, the passing of time which separates and reunites, communion with nature and the value of life for life's sake.

The same existential moods may be found in the paintings of Felicjan Kowarski, especially in such works as *The Wanderers* and *The Withered Tree* (1928) in which he portrayed solitude, the feeling of loss, a vain peering ahead into a future that promises nothing, and exhaustion with the pilgrimage of life.

This philosophy, however, was not the monopoly of only poets, writers and artists. It was just as characteristic of all who tried in a rational way to find the truth about the world and the joy of life.

The current of this relentlessness and anxiety, called "troubles with existence", appears frequently throughout the pages of the diary of Henryk Elzenberg, a philosopher who kept notes from the period prior to World War I. The diary developed the question: "Where is the so-called Ego?" In 1937 this question collided dramatically with another on man's historical situation and the meaning of historical changes. "In the long run, this is not an issue of great structures — of institutions, homelands, religions, spiritual trends — but it is a matter of live people in given moments and places being what men deserve to be"; and the only meaning of that objective social world lies in serving actual people. "In concrete achievements by concrete beings, "the meaning of existence is fulfilled."

In various circles of artists and intellectuals these existential experiences developed in different ways. Resulting from personal emotions, they remained free from any attempt at influencing society and produced the feeling of solitude. They were more of a poetical and intuitional rather than of a regional character. Sometimes they gave birth to an image of life which was happy, thanks to creative work in the fields of philosophy, poetry and art. Sometimes they led to utopias; at other times they became attempts of forming private philosophical systems; sometimes they consisted of the knowledge of many various systems, mixed with the joy of not being compelled to choose between them once and for all.

Jarosław Iwaszkiewicz adequately defined such an attitude toward the world when in later years he wrote: "I'm no intellectual; I do not speculate; I distrust doctrines; I hate preaching truths and slogans *urbi et orbi* . . . All I do is to make the experience last; I don't philosophize." A good many artists, poets, writers and intellectuals adhered to this formula, and such an individualistic and existentialist concept of "finding one's self in the world" during these difficult years was characteristic of those artists and intellectuals who avoided direct political involvement.

ELITE CULTURE AND MASS CULTURE

The state which emerged in 1918 inherited various school systems and varying standards of education. The former Prussian zone had the highest level of school attendance, although providing a German education. To create a Polish school organization meant virtually to begin everything anew. The vast expanses of the former Russian zone had the lowest level of school attendance: huge numbers of children received no education and provisions were made for only a few years' schooling in the existing system. The situation in Galicia was better, but even there it was rather difficult to speak of universal primary education; what is more, its standards did not much exceed the standards of the traditional dame schools.

The improvement of this state of affairs and a desire to create conditions for higher standards of general education stood foremost in the minds of society, the teachers and the administration.

Poland regained its independence in early November 1918. Already on 20 November a government declaration proclaimed "the foundation of a general, lay, free school equally accessible to all regardless of their financial status. Personal ability is the only criterion in gaining the privilege of education."

The so-called Teachers' Parliament which convened in Warsaw in April 1919 set up a project for the democratic reform of education.

This program of education, bold and far-reaching, exercised a particular influence on all later educational projects. The principle of a unified system of compulsory primary education stood in sharp contrast to the selective systems of education accepted in the capitalist world.

The implementation of this principle was not easy and, particularly during the first years of independence, a bitter war was waged with the defenders of an eight-year "gymnasium," built on the basis of the four-year primary school, as an institution of the social élite. All attempts at encroachment on that status quo were considered an assault against culture and proof of "barbarism."

The efforts to produce conditions for raising the level of general education within the seven-year school were also not easy. A high level of expenditure and huge organizational effort were necessary in order to produce the success achieved in this field. At the end of the 1920's the realization of the principle of compulsory universal education for seven years was in full swing.

And although the recession which began in the early 1930's prevented thousands of children from going to school, in 1935 the extremely slow process of removing obstacles and limitations again began, proof that the pressure of public opinion and the demands of the teaching community were not without significance.

And indeed, despite all the difficulties and controversies, primary schools earned an important and lasting place in the social landscape of Poland between the wars. The traditional image of a "triangle of forces" — the manor-house, the manse, the village — underwent a radical transformation from the time when in tens of thousands of villages, school buildings were erected and schools and teachers became partners and antagonists of the traditional forces. Rarely operating hand in glove with the lord of the manor if perhaps slightly more often with the parish, they usually backed the peasants although, of course,

numerous conflicts arose between the "lord's school" and "peasant reality" during this time.

Along with a generally victorious struggle for universal long-term education, the social position of teachers improved and awareness of their professional dignity and the strength of their trade union organization increased. On Polish soil, prior to 1918, only "gymnasium" (secondary school) teachers enjoyed some degree of respect in the community, especially in Galicia. Teachers of primary schools of all kinds were accorded a very low position in the contemporary social hierarchy. Their situation in the Prussian part of the country was somewhat different, but the educational system there was not Polish but German.

After the restoration of independence, the role of primary school teachers was improved. From the very first months of independence, this large group displayed particular energy and activity; aware of their responsibility for the state of Polish education, they championed projects on school organization and presented their demands to the authorities. Within the teaching community an awareness ripened and developed regarding the significance and dignity of the teaching profession, of the need to improve continually the performance of their work, of the will to bring themselves to perfection in every respect.

All of this, despite the difficult financial situation of the teaching community, produced an already irreversible situation in the attitudes and feelings of identity of the teaching profession as a whole, which made teachers into a solid, coherent group, imbued with a consciousness of vocation, aware of their social duties and social significance, active in school and in society, bold in conducting all sorts of campaigns to promote the good of the school and the good of democracy.

Thus the organization of education, the functioning of the schools, and the activity of the teachers produced a lasting contribution to the forthcoming development of Polish culture.

The success of underground education during the Nazi occupation was chiefly due to the very same patriotic and responsible attitude of the teachers. The same can be said of the situation which saw the successful reconstruction and reorganization of education after 1945, for teachers were experienced in work and responsibility.

The educational system, however, did not meet all the demands, particularly of the peasant and worker sections of society. Their needs gave birth to extra-school activity among young people and adult groups, under the auspices of such organizations of long standing as Polish Alma Mater, the Popular School Society, or the Popular Reading-Room Society, but mainly the newly founded civic organizations joined with the peasant and worker movements.

The activity and courage of the leaders of these institutions, despite the political situation and sometimes despite police chicanery, opened up new ways for extensive and intensive schooling. At the same time they created a new atmosphere for the intellectual and artistic life of the masses, as well as new types of communities in which anyone who wished to improve his or her education or just share with others some reflection about the world and himself could take part.

This was particularly characteristic of the peasant community. In the words of one of the "peasant philosophers," Józef Niećko, "the international urban culture will have to give way to a specifically Polish, absolutely free culture."

Similarly, Ignacy Solarz set up the great objectives of the "village universities": "Through freedom of spiritual growth, through individual ripening of social thought and emotion, we intend to influence collectively the course of human history."

The Peasant University at Gać Przeworska, directed from 1932 by Solarz, won particular renown as a nursery of radical peasant thought.

The history of workers' education developed in a different way. It was linked to proletarian ideology, to industrial and urban conditions of life and work, and to modern components of civilization. The Society of Workers' University (TUR), founded in 1923 in order to "foster education and culture, assist in the development of the mind and in the working out of an independent philosophy among labor," became a center of this civic and cultural activity.

The development of this organization was very fast, and in the 1930's it consisted of 200 branches with an operational range embracing all forms of educational and cultural activities, from scientific research through artistic and theatrical productions among adults as well as youth groups, organized in the OMTUR (Youth Organization of the Society of Workers' University) and the Red Scouts. On the initiative of TUR the following great cultural and political events were organized: the Days of Workers' Culture in Cracow in 1936 and the Young Workers' Convention in Warsaw in 1937.

In these diversified forms of voluntary educational and cultural activities, both in town and country, the emancipation of individuals and of local communities was taking place concurrently with liberation from the intellectual and emotional bonds and limitations of cultural reality. Their objective was a final transformation of life.

The significance of these objectives and the large scope of this activity played an important role in the wide mobilization of a remarkable group of scholars, mostly sociologists and teachers, headed by Helena Radlińska and Florian Znaniecki. The Institute for Adult Education, the only institution in Poland between the two world wars interested in educational issues, together with the School of Social and Educational Work of the Polish Open University, played a remarkable part in the preparation of personnel and in inspiring new forms of educational activity among various social groups.

An important expression of these experiences and aspirations was Znaniecki's chief thesis, according to which, not children and young people, but adults, due to the wealth of their experience and to their intellectual and emotional maturity, represent the most responsive material for both educational activity and self-improvement.

The task of making these concepts materialize was not an easy one; nevertheless, it was characteristic of this period in Polish culture, and proof of the tendencies of the working masses, of their striving after social emancipation and after full participation in culture.

The cultural issues stood, in fact, at the center of all interests of the era. And it is one of the characteristics of the time that they were undertaken simultaneously from two absolutely independent poles.

One viewpoint emerged from those for whom culture was synonymous with elitist values; the other from those who considered culture a matter of universal dissemination. The fact that Zenon Miriam-Przesmycki held the post of Minister of Culture was significant for those elitist and spiritual concepts in which the tendencies of a good many artists of the period found their expression. Their language was rather hermetically sealed, reaching back to the tradition of Young Poland expressionism as well as to the pathos of the romantics.

On the other hand, a counter-current developed, aiming at a wide democratization of culture, at founding a cultural idiom belonging to the entire nation. This was the line taken by the progressive, radical intelligentsia, backed by the emancipationist tendencies of the masses. The development of material and technical means of disseminating culture went along the same lines: the advancement in the fields of press and publishing, the growing influence of film, and ever-spreading network of libraries and reading-rooms.

Radio, too, started to play its role as a supplement to the network of libraries which allowed easy access to cultural materials. Broadcasting was inaugurated in 1926, but only with the construction of the radio station at Raszyn in 1930 was it possible to relay radio programs throughout the whole country. During the 1930's a comprehensive system of local stations was created: in Cracow, Łódź, Vilna, Lvov, Poznań, Katowice, Toruń and Baranowicze. Radio programs were enriched by introducing many popular science subjects, literature, poetry, and radio plays. The radio program, "Theater of the Imagination," enjoyed great popularity, as did local artistic programs, some of which were broadcast on the national network. The social and artistic role of radio was highly esteemed, as evidenced, for example, by the fact that the consultative Literary Board of Polish Radio comprised the most distinguished writers of the time (Wacław Sieroszewski, Zofia Nałkowska, Juliusz Kaden-Bandrowski, Tadeusz Boy-Żeleński, and others). People in Poland made an ever-increasing use of radio. In 1938 Poland ranked eighth in Europe in the number of radio subscribers, and in that same year the mailbox of Polish Radio received 300,000 letters from listeners.

The influence of literature went hand in hand with that of film. The beginnings of the film industry dated from the period immediately preceding World War I. After regaining independence, Polish movie-makers produced a host of comedies and melodramas, but also "serious" pictures such as *Pan Tadeusz* after Mickiewicz (1928) *The Enslaved Souls* after Prus (1930), *The Promised Land* after Reymont (1927), *Early Spring* after Żeromski (1928) and *Hurricane* after Gąsiorowski (1928). Karol

Irzykowski acknowledged the social and artistic significance of film, publishing as early as 1924 his pioneering book, *The Tenth Muse*.

The first movie theater with sound equipment was opened in 1929, and from that date on the Polish film industry started slowly to change from silent to talking pictures.

In 1929 a group of movie artists founded Start, an association whose objective was to produce artistic and socially significant pictures; they tried to continue the tradition of such directors as Eisenstein and Pudovkin. Obstacles of a political nature, however, frustrated the realization of the project.

But, despite all these efforts, film never achieved the status of a truly great art for a mass audience. The peasant population remained almost completely excluded from its influence; and the small towns did not possess the network of theaters equipped with adequate technical facilities. Books and newspapers had to remain the only mass medium accessible to the general public.

It was characteristic and typical of the literary culture of the era that sensational books — the thrillers and the yellow press — did not exert greater social influence. The primary aim of both public opinion and publishers was ambitious literature of high artistic merit.

From the moment Poland regained its independence, theater, which during the whole period of foreign rule continued to be such a great and important instrument in shaping the national identity, was in a better position to further its influence. New theaters were founded, expecially in regions which had previously belonged to Prussia; and a pioneering drama movement started not only in Warsaw and Cracow, but also in Łódź and in Vilna. During this entire period Arnold Szyfman directed the still prestigious Teatr Polski in Warsaw.

Particularly significant and influential were efforts at finding a new understanding of the social and artistic role of theater. In 1919 Juliusz Osterwa, with Mieczysław Limanowski, founded the Reduta Theater in Warsaw, and moved it to Vilna in 1925. Theirs was a theater of psychological realism, of fine words and style, and of earnest acting. Accustomed to playing in a small house and in an intimate manner in Warsaw, the ambition of its creators was to reach a mass audience. To accomplish this social mission the Reduta ensemble played in small-town market-places and in far-off, unknown villages of the Vilna region. Never before had great dramas, like *El principe constante* by Calderón in Słowacki's free translation, been viewed by audiences numbering hundreds of thousands of ordinary people, as they were during those artistic pilgrimages of the Reduta.

Different in character was the Bogusławski Theater, directed by Leon Schiller in 1924—26. Schiller staged great social dramas like *Prince Potemkin* (1925) by Miciński, *The Rose* (1926) by Żeromski, and *The Un-Divine Comedy* (1926) by Krasiński. Schiller and Horzyca, like Zelwerowicz and Jaracz were creating great Polish theater through their production of national plays by Mickiewicz, Słowacki, Norwid and Miciński.

213 In his inaugural address during the opening of the Ateneum Theater in Warsaw, housed in the building of the Railwaymen's Union, Stefan Jaracz said: "We want it to be a living theater." That was the objective of the entire theatrical movement in Poland during the period.

Alongside the professional theater amateur acting developed. Jędrzej Cierniak was an indefatigable organizer of popular theater. The Association of Popular Theaters, founded in 1919, had a large field of operation. The Institute of Popular Theater included nine regional Unions of Popular Theaters stretching out across almost all of Poland. Cierniak, the organizer and force of inspiration behind the movement, estimated the number of theatrical groups in the mid-1930's at 26,000. They staged more than ten thousand productions annually.

The non-professional workers' theater had a staff of enthusiasts of its own, and an entire group of poets, playwrights, committed actors and theoreticians.

But life in the workers' theater was not easy. There were continual new developments, which disappeared just as quickly; numerous houses were closed by order of the police. Other groups had to struggle with financial and space difficulties. The following theaters lasted somewhat longer and were very popular: the Workers' Stage and Lute, which operated in Warsaw between 1919 and 1921, under the management of Antonina Sokolicz; the Workers' Stage in Łódź, directed by Witold Wandurski between 1925 and 1928; and the TUR Theater in Sosnowiec, managed by Adam Polewka during the 1929—30 season. These theaters produced great social dramas from a classical repertoire, modern plays containing a social message (*The Weavers* by Gerhart Hauptmann), together with some "purely poetical" plays.

The amateur workers' theater gave vent to anger and visions. Lech Piwowar, one of the outstanding leaders of the movement, declared: "The worker will not leave theater outside the range of his burning truths."

POLAND AND THE WORLD

The regaining of independence in 1918 opened new possibilities for the reception of foreign culture in Poland and for the role of Polish culture in the world. The notions of "poor Poland and the hapless Polish nation" were still there, coupled with enthusiasm for Poland's fight for her own and other nations' freedom. That was the spirit of Bourdelle's design for the statue of Mickiewicz made in 1908—09 but not erected until 1919, when new opinions and new criteria were already appearing.

What did we have to offer the world?

First and foremost, science. Polish mathematics, centered in Lvov, Cracow and Warsaw, soon crossed the frontiers of the country and gained international fame, for the most part due to the works of Stefan Banach, Wacław Sierpiński and Kazimierz Kuratowski. Logic, a closely related subject and the theme of the work of Stanisław Leśniewski, Jan Łukasiewicz and Alfred Tarski, became a Polish scientific speciality. The internationally significant research achieved during the period of the partitions by Polish physicists and chemists, was maintained through the research carried on by Stefan Pieńkowski, Wojciech Rubinowicz, Czesław Białobrzeski and Wojciech Świętosławski. Medical and technical disciplines also had important achievements of their own. Jan Czekanowski's school was considered significant in European anthropology, as was the activity of Jerzy Kuryłowicz and Kazimierz Nitsch in linguistics. Unfortunately, Bronisław Malinowski, an ethnologist of world renown, did not return home after World War I, but continued to work in England; whereas Florian Znaniecki, creator of humanist sociology, returned from the United States and continued his work in Poznań.

Literature, unlike science, could not cross the boundaries created by the Polish language, although the Nobel Prize bestowed on Reymont for his novel *The Peasants* in 1924 revealed to the world the writer and his agrarian country, which were until then understood by foreigners in terms of exoticism.

Some success was noted in the sphere of the fine arts. During the 1925 Exhibition of Decorative Arts in Paris, Polish art had great triumphs. But the greatness of Tadeusz Makowski, a painter who lived and worked in France, was recognized only after the artist's death.

The music of Karol Szymanowski reached beyond the frontiers of the country and became a world event, mostly due to its linking of modern expressiveness with folk traditions. His ballet, *Harnasie* produced in 1936 at the Paris Opéra, was enthusiastically acclaimed; it was choreographed by Serge Lifar, who also danced in the production.

Occupation

THE DEFEAT OF 1939
AND THE WILL TO RESIST

The disputes about Poland's proper place in Europe and about the interpretation of her historic path were not yet completed, when the Nazi invasion began in September 1939. The Polish army, and the civilian population of the towns, especially Warsaw, were forced to surrender after stubborn, courageous and sometimes even victorious fighting. The years ahead were not like the military occupation during World War I; it was a period marked by the systematic planned extermination of the nation as a whole.

About one million Poles were banished from the territory incorporated into the Reich; over a quarter of a million were removed from the so-called General Government; particularly brutal were the deportations from the Zamość region. About one million Poles were sent to forced labor in German industry and agriculture. Arrests and executions were everyday occurrences. There was a steady growth in the number of camps designed for the biological annihilation of the inmates. Thousands of Poles were placed there.

But the resistance displayed against the invaders throughout those difficult years by all sections of the nation was remarkably strong and widespread — both spontaneously and in an organized fashion.

Already in late September 1939, an Underground Military Organization was set up, concurrently with the forming of various local conspiratorial groups. Some units of the Polish Army did not surrender and continued fighting in the forests. A detachment commanded by Major Henryk Dobrzański (Hubal), which continued fighting until June 1940, became a national legend. A movie, relating the story of the tragic heroism of this lonely commander and his soldiers, paid tribute to their courage and sacrifice, inaugurating a number of discussions on the sense of this heroic struggle in isolation and without the slightest hope of victory.

Military resistance movements during the occupation were not consolidated. Numerically of greatest strength was the Armed Struggle Union (ZWZ) founded in January 1940 and reorganized two years later into the Home Army (AK). In March 1940, the peasant movement established the Peasant Guards, renamed later the Peasant Battalions. In 1942, the communists organized the People's Guard. In all of these formations, young people formed the major element.

In the summer of 1942 the Germans began to put an end to the Warsaw Ghetto. A considerable part of its Jewish population was murdered on the spot; the survivors were carried off to the extermination camps at Treblinka and Majdanek.

Janusz Korczak, a great educationist, an outstanding writer, and a founder of orphanages, displayed exceptional human dignity and defiance in the face of violence, personally leading the death march of his children from the ghetto to the deportation trains; he chose to die with them of his own free will and led his pupils to their death with a smile of love on his face. Polish artists — Xawery Dunikowski in sculpture and Antoni Słonimski in verse — have paid tribute to his sacrifice. A few months later, when the remnants of the Jewish ghetto population tried to resist, the Germans completely annihilated the people, together with that part of the city.

The Warsaw Uprising of 1944 provided the great and heroic finale of the resistance movement. It was initiated by the leadership of the Home Army, but joined by all underground military groups, as well as all inhabitants of the capital who were carried away by a will to fight the enemy and by the hope of victory.

The poets of the generation that spent the prime of its youth in the ranks of the resistance movement and in insurrection, expressed their patriotic experiences in poetry. As Andrzej Trzebiński, one of these poets, who was shot in 1943, noted: "History will engulf us: the young boys of twenty." Another poet wrote: "We have to die now, so Poland can learn how to live again." Wacław Bojarski, Tadeusz Gajcy (both killed in action) and, above all, the "Słowacki of his generation," Krzysztof Kamil Baczyński (killed on the third day of the Warsaw Uprising), recreated by means of their acts and words in the course of those difficult years, during the days of fighting against great odds, a new version of Polish romanticism, oriented, like its predecessor, toward youthful life, love and nature, devoted to brotherhood and poetical sensitivity and just as tragic as the first.

While the resistance movement of the unvanquished nation went on in the city streets and in the forests of Poland, while thousands of Poles were being held captive in prisons and concentration camps — at the gates of death — Polish soldiers continued their struggle for freedom on foreign battlefields.

After the September defeat dispersed groups managed to reach Western Europe to participate further in a war which was already over on Polish soil. Polish units took part in the defense of Norway against the Nazi invasion at Narvik; they fought together with French units, up to France's defeat. Partially evacuated to Britain, then the last redoubt to withstand Nazism, they contributed in great measure to the 1940 victory in the Battle of Britain. The 303rd Airborne Squadron became the well-known symbol of Poland's contribution.

Other units fought in Africa and distinguished themselves during the 1941 defense of Tobruk. Polish units participated in the liberation of Italy in 1944. During that same year other Polish forces participated in the landing in Normandy, in the battles at Falaise and Chambois, and later, in the recapture of Breda and Arnhem in the Netherlands.

The most famous passage of arms of the Polish Armed Forces was the capture of Monte Cassino in May 1944. The cemetery of fallen Polish soldiers on Hill 593 contains a massive Virtuti Militari Cross made of stone at the entrance. The inscription on the huge slate reads: "Go, tell the Poles, thou who passest by, that here obedient to their laws we lie."

Hitler's assault on the USSR provided hope of organizing Polish armed forces on that front as well. However, the first Polish units formed there were soon moved to the Middle East where they became the basis for the II Polish Corps and participated in battles on the Western Front. From 1943, the Polish Army in the USSR was again mobilized and in the battle of Lenino began its path to glory, leading through Gdańsk to the Pomeranian Line, to Kołobrzeg, the Nysa and, finally, to Berlin.

THE DEFENSE OF NATIONAL CULTURE

The years of occupation witnessed the systematic annihilation of the Polish nation, its life and culture, by the Nazis and years of defiant and victorious defense on the part of the vanquished. As early as October 1939, at a conference held by Goebbels, the Nazi Propaganda Minister, and Hans Frank, the Governor-General of the occupied Polish territory, there came a statement that "the Poles should be provided with education only to the extent that will make them realize that as a nation they do not have any prospects."

In November the Governor-General was present at an interview with Hitler, who endorsed the decision to destroy the Royal Castle in Warsaw and explained that Warsaw would not be rebuilt. Further executive decisions were related to the confiscation of works of art, state and privately owned collections and books, including sacral art. Hundreds of German experts, some of them outstanding scholars, searched for works of art in Poland and prepared lists of the objects to be removed "to add to German art collections." On the other hand, Polish national art was being systematically destroyed: The Prussian Homage by Jan Matejko was cut to pieces; the German search for his Battle of Grunwald fortunately failed.

The destruction of Polish libraries and archives, and archeological, natural science, and ethnographical collections and publications was also systematically carried out. This German policy of cultural terrorism was also reflected in confiscations, appropriations and common robbery of property, and the annihilation of people involved in culture — artists and scholars, who were held in jails or sent to death-camps. The fate of the Jagiellonian University professors, deported to a concentration camp, was an ominous forecast of the policy of destruction of national culture and of its authors.

And yet these same occupation years constituted a period of unusual activity in Polish culture. Bereft of all cultural or educational institutions, the Poles were deprived of education above the primary or vocational level, and even what remained was only semi-legal; they had no universities, no press, no theaters, no philharmonics, radio, film; all cultural centers, libraries, and reading-rooms were closed.

And yet, all these institutions existed in the underground. Polish cultural life was creative and rich. It was not concentrated merely in the big cities; it continued to develop, in spite of the extermination policy of the invaders. Poles managed to keep up not only their current cultural life, but also worked out projects for its comprehensive organization and development after the war.

Books continued to appear, mostly under a fictitious year and place of publication and, in same cases, thanks to these means, they were openly sold in the bookstores.

They were books on political, historical, cultural subjects, anthologies of poetry and war-jokes, books on fundamental philosophical issues and on socio-political matters. Translations of outstanding western writers and philosophers were in steady circulation. A whole series of books appeared about the western territories which were to be returned to Poland.

The intensity of this movement may be judged by the fact that during the occupation about 900 underground periodicals appeared, most of them of a political nature, but 39 of a purely literary character.

And, most amazing of all, an underground theater came into being. A Theater Council was functioning and preparing projects for the future; plays were produced in most difficult, unusual circumstances: in private homes, in attics and cellars, in the forests among guerilla detachments, and in monastery crypts. Some of these productions, like for example, those of Tadeusz Kantor in Cracow (Balladyna and The Return of Odysseus), became significant events in Polish cultural life. Widely acclaimed and much easier to organize were poetry evenings with outstanding artists participating.

Musical concerts were in a slightly better situation. Although Chopin's music, since it was prohibited by the German authorities, had to go underground, classical music, mostly, of course, piano works, found refuge in a number of coffee-houses.

Those who planned for and reflected on the future, tried to include all branches of cultural life. Large groups of experts were preparing projects for the reform of education, of a library law, of an archives act, of the organization of unions of artists; there were discussions on different methods of stage productions of such works as Moniuszko's *Halka* or *The Legion* by Stanisław Wyspiański, which were planned to inaugurate the activity of Warsaw theaters after the liberation.

This difficult but rich cultural life under the occupation produced a twofold experience. It proved how important in the development and propagation of culture are institutional organizations and a systematic policy of the state. It also proved for the second time after Polish experiences in the nineteenth century that culture, in the final analysis, involves a personal need and the passion of the people, that the promotion of culture is an expression of the will of the people, who in spite of all the terrors that life brings, keep looking for the "fragile" values which, nevertheless, are able to resist violence. Perhaps at this time, as never before, men understood that cultural values are priceless and inevitable in human life, even or perhaps, particularly, when that life is threatened by destruction.

FAITS ACCOMPLIS AND HUMAN VALUES

In the course of these difficult years, under conditions of conspiratorial activities in uninterrupted danger, amidst acts of despair and hope, and of the mobilization of spiritual forces for the future, important changes were going on in attitudes toward the world at large.

All previous philosophical trends survived but were undergoing modifications. During various meetings, in the underground press, inside the ideological organizations, old dogmas were preached, expressed and fostered. Social consciousness was awakening: the currents of Catholic thought and messianistic metaphysics, rationalism and irrationalism, nationalist ideology of various shades, and popular faith in the future of a "peasant Poland," viewed as "the home of the village and the sun" — all were entangled in various contests and alliances. Philosophical and artistic writings, devoted to general universal problems, appeared in ever-increasing numbers in hundreds of underground periodicals.

The experience of war and defeat impressed its own hallmark on this wealth and variety of intellectual life. A settling of accounts with European fascism, the Polish pre-war government and nationalist ideology was taking place; and there was a great opening of minds to the prospects for revolutionary ways of rebuilding post-war Poland.

The basic philosophical problem was man versus history, as well as the conflict between values due to which human life gains dignity and real historical events where violence prevails. In quest of a solution to these agonizing issues, many underscored the condition of man, his guilt and responsibility; others analyzed the objective arrangement of social forces which, for the time being, made certain the victory of history over humanism. However, this pessimistic view did not predominate. A more powerful trend was that of heroism, so characteristic of those years. Joseph Conrad was the writer to appeal to the time and circumstances, although his novels portrayed an exotic environment and bygone days. The mystery of evil became the problem of human responsibility and of human guilt. Therefore, the issue of personal involvement remained the gist of the intellectual and moral disputes of those years.

The same reason could explain the popularity of existentialism, a philosophy consistent with the fundamental intellectual experience of the era, that thinking is the expression of the tragedy of individual existence.

Involvement, as authentic human existence, meant "the acceptance of destiny," seen as a set of conditions and aims in life laid down by a given time and place and, at the same time, a revolt against the forms of life which destiny wanted to impose.

And all the time the question kept returning: what is man — a being that creates all great and wonderful things in the world, and nevertheless destroys everything that is human? What is human culture? The great tradition of the European concept of culture was eagerly defended; but it was also thought desirable that culture should be universal, living, authentic and real. How was one to draw a line between a living and a dead culture, how was one to connect — or oppose — culture to civilization, how was one to define man in categories both of real life and of culture? These questions were again touching the very core of individual experience.

In those circumstances the concept and deep meaning of alienation became apparent. That was the point of departure for a prolonged and spirited discussion which followed the Personalist Manifesto by Emmanuel Mounier. Very few people accepted these views as an expression of Catholicism which tried to meet the requirements of a new era; for the majority, the philosophy signified a critique of bourgeois culture and was a defense of human personality, both against individual egoism and against the pressure of leaders who attempted to intoxicate the masses with fanaticism.

But it was another conviction that was undoubtedly the most important. The experiences of those years have remained not only in the form of concern with the future of the world, but as the truth about human involvement. Those cruel years have taught us that we should not always trust ourselves because we are products of the already dying past; but neither should we trust a world governed by power and violence which subjugate people. They have taught us the seemingly paradoxical truth that we are true to ourselves and to history when in spite of ourselves and in spite of reality we create the world and   216 ourselves anew. It was a way which led to the future, through meditation about the history of mankind and about human responsibility, through differentiation of superficial and authentic existence, through dramatic dialogue with the world, and through involvement in human affairs. This was the essence of life under occupation: people, after all, continued to believe in man and in the world he created with his own hands.

Parallel roads into the future were those determined by the tradition of Marxist thought, of the pre-war revolutionary practice of clandestine left-wing political organizations, the communists in particular. Another justification for hope was found in Marxist analysis of the mechanism leading to Hitler's success in Germany and in the world; this required political commitment of a different kind from the metaphysical and moral commitment of the former.

But shortly after the liberation, it became apparent that revolutionary theory and practice were not the only ways leading to socialist Poland; there was another one: personal, reflective and existentialist.

People's Poland

THE YEAR 1945: NEW BOUNDARIES AND NEW HISTORICAL CONSCIOUSNESS

In Chełm on 22 July 1944, on the first piece of Polish soil liberated by the Red Army and the Polish soldiers, the Polish Committee of National Liberation issued a famous Proclamation, the manifesto of independence regained.

War between the Allies and Hitler's armed forces was to last another year. It ended only on 9 May 1945. During that year a Soviet offensive gradually liberated Poland. In mid-1944 Soviet and Polish armies reached the Vistula; in January 1945 Warsaw in ruins was returned to Poland.

A special order, issued by the Polish Army Headquarters on 9 May 1945, paid tribute to the Polish soldiers who contributed to the victory and to the liberation of Poland and it set up new targets: "After winning the war, the nation has to win and safeguard a proper peace for our country."

The realization of that program had to be conducted under new conditions. Poland regained her independence within new boundaries. In the West its territory included Szczecin and Pomerania, the Lubusz region, Wrocław and Opole, together with Lower and Upper Silesia, and the state boundary ran along the rivers Odra and Lusatian Nysa. In the East ethnically Polish lands were included, but the boundary left all the territory East of the Bug and Niemen Rivers, with the cities of Vilna, Grodno, Brest on the Bug and Lvov, to Lithuania, Byelorussia and the Ukraine.

A great and difficult process was beginning, that of the birth of a new era in Polish history. The war was still going on when, in the spring of 1945, throngs of Poles, the bitterness of departure mixed with a hope of a new life in their hearts, set off on the road leading from the area beyond the Bug, from Vilna and Lvov to the regained lands in the West.

This great exodus of millions of people into the new and at the same time ancient Polish lands became an unusual education for the whole nation, a historic education on a massive scale. The lands on the Odra and the Baltic, regarded in the social consciousness as Polish soil in terms of history, nonetheless, lacked the elements of individual and family memories. On entering them one was crossing the frontier of individual biography and entering into the realm of national history and the new policy of the state.

Settling the territories on the Odra and the Baltic became an act of establishing contact with a thousand years of Polish history and, simultaneously, an act of confirming the correctness of the policy of the Polish Workers' Party and the principles of the alliance with the Soviet Union. This alliance formed a completely new factor in the political consciousness, due to which the two experiences of regained independence, in 1918 and in 1945, differed so basically.

They also differed substantially because of the fundamental changes in ethnic structure that was an inevitable consequence of the new state frontiers. For the first time since the Piasts, Poland had become a nationally uniform state; the issue of national minorities had disappeared, and with it the old contradictions and causes of strife. The Polish state which returned to the old Piast territories renounced eastward expansion, abandoned the mystifying theories of the "bulwark of Christendom" or the "bastion of Western civilization," concluded centuries of conflict with the Lithuanian, Byelorussian and Ukrainian nations and achieved, within its new frontiers, an absolutely new substance of national identity. The return of ancient Piast lands directed the historical consciousness to the early traditions of the nation and the state. The significance of this act was confirmed in 1946 by the foundation of the Board of Research on the Origins of the Polish State. This extensively planned research, conducted mostly by archeologists, historians and linguists, threw new light on the prehistoric and early Piast eras of Poland. It gradually extended to later epochs and formed the basis for the concepts of the great celebrations of the millennium of the Polish state, proclaimed in 1958 by the Polish Seym. These celebrations, combining academic research and popularization of its results, took place between 1960 and 1966. They included the whole country; various events were held in large cities, like Warsaw, Cracow, Gdańsk, and Poznań, in the Białystok region, Warmia, Upper Silesia and Opole, Silesian areas on the Odra and a host of such small towns as Żnin, Giecz, Wiślica and Wolin.

The program of these celebrations emphasized the pre-history of Polish lands and the formation of the Polish state during the tenth century, as well as Poland's role in the medieval era; it recalled Poland's struggle with the Teutonic Knights and the 550th anniversary of the battle of Grunwald; it attracted attention to the greatness of Polish Renaissance culture and to the achievements of the Polish Enlightenment, and, lastly, to the struggle for freedom, and the rise and development of People's Poland.

These research projects, discussions and celebrations drew attention to a wide range of valuable national traditions. Ideological and artistic merits of traditional Polish culture were revealed; the role of the masses and their participation in the creation of culture was analyzed; and new and previously unknown aspects of the social and national liberation struggle were demonstrated.

And not only words served the cause of historical consciousness. It was accompanied simultaneously by a great campaign of reconstruction and renovation of historic monuments on an unbelievable scale. Old town complexes in Warsaw, Gdańsk, Wrocław, Opole, Lublin and hundreds of other sites destroyed during the war, were reconstructed, or even newly built up again from ruins; castles and palaces, churches and monasteries, city halls and burgher houses were rebuilt. Every valuable relic was reconstructed, even when it belonged to a hostile historical tradition, like the great Teutonic Knights' castle at Malbork. In consequence many Polish historic sites were saved and the consciousness of generations was linked with the national tradition under conditions of everyday life.

This great program of reconstruction is still under way. The Royal Castle in Warsaw is still under reconstruction, as are the Piast Castle at Brzeg and hundreds of mansions and country residences, which, after renovation, will serve new social aims, providing in these changed conditions an element of traditional beauty.

BITTER AND CRITICAL POST-WAR REFLECTIONS

Apart from these political and historical issues, the social consciousness oriented toward the future also carried with it a disturbing complex of memories which stemmed from experience of the war and prison camps, and painful reflections on that cruel reality persisted. How was it all possible? What factors could have released the blind forces of hatred and cruelty which caused people to annihilate other people? Would there remain any hope for the progress of civilization after such experiences of the war and prison camp? What human values could retain their significance? Would not the smoke from camp crematoria poison forever the atmosphere of our world? Years after the end of the war Polish thoughts returned to the problem of German fascism, viewed in the broader context of the war and death-camp experience. This moral reflection formed one of the basic elements in the culture of the era.

Writers and artists, above all, would speak with that voice of conscience. Immediately after the war there appeared a whole series of novels and short stories related to the inhuman world of the occupation, of prisons and camps. This great tragic series of memoirs, condemnations, and reflections were inaugurated by Seweryna Szmaglewska's *Smoke Over Birkenau* (1945). Several books long held special significance: *The Medallions*

(1946) by Zofia Nałkowska, together with two books by Tadeusz Borowski, *Farewell to Maria* (1948) and *The World of Stone* (1948).

The same austere style of moral reflection could be found in lyrical poetry, particularly in Mieczysław Jastrun's *A Human Thing* (1946) and in Tadeusz Różewicz's early works, *Disquietude* (1947) and *Red Glove* (1948), in Antoni Słonimski's *Age of Defeat* (1945), and in Tadeusz Hołuj's *Poems from the Camp* (1946). Widely acclaimed throughout the world was the manifesto of Polish solidarity with every nation scourged by the iron and fire of Nazi hatred: Antoni Słonimski's poem, "He Is My Fellow Countryman" which described a tortured man in Bohemia, Yugoslavia, Norway, Russia, the Ukraine, France and Greece. The Pawiak and Montelupi prisons, Dachau, Sachsenhausen, Buchenwald, Mauthausen-Gusen, Ravensbrück, Stutthoff, Auschwitz-Birkenau, Gross-Rosen, Bergen-Belsen, Majdanek — these names have impressed themselves in the nation's memory as battlegrounds in the struggle for human life and dignity, under conditions of extermination and death. The heroic act of sacrifice by which Father Maximilian Kolbe offered his life to save that of another Auschwitz inmate appeared to the whole world as a symbol of the great nobility of man. But, in fact, all this time a tragic fight was going on in the camps between the world of values and the world of violence. Underground political activity, the organization for cooperation and mutual help which defended the sick and the weakest, the possibility of bettering conditions through detection of cracks in the system of outrage aimed at total annihilation and, most of all, the strengthening of belief in the invincibility of the mind — all these saved many and helped all. One of the elements in that resistance was art — painting, sculpture, poetry, music and singing, even theater.

A survivor from a camp, a poet, noted in his book *Man is Naked* (1960): "Strange, incomprehensible . . . art in the camps existed side by side with crime, and flourished against all logic. It became a potent agent of resistance against terror, helped prevent a complete brutalization of the inmates, gave birth to belief in man and the invincibility of human ideals."

Father Konstanty Michalski, a professor at the Jagiellonian University, an outstanding historian of medieval philosophy, analyzed the two dimensions of the human soul in his book, *Between Heroism and Bestiality* (1949). The problems of the German nation were dealt with by Leon Kruczkowski in his drama *The Germans* (1949). He treated the issue in deeply human terms, free of the accusations and resentment that one might expect from a representative of a nation that was to have been destroyed; the author exposed the weaknesses of German intellectuals in the face of fascist ideology, their delusion that peace of mind and human dignity might be found in solitude, in renouncing all personal responsibility. The play, produced many times both in Poland and abroad, was an expression of deep concern with the responsibility of intellectuals for the world's future. It was, like Sartre's *Les Séquestres d'Altona,* a voice of conscience.

The theme of occupation and the camps also found   218

expression in films. The first of these were *Forbidden Songs, The Last Stage* by Wanda Jakubowska and *Border Street* by Aleksander Ford, the last of which told of the extermination of the Jews of the Warsaw ghetto.

What lasting effects these subjects produced on the national consciousness can be seen by various works later produced. While the dramatic, tragic and cruel events of those years were passing into oblivion, moral considerations, full of concern and accusation, continued to remain alive, even gaining in range and depth. The novels of Tadeusz Hołuj, Tadeusz Konwicki, Andrzej Kuśniewicz, Hanna Malewska and numerous other writers, followed a similar line of approach.

The fine arts also expressed camp and war memories and reflections. Władysław Strzemiński and Henryk Wiciński sketched from life studies of human cruelty and despair during the war. During the war and later, Felicjan Kowarski created his moving paintings and drawings: *The Israelite Woman, Famine in the Ghetto, On the Doorstep* and *The Refugees*, reminiscent in general atmosphere of Grottger's visions of Polish destiny, expressed however by a new, almost brutal, means. His *Don Quixote*, painted in 1944, reverted to the romantic tradition of the lonely, hopeless fight, confirmed once again by the Warsaw Uprising.

Xawery Dunikowski continued to return to prison camp themes between the years 1948 and 1955. His cycle *Auschwitz*, in which he went back to memories of the camps, is a work of art unique in character which understood and bore witness to the beauty of life and the cruelty of brute force: *Christmas at Auschwitz, The Road to Liberty,* which leads through the barbed wires to death and, most of all, unusual in their lyrical expression, *The Vision* and *Dying Amaryllis*, picture of a crucified man withering like a flower.

The experience of war and occupation found expression in the drawings by Tadeusz Kulisiewicz, in the series *Ruins of Warsaw* (1945); in Jonasz Stern's compositions from the late 1940's, full of dramatic expression; such paintings by Andrzej Wróblewski as *The Shadow of Hiroshima* (1957); and in the work of Bronisław Linke, which exposed an almost surrealistic folly of the world of wars, cruelty, violence and absurdity.

The work of Waldemar Cwenarski, who died prematurely, also belongs to this same trend, particularly his *Self-Portrait* (1952), which offered a shocking synthesis of the war and occupation experience, of the painful fate of man, crushed by the machine of history.

Sculpture, too, was deeply involved in the same area of reminiscences, accusations and hopes. The works of Franciszek Strynkiewicz were a moving document of annihilation, especially his small sculpture, *Auschwitz* (1944); it portrayed a woman falling from deathly exhaustion who, nevertheless, tried to save from death a child she was holding in her arms.

The main trend in sculpture was that of monumentalism: for example, Tadeusz Łodziana's Memorial Mausoleum of the Victims of Fascism at Radogoszcz in Łódź (1959), or Gustaw Zemła's Monument to Silesian Insurgents in Katowice.

The subject of the last war returned during the late 1960's. Władysław Hasior's great compositions, *Monument to Hostages Executed in Nowy Sącz* (1966—68) and *An Iron Organ* (1966) were dedicated to the memory of the members of the Podhale partisan movement. Monumental sculptures commemorated the sites of death camps; significantly, they usually were the work of teams of artists. Thus, the International Memorial to the Victims of Fascism at Auschwitz was designed by Polish (Jerzy Jarnuszkiewicz and Julian Pałka) and Italian (Pietro Cascella and Giorgi Simoncini) artists. The Monument in Honour of the Victims of the Death Camp at Treblinka was the work of Franciszek Duszenko, Adam Haupt and Franciszek Strynkiewicz. The Majdanek Memorial was created by Wiktor Tołkin and Janusz Dembek.

The paintings and stage designs of Józef Szajna stemmed similarly from the world of memories of the camps.

Music conveyed similar recollections of the experiences of war and the camps. Some works directly referred to the events of those years, like *The Peace Cantata* by Stanisław Skrowaczewski, *Cantata in Honor of Peace* by Alojzy Dąbrowski or *The Warsaw Symphony* by Bolesław Woytowicz. Others were inspired by these events, by the awareness of the tragedy of existence, the sinister fate of the war, revenge, annihilation and by the fragile hope for the light of humanism. Such a spirit prevailed in the *Stanzas* by Krzysztof Penderecki (1959), based on classical pronouncements on man, and especially in his *Threnody for the Victims of Hiroshima* and his oratorio *Dies Irae*, written for the unveiling ceremony of the Auschwitz Memorial in 1966. Similar in their reflective and emotional mood were Witold Lutosławski's compositions, *Musique Funèbre, Béla Bartók in Memoriam*, conveying the universal human feeling of mourning, or his *Trois poèmes d'Henri Michaux* (1963). Stanisław Wiechowicz composed, to the words of Jerzy Ficowski, an oratorio cantata. *A Letter to Marc Chagall*, which recalled the martyrdom of Polish Jews. Tadeusz Baird, in his *Exorta* (1960), used old Hebrew texts to show the fear of the people and the horrors of the times of violence.

This examination of conscience embraced not only universal problems of violence and responsibility, but also an absolutely different one, of a purely national character. Poland's past gave the impulse to reflection and soul-searching concerning the historic path of development of the nation, and of the Polish national character in particular. Many questions were put forward, especially on the fall of inter-war Poland, and the Warsaw Uprising and its failure. What caused such a course of events? Was it our fault? Did we repeat the errors of our forefathers, or did we act consistently with our national character?

The great examination of the national conscience started immediately after the liberation and lasted for many years, leaving its mark on the changes in the social consciousness of the era. It was a matter of judgment, proclaimed by reason and duty, on the Polish way of life and on heroism, courage and sacrifice, as well as on political gullibility and folly. The moral and political problems of the Warsaw Uprising, in particular, became the main focus of passionate dispute.

This critical evalution of Poland and the Poles found its expression in such films as *Kanal* by Andrzej Wajda (1957) and *Eroica* by Andrzej Munk (1958). *Eroica* provoked violent attacks for its effort to unmask "cheap heroism" as well as for the criticism of the national homage paid to all who died, or were ready to die, for Poland, irrespective of political consequences.

A number of movies were connected with the theme of accusation. The same was true of literature, as is evident from the works of Kazimierz Brandys, Paweł Hertz, Stanisław Dygat and Jerzy Putrament. The issue was also picked up by historians. Years later these condemnations led to controversies and protests. Zbigniew Załuski's books, especially *The Seven Polish Deadly Sins*, were widely acclaimed as a defense of the Polish heroic tradition, showing how greatly in spite of accusations, this line of action was "reasonable."

In his *Pass to History* (1963), Załuski further undertook to find values in the past decades like "self-confidence, belief in reason and the ability to act effectively, and belief in the national ability not only to fight, but to win as well." His works served the purpose of giving "knowledge of the circumstances of successful fight and sacrifice," to disperse "the shadows of our national soul," which have stemmed from the false conviction the "we had always been doomed to defeat."

The same issue, but seen from another perspective, was treated by Melchior Wańkowicz. His consideration of the Polish war epic, from Westerplatte through Hubal's partisan warfare, to Monte Cassino, led him, in the end, to contrast "the culture of the imponderabilia of the gentry" and the "culture of the realia of the peasantry", that is, two different cultures which find expression in different styles of fighting and heroism. Within these categories he considered the reasonable and "honorable" surrender of Major Henryk Sucharski, the Westerplatte commander, a peasant from Wola Gręboszewska, as opposed to the hopeless, futile though heroic-to-the-death resistance chosen by Major Dobrzański (Hubal), a member of the gentry, who waged partisan warfare against the Germans months after the fall of the Polish state. According to Wańkowicz, these were the two truths about Polish heroism, and both were accepted by the national consciousness. The arrival of Major Sucharski's ashes from Italy, where he died, was the occasion for a national demonstration; and the film about the defense of Westerplatte equalled in popularity the film about Hubal's campaign and subsequent death; both were watched with deep emotion by millions of movie-goers, although more than a quarter of a century had elapsed since the events that were covered.

THE ROAD TO SOCIALIST POLAND

The everyday life of the community was devoted to reconstructing the ruined country and linking this work with the great program of effecting a socialist revolution.

The Manifesto of the Polish Committee of National Liberation of 22 July 1944, proclaimed in posters, published in the press and broadcast by radio stations, was moving westward throughout the towns and villages along with the front line. The army of liberation was bringing with it an image of a new Poland. It was an image of a Poland still fighting the Germans but already mobilizing her resources for reconstruction, of a Poland embarking on the road to democracy and social justice. The Manifesto promised restoration of all democratic freedoms; the equality of all citizens regardless of race, creed, nationality; freedom for political and labor organizations; and of the press and conscience. The only restriction was that they must not "serve the enemies of democracy." With regard to social reforms the Manifesto promised "to satisfy the age-old demand of the Polish peasantry for the soil" by the immediate "inauguration of agrarian reform on all liberated territory." The Manifesto did not use the word "socialism"; it did not refer to a "socialist Poland," but to a "Poland free, strong, independent, sovereign and democratic."

That new Poland which first emerged directly behind westward advance of the front line, became increasingly in the years that followed a state of the workers, of peasants and of the working intelligentsia. Introducing a program of social reform was not an easy task. The fight to consolidate the popular government and to increase its influence continued for several years.

During those difficult years, conditions were created and stabilized for the establishment and development of a People's Poland. This was supported not only by the workers, but by the masses of the peasantry, which had gained land and the right to work because of the new agrarian policy; this line was also supported by an ever-increasing number of the Polish intelligentsia, always true to their democratic and radical traditions. Under the pressure of social forces, new forms of Polish life were being shaped; they found expression in the central administration, in the system of people's councils; but, most important, in the agrarian reform and the nationalization of industry. New forms of economic and social life were thus being created at a faster rate than the changes in social awareness.

The beginning, 1944—45, was not easy. In a country with economic development so retarded that during the years between the wars both the gross national income and the standard of living indices placed Poland at the very lowest level among European nations, in a country devastated by the war so severely that a substantial part of its citizens lost even the roofs over their heads and their means of subsistence (the overall loss in national fixed assets was almost five times greater than during World War I), in a country with a decimated population and millions of its citizens newly resettled in the West, the task of economic reconstruction appeared truly enormous.

These goals were attained at different levels in the various regions. As early as 1949 the gross national income was higher than in 1938, and in 1968, it was four and a half times greater. The real meaning of these achievements may be assessed in a broader historical perspective. Taking 1950 as 100 we can compile a national product index showing that it equalled 32 in

1865, 75 in 1913, 58 in 1929, 63 in 1938, and 246 in 1967.

It was not simply a matter of material results. Just as significant were the changes in the social consciousness. In the final analysis, the decisive factors for the growth of reconstruction and development were the creative forces of the community. The national planning and the policy of the state were gaining active support from the working masses who continued to mature in their role as rulers of their country.

The socialist revolution had taken power from the hands of the propertied class and placed the country in the hands of the working people. The fact that they became joint rulers of the state deeply influenced both their work and their social attitudes.

Previously, in the history of Poland, neither work nor voluntary social work had developed rich or lively traditions. For ages Poland had been a country of primitive farming and insufficient industrialization. Only in People's Poland did industry develop and farming undergo a steady process of modernization. But progress required an ever-developing culture and discipline of work, an ever-greater efficiency of planning and organization of collective work, and an ever-growing amount of scientific and technological knowledge combined with the ability to follow up its new achievements.

Concurrently, the basic motivation for work was changing. With the removal of compulsion, characteristic of the capitalist economy, and with the limited possibilities of achieving profit by means of exploiting the work of others, significantly greater attention was paid to motivations of direct interest and personal involvement in professional activities.

Under these circumstances, for the first time in Poland's history, new links between the interests of the individual and the interests of the whole were being created. The scales of these two interests were still unevenly balanced and fairly often self-denial and sacrifice in the interest of the community were more strictly exacted than considerations of individual well-being; and, particularly at the beginning, emphasis on investment limited the funds that were made available for collective and individual consumption. But generally, conformity between personal and social interests was gaining ever greater significance. Growth in material well-being, together with the development of social welfare, gave the masses a feeling of unity. It manifested itself in the form of a conviction that "we are marching together," that "we are moving forward" along the road of a properly planned development of the country, that each one of us is a participant in a great and important common cause, and that no one is left alone to cope with life's difficulties.

The socialist revolution also opened up new avenues of development in the spheres of political and social democracy. In the socio-economic field this was effected above all through nationalizing the means of production. The working masses took control over decisions concerning the development and utilization of the country's material resources, together with the just distribution of national product, the ending of man's exploitation by man,

and a decrease in income differentials. The general growth in living standards formed a basis for all citizens to strive for a more human existence, and generally equal participation in the social life and culture. An end was put to unemployment and to treating people in terms of mere labor force categories. All working people, whatever their trade and profession, became citizens of the country.

The political system called on all to participate in the government of the country, and in this way, socio-economic democracy was supplemented by political democracy based on the principle of government by the people. Various forms of this principle previously unknown in our history, especially during the period of the so-called "bourgeois democracy," were put in operation in different branches of life. Because of the innovative character of these processes, they were introduced slowly; systematic efforts were made to safeguard an increasing measure of influence of the masses of the working population on the course of state and social affairs; a constant search took place, and continues, for such forms of administration as would favor the development of social initiatives and an increase in the feeling of responsibility of the citizens for the country as a whole, and for its future development, both general and regional. The role of the trade unions and of workers' self-governing councils, together with the increasing powers of the people's councils, constituted important elements in the development of popular rule; it was concurrently strengthened through the political activity of political parties, of civic organizations, of the Front of National Unity, as well as by organized discussions and social criticism which provided opportunities for testing public opinion and for putting forward suggestions regarding improvements in all branches of life of the community.

However, despite the achievements and the changes in social consciousness, the road to socialism proved difficult, crammed with inner tensions and contradictions. The Polish mind, shaped for ages by a tradition based on the gentry-landowner-intelligentsia had to undergo a revision. In his great historical trilogy, *The Fame and the Glory* (1956—62) Jarosław Iwaszkiewicz exposed the trauma of these changes which spanned the time from World War I through the twenty years between the wars, to World War II and to the beginnings of People's Poland. However the author left untouched the particularly difficult situations which arose in the political field during the very first years after the liberation. The most important question was the involvement of various social groups and of individuals in the development of People's Poland. From the first days of liberation of Polish soil by the Red Army and by units of the Polish First Army, a rift became evident between the attitudes of the followers of the Polish Workers' Party program and those connected with other political organizations: socialist and peasant parties and, most of all, the nationalists and Catholics. The process of political unification proceeded slowly. The merger of the Polish Workers' Party with the Polish Socialist Party took place in 1948, and the process of the unification of all peasant parties and organizations was completed in 1949. Similar processes in the Catholic movement took much longer.

These processes, formally manifested in changes in political organizations, in reality took place in the minds and the attitudes of individuals. Millions of Poles had to reorient laboriously their national consciousness which was being shaped anew by new state boundaries, a new social system, and a new form of government by the people. It was not easy to sever ties with traditional concepts and political notions of the previous historical path of development, to discontinue activities carried over by pre-war political party organizations from the period of the occupation. The process of these alterations of mind and attitude was, moreover, hindered during the post-war years, during the so-called "era of mistakes and deviations," by false accusations and distrust which led to the imprisonment of many a good patriot.

It was the younger generation, who had behind them active participation in the Home Army during the occupation, that was particularly severely affected. These dramatic conflicts found expression in Jerzy Andrzejewski's novel *Ashes and Diamonds* (1948). It was reprinted many times and remained so popular that ten years after its publication Andrzej Wajda made a film of it, thereby widening even further the social impact of the book. Bohdan Czeszko also dealt with this subject in some of his works. A collection of his stories *Early Education* (1949) and particularly his novel, *Generation* (1951), depicted the difficult process of achieving moral and political maturity in conspiratorial activity during the occupation, in the course of insurgent and revolutionary struggles.

With her usual sharp eye for social processes Maria Dąbrowska in her story *Third Autumn* (1954), presented the conflict between a civic leader and a stolid, bureaucratic administration, projecting against this background the values of social duty and of individual initiative and self-denial. In another story, *A Country Wedding*, Dąbrowska portrayed the difficult transformation of the Polish villages.

During the same era, Konstanty Ildefons Gałczyński's works with their allegories, irony, absurdity, satire and grotesquery, gained special favor with the public. They were published in the Cracow weekly *Przekrój* and some of them, especially his *The Green Goose Theater* and *Aesop Freshly Painted* (1951), were a sharp satire on Polish reality and on the weaknesses of the Polish intelligentsia.

In his *Poem for Adults* (1955), Adam Ważyk continued the line of bitter accusations, exposing the hiatus that existed between the words of the propagandists and reality, the inhuman living conditions of young people from all over Poland employed in building Nowa Huta, the false and arid spiritual education, the hypocrisy of the new moralists, the destruction of the revolutionary spirit by endless routine combined with materialistic calculation.

This was an era of "mistakes and deviations," and the young generation of journalists and critics were beginning to see the state of affairs with an unflinching eye. Simultaneously a wave of dissatisfaction grew among the workers, precipitated by economic and social policy.

When the 20th Congress of the Communist Party of the Soviet Union (1956) criticized the "cult of personality", the tendency to change the organization and style of administration, to link society more closely with the party and authorities gained new momentum. After the workers' manifestations in Poznań, in the fall of 1956, the plenary session of the Central Committee of the Polish United Workers' Party elected Władysław Gomułka its new First Secretary and established new principles of economic and social policy.

Gomułka defined these principles in the following manner: "The essential meaning of the 8th Plenary Session of the Central Committee of the Polish United Workers' Party lies in the fact that it has corrected party policy in such a way as to make the building of socialism a living, creative effort of the working class and of the working masses. We want to direct the building of socialism in such a manner that the working class and the working masses will know what they are fighting for today, and what their fight will bring them tomorrow; and that they believe deeply in socialism."

These new tendencies were reflected in the famous Roll-Call of the Fallen Fighters announced by the Polish Army Headquarters on the twelfth anniversary of the end of the war, 9 May 1957. It recalled all the people who fought for Poland, both at home and on all fronts of World War II.

This acceptance of the many ways of military service and sacrifice became from that time on a great source of national reconciliation. Literature, art and films now naturally turned to these heroic struggles, overcoming previously imposed censorship.

These patriotic emotions also found expression in monumental sculptures. Although Dunikowski's designs for monuments — for example, the two versions of his monument in honor of the Heroes of Warsaw (1956 and 1957/58) — were never constructed, some, like the Monument to Silesian Insurgents on Mount St. Anne, met with immense social acclaim. Some sculptors turned even further back to the knightly past, like Jerzy Bandura, designer of the Grunwald Victory Memorial (1956). A number of films dealt with armed struggle waged both at home and abroad, including films by Jerzy Bossak, Wanda Jakubowska, Jerzy Passendorfer, Bohdan Poręba and many others.

Literature, too, continued to create war epics, as evidenced in the works of Ksawery Pruszyński, Melchior Wańkowicz, Wojciech Żukrowski, Jerzy Putrament and Jan Dobraczyński.

Of course, the national reconciliation was being effected not only in art and not only in regard to the past; it also embraced the everyday lives of millions of people.

Hundreds and thousands of workers in Poland in their everyday work were now facing tasks they had not met before: the necessity of assuming responsibilities with which they had not been burdened previously. And hundreds and thousands of workers were acquiring completely new working methods in their jobs, making use of new implements, applying a new kind of organization. But people were not changing and improving exclusively, in the narrow sense, their professional qualifications and technical skills. Simultaneously with improvement in that field, man himself was changing and growing. Mastering new technologies, joining in the new organization of work, and undertaking new tasks, transformed man not only in regard to his specialist skills; these were also helping to remake his mind, to develop his ability to learn, to observe, to think critically, to work in accordance with his particular moral properties. The man who improved his qualifications to perform harder jobs and to perform them better than he did before, was becoming a different worker from the one who once was bogged down in routine; and because of this, he was developing differently in his life, as were his interests, his main aspirations and methods of evaluation. A man who was learning to work collectively was not only becoming a different worker from the one that used to stick stubbornly to individual methods of work, but was becoming, at the same time, a different man, a socialized one, with new, socialist attitudes toward other men. A man who was learning to undertake new tasks in his professional life and who approached them with enthusiasm and joy was becoming a new man, who grew together with the reality that he was creating.

Memoirs written at this time by people from various sectors of society, representing various trades and various levels of education, coincidentally related experiences concerning work and hope, aspiration and development. They displayed a fight for survival, reconstruction and reform, for new work, for collaboration in economic progress as a struggle for a new, truly human experience, both individual and social.

Such prospects opened up spontaneously in Poland for hundreds and thousands of people, above all, for the young peasant generation who found access not only to a wide variety of non-agrarian professions and trades but to new possibilities and obligations to fight for a new type of village community, for a cooperative economy, a socialist culture and the end of rural backwardness, and the overcoming of their isolation from the great and common goals of the whole nation.

Experiences relating to the nation's historic path of development formed the main contents of these changes. Though the situations and the particular goals were changing, and although the plans and endeavors frequently underwent revision, and errors were committed to be made up for, the overall main current remained the same: that is, the construction of socialism, the creation of a "Polish nation as a community of free working people." Independent of varying circumstances, a deep and fundamental process was continually under way, the historic process aimed at a basic orientation of human consciousness and attitudes, at creating new concepts and new ideals. And it gained momentum from year to year.

However, in 1969—70 faults and errors in economic policy came to light, mostly in respect to investment, which together with the lack of flexibility in planning and insufficient care for the material needs of society, deficient welfare, and an arbitrary mode of reaching decisions, led to a loss of contact with the masses and, consequently, to a neglect of such principles of democracy as participation in government and in responsibility. Under pressure from workers in Gdańsk and Szczecin, in December 1970, changes were effected in the party leadership. Edward Gierek was chosen first secretary.

A new phase in the development of socialist Poland began. The creation of socialism for the people and by the people became the leading principle. A national policy defined in the course of numerous consultations with the citizens led to linking economic development with social development — in order to harmonize the goals of investment with consumer requirements.

Defining new principles of policy at the 6th Congress of the Polish United Workers' Party in December 1971, Edward Gierek remarked: "The overall goal of the economy consists of a systematic improvement in the national standards of living of working people and of creating conditions for all-round individual development as well as of strengthening socialist social ties. An increase in consumption, an improvement of the material and cultural life of the working people, is the basic foundation of the concept of the socio-economic growth of Poland, which has been worked out by the Party. In such a definition of targets and motivating forces for further construction of socialism, our Party sees the basic element of its tie with the community."

These future prospects involved a grand program of "building a second Poland" both in a literal sense — that of constructing apartments for millions of inhabitants — and metaphorically. It aimed at a modernization of the national economy in industry and farming; the intensification of work in output and quality; the speeding up of the application of scientific and technological progress; the modernizing of management and organization; the modernization of thinking and attitudes; and the democratization of life. An absolutely new language appeared, which attempted to define the new situation and enumerate the tasks for today and tomorrow: interaction between economic and social policy, the acceleration of growth, the scientific and technological revolution, the quality of work, the intensive economy, tangible improvement in material conditions, innovation and modernization, a creative attitude, the quality of life, etc.

Unfortunately very soon, in fact as early as the mid-1970's, reality became increasingly removed from this program of slogans and promises. With every passing year the living conditions of the masses of the population were deteriorating, agricultural production was falling short of the nutritional demands of the nation, and forced industrialization, carried out with the help of huge foreign loans, was not bringing expected results. Society, and in particular the working class, which thanks to progress in education had become more mature and conscious of its role, could not reconcile itself with the authoritative and arrogant style of government; links between the country's state and political authorities and the people became increasingly superficial; part of the ruling apparatus used the position they held in society for their private gains and conducted a glaringly consumption-motivated style of life. Thus socialist ideals and norms of coexistence were betrayed by those who had been called upon to demonstrate and implement them.

223

This complex crisis deprived the government and the party of society's confidence and caused more and more general criticism and disappointment. In mid-1980 the working class first on the seacoast, especially in Gdańsk and Szczecin, and later in Silesia demonstrated their dissatisfaction in a wave of protest strikes and forced the party and administrative authorities radically to review methods of government and to change the composition of the supreme party authorities, with Edward Gierek in the lead. This spontaneous social movement of criticism and hope, organized under the slogan of Solidarity, rapidly attracted millions of supporters for whom the original program — that of forming independent autonomous trade unions in order to defend the rights and interests of the working people — was just the first stage of the campaign to show much broader prospects of improvement of the country, that is the implementation of demands of democracy and self-government and, on this foundation, the revival of mutual confidence between the government and society. In this spirit the new party and government authorities concluded a number of agreements with representatives of the workers and peasants with a view to overcoming old errors and renewing socialism in the spheres of the economy, politics and public morality. The Extraordinary Congress of the Polish United Workers' Party defined these errors and neglect and pointed out the way of renewal and national reconciliation.

The implementation of this program proved, however, far from easy. The extreme elements in Solidarity pressed on to decisive confrontation with the government, while party dogmatists questioned the political method of relaxing tensions which was pursued by the government and the party authorities. At the same time, aggravated relations between West and East, in particular between the United States and the USSR, turned our country into an area of imperialist political offensive and diversion. Internal peace in Poland and even the very existence of the state were threatened. In these conditions the introduction of martial law in December 1981 brought desired appeasement and as a result was abolished in July 1983. Simultaneously, consistent efforts by the government and the entire administration, led by the new secretary of the Polish United Workers' Party and Prime Minister, General Wojciech Jaruzelski, helped to overcome economic catastrophe and build new bases for national reconciliation, aimed at resurrecting the faith in the justness of the socialist road of development for Poland under the existing conditions of a world of great military blocs and of contradictions and conflicts.

Reconstruction of this faith, which adds meaning to human activity and also to people's private lives, is a difficult task of the coming years. For the dimensions of economic catastrophe and political crisis not only undercut confidence in the government and the party but also bred dramatic doubts as to whether it is still possible to believe in the prospects of durable improvement of socialism and implementation of its values after so many bad experiences, the so-called distortions of socialism (in 1956, 1970, 1980). At the same time, hopes for a new

shape of Poland, awakened within the Solidarity movement, were frustrated in the course of intensifying processes of anarchy in public life, and also in strivings to take over power in order to carry out dangerous political speculations growing out of an increase in international tension. In these conditions of criticism and disappointment there appeared an ideological void of social frustration and political cynicism. Such attitudes of resignation and indifference, especially among young people, are changed slowly and with difficulty. In everyday activity for the well-being of the country and in an atmosphere of common efforts aimed at national revival, new possibilities of individual commitment are appearing.

The political history of building a socialist Poland has been complex and has abounded in tensions and crises. However although these breakdowns of political development were difficult and painful, the nation's cultural development has not been interrupted nor damaged. Of course, under more favorable circumstances, it would have been more intensive but even in these conditions of conflicts and programs for renewal Poland's cultural life has preserved its continuity and richness. Proof of it is the intensity of ideological problems and their diversity, the development of all fields of art, the results of national education and growing needs in the sphere of cultural dissemination. In the forty years of People's Poland culture has been a grand manifestation of the nation's life and development, exactly as it happened repeatedly in Polish history. And this is what counts most.

MARXISM AND VIEW OF THE WORLD

After the restoration of her independence, in the course of a difficult social struggle, Poland was being transformed into People's Poland. This created particularly favorable conditions for the development of Marxist thought, which had to cope with new and serious tasks.

The radical Polish intelligentsia, having already mobilized its forces during the occupation, launched amidst these new conditions of national life a great ideological offensive aimed at winning and transforming the social consciousness. In 1945, the journal *Kuźnica* (Forge), published in Łódź under the editorship of Stefan Żółkiewski, became an instrument of that offensive. The periodical attracted a large group of journalists and scholars.

The intellectuals associated around *Kuźnica* drew, according to the suggestion of its title which referred to Kołłątaj's Forge, on the tradition of Polish radical thought, connected philosophy to political revolutionary activity and, by the same token, undertook a great program for the reconstruction of the mentality of the Polish intelligentsia. "Marxism for those people," wrote Stefan Żółkiewski, "was an authentic intellectual experience of their own, chosen out of conviction." In their view, Marxism made possible a true diagnosis of the problems of pre-war Poland and the reasons for her defeat, as well as an understanding of the mechanisms by which fascism emerged in Europe, and of the forces which

312. Jan Koszczyc Witkiewicz,
Experimental Center of the Higher School
of Commerce in Warsaw. 1928—30

313. Zdzisław Mączeński,
Ministry for Religious Denominations
and Public Education in Warsaw. 1931

314. Antoni Dygat,
Bonds and Stock Printing Office in Warsaw, 1925—29

315. Barbara and Stanisław Brukalski, Estate of the Warsaw Housing
Cooperative at Żoliborz in Warsaw, 1925—39

316. Roman Piotrowski, Residential house for employees
of the Social Insurance Company in Gdynia, 1935

317. Rudolf Świerczyński,
National Economic Bank in Warsaw, 1929

318. Xawery Dunikowski,
Sarcophagus of Boleslaus the Bold, 1916—17

319. Jan Szczepkowski,
Nativity shrine
(reconstruction), c. 1925

320. Edward Wittig,
Polish Nike, 1918

321. Henryk Kuna, *Rhythm*, [1925]

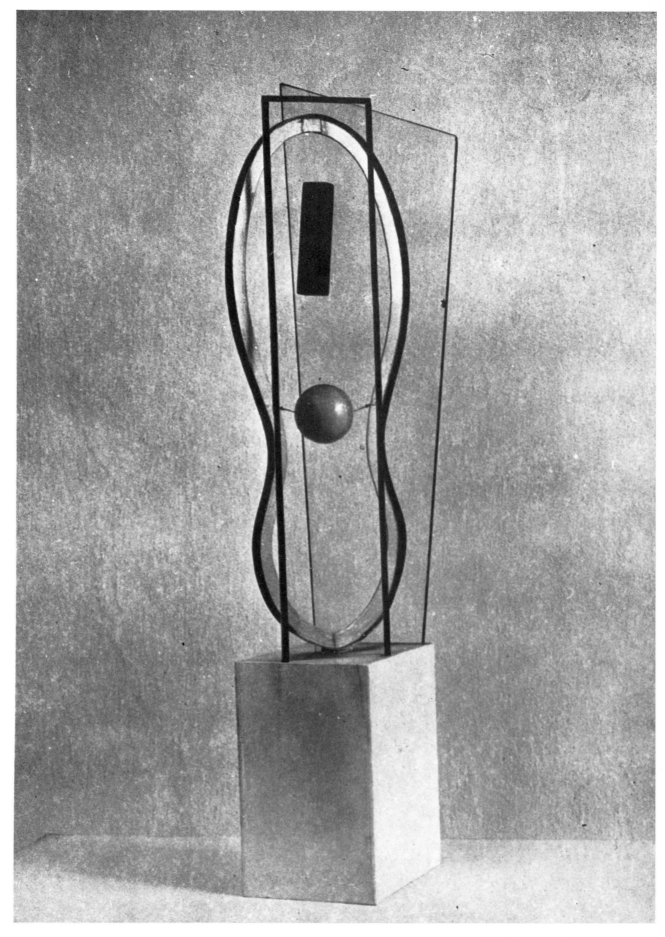

325. Katarzyna Kobro,
Suprematist Sculpture, c. 1924

324. Stanisław Szukalski,
Boleslaus the Bold, c. 1930

326. Zbigniew Pronaszko,
Nude, 1917

327. Andrzej Pronaszko,
Flight into Egypt, 1918—21

328. Leon Chwistek,
Butterflies, 1920

329. Leon Chwistek,
Industrial City, 1921

330. Stanisław Ignacy Witkiewicz,
Composition (Temptation of Adam), 1920

331. Stanisław Ignacy Witkiewicz,
Composition, 1921—22

332. Józef Pankiewicz,
Flowers in a Blue Vase, 1933

333. Felicjan Kowarski,
Withered Tree, 1930

334. Felicjan Kowarski,
Wanderers, 1930

335. Tytus Czyżewski,
Spain, 1923

336. Tadeusz Makowski,
    Village Yard, 1928

337. Tadeusz Makowski,
    Jazz, 1929

338. Zygmunt Waliszewski,
    Feast (small), 1933

339. Zygmunt Waliszewski,
    Don Quixote on Horseback, 1934

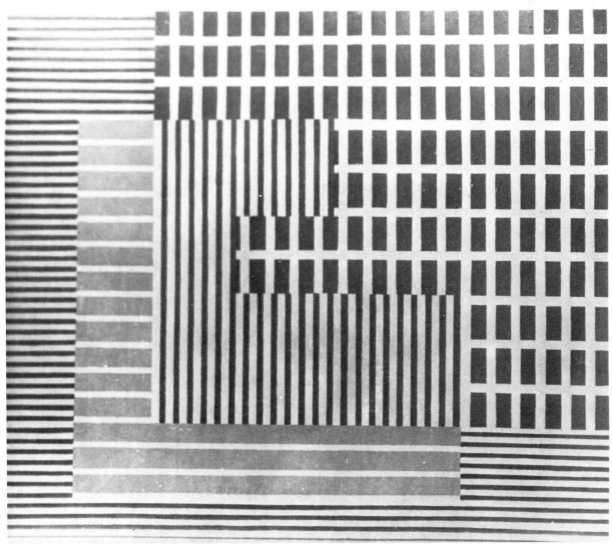

340. Henryk Stażewski,
Counter-composition, 1930—32

341. Władysław Strzemiński,
Łódź City Scape, 1932

342. Jan Cybis,
Peonies, 1936

343. Franciszek Józef Bartoszek,
Smithy, 1937

344. Jerzy Hulewicz,
Composition, 1920

345. Jonasz Stern,
Nude, 1935

346. Eugeniusz Zak,
Landscape, c. 1917

347. Mieczysław Szczuka,
Self-portrait

348. Karol Hiller,
Coal Basin, 1933

349. Leon Wyczółkowski,
Polish Knights Riding in the Rogalin Woods, 1925

350. Władysław Skoczylas,
Highland Robbers' Dance

351. Tadeusz Kulisiewicz,
     Women from Szlembark, 1939

352. Zofia Stryjeńska,
     Mountain Pasture

353. Stanisław Osostowicz,
Peasant Epic, 1930

354. Stanisław Ostoja Chrostowski,
Illustration to *Pericles, Prince of Tyre*, 1937

355. Tadeusz Gronowski,
    Poster advertising Radion washing powder

356. Zofia Stryjeńska,
    Kilim rug, after 1925

357. Eleonora Plutyńska,
Kilim rug *Squares*, 1929

358. General view of the ruins
of the Old Town in Warsaw in 1945

359. Bird's eye view
of the reconstructed Old Town in Warsaw

360. Gdańsk in 1945

361. Reconstructed Main City in Gdańsk

362. Ruins of Wrocław in 1945

363. Reconstructed Wrocław

364. Reconstructed castle in Szczecin

365. Marek Leykam,
     Department store in Poznań, 1950—52

366. Romuald Gutt,
     Central Statistical Office in Warsaw, 1948—50

367. Tadeusz Ptaszycki and team,
Central Square in Nowa Huta

368. Zbigniew Karpiński, and Jerzy Kowarski.
East Side of Marszałkowska Street in Warsaw, 1961—69

369. Intersection of the Łazienkowska
and Wisłostrada throughways in Warsaw, 1974

370. M. Budzyński and team,
   Ursynów North housing development in Warsaw

371. Tanks for liquefied gas
   in the Petrochemical Plant in Płock

372. Sports and Entertainment Hall
    and *Monument to Silesian Insurgents* in Katowice

373. Xawery Dunikowski,
    Monument to Silesian Insurgents on Mount St. Anne near Opole, 1949—52

374. Natan Rappaport,
Monument to the Heroes of the Jewish Ghetto in Warsaw

375. Franciszek Duszenko, Adam Haupt and Franciszek Strynkiewicz,
Monument in Honour
of the Victims of the Death Camp at Trebinka, 1964

376. Maria Albin Boniecki,
Coping of the *Monument of Three Eagles* at Majdanek in Lublin

378. Marian Wnuk,
Monument to Women of the Nazi Occupation Period, 1964

377. Władysław Hasior,
Design of a *Monument to Hostages Executed
in Nowy Sącz*, 1966—68

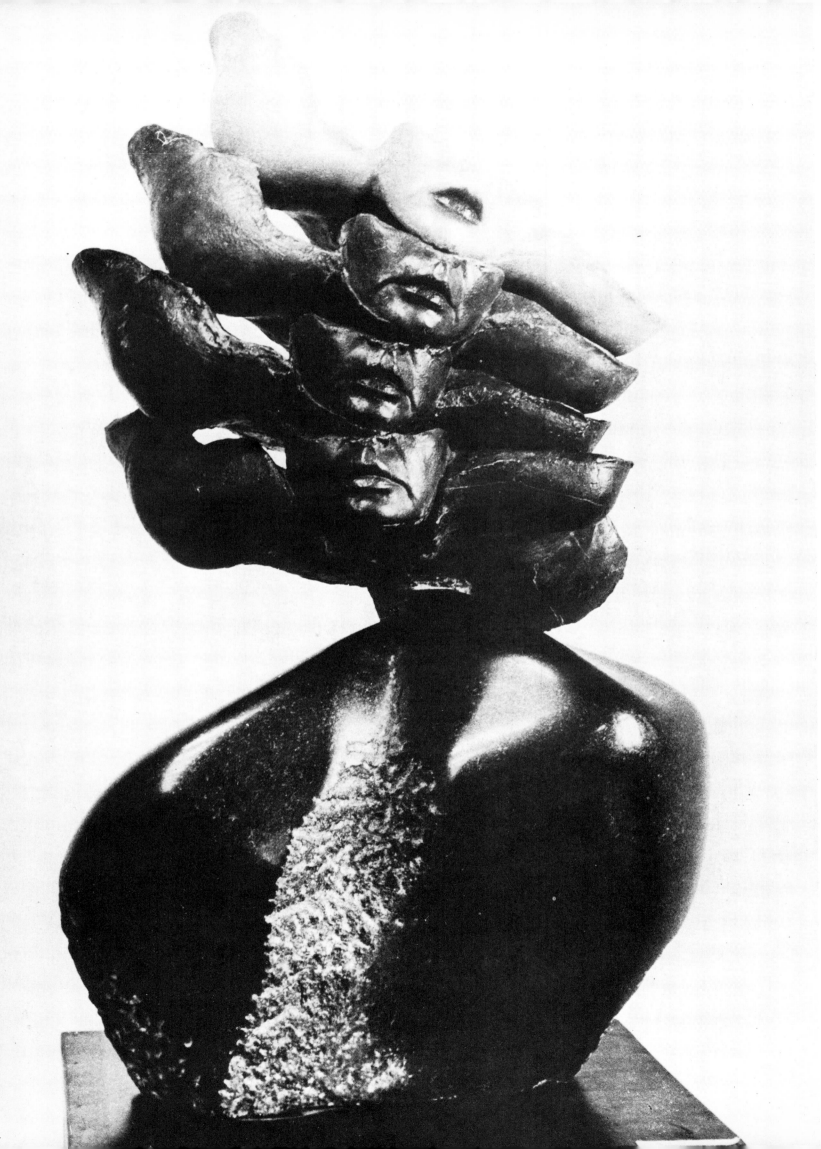

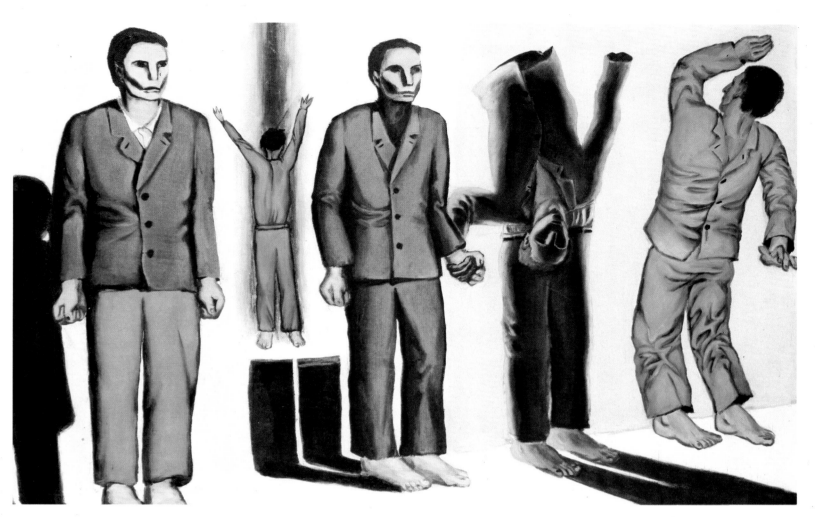

380. Andrzej Wróblewski,
Execution VI, 1949

379. Alina Szapocznikow,
Multiplied Self-portrait, 1965

381. Eugeniusz Eibisch,
Sisters, 1949

382. Marian Bogusz,
Mr Brown Sends His Regards to Fighting Palestine, 1948

383. Juliusz Krajewski,
    Stakhanovite, 1949

384. Helena Krajewska,
    Youth Brigade on the Building Site, 1949

385. Wojciech Weiss,
    Manifesto, 1950

386. Aleksander Kobzdej,
    Pass me a Brick, 1950

387. Tadeusz Brzozowski,
Prophet, 1950

388. Wojciech Fangor,
Korean Mother, 1951

389. Tadeusz Kantor,
Open Space

390. Marian Bogusz,
Honegger's Liturgical Symphony, 1955

391. Kazimierz Mikulski,
View from My Window, 1977

392. Henryk Stażewski,
     Coloured Relief 7, 1960

393. Andrzej Wróblewski,
     Queue Is Going on, 1956

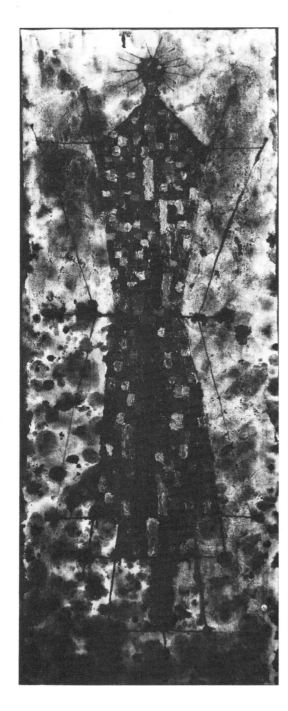

394. Jan Lebenstein,
Figure in a Brown Frame

395. Władysław *Strzemiński*,
After-image of the Sun, 1948—49

396. Stefan Gierowski,
Painting CC, 1966

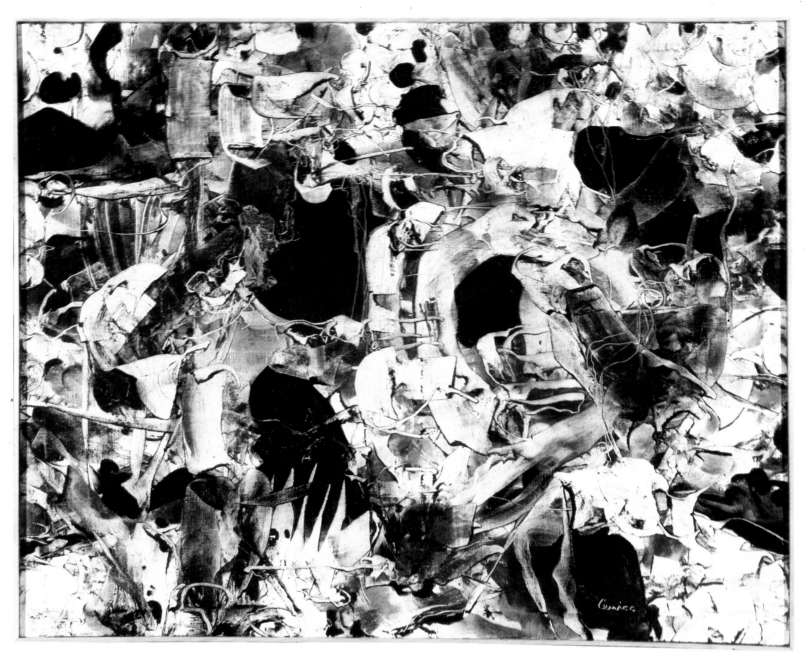

397. Alfred Lenica,
  Lost Photo, 1964

398. Józef Szajna,
  Epitaph IV, 1967

399. Władysław Hasior,
Polish Banners, 1967—70

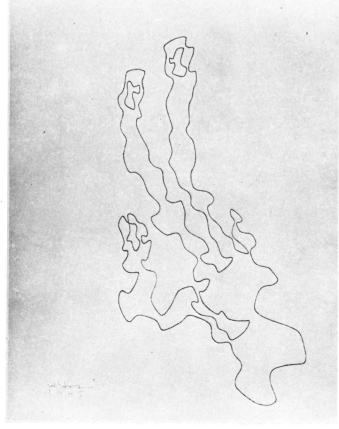

400. Władysław Strzemiński,
Drawing from the series *Hands That Are not with Us*, 1945

401. Maria Jaremianka,
Rhythm VII, 1958

402. Adam Marczyński,
Circus, 1955

403. Mieczysław Wejman,
Cyclist VIa, 1968

406. Waldemar Świerzy,
    Poster for the Mazowsze song and dance
    company, 1961

404. Tadeusz Trepkowski,
    Poster for the Peace Cycling Race, 1950

405. Tadeusz Trepkowski,
    Poster for the International
    Frederic Chopin
    Piano Competition

MAZOWSZE

407. Franciszek Starowieyski,
Movie poster

408. Franciszek Starowieyski,
Theater poster

409. Józef Szajna,
     Production of *Dante*, 1974

410. Tadeusz Kantor,
     Production of *The Dead Class*, 1975

411. Magdalena Abakanowicz,
Tapestry *White*, 1964

led to victory in 1945. In those circumstances Marxism became an arm to fight with, not only for new political ideology but for a new philosophy of life.

The battlefront of the fight for this new philosophy waged by *Kuźnica* covered several important sectors. It was a fight against the Catholic standpoint which enlisted great support throughout the community, particularly among the intelligentsia. It was a fight against various strains of the metaphysical philosophy which continued the old Polish messianistic and romantic tradition, against positivism and neo-positivism, and particularly against the concepts of what was termed the Lvov-Warsaw school, which had numerous adherents among professors of logic and philosophy. It attacked the various trends in idealistic philosophy, like phenomenology, existentialism and personalism, which were winning wide popularity at the time. The agrarian ideology which, towards the end of 1945, stated that "the trend to industrialize our civilization reverses the development of mankind and digs a grave for true human culture", was also attacked by the Forge in the name of technological advancement and the industrialization of the country.

Other magazines collaborated with the action of the Forge. A considerable role was played by the major project for wide distribution of Marxist literature. The classic works of Marxism were published in hundreds of thousands of copies in Polish translations, as were numerous studies by Soviet authors. Simultaneously a body of Polish Marxist philosophers was emerging and operating.

The scientific and popularizing activity of Adam Schaff, especially in his *Introduction to Marxist Theory*, published in 1947 with many later reprints, and several of his other studies, exerted a great social influence. Several generations of students were brought up on these books.

Particularly important among the goals of this Marxist offensive was its effort to reform academic thinking. The First Congress of Polish Science called in 1951 was of decisive significance. The President of the Polish Academy of Sciences, Jan Dembowski, an outstanding biologist, reiterated that for Polish scholars to absorb dialectical methodology was not enough; most important and necessary was the next step, "the real application of its principles to scientific practice," the skillful and creative practical application of scholarly research, and cooperation in the shaping of a scientific outlook.

This task was to be carried out by full-time school education and specialized institutions such as TUR (The Society of Workers' University) reactivated in late 1944, the Association for Popular Knowledge (TWP) in existence since 1950, the Association for the Secular School (1957) and the Society of Atheists and Freethinkers (1957).

Marxist ideology as a philosophy of life could not remain stagnant during this period of significant social and political changes at home and abroad, coupled with the great upheavals in science. Heated discussions, especially during the late 1950's, dealt with dogmatic petrifications in Marxism, while the fight against what were called revisionistic concepts was still going on.

From this point of view attacks were made on Leszek Kołakowski's criticism of "the priest" and defense of "the jester," his concept of rationalism, his concept of the significance of the individual conscience and individual responsibility, and his vision of a socialism of committed people. A great wave of criticism was aroused by Adam Schaff's book, *Marxism and the Human Individual*, published in 1965, which continued the line of reflection already inaugurated in his work *The Philosophy of Man* (1961). The author emphasized that "the focal issue in any socialism, either utopian or scientific, is that of man and his affairs, and not abstract man, not man in general, but a particular human individual." He raised the problem of a comprehensive development of man, of man's role in a community constructing a socialist system; the question of the constant battle against alienation along the path opened up by the ideals of "Marxist humanism."

Adam Schaff's adversaries pointed to deviations in his dialectic from the concept of objective social development, from the revolutionary principle of the dictatorship of the proletariat expressed in the form of a state of the people, from the strategy and tactics of party procedures in the field of social change. In this polemic, similar to that in the late 1940's, a different understanding of some principles of Marxism could be detected; the differences were deeply rooted both in history and in the Polish tradition of a revolutionary movement perceived as collective action born of the will and the imagination of individuals.

Development of Marxist thought was also going on in the fields of the humanities and anthropology. The problems of man in a society building socialism, particularly problems of personality development and of attitude to life and other people, became especially important in the everyday life of the masses. Sociologists and experts on ethics, psychologists and pedagogues, were particularly sensitive to social needs of this kind which, incidentally, had had in Poland a long and important tradition. Patterns of and hopes for a full life of the individual and of the community accumulated in that tradition were still considered worth realizing.

Under these conditions a wide variety of thoughts and considerations related to a philosophy of life were emerging in a way very characteristic of the whole era of People's Poland.

In the course of these discussions the notion of "socialist humanism" was formulated and from that point of view an attempt was made to find a "human cause" of the proletarian revolution. It was not a question, wrote Jan Strzelecki as early as 1946, "of humanity, but of living people, of their way of life, maturity, attitudes in relation to values, and of their aspirations." It was not enough to define socialism in terms of the "pressure of socio-economic" situations; it was a matter of basic moral values as motivations for revolutionary action and hope.

Maria Ossowska devoted her books to these moral historical and supra-historical issues, from *The Fundamentals of Moral Science* and *The Motivation of Behavior*, published during the first years of independence, to her last works, particularly *The Knightly Ethos and Its Variations* (1973). Stressing the diverse conditioning of historical and social morality, Ossowska, however, expressed conviction that there were some universal moral norms found irrespective of human groupings, based on the needs and strivings discernible in human nature, and that it was therefore possible to describe man as *homo moralis*. This issue provoked lively discussions and led to the development of theoretical ethics and metaethics which was one of the characteristic phenomena of the era.

Prospects for the future were widely disputed. Socialism was a system in *statu nascendi*. What was to be its future form? Many authors and scholars were trying to formulate various expectations. The statements of Stanisław Ossowski may be considered most representative. Continuing the line of thought he first developed during the occupation, Ossowski analyzed the roads leading "to new forms of social life", in which human commitment to the common cause and human ability for self-government were supposed to increase.

He often returned to the subject. In *Class Structures in Social Consciousness* (1957), he emphasized the significance of the conflict between society and bureaucracy, between spontaneous action and centralized administration. In one of his last publications *On the Peculiarities of the Social Sciences* (1962), Ossowski tried to prove that central planning, unavoidable in this modern era, may be linked to the "polycentric character of social life" and that thanks to "sociological imagination," it was possible to reach "a solution to the conflict between the efficacy of a uniform leadership and the humanistic values of polycentrism." Within that framework people could achieve the possiblity of active social participation, together with that of individual development. The old hopes of Polish revolutionaries of the romantic era, and of the socialist leaders from the turn of the nineteenth and twentieth centuries, again came to life in these visions of a democratic future. Other philosophies of life adumbrated in the 1960's and 1970's were expressed by empirical and pragmatic sociology which was directed towards reality and its rational improvement. A large group of scholars headed by Jan Szczepański step by step exposed the hitherto hidden face of industrial and agrarian Poland on the march along her road to democratization and increasing well-being. An analysis of that reality, particularly of socialist industrialization, pointed out both the growth factors in progress and those inhibiting development, attacked conservative thinking, and acknowledged the right of the masses to participate in administration, in consumption and in culture. The appropriate model of the future community was thus being shaped, liberated from blind mechanisms, inefficient bureaucratic administration and inexperienced political staff; it was a model of society which "edifies" by means of rationally organized work, truly "human" relationships and culture based on material well-being — a wisdom about life attained through practice in action and coexistence.

Psychology, and psychopathology in particular, provided another avenue for directing attention to the particular human individual.

As the cruel years of war and occupation were receding into the past, as the characteristics of life of the first post-war period of reconstruction and revolutionary struggle changed, with the growth of a consumer climate and aspirations, new and difficult problems of a balanced spiritual life were emerging with greater force: this had already been disturbed by the burden of memories and, later, by the processes of modern, industrialized and urbanized, mass civilization. Now people were beginning to look for the meaning of their existence and for the sources of personal happiness, personal harmony, and the significance of life in terms of the individual. Evidence of these needs can be found in the enormous popularity of Antoni Kępiński's books. In his numerous studies, which for the most part appeared only after the author's death, he exposed the profound conflicts of the modern man, his "troubles" with his own self. Obliterating the strict line between "the sick" and "the sound," he wanted to help both groups. "Schizophrenia," he wrote, "reveals an unusual wealth of human nature." In the "schizoid world" all human relationships, conflicts and aspirations become more acute; for example, the need for metaphysics and sex, for lies and truths, for authenticity and semblances, for envy and power, for emotional ambivalence, fear and extreme situations, for autism and efforts to overcome the "ego"; the need to conquer the spatio-temporal structures of everyday life, the role of imagination and delusions, the desire to create the world, and the defeats leading to feelings of chaos and void. Kępiński also demonstrated the variety of fears which oppress men, the need of trust and patience, of contacts developed through psycho- and socio-therapy. In a similar way he analyzed melancholy, both as "illness" and as a regular human condition.

Educational theory also showed the way towards individual human beings although emphasizing different aspects of the matter. According to Polish tradition, it was connected to the widespread educational and instructional movement and the activity of teachers, aiming at the future and striving to shape man to the measures of his times. The hopes of the people were expressed in these actions, the belief that it would be possible to overcome contradictions between individual development and social requirements, between work and participation in culture, between "practice" and "poetry."

On this basis, during the 1970's, an alliance was formed between the scholars committed to problems of social progress on the one hand and the humanists interpreting cultural traditions in terms of modern requirements on the other. This alliance became a method of exploring and creating the quality and way of life. The term acquired a rather general meaning, that of precept for social and individual actions, of a trend in criticism of bourgeois consumer society. It was also an important element in the theory of developed socialist society.

From its very beginning, the program of socialist humanism was linked to the image of new technical means of operation aimed at satisfying human needs. It was not connected with the romantic tradition, but rather with positivism, striving to act concretely in the direction of efficient organization and the improvement of reality, to establish a philosophy of life which was to define the meaning of human life and rational behavior.

In Poland as it entered on the road to modernization — in this country of rapid industrialization and a nascent scientific and technological revolution — this trend of deliberation and research directed to material as well as social reality, to effective and efficient action, to professional tasks, to men's responsibility for everything in everyday life, rationally organized within the framework of work and cooperation, was steadily gaining great significance. This philosophy of life was very popular among the intelligentsia, especially the technical intelligentsia who were not interested in metaphysical and philosophical problems; among the younger generation who sought modern possibilities to act and were averse to debating existentialist and psychological matters; and among the educational leaders who directed their efforts not toward the "shaping of souls" but toward perfecting their skills. It could be found, and put down its strongest roots, in concrete plans for and the actual organization of everyday life. These aspirations and methods of evaluating life appeared in the memoirs and diaries of technicians and engineers, in the statements made by innovators and inventors, in the declarations of leading workers, in discussions conducted by young working people.

This provided the broad social basis for the intensification of activity of the Chief Technical Organization (NOT), as well as development of research in the field of scientific organization and management of work, research which was believed to constitute one of the chief agents in the modernization of the economy and administration.

The activity of Tadeusz Kotarbiński expressed and inspired such needs. The ideal of "good work," which was one of the main themes of his philosophy, met, unlike many other philosophic ideas of the time, with deep social acclaim and consequences. His monographs and articles, which he started publishing in the late 1940's, particularly his *Treatise on Good Work,* published in 1955 and reprinted many times, exerted a great influence.

Elaborating his notion of praxiology, Kotarbiński wrote that, on the one hand, it was connected to the theory of rationalization of work and scientific management and, on the other, to methodological problems focused on the implementation of thought in action.

Such an interpretation of praxiology became a way of approaching the world, an expression of a philosophy which "emphasized its causative, adaptive attitude to reality contrasted with passive, contemplative thinking."

As a supplement to this knowledge of "cool precepts," there were "hot reflections," dealing with problems of responsibility in action, particularly with regard to human interrelationships and obligations. Numerous statements that Kotarbiński made on the subject were collected in his book, *Meditations on an Honest Life* (1966), which even found its way into several theatrical productions staged by students. These reflections answered the basic question: how to live? Above all, they underscored the obligation of loving other human beings, understood as real and concrete assistance to the needy, the wronged, and the weak.

The praxiological outlook developed in Kotarbiński's philosophy also manifested itself in various film produc-

tions. Numerous documentary films, avoiding the field of history and heroism and abandoning psychological and romantic tales, turned to dramatizing the activity of the people who were creating a new material reality in a rational and hard way. The very titles of these films gave evidence of the new elements which projected the image of the world and of the new aims of the people: *Chronicle of a Great Building Site, Earth and Coal, The Dam, The Time of Change, Energy, Bread Is Always Born, Rafts Afloat* and *I Was Building a City.*

Concurrently with this, the film world penetrated deeply into controversial situations which resulted from the industrial, scientific and technological civilization, the situations determining and complicating human destinies and human interrelations. Particularly characteristic of the trend were the films by Krzysztof Zanussi: *The Structure of a Crystal* and *Illumination.* A meaningful supplement to Kotarbiński's thesis of good will was the criticism of man's indifference to man, expressed in such films as Zanussi's *Next Door* or Krzysztof Gradowski's *Atrophy of the Heart.*

That world, seen objectively through human actions, rational, utilitarian and effectively planned and executed, appeared as the great responsibility of man, not only for "created objects" but also for human relationships.

Together with this outlook and concurrently with the ideal of "golden hands," appeared another one, slightly suppressed, a little too traditional for some people, but for others more modern than formerly supposed — the ideal of the "golden heart."

Catholicism reached above the mundane issues of a philosophy of life developed in these diverse aspects. Catholic circles promptly adjusted their activity to the new situation. As early as March 1945, they inaugurated the publication of the *Tygodnik Powszechny,* which has remained to this day the main organ of traditional Catholicism. The Catholic monthly *Znak* has been published since 1946 and is the most significant organ of Catholic thought. The Catholic University of Lublin (KUL) was re-opened. Laski again radiated its religious atmosphere far and wide.

Catholic literature (Władysław Grabski, Antoni Gołubiew, Jan Dobraczyński, Hanna Malewska) was more eager to deal with history than with contemporary psychological and moral issues. Virtually the only exception was Jerzy Zawieyski, who in his numerous novels and plays continued to show contemporary perplexities and to look for "the way home" through the labyrinths of the difficult world. From a viewpoint of devotion he tried to define the character of a Christian life and Christian commitment, the situations which necessitated moral choice, the problems of good and evil, of guilt and responsibility. In a world of cruelty and hatred, he was looking for love and brotherhood.

The theme of man and his world was also discussed in philosophical writings. Studies by Cardinal Karol Wojtyła dealt with the analysis of personality; Lublin university was interested in philosophical anthropology and in the history of Catholic philosophy, with special emphasis on the anthropological aspect. Stefan Świeżawski's edition of

St. Thomas Aquinas' Treatise on Man in 1956 formed a basic expression of that trend.

In Warsaw in November 1945, Bolesław Piasecki founded the weekly, *Dziś i Jutro,* with the aim to "build a bridge between Catholicism and the circles who preached the ideas of radical social reform." During several years of ideological and organizational struggles, the activists and writers from *Dziś i Jutro* implemented their program and founded the PAX Association, which received authorization in 1952 to operate in Warsaw, and in 1957 throughout the whole country. The PAX Publishing Institute, operating from 1949, published widely, ranging from editions of the Bible and the Fathers of the Church (St. Augustine and St. Gregory), to contemporary Catholic literature (Georges Bernanos, Daniel Rops and others).

During these years PAX was busy shaping its ideology, which was supposed to prove "on the ground of socio-political facts that the Christian attitude is not connected to the capitalist system" and it was therefore possible for Catholics to cooperate with Marxists in building a socialist Poland, reserving by the same token the right to continue a dialogue between the followers "of the materialistic and non-materialistic viewpoint."

However, the religious life and religious concepts of the world reached farther and wider, outside the organization of the Catholic Church and the socio-political orientation of PAX. In that period, as in former times, there existed an extra-institutional current of religious experience. Continuing Polish traditions of non-denominational religious feeling, music and painting expressed the religious experience and religious needs of the people. Of exceptional significance was the work of Krzysztof Penderecki who, like Karol Szymanowski in the preceding era, expressed this theme in musical terms. His oratorio *Dies Irae* (1966), recalled the drama of Auschwitz; the great work, *Passio Et Mors Domini Nostri Jesu Christi Secundum Lucam,* performed for the first time im Münster in 1966, and repeated at Wawel, in Cracow, was a thoroughly modern tale of Golgotha. Similarly innovative from both a psychological and musical viewpoint were *The Psalms of David* (1959), *Psalmus* (1961), and finally *Utrenye* (1971).

Penderecki's opera *The Devils of Loudun* (1969), presented the religious emotions leading to hysteria in a convent, the inquisitional severity of the Church, the intrigues of secular rulers and was yet profoundly human, true to the integrity of experience, to the tragic end to the road of life, which was supposed to lead plain honest people to God.

The art of Władysław Hasior also differed from the conventional clichés of expression regarding the religious experience. Tragically involved in the realities of war and the extermination camps, his art portrayed processions of people marching with national and church banners throughout the world, the "broken heaven", "the shaking of the heavens", village roadside shrines with figures of Our Lady and Christ, sometimes treated as old theater props, sometimes as touching mementos of a lost belief in heaven — it pictures "the angels of old" who might still be keeping guard over the people.

Society's religious needs and experiences, expressed in this diversity and wealth of both church and secular forms, were unexpectedly consolidated towards the end of the 1970's by the election of a Pole to the office of Pope. This event, which was of international significance, was particularly important for Polish society which for ten centuries had been associated with the church and its organization in Rome. For the personality of John Paul II combined the religious with patriotic feelings which for centuries were linked together in Poland, while the Pontiff's philosophical and literary output showed broad horizons of anxieties and hopes of modern man and was, in particular for the intellectuals, an evidence of a union between religion and cultural values.

John Paul II's two visits to Poland, in 1979 and in 1983, were a source of deep experiences for millions of believers who from papal sermons and from religious community drew hope and courage. Especially the second pilgrimage, which took place in the period when the country was making its first steps on the way to overcoming economic crisis and social tension, became an appeal for life in truth, work and community, an appeal which determined both the Church's policy and the everyday attitude and activeness of millions of Catholics. Religious experiences, which reached their apex at the Jasna Góra Monastery in Częstochowa, were to become a factor of the nation's moral revival and of the creation of mutual trust between the governed and the governing. The second millennium of Polish culture, like the first one, opened, in the consciousness of Catholics, with an intensification of religious feelings which are to help rebuild and defend the state, the common home of all Poles. A significant expression of these convictions was the growth of the church network through the construction of hundreds of new churches which were to constitute not only the material and organizational evidence of the role of the clergy, but also to become centers of the nation's religious and moral revival, a new stage in the Christianization of Poland. The same aim was to be served by the canonization of a Polish saint, Father Maximilian Kolbe, and three beatifications.

CRY OF THE HEART

The attitudes to life of Marxism and humanism, rationalism and pragmatism, the ideals of "good work" and Catholic images of duty were solemn and austere. But still, within the framework of the problems associated with a philosophy of life, there remained areas not treated in that way. These were areas of emotion and sensitivity, dreams and desires, sometimes of rebellion and contestation, sometimes of bitterness and scorn, which masked attachment and faithfulness.

The problem of a philosophy of life now appeared in a new light. Since exploitation and oppression had ceased in contemporary Poland, people could look forward to full human lives. As soon as the difficult initial period of the struggle for socialism was at an end, as soon as the years of war and occupation, of the uprising, became only a painful memory, and as the most difficult era of reconstruction which required unusual sacrifice was receding into the past, when the time "to temper the steel" was over, then vistas of a fuller life began to open up. The issues of the "heart" started to play an important role, particularly from the 1950's on.

The first and earliest attempt in that direction was Jerzy Szaniawski's play, *The Two Theaters,* published in 1946, produced by almost every theater immediately after the liberation and revived many times in later years. The director of the Small Mirror Theater decided to stage only realistic plays and to interpret human dreams in a rational way. But reality, like imagination, created dramatic and irrational situations. A second theater of "dreams" revealed another dimension of reality concealed in the human consciousness: of suffering, remorse, hope, suppressed by the necessities of life. This second theater "made the heart of the sleeper beat with a violent pulse, to flood his face with tears and make his hair stand on end."

The poetry of Konstanty Ildefons Gałczyński took a great step forward along that road. His poems, in which the world of poetic imagery was combined with daily reality, personal experiences with the social tasks of the people, and lyrical emotions with jokes and with the grotesque, met with ever greater acclaim during a time when the populace was no longer required to fight for People's Poland but could live in it instead. The tune of "things Polish," which was heard in his poems painting the charms of Polish landscape and history, the world of Wit Stwosz and Niobe, but also the soldiers of Westerplatte, the melancholy of the Mazurian Lakes and the marvels of a country under reconstruction — all these things appealed directly to the heart.

The readers of Gałczyński's poems were also enchanted by his gift of arousing emotions, offering melancholy and sentimental reflection, all treated in a detached manner, in a half-serious, half-joking manner, enveloped in good-humored irony, a satirical smile, surrealist nonsense, which reigned in his *Green Goose Theater* and *Correspondence with a Violet.* To other readers he was a poet who wrote movingly about daily life and work, "geraniums in windows", "an enchanted cab" carrying people through the world, about how "work throbs" and "poems, houses and symphonies" are created, and how important it is to make everything on earth "beautiful and just, and put bread and flowers on every table". Gałczyński's poetry expressed in fullest measure these various emotional needs and the atmosphere associated with them.

Similar in nature, but different in their range and manner of expression was the poetry of Tadeusz Różewicz and Zbigniew Herbert. The former, like Gałczyński, attempted to create poetry for the people, a poetry of understanding and a smile, and of common experience, of family life under the care of one's mother and of dreams come true. This trend toward simplicity and peace, however, was threatened by the reality of the cruel world, by painful memories and ever-present fears of war and of imposed patterns of life.

And although one collection of Różewicz's poems was entitled *The Smiles,* it was a bitter smile in the face of a cruel world to which only "a stony imagination" could bear witness. Will man ever be able to master that world and make it human? Or will he not be able, or even willing, to do it? One collection of his stories was entitled The *First Examination.* These were stories of people who had not yet found themselves through their responsibility to the world. They lead a life that was perhaps only recorded in the *Card Index* (1961); a sterile, satisfied life as shown in *Our Little Stability* (1962), the title of which became a symbol of the struggle against the consumer approach to life that snobbish art had not overcome; and in his *The Laocoon Group,* which exposed the false life of artists and their public. In these circumstances maybe only *Death in Old Scenery* (1970) remains open to men.

A different tone was struck in Zbigniew Herbert's poetry. "The beehive of the heart is empty," he wrote with bitterness. Only reason remains to man; but its great challenge leads him to inevitable defeat. *The Ray of Light* (1956) was a road sign and a goal, an appeal for heroism. However, "Nike is dubious" and "the world offered a stone instead of flowers"; whereas anything of value is fragile. To live consciously means to lead a hard life. In *The Cave of the Philosophers* (1970) Socrates asserts: "I've never given up sobriety. And never have been ashamed of the dizziness born of full awareness." Such a life, however, means the acceptance of death in the midst of the mob. Thus, *Mr. Cogito* (1974), because of his courageous thinking, set out on the road of conflicts, because, as he confesses with bitterness and with the heroism of defeat: "You didn't go mad in order to stay alive."

Tragic and ironic works introduced yet other notes. A special meaning among post-war novels was achieved by Bohdan Czeszko in his *Threnody* (1961) which exposed life as a march to death and nothingness, and war and struggle as chaotic, unnecessary action undertaken by a detachment which goes to the front and is wiped out although the war is almost over.

Simultaneously with these various currents of lyricism and tragic images of the world which presented the fate of the people and the nation, there appeared a counter-current closely related to them. Gałczyński also formed part of this trend which later, with its variety of grotesque, irony and contempt, became one of the most characteristic phenomena in the Polish culture of the era.

Sławomir Mrożek's plays, particularly his *Policemen* (1958) and *Tango* (1964), were theatrical events portraying the conflicting experience of greatness and of mediocrity, desires and falsehood, the authenticity of life which is violated time after time.

A parody of the romantic and neo-romantic approach, the grotesque quality of the modern world, the tragic real conflicts and a parody of the struggle for progress under the rule of the police, the mad tango which was a contemporary version of the traditional power over human beings of the straw figure from Wyspiański's *The Wedding* — this was the world Mrożek portrayed and fought with in his plays. In *Tango,* as earlier in *The Wedding,* Polish life was caged in the rhythms of dance, a vicious circle, lacking any idea, any faith, any hope.

Experience of that sort gave rise to a renaissance of former literary surrealism, grotesque and satire.

The rediscovery of Gombrowicz, Schulz and, above all, Witkiewicz (Witkacy) was already evident under the occupation, but only in the late 1960's did Polish theaters become submerged by a wave of surrealist "derisive" art. Witkacy was staged in all theaters; almost all of his dramas were played in various productions to an astonished, sometimes even shocked, new audience. Gombrowicz's plays, never staged before, were also shown.

Concurrently with this trend, however, came another — a great revival of Romanticism. The greatest works of the Polish romantics returned to all Polish theaters. The staging of Mickiewicz's *Forefathers' Eve* seemed to become a passion with theatrical directors in People's Poland. The interpretations of Romanticism put forward by the Young Poland movement, in particular by Wyspiański, are still alive today. His dramas, *The Wedding* and *Deliverance*, revived frequently at various theaters, still register in the contemporary social consciousness an important settling of accounts with the guilts and virtues of Romanticism. *November Night*, which in the Cracow production indicated unity of aims and spirit between the conspirators from the November Insurrection of 1830 and the Warsaw insurgents of 1944, proved how inexhaustible was the romantic source of Polish experience and Polish thought. The same was true of the success of Ernest Bryll's play, *The November Matter*.

These experiences led to the return of the great disputes concerning the values of romanticism. No place could be found for them during the early post-war years. Poland was then being rebuilt from ruins by arduous work and self-denial, her social structure reformed in the course of a bitter fight with her enemies. The Warsaw Uprising had been severely condemned because of its obvious political aims, and a veil of silence had been drawn over the mourning for hundreds of thousands of people who had lost their families and their city in that battle. Survivors of Hitler's prison camps brought with them an image of the "stone world," at the same time cruel in cynicism and sophisticated in tortures. Smoke from the crematoria covered the sky. There was no sense in looking for God, or justice, or charity, or traditional heroism: "We will leave behind iron junk, and the hollow, scornful laughter of generations," Tadeusz Borowski, an inmate at Auschwitz, wrote. Where was there room for romanticism here? Even his suicide was far from the romantic self-inflicted death born of the feelings of a "disenchanted heart" and a "betrayal of dreams."

In that climate the chapter of the Romanticism of the century of the partitions seemed closed once and for all, alien and useless, even incomprehensible. From the book of history only those pages were read which spoke of science and rationalism, of work and technical progress, of good management and education, only those which were forerunners of a materialistic philosophy and the revolutionary road which led to socialist change. From this vantage point Polish Enlightenment and Polish Positivism seemed especially close.

But characteristically enough, despite criticism or perhaps because of it, Romanticism appeared on the scene again. It was noted that Romanticism, and not the ideology of organic work, had been the inspiration of all the revolutionary movements of the nineteenth century; even if as in the first decades of that century, this had been a movement of "revolutionary noblemen", it had nonetheless developed into a theoretical and practical program for "the revolutionary-democratic struggle." Large-scale research in preparation for the Centennial of the 1848 Springtime of Nations exposed these very aspects of Polish Romanticism.

These various experiences — reflected in lyrical poetry, in the grotesque, in tragedy, irony and the absurd, in the criticism of Romanticism and in its comeback — shaped a certain philosophy of life, a kind of personal and existentialist experience characteristic of the people of the era, involved deeply in life yet often lost in it. In this way a certain aspect of modern life was disclosed, different from that currently accepted but nevertheless important for the overall cultural transition.

Not all of human life could be defined in terms of an alliance between scientific and technological development and social progress, in the framework of a universal rationalist and pragmatic program of education. It was evident that modernity could not be defined clearly and unequivocally by an increase in the material standard of living, by an increasingly effective equality of chance, a more just division of the national product, the development of computer science and managerial efficiency, by an intensification of the processes of professional work.

Questions were emerging: Was it possible to translate the issue of modernity into the language of human felicity? Was there some special modern form of happiness and was its social range widening? Could it not be that the modern methods of institutionalization of life, of organization and management, the prospects of popularization of computer science were factors bringing about the disintegration of personality and community? And did not modern conditions reduce the possibilities of individual self-realization, even though social needs of this kind were increasing?

The agonizing questions of the post-war and post-occupation period continued to return. Did it pay to live in a world, where it was impossible to forget the cruelties of the war which had ended not so long before and was still a living threat; to forget the genocide perpetrated in the concentration camps, in Hiroshima; or the wave of terrorism and vengefulness which was destroying political figures in various countries, or the hundreds of thousands of people dying of starvation while the whole world looked on, or the millions of starving children deprived of education and medical care? Was it worthwhile to live in a world stricken with fear about the progress of science, previously looked upon as the paramount triumph of man over nature, but which now enabled criminals and madmen to destroy mankind by means of nuclear arms, chemical weaponry, or a future dictatorship based on interference in eugenics? In a world where universal trust in the beneficial mechanism of progress was breaking 230 down, and the defensive forces of the endangered biological environment of man had proved to be so weak and fragile? In such a world in which the mechanisms of power and the structure of the establishment rarely permitted the triumph of justice and truth, while opening up roads to action and success for the ruthless and the sly? These conditions created complex problems for man's inner life and it was with them that the art of the era had to deal.

The most significant developments were the STU Theater, a, student group from Cracow, the songs of Ewa Demarczyk, and the art of Hasior. All of them recalled the cruel years of destruction of all things human, reminiscences which could not be erased from memory or from the heart, still filled with terror and melancholy. That world, at one time so real and still agonizing, remained in Hasior's work, much like the nightmares of Goya, whose life was similarly influenced by his country's history. Through flaming meadows of blood — the title of one of Hasior's unusual multi-plane creations, compositions, referring to one of Baczyński's poems — the path of modern man is paved with thorns. In the shadows of that world with red waterfalls, black landscapes and dark songs, the helpless witnesses to destruction appear: the cross and Christ.

That subject leads directly to the "vivisection of the Polish soul," namely to the production *Exodus,* staged by the STU Theater, which tells the story of the forsaking of unauthentic life, the life of masks in a false world. The core of the matter is "that the shell of dirt, masks, costumes and daily worries should not kill the fundamental question: What am I? How do I live?" And the fire which consumes the wings of the guardian angel who, while surrounding with solicitude man's loneliness, promises him nothing; this fire — an ancient symbol of light and warmth and also of annihilation — turns into a symbol of purification and liberation. It is the same fire which burns in Hasior's creations, in his somber reminders of violence and cruelties that were committed by the German Teutonic Knights, in his monuments placed high up in the mountains which, like live torches left over from the holocaust, are at the same time lights in the darkness, conveying hope in spite of all doubts; in his mysteries of candles burning around coffins in circles one has to cross; in his images showing that man has to burn.

A leading role in these efforts to organize the national imagination was played by the STU Theater in Cracow. Its founder, Krzysztof Jasiński, dreamed of a popular theater present everywhere, a mass theater. He created a Wawel Cantata, turning Wawel into a "national stage" and seating his audience across the River Vistula; he created the Auschwitz Cantata and the great background to the unveiling of the Lenin Memorial in Nowa Huta. He dreamed of a great theatrical pilgrimage which would progress through Poland and for Poland and which would liberate the people from the deadlock of "a petrified life." In reference to the collection of Tadeusz Borowski's stories, *The World of Stone,* the motif of stone became one of the leading subjects of poetry, which searched for ways of liberation, including that by Różewicz and Herbert.

The road of the heart was believed to lead through a stony labyrinth. This traditional road, forgotten by the people who thought only of advantages and scorned by noisy rationalists, was taken by the kind of art which is discussed here, especially by poetry sung by Ewa Demarczyk. When she sings Baczyński's poems, the audience is always deeply moved, because those events are still alive for everyone; there is still a link between those who survived and those who had died, and those who are still dying somewhere on earth. Conscience awakens when history challenges human happiness; when love clashes with heroism, and sacrifice tries to put an end to violence and cruelty. In this image of the world of tragic memories and dramatic conflicts, we hear the voice of bitter reflection on human fate, somehow mollified by the tenderness of the heart for the weak and hapless. This is what we find in the poetic texts chosen by Ewa Demarczyk, in her expressive, moving intonations which soften the sharp thorns of life, in the enchanging warmth and kindness of the heart. Is it not so that each of us — in the words of the poet — "constantly carries a hump on his back," and with that hump "continues to dance and beg?" And does not each of us, in the words of another poet, at least for one tiny moment of joyful abandon want to embrace the whole world like the madonna of his happy years? How many people can hear Hercowicz, the violinist of the heart, play his eternal sonata when "night and snow reigns" in the indifferent and hostile world out of doors?

This is the other dimension of the world we find in the songs of Ewa Demarczyk: the man who has a heart.

In his film *Atrophy of the Heart* (1970) Krzysztof Gradowski relates a story of an old woman nearing her death, as if alone yet in the presence of neighbors, friends and family, no one of whom has a heart. The Ochota Theater called the man of the heart *homo mollis.* But does not history confirm that such "softness" is strength?

REALISM AND THE VARIETY
OF CURRENTS IN THE ARTS

Art, particularly poetry, accompanied the changes and the conflicts, the hopes and the social plans. It expressed enthusiasm and also pronounced judgment on the course of public affairs. Some of the works, even the poetic ones, became significant political agents in the change and, while preserving the merits of beauty, gained the character of social manifestoes of a new order.

The prophetic words of Stefan Żeromski came true, although during his lifetime they seemed premature. In his *Dream of the Sword,* Żeromski wrote: "The socialist idea has not been popular with our nation. It was imported from the West and imposed on us. However, the astonishing fact is that the entire Polish nation has accepted it for its own."

Literature, both prose and poetry, fulfilled Żeromski's hopes and put themselves at the service of People's Poland. These tendencies were expressed in Mieczysław Jastrun's famous article, "Beyond Historic Reality," published in one of the first issues of *Kuźnica* in 1945.

Jastrun attacked literature which "tries to ecape historic responsibility, the horrors of historic reality that was about to destroy the country and set fire to ages of our culture." This was the approach of humanism fighting for the future of Poland and the world.

Julian Tuwim, on returning from abroad, brought with him *The Polish Flowers;* in a long litany of wishes, he defined the shape of a new Poland, ruled "by wise and good people," whose interest is the happiness and freedom of all the people.

Adam Ważyk in his famous poem, *The People Will Enter the City,* recounted the reconstruction of Warsaw and the building of a new Poland in a remarkably astute way.

Władysław Broniewski, who at the beginning of the war stated that "there are accounts for injuries to be paid in Poland," hopefully embraced and welcomed the liberation. In his poem, *The 22nd of July,* he paid homage to the soldiers who had liberated the country, and the workers who were busy with the construction of a new life.

In literary practice this enthusiasm was transformed into a great plan for the development of a new socialist literature. During the late 1940's, in the course of various bitter disputes concerning cultural and artistic policy, a program for socialist realism in literature and art was drawn up. At a writers' convention in Szczecin in 1949, a proposal was accepted that literature should "assist in the construction of socialism in Poland" and that it should do so according to the principles of realism, which contrary to bourgeois realism, should achieve a socialist character. The prolonged arguments which were inaugurated by this congress dealt with the essential contents of the concept and with the artistic program it designated. The disputes also touched upon specific efforts to put these ideas into practice.

The great discussion about the poetry of Mayakovsky in 1950, and of Gałczyński in 1951—52, together with polemics published by *Życie Literackie* in Cracow in 1951, brought down the barriers of schematism and didacticism and opened up broader ways to literary work. Starting from the early 1950's, poetry and prose began to flourish in various forms.

The poets, as Julian Przyboś said in 1954, wanted "to create the lyrical poetry of socialist man, and to express experiences and sensitivity hitherto unknown."

The fine arts also tried to express these changes in various attitudes and strivings. Painters sought new roads to a new Polish reality and, like the poets, had to cope with both artistic tradition and the schematic treatment of this new reality. This search for new approaches was, almost symbolically, inaugurated by a painter of the older generation, Wojciech Weiss, with his famous oil-painting (1948), portraying a group of workers reading the July Manifesto.

A significant influence was exerted by the works of the following great artists: Xawery Dunikowski, Felicjan Kowarski and Władysław Strzemiński, artists who were at the zenith of their careers in People's Poland and were opening up ways for new painting and sculpture. The methods they employed were those of monumental realistic art, which revealed the destiny of man and at the same time of an art which penetrated the existential experience of man, art of a new vision, perhaps even of a new liberation.

Dunikowski's work showed the possibilities of monumental, patriotic and historical memorial sculpture; his Monument to Silesian Insurgents on Mount St. Anne, and designs for the Monument to Warsaw Insurgents were imposing compositions which attempted to prove the invincibility of man. The artist criticized abstract art when he said that "the new art will be superhuman, will feel and show infinity; it will be born of a perfect understanding of nature, and will penetrate the very essence of man." Concurrently, Dunikowski's paintings, *The Auschwitz Cycle,* achieved that essence in a different manner, by contrasting the cruelty of violence with the lyrical relationship between men and nature.

Kowarski also worked within the framework of this monumental and social art, expressing at the same time the tragic destiny of man. The period of the occupation gave rise to the paintings and drawings of the series entitled *Ghetto. Electra,* painted in 1947, conveyed the same atmosphere. The Polish tradition may be seen in *Don Quixote,* created during the year of the Warsaw Uprising. But his famous canvas, *Proletarians* (1948), drew on another Polish tradition — the tradition that created the modern era.

Strzemiński, at this time, produced series of drawings, *Hands That Are not with Us* (1945), including such pictures as *The Unemployed, The Factory* and *The Tenement;* he continued his interest in the theory of vision; his plans for making the city of Łódź functional (1947) envisaged a modern reconstruction of the city thanks to cooperation amongst architects, urban planners, painters and sculptors. Simultaneously, he undertook studies which combined optics and painting, and studies on man's visual powers which had not been utilized thus far. He created solar compositions.

Independent of the work of these three great older artists (Kowarski died in 1948, Strzemiński in 1952, Dunikowski in 1964), the younger generation of painters showed signs of unusual activity.

During the early months after the liberation, they proceeded along different roads, which were represented at the Exhibition of the Group of Young Artists in Cracow in June 1945, and at the Spring Salon in Warsaw in 1946. Henryk Stażewski, Maria Jaremianka, Władysław Strzemiński and Tadeusz Kantor created abstract, avant-garde art; Andrzej Wróblewski, Jerzy Nowosielski, Tadeusz Brzozowski and Kazimierz Mikulski revealed the truth about man by means of the grotesque, metaphor, idealization and allusion.

The exhibition provoked discussion in which different views clashed. Some championed traditional realistic art; others formulated concepts of socialist realism; while still others revolted against treating art as some sort of documentary illustration to the history of culture and demanded a more profound and novel look at reality and man. Some supported the program of colorism; others advocated avant-garde formulae. Fairly quickly there emerged a large group of painters and sculptors professing socialist realism. Particularly active in this field were Juliusz Krajewski, creator of such paintings as *The Female Stakhanovite* and *Land to the Peasants;* and Helena Krajewska *(The Youth Brigade on the Building Site).* Their paintings although sharply criticized portrayed conditions of work and life in Poland. During the 1950's Tadeusz Kulisiewicz created two series of drawings: *Soldiers of Revolution and Peace* and *Fighters for Freedom and Democracy.* In 1950 Aleksander Kobzdej exhibited his well-known painting, *Pass me a Brick,* which portrayed the work of bricklayers, and *The Female Brickmaker* in which however the realistic convention was no longer strictly adhered to.

However, not all the artists accepted this interpretation of a program designed to link art to contemporary Polish life. In painting, as in poetry, a conviction was born that greatness and wealth and the dramatic conflicts of life required innovative art, utilizing new strong means of expression. This type of experimentation was to be found first in the work of Marek Włodarski who, continuing his pre-war style and method, painted such pictures as *Barricades* and *Mutiny on the Battleship Potemkin.* He also attempted as, for example, in his *Building Site* (1948), to portray with unusually suggestive force, yet in absolute contrast to the requirements of realism, an image of the new workers' homeland.

The great display of painting, sculpture and architectural designs at the Exhibition of the Regained Territories in Wrocław in 1948, became a great manifestation of art in quest of an alliance with modern times. Above it toward a 106 meter high steel spire. Screens made of enamel-painted glass six meters high were erected according to a project by Stażewski and Urbanowicz. A huge mural represented the four riders of the apocalypse. A ship's propeller was acclaimed "the best sculpture of the exhibition." In the coal and quarrying exhibition hall, art conveyed the darkness of the mine and the roughness of the stone. This current of art opened to reality, to matter and space, realistic in molding the world and not reflecting it passively, became an important artistic and social experience in the years to come.

In 1957 Oskar Hansen, in his exhibition of sculpture and architectural design, presented the concept of "dynamic space," the main feature of which was "occurring in time, not lasting." Wojciech Fangor and Stanisław Zamecznik shared this concept with Hansen. At the second Exhibition of Modern Art in Warsaw (1957) they showed their study of space, the purpose of which was "to open art for man and man for art." Questioning the validity of opposing man "as a closed, finite individuum to the closed, finite construction of the painting," they showed roads of "relativity" and demanded that "art reach out for things impossible."

Several artistic events played an important role in these endeavors: the Biennale of Spatial Forms in Elbląg (1965), the exhibition Space and Expression in Zielona Góra (1967), and the Symposium of Spatial Forms at Ustka (1972). A symposium of artists and scholars sponsored by the Azoty fertilizer plant at Puławy (1966) dealt with the links between art, technology and science. At its exhibitions and in its discussion a conclusion was reached that "statistical data, visual codes and statistical analysis create a world in which technology and creativity meet."

At the El Gallery in Elbląg and at Puławy, under the sponsorship of the Azoty plant, compositions of "impossible art" were created, which transcended traditional limits. Concurrently with this "opening" of realistic art to material and spatial reality and to the tasks of its transformation, another similar process was underway, that of "an opening to human matters." At Puławy one of the captions leading into the exhibition read: "And what about the psyche?" The question was significant, indeed, and opened up large and difficult territories for realism.

From the beginning the practice of realism transcended the limits of depicting reality and treated it in such a way as to demonstrate its deeper layers, its creative and destructive forces. Immediately after the war, these trends could be discerned in the works of Tadeusz Kulisiewicz, especially his series *Warsaw,* and of Bronisław Linke, Alfred Lenica, and Juliusz Studnicki. During the 1950's the socially committed painting of Andrzej Strumiłło surpassed the limits of socialist realism, expressing dramatic and revolutionary experiences in a new artistic style, as evidenced by his extremely impressive painting, *The Right to Work* (1952). Many works of documentary realistic art went beyond the borderline of mere information. This was true of Kobzdej's drawings from his Chinese and Vietnamese trips. The same can be seen in Wojciech Fangor's *Korean Mother,* or Tadeusz Kantor's *Washerwoman,* profoundly true and yet absolutely free of any realistic convention. This trend, leading to a particular type of realism born under the pressure of reminiscences from the brutal years, was exceptionally significant. Both the writer Tadeusz Borowski, who committed suicide in 1951, and the painter Andrzej Wróblewski, who died in the Tatra Mountains in 1957, were proponents of this trend.

During the 1950's Wróblewski painted his works as documents of the "times of contempt," documents of daily life. But his form of realism underscored ever more strongly the dramatic existential conflicts and bordered on the grotesque, and the cruel but true deformation of reality. In his painting we find, under the guise of a realistic image of the world, painful aspects of existentialism. This was a specific form of realism marked by war and the occupation, an image of a shattered world, of Executions, of Submerged Cities and of Headless Fish. It exposed a world which poets considered to be "stony", in terms of daily waiting for distant death; his paintings *Queue Is Going on* and *Man-Chair* were in this vein strikingly similar in tone to Ionesco's world-image as developed in *The Chairs.*

Even more clearly and dramatically this process of reaching beyond documentary realism to the interplay of forces, tensions, defeats and folly, is visible in the art of Waldemar Cwenarski. He painted a cruel world, of death and camp torture, in which *Etudes* were funeral music and the modern *Pietà* was an image of a murdered man,

233

lying on the lap of his mother whose arms are out-stretched.

A number of artists working alone belonged to this wave: their figurative compositions bore the accents of dramatic agony and the sophisticated deformation of people and the world. Such were the works of Zdzisław Beksiński, the recluse from Sanok, of Zbigniew Makowski, Kiejstut Bereźnicki, Benon Liberski and Eugeniusz Markowski, all of whom were solitary, seeking and lost.

Tadeusz Brzozowski, in the simplest manner possible, expressed the way and the vocation of the artist when he explained his creed during the 1956 Warsaw exhibition. He said that his art did not serve the aim of contemplating beauty but of personally experiencing human affairs. His work, filled with the gloomy accents of terror, grotesque, tragedy and deformation, forms at the same time a link with the folk tradition as exemplified in his *Prophet,* a modern paraphrase of the old theme of the *Sorrowing Christ* with camp life reminiscences.

Graphic art covered a wide range of "human affairs." In various forms it depicted surrounding reality in order to show the man lost in it. It used beautiful and shocking metaphors in order to reveal perspectives of freedom. It searched for the truth of life, reaching beyond documentary record and surrealist expression. Hundreds of graphic artists created the art of "small forms," intimate and familiar. Dozens of painters cultivated the graphic arts.

In the 1950's Jerzy Nowosielski joined in the surrealist movement, adding to it a special imaginative and emotional element of his own. Nowosielski's painting, thoroughly original, full of lyricism and unusual links between the monumentalism of his world and "the pettiness of the lost man" was a great artistic event. On the other hand Kazimierz Mikulski created an absolutely different version of surrealism. In images full of a particular atmosphere and lyric emotion, similar to that of Gałczyński's poems, he portrayed a world of sentiments, of dreams, and of visions. The mere titles of his compositions testified to his style: *At Evening We Hear the Whistling Trains, Meeting the Moon in the Suburbs, Magic Shop, Twilight Every Saturday* and *Portrait of a Cellist.*

Ideological restlessness and artistic experimentation were naturally reflected in changes in the arts, especially in painting and music. Never before had art been so daringly innovative in the realm of artistic techniques and, at the same time, so profoundly humanistic in experience and expression. A particular characteristic of Polish culture of the era was the wealth of trends, of attempts and achievements, the variety of suggestions tied in diverse manner to the Polish situation and to prospects for development.

A great explosion of avant-garde painting took place at the turn of the 1950's and 1960's, beginning with the second Exhibition of Modern Art in 1957. During this period Wojciech Fangor and Stefan Gierowski created their most important works. The painter, Jan Tarasin, published a treatise, *On Objects* (1959). Jerzy Tchórzewski was searching for a new formula for light.

Zbigniew Makowski concentrated his vision on the border between the open and the hidden world. Others turned to factural painting. Some pictures were virtually battlegrounds. In Cracow, Poznań, Wrocław, Lublin and Sopot numerous groups of artists were forming, with little organization and varying programs, but always very alive and committed.

The exhibition entitled Metaphor, organized in Warsaw in 1962, opened further vistas for that sort of painting. It became an expression of a new concept of avant-garde art, which stood in opposition to abstract painting. The compositions of Władysław Hasior and Jerzy Stajuda provoked particular response. Hasior inaugurated a new chapter in the development of Polish art, its relation to national life and its means of expression. Utilizing all sorts of refuse and garbage-type elements of reality, and adding folk consciousness and folk imagery, he produced great metaphors-myths of modern, disintegrated life. Bruno Schulz in his *Treatise on Tailors' Dummies* in 1934, and reprinted in Cracow in 1957, had already partially predicted such images of the world, as "the poverty and cheapness of its material." Similarly Miron Białoszewski saw reality as a collection of *objets trouvés* which were "the articles of truth" and "groupings of broken things." Hasior would light the fires of pathos and greatness over this world of ruin.

Art began to be shown in new ways, and was taken out of the exhibition halls and museums. Kantor, in 1956, reaching back to his theatrical productions of the occupation era, opened up in Cracow a stage which transcended the scope of traditional theater. In Warsaw Miron Białoszewski inaugurated his own theater of the poetry and metaphysics of *objets trouves* where Jan Lebenstein worked and developed as an artist. Continuing the line of experiences which connected theater to the visual arts, Józef Szajna introduced his "condensed scenic images," "elevated action" and "interplay of contradictions and clashes."

In this diversity of attempts artists were searching for the full measure of human experience, authenticity of emotions and roads leading to human freedom and fellowship. These searches and strivings were expressed in a most characteristic way by the students' theaters, from the Gdańsk Bim-Bom to the Cracow Cellar; and during the 1970's by the great paratheatrical shows of Kantor (for example, *The Panoramic Sea Happening* or *The Letter),* by the STU Theater, and by the numerous happenings which put to the fore the drama of choice which is a permanent necessity of life. From this point of view the Convention of Dreamers called in Elbląg in 1971 was indeed appropriate.

The changes in approaches to life and the world, to sensibility and imagery, to visual and emotional experiences, found expression not only in the fine arts of the period, but also in music.

Whereas painting was looking for new artistic directions from the early years after the liberation, Polish music remained true to the classicist program much longer, to the tradition of Szymanowski and folk inspirations. Only towards the end of the 1950's did it widen its sphere of

234

search for a new musical language and its enrichment. The process of overcoming neo-classicism, of undertaking attempts in the field of the twelve-note scale was inaugurated, for example, in the works of Kazimierz Serocki and Tadeusz Baird. Their music was frequently tied in to modern lyrical poetry, as evidenced by such works as *The Eyes of the Air* by Kazimierz Serocki (to words by Julian Przyboś); *Sonnets and Verses* by Bolesław Szabelski; *Stanzas* by Krzysztof Penderecki; or *Soliloquies* by Henryk Górecki. Also connected with poetry were the compositions of Witold Lutosławski, Stanisław Wiechowicz, Tadeusz Baird and many others. Vocal lyricism was one of the outstanding achievements of that music. The 1960's were marked by a widespread search for a new musical language.

In these formal explorations there was also harmony between the new painting and the new music. Just as in painting, the traditional bourgeois realist style and impressionism, representational art, were no longer obligatory, so in music the former classical and neo-classical accepted forms ceased to be universal, although many composers continued to work within these conventions.

Numerous attempts at finding a new musical language were made. Aleatorism assumed fortuitous artistic activity and was looking for new values of sound. Performing artists were also gaining greater freedom of interpretation in relation to composers whose works were registered more as suggestions rather than obligatory sets of directives. Attempts were being made to create new sound by the utilization of the wealth of electro-acoustical means. Musical language, like that of painting, was in this way gaining new possibilities of expression.

Important changes took place in musical sonoristics, particularly during the 1960's. Music by Polish composers gained a new force with its volume of sound, new dynamics, new beat and new means of sound transformation. The works of Penderecki, Lutosławski, Schäffer, Kotoński, Baird, Szabelski and Górecki continued to create this completely new world of music.

Thanks to their music, reality gained a new sound, just as avant-garde painting had created for it a new appearance. One may even define it more clearly, stating that new acoustical and visual means turned into a new environment for man in his quest for self-expression, finding himself in his own and yet new and unexpected, wealth.

PROSPECTS FOR POPULAR AND EVERYDAY CULTURE

The historic breakthrough which took place in the years 1944—45 defined new objectives for national education.

These tasks, appearing more and more clearly as socialism in Poland continued to develop, mobilized all educational institutions to intense activity. In this field, as in so many others, the years 1944 and 1945 were crucial years. Together with the abolition of private ownership of the means of production, and with the agrarian reform, which transferred the land to the state and the peasants, the first reform in the educational system designed to remove all class obstacles to free access to education was introduced. The principles of this reform were defined by the National Educational Congress called in June 1945 in Łódź by the Ministry of Education.

It inaugurated the great task of introducing universal education. In the following years primary education, unlike that in pre-war times, became truly universal and uniform. Children in the town and the countryside were given identical education, compulsory for all. During the next few years education beyond the primary level became increasingly universal, not only in vocational schools, but in the general grammar schools as well. For the children of workers and peasants, access to higher education became widely assured, and more institutions of higher education were founded.

In 1961, the Seym passed a bill regarding the development of a system of education, introducing eight years' compulsory attendance in primary school. This was the basis for all other stages of education. The post-primary schools were not compulsory, but an ever-increasing percentage of primary school leavers continued their education in various types of schools. As a result of this campaign, the level of education of the younger generation was becoming ever higher and was increasingly different from that of the older generation. Some levelling of these differences occurred, due to the growing opportunities in extra-mural vocational education and to various institutions for the promotion of culture.

In this way a breakthrough in the national life was achieved, based on the fact that the socialist revolution in Poland, which overthrew the class structure and conducted a democratic reform of education, stimulated a general demand for education and culture, opening, at the same time, possibilities for fulfillment which, in turn, acted as stimuli to a further increase in educational and cultural interests.

The solemn declaration accepted by the Seym in honor of the Bicentennial of the Commission for National Education, called for a reform of education in the nearest future. The immediate task, defined in the declaration, set a goal of a comprehensive ten years' instruction program for children through universal grammar schools.

The introduction of this reform was to signify a great breakthrough in the social and cultural life of the nation. For the first time in the history of Poland the huge gap between fully educated and partly educated people would cease to exist. For the first time the younger generation would achieve a uniform and sufficiently comprehensive education to go through life, participating in everything of importance in professional work, civic activity, cultural experience and in the development of their personalities.

Unfortunately, the deepening economic crisis made it necessary to interrupt the introduction of this reform. However under these new, more difficult conditions, the aims which guided it were not forsaken. The project of forming comprehensive ten-year schools was abandoned, but within the present educational system of an eight-year compulsory primary education and a four-year general education or vocational training, efforts were made for systematic universalization of secondary education. These efforts have been crowned with success since the percentage of primary school leavers who undertake secondary education is constantly growing and in some regions of Poland is as high as 90 percent. Also worthy of attention are the achievements of higher education which supplies highly qualified specialists to the economy and culture. More than a million and two hundred thousand graduates have taken up jobs in various professions and at present they constitute a high proportion of those employed.

The development of education became a basic factor in the widening of the social range of cultural participation in People's Poland.

In creating this new character of cultural life a number of other factors worked together with education: the fast growth of publishing institutions, the better circulation of books, due to the improvement in sales organization and a more efficient network of libraries and reading-rooms, the development of a daily and weekly press, the advancement of radio and television as well as films and general progress in mass post-primary education.

The basic outlines of a cultural policy under new conditions were included in a speech by President Bolesław Bierut in November 1947. Bierut emphasized that "promotion and modernization of cultural activity" was among the most important tasks and opposed the view that the participation of working people "required a lowering in the standards of cultural and artistic creation." He suggested the implementation on various levels of cultural and broadly educational campaigns which would promote cultural needs.

During these years remarkable progress was achieved in forms and methods of operation, as well as in the contents of that common and popular culture.

It was first effected in the area of production and distribution of books and magazines. Although numerous newspapers and magazines were published in pre-war times, their circulation was relatively low. The average circulation of a daily newspaper reached about 10,000, and only two of the most popular pre-war papers achieved a circulation of 100,000 copies each. In People's Poland those numbers increased more than tenfold, with some of the papers achieving a circulation of more than one million.

Exceptionally large numbers of books were printed, in particular Polish and foreign classics. Between 1944 and 1975, 15,500,000 copies of the works of Henryk Sienkiewicz were printed, 14,800,000 copies of the works of Bolesław Prus, 14,400,000 copies of the works of Maria Konopnicka, 13,700,000 copies of the works of Ignacy Kraszewski, 12,500,000 copies of the works of Adam Mickiewicz, and 11,000,000 copies of the works of Stefan Żeromski. Among foreign authors, Jack London held the record with 4,200,000 copies, followed by Maxim Gorky with 3,200,000 copies, Honoré de Balzac with 2,800,000 copies, Ernest Hemingway with 2,700,000 copies, Hans Christian Andersen with 2,600,000 copies, Leo Tolstoy with 1,900,000 copies and Thomas Mann with 1,000,000 copies.

The era was characterized not only by progress in the traditional methods of the promotion of culture, that is by publications; but also the type of culture itself underwent a transformation. New technical devices were created to ensure its circulation within the community. In the late 1960's radio broadcasts of the Warsaw I Radio Programs were heard over 95 percent of the country; other programs reached about 50 percent of the territory. The potential range of television programs covered 68 percent of the territory and were watched by 81 percent of the population. Statistical data showed remarkable yearly increases in the number of listeners and viewers. Thus a specific closed world of information and cultural values was born, in which all citizens were able to participate.

The cinema became an institution of enormous, almost universal, range. Its beginnings after war-time destruction were difficult, both in respect to the work of those making the films, and to the audience. Almost 75 percent of movie theaters were damaged. Reconstruction and expansion progressed very quickly. Both the number of houses and size of audiences steadily increased. In the 1960's films were already accessible to millions of viewers. The total film audience in 1975 was 165 million, which meant that the average movie-goer went to the movies five times a year, and when the films shown on television are taken into account, the social range of films becomes enormously wide. It created a new quality of cultural life and introduced new elements to the collective and individual imagination.

Not so universal, though nonetheless significant for the social consciousness, was the theatrical scene. The theater began its activity in post-war Poland with the production of Fredro's *Maidens' Vows,* staged in July 1944 by the Theater of the First Army. As the liberation of the country progressed, new theaters were opened in Lublin, Białystok, Rzeszów, Warsaw, Cracow, Łódź, Bydgoszcz, Katowice, Częstochowa, Sosnowiec, Kalisz, Kielce and Poznań. In May 1945, on the day the war ended, 16 professional theater companies were active. Others were opened during the following months in Gdańsk, Szczecin, Olsztyn, Toruń, Wrocław, Opole, Jelenia Góra and in other towns. The number of theaters soon swelled to more than 50. Ten years after the war the total size of theater audiences reached almost nine million annually. Several thousand small towns and villages with no permanent companies of their own were reached by touring ensembles.

In this way, the great Polish theatrical tradition was continued, in towns which never before had had a theater of their own; and by means of television screens, which introduced this art form into the lives of millions of viewers living in districts remote from the centers of cultural life. This probably accounts for the fact that the amateur theater movement, active before the war, was not revived. Similarly, attempts to revive the workers' theater failed, despite many attempts to raise interest among the working class. Professional theater became a national theater. Only student companies, the great event of modern times, developed along a road of their own and achieved, especially during the 1950's and 1960's, an exceptional position, particularly in Gdańsk and later in Warsaw. The national theater had many faces. New audiences, mostly from among the younger generation, were attracted to Adam Hanuszkiewicz, who taught them a modern view of tradition and contemporary reality. In Cracow the director Konrad Swinarski started a new phase in methods of presenting the great Polish dramas. The limitations of traditional staging were broken by Józef Szajna who used the visual arts to support the spoken word, in order to achieve violent, even brutal, expression. Jerzy Grotowski's Laboratory Theater became world famous: here the traditional borderline of theatricality was transcended in another direction, involving the actors and their audience in processes of shock and cathartic therapy. It was from the very beginning characteristic of Polish mass culture that one could see its connection with intellectual values.

Together with the enormous increase in the range of culture brought about by films and television, by the living word of artistic and literary radio broadcasts and by the theater, progress was achieved in regard to the participation of ever greater numbers of people in intellectual culture. A similar development was seen in connection with the advancement of science and technology, with the increasing needs of improving professional qualifications and of a better understanding of social reality.

These trends and aspirations were manifested and strengthened by an extensive action of popularization of the results of scientific research and achievements in technological progress. Thus, ever widening sectors of society were granted the opportunity of actively participating in the advancement of learning.

In 1950 the Association for the Dissemination of Knowledge was founded. Its main focus was a widely conducted round of lectures which reached out into the entire country. By the late 1950's the Association began to organize permanent forms of education. This soon resulted in about 2,000 popular lecture series with various specializations depending on the local needs and tastes of their audiences. Widespread popularization is now being conducted by societies which reach out to people interested in various branches of knowledge, particularly in such fields as astronomy, archeology, linguistics and ethnography. Magazines and books devoted to the dissemination of science enjoy great popularity among ever-widening circles of readers.

Of decisive significance in this field, however, was the social change effected in work itself, as a result of which an ever-growing number of people performed specialized jobs, based on scientific studies and requiring constant upgrading in their skills. During the 1970's the awareness of the need for a permanent education became one of the characteristic traits of general culture.

The accumulation of these factors of a double nature — that is, artistic-visual and scientific-abstract — greatly influenced the consciousness, imagination, emotions and attitudes of the people. They were more and more taking part in everything that was going on in Poland, and to a certain degree, in the world. Culture, under these conditions, has become not only an individual experience of chosen works, but also an objective social reality in which people participate. This participation has been, and

continues to be, varied: both direct perception of facts and events, and reflection which produces definite action. Thus, differences were obliterated between the traditional meaning of the "realm of culture" and social reality, between the world of "masterpieces" and that of human work, and between weekdays and holidays.

The Congress of Polish Culture in 1966 recapitulated existing cultural achievements and laid out a plan for further development. A resolution passed by the Congress underscored the merits of the millennial heritage of Polish culture, its role in the nation's history, its contemporary renaissance, especially on the ancient territories of Wrocław, Opole, Szczecin and Olsztyn. It also emphasized the interrelation between art, science and technology and the link between the work of artists and a mass audience. The resolution pointed out further prospects of development, growing out of the new experience of social life and culture in People's Poland.

The old contradictions between culture and life is slowly being overcome, and a new structure of culture and its dynamics has been outlined. Contact with culture has ceased to be exclusively an exceptional occurrence, for special occasions, but is now an everyday affair. Not only books and film, but music, theater and the fine arts, are natural components of the daily life of the people. The increase in the amount of free time, although not as yet a universal phenomenon, is nonetheless tangible in the life of different groups of society, particularly in some age categories, and makes possible a new organization of the daily routine. Modern means of popularization and reproduction of works of art enable them to last and circulate in various forms.

However, the widening of the roads linking everyday life to culture is not only due to increases in individual free time and to the mass media, but also to the purposeful activity of the state and the varied initiatives of the artists themselves. Thanks to this, the fine arts are becoming one of the major agents in shaping the material environment of the people. Hand in hand with urban planning and architecture, the fine arts shape anew towns and districts, the landscape which surrounds people in their work and homes. Drawing on the wealth of form and tradition — from folk art to industrial design, artists create man's daily surroundings in which the material conditions of existence are shaped not only according to the requirements of life's necessities, but also according to the canons of beauty. Sometimes, as is the case with the Elbląg experiment, art goes out into the streets, concrete evidence of the link between the work of artists and technicians, a symbol of modern times in which people can shape matter.

This is the meaning of the actual process of renovation and restoration of monuments and old works of art, of castles, palaces, churches, monasteries and of old town quarters, which introduces into modern material reality things which up to now have survived only in old drawings and documents from archives.

In this process of transposing culture from the level of celebration into the real shape of daily life, science and technology have been of particular significance. For ages scientific and technological culture, like culture generally, stood in opposition to the daily life of the masses, who were condemned to hard physical labor. Science and technology, produced somewhere beyond their everyday experience, were simply a collection of imposed means, the only purpose of which was to increase productivity and which did not effect human values and human responsibilities.

The work of millions of people today, in industry, in agriculture, in various trades and professions, is increasingly being pervaded by science, not only in the sense that the results of scientific research are applied in practice, but also that the best and most innovative forms of practical work constitute one of the major agents in the development of scientific and technological know-how.

The culture of intellectual and scientific activity and human work are connected more closely in all trades and professions. Similarly, a technological culture is developing directly out of the practical activity of the people; and it is here that rich resources for further advancement are to be found.

Thus art, science and technology are becoming a more powerful force in shaping people's dialy surroundings. For this reason the old contradictions between culture and everyday life no longer exist. Conditions have been created for life to become cultural and for culture to become alive.

POLAND AND THE WORLD

Drawing conclusions from its terrible war and occupation experience, Poland called on all nations to fight for peace. The World Congress of Intellectuals in the Defense of Peace took place in Wrocław in 1948; two years later, a Congress of Defenders of Peace was also convened in Poland. Several years later, Adam Rapacki, the then Polish Minister of Foreign Affairs, presented his famous plan for creating an atom-free zone in Central Europe. This initiative later became the main arms in defense of peace throughout the whole world. Many plans that Poland put forward on an international scale played important roles and confirmed the significance of Poland in the world's fight for peace. The concepts of "Poland" and "peace" became one, not only to the Poles but to the entire world.

Poland's participation in world culture was shaped by that global outlook. A remarkable characteristic of this participation was its steadily increasing range. Between the wars it was limited to the West, North and South European countries and to North America. The year 1945 opened up possibilities for getting acquainted with Soviet culture in music, film, theater, literature; and opened Polish windows onto the whole world. Continents and countries, previously known only to a small group of travelers and explorers, were becoming unexpectedly near and important. Thus, the culture of Asiatic nations, especially of India and Vietnam, and that of Latin American nations — Peru, Chile, Brazil, Mexico — as well as of African nations, became an element in Polish cultural life and of Polish artistic and scientific activity.

That activity was winning Poland a place in the world. For what counts in world culture is that which is great and new, and the voices of nations which can be heard and understood by other nations. Polish science and Polish art transcended the borders of one country and they were becoming global.

Polish scholars strengthened and extended the position of their country's science in the world. Significant results were achieved especially in mathematics, a field eagerly cultivated in Poland. As a result of this research the Stefan Banach International Mathematical Center was founded in Warsaw in 1972. Leopold Infeld, who has worked together with Einstein, and a numerous group of young physicists, mostly in Warsaw and Cracow, continued to maintain the high standards of Polish physics. The situation in other branches of the natural sciences, particularly in chemistry, was similar.

Polish philosophy achieved a remarkable position, particularly due to the work of Tadeusz Kotarbiński, Władysław Tatarkiewicz and Roman Ingarden. In economics the activity of Oskar Lange and Michał Kalecki led to significant results and contributed to the establishment of the line of development of that discipline in the world.

International significance was also attained by a new science — sozology — the conservation of nature and its resources. Deeply rooted in the tradition fashioned by the work of Walery Goetel and Władysław Szafer in the first half of the twentieth century, this new branch of learning has attained new possibilities for development in which the various branches of biology play an active part. Through research in this area, Poland has joined international programs dealing with the conservation of the environment.

The fine arts have also found their way into the world. At various international exhibitions, for example the São Paulo or the Venice Biennales, Polish art has met with wide acclaim. Artistic tapestries, which continue old Polish traditions, have become objects of admiration at many exhibitions. Polish posters have won numerous awards for their artists. From 1966, Poland has organized the International Poster Biennale. A special Poster Museum was founded at Wilanów.

Conservation of antiquities and renovation and reconstruction of works of art and historic monuments are also specialties of Polish artists. Poland has followed an ambitious program of conservation and reconstruction of the most valuable remnants of the past; inventory and historical research in this field has developed, making possible a rational approach to conservation, safeguarding the requirements of authenticity and the true reconstruction of ruined relics. The rebuilding of old town quarters, first begun in Warsaw and Gdańsk and later conducted in dozens of other Polish cities, of churches, monasteries, castles and palaces, served sometimes as models to other countries.

The extent of Polish cultural influence was singularly visible in the field of music. Previously unknown, the song and dance ensembles Mazowsze and Śląsk have attracted millions of people throughout the world, with their Polish folk melodies and colorful costumes. Similarly, and for the first time since Szymanowski, Polish music has been recognized worldwide, with the compositions of Lutosławski, Baird and Penderecki.

Polish participation in world culture takes the form of cooperation with international organizations like the UN and its agencies, FAO, ILO, WHO and UNESCO. In all these bodies Poland's political judgment, readiness to engage in difficult tasks and ability to act effectively and rationally finds a wide field of action.

Poland's position in world culture may be measured by the variety of events organized in our country: the International Book Fair in Warsaw, the International Short Film Festival in Cracow, the Wratislavia Cantans Oratorio and Cantata Festival in Wrocław, the International Chopin Piano Competition in Warsaw, the International Henryk Wieniawski Violin Competition in Poznań, the International Biennale of Graphic Arts in Cracow, the International Poster Biennale in Warsaw, and many others.

Cultural cooperation has also developed as the result of numerous cultural agreements signed with many countries. These agreements have paved the way for Polish art in the world: for literary translations, for theater tours, for motion pictures and concerts. Various festivals of Polish culture are organized in many countries. These presentations show how Polish culture is rooted in the needs and demands of the masses and how it is appreciated by them. Thanks to this, it has become an important element of their endeavor to improve the quality of life. This striving reaches deeper than mere prosperity and consumption. Based on the improvement of the material conditions of existence for a wide section of society, it shows how prosperity can serve a purpose.

The fact that cultural activity in Poland has always been so inextricably linked with its wide dissemination, with the widening of the range of its social impact, attracts the attention of many nations who are seeking ways to make culture universally available.

Poland's new position in the world has been especially noticed by millions of Poles living abroad. They have tried to establish, individually and collectively, closer contacts with their native country, feeling pride in its achievements. In their appeal issued in Szczecin in 1961, Poles residing in other countries expressed joy and pride, and called up on all Poles to engage in the cause of friendship between all nations and of peace: "We devote all our energy to the great cause of friendship among nations, because it serves peace, and peace serves the holy cause of Poland."

Index of Names

Abakanowicz, Magdalena *ill. 411*
Abbot, George 70
Abramowski, Edward Józef 162, 166, 173, 186, 189
Adam of Bochynia 53
Adam of Bremen 16, 35
Adelgoz, Archbishop of Magdeburg 16
Aigner, Piotr 128, 140, 175, *ill. 196*
Alaric, King of Visigoths 35
Albert, Brother *see* Chmielowski, Adam
Albert, mayor of Cracow 19, 28, 33
Albertrandi, Jan Chrzciciel 135, 174, 185
Albrecht Hohenzollern, Prince of Prussia 153
Alembek family 98
Alexander the Jagiellonian, King of Poland *ill. 59, 60*
Alexander I, Emperor of Russia 163
Althusius, Johannes 104
Altomonte, Martin 102
Anczyc, Władysław Ludwik 160, 187, 188
Andersen, Hans Christian 236
Andrzejewski, Jerzy 206, 222
Anne the Jagiellon, Queen of Poland 95, 101
Antoni of Wrocław *ill. 105, 106, 107*
Apollinaire, Guillaume 178
Appiani, Galeazzo *ill. 83*
Aqua, Andrea dell' 92, *ill. 136*
Aquinas, Thomas, *see* St. Thomas Aquinas
Argenson, René d' 104
Ariosto, Ludovico 102
Aristotle 24, 36, 89, 91
Arminius, Jacobus 105
Asnyk, Adam 150, 185
Aszpergerowa, Aniela 188
Attila, King of Huns 35
Augustus II, King of Poland 80, 82, 85, 86
Augustus III, King of Poland 93, 139
Augustynowicz, Tomasz 194

Bacciarelli, Marcello 113, 128, 129, 131, 140, *ill. 210, 212, 213, 214, 215, 216*
Bacon, Francis 90, 104, 140, 141
Baczyński, Krzysztof Kamil 214, 231
Badurski, Jędrzej 115
Baier, Melchior *ill. 86*
Baird, Tadeusz 219, 235, 239
Baka, Józef 126
Bakfark, Valentin 55
Bakunin, Mikhail 192, 193
Balicki, Zygmunt 191, 202
Bałucki, Michał 187
Balzac, Honoré de 236
Balzer, Oswald 152
Banach, Stefan 213, 238
Bandrowski, Juliusz Kaden 209, 212
Bandura, Jerzy 222
Barbaro, Giosafat 36
Barclay, John 104
Barss, Franciszek 136
Barszczewski, Leon 194
Bartók, Béla 219
Bartoszek, Franciszek Józef *ill. 343*
Baryczka family 98
Baryka, Piotr 96
Báthory, Stephen *see* Stephen Báthory, King of Poland

Bauch, T. 139
Baudouin de Courtenay, Jan de 195
Baworowski family 186
Bayle, Pierre 105
Bazylik, Cyprian 60, 67
Bechon, Charles 140
Behem, Balthasar 18, 28, 56, *ill. 93, 94*
Beksiński, Zdzisław 234
Bella, Stefano della *ill. 177*
Bellotto, Bernardo, called Canaletto 130, 131, 140, *ill. 167, 218, 219, 220*
Bem, Józef 192, 195
Benedykt of Koźmin *ill. 100*
Beniowski, Maurycy August 133, 144, 172
Benisławska, Konstancja 126
Bensheimer, J. *ill. 178*
Berent, Wacław 162, 173
Bereźnicki, Kiejstut 234
Bernanos, Georges 228
Berrecci, Bartholommeo *ill. 77, 80*
Berwiński, Ryszard 171, 193
Béze, Théodore de 70
Białozor, Mateusz 116
Białobłocki, Bronisław 162, 169, 181
Białobrzeski, Czesław 207, 214
Białoszewski, Miron 234
Biegas, Bolesław 178
Bielski, Joachim 42
Bielski, Marcin 42, 54, 60, 61, 64, 68, 112, *ill. 61, 114*
Biem, Marcin 71
Biernat of Lublin 52, 53, 55, 63, 68, 73, *ill. 118, 119, 120*
Bierut, Bolesław 236
Birkowski, Fabian 88, 92
Bismarck, Otto von 185
Blanchard, Jean Pierre 116
Blandrata, Giorgio 72
Bliziński, Józef 187
Blocke, Abraham van dem 94, 95
Blocke, Izaak van dem 94, *ill. 108*
Blocke, Wilhelm van dem 95, *ill. 69, 92*
Blühdorn, Leonia *ill. 265*
Bobrzyński, Michał 152
Bodel of Arras, Jehan 35
Bodin, Jean 104
Boguslaus XIV, Prince of Pomerania 79
Bogusławski, Wojciech 133, 136, 137, 138, 187, 213
Bogusz, Marian *ill. 382, 390*
Boguszewski, Krzysztof *ill. 149*
Boguszowicz, Szymon 100
Bohdanowicz, Karol 194
Bohomolec, Franciszek 43, 112, 130, 135, 137
Boileau-Despréaux, Nicolas 141
Boim, Jerzy 95
Bojanowski, Jan 102
Bojarski, Wacław 214
Bojko, Jakub 189
Boleslaus (I) the Brave, King of Poland 12, 13, 16, 18, 20, 21, 23, 24, 28, 31, 32, 112, 153, 154, *ill. 22*
Boleslaus (II) the Bold, King of Poland 13, 14, 20, 21, 24, 178, *ill. 318, 324*
Boleslaus (III) Wrymouth, Prince 13, 14, 20, 21, 32, 34, 37
Boleslaus (V) the Bashful, Prince 22

Boleslaus of Legnica, Prince 27
Boleslaus the Pious, Prince 22
Bolesławiusz, Klemens 90
Bolívar, Simón 192
Bona Sforza, Queen of Poland, wife of Sigismund I 60, 71, 75
Boner, Seweryn 68
Boner family 58
Boniecki, Maria Albin *ill. 376*
Borlach, J. G. *ill. 191, 192*
Borowski, Tadeusz 218, 230, 231, 233
Bosak, Józef Hauke *see* Hauke-Bosak, Józef
Bossak, Jerzy 222
Botev, Khristo 193
Boucher, François *ill. 238*
Bourdelle, Antoine 213
Bovio, Gianbattista 72
Boy, Adolf *ill. 178*
Boy-Żeleński, Tadeusz *see* Żeleński, Tadeusz Boy
Boznańska, Olga 178
Brandt, Józef 153, 180
Brandys, Kazimierz 220
Branicka, Elżbieta 136
Branicki, Jan Klemens 93
Braun, Georg *ill. 111, 112*
Brenna, Vincenzo 140
Bretislav, Prince of Bohemia 14
Brodowicz, J. M. 156
Brodowski, Feliks 206
Brodowski, Józef *ill. 260*
Brodziński, Kazimierz 168, 179
Bromirski, Andrzej 141
Broniewski, Władysław 209, 232
Brożek, Jan 73, 97
Brühl, Alojzy Fryderyk 136
Brukalska, Barbara *ill. 315*
Brukalski, Stanisław *ill. 315*
Brun, Andreas Le 113, 131, 140
Bryll, Ernest 230
Brzóska, Stanisław 164
Brzoza, Jan 165
Brzozowski, Stanisław, 162, 163, 169, 181, 203, 206
Brzozowski, Stanisław, poet 177
Brzozowski, Tadeusz 232, 234, *ill. 387*
Brzozowski, Wincenty 177
Buckle, Henry Thomas 169
Budny, Szymon 51, 56, 67
Budzyński, Marek *ill. 370*
Buffon, Georges Louis Leclerc 123, 140
Bujak, Franciszek 207
Buonaccorsi, Filippo (Kallimach, Callimachus) 43, 49, 54, 57, 69, 70
Burattini, Livius 103
Buridan, Jean 36
Burke, Edmund 143
Bursius (Burski), Adam 89, 90, 105
Burski, Adam *see* Bursius (Burski), Adam
Bylica, Marcin 36, 73, *ill. 64, 65*

Caesar, Gaius Julius 35, 71
Cagliostro, Alessandro 140
Calderón de la Barca, Pedro 213
Callimachus *see* Buonaccorsi, Filippo
Callot, Claude, *ill. 165, 166*

240

242

LIST OF
ILLUSTRATIONS

copy of his *Commune incliti regni Poloniae privilegium,* woodcut, 1506. National Library in Warsaw. Photo: M. Musiał (Interpress).

60. Seym debate attended by King Alexander. Woodcut from *Commune incliti regni Poloniae privilegium,* 1506. National Library in Warsaw. Photo: M. Musiał (Interpress).

61. *Battle of Grunwald in 1410,* woodcut from Marcin Bielski's *Chronicle,* 1597. National Museum in Warsaw. Photo: J. Morek (Interpress).

62. Mother of God with the Infant Jesus. Detail of a baptismal font in SS. Peter and Paul's church in Legnica. Photo: T. Zagoździński (Interpress).

63. Marcin Marciniec, Reliquary of St. Stanislaus, 1504, Treasury of Wawel cathedral in Cracow. Photo: S. Michta.

64. Arabian astrolabium of Marcin Bylica, made in Córdoba in 1054. Museum of the Jagiellonian University in Cracow. Photo: W. Kryński and T. Prażmowski (Interpress).

65. Marcin Bylica's torquetum, 1493. Museum of the Jagiellonian University in Cracow. Photo: W. Kryński and T. Prażmowski (Interpress).

66. Castle gate in Brzeg, 1551—53, designed by Francesco Parro (Pario) and with sculptures by Andreas Walther I. Photo: M. Musiał and K. Szeloch (Interpress).

67. Andreas Walther I, Piast images. Detail of the castle gate in Brzeg, 1551—53. Photo: M. Musiał and K. Szeloch (Interpress).

68. Georg of Amberg, Castle gate in Legnica, completed in 1533. Photo: T. Zagoździński (Interpress).

69. High Gate in Gdańsk, 1586—88, designed by Johannes Kramer and with sculptures by Wilhelm van dem Blocke. Photo: W. Kryński and T. Prażmowski (Interpress).

70. Interior of the Grand Debating Chamber in the City Hall of the Main City in Gdańsk, 1593—1611. Photo: G. Rogiński (Interpress).

71. Kasper Fotyga, City hall in Szydłowiec, 16th cent., with parapet dating from 1601. Photo: J. Morek (Interpress).

72. Giovanni Battista Quadro, City hall in Poznań, 1550—60. Photo: W. Kryński (Interpress).

73. Orsetti house in Jarosław, 1580 and 1640. Photo: J. Morek (Interpress).

74. Bernardo Morando (from 1591) and Jan Jaroszewicz (from 1622), City hall in Zamość. Photo: K. Niedenthal (Interpress).

75. Cloth hall in Cracow, with parapet dating from 1556—60. Photo: W. Kryński (Interpress).

76. General view of the Wawel Castle in Cracow. Photo: W. Kryński and T. Prażmowski (Interpress).

77. Francesco Fiorentino and Bartholommeo Berrecci, Arcaded loggias at Wawel Castle, 1507—36. Photo: W. Kryński and T. Prażmowski (Interpress).

78. Deputies' Chamber in Wawel Castle, 1530's. Photo: J. Rosikoń (Interpress).

79. Southern view of the royal cathedral at Wawel. Photo: W. Kryński and T. Prażmowski (Interpress).

80. Bartholommeo Berrecci, Sigismund chapel at Wawel cathedral, 1519—33. Photo: J. Ochoński (Interpress).

81. Courtyard of the royal castle in Niepołomice, 1550—71. Photo: W. Ochnio and Z. Wdowiński (Interpress).

82. Santi Gucci (?), Courtyard of the castle in Baranów, 1591—1606. Photo: J. Grelowski (Interpress).

83. Galeazzo Appiani, Castle in Krasiczyn, 1598—1633. Photo: J. Morek (Interpress).

84. Wawrzyniec Lorek, Manor-house in Pabianice, 1565—70. Photo from the collection of the Monument Documentation Center.

85. Fortified mansion in Szymbark, 1585—90. Photo from the collection of the Monument Documentation Center.

86. Silver altarpiece in the Sigismund Chapel of Wawel cathedral, 1535—38. Bas reliefs by Melchior Baier modelled on Peter Flötner and partly on Albrecht Dürer's woodcuts. Photo: W. Kryński and J. Ochoński (Interpress).

87. *Adoration of the Shepherds.* Panel of the silver altarpiece in the Sigismund Chapel of Wawel cathedral, 1535—38. Photo: W. Kryński and J. Ochoński (Interpress).

88. *Adoration of the Magi.* Panel of the silver altarpiece in the Sigismund Chapel of Wawel cathedral, 1535—38. Photo: W. Kryński and J. Ochoński (Interpress).

89. Jan Michałowicz of Urzędów, Gravestone of Filip Padniewski in Wawel cathedral, 1572—73. Photo: W. Kryński and J. Ochoński (Interpress).

90. Gravestone of Jan Grot (d. 1579) and his son (d. 1580) in the Dominican church in Cracow. Photo: W. Kryński and T. Prażmowski (Interpress).

91. Bernardino de Gianotis and Giovanni Cini, *Opatów Lament.* Bas relief on the sarcophagus of Krzysztof Szydłowiecki in the collegiate church in Opatów, 1533—41. Photo: J. Morek (Interpress).

92. Wilhelm van dem Blocke, Cartouche with the emblem of Poland. Detail of the sculpted decoration on the western front of the High Gate in Gdańsk, 1586—88. Photo: G. Rogiński (Interpress).

93. Bell-founder's workshop. Miniature from *Balthasar Behem's Codex,* early 16th cent. Photo: T. Prażmowski (Interpress).

94. Goldsmith's workshop. Miniature from *Balthasar Behem's Codex,* early 16th cent. Photo: T. Prażmowski (Interpress).

95. Stanisław Samostrzelnik, Miniature from *Liber geneseos illustris familiae Schidloviciae,* before 1532. Library of the Polish Academy of Sciences at Kórnik. Photo: J. Morek (Interpress).

96. Unknown painter, *Battle of Orsza* (detail), c. 1515—20. National Museum in Warsaw. Photo: W. Kryński (Interpress).

97. *Portrait of Sigismund the Old* from Pawłowice, c. 1540. State Art Collections at Wawel Castle in Cracow. Photo: W. Kryński and T. Prażmowski (Interpress).

98. *Portrait of Sigismund Augustus,* 1547. Wawel cathedral in Cracow. Photo: W. Kryński and T. Prażmowski (Interpress).

99. Late 16th cent. Polish painter, *Portrait of Stephen Báthory.* National Museum in Cracow. Photo: W. Kryński and T. Prażmowski (Interpress).

100. Unknown 16th cent. Polish painter, *Portrait of Benedykt of Koźmin,* c. 1550. Museum of the Jagiellonian University in Cracow. Photo: J. Ochoński (Interpress).

101. *Portrait of Sebastian Petrycy of Pilzno,* after 1626. Museum of the Jagiellonian University in Cracow. Photo: W. Gomuła.

102. *Musician.* Detail of a polychrome, c. 1530. Parish church in Grębień. Photo: E. Kozłowska-Tomczyk (Art Institute of the Polish Academy of Sciences).

103. Hans Dürer after *Tabula Cebestis* by the moralist Cebes, *Youth.* Detail of the frieze *History of Man's Life* in the Deputies' Chamber of Wawel Castle, 1532. Photo: W. Kryński and T. Prażmowski (Interpress).

104. Hans Dürer after *Tabula Cebestis* by the moralist Cebes, *Dances.* Detail of the frieze *History of Man's Life* in the Deputies' Chamber of Wawel Castle, 1532. Photo: W. Kryński and T. Prażmowski (Interpress).

105. Antoni of Wrocław, *Infantry Parading before King Sigismund the Old.* Detail of the fricze in the Troops Review Hall of Wawel Castle, 1535. Photo: W. Kryński and T. Prażmowski (Interpress).

106. Hans Dürer and Antoni of Wrocław, *Before a Fight.* Detail of the frieze in the Tournament Hall of Wawel Castle, 1534—35. Photo: W. Kryński and T. Prażmowski (Interpress).

107. Hans Dürer and Antoni of Wrocław, *Sword Fight.* Detail of the frieze in the Tournament Hall of Wawel Castle, 1534—35. Photo: W. Kryński and T. Prażmowski (Interpress).

108. Izaak van dem Blocke, *Allegory of Gdańsk Commerce,* 1608. City Hall of the Main City in Gdańsk. Photo: W. Kryński and T. Prażmowski (Interpress).

109. Antoni Möller, *Building the Temple of Solomon* (detail), 1601 (?). Cita Hall of the Main City in Gdańsk. Photo: G. Rogiński (Interpress).

110. Bernard Wapowski, *Mappa ... Poloniae ac Magni D(ucatus) Lithuaniae* (detail), 1526. Archive of Ancient Documents in Warsaw. Photo: M. Musiał (Interpress).

111. View of Cracow in the late 16th cent. Illustration from J. Braun and F. Hoggenberg's *Civitates orbis terrarum,* Cologne 1597—1618. National Museum in Warsaw. Photo: J. Morek (Interpress).

112. View of Warsaw in the late 16th cent. Illustration from J. Braun and F. Hoggenberg's *Civitates orbis terrarum.* Cologne 1597—1618. National Museum in Warsaw. Photo: J. Morek (Interpress).

113. *Holy words and lordly matters...,* title page of Mikołaj Rej's

252

216. Marcello Bacciarelli, *Prussian Homage*, 1785—86. National Museum in Warsaw. Photo: National Museum in Warsaw.

217. Jan Chrzciciel Lampi, *Portrait of Stanislaus Augustus Poniatowski*, c. 1791. Czartoryski Collections of the National Museum in Cracow. Photo: W. Kryński and T. Prażmowski (Interpress).

218. Bernardo Bellotto called Canaletto, *Election of Stanislaus Augustus at Wola*, 1778. National Museum in Warsaw, collections of the Royal Castle. Photo: G. Rogiński (Interpress).

219. Bernardo Bellotto called Canaletto, *View of Warsaw from Praga*, 1770. National Museum in Warsaw, collections of the Royal Castle. Photo: J. Morek (Interpress).

220. Bernardo Bellotto called Canaletto, *View of Warsaw from the Terrace of the Royal Castle* (detail), 1773—74. Warsaw. Photo: W. Kryński (Interpress).

221. Kazimierz Wojniakowski, *Society Gathering in a Garden*, 1797. National Museum in Warsaw. Photo: National Museum in Warsaw.

222. Jean Pierre Norblin, *Trip to the Lake*. Painted decoration from Izabela Czartoryska's residence at Powązki in Warsaw, [1785]. National Museum in Warsaw. Photo: Żółtowska.

223. Jean Pierre Norblin, *Bathing in a Park*. Painted decoration from Izabela Czartoryska's residence at Powązki in Warsaw, [1785]. National Museum in Warsaw. Photo: W. Kryński (Interpress).

224. Franciszek Smuglewicz, *Ratification of the Agrarian Law Granted to the Peasants in Pawłów by Paweł Ksawery Brzostowski in 1769*. National Museum in Warsaw, branch at Wilanów. Photo: National Museum in Warsaw.

225. Jean Pierre Norblin, *Proclamation of the Third of May Constitution of 1791*. Library of the Polish Academy of Sciences in Kórnik. Photo: Interpress.

226. Kazimierz Wojniakowski, *Passing of the Third of May Constitution*, 1806. National Museum in Warsaw. Photo: National Museum in Warsaw.

227. Kazimierz Wojniakowski, *Portrait of Thaddeus Kosciuszko*, after 1794. National Museum in Poznań. Photo: W. Kryński and T. Prażmowski (Interpress).

228. Krzysztof Lubieniecki, *School Teacher*, 1727. National Museum in Warsaw. Photo: National Museum in Warsaw.

229. Stanisław Staszic, *Warnings to Poland*, 1790, title page. Photo: National Museum in Warsaw.

230. Daniel Chodowiecki, *Stanislaus Augustus Extending his Protection to All Estates*, allegorical etching. National Museum in Warsaw. Photo: National Museum in Warsaw.

231. Jean Pierre Norblin, *Diet in Church*, (1808). National Museum in Poznań. Photo: W. Kryński and T. Prażmowski (Interpress).

232. Jean Pierre Norblin, *Fighting in Miodowa Street in Warsaw*. National Museum in Warsaw. Photo: W. Kryński (Interpress).

233. Jean Pierre Norblin, *Market in the Slaughterers' Gate in Warsaw*. Czartoryski Collections of the National Museum in Cracow. Photo: W. Kryński and T. Prażmowski (Interpress).

234. Jean Pierre Norblin: *Distribution of Meals at the Sigismund Column at Castle Square in Warsaw*. National Museum in Warsaw. Photo: National Museum in Warsaw.

235. Jean Pierre Norblin, Design of stage sets for a play on peasant themes produced in the court theater in Puławy, 1802. National Museum in Warsaw. Photo: National Museum in Warsaw.

236. Józef Richter, *View of the Sibyl Temple in Puławy*, watercolor, c. 1830. National Museum in Warsaw. Photo: National Museum in Warsaw.

237. Józef Richter, *View of the Palace in Puławy*, watercolor, 1830. National Museum in Warsaw. Photo: National Museum in Warsaw.

238. Francois Boucher, Coat-of-arms of King Stanislaus Augustus surrounded by personifications of Peace and Justice. Design for the coping of the royal throne. Print Room of the Warsaw University Library. Photo: Library of Warsaw University.

239. Franciszek Smuglewicz, *Ladislaus Jagiello and the Elders Debating on Plans of a New Town*. National Museum in Warsaw. Photo: National Museum in Warsaw.

240. Zygmunt Vogel, *Palace-on-the-Lake in the Royal Łazienki Park*, watercolor. National Museum in Warsaw. Photo: National Museum in Warsaw.

241. Zygmunt Vogel, *View of the Palace in Puławy from the River*, watercolor, 1796. National Museum in Poznań. Photo: W. Kryński and T. Prażmowski (Interpress).

242. Zygmunt Vogel, *View of the Officer Cadets' Palace, Also Known as the Kazimierzowski Palace*, watercolor. National Museum in Warsaw. Photo: National Museum in Warsaw.

243. Zygmunt Vogel, *Załuski Library*, watercolor. National Museum in Warsaw.

244. Jan Wahl, *Warsaw Councillors Taking an Oath of Loyalty to the King*. Graphic Art Collection of the Warsaw University Library. Photo: Library of Warsaw University.

245. Michał Stachowicz, *General Thaddeus Kosciuszko Taking an Oath in Cracow on 24 March 1794*. color drawing, 1797. National Museum in Cracow. Photo: W. Kryński (Interpress).

246. Aleksander Orłowski, Design of the statue of Prince Joseph Poniatowski in general's uniform, watercolor, 1818. National Museum in Cracow. Photo: W. Kryński and T. Prażmowski (Interpress).

247. Aleksander Orłowski, *Battle of Racławice*, [1797]. Czartoryski Collections of the National Museum in Cracow. Photo: W. Kryński and T. Prażmowski (Interpress).

248. Aleksander Orłowski, *On the Ramparts*, 1798. Ossoliński Library in Wrocław. Photo: National Museum in Warsaw.

249. Philibert Debucourt, after Horace Vernet, *Death of Prince Joseph Poniatowski in the Elster*, aquatint. National Museum in Warsaw. Photo: W. Kryński (Interpress).

250. Vase produced in the Belvedere manufactory. National Museum in Warsaw. Photo: National Museum in Warsaw.

251. Soup toureen with a cover from the manufactory in Korzec. National Museum in Warsaw. Photo: National Museum in Warsaw.

252. Jan Gładysz, *Portrait of Stanisław Staszic*, c. 1820. National Museum in Poznań. Photo: W. Kryński and T. Prażmowski (Interpress).

253. Walenty Wańkowicz, *Portrait of Mickiewicz*, 1828. National Museum in Warsaw. Photo: National Museum in Warsaw.

254. Wincenty Kasprzycki, *Bankowy Square in Warsaw*. National Museum in Warsaw, on loan in the Historical Museum of the City of Warsaw. Photo: National Museum in Warsaw.

255. Wincenty Kasprzycki, *Fine Arts Exhibition in the Rooms of Warsaw University*, 1828. National Museum in Warsaw. Photo: National Museum in Warsaw.

256. Marcin Zaleski, *Capture of the Arsenal*. National Museum in Warsaw, on loan in the Historical Museum of the City of Warsaw. Photo: W. Kryński (Interpress).

257. *Kopernik Square in Warsaw with the Staszic Palace, headquarters of the Warsaw Learned Society*, after 1832. National Museum in Warsaw, on loan in the Historical Museum of the City of Warsaw. Photo: W. Kryński and G. Rogiński (Interpress).

258. Piotr Michałowski, *Somosierra*, c. 1837. National Museum in Cracow. Photo: S. Michta.

259. Piotr Michałowski, *Equestrian Portrait of Hetman Stefan Czarniecki*, c. 1846. National Museum in Cracow. Photo: W. Kryński and T. Prażmowski (Interpress).

260. Józef Brodowski, *View of Wawel*, 1825. Museum in Tarnów. Photo: J. Morek (Interpress).

261. Jan Nepomucen Głowacki, *Morskie Oko Lake*. National Museum in Cracow. Photo: W. Kryński and T. Prażmowski (Interpress).

262. January Suchodolski, *General Henryk Dąbrowski Entering Rome at the Head of the Polish Legions*, c. 1850. National Museum in Warsaw. Photo: National Museum in Warsaw.

263. Józef Simmler, *Death of Barbara Radziwiłłówna*, 1860. National Museum in Warsaw. Photo: National Museum in Warsaw.

264. Henryk Rodakowski, *Portrait of General Henryk Dembiński*, 1852. National Museum in Cracow. Photo: W. Kryński and T. Prażmowski (Interpress).

265. Henryk Rodakowski, *Portrait of Leonia Blühdorn*, 1871. National Museum in Warsaw. Photo: National Museum in Warsaw.

266. Juliusz Kossak, *Mickiewicz and Sadyk Pasha*, 1890. National Museum in Poznań. Photo: W. Kryński and T. Prażmowski (Interpress).

267. Leopold Loeffler, *Return from Captivity*, 1863. National Museum in Warsaw. Photo: National Museum in Warsaw.

268. Franciszek Kostrzewski, *Wharf for Steamships in Powiśle in*

253

Warsaw, c. 1853. National Museum in Warsaw, on loan in the Historical Museum of the City of Warsaw. Photo: National Museum in Warsaw.

269. Franciszek Kostrzewski, *Circus at Saska Kępa in Warsaw*, 1852. National Museum in Warsaw. Photo: National Museum in Warsaw.

270. Franciszek Kostrzewski, *Drawing-room of Wacław and Nina Łuszczewski in Warsaw*, 1854. Historical Museum of the City of Warsaw. Photo: M. Musiał (Interpress).

271. Józef Szermentowski, *Return from Pasture*, 1876. National Museum in Cracow. Photo: W. Kryński and T. Prażmowski (Interpress).

272. Wojciech Gerson, *Cemetery in the Mountains*, 1894. National Museum in Warsaw. Photo: W. Kryński and T. Prażmowski (Interpress).

273. Władysław Malecki, *Storks*, c. 1874. National Museum in Cracow. Photo: W. Kryński and T. Prażmowski (Interpress).

274. Aleksander Kotsis, *Homeless*, c. 1870. National Museum in Warsaw. Photo: National Museum in Warsaw.

275. Aleksander Kotsis, *Last Chattel*, 1870. National Museum in Warsaw. Photo: National Museum in Warsaw.

276. Artur Grottger, *Evening Prayer*, 1864—65. National Museum in Cracow. Photo: W. Kryński and T. Prażmowski.

277. Jan Matejko, *Skarga's Sermon*, 1864. National Museum in Warsaw. Photo: National Museum in Warsaw.

278. Jan Matejko, *Prussian Homage* (detail), 1882. National Museum in Cracow. Photo: W. Kryński and T. Prażmowski (Interpress).

279. Antoni Kozakiewicz, *Winter*. National Museum in Warsaw. Photo: National Museum in Warsaw.

280. Tadeusz Pruszkowski, *Death of Ellenai*, 1892. National Museum in Wrocław. Photo: M. Musiał (Interpress).

281. Maksymilian Gierymski, *Insurgent Guard in 1863*. c. 1873. National Museum in Warsaw. Photo: W. Kryński and T. Prażmowski (Interpress).

282. Aleksander Gierymski, *In the Summer-house*, 1882. National Museum in Warsaw. Photo: National Museum in Warsaw.

283. Aleksander Gierymski, *Peasant Coffin*, 1894—95. National Museum in Warsaw. Photo: National Museum in Warsaw.

284. Aleksander Gierymski, *Sand Diggers*, 1887. National Museum in Warsaw. Photo: W. Kryński and J. Grelowski (Interpress).

285. Stanisław Witkiewicz, *Foehn*, 1895. National Museum in Cracow. Photo: W. Kryński and T. Prażmowski (Interpress).

286. Józef Chełmoński, *Autumn*, 1897. National Museum in Poznań. Photo: W. Kryński and T. Prażmowski.

287. Stanisław Lentz, *Pay Day*, 1885. Episcopal Curia in Lublin. Photo: K. Szeloch (Interpress).

288. Stanisław Lentz, *Strike*, 1910. National Museum in Warsaw. Photo: National Museum in Warsaw.

289. Jacek Malczewski, *Death of Ellenai*, 1883. National Museum in Cracow. Photo: T. Prażmowski and W. Kryński (Interpress).

290. Jacek Malczewski, *Melancholy*, 1894. National Museum in Poznań. Photo: W. Kryński and T. Prażmowski (Interpress).

291. Jacek Malczewski, *Thanatos II*, 1899. Museum of Art in Łódź. Photo: J. Grelowski (Interpress).

292. Jacek Malczewski, *Workers on Their Way to the Factory*. Private collection. Photo: J. Morek (Interpress).

293. Stanisław Wyspiański, *Self-portrait with Wife*, 1904. National Museum in Cracow. Photo: W. Kryński and M. Sielewicz (Interpress).

294. Stanisław Wyspiański, *Rhapsody*, pastel, c. 1903. Upper Silesian Museum in Bytom. Photo: J. Morek (Interpress).

295. Leon Wyczółkowski, *Fishermen*, 1891. National Museum in Warsaw. Photo: W. Kryński and T. Prażmowski (Interpress).

296. Leon Wyczółkowski, *Beetroot Digging I*, 1895. National Museum in Warsaw. Photo: National Museum in Warsaw.

297. Władysław Podkowiński, *Ecstasy*, 1894. National Museum in Cracow. Photo: National Museum in Warsaw.

298. Jan Stanisławski, *Cloud*, c. 1903. National Museum in Warsaw. Photo: National Museum in Warsaw.

299. Józef Mehoffer, *Strange Garden*, 1903. National Museum in Warsaw. Photo: W. Kryński and T. Prażmowski (Interpress).

300. Ferdynand Ruszczyc, *Soil*, 1898. National Museum in Warsaw. Photo: W. Kryński and T. Prażmowski (Interpress).

301. Witold Wojtkiewicz, *Children's Crusade*, 1905. National Museum in Warsaw. Photo: W. Kryński and T. Prażmowski (Interpress).

302. Witold Wojtkiewicz, *Ash Wednesday*, 1900. National Museum in Cracow. Photo: W. Kryński and T. Prażmowski (Interpress).

303. Józef Richter, *Palace in Tulczyn*, watercolor, 1836. National Museum in Warsaw. Photo: National Museum in Warsaw.

304. Fryderyk Krzysztof Dietrich, *Teatralny Square in Warsaw with the Theater Building designed by Corazzi*, aquatint. National Museum in Warsaw. Photo: National Museum in Warsaw.

305. Teofil Kwiatkowski, *Chopin Polonaise or Ball in Hôtel Lambert*, gilt gouache, 1849. National Museum in Warsaw. Photo: National Museum in Warsaw.

306. Teofil Kwiatkowski, *After a Battle*, gilt watercolor, 1869. National Museum in Warsaw. Photo: National Museum in Warsaw.

307. Wojciech Gerson, *Jan Wilczek in Wilanów Asking John Sobieski to Come to the Assistance of Vienna against the Turks*, 1889. National Museum in Warsaw. Photo: National Museum in Warsaw.

308. Juliusz Kossak, *Cracow Wedding*, watercolor, 1895. National Museum in Warsaw. Photo: National Museum in Warsaw.

309. Artur Grottger, *Comet*, drawing from the series *War*, 1866—67. National Museum in Warsaw. Photo: National Museum in Warsaw.

310. Artur Grottger, *Polish Peasant and the Gentry*, drawing from the series *Warsaw*, 1861. National Museum in Warsaw. Photo: National Museum in Warsaw.

311. Witold Wojtkiewicz, *Protest March*, ink drawing, 1909. National Museum in Warsaw. Photo: National Museum in Warsaw.

312. Jan Koszczyc Witkiewicz, Experimental Center of the Higher School of Commerce in Warsaw, 1928—30. Photo: J. Morek (Interpress).

313. Zdzisław Mączeński, Ministry for Religious Denominations and Public Education in Warsaw, 1931. Photo: J. Morek (Interpress).

314. Antoni Dygat, Bonds and Stock Printing Office in Warsaw, 1925—29. Photo: J. Morek (Interpress).

315. Barbara and Stanisław Brukalski, Estate of the Warsaw Housing Cooperative at Żoliborz in Warsaw, 1925—39. Photo: J. Morek (Interpress).

316. Roman Piotrowski, Residential house for employees of the Social Insurance Company in Gdynia, 1935. Photo: K. Szeloch (Interpress).

317. Rudolf Świerczyński. National Economic Bank in Warsaw, 1929. Photo: J. Morek (Interpress).

318. Xawery Dunikowski, *Sarcophagus of Boleslaus the Bold*, 1916—17. X. Dunikowski Museum at Królikarnia in Warsaw. Photo: National Museum in Warsaw.

319. Jan Szczepkowski, *Nativity shrine* (reconstruction), c. 1925. National Museum in Warsaw. Photo: National Museum in Warsaw.

320. Edward Wittig, *Polish Nike*, 1918. National Museum in Warsaw. Photo: K. Zakrzewska (Art Institute of the Polish Academy of Sciences).

321. Henryk Kuna, *Rhythm*, (1925). National Museum in Warsaw. Photo: National Museum in Warsaw.

322. Zbigniew Pronaszko, *Pietà*, 1921. Museum of Art in Łódź. Photo: J. Grelowski (Interpress).

323. August Zamoyski, *Head of Verka*, 1936. National Museum in Warsaw. Photo: W. Mądroszkiewicz (Art Institute of the Polish Academy of Sciences).

324. Stanisław Szukalski, *Boleslaus the Bold*, c. 1930. Upper Silesian Museum in Bytom. Photo: J. Morek (Interpress).

325. Katarzyna Kobro, *Suprematist Sculpture*, c. 1924. Museum of Art in Łódź. Photo: J. Grelowski (Interpress).

326. Zbigniew Pronaszko, *Nude*, 1917. National Museum in Cracow. Photo: W. Kryński and T. Prażmowski (Interpress).

327. Andrzej Pronaszko, *Flight into Egypt*, 1918—21. Museum of Art in Łódź. Photo: J. Grelowski (Interpress).

328. Leon Chwistek, *Butterflies*, 1920. National Museum in Warsaw. Photo: W. Kryński (Interpress).

329. Leon Chwistek, *Industrial City*, 1921. National Museum in Warsaw. Photo: National Museum in Warsaw.

330. Stanisław Ignacy Witkiewicz, *Composition (Temptation of Adam)*, 1920. National Museum in Warsaw. Photo: National Museum in Warsaw.

331. Stanisław Ignacy Witkiewicz, *Composition*, 1921—22. Museum of Art in Łódź. Photo: J. Grelowski (Interpress).

332. Józef Pankiewicz, *Flowers in a Blue Vase,* 1933. National Museum in Warsaw. Photo: W. Kryński (Interpress).

333. Felicjan Kowarski, *Withered Tree,* 1930. National Museum in Warsaw. Photo: J. Morek (Interpress).

334. Felicjan Kowarski, *Wanderers,* 1930. National Museum in Warsaw. Photo: National Museum in Warsaw.

335. Tytus Czyżewski, *Spain,* 1923. National Museum in Warsaw. Photo: T. Prażmowski (Interpress).

336. Tadeusz Makowski, *Village Yard,* 1928. National Museum in Warsaw. Photo: National Museum in Warsaw.

337. Tadeusz Makowski, *Jazz,* 1929. National Museum in Warsaw. Photo: J. Morek (Interpress).

338. Zygmunt Waliszewski, *Feast* (small), 1933. National Museum in Warsaw. Photo: J. Morek (Interpress).

339. Zygmunt Waliszewski, *Don Quixote on Horseback,* 1934. National Museum in Warsaw. Photo: National Museum in Warsaw.

340. Henryk Stażewski, *Counter-composition,* 1930—32. Museum of Art in Łódź. Photo: J. Grelowski (Interpress).

341. Władysław Strzemiński, *Łódź City Scape,* 1932. Museum of Art in Łódź. Photo: J. Grelowski (Interpress).

342. Jan Cybis, *Peonies,* 1936. National Museum in Cracow. Photo: J. Kryński and T. Prażmowski (Interpress).

343. Franciszek Józef Bartoszek, *Smithy,* 1937. National Museum in Warsaw. Photo: K. Zakrzewska (Art Institute of the Polish Academy of Sciences).

344. Jerzy Hulewicz, *Composition,* 1920. Upper Silesian Museum in Bytom. Photo: J. Morek (Interpress).

345. Jonasz Stern, *Nude,* 1935. National Museum in Cracow. Photo: W. Kryński and T. Prażmowski (Interpress).

346. Eugeniusz Zak, *Landscape,* c. 1917. Museum of Art in Łódź. Photo: J. Grelowski (Interpress).

347. Mieczysław Szczuka, *Self-portrait.* National Museum in Warsaw. Photo: National Museum in Warsaw.

348. Karol Hiller, *Coal Basin,* 1933. Museum of Art in Łódź. Photo: J. Grelowski (Interpress).

349. Leon Wyczółkowski, *Polish Knights Riding in the Rogalin Woods,* 1925. National Museum in Warsaw. Photo: National Museum in Warsaw.

350. Władysław Skoczylas, *Highland Robbers' Dance.* National Museum in Warsaw. Photo: National Museum in Warsaw.

351. Tadeusz Kulisiewicz, *Women from Szlembark,* 1939. National Museum in Warsaw. Photo: National Museum in Warsaw.

352. Zofia Stryjeńska, *Mountain Pasture,* illustration to Stanisław Mierczyński's *Muzyka Podhala.* National Museum in Warsaw. Photo: National Museum in Warsaw.

353. Stanisław Osostowicz, *Peasant Epic,* 1930. National Museum in Warsaw. Photo: National Museum in Warsaw.

354. Stanisław Ostoja Chrostowski, Illustration to *Pericles, Prince of Tyre,* 1937. National Museum in Cracow. Photo: W. Kryński and T. Prażmowski (Interpress).

355. Tadeusz Gronowski, Poster advertising Radion washing powder. Poster Museum at Wilanów in Warsaw. Photo: M. Sielewicz.

356. Zofia Stryjeńska, Kilim rug, after 1925. National Museum in Warsaw. Photo: J. Morek (Interpress).

357. Eleonora Plutyńska, Kilim rug *Squares,* 1929. Central Museum of Textile Industry in Łódź. Photo: J. Grelowski (Interpress).

358. General view of the ruins of the Old Town in Warsaw in 1945. Photo: Central Photographic Agency.

359. Bird's eye view of the reconstructed Old Town in Warsaw. Photo: J. Morek (Interpress).

360. Gdańsk in 1945. Photo: Central Photographic Agency.

361. Reconstructed Main City in Gdańsk. Photo: K. Kamiński (Interpress).

362. Ruins of Wrocław in 1945. Photo: Central Photographic Agency.

363. Reconstructed Wrocław. Photo: W. Kryński (Interpress).

364. Reconstructed castle in Szczecin. Photo: T. Prażmowski (Interpress).

365. Marek Leykam, Department store in Poznań, 1950—52. Photo: T. Prażmowski (Interpress).

366. Romuald Gutt, Central Statistical Office in Warsaw, 1948—50. Photo: J. Morek (Interpress).

367. Tadeusz Ptaszycki and team, Central Square in Nowa Huta. Photo: W. Kryński and T. Prażmowski (Interpress).

368. Zbigniew Karpiński and Jerzy Kowarski, East Side of Marszałkowska Street in Warsaw, 1961—69. Photo: J. Morek (Interpress).

369. Intersection of the Łazienkowska and Wisłostrada throughways in Warsaw, 1974. Photo: J. Morek (Interpress).

370. M. Budzyński and team, Ursynów North housing development in Warsaw. Photo: J. Morek (Interpress)

371. Tanks for liquefied gas in the Petrochemical Plant in Płock. Photo: L. Łożyński (Interpress).

372. Sports and Entertainment Hall (M. Krasiński, M. Gintowt and team, 1972) and *Monument to Silesian Insurgents* (G. Zemła) in Katowice. Photo: M. Musiał (Interpress).

373. Xawery Dunikowski, *Monument to Silesian Insurgents* on Mount St. Anne near Opole, 1949—52. Photo: M. Musiał and K. Szeloch (Interpress).

374. Natan Rappaport, *Monument to the Heroes of the Jewish Ghetto* in Warsaw. Photo: J. Morek and L. Łożyński (Interpress).

375. Franciszek Duszenko, Adam Haupt and Franciszek Strynkiewicz, *Monument in Honour of the Victims of the Death Camp at Treblinka,* 1964. Photo: B. Różyc (Interpress).

376. Maria Albin Boniecki, Coping of the *Monument of Three Eagles* at Majdanek. Photo: L. Łożyński (Interpress).

377. Władysław Hasior, *Monument to Hostages Executed in Nowy Sącz,* 1966—68. Museum of Architecture in Wrocław. Photo: A. Twardowski (Museum of Architecture in Wrocław).

378. Marian Wnuk, *Monument to Women of the Nazi Occupation Period,* 1964. National Museum in Warsaw. Photo: A. Czudowski and H. Weinberg.

379. Alina Szapocznikow, *Multiplied Self-portrait,* 1965. National Museum in Warsaw. Photo: J. Grelowski (Interpress).

380. Andrzej Wróblewski, *Execution VI,* 1949. National Museum in Warsaw. Photo: J. Morek (Interpress).

381. Eugeniusz Eibisch, *Sisters,* 1949. National Museum in Warsaw. Photo: W. Kryński (Interpress).

382. Marian Bogusz, *Mr. Brown Sends His Regards to Fighting Palestine,* 1948. Museum of Art in Łódź. Photo: J. Grelowski (Interpress).

383. Juliusz Krajewski, *Stakhanovite,* 1949. National Museum in Warsaw. Photo: National Museum in Warsaw.

384. Helena Krajewska, *Youth Brigade on the Building Site,* 1949. National Museum in Warsaw. Photo: National Museum in Warsaw.

385. Wojciech Weiss, *Manifesto,* 1950. National Museum in Warsaw. Photo: National Museum in Warsaw.

386. Aleksandar Kobzdej, *Pass me a Brick,* 1950. National Museum in Wrocław. Photo: M. Musiał and K. Szeloch (Interpress).

387. Tadeusz Brzozowski, *Prophet,* 1950. National Museum in Warsaw. Photo: J. Morek (Interpress).

388. Wojciech Fangor, *Korean Mother,* 1951. National Museum in Warsaw. Photo: National Museum in Warsaw.

389. Tadeusz Kantor, *Open Space.* Museum of Art in Łódź. Photo: J. Grelowski (Interpress).

390. Marian Bogusz, *Honegger's Liturgical Symphony,* 1955. Regional Museum in Bydgoszcz. Photo: G. Rogiński (Interpress).

391. Kazimierz Mikulski, *View from My Window,* 1977. National Museum in Cracow. Photo: W. Kryński and T. Prażmowski (Interpress).

392. Henryk Stażewski, *Colored Relief 7,* 1960. Museum of Art in Łódź. Photo: J. Grelowski (Interpress).

393. Andrzej Wróblewski, *Queue Is Going on,* 1956. National Museum in Warsaw. Photo: National Museum in Warsaw.

394. Jan Lebenstein, *Figure in a Bronze Frame.* National Museum in Warsaw. Photo: National Museum in Warsaw.

395. Władysław Strzemiński, *After-image of the Sun,* 1948—49. National Museum in Cracow. Photo: W. Kryński (Interpress).

396. Stefan Gierowski, *Painting CC,* 1966. National Museum in Warsaw. Photo: J. Morek (Interpress).

397. Alfred Lenica, *Lost Photo,* 1964. National Museum in Cracow. Photo: W. Kryński and T. Prażmowski (Interpress).

398. Józef Szajna, *Epitaph IV*, 1967. Studio Theater Gallery in Warsaw. Photo: S. Okołowicz.

399. Władysław Hasior, *Polish Banners*, 1967—70. Photo: A. Bujak.

400. Władysław Strzemiński, Drawing from the series *Hands That Are not with Us*, 1945. Museum of Art in Łódź. Photo: J. Grelowski (Interpress).

401. Maria Jaremianka, *Rhythm VII*, 1958. National Museum in Cracow. Photo: W. Kryński and T. Prażmowski (Interpress).

402. Adam Marczyński, *Circus*, monotype, 1955. Photo: W. Mądroszkiewicz (Art Institute of the Polish Academy of Sciences).

403. Mieczysław Wejman, *Cyclist VIa*, etching, 1968. National Museum in Cracow. Photo: W. Kryński and T. Prażmowski (Interpress).

404. Tadeusz Trepkowski, Poster for the Peace Cycling Race, 1950. Poster Museum at Wilanów in Warsaw. Photo: M. Sielewicz.

405. Tadeusz Trepkowski, Poster for the International Frédéric Chopin Piano Competition. Poster Museum at Wilanów in Warsaw. Photo: M. Sielewicz.

406. Waldemar Świerzy, Poster for the Mazowsze song and dance company, 1961. Poster Museum at Wilanów in Warsaw. Photo: M. Sielewicz.

407. Franciszek Starowieyski, Movie poster. Poster Museum at Wilanów in Warsaw. Photo: M. Sielewicz.

408. Franciszek Starowieyski, Theater poster, 1974. Poster Museum at Wilanów in Warsaw. Photo: M. Sielewicz.

409. Józef Szajna, Production of *Dante*, 1974. Studio Theater in Warsaw, Photo: S. Okołowicz.

410. Tadeusz Kantor, Production of *The Dead Class*, 1975, Cricot 2 Theater in Cracow. Photo: M. Socha (Interpress).

411. Magdalena Abakanowicz, Tapestry *White*, 1964. Central Museum of Textile Industry in Łódź. Photo: J. Grelowski (Interpress).